GN
857

D0844879

HUMAN BY NATURE

*Between Biology
and the Social Sciences*

BELL LIBRARY
TEXAS A&M UNIVERSITY
CORPUS CHRISTI

HUMAN BY NATURE

Between Biology and the Social Sciences

Edited by

Peter Weingart
*University of Bielefeld,
Germany*

Sandra D. Mitchell
*University of California,
San Diego*

Peter J. Richerson
*University of California
at Davis*

Sabine Maasen
*Max Planck Institute for
Psychological Research,
Munich*

LEA LAWRENCE ERLBAUM ASSOCIATES, PUBLISHERS
1997 Mahwah, New Jersey   London

Copyright © 1997 by Lawrence Erlbaum Associates, Inc.
All rights reserved. No part of the book may be reproduced in any form, by photostat, microform, retrieval system, or any other means without the prior written consent of the publisher.

Lawrence Erlbaum Associates, Inc., Publishers
10 Industrial Avenue
Mahwah, NJ 07430

Library of Congress Cataloging in Publication Data

Human by nature: between biology and the social sciences
/ Peter Weingart ... [et al.].
    p. cm.

Includes bibliographical references and index.
ISBN 0-8058-2154-6 (alk. paper)
1. Culture.   2. Sociobiology.   3. Human beings —
Animal   nature   4. Nature and nurture.   I. Weingart,
Peter.
GN357.H86   1997
304.5—dc20

                                96–45735
                                CIP

Books published by Lawrence Erlbaum Associates are printed on acid-free paper, and their bindings are chosen for strength and durability.

Printed in the United States of America
10 9 8 7 6 5 4 3 2 1

CONTENTS

PART III: ANALOGIES

PREFACE

Human By Nature—Between Biology and the Social Sciences is an unusual book with an unusual history that deserves a short narrative. When I first conceived of the project to convene biologists and social scientists for an academic year at the Center for Interdisciplinary Research (ZiF) to discuss their differences and agreements, and perhaps also their mutual agnosticism, the working title of the project was meant to be provocative: *Biological Foundations of Human Culture*. For political-historical and methodological reasons, this theme invites skepticism or worse. Social scientists would not only point to the catastrophic consequences of "biologization" during the Nazi regime in Germany; they would also warn against reductionist effects of any attempt to explain social phenomena in terms of biology. The sociobiology debate still looms large.

However, this was precisely the challenge, and even the adventure: to delineate a theme that among social scientists is fraught with historical and political taboos, but that would provide an opportunity to open the way to a host of new insights from other disciplines into human cultural evolution.

To be sure, the challenge of being open to unfamiliar views—to listen and learn one another's "language"—confronted all the scholars who met at the ZiF during the academic year 1991–1992. They came from disciplines as different and far apart as biology, sociology, anthropology, economics, human ethology, psychology, primatology, history, and philosophy of science. All of these disciplines have their entrenched biases and established preconceptions about their subject matters. Thus, interdisciplinary research, as it is promoted by the ZiF in Bielefeld, Germany, is also a social and psychological adventure. Throughout the academic year, the scholars were an interdisciplinary experiment *in vivo*. The assumption of this experiment was that the scholars—while working and residing at the ZiF—would be united intellectually as well as socially, a connection that might eventually enhance interdisciplinary communication even after the research group had dispersed again.

The research group on *Biological Foundations of Human Culture* met regularly on *jours fixes*, workshops, colloquia, and conferences. More often than not, scientific discussions continued on the way to the laundry, at a birthday party, or over dinner. Although initially, as is common, we experienced a Babylonian confusion of disciplinary languages, the thematic unity and social proximity gradually led to the realization that methods could be transferred, terms borrowed, explanations integrated, and intellectual unity achieved, after all.

Thus, a consensus emerged. The issue of human culture poses a challenge to the division of the world into the realms of the "natural" and the "cultural," and hence to the disciplinary division of scientific labor. In our view, the appropriate place for the study of human culture is located between biology and the social sciences.

The problem, then, was to find a common methodological ground to bridge the gap between different disciplinary approaches to the study of specific aspects of human culture. In discussing phenomena such as the evolution of social intelligence, of psychological dispositions such as trust and the detection of cheating, or basic social institutions such as the family, we explicitly avoided biological and sociological reductionisms. Instead, a pluralistic perspective was considered a prerequisite of the project by all participants. We adopted the model of "integrative pluralism" as its methodological strategy. This took into account both today's highly specialized and effective (sub-)disciplinary research and the possibility of integrating the respective findings on a case-by-case basis. With this model, an ambitious program was launched indeed.

What followed may best be described as interdisciplinarity in the making: After we decided on a general structure of the book that was to be the product of its work, and had given full editorial power to the four editors, subgroups were established. According to the particular object of its study and the different explanatory approaches involved, each subgroup had to find its own way of interdisciplinary collaboration. Each submitted a contribution to the present volume reflecting one of several types of fruitful cooperation (i.e., the fully integrated chapter, the multidisciplinary overview, or the discussion between different approaches). These variations notwithstanding, the orientation toward interdisciplinary dialogue was produced by a complex process of writing and editing contributions—a process that was supposed to favor discussion among the authors of a chapter and the rest of the group as much as possible.

Each group chose a lead author who collected single-authored or coauthored contributions to the chapter and suggested a structure for the chapter as a whole. After the authors and the book's editorial board agreed, the lead author acted as "interface" between his or her authors and the editorial board. (To honor this—certainly not always pleasant—task, the lead author is always mentioned first in the list of authors of a chapter; the other authors are in alphabetical order. The authors responsible for individual sections of a chapter are indicated under the headings of their sections.)

Chapters were exchanged among authors, lead authors, and editorial board several times—stimulating a lot of discussion and bringing about ever new aspects of the problems involved. This procedure ensured that even where sections were single-authored, a great deal of interdisciplinary debate and critique had preceded their final state. This highly complex arrangement was designed to lend the utmost coherence to a multi-authored book. Although the reader will have to judge if we have been successful in this respect, for those involved, it was a worthwhile experience, and for some of us it still is. Many interesting ideas for further study have emerged, and scholars from different, but pertinent areas came to know each other. Although we do not claim to have mastered all the challenges involved, we consider this volume a promising first step on the long road to an interdisciplinarily informed understanding of human culture. The dialogue has only just begun. If this book stimulates multidisciplinary interest and interdisciplinary exchange, the adventure may go on, and we may hope that social scientists and biologists alike will join in investigating the nature of human culture inspired by the ideal of integrative pluralism.

Attention should be drawn to several publications that have emerged from the research group as a result of conferences devoted to specific topics pertinent to its theme but beyond its own competence. One addresses the question of *Nonverbal communication: Where nature meets culture;* another dealing with *Communicating meaning: The evolution and development of language.* A meeting was held on historical issues concerning the transfer of metaphors between biology and the social sciences, the proceedings of which are entitled *Biology as Society/Society as Biology: Metaphors.*

An effort like this requires substantial intellectual, technical, and financial help. Hence, I first want to thank those colleagues who early on helped me with their advice on potential members of the group, issues to be addressed, and mistakes to be avoided. They are too many to be mentioned by name. Second, I want to thank the ZiF staff for providing the conducive atmosphere in which the group and their families could live and work. In particular, I am indebted to Dr. Gerhard Sprenger who shared with us his more than 20 years of experience in organizing and hosting research groups at the ZiF. Special thanks go to Ms. Lilo Jegerlehner for preparing the final manuscript after going through seemingly endless revisions. Her patience and precision have been most valuable assets in finalizing this multi-authored manuscript. Also, we would like to thank Ms. Adelheid Baker in assisting with the copy-editing. Finally, speaking on behalf of the group as a whole, I thank ZiF as an institution for making this endeavor possible.

Bielefeld, April 1997   Peter Weingart

GENERAL INTRODUCTION

It has been twenty-two years since E. O. Wilson (1975) wrote *Sociobiology: The New Synthesis*, which contained a final chapter advocating the consideration of humans "in the free spirit of natural history, as though we were zoologists from another planet completing a catalogue of social species on earth" (p. 547). Wilson's chapter ignited the "sociobiology controversy." Its claims for the relevance of evolutionary ideas from biology to the study of humans coincided with a highly politicized involution of the social sciences that turned a previously quiet disciplinary boundary into an intellectual Western front. The confrontation was conducted with strong words and naive dichotomies on all sides: nature versus nurture, reduction versus autonomy, atomism versus holism, evolution versus progressivism. The intensity of the debate revealed the value-laden, easily politicized nature of the relationship between biology and the social sciences. The apparent ignorance of the history of this relationship and the newness of this particular expression led to ideological furor on both sides.

In fact, by and large social scientists have ignored the biological sciences as irrelevant for their concerns. This attitude has its origins in the gaining of disciplinary independence of both biology and sociology (as well as economics and anthropology) around the turn of the century, and the different paths taken by their theoretical development. Ever since the constitution of sociality as an independent subject matter, scholars in the social sciences have been wary of biological theories for fear of reductionism. As a consequence, social scientists avoided meeting the challenge of seriously considering the biological foundations of culture.

In addition to being merely oblivious, however, there is also a more aggressive repudiation of anything smacking of "biologization." This attitude has its origins in recent history—namely, the unholy union of biological determinism and racism in the form of Nazi race policies that served to justify horrific practices.

As a result of this configuration of disciplinary perspectives, social values, and political convictions, social scientists overlooked the real advances in the application of evolutionary ideas to animal behavior surveyed in E. O. Wilson's (1975) substantive chapters. They also did not take note of their colleagues, who were traveling among the disciplinary

1

territories and beginning to make serious use of biological ideas to understand human culture. Among these were Donald Campbell (psychologist), Napoleon Chagnon and William Irons (anthropologists), Richard Nelson and Sidney Winter (economists), Richard Alexander (biologist), and Luigi Cavalli-Sforza and Marcus Feldman (biologists). Much theoretical and empirical work has been undertaken since then. The time of the initial optimism and the furor it evoked has passed. Some of the promissory notes of the power of biological explanatory strategies have been cashed in, some had to be withdrawn, and others remain outstanding. The results of the last two decades of work are summarized in Barkow, Cosmides, and Tooby's (1992) *The Adapted Mind,* Smith and Winterhalder's (1992a) *Evolutionary Ecology and Human Behavior,* Durham's (1991) *Coevolution* as well as over 200 books, papers, and cited reviews, such as Durham (1992) and Borgerhoff Mulder (1987).

Now that the climate is calmer and the debate can be grounded on work done, rather than on promises and claims, the time has come for a critical assessment of the achievements and the potential for closer, constructive interdisciplinary interaction between biology and the social sciences. In this spirit, the scholars represented here convened to explore the opportunities for collaboration in the study of culture, to stake out their agreements, and to specify their differences. The results of this effort are reflected in this book.

PREPARING THE GROUNDS FOR INTERDISCIPLINARY DIALOGUE

A. Human Uniqueness Reconsidered

This volume addresses the reservations voiced by social scientists at the mention of biology by reconstructing some of the historical, political, and philosophical contexts that generate and justify them. From their beginning, the social science disciplines have invited biological theories and metaphors into their domains. But the nature of those borrowings, and the responses to them, have varied from sociology to economics, from psychology to anthropology (see chap. 1). How the new forms of interaction described here might be met can be better understood by acquaintance with this theoretical history.

The political abuse of the biological sciences' authority by the Nazi race policies should give pause to those who are propagating anew our biological foundations as an explanation of human differences and universals. However, historical experience shows there has been the same corruption of scientific authority on the opposite side of the political spectrum—extreme environmentalism—as in the case of Lysenko. Both examples point to the underlying, more general phenomenon: No scientific discourse is completely detached from the political or the social. Scientific reasoning is both influenced by, and has effects on, political thought and action, as well as social values. In addition, there is no unequivocal relationship between scientific theories and political credo, as the multiple uses of Darwin's theory demonstrate. Rather, there is a shifting of boundaries in the time-bound and discipline-specific definition of what is considered to be *natural* or *social* about human beings (see chap. 2). What at one time, or for some disciplines, counted as thoroughly natural, might later, or by other disciplines, be conceived of as (either thoroughly or partly) socially constituted. With the emergence of the social sciences as independent disciplines, this distinction became ever more crucial. Above all, the relationship between biology and the social sciences has been troubled by simplified and false dichotomies partly originating in biology, partly in misunderstandings on the part of the social sciences. These dichotomies, which divide research and reify differences, are particularly pronounced with respect to the different disciplinary realms of nature and culture.

At the basis of dichotomous thinking is the notion of human uniqueness with its deep roots in Judeo-Christian religion. Human and social scientists have used the thesis of human uniqueness as an argument for ignoring biology. It is claimed that entirely different theoretical constructs are required to understand humans, and thus the natural sciences are of little relevance. Prior to Darwin, human distinctness was an assumption shared by almost all European intellectuals. From a creationist perspective, the uniqueness of each type of creature, and hence the unbreachable boundaries between them was secured by God's design. Darwin's theory drew aggressive opposition not least because it challenged the "uniqueness" paradigm. The Darwinian revolution replaced unbridgeable categorical gulfs with the idea that all organisms were united in common origins and by the influence of common natural processes. What had once seemed the natural and basic units—species—became exceedingly problematic, as indeed they still are for systematists. Given a theory of a single, shared origin, and subsequent diversification through history, the boundaries between species become blurred by the dynamics of evolution. No longer are they sharp and absolute. Rather, they are established by various means, being continually challenged and reestablished, becoming stronger and weaker in the process. All things are ultimately connected and situated in a phylogenetic continuum.

What can be meant, then, by pointing to human uniqueness from an evolutionary point of view? A number of characteristic properties of our species are found only in relatively rudimentary form in other species. Indeed, most observers hold that human behavior is highly distinctive, despite our close relationship with the higher primates, as measured by raw genetic distance. Systematists typically honor the apparently large behavioral difference between humans and the great apes with a separate family, the *Hominidae,* for us.

However, problems arise when what is identified as a mark of species distinction is reified into an essential difference. Every species, including *Homo sapiens*, is subject to, and a product of, the evolutionary processes of mutation, selection, drift, and the like (see Part II). Like every species, *Homo sapiens* is unique, if what we mean is that it is sufficiently distinct to be identified as a separate species. What features it has that diverged from its nearest ancestor are the grounds for the distinction and mark its uniqueness. Thus, just as we may ask how domestic dogs are unique, relative to wolves, we can ask how humans are unique, relative to their primate relatives (see chaps. 4, 5). Humans are, in this sense, just "another unique species" (Foley, 1987). But this recognition does not preclude, but indeed presupposes, both a historical connection and many shared features between related populations (Dupré, 1991; Konner, 1991). The assertion of a strong form of the uniqueness argument echoes back an earlier essentialism (Hull, 1965; Mayr, 1959), and closes off connections between the social and natural sciences.

A basic feature of biological phenomena is the combination of uniqueness of the variants within a framework of phylogenetic continuity. The marking of boundaries within a continuum entails a classification problem whose solution may sometimes be interpreted with more ontological emphasis than is warranted. Darwin struggled with the conceptual change required in the notion of "species," which accompanied embedding it in an evolutionary framework. Indeed, the "species problem" (i.e., reaching agreement on a set of criteria for distinguishing separate species) has not yet been "solved" univocally for the various biological contexts (see Ereshefsky, 1992).

The dynamic processes, which explain the continuity, are responsible for generating variation in morphology, behavior, habitat, and so on. The closer two populations are, the more severe the competition is between them in the struggle for existence, and hence the greater the pressure for diversification. Being different allows new habitats to be accessed, and perhaps the successful escape from the direct competition for food. As Darwin argued, any slight heritable advantage a variant displayed would be preserved. As natural selection pushes populations to ever greater diversification, the ability to interact reproductively may diminish until, at least on one definition (Mayr, 1942), with the onset of reproductive isolation, a new species is created. For Darwinians, species are just extended versions of varieties. Populations we call species are classified according to "diagnostic features," not essentialist logos.

> Evolution is continually going on; the traits of lineages continually change. What will define a group at one time may not define it at another. The traits defining groups are temporally contingent, not essential. The phylogenetic group Vertebrata may happen to be defined, at present, by the possession of bones, but that may no longer be true in a million years' time. (Ridley, 1986, p. 86)

Seen within an evolutionary framework, there are reasons to maintain a concept of human uniqueness in that transient sense. The differences that evolved in humans have a significance beyond mere reproductive isolation from ancestors. Human behavior is much more substantially influenced by culture than is the behavior of any animals we are aware of (see chap. 4). However impressive the social activities of animal species are, they lack the capacity to attach representational meaning to a situation or context, and, hence, the capacity for interpretation (see Wolfe, 1993). Human use of symbols for communication is elaborate by animal standards (see chap. 5). Human societies are large to very large, and involve unusual degrees of cooperation, coordination, and division of labor. Their organization in relatively stable social institutions is the subject matter of sociology (see chap. 6). Entire local subpopulations are typically organized into more or less bounded, coherent groups, which are called *societies* or *cultures*, marked by culturally coded boundaries. The behavioral repertoire of human societies is very diverse. As a consequence of technical and social adaptations, humans have managed to become the most widespread vertebrate on earth—a phenomenon within the purview of anthropology (see chap. 7).

In addition, human societies have developed complex social structures as a result of multiple causes acting at multiple levels (see chap. 11). Each of these features has some parallels in other organisms, but the combination and degree of exaggeration of these features indicate that the ways in which humans are unique are crucial to the construction of explanations of their behavior. As is argued later (see Part III), the capacity for culture, although evolved by means of natural selection similar to other features of other species, introduces new complexities and processes of transmission (see chap. 9), which must be taken into account to understand cultural variations and cultural phylogenies (see chaps. 10, 11).

B. Beyond Dichotomies

The debate over human uniqueness is reflected in other dichotomies. By arguing from a nonessentialist approach to human uniqueness, these related dichotomies need to be abandoned accordingly.

Causation: Nature Versus Nurture. The classic division of explanations of human behavior into nature or nurture entails the separation of the causal processes of genes and learning, biology and culture. This is a simple analytical distinction. All phenotypic characters, be they morphological or behavioral, are the joint product of genetic templates and environmental input. We make such distinctions to understand how processes interact, and their reification into axes of polemical debate and disciplinary posturing is a horrifying error. Whether some individuals speak English or German is the result of the linguistic environment in which they were reared, but that they speak any language at all has a genetic basis. Whether an individual suffers the disastrous symptoms of developmental and mental retardation associated with PKU disease is a function of whether phenylalanine is part of his or her diet. However, given that phenylalanine is a dietary staple in all human populations, it is the difference in genes that explains why some suffer from PKU disease and others do not (Burian, 1981–1982). There are plenty of well-documented examples of how genes and environment interact; in general, our understanding is more limited by methodological than conceptual problems.

One reason this rather obvious solution has not ended the nature–nurture debate is that the distinction is flawed in the case of humans. Human culture fits poorly in either category. On the one hand, culture is learned, imposed by the environment, and hence is nurturelike. On the other hand, culture is a means for transmitting enduring traditions of behavior whose origins can be discovered in the remote past. Socialization imposes the collective past on the present behavior of individuals almost as firmly as genes do, although by a rather different process. As is often said, culture is a Lamarckian system for the inheritance of acquired variation that mixes and matches the properties of nature and nurture in a most confusing way. Thus, the minimum set of analytical concepts in the human case is environment, biological inheritance, and culture. In the human case, it is often necessary to subdivide environmental effects into social and physical subcategories, not to mention a host of more detailed distinctions.

The recognition of the complex interactions among genes, culture, and environment allows a more sophisticated evaluation of the relative importance of various causal contributions to the origin, maintenance, ubiquity, and absence of particular traits. The causal players are varied, and their roles on any given occasion may be more or less explanatory.

Explanation: Reduction Versus Autonomy. The antinomy between reduction and autonomy bears witness to a methodological heritage advocating grand unification as the goal of the end of all science. Referring to Newton's unification of celestial and terrestrial mechanics by means of four simple laws and the chemical revolution as models, philosophers and scientists alike have promised unity through reduction (Weinberg, 1992). Sociology would be replaced by psychology, psychology by biology, and biology in turn by chemistry and chemistry by physics, until all explanations would emerge from the most basic entities interacting according to the most fundamental laws. However, although the promises of fundamentalism and unification may be psychologically comforting, they are neither philosophically necessary nor methodologically practical (see chap. 3). The commonly perceived, single alternative to reduction has been complete disciplinary autonomy: Scientific practice is legitimated by the absolute disconnection of its subject matter from the domains of other sciences. Social facts are *sui generis*, making the gap between biology or psychology and social studies vast and unbridgeable. Such a strong defense against reduction entails an isolationist stance when it presupposes the dichotomy of possibilities as exhaustive. It confounds the narrowly reductionistic agenda with the broader supposition of the scientific project as a whole that nature is seamless.

The seamlessness assumption is as robust as the reductionist program is weak. It is sufficient that humans are descended from apes, and that we live in the world to argue that biological and other natural processes have affected the history and ongoing processes of human societies, and that the social sciences thus cannot isolate themselves from the natural sciences. (The reverse is true as well; human agriculture affects weather patterns, the phenomena studied by the physical science of meteorology. Medical interventions can and have altered the evolutionary trajectories of viruses, a process under biological investigation.) It is a much stronger claim that social science can be subsumed by the more general laws of biology, and these in turn by those of chemistry and physics. Given seamlessness, but not reduction, there can be pluralism without isolationism; there are many paths to understanding the social world that can benefit from information and interaction at the crossroads.

Ontology: Atomism Versus Holism.   The debate over the adequacy of an atomistic or holistic ontology goes back to antiquity, when it was posed as the dilemma between indivisible entity and continuum. Atomism supports an ontological reduction to fundamental entities, based on the assumption that natural processes are strictly determined according to combinatorial natural laws. The influence of atomism is most apparent in physics and chemistry. In contrast, holism has its roots in biology, where it constitutes the paradigm of living organisms as a unity of self-organizing, open systems, not as a mere aggregation of parts. The term *holism* was coined by J. C. Smuts and introduced into theoretical biology by J. S. Haldane, and further supported by systems theory approaches to biology. The growing interest in complexity and chaos theories in biology have focussed increasingly on nonadditive effects.

A similar tradition developed in the social sciences, where first, under the influence of Spencer and Darwin, organismic concepts were used to denote the holistic or independent nature of social relationships. Durkheim then coined the term of *social facts* to demarcate phenomena like social cohesion, solidarity, mutual expectations, and so on as being beyond explanation by (or reduction to) the acts of individuals.

The dichotomy is thus reflected in the relationship both between biology and the social sciences (as these domains represent a part–whole relationship) and within each discipline. Within biology, it is reflected in the debate between adherents of a strong genetic determinism and those of epigenetic explanations of morphological processes, extending all the way to ecological systems theories. In the social sciences, the analogous debate is between microstructural "individualists" and macrostructural systems theorists (see chap. 11). It is clear that the most extreme conflicts would arise between propagators of genetic determinism (real or imagined) on the biological side and of sociality as a fact *sui generis*.

Both in the natural sciences, with physics leading the way, and in the social sciences, it is becoming increasingly clear that the dichotomy generated by these extreme perspectives is false, not least because numerous phenomena have escaped its description. Ontological and methodological pluralism warrants thinking in terms of different levels of abstraction and different perspectives of observation.

Theory: Evolution Versus Progressivism. The strongest influence of evolutionary ideas on the social sciences has emanated from Spencer's notion of evolution with its definitely progressivist tinge. Darwin's nonteleological reformulation of evolution was more often than not interpreted—and thus misunderstood—as progressivist, especially in political discourse and when applied to human society. Therefore, within the social sciences, Spencer's thesis was denigrated as "evolutionism."

The ensuing skepticism toward Darwinian evolutionary theory, and its later modernizations in the social sciences, may have originated in the added complexity of social analysis: the difficulty to clearly delineate the units of selection and the selective environment due to multiple recursive links. Today, as the ideological implications of the dichotomy have vanished, it does not seem that the progressivist misunderstanding of evolutionary theory still has a serious following. Biology and the social sciences can both tap the potential of the evolutionary explanation of stochastic biological and sociocultural processes.

BIOLOGICAL RESOURCES: HOMOLOGY AND ANALOGY

Although the studies in this volume all make use of biological resources, they deploy two different strategies. Part II assembles studies that follow a homological line of reasoning ("humans *are* animals"), and Part III explores the potential of analogical reasoning ("humans are *like* animals").

A. Homology

Humans are the product of evolution. On this level, some features of our morphology and behavior may be homologous with features of other species (see Part II). *Homology* refers to the similarity of structures in different populations. Sometimes it is used just to identify similarity without implication regarding the cause of the similarity. More commonly, it is taken to pick out those structures that are similar as a result of inheritance from a common ancestor (Jepsen, Mayr, & Simpson, 1963).

The abilities and limitations that our morphology imposes on us may be remnants of ancestral adaptations, features designed for other environments. In addition, the evolutionary processes that shape morphology and behavior might be understood by a comparative analysis. One can study homologies through time, as well as across species or populations. Some institutions are characteristic of human societies: The family, economic division of labor, and communication are found in various forms in other animal societies. Do similar environmental challenges shape such institutions? For example, we might ask why females are responsible for primary parental care in some populations, but not in others? Why are the taboos against incest ubiquitous? A comparative analysis illuminates the similarities, as well as the differences that contribute to the explanation of the traits under investigation.

Given our explicit acknowledgment of the ways in which human societies differ from other biological groups in terms of the introduction of cultural processes and increased complexity, how can biological explanations fashioned specifically for nonhumans be applied to humans? Two assumptions are required to explain human behaviors like incest taboos or family structure in terms of their consequences on biological fitness. The fitness of a trait or behavior has been generally interpreted in biology as referring to the consequences on individual reproductive success. However, developments within biological theory—primarily the introduction of inclusive fitness measures—have suggested that the bearer of fitness is not an individual organism, but rather a "gene" (Dawkins, 1982). But the genetic bases of the human social behaviors investigated by the homology approach are not well known, and are unlikely to be directly connectable to stretches of DNA.

Nevertheless, this gap can be and has been bridged by the regular appeal to the "phenotypic gambit" (Grafen, 1991). This strategic assumption ignores the genetic mechanisms underlying a trait in studying the evolution of it (i.e., it assumes for any trait under study that there is some mapping onto the genetic level, and hence one can presume fitness consequences will have evolutionary effects). This assumption is not unproblematic, but it is widely made, and has directed research in behavioral ecology for more than 20 years. Of course, the black boxing of genetic mechanisms is open to criticism, and chapter 11 raises some. Nevertheless, by treating the genetic basis as unproblematic, investigations can then focus on the role that natural selection and the environment have or could have in the generation and maintenance of social behavioral traits, *ceteris paribus*. In contrast, if one focuses on the details of the genetic mechanisms, the power of nonstandard transmission or nonadditive relations on traits can be exposed. Ideally, in cases where there are reasons for thinking that the genetic basis is in fact problematic, we would recommend an integrative strategy to put the results of the two strategies together in explaining a particular instance. This would be the case for human and nonhuman traits alike.

There is another assumption, however, that is required to make the move from genetic fitness to explanatory role, and it is especially pertinent to human social behavior. This additional assumption, the "natural origin" argument, also has a long history (see Boyd & Richerson, 1985; Chagnon & Irons, 1979; Durham, 1990). That is, even the most clearly culturally variable behavior that is not directly genetically controlled (hard wired), can be treated "as if" it were. This is based on the assumption that any cultural learning mechanism to have survived an initial selective competition, and hence evolved, would have to have led to behaviors that increase genetic fitness. How tight the "leash" of genes holds onto learned behaviors is, quite clearly, also controversial. But again, by making this assumption explicit, one can see where and how criticisms of the scientific explanations generated by appeal to it can be rigorously, and not frivolously, criticized.

Thus, the homology strategy is one that seeks explanations of human social behavior by appeal to the theoretical resources developed in the biological investigation of nonhuman behavior. In applying models of inclusive fitness maximization in this domain, two assumptions are required: the phenotypic gambit, which bridges the unknown proximate genetic and developmental mechanisms leading from genes to behavior, and the natural origin argument, which justifies the collapsing of the proximate cultural learning mechanisms to extend the genetic connection to learned behaviors as well. Some authors in this collection embrace these assumptions (see chaps. 7, 8), whereas others directly challenge them (see chaps. 9, 10, 11). A pluralistic approach suggests that much can be learned from a variety of simplifying starting points, while holding out the hope that local integrations can be developed (see chap. 3). Human culture is a complicated mixture of interactions of various causal mechanisms. Some features may be explicable with relatively simple assumptions (i.e., most likely cultural universals—things so basic to us qua human beings that the cultural mechanisms do not intervene). Other features are not so easily explicable (i.e., they are more culturally or environmentally sensitive). This book presents tools for these different kinds of explanatory pursuits, and clearly does not endorse the view that one project, or one strategy, is adequate to investigate all the features of human culture with which we are concerned.

B. Analogy

Evolution is a historical process. Therefore, long-term consequences are subject to historical "accidents" or contingencies, such as which variations happened to be available for selection to fine-tune environmental exigencies at a given time. As complexity builds on simpler forms, some early "decisions" may constrain later possibilities. Human cultures also are historical entities, changing over time, but they also carry with them vestiges of their past. For these reasons, it is plausible to suggest that the mechanisms by which cultural change occurs may be analogous to biological processes (see Part III). Transmission of information occurs, whether it be encoded in genes or ideas. Thus, another resource that biology offers is a theoretical structure from which to build analogous models for cultural change and stasis. The analogical strategy acknowledges from the outset that the relation between the two domains is one of similarity, not identity, so that such an investigation illuminates the differences between biological and cultural processes, as well as the similarities. (For a more detailed explication of this approach, see chap. 9.)

Our book is not a direct debate with critics on the hypothetical possibility or desirability of integrating the social and natural sciences. Rather, by presenting positive examples, it tries to show how addressing the human special case in the light of processes and methods borrowed from biology generates interesting and soluble problems. It is only by interdisciplinary interaction that the development of sophisticated models for understanding human cultural phenomena is made possible.

We have engaged in the interdisciplinary effort that resulted in this book, not to fuel the fires of old battles, nor to play into the hands of limited dichotomies, but rather to illustrate the promise that lies in making use of the components contained in the scientific toolbox tendered by the biological sciences. Both biologists and social scientists are invited to explore the usefulness of, and develop further, adaptationist, coevolutionist, and developmental explanatory strategies with respect to their explanatory projects. Success lies not in adopting isolationist stances to defend disciplinary boundaries, but rather in recognizing diversity and the opportunity this offers for a constructive exchange. The future lies in integrative pluralism, calling for both creativity and commitment to the tasks ahead.

PART I

CONTEXTS

INTRODUCTION: BRIDGES BETWEEN BIOLOGY AND THE SOCIAL SCIENCES

In Part I, the various perspectives on the biological foundations of human culture found in Parts II and II are set into three different contexts: (a) historical disciplinary development, (b) sociopolitical history, and (c) philosophical and methodological reflection. The reasons for this threefold contextualization are as follows.

The discussion of disciplinary history sheds light on what have often been long and intricate conflicts over the demarcation of disciplinary boundaries, in particular between the biological and social sciences. Any attempt to cross the boundary between biology and the social sciences makes visible the connections and reveals the blind spots created by these disciplinary divisions. Past history is still present in the definition of concepts, the images created by them, and, above all, in the resistance to interdisciplinary interactions. For these reasons, awareness of the sources of potential misunderstandings can help focus attention on real, rather than spurious, disagreements.

Likewise, the sociopolitical context has played, and continues to play, an enormously important role in shaping the discourses on "biology" and "society." Biological categories such as *race*, and *inheritance* or *genetic makeup* or metaphors such as the *struggle for existence* have assumed ideological functions in the political arena and at times have been invoked to legitimate discrimination and oppression, taking such extreme forms as mass murder.

Reactions to the most notorious associations of biological science and social policy have intervened in scientific debate in attempts to give political and public support to a variety of positions and counterpositions. In this process, the demarcation line between biology and the social sciences is fortified by societal memory, and appears even more insurmountable than ever before. To engage in interdisciplinary programs that presume that biology has something important to contribute to social science, one must understand the ways in which ideology has traveled between science and policy.

Finally, an overly strong defense of the autonomy of the social sciences which precludes any fruitful interactions with the biological sci-

15

ences, is predicated on the false dichotomy between reduction and isolation. This image of science emerges from a methodological goal of global unification. A third, pluralistic conception of the place of the various scientific theories and their integration in explanation provides the methodological foundation to support the types of strategies described in the remainder of the book. There is much to be gained from interdisciplinary transactions, but to reap the benefits both the promise and the problems must be acknowledged.

Part I attempts to smooth the ground to building bridges between the biological and social sciences. The discussions that follow represent a variety of efforts, incorporating differing assumptions about how to do just that. The more abstract and programmatic messages of Part I have not all been integrated into the analyses that make up the remainder of the book. We believe that progress in this important domain of science is made through the continuing dialogue among these positions, in conjunction with reflection on their historical, sociopolitical, and methodological presumptions and implications. This book is a contribution to that dialogue.

1

LOOKING BACK: HISTORICAL AND THEORETICAL CONTEXT OF PRESENT PRACTICE

Jonathan H. Turner
University of California
Riverside

Monique Borgerhoff Mulder
University of California
Davis

Leda Cosmides
University of California
Santa Barbara

Bernhard Giesen
Justus-Liebig University
Giessen, Germany

Geoffrey Hodgson
University of Cambridge
Cambridge, UK

Alexandra M. Maryanski
University of California
Riverside

Stephen J. Shennan
University College London
London

John Tooby
University of California
Santa Barbara

Boris M. Velichkovsky
Dresden University of Technology
Dresden, Germany

The various social sciences emerged as distinct modes of inquiry in the latter part of the 19th century. Enlightenment thinking about the inevitable march of human progress was coupled with a metaphorical use of concepts and terms from the other established sciences of physics and biology. The transfer of metaphors between areas of inquiry, back and forth and back again, has characterized scholarly discourse on nature, society, and humans. As this volume seeks to demonstrate, this discourse has entered a new, and potentially revolutionary, phase. Yet in the past, images and concepts that described one phenomenon were borrowed as analogies to describe the other. When the discrepancies between the images of such analogies and the objects they were supposed to represent, as well as the implicit values attached to them, became apparent, biology and the social sciences diverged. Thus, the question of the role of biological thinking in the social sciences is as old as the social sciences.

However, the past borrowings from biology by the various disciplines and subdisciplines do not afford a unitary interpretation of evolutionary theory, nor do they display uniformity of impact. As is explored in this chapter, the fate of biological ideas in sociology, anthropology, archaeology, economics, and psychology has been uneven: Sometimes they flourished in a discipline, and other times they languished at the margin. In anthropology and sociology, biological arguments greatly influenced the early phases of these disciplines. Indeed, many ideas from the pre- and post-Darwinian period were incorporated into the emerging conceptual cores of sociology and anthropology. But even in these cases, the influence of biology was to wane, even in fields such as anthropology which, in America at least, had kept its biological wing within the discipline. Other social science disciplines, such as economics, political science, and psychology, have all flirted with biological ideas, but have nonetheless kept them somewhat at the margins. Even psychology, which Darwin had entered and in which physiology and neurology have always been components, has not been greatly influenced by biology until recently. Still, there is a new rapprochement with biology in all of the social sciences. If this new spirit of interdisciplinary inquiry is not to falter, as have past periods of interchange, we need to know something of what occurred in the past, where concepts were borrowed back and forth between the social and biological sciences.

However, more than mere historical curiosity guides this review of the history of interchange between the social sciences and biology. If the current receptiveness to true conceptual interchange is to remain on track, it is important to understand where it went wrong in the past and, perhaps equally important, where it was on track, but somehow became sidetracked and pushed to the margins of a discipline. If we do not know what occurred in the past, we are potentially doomed to make the same mistakes as our scholarly forbearers.

There are additional reasons to be concerned with history. One is that current approaches within the social sciences are still subtly influenced by their past connection to biology, although this connection has often been lost as new vocabularies have been adopted within each of the social sciences. Yet another is to document the loss of early insights that have had to be rediscovered in the present era, and hence, to warn against a similar loss in the future. Another reason to examine history is to reveal that the borrowing of ideas from biology was not just one way. Biology borrowed from the social sciences, as is most evident in Darwin's use of Malthus' essay on population, Hughlings–Jackson's reliance of Spencer's views on differentiation and hierarchy, and, more recently, Maynard Smith's adaptation of game theory to evolutionary equilibria. A final reason to pay attention to history is to learn that the social science disciplines were not always so well insulated from each other, and that if biology and the social sciences are to once again influence each other, the boundaries among the social sciences disciplines need to be reexamined to see what they once had in common.

We need not adopt E. O. Wilson's somewhat arrogant belief that sociobiology would be the basis for the "new synthesis" to recognize that the use of biological ideas within the social sciences may represent an important way to bridge disciplinary boundaries. Hence, there are good reasons to look back at the history of the social sciences and their involvement with biology before we look forward to the creative use of biological concepts and models in the social sciences today.

The purpose of this chapter is not to present a comprehensive history of these disciplines. Rather, it offers reflections by contemporary theorists on the past and current impact of biology in each of their disciplines. The situating of contemporary attempts to bridge disciplinary gulfs between social sciences and biology within their respective contexts is necessary both for understanding the significance of the current foray into what have been embattled territories and for eluding the traps of potential confusion and misunderstanding.

BIOLOGY AND SOCIOLOGY

Jonathan H. Turner, Alexandra M. Maryanski,
and Bernhard Giesen

Sociology and economics share common roots in the work of Adam Smith (1776 [1937]), who posed the central problem that was to guide the use of biological metaphors in sociology as they were blended with Newtonian physics and Enlightenment philosophy. For Smith, the key dilemma of modern society was the division of labor: If societies were to reveal ever more specialization of activities, what force was to hold this

diversity together? A similar question consumed the French Philosophers. In the first decades of the 19th century, Auguste Comte (1830–
1842) merged the British and French wings of the Enlightenment into a
discipline that, in deference to Newtonian mechanics, he initially termed
social physics and later *sociology*. In seeking to forge sociology as a "positivistic" social science, Comte turned to biology. Sociology was to arise
out of biology in the hierarchy of the sciences, and, once developed, was
to inform biology. But aside from superficial analogies between society
and organisms, Comte's linking of sociology with biology seems to have
been primarily a legitimating ploy to make sociology respectable—by as-
sociating it with what was fast becoming the most respected of all the
sciences.

It was Herbert Spencer (1874–1896 [1898]) who systematically incorporated biological concepts into sociology and, in so doing, articulated three lines of biosocial thinking. One was a sophisticated developmentalism, or stage model of human history ranging from simple to complex societal forms. Another was a revived organicism, or the drawing of
analogies between organic and superorganic (societal) bodies. A third
was selectionism, or the view that a driving force behind the evolution of
superorganic bodies was conflict and selection of the fittest. Each of
these modes of thinking about society was to be developed more fully in
the post-Darwinian era, but the seeds for all three were clearly evident in
Spencer's synthetic philosophy. Spencer is a key figure in establishing the
basic way sociologists and other social scientists still use biological and
evolutionary thinking.

Spencer's initial borrowing from biology involved an analogy between the growth of an organism and the development of a society. Before Darwin, evolutionary thinking often focused on how a single cell
becomes a multicellular organism, and hence developmental and evolutionary ideas were often fused. In particular, the embryology of van
Haller, Bonnet, Wolf, and, most important, Karl Ernst von Baer was critical of Spencer's analogy to organismic development. Spencer's view that
societal evolution involves a movement from "homogeneity" to "heterogeneity" was taken from von Baer's work on embryology and cell theory.
It was then blended with notions from physics about "matter," "motion,"
and "force" to form a general "law of evolution" for all domains of the
universe—organic, superorganic, psychological, inorganic, and ethical.
Thus, by employing an embryological, rather than Darwinian, analogy,

Spencer saw, as a process of growth and differentiation, a conceptual emphasis followed by virtually every sociologist since Spencer.

Only well after Darwin did evolutionism become associated with the notion of "descent with modification" through selection processes as these affect heritable variation. With Darwinian theory, the emphasis was on speciation through competition and selection, whereas with pre-Darwinian thinking, the concern was about growth and development. Ironically, the most Darwinian sounding ideas in Spencer's philosophy (i.e., competition and the "survival of the fittest") predate his major scientific treatises on biology (H. Spencer, 1864 1867 [1887]), psychology (H. Spencer, 1854–1855), and sociology (H. Spencer, 1873, 1874–1896 [1898]). As Spencer moved into sociology in the 1870s, he was more apt to emphasize organicism and developmentalism. Yet curiously, it is H. Spencer's (1852 [1888]) early, more philosophical tracts on "survival of the fittest" that are most remembered. Even when H. Spencer (1874–1896 [1898]) employed selectionist arguments in his sociology, these are group-selectionist in tone: Better organized societies are more "fit" and can conquer, annex, and assimilate less organized societies, and thus over the long course of human history, war has been a force in increasing the scale and complexity of societies. In these arguments, societies are the units of competition, selection, and adaptation. This position is still dominant in modern theorizing in sociology that employs selectionist models.

Spencer's other modes of thinking are also still prominent. His analogies between organisms and society ultimately represent the logic of modern functionalism (J. H. Turner & Maryanski, 1979), where a sociocultural part is analyzed with respect to its functions for the operation, maintenance, and adaptation of the larger social whole. In his more functional analyses, which are explored in more detail in chapter 6, he implicitly introduced another kind of selectionist argument: The potential for disintegration or "dissolution" of a population creates selection pressures *for* new kinds of social structures in the absence of density and competition among structures (i.e., selection often works without an existing range of variation on which competition and selection can operate).

Spencer's construction of an evolutionary stage model, where basic types of historical societies are arrayed along an assumed evolutionary continuum from simple to complex, is still the dominant way sociologists think about evolution (e.g., G. Lenski, 1966; G. Lenski, J. Lenski, & Nolan, 1991; Maryanski & J. H. Turner, 1992; Parsons, 1966, 1971; Sanderson, 1990; J. H. Turner, 1972, 1984). Indeed, Spencer's model is by far the best of all the 19th-century models constructed by sociologists and anthropologists.

In the late decades of the 19th century, and well into the first two decades of the 20th-century, some sociological theorizing became intertwined with Darwinian metaphors, although it should be emphasized, once again, that the most prevalent mode of evolutionary thinking in sociology was, and still is, the non-Darwinian stage model, which, it can be argued (e.g., Nisbett, 1969), represents the continued influence of Enlightenment thinking about human "progress" (especially the French who provided the vision of progress for Saint-Simon, Comte, de Tocqueville, and Durkheim, but also the lineage of German idealism from Hegel through Marx and on to Habermas and his disciples in contemporary social theory). Notions of competition and selection were often blended with organicism in Europe, particularly after the widespread translation of Darwin's *The Descent of Man,* published in 1880 (cited in Barnes, 1925). Beginning in the 1870s, Lilienfeld (1873–1881; 1898), Schäffle (1875–1878), and Worms (1896) all sought to extend Spencerian organismic analogies to social systems. Although Lilienfeld went so far as to argue that society *is* an organism, most of these thinkers simply repeated Spencer's views that societies and organisms reveal some common processes (e.g., growth and development, size and differentiation, structural and functional interdependence). These analogies were undergirded by a view of societal development (i.e., growth, differentiation, interdependence, decline, and death) as being driven by competition and selection. True to Enlightenment thinking, scholars like Schäffle could conclude that "the progressing formation of society (civilization) is the highest result of perfecting selection of human struggles for life." (p. 3)

Other Europeans, such as Gumplowicz (1875), pursued a more explicitly Spencerian, geopolitical argument: As humans evolved, they formed heterogeneous groupings, which, inevitably, came into conflict over resources; the conquered were often exterminated, but eventually the state was created for political subjugation; once the state existed, internal conflicts increased, leading to assimilation of diverse groups to mitigate such conflicts. Thus, in Gumplowicz's view, societal evolution had revolved around war, internal conflicts, state formation, amalgamation, and assimilation. Others (e.g., Ratzenhofer, 1881) pursued these ideas, although they saw selection for the political state primarily as a response to internal conflicts.

These approaches all appeared in early 20th-century texts of the first generation of American sociologists (e.g., Ward, 1903; Small, 1905). It was William Graham Sumner's student and colleague, Albert Galloway Keller (1915), who, in his *Societal Evolution*, sought to use Darwinian concepts as replacements for Spencer's ideas about evolution as movement from incoherent homogeneous to coherent heterogeneous. Instead, Keller proposed that notions of variation, selection, transmission, and adaptation should be used in the analysis of societal evolution. Drawing on Sumner's (1906) conception of "mores," as well as his ongoing collaborative work with Sumner (Sumner & Keller, 1927), Keller anticipated modern coevolutionary theory's emphasis on cultural symbols and memes, arguing that certain variations in mores are selected and then transmitted (through imitation and education) when they increase the adaptation of groups (rather than individuals) to an environment.

Accompanying this kind of sophisticated analysis in both Europe and the United States was, unfortunately, a more sinister ideological argument: Social Darwinism (Hofstadter, 1945). Keller's mentor, Sumner (1914), was the most vociferous advocate of the view, initially articulated by H. Spencer ([1852]1888) in *Social Statics* and picked up by Gumplowicz and others in this German–Austrian lineage, that unregulated competition among individuals should be allowed to proceed, sorting out the fittest from the least fit, with inequalities being the natural outcome of this competition and selection. Moreover, to maximize societal fitness, this basic law of nature should not be subverted by uncalled-for social intervention and amelioration. The advocates of eugenics emerged from this ideological movement, and even important figures in genetics such as R. A. Fisher (1930) incorrectly used Spencer's words to propose arguments in favor of "unnatural selection" (or selective breeding of the fit; see chap. 2).

All of these models fell into intellectual oblivion, except for the persistence of the organismic analogy in modern functionalism. Drawing heavily on Spencer's views about size and differentiation, Durkheim ([1893]1933) added an explicitly Darwinian dynamic: Differentiation is the result of competition and selection, which, in turn, are generated by increased moral (rates of interaction) and material (population size, ecological concentration) density. But in human populations, such selection does not lead to the "death" of the less fit, but rather to their differentiation into specialties more suited to their talents. Thus, the driving mechanisms behind evolution from simple to complex structures are niche density, competition, and selection. It is from these Durkheimian metaphors that human ecology as a theoretical perspective emerged in post-World War I American sociology, and it is in this theoretical school that Darwinian thinking exerts the most influence in sociology today.

In essence, there are two levels of ecological work within sociology: At the mesolevel, there is organizational ecology and urban ecology; at the macrolevel, there are societal analyses from an ecological perspective. At the mesolevel, all these models proceed from the assumption that the aggregation of a population generates competition for resources, especially land and space, under conditions of high density or concentration (Burgess, 1925; C. Harris & Ullman, 1945; Hoyt, 1939; McKenzie, 1933; Park, 1916, 1936; Park & Burgess, 1925; Wirth, 1928; Zorbaugh, 1926). Such competition was seen to create a high-velocity real estate market that, reciprocally, fuels competition over land use (McKenzie, 1933), leading to spatial differentiation. Differentiation and competition eventually push the boundaries of the urban region outward (suburbanization) as "less fit" users of space seek less costly land resources.

Later extensions and adaptations of this basic ecological model add some useful refinements (see, e.g., Berry & Kasarda, 1977; Frisbie & Kasarda, 1988), and in many ways, these extensions have obscured the underlying Darwinian dynamic. By contrast, although urban ecology has increasingly obscured its Darwinian-inspired origins, where emphasis is on density, competition, and selection, the other mesolevel approach—organizational ecology—has given special emphasis to these processes and, in fact, has sought to supplement Durkheim's metaphoric use of Darwinian ideas, with the explicit adoption of concepts from bioecology (Hannan & Freeman, 1989).

The units of analysis in Hannan and Freeman's approach are populations of organizations revealing similar forms in terms of their structure of positions, patterns of activity, products and services, norms, and reliance on external resources. A population or subpopulation of organizations in a larger and more inclusive social system is the analogue of a "species" in bioecology because its member organizations evidence similar characteristics and dependence on particular kinds of environmental resources. Following earlier ecological work in sociology (e.g., Hawley, 1950), a basic assumption in their approach is that there is an "isomorphism" between the diversity of subpopulations of organizations, on the one hand, and the variability of resource environments, on the other. This isomorphism between types of organizational structure and configurations of material and nonmaterial resources can be the result of adaptation through learning and reorganization (because organizations are teleological units capable of adaptation to changed circumstances).

Those organizational forms most "fit" in an environment are those whose characteristics place them at an advantage in competition with other organizations for resources in this environment. As a result of their competitive advantage, they are more likely to be "selected" for survival in that resource environment. In their words, "if two populations of organizations sustained by identical environmental resources differ in some organizational characteristic, that population with the characteristic least fit to environmental contingencies will tend to be eliminated" (Hannan & Freeman, 1977, p. 943). Subpopulations of organizations occupy environmental "niches" involving a particular profile or configuration of resources. Those most "fit" to secure these resources will "survive" and those less fit will "die". Or if adaptation and change are possible, they will alter their structure and/or move to another resource niche. Hence, organizations are isomorphic with their environment.

The total level of resources is a crucial aspect of the environment, niches, competition, and selection. The greater the available resources, the less exploited is an environment, and the faster the proliferation of organizational units to secure these underutilized resources. Thus, in expanding resource environments, the number of units in a population of organizations increases. If this expansion of resources creates new niches, or alters the profile of resources in old niches, the level of differentiation ("speciation") among types of organizational units should increase.

New types of organizations face problems of legitimating themselves, however. These problems influence their access to material resources, and hence their survival in a given environment. As a result of growing legitimacy, the costs of founding an organizational form decrease; as costs are lowered, organizational units can proliferate even more. Such proliferation of numbers within a subpopulation of organizations increases their density, with the result that competition and selection begin to rise. Thus, when density is low, legitimating processes are most salient; but as legitimacy is achieved and encourages increases in the number of organizations of a particular type, competition and selection become more significant in shaping the structure of an organization. Therefore, although increased density facilitates legitimacy, it escalates competition and selection. Hannan and Freeman (1987, 1988; see also

Carroll, 1984) employed this logic to predict the pattern of foundings and failures of organizational types. Foundings increase rapidly at an accelerating rate (as a consequence of underutilization of resources in a niche and increasing legitimation) up to the point of high density, when the number of organizations of this type should begin to decline (as a result of increased competition for resources and selection).

This line of ecological work has stimulated many variants (e.g., McPherson, 1981, 1983, 1990), but the essential argument remains the same: Types of organizations are the equivalent of a species in the biotic world. The prevalence or decline of a given type of organization is related to the level of resources in its niche, the density of organizations in this niche, and the resulting competition and selection among organizations in a niche.

Along with the proliferation of urban and especially organizational ecological approaches, there have been efforts to "upsize" ecological theory back to the macrolevel originally pursued by Spencer and Durkheim (Hawley, 1986; J. H. Turner, 1994a, 1994b, 1995). The key figure here has been Amos Hawley (1944, 1950, 1971, 1973, 1978, 1981, 1986) whose early work continued the urban ecological tradition of his mentor, McKenzie (1933). From the beginning, Hawley sought to move beyond the Durkheimian metaphor and, thereby, to incorporate ideas from bioecology into the analysis of the dynamics organizing human populations.

For Hawley, the basic units of human organization are "corporate" units (goal-oriented structures organizing and coordinating individuals' activities) and "categoric" units (classifications of individuals in terms of distinguishable characteristics). Therefore, ecological analysis must explain the dynamics of corporate and categoric units that enable a population to become organized for survival in an environment. In pursuing this explanatory goal, Hawley introduced the notion of "mobility costs" for moving people, material, and information about a population. Such costs are an inverse function of communication and transportation technologies, and they ultimately determine how many corporate units can organize a population. If mobility costs are high, relatively few corporate units revealing little differentiation or spatial dispersion can survive. Because of this, few categoric units can be created or sustained. If a societal system is exposed to information from other populations, it is likely that new technologies will be adopted, thereby lowering mobility costs and increasing the number and differentiation of corporate and categoric units, up to the limits of complexity allowed by a particular type and level of technology.

To the extent that Darwinian ideas are still employed by Hawley, the focus is on how competition for resources affects patterns of growth and differentiation in a population. Population size, density of settlement, and extensiveness of markets all escalate competition for resources, which then increase the number of corporate units seeking resource niches and the number and size of categoric units. Corporate units generate categories (e.g., job classifications, education levels), but more important is the effect of threat arising from competition on the formation of large categoric units (e.g., by ethnicity, region, social class) which can disrupt balances of power. Such potential leads to a complex set of dynamics revolving around co-optation of categoric units into existing networks of power, which, in turn, have effects on the overall level of political regulation among members of a population. The details of this analysis are beyond this brief overview, but to the degree that ecological analysis can be used at a macrolevel of analysis, the focus is on how competition for resources affects balances of power. If competition and selection generate threats to significant numbers of individuals, these threats create large categoric units that can potentially become mobilized as a corporate unit to challenge centers of power.

As the vagueness of Hawley's macrolevel ecological approach testifies, the adoption and adaptation of Darwinian ideas to sociological analysis works best at the mesolevel, particularly for the analysis of competition and selection among types of organizations. Urban ecology is also amenable to this kind of analysis. However, once one moves beyond the narrow forces of the competition for land and space, it becomes more difficult to delineate resource niches, units and populations, and densities, which, in the end, are the key forces behind competition and selection.

Recently, Darwinian-inspired ecological arguments have been extended to new topics. For example, in a vein reminiscent of Keller in the United States, Wuthnow (1987) has sought to analyze the rise and fall of religious movements in terms of variation, competition, and selection among ideologies. In England, Runciman (1989) attempted to reconnect a stage view of societal evolution to a model of competition and selection among the "practices" within units he termed *syntacts*. Syntacts are "carriers of mutant or recombinant practices" that compete for ideological, economic, and coercive advantage, and, in so doing, transform societies.

Both of these approaches are highly metaphorical, borrowing images of Darwinian selection with little precision.

A more detailed (although still analogous) use of Darwinian concepts can be found in several European attempts to reconstruct key problems of social theory in a selectionist way (Giesen, 1980, 1991; Schmid, 1982; Schmid & Wuketits, 1987). Attacking the general evolutionism of the Hegelian tradition, but also the straightforward reductionism of radical sociobiology, these reconstructions treat the Darwinian paradigm as an analytic model that can be separated from its material-biological interpretation and transferred to the domain of sociology. For example, social rules are considered to be the analogues of biological genes; they are recombined in processes of social interaction, and are selected by the particular social situation to which they apply. In contrast to rational choice models of social evolution (e.g., Axelrod, 1984; Boulding, 1978), however, the individual actor and his or her preferences are no longer the reference for processes of selection. The single actor perspective is replaced by a Durkheimian or Hobbesian orientation: A social rule is selected because of its superior ability to cope with the complexity of a given situation. These selectionist reconstructions of classical social theory claim to account for the differences between the material domains of sociobiology and biology—thus leaving the core assumptions of sociological ontology untouched—but also to bridge the gap between the disciplines by an interdisciplinary theoretical heuristic.

In summary, the post-Darwinian period produced a variety of models that were seriously flawed. Because of this, selection arguments receded in sociology. The only persistent Darwinian model has been human ecology, which emerged with Durkheim's adoption and adaptation of Spencer. There has been a recent effort to extend this kind of ecological analysis to ideological competition and societal evolution. The latter effort is reminiscent of models in the late 19th and early 20th centuries, which also sought to connect Darwinian notions of selection to an analysis of the stages of societal development. Yet today the dominant evolutionary model in sociology is primarily a non-Darwinian analysis of societal types in terms of such macrolevel forces as technology, production, power, and inequality, although a recent theory by J. H. Turner (1995) sought to synthesize selectionist and non-Darwinian analyses.

It is in this context that the failure of sociobiology to take hold in sociology must be viewed. Drawing from Fisher, who invoked Spencer, but owing the most basic argument to G. Williams (1966) and others (e.g., Hamilton, 1963, 1964; Trivers, 1971), the essentials of sociobiology in sociology include the following: (a) genes seek to increase their presence in the gene pool, (b) those behaviors that promote fitness (i.e., the capacity to pass on genes) will be selected, and (c) social behaviors and patterns of organization among humans are to be explained in terms of their capacity to maximize the fitness of genes. A few well-known sociologists (e.g., van den Berghe, 1973, 1977/1978, 1981, 1986; Lopreato, 1984) in the United States tried to employ such key ideas in sociobiology as reproductive fitness, kin selection (or inclusive fitness), and reciprocal altruism to sociological phenomena. Indeed, sociobiology is often derided and scorned, but more often it is simply ignored as either extremist or irrelevant to sociology's interests.

There are several reasons that sociobiology has not had great influence in sociology. First, it is seen as radically reductionist, shifting attention from group structures and group selection to individuals and genes. As such, sociologists typically see sociobiology as ignoring those "emergent" sociocultural phenomena that reveal their own dynamics and that require their own modes of explanation. Second, sociobiology is viewed as simplistic, trying to explain complex, emergent phenomena in terms of ideas about genic fitness. Even those who argue that sociological explanations should be simple and parsimonious recoil at the thought of explanations revolving around a couple of extensions of fitness assertions (e.g., inclusive fitness and reciprocal altruism). Third, sociobiology is viewed as producing glib, ad hoc, and easily constructed stories about how a phenomenon promoted genic fitness in the evolutionary past (Maryanski & J. H. Turner, 1991).

For at least these reasons, then, sociobiology has made few inroads into sociology. Although there now appears to be some interest in introducing biological models back into sociology, above and beyond the models of human ecology, it is unlikely that even a more muted form of sociobiology will enjoy much success.

A more recent alternative to sociobiology is a set of approaches emphasizing that cultural phenomena operate in terms of Darwinian principles. Early versions of this argument (e.g., R. D. Alexander, 1977; Dawkins, 1976; Lumsden & E. O. Wilson, 1981) still insist that cultural evolution is highly circumscribed by considerations of genic fitness, and so they are not likely to have much influence on sociology for the reasons noted earlier. Coevolutionary approaches from anthropology, however, have more potential because they only assert that isomorphisms between the processes of biological and cultural transmission can be the basis for constructing theoretical models. Such an approach does not aver that cultural transmission is reducible to genic processes, although a number of coevolutionary approaches propose interactions between genetic and cultural transmission (e.g., Cavalli-Sforza & Feldman, 1981; Durham, 1991). Other approaches, such as the dual inheritance models of Boyd and Richerson (1985), only emphasize that because culture is transmitted, it can be studied employing the same Darwinian *methods* used to study genetic evolution (Richerson & Boyd, 1992).

This emphasis on Darwinian ideas (i.e., variation, competition, selection, and transmission of traits) is as old as Keller's (1915) effort to examine the evolution of mores in Darwinian terms, or as recent as Wuthnow's (1987) analysis of the competition among religious ideologies. (The more general argument that Darwinian dynamics also operate on sociocultural processes echoes the conceptual thrust of the long-running human ecology school.) With the exception of a few scholars (e.g., Hannan & Freeman, 1977; Hawley, 1950), the use of Darwinian ideas has not been very precise; instead, only metaphorical analogies to Darwinian ideas are generally made. In contrast, as is examined shortly in the review of anthropology, coevolutionary and dual inheritance models are more precise, using Darwinian ideas to build elegant models, rather than imprecise metaphors.

In summary, sociology was born as a self-conscious discipline by drawing parallels to biological processes—at first analogies to organisms and later to Darwinian selection processes. Yet despite this early connection, biology has not served as a great source of theoretical inspiration for the discipline, save for human ecology and modern-day functionalism (which has long repressed its roots in the organismic analogy). With a few exceptions, evolutionary models are clearly non-Darwinian, and owe more to Enlightenment thinking about stages of human progress than to Darwinian selection. Part of the reason for this lack of real influence of Darwinian concepts has much to do with the extremes of Social Darwinism and the eugenics movement in the early decades of this century, which caused subsequent generations of sociologists to stay away from concepts and models with such unsavory connotations (see chap. 2). The emergence of sociobiology did not help this situation because of its extreme reductionism (at least in the eyes of most sociologists, see Freese, 1994). Hence, biology has not made significant inroads into sociology in recent decades. Coevolution and dual inheritance models offer some hope for a rapprochement of Darwinian and sociological models beyond the narrow confines of the human ecology school.

BIOLOGY AND ANTHROPOLOGY

Monique Borgerhoff Mulder, Alexandra M. Maryanski,
and Jonathan H. Turner

Sociology and anthropology share common origins, although the concern of anthropology with preliterate cultures increasingly led to the separation of the disciplines, despite the fact that early pioneers such as Radcliffe-Brown and Malinowski saw their work as sociology. Anthropology, at least in the United States, differs from sociology in that biological and archaeological components were kept organizationally attached to the social or cultural wing of the discipline.

This connection of the "physical" side of anthropology to the "social" or "cultural" side created problems during the formative beginnings of the discipline. Before Darwin, the physical side focused on the question of "race" and especially on documenting the biological superiority of white Europeans. Much of the effort to "scientifically" establish the superiority of Europeans focused on the measurment of skulls, postulating that absolute cranial size, narrow or wide skulls, size of frontal lobe, and other features distinguished the races. The leader of this movement, Paul Broca, established the *Anthropological Society* in Paris during the same year that Darwin's ([1859]1964) *On the Origin of Species* was published. After Darwin, and along with the growing acceptance of an evolutionary view, a new justification for such racist thinking emerged: Whites were the most evolved humans, and hence most distinct from apes (with Africans being viewed as the closest). These kinds of arguments were to prove compatible with Social Darwinism, as well as the eugenics movement. As a result, when the racism and ethnocentrism contained in these ways of thinking were destroyed by Boas (1911) and Klinebeg (1935), the use of biological theory to interpret sociocultural processes remained under a cloud of suspicion in anthropology and sociology for several decades.

Parallel to the use of biological theory to buttress the ethnocentrism of white Europeans came the development of stage-model evolutionism in the cultural wing of the discipline. For example, in England Tylor (1871) saw societies as evolving from "the simple savage" to the "complex Englishman." Tylor (1888) also saw a "psychic unity of mankind," in which institutions "succeed each other in a series substantially uniform over the globe, independent of what seemed the comparatively superficial differences of race and language, but shaped by a similar human nature acting through successively changing stages in savage, barbaric and civilized life" (p. 54). In America, L. H. Morgan (1877) echoed these sentiments when he argued that, "since mankind were one in origin, their career has been essentially one, running in different but uniform channels upon all continents, and very similarly in all tribes and nations of mankind down to the same status of advancement" (p. 7). Although these developmental approaches were not blatantly racist, the portrayal of stages in these models suffered from heavily evaluative terms like primitive, savages, barbarism, and civilization. No one questioned the assumption that European society was the most advanced stage of human evolution.

The mechanisms driving movement from one stage to another were not systematically theorized. Independent invention and diffusion were the favorite explanations; for the most part, they did not invoke Darwinian ideas of selection, adaptation, and descent. Some evolutionists focused on particular institutions, like kinship (e.g., Bachofen, 1861) or law (Maine, 1861), as crucial evolutionary forces. Compared to Spencer's model, they seem conceptually and empirically inadequate.

Outside the Anglo-American line, the "culture history school" in Germany, including such scholars as Leo Frabenius, Robert Graebrer, Friedrich Ratzel, and Wilhelm Schmidt, all attacked simple models of unilinear evolution, arguing instead that complexes of culture develop and then diffuse. Instead of "armchair" speculations about straight-line stages of human progress, the contingent and unique history of a culture must be examined.

The ethnocentrism of stage models of evolution and the undocumented assumption that diffusion was a driving mechanism of evolution and cultural history both came under attack from Franz Boas (1911). For Boas, who came to Columbia University in 1896 and trained the first generations of American anthropologists, the goal of anthropology was to describe the characteristics of "each culture" and to reconstruct its history, although the latter proved rather difficult for populations without written records. As Boas pushed stage-model evolutionism and diffusionism to the margins of anthropology, he inadvertently fostered a number of alternatives. First, he helped keep physical and cultural anthropology together in America, ensuring that a nonracist approach to biology could be part of the anthropological approach. Second, his students' interest in the ethos, or *Weltanschauung,* of each culture initiated an interest not just in "culture and personality," but also in cultural transmission processes. The first efforts in analyzing culture and personality were Freudian, later ones less so. But when these died out, the issue of transmission of cultural patterns remained, and it was here that more systematic incorporation of biological models could occur. Third, by rejecting evolutionists' and diffusionists' claims, and by focusing attention on the history of a population as a means to explaining its culture, concerns with the effects of habitat, environment, and ecology began to increase, especially because history was impossible to reconstruct among preliterates, and this set the stage in later decades for cultural ecology and, eventually, more sociobiological approaches. Finally, without stages of evolution or diffusion as an explanatory tool, a door was opened for functionalism to be incorporated into anthropology.

The last development reinvigorated an approach that was dying in sociology by the turn of the century. In fact, had Radcliffe-Brown and Malinowski not turned to functional explanations, this approach would have died with Durkheim (J. H. Turner & Maryanski, 1979). In saving functionalism, the organismic analogy was kept alive. With Malinowski (1944), biological needs for survival, or what he termed *vital sequences,* were the "primary needs" on which social structure is first built, later to be supplemented by emergent, "derived needs" that came when structure and symbols are elaborated. But Malinowski and later Parsons (1951) made biological forces once again a parameter of sociocultural organization.

By the middle of the century, the biological models were more systematically incorporated into cultural anthropology, as the explanatory power of alternative approaches seemed limited. Leslie A. White (1959) sought a return to stage-model evolution in a much more sophisticated form, and suffered for his efforts by heated critiques from the Boasians. It was perhaps Julian Steward (1955) who made the connection between evolutionary biology and cultural anthropology. Influenced by his training in evolutionary biology, Steward proposed that the environment, together with the technological achievements of the social group in question, determine the payoffs to various patterns of human action. Hence, a modern, if somewhat loosely defined, notion of adaptation lay at the heart of Steward's account of cultural change. Like his intellectual forbears, however, Steward never came up with a clear explanation or precise mechanism for adaptive optimization that linked material conditions to cultural change. As noted by Bettinger (1991), this is reflected in his tendency to downplay materialist considerations as he became increasingly concerned with the study of cultural change.

The evolutionary core of cultural ecology was incorporated into two schools of American anthropology emerging in the 1960s: (a) the reincarnation of functionalism in a more ecological guise (e.g., Vayda & Rappaport, 1968), and (b) the rise of cultural materialism (e.g., M. Harris, 1979). Proponents of the former theoretical persuasion, in particular, borrowed models from biology (e.g., Wynne-Edwards, 1962) and ecology (e.g., Odum, 1959). However, the opportunity for a genuine transfer of Darwinian ideas between the biological and social sciences occurring at that time was again lost, primarily because of the excessive reliance of the functionalists on group selection and systems theory—concepts that were already losing credence within biology in the 1960s. As many have discussed in detail (e.g., Orlove, 1980; E. A. Smith; 1984), this newer functionalism was as riddled with tautology as were the older functionalism of Spencer and Durkheim and the mid-century functionalism of Malinowski and Radcliffe-Brown.

Hence, the rise of evolutionary ecology and sociobiology within anthropology in the late 1970s ironically owes much more to the insights of Steward than to the more recent, and more explicitly biological and ecological, schools of neofunctionalism and cultural materialism. Informed by a neo-Darwinism emphasizing individual-level selection, as well as a host of new theories developed for the study of foraging, nepotism, reciprocal altruism and parental care, several anthropologists began to pursue functionally inspired ecological work (e.g., R. D. Alexander, 1979; Chagnon & Hames, 1979; E. A. Smith, 1984).

The introduction of sociobiology into anthropology occasioned hostility for reasons now well rehearsed (e.g., Caplan, 1978; Sahlins, 1976). These revolved around two issues: the conflation of scientific matters with ideological ones, and the legitimacy of hypothetico-deductive and deterministic approaches within anthropology. Analysis of the disputatious exchanges within anthropology reveals that, in a very real sense, the implications of sociobiology for anthropology were misunderstood. There was widespread confusion (e.g., M. Harris, 1979; Sahlins, 1976) over whether conventional theories of economics, culture, consciousness, learning, and rationality generated alternative or compatible hypotheses with those of sociobiology. This arose, in part, because of (a) a general aversion to evolutionary thinking, associated no doubt with the notorious excesses of Social Darwinism; (b) a poor specification of the causal roots whereby evolutionary processes might influence human behavior (Kitcher, 1985); and (c) disagreement among sociobiologists as to the implications of cultural influences on behavior (e.g., Daly, 1982).

Yet sociobiology, and especially the closely related fields of human behavioral and evolutionary ecology, presently holds a legitimate position within anthropology (Cronk, 1991; L. Lieberman, 1989; E. A. Smith, 1992). This position can be attributed to four principal factors. The first is that anthropology as a discipline has long been concerned with cross-cultural variation as arising from adaptation to different environmental challenges. Although Steward had a somewhat loose definition of *adaptation*, at least compared with that of modern evolutionary biologists, he saw the adaptation of behavior to ecological contingencies as lying at the heart of sociocultural evolution. Therefore, one of the central tenets of evolutionary ecology was not entirely foreign to anthropologists. Furthermore, archaeologists, many of whom were committed to a comparative, materialist, evolutionary stance, were receptive to some of the branches of adaptationist reasoning, especially optimal foraging theory (e.g., Bettinger & Baumhoff, 1982).

The second reason that sociobiology, and in particular behavioral and evolutionary ecology, has met with some success within anthropology is its empiricism. Stimulated by early field and comparative studies (e.g., R. D. Alexander, 1979; Chagnon & Irons, 1979; Daly & M. Wilson, 1983; Symons, 1979; Winterhalder & E. A. Smith, 1981), a host of empirical work that tested sociobiological and evolutionary ecological hypotheses accumulated throughout the 1980s (Borgerhoff Mulder, 1988a). These focused on two areas: (a) mating and parental behavior, with detailed investigations of such old anthropological chestnuts as marriage, family, inheritance, mate choice and nepotism (e.g., Betzig, Borgerhoff Mulder, & Turke, 1988); and (b) resource acquisition, with studies on foraging, food sharing, and territoriality (e.g., E. A. Smith & Winterhalder, 1992a). This empirical work makes an increasingly significant contribution to contemporary anthropology. Inspired by a variety of theoretical frameworks, authors not only utilize the data and codes developed by sociobiologists (e.g., D. R. White, 1988), but test hypotheses derived from cultural ecology against those of sociobiology (e.g., E. A. Roth, 1993). Appreciation of the empirical contribution of sociobiology is fostered, in part, by the broader reaction against antiempiricism, so prominent within anthropology these days, and against the deconstructionist stance of critical theorists. Indeed, the situation in contemporary anthropology is reminiscent of C.P. Snow's *Two Cultures* (see Carrithers, 1990; Lee, 1992). In the current, somewhat hostile antiscience climate, then, empirically oriented anthropologists unite in getting down to the business of exploring diversity and testing hypotheses, as recent volumes of the journal *Current Anthropology* attest.

The third factor contributing to the gradual acceptance of Darwinian thinking was that the early sociobiological position papers emphasizing neo-Darwinian individual-level selection dovetailed quite nicely with the pioneering work of Barth (1967) and Britain's Manchester School. Barth and his followers explicitly focused on how political organization emerges from the decisions made by individual actors operating under different constraints. This methodological individualism developed into rational choice theory (Elster, 1986). Like evolutionary ecologists, rational choice theorists draw their models from neoclassical economics; they also generally assume that actors are both selfish and rational. Evolutionary ecologists rely heavily on rational choice theory as providing a mechanism for adaptive optimization (E. A. Smith & Winterhalder, 1992b), because it is through such individual choices that predictable behavioral outcomes occur in different social and ecological contexts. Finally, and undoubtedly more contentiously, evolutionary ecologists suspect that the preferences that individuals express for options with high payoffs ultimately depend on a history of natural selection.

The fourth factor that has already contributed somewhat to the success of sociobiology within anthropology is the challenge raised by evolutionary psychologists. As discussed in chapter 7, the causal factors whereby evolutionary processes might influence human behavior have been rather poorly specified by sociobiologists, generating considerable misunderstanding among critics over how sociobiological theories articulate with those of ecological anthropology, cultural ecology, and psychological anthropology. Humans were predicted to behave "as if" they were maximizing their fitness, with little or no consideration of how they reached the optimal decision. Hence, with the amendment of evolutionary psychology (see chap. 6), sociobiological analyses may extend their analytical objective from that of the actor's acts to that of his or her goals, beliefs, and motives. In addition, early studies paid little attention to the constraints on optimality, either phylogenetic, psychological, or environmental. As an understanding of such constraints develops, sociobiological theory should become more acceptable to anthropologists (see also Harpending, Rogers, & Draper, 1987).

In summary, sociobiology and the related fields of evolutionary and behavioral ecology have done much better in anthropology than in sociology. The reasons for this success include: (a) their power in exploring what is, in effect, the *raison d'être* of sociocultural anthropology—diversity—through their reliance on concepts that were not entirely foreign to anthropologists—adaptation and strategic behavior; (b) their strong empirical bent, attractive at least to the "antiscience" anthropological coterie in these times of heady postmodernism; (c) their close links with methodological individualism and rational choice theory; and (d) their increasingly sophisticated treatment of mechanism, causality, and constraint.

Early sociobiologists recognized that genes may not be the only replicators driving the evolution of smart animals. For example, Richard Dawkins (1976) hedged his bets in the last chapter of *The Selfish Gene*, as have many contemporary sociobiologists in recent years. Dawkins posited a "new replicator" that he termed *memes*. The basic tenets of sociobiology—genic selection, inclusive fitness, and reciprocal altruism as these produce strategies and "survival machines" for genes—can explain how humans came to exist, but culture begins to supplement and supplant biology as the major replicating mechanism. Memes are those new cultural units that exist inside brains and that, via socialization, are passed on and preserved in a "meme pool." Dawkins recognized that meme evolution will now begin to accelerate, because, "once genes have provided their survival machines with brains which are capable of rapid imitation, the memes will automatically take over" (p. 21). It might even be possible for memes to rebel against their creators—the selfish genes. Similarly, other biologically oriented social scientists have begun to talk in terms of "coevolution," operating at both the genetic and cultural levels.

As noted in the discussion of sociology, coevolutionary approaches all emphasize that evolution involves Darwin's emphasis on descent with modification, in which a set of elements is related by inheritance. In coevolutionary approaches, this process of inheritance operates at both the biological and sociocultural levels, and thus biological and sociocultural evolution are guided by similar evolutionary processes. Yet the isomorphism with biological forces varies in different coevolutionary approaches. For some (e.g., Durham, 1991), biological evolution is but one type of a more general evolutionary process that also includes cultural evolution. For others (e.g., Boyd & Richerson, 1985, 1990), biological processes can provide the conceptual leads to develop distinctive models for understanding the evolution of traits in sociocultural systems. There are also differences in how much the biological and cultural inheritance systems influence each other. For some who remain sympathetic with sociobiology (e.g., R. D. Alexander, 1979; Lumsden & E. O. Wilson, 1981, 1983), much sociocultural inheritance is circumscribed by biology. For others much less committed to sociobiology (e.g., Boyd & Richerson, 1985; Cavalli-Sforza & Feldman, 1981), the two systems of inheritance—the genetic systems of biology and the traits of sociocultural systems—are distinctive, although understandable with similar models emphasizing variation and selection processes. Boyd and Richerson were the first to use the term *dual inheritance*, in connection with the development of a more detailed set of models to explain cultural transmissions (see chap. 10). Because culture is transmitted, it can be studied using the same Darwinian methods employed to study genetic evolution (Boyd & Richerson, 1992; Durham, 1991, 1992).

Perhaps because of the maintenance of the biological component in anthropology, along with the long flirtation with functionalism, the recent application of biological ideas has proceeded furthest in cultural anthropology. Although sociologists have rejected the extremes of sociobiology and have remained largely indifferent to coevolutionary models, these approaches have provided a new theoretical spark to anthropology, which, as a whole, has become atheoretical and antiscience. Into this vacuum has swept biology, whereas in the other social sciences, the existence and acceptance of non-biological theories have kept biological ideas at the margins.

BIOLOGY AND ARCHAEOLOGY

Stephen J. Shennan

Like many other subjects, archaeology began to emerge as an academic discipline in the 19th century, in an intellectual environment heavily influenced by the evolutionist ideas of such authors as Spencer, Darwin, and L. H. Morgan. One of its most important roles was to document the history of progressive civilization—visible, for example, in the technological succession from Stone through Bronze to Iron Age. However, these evolutionary concerns did not last, or, rather, they became transmuted. As knowledge of archaeological material increased, it came to be seen that enormous geographic variation existed, and a concern with documenting the stages of human progress gave way to an interest in the explanation of this variation. The result was an "ethnic" model of the prehistoric past in which regional differences were seen as relating to different peoples, and changes were largely explained in terms of their migration. Those peoples seen as expanding over the widest area were held to be representatives of "races" which were successful in the process of evolutionary competition. Many of those involved in archaeology, however, simply jettisoned virtually all theoretical baggage and studied the material for its own sake, but with an emphasis on defining culture areas and tracing cultural traditions.

Outside the Soviet Union, it was only in the 1960s and 1970s that evolutionary ideas returned explicitly to archaeology. This was the result of North American neo-evolutionary anthropology, and especially the work of L. A. White (1959) and Steward (1955). White's legacy, via the enormous influence of his student, Elman Service, was an archaeological emphasis on progressive social evolution, and especially the rise of the state. Steward's ecological anthropology viewed this process as arising from the overcoming of adaptive challenges, especially those posed by an increasing population size. These concerns, although still current in some archaeological research, have been widely rejected since the beginning of the 1980s. The first published sign of dissatisfaction from a Darwinian point of view was Dunnell's (1980) paper, which suggested that a selectionist perspective provided a more appropriate theoretical framework for archaeology than the progressive models derived from L. A. White (1959) and Service (1962). The latter lacked convincing explanatory mechanisms. Since then, there has been a steadily growing interest in such selectionist models, closely connected to their development in anthropology more generally.

In fact, one can review the whole history of archaeology from a Darwinian perspective, although it is not usually done. The late 19th and early 20th centuries interest in describing and explaining regional cultural history and its variations can be seen as a concern with tracing the history of descent with modification. However, the approach paid no attention to adaptive processes. The neo-evolutionary archaeology of the 1960s and 1970s discarded the study of descent with modification in favor of a concern with adaptation, based on an implicit notion of group selection within a functionalist framework. This position was subsequently criticized by Gould and Lewontin (1979) and Elster (1983) among others. In neo-evolutionary models, the motor for change or the reasons for stability came from the "environment," broadly construed, to which past populations responded.

The 1980s saw attempts to reunite the two strands of descent with modification and adaptation from a more rigorously selectionist perspective. This meant a new concern with cultural transmission, on the one hand, and with the specification of costs and benefits in social interactions, on the other, especially in the context of conflicting interests.

An example of such a cost–benefit model is Kohler and van West's (1992) study of the emergence and disappearance of food-pooling cooperation in the North American southwest A.D. 900–1300. Given a situation in which agricultural production is variable, both spatially and temporally, they showed by an analysis of harvest size in relation to the marginal utility of the product to consumers that it would be in the interest of individual households to share food when average production was high, not when it was low. They then used detailed climatic records as a proxy measure for variation in agricultural production, and showed that evidence for sharing, in the form of aggregations of population with storage facilities, was largely restricted to periods favorable to agriculture, suggesting that, when conditions deteriorated, households defected from the arrangements and the pooling system collapsed. However, a model based entirely on the self-interest of the participants generates patterns in the settlement of the region, in terms of aggregation and dispersal, which correspond closely to those actually found. The success of such a self-interest model is, at first sight, surprising in the light of the ethnographically known patterns of social organization in the southwest, which are strongly group-oriented. However, there is also a contrast in settlement processes. Although the period from A.D. 900-1300 was characterized by cyclical patterns of aggregation and dispersion, since that time, aggregated village settlement has been uninterrupted in the areas actually occupied. The reason for this, Kohler and van West suggested, was the emergence of new sharing rules emphasizing village-level activities, combined with new sanctions against defection.

Studies like Kohler and van West's are in many ways an obvious step from the previous functionalist adaptive concerns. But since the discrediting of culture history in the 1960s left cultural transmission without a viable theoretical framework, it had not been on the archaeological agenda. In this respect, the key development of the 1980s has been the emergence of "dual inheritance" theory (especially Boyd & Richerson, 1985;

Cavalli-Sforza & Feldman, 1981), with its account of the mechanisms of cultural transmission and the factors affecting these mechanisms. This approach has a considerable number of implications for archaeology, both in its study of the history of changing material culture and more generally.

In the first place, it is clear that archaeologists will have to change their whole approach to the study of their material. In the past, archaeology has been based on the construction of "types,"—archetypal forms or essences seen as existing in the minds of the makers, reproduced in the real world, and therefore subject to its contingencies. Thus, the reality is the "mental template" and the variation is so much noise, which may be ignored in the type definition. In the light of transmission theory, the concern with essences now has to be replaced by a conceptualization in terms of populations of traits affected by selection and by nonselective processes such as drift and linkage.

An example of a study based on such an approach is that by O'Brien and Holland (1992), who examined the changing frequencies of grit, shell, and limestone tempered vessels from the North American midwest during the later Woodland period. Initially, grit was the most common type of temper, although other materials were occasionally used as well, including limestone and shell. For about 300 years after its first appearance, shell remained a minor component of the temper before suddenly increasing A.D. 900–1000 and taking over as the predominant temper type. It appears that shell enhances the workability of the flood plain clays of the region, which were the raw material for pottery throughout the period, but until A.D. 900 were largely tempered with grit. Shell also increases the strength of the pot, as well as being a better preventer of cracks during firing. However, use of shell temper requires the control of firing temperatures below 700°C. Once the ability to control firing temperature was achieved, shell tempering spread rapidly. In this case, we see a process of descent with modification operating on pottery tempering, leading via a selective process to changes in the frequencies of the different temper types in the population as a whole. In effect, once firing temperatures could be controlled, a process of directly biased transmission led to a rapid increase in the use of shell tempering, as potters perceived the successful consequences of the use of this material by others and therefore adopted it themselves. Thus, shell tempering is an adaptation for strength, stability, and facility in handling pottery. That is, selection occurred for these functional consequences of shell tempering, and it was adopted preferentially as a direct result of the selection process. Therefore, we have a postulated "causal history" (S. D. Mitchell, 1989), in which the mechanisms are derived from the experimental technological study of pottery, and the phenomenon is identified by the observation of differential patterning in frequency changes in temper use through time.

Other recent studies have used dual inheritance theory in a much more generalized manner. In a recent article on the role of ritual in foraging societies, Aldenderfer (1993) has suggested that ritual appears to have an analogous role to reciprocal altruism and kin-based reciprocity, in that it produces group functional behavior that may be advantageous in competition between rival groups by virtue of creating and maintaining a conformist tradition. However, there are pressures in the opposite direction because all societies contain inequalities and individuals will compete for prestige and status. This is satisfactory if there is a means to escape the stresses that may arise, but under conditions of circumscription, stresses may be created that threaten both individual and group benefits. Ritual may be called into question if existing practices cannot cope with new conditions. If individuals find that their expected benefits from participation in ritual do not appear, or the costs begin to exceed the benefits, this may lead to the emergence of cultural variants modifying existing ritual practice, and to a situation where group-level selection is no longer protected from the effects of individual selection. In these circumstances, those who hold ritual power may lose it, and the prestige that goes with it, and those who have been cooperating face the loss of group-level benefits. Aldenderfer went on to explore the possible implications of such a situation, particularly as they concern the ability of holders of ritual power to extend it in other directions. On this basis, he proposed a model of social change that has ritual as its core.

Aldenderfer's (1993) study dealt with a broader subject of greater general archaeological and anthropological interest than that of O'Brien and Holland (1992), but did so at the expense of specificity, at least as far as the evolutionary models are concerned. Dual inheritance theory provides little more than a general theoretical framework that offers an interesting slant on the topics being examined (see C. S. Spencer, 1993, for a study that is rather similar in this respect). Additionally, there is always a danger, that Aldenderfer avoided, of slipping back into the sloppy adaptive functionalism of the 1960s and 1970s. Moreover, although he dealt with a topic of archaeological importance, he did not actually use archaeological data.

Archaeological data by their very nature provide little information about the mechanisms of transmission processes. This must come from experimental and ethnographic studies in the present. Nevertheless, as O'Brien and Holland's (1992) study shows, patterns can be distinguished in the archaeological record that can convincingly be argued to arise from some specific processes rather than others. Such studies can be made more rigorous by the application of mathematical/computer-based modeling techniques, rather than informal comparisons.

Furthermore, the archaeological record provides the only long-term record of the histories of cultural descent with modification and the factors that may have influenced it. The question is, how much interest do these histories have if they remain exclusively at the level of documenting changing temper use in prehistoric pottery? In recent years, archaeology's claim to be a subject of general interest has lain in its efforts to produce a history of society. But what is largely missing from recent evolutionary models is the social, which has been squeezed out between the cultural and the genetic.

What follows is a sketch of some links between social and cultural processes, and an indication of some ways in which they might be investigated archaeologically. Any model of such processes has to take into account the fact that people's interests and the "interests" of their cultural attributes do not necessarily coincide. Cultural traits are not just aspects of people's phenotypes as interactors, but have their own "life" as replicators (see S. D. Mitchell, 1987). As is seen here, archaeology can provide information about both the replicators and the interactors, although some of the discipline's unsuccessful research programs in the past arose from a failure to distinguish the two. The starting point of this sketch is some recent work in anthropology and in the analysis of cooperation processes.

Brunton (1989) developed an argument for the cultural instability of egalitarian societies based on Woodburn's distinction between "immediate-return" and "delayed-return" foragers. Recent ethnographically known hunter–gatherer groups who operate immediate-return foraging systems tend to be strictly egalitarian, in that there is an automatic entitlement to equality of social outcomes. This is in contrast to "other acephalous societies, such as those in Melanesia, where equality has to be earned through fierce competition, which inevitably results in a substantial degree of de facto inequality" (Brunton, 1989, p. 673). Egalitarian societies, which are very unstable in their group membership, also tend to be culturally fluid, Brunton argued—susceptible to acculturation, and relatively limited in their collective representations. This arises because of the structural nature of genuine egalitarianism because it can never provide a basis for ensuring a correct version or interpretation of that which is communicated. Any attempt to distinguish what is valuable and what is not requires an act of evaluation, which implies inequality. To the extent that evaluation, and exclusion on the basis of evaluation, takes place, egalitarianism is compromised. To the extent that egalitarianism is thoroughgoing, such cultures can be little more than heaps of randomly associated elements, whose persistence is always fortuitous (Brunton, 1989).

On this view, authority relations are necessary for the transmission of culture, and egalitarianism can only be maintained by according little value to cultural products, which indeed accounts for the general indifference to such products in the egalitarian societies discussed by Brunton. In fact, the rarity of such societies is not surprising because they are weak in political terms, and they have no basis to defend their values against the cultural subversion of egalitarianism. This may or may not matter to the human groups concerned, although if such egalitarian arrangements do persist, it raises interesting questions about the factors that make this possible. It may be that group fluidity is more important than continuity.

Delayed-return economies, whether agricultural or based on foraging, involve returns on labor that take place over a considerable period of time and require long-term claims on resources and relationships, including systems of rights and obligations. Furthermore, "inter-generational inequality, as well as inequality between household heads in terms of power, wealth and status are commonly present" (Brunton, 1989, p. 674). In these circumstances, group continuity is important. Such circumstances are also ideal for some degree of coherent cultural continuity, in that the inequalities present provide a basis for necessary cultural evaluation processes. Moreover, group membership is longer lasting, and thus provides a better basis for the consistent transmission of particular sets of cultural practices (Braun, 1991).

Nevertheless, even allowing for the greater tendency toward group continuity implicit in delayed-return systems, the possibility of group fission in the face of cooperation problems is always present, with potentially undesirable consequences. Simulation studies of the maintenance of cooperation in the face of social dilemmas have shown that it will be pro-

moted in situations where individuals have a long future expectation of
cooperation, and where groups have structures that are fluid but hierarchical, not necessarily in the manner of a conventional social hierarchy,
but in the sense that members of a large group do not interact equally
with one another. They interact closely with members of a small group,
and small groups interact with one another via representative individuals
and organizations (Glance & Huberman, 1993). This corresponds closely
to the notion of "sequential hierarchy," coined by G. A. Johnson (1982).

Groups based on such forms of organization tend to be perpetuated
through time more successfully than those that are not. At the same time,
their particular sets of cultural practices are also successfully perpetuated.
Furthermore, those practices that are conducive to group continuity are
more successful, creating a positive feedback loop in favor of group continuity and social practices that encourage it. But group continuity is not
the only relevant factor. There is also the question of the positive and negative social evaluation of particular practices as discussed by Brunton.
Even if group continuity is an important aspect of this, it requires some
notion of inequality among group members as to who are the arbiters of
these standards—often older males. Here again, positive feedback loops
can develop. For example, existing inequalities connected, with the operation of delayed-return foraging systems could be associated with cultural evaluation, and the prestige and status of these arbiters could increase
as a result of their role as guardians of cultural tradition. At the same
time, those practices are likely to be more successful, and thus more conducive to increasing the arbiters' prestige.

The group continuity loop and the prestige/status loop are potentially
incompatible with one another. The unbridled expansion of prestige and
associated inequality may be detrimental to some group members' interests, and thus can lead to group fission (see Aldenderfer, 1993). Furthermore, although both group continuity and the growth of prestige are positively associated with the propagation of cultural practices through time,
the factors involved may be different. The kinds of attributes successfully
replicated by virtue of their prestige may not particularly require group
continuity for their replication, nor will they necessarily be restricted by
group boundaries; speed of spread may be an alternative to group longevity. How the implications of such incompatibilities play themselves out
over time is a contingent process: The extent to which regularities are
present at a larger scale than microlevel transmission and interaction processes remains an open question.

Archaeology as it is currently practiced could potentially throw a great deal of light on the history of such processes, but has not yet been used for this purpose. In the first place, it provides an extensive record of the spatial and temporal distributions of a great range of material cultural attributes. These were the raw material of the cultural history discussed earlier, but from the current point of view they provide information on the transmission/replication history of the material attributes concerned. However, to make use of this information to investigate the social inter-action–cultural transmission mutual causal processes discussed earlier, one must also have information about the social life of the interactors, as well as the history of the replicators. In the last 30 years, the kind of ar-chaeology concerned with documenting the history of social evolution—in the sense of the emergence of different types of society—has made a great deal of progress in the reconstruction of prehistoric social and econ-omic organization. Its methods and results can be used in the kinds of in-vestigations that a Darwinian approach to cultural transmission and the factors affecting it require; important aspects of the lives of social inter-actors can be reconstructed.

One example is the study of prestige and social inequality. In certain regions at certain times, the presence of individual inhumation burials with varying quantities and qualities of grave goods makes it possible to infer patterns of social differentiation and link certain items with people of higher status. The higher status individuals may also have had differ-ent living conditions, as evident from the results of various kinds of sci-entific analysis of their bones. Once one has inferred that certain items are associated with prestige or higher status and others are not, one can examine their spatial distributions and see how these vary. It is clear that types associated with prestige in general have far wider distributions than those that are not. However, they also tend to have shorter life spans, in the sense of the length of time they are in circulation before they fall out of use. In the specific case of later prehistoric Europe, it is clear that some of these differences are associated with gender. The majority of prestige items with wide distributions are linked to males rather than fe-males—a situation that raises interesting questions concerning different "strategies" for replicative success in male and female cultural attributes; female attributes may be favored by group continuity and male ones by the growth of prestige. It is of some interest in this connection that the Neolithic and Bronze Age prehistory of Europe shows broad patterns of periods when localized patterns of cultural variation seem to be dominant, alternating with others when widespread distributions are more apparent. The success of female versus male cultural propagation may be relevant to this, but this is only one of many issues on which a Darwinian perspective can potentially throw light.

In conclusion, however, it is worth commenting on an issue that, at first sight, seems far removed. One of archaeology's least satisfactory, but most tenacious, theoretical assumptions—deriving from its cultural historical origins—has been its assumption that "cultures" equal "peoples." This view is now attracting renewed interest as a result of such nationalistic developments as those following the collapse of the Soviet Empire. The application of a Darwinian approach to archaeology, in which interactors are distinguished from replicators and archaeological distributions are examined in the light of the complex interplay between them, is of relevance not just to the development of the theory itself. It is also relevant to the capacity of archaeology as a discipline to avoid becoming an ideology for nationalists seeking historical legitimation by projecting their "peoples" into the prehistoric past through their identification with archaeological distributions.

BIOLOGY AND ECONOMICS

Geoffrey Hodgson

Adam Smith, the founder of modern economics, was more influenced by Newtonian physics and astronomy than by biology. Nevertheless, there are traces of the biological metaphor in his works (A. Smith, [1759] 1976a, [1776]1976b). The most important example is his central use of the concept of the "division of labor," which was coined by Mandeville (1970) in his *Fable of the Bees* to represent the division of types and tasks in the hive. The idea is passed on directly to Smith and the classical economists, and from there to sociology, where it became the central metaphor for the organismic analogy and for the emphasis in functional sociology on growth and differentiation.

In addition, Thomas Robert Malthus was affected by visions of the natural world. On the first page of his *Essay on Population* (1798), Malthus observed the "crowding and interfering with each other's means of subsistence" among plants and animals. Such considerations about nature influenced his thinking about political economy. Given the Malthusian influence on Charles Darwin, it is appropriate to suggest that some proto-evolutionary ideas traveled from biology to Malthus and the social sciences, only to return later and influence Darwin and biology in a refined form. Moreover, there is no doubt that Malthus' essay influenced Herbert Spencer's ([1852]1888) political essays and his first book, *Social Statics*, where the phrase "survival of the fittest" was used. Indeed, in the preface to *On the Origin of Species*, Darwin ([1859]1964) cited and credited Spencer's work. Thereby, the early development of the natural sciences and economics involved substantial interdisciplinary dialogue.

Overall, however, the influence of pre-Darwinian biology on economics is not that pronounced. The single major exception is Alfred Marshall, who was profoundly influenced by the biology of Herbert Spencer (Hodgson, 1993a, 1993b; Thomas, 1991). This influence is evident in his direct adoption of the Spencerian law of evolution as involving increasing heterogeneity, which Spencer took from von Baer, and in his widespread adoption of the idea of "use and disuse," which Spencer took from Lamarck.

Marshall made a distinction between "economic statics" and "economic dynamics," indicating that, like Comte before him, the metaphors of classical physics were appropriate for the former and biology for the latter. His *Principles of Economics* (1890) concentrated largely on statics, and he planned a second volume to explore the dynamic aspects. Unfortunately, this was never written.

The example of Marshall's appeal to biology is thus an ironic one. Much more than his contemporaries, he saw the limitations of the mechanistic metaphor, and perceptively saw biology as providing a more appropriate alternative. Yet his work remained almost entirely in a static and mechanistic mode, even when he found inspiration in biology, it was in the rather mechanistic and pre-Darwinian ideas of Spencer, whose law of evolution blended simplistic views of Newtonian mechanics with organismic growth and development.

The most important influence of Darwinian evolutionary theory in economics was on Thorstein Veblen (1899, 1919). Just before the end of the 19th century, Veblen (1898) asked in a famous article: "Why is economics not an evolutionary science?" In asking this question, Veblen made a direct appeal to biological science for inspiration, but subsequently, and until very recently, his example has rarely been replicated.

Veblen saw the evolutionary metaphor as crucial to the understanding of the processes of technological development in a capitalist economy. He explicitly characterized his own economics as post-Darwinian, and argued that economics should embrace the metaphor of evolution and change, rather than the static ideas of equilibrium, which had been borrowed by the neoclassical economists from physics. Veblen had two primary reasons for the adoption of a Darwinian and evolutionary metaphor. One relates to the idea of cumulative causation and an opposition to depictions of the economic process that are consummated in equilibrium. The other is based on the formation of analogies to both the gene and the processes of natural selection in the social world. He stated, "The evolution of social structure has been a process of natural selection of institutions" (Veblen, 1899, p. 188).

However, Veblen was faced with a biology at a stage of development at which the mechanisms of evolution were only partly understood. Consequently, and given his own personal aversion to intellectual "symmetry and system-making" (Veblen, 1919, p. 68), there was little chance that Veblen would be able to build an economic theory on the Marshallian scale. Yet Veblen was relatively successful in establishing the basis of Darwinian economics. First, his principle of "idle curiosity" became the ongoing source of variety or mutation in the evolutionary process. Second, the institution became the unit of relative stability and continuity through time, ensuring that much of the pattern and variety is passed on from one period to the next, so that selection has relatively stable units on which to operate. Third, mechanisms are identified through which well-adapted institutions are imitated and replicated, and the less adapted become extinct, analogous to the "struggle for existence."

Hence, a principal component of this achievement is its embodiment of the idea of the cumulatively self-reinforcing institution as a unit of evolutionary selection, subject to the procedures of mutation and selection. The nature of the evolutionary process governing these elements is selective rather than purely developmental, and phylogenetic rather than simply ontogenetic. Veblen's writings stand out as the most successful attempts, at least until the 1970s, to incorporate post-Darwinian biological thinking into economics and social science.

For a long period after the deaths of both Marshall and Veblen in the 1920s, biological and evolutionary ideas made limited impact on economics. Arthur Pigou and other inheritors of the Marshallian tradition regarded the use of biology as an idiosyncratic diversion. Institutionalists such as John Commons echoed Veblen, but little attempt was made by subsequent institutionalists to develop the links between economics and biology. Strikingly, this is true for Joseph Schumpeter as well, although

Schumpeter is celebrated today as a mentor of evolutionary economics, and his name is explicitly connected with its modern developments. However, Schumpeter's own notion of economic evolution is distanced explicitly from evolution of a biological kind, and excludes any suggestion of a Darwinian process of selection (Schumpeter, 1939, 1954).

The most important subsequent use of Darwinian ideas in economics was by Alchian (1950), with his adoption of the idea of "natural selection" in theory of the behavior of firms. This was subsequently developed by Friedman (1953) in an effort to support the neoclassical hypothesis of profit maximization. Later, other economists (e.g., Williamson, 1975) appealed to the idea of competitive "natural selection" in an attempt to support the notion that survival means efficiency. No doubt, these modes of analysis influenced, and were influenced by, the emergence of organizational ecology in sociology, where the unit of analysis became populations of organizations in a resource niche (Hannan & Freeman, 1977).

The most important recent work on the application of ideas of evolutionary selection to economics is the pioneering volume by Nelson and Winter (1982). Although the authors described this work as "Schumpeterian," its explicit use of biological analogies puts it closer to Veblen, and perhaps Hayek, than Schumpeter. This volume is mainly responsible for a revival of evolutionary economics in the 1980s and 1990s.

Another recent influence of biology is found in the work of Friedrich Hayek. Although traces of Hayek's evolutionism can be found as early as the 1930s, it did not appear in a fully developed form until the 1970s (Hayek, 1982, 1988). Hayek's employment of evolutionary thinking is largely used in support of a pro-market and noninterventionist policy stance.

Despite these incursions from biology, the influence of biology on economics remains on the fringes. This conclusion is particularly apt for sociobiology which has had little impact on economics, although there are a few exceptions. The first is the work by contemporary economists Becker (1976), Hirshleifer (1987) and Tullock (1979). They proclaimed themselves "economic imperialists," and declared that common "economic" principles bind biology to economics. These principles include scarcity, self-interest, and competition. The Becker–Hirshleifer–Tullock school saw these ideas as universal and applicable to both the economic and biological spheres. The inspiration drawn from sociobiology is that the process of natural selection should result in the emergence of something like "rational economic man," providing the bridgehead for the maximizing postulates of economics across to biology and other social sciences.

There is a second instance where sociobiology has interchanged ideas with economics. Evolutionary biologists such as John Maynard Smith and others have made use of game theory, which was originally developed in economics by von Neumann and Morgenstern (1944). Notably, after developing the concept of an evolutionary stable strategy within game theory, this concept was then transferred back to economics in the work of Sugden (1986).

In many ways, the Becker–Hirshleifer–Tullock arguments are redolent of the Social Darwinists, and many of the earlier criticisms of this current are still relevant in regard to this contemporary work. However, such criticisms are rarely made. Furthermore, the postulated link between economics and sociobiology is ignored by most economists because they simply assume the existence of individual preference functions, without trying to found them on any theory, including that provided by sociobiology, as well as those found in psychology, sociology, and anthropology.

An important exception, however, is the work of Hayek (1982, 1988). His work is more interdisciplinary, and he is a strong advocate of the preeminence of cultural, rather than genetic, evolution. His criticism is essentially that cultural evolution works much more rapidly than genetic evolution and swamps its effects. Other rare criticisms are found in the work of Witt (1991). Still, given that most economists take individual preferences as given, and explicitly reject any inquiry into the processes governing their formation, it is a matter of little importance to them as to how they are determined, whether by genes or by culture. Accordingly, thus far dual inheritance or coevolutionary approaches have had little impact on economics (see Boyd & Richerson, 1985). Although biology offers no ready-made solutions, it provides a metaphor that has to be employed with discrimination and care. In particular, the idea of a hierarchy of levels and units of selection seems to be eminently transferable to economics and the social sciences in general through the incorporation of hierarchies of habits, routines, and institutions. Although economic analogies to units mechanisms and processes of evolution are limited, they can be applied to socioeconomic evolution in a nonreductionist way.

BIOLOGY AND PSYCHOLOGY

Leda Cosmides, John Tooby,
Jonathan H. Turner, and Boris M. Velichkovsky

The founders of scientific psychology, Wilhelm Wundt and William James, saw it as "the science of the mind," although today one would have difficulty reconciling this early vision with what has become a large and highly diverse discipline. Decades before Wundt and James, Herbert Spencer wrote the first of his scientific treatises, *Principles of Psychology* (1854–1855), where he first utilized a non-Darwinian, progressive principle of evolution that was to be more fully developed later in *First Principles* ([1862]1898). Here, too, emphasis was on the mind, or the "mental faculties," of organisms as they became more complex in the course of progressive development. Although this work was indifferently received and soon passed into obscurity, such universities as Cambridge and Harvard used *Principles of Psychology* as a text in the 1870s and 1880s. Yet, unlike economics and sociology, psychology developed as a discipline primarily after Darwin, and indeed, unlike other social sciences, Darwin himself ventured into the field. Thus, the history of Darwinism in psychology began with Darwin, as did the controversy about whether the theory of evolution by natural selection and other biological conceptions could be applied to psychology.

One of the most productive fields of interaction of these two disciplines has become neuropsychology, which investigates the brain's mechanisms for psychological processes. Although the term *neuropsychology* was introduced into scientific discourse as late as 1949 (Hebb, 1949), the majority of important discoveries, theoretical insights, and actual controversies in the field goes back to the second half of the 19th century. Under the direct influence of Spencer's ideas on the evolution of the brain in a series of steps, each of which brought about the capacities for new forms of behavior, the English neurologist John Hughlings-Jackson (cited in Taylor, 1959) worked out (in hundreds of case studies dispersed across medical journals of that time) a theory of the functional hierarchy of the brain's functions. He differentiated three such phylogenetic levels, from the spinal cord to the frontal cortex. The latter level of this hierarchy was described as responsible for the highest psychological functions, such as conscious monitoring of activity, thinking, and personality. This was a modern conception both from the point of view of contemporary scientific psychology as well as biology. It proposed that the entire period of human evolutionary existence could be considered as the "age of the frontal lobe" (Deacon, 1992; Tilney, 1928). Another aspect of his theory, which makes it very modern, was Jackson's insistence that every major part of the brain is involved in a specific activity (e.g., language), with each part making some unique contribution to such distributed across the whole of brain processing (see Kolb & Whishaw, 1990).

Yet, more mechanistic views dominated the scene. By the beginning of the 20th century, psychological textbooks were filled with almost unrestricted speculations about dozens of specialized "centers" within the brain and interconnections among them. These views were especially supported by Broca's and Wernicke's discovery of a relatively narrow "language core area" around planum temporale of the left cerebral hemisphere (see e.g., Kolb & Whishaw, 1990; Luria, 1980, for further discussion). A more or less deliberate splitting of neuropsychological mechanisms into "centers" (or "modules," as they might be called today) was a reproduction of ideas from phrenology, leading to a direct classification of human abilities and personality traits in the topography of the brain.

Since Descartes, educated opinion was quite willing to hold that the physical body was a machine, subject to physical law, and that animals were automatons. It was mental phenomena, such as reason, emotions, goal-seeking, language, and culture, that were believed to exist only in humans, and hence were separated off by religious belief and Cartesian dualism into the extranatural domain of the soul, the mental, and the psychical (Descartes, 1977). In contrast, like Spencer before him, Darwin believed that mental faculties were explicable in the same evolutionary terms that accounted for the origin of species and the acquisition of their physiological characteristics—a position that even Alfred Russell Wallace, co-originator of the theory of natural selection, was not willing to endorse. In fact, by 1904, Wallace had become convinced that human mental faculties required supernatural explanation (Wallace, 1904). If human mental processes represent an essence or spiritual agency that make them qualitatively different from physical processes, then there would be an abyss between the mental and the physical that evolutionary explanations could not bridge (Darwin, 1873). To convince a disbelieving world, Darwin had to refute this dualistic claim.

The form that Darwin's argument took had a large impact on the history of evolutionary thought within psychology. There are two interwoven threads of explanation in Darwinism: (a) phylogenetic explanations emphasizing descent, and (b) adaptationist explanations stressing selection. That is, some take an "evolutionary perspective" to mean a *phylogenetic* perspective, or the search for phylogenetic continuities implied by the inheritance of homologous features from common ancestors. Others take an "evolutionary perspective" to mean an *adaptationist* perspective, or the search for niche-differentiated adaptive design created by natural selection. Phylogenetic and adaptationist analyses are both components of an evolutionary approach, and both have value, but their relative validity may depend on which psychological mechanism is being investigated and at what level. Adaptationist approaches are often more appropriate for investigations at the cognitive level, whereas phylogenetic approaches are often appropriate for investigations at the neuroscience level (Tooby & Cosmides, 1989c).

One would expect both strands of Darwin's thought to be represented in theories of psychology. Instead, insofar as psychology has been Darwinian at all, the adaptationist thread has been largely ignored. Only phylogeny has been given an important explanatory role. This is a legacy from Darwin himself; he was trying to combat the dualist idea that the human mind was composed of different "stuff" than the physical body, rendering it exempt from evolutionary explanations (see Fridlund, 1992, for discussion). For example, in *The Expression of the Emotions in Man and Animals* (Darwin, 1873), Darwin showed how expressions of anger in humans were similar to those in other primates—mere tweaks on a basic design. He argued that these similarities only made sense if they were forged by a common descent—by a close evolutionary ancestry. Obviously, a phylogenetic approach was necessary to convince skeptics that minds were part of the natural world, and therefore subject to natural selection. Adaptationist analyses could not help him make this point because they tend to emphasize qualitative differences between the minds of different species. The dualists were already convinced that human minds were qualitatively different from those of other animals; an adaptationist approach would only have added fuel to the dualist fire (Degler, 1991).

This emphasis on phylogenetic analyses of the human mind gave rise to what became known as the "doctrine of mental continuity." Drawing inspiration from Darwin, animals were anthropomorphized while humans were "zoomorphized" (Krementsov & Todes, 1991). Little difference was seen between animals and humans, with human behaviors being observed in animals and vice versa. Thus, toward the latter third of the 19th century, such scholars as Romanes, Lubbock, Brehm, Lewes, Fouchet, and others drew analogues and asserted homologies. For example, Romanes (1898) posited a long list of emotional states common to humans and animals. These sentiments were echoed in others such as Sutherland (1898), who postulated even longer lists of homologies between animals and humans. By the turn of the century, one could find a plethora of popular publications that posited such things as judicial and educational systems, states, factories, arts and crafts, families, and war among nonhuman animals (Krementsov & Todes, 1991). Although popular for a time, such analogizing soon fell into disrepute as the study of behavior in both animals and humans became more precise and specialized.

At the birth of experimental psychology in the 1880s, there were a few adaptationists. The most famous were William James and William McDougall. In their view, the human mind is a collection of "faculties" or "instincts": complex, functionally specialized mechanisms, each of which evolved to solve a different adaptive problem, some of which are qualitatively different from the faculties of other animals. Nevertheless, most experimental psychologists of the time were phylogeneticists. In fact, by the 1920s, Darwin's doctrine of mental continuity had been over-literalized by most experimental psychologists into the idea that the minds of humans and other animals exist on a linear continuum, with only quantitative differences in their capacities—different sized memory stores, different proficiencies in forming associative links between stimuli, and so on (see Hodos & C. B. G. Campbell, 1969; Lockard, 1971, for a critical discussion of this issue; see Macphail, 1987, for a postbehaviorist defense of the doctrine of mental continuity).

The adaptationist faculty psychology of James and McDougall did not catch on. James admired the German experimental psychology of his day, but had no taste for it himself, so he did not leave a legacy of empirical research implementing his program (or students trained in such). McDougall's views were dismissed for reasons that appear largely political (Cosmides, 1979). W. James' (1890) *Principles of Psychology* and McDougall's (1908) *Introduction to Social Psychology* seem modern today because they advocate what cognitive scientists such as Chomsky (1980) and Fodor (1983) call a "modular view of mind." James and McDougall both thought that: (a) one can precisely characterize the mind, and not just behavior; (b) the mind is a collection of complex, functionally specialized mechanisms, or what Chomsky calls *mental organs* and Fodor calls *modules;* (c) these specialized mechanisms—these "instincts"—make learning possible; and (d) human thought and action are so flexible because these instincts are sophisticated and large in number. Yet James and McDougall lacked a good language for describing the mind. Hence, it was easy for critics to argue that "mind" was a woolly concept that had no place in a science of behavior, which should restrict itself to analyzing the relationship of publicly observable stimuli and responses (a view lent philosophical support from the logical positivists). Critics also argued that too many instincts were being posited, violating the principle of parsimony (a version of parsimony that was derived from physics, not biology). In addition, they argued that there was no sound basis for positing one instinct rather than another, and that every time a new behavior was observed, a new instinct was posited to explain it (Dunlap, 1919, 1922; G. C. Field, 1921; Kuo, 1921).

There was certainly something to this last criticism. First, faculty psychology was developed before the "modern synthesis" of the 1930s (the melding of Mendelian genetics with natural selection theory). The modern synthesis gave birth to more precise techniques for identifying and analyzing adaptive problems, which were not available to James and McDougall. So, when they were writing, the implications of Darwin's theory and genetics were not as clear as they are now. Second, some of McDougall's followers did seem to abuse his approach by making up instincts willy-nilly. This was perhaps an unfair criticism to raise against McDougall, who tried to define empirical criteria for positing an instinct, which included converging lines of evidence from physiology, comparative psychology, and psychopathology.

McDougall's dialectical opponent became John B. Watson, the founder of the behaviorist school of psychology. Watson scoffed at the mentalism of introspectionists and viewed their methods as unscientific. In essence, Watson was arguing that the mind has neither inherent content nor functionally specialized faculties or instincts. All mental content derives from the external world, via an associationistic process of learning that links stimuli with responses. These processes are "equipotential": i.e., they do not privilege some stimulus response pairings over others. As a result, it is equally easy to link any stimulus with any response. Differences between people in personality and ability will ultimately prove traceable to different histories of conditioning. According to Watson, Pavlov (1960) in Russia and Thorndike (1932) in the United States had discovered the only "mental" processes that humans and other animals possess: A process that causes classical conditioning and a process that causes instrumental (i.e., operant) conditioning. Because humans and other animals all learn via these two simple general-purpose processes (he argued), one can get more insight into human behavior by studying rats, pigeons, and other animals; after all, the contingencies of their environments can be experimentally controlled in a way that is not possible (or ethical) with human subjects.

With its rigid and overliteral insistence on Darwin's doctrine of mental continuity, behaviorism dominated experimental psychology in America from the 1920s to the 1970s. Paradoxically, this view, which had its roots in Darwin's arguments for phylogenetic continuity, fostered a deeply anti-Darwinian belief that learning and environmental influences somehow insulate behavior from evolutionary shaping and analysis (Boakes, 1984; Skinner, 1953). Most psychologists thought that, aside from the insight that human learning is continuous with animal learning, the theory of evolution could do nothing to illuminate human behavior. Antimentalism and the equipotentiality assumption became the two pillars of behaviorism.

Watsonian behaviorism was made even more radical in the 1950s by Skinner (1953), who declared that the "mind" should be treated as a black box. No statements about the structure of the mind should be made—in principle, characterizing mental processes as associationistic was as philosophically forbidden as claiming that the mind contained instincts, faculties, memory images, or emotional processes. All that was needed for a science of behavior was the reinforcement history of an organism and the phylogenetic history of a species, which provided it with its "genetic endowment"—most notably, the ability to be classically and operantly conditioned.

Several schools of thought (all European in origin) challenged American behaviorism, and all of these schools have links to evolutionary and biological thought. These schools were (a) the Berlin branch of Gestalt psychology, (b) the cultural-historical school of Russian psychology, (c) the genetic epistemology of Jean Piaget, and (d) the ethological school developed by Niko Tinbergen and Konrad Lorenz.

Gestalt psychology may have been the most important school of psychological science in the first half of the 20th century. Its leading figures (e.g., Wertheimer, 1925; Köhler, 1947; Koffka, 1935) were physicists. They attempted to use concepts and methods of contemporary physics for the analysis of psychological problems. Basically, they operated with the notion of fields of forces, applying methods of subdisciplines of physics such as crystallography and thermodynamics. This was an overtly antilo-calizationist approach: "The whole is more than the sum of its parts." At about the same time, Lashley (1963), a neurologist deeply influenced by Gestalt psychology, performed a series of neurological experiments on animals that persuaded him that there is a lack of any narrow localization of psychological functions within the neocortex. He introduced the term *equipotentiality* into psychological literature.

Another American student, influenced by this European school, was Gibbson (1979). After many ingenious studies demonstrating context de-pendency of our perception of the world, Gibbson concluded that the or-ganization of environmental context (not any type of learning, as in be-haviorism) is the main determinant of our subjective perception of ob-jects within the environment. Gibbson founded a school called *ecological psychology*. One of its methodological postulates is: "Do not ask what is inside of your head, but ask what is your head inside of" (Mace & J. James, 1977).

Vygotsky (1985) and Luria (1932) in the Soviet Union discovered another grave limitation of behaviorist analysis. Devoted followers of an evolutionary approach (broadly construed), they stressed the importance of cultural, not just physical or biological, environment for all so-called "higher psychological functions." Compared with natural (i.e., genetically determined or acquired in the course of conditioning) functions, the higher psychological functions, such as deliberate recollection or purposeful problem solving, are under conscious control and include his-torical "tools" as mediated components. They argued that the sociocultu-ral environment supports human behavior and cognition. All these high-er, culturally mediated psychological functions are specific only to hu-man beings, and hence it is at this point where continuity ceases to exist. In his neuropsychological work, Luria (1980) showed that these higher psychological functions rely heavily on the mechanisms of phylogeneti-cally new, prefrontal parts of the brain. Luria (1970) and Bernstein (1947) proposed modern versions of levels classifications, more detailed than in the case of Hughlings-Jackson, but following the same evolution-ary design. Recently, similar approaches have also been proposed within experimental psychology and cognitive science (see Lockhart & Craik, 1991; Velichkovsky, 1994, for an application of the levels approach to the problems of cognitive psychology).

Piaget considered himself a biologist, studying the ways in which or-ganisms adapt to their environment (Boden, 1980). Seeking a middle ground between Lamarck and Darwin, between empiricism and rationalism, between behaviorism and Gestaltism (Boden, 1979; Piaget, [1940]1967), Piaget proposed that organisms can adapt to their environment because they possess two very general processes: assimilation and accommodation. According to Piaget, these innate processes are evolved adaptations that guide learning (among other things), and all animals have them in one form or another (phylogenetic continuity), operating uniformly across a wide variety of domains and causing cognitive development to proceed in discrete stages. Piaget thought the resulting mental structures and the processes that govern their transformation could be characterized precisely. But Piaget, like James and McDougall, lacked a convenient language for doing so. When the cognitive revolution provided a convenient language for talking about the mind, Piaget's views gained influence. But before that time, Piaget was relatively ignored by the American behaviorists, who dismissed him as a mentalist.

The ethologists, by contrast, played a major role in the demise of American behaviorism. Tinbergen (1951) and Lorenz (1965), who eventually won the Nobel prize for their work, argued that an animal's behavior should be studied in its natural habitat. Natural selection theory says that form follows function, and therefore the only way one can understand the form a behavior takes is to see what adaptive function it fulfills in that animal's niche. Different animal species have different niches; consequently, different species can be expected to have evolved different functionally specialized, psychological mechanisms (e.g., different instincts, reflexes, fixed action patterns, imprinting processes, etc.). Ethological demonstrations that animals possess functionally specialized mechanisms challenged the behaviorist assumption that learning mechanisms are equipotential (e.g., Lorenz, 1965; Tinbergen, 1951). In an article entitled "The Misbehavior of Organisms," which was a play on the title of Skinner's book, *The Behavior of Organisms,* K. Breland and S. Breland (1961) declared the ethologists were right. The Brelands' attempts to train animals using classical and operant conditioning were constantly foiled by the animal's "instincts"—its functionally specialized adaptations.

This latter finding sent shock waves through the behaviorist community, but experimental psychologists did not seriously question the equipotentiality assumption until it was decisively shaken by Garcia and Koelling in 1966. Using classical conditioning, they showed that it is difficult—perhaps impossible—for a rat to learn to avoid flavored water, even when it receives an electric shock immediately after tasting it. Yet in just one trial, the rat can learn to avoid the flavored water when tasting is followed by (experimentally induced) nausea, even when the nausea occurs 2 hours after the flavored water was tasted. During the 1970s, evidence against the equipotentiality assumption kept accumulating. By the end of the decade, the equipotentiality assumption was virtually dead in the field of animal behavior (Herrnstein, 1977).

Thus, the first pillar of behaviorism was seriously damaged. The second pillar—antimentalism—was destroyed by the advent of the computer. Computers are physical systems that process information, but they can parallel (although usually in a very modest way) human cognitive processes that cause reasoning, memory, knowledge, skill, judgment, choice, purpose, problem solving, foresight, and language. The computer is an existence proof: "Mental" activities can occur in a physical device, with no need to posit spirits, souls, or ghosts in the machine. One can characterize its data structures and the internal processes that transform them with precision. As computers became more common—and psychologists began to understand what these tools in their laboratories were capable of doing—behaviorist arguments against mentalism began to ring hollow. Finally there was a convenient and precise language for describing mental phenomena: the language of information processing, which is used to describe what a computer does. One has described the "mind" when one has described what the brain does in information-processing language. Cognitive psychology was born. Several of its paradigmatic texts, such as *Cognitive Psychology* by Neisser (1967), were published in the 1960s.

The equipotentiality assumption became increasingly questioned after the cognitive revolution was well under way. The new cognitive psychologists were primarily interested in "higher" mental processes, which were presumed absent from other animals. Moreover, they associated studies of animal learning with the dreaded behaviorism. As a result, they paid little attention to the animal behavior literature, which was exploding with ethological and evolutionary critiques of the equipotentiality assumption. They also ignored the game theoretic analyses of the evolution of social behavior, which began pouring out of biology departments in the 1970s, traveling under names such as *sociobiology* and *behavioral ecology* (Hamilton, 1964; Krebs & N. B. Davies, 1984; Maynard Smith, 1982; Trivers, 1971, 1972, 1974; G. Williams, 1966). While the cognitive psychologists were not looking, the study of animal behavior became an adaptationist discipline.

The recent adaptationist approach involves a return to concern with the organization of "mental faculties" evident in James' and McDougall's approach. But this time around, efforts are informed by the modern synthetic theory of evolution and the implications of the information sciences spawned by the advance of computer technology. Thus, over the last two decades, a growing number of cognitive scientists have realized that general-purpose computational systems with no inherent content are weak problem solvers. Consequently, many are now arguing that the mind must contain a large number of complex, domain-specific, functionally specialized computational mechanisms: modules, mental organs, or instincts (for discussion, see Chomsky, 1980; Fodor, 1983; Marler, 1991; Pinker, 1984, 1994; Pylyshyn, 1987; Tooby & Cosmides, 1992). At the same time, animal behavior researchers have been trying to educate cognitive psychologists about the considerable body of research demonstrating that functionally specialized cognitive adaptations are ubiquitous in the animal world (e.g., Carey & R. Gelman, 1991; Gallistel, 1990; Rozin, 1976). This line of evolutionary psychology proposes that theoretical analyses drawn from evolutionary biology can guide the search for complex, functionally specialized cognitive adaptations in humans because they can provide a way of deciding what kind of modules, mental organs, or instincts are likely to have evolved (see, e.g., Barkow, Cosmides, & Tooby, 1992).

However, this search for functionally isolable (but not necessarily spatially located) units of processing in the mind and brain has not remained without criticism. An approach within artificial intelligence (i.e., "connectionism") has formed an important theoretical school of contemporary psychology and related fields. Connectionism is based on the theory of parallel computation and adaptation effects in large neural networks (McClelland, Rumelhart, & PDP Research Group, 1986). This is a different type of computation than is typical of a common computer. The latter, a serial processing model, brought about the paradigmatic metaphor of the symbol information-processing models of cognitive psychology.

Modules can, of course, operate in parallel, and there are some modular connectionists (e.g., Jacobs, Jordan, & Barto, 1990). But connectionism as a form of equipotential empiricism has run into the same problems as its behaviorist and associationist precursors (e.g., Pinker & Prince,

1988). As a result, much recent work in connectionism assumes more domain-specific architectures. Nevertheless, the interactionism of distributed parallel processing has led some neuropsychologists to reject the more "modular" theories of the last two decades (Farah, 1993; Hinton & Shallice, 1990; but for an apparent reversal of her position, see Farah, K. Wilson, Drain, & Tanaka, 1995). This can be considered the legacy of Hughling-Jackson, Lashly, and Luria, insofar as they all stressed the coordination of the functioning of different "blocks" of the brain.

Also, the Vygotskian cultural-historical approach, with its insistence on cultural determination of specifically human psychological processes, has gained in international and interdisciplinary importance (see Scribner & Cole, 1991). An interesting outgrowth of increased concern with cultural/historical context has been a new approach called *cognitive culture theory*. Advocates of this approach have been trying to link cultural processes to the domain-specific architecture of evolved cognitive mechanisms (Atran, 1990; Boyer, 1994; Hirschfeld, 1996; Sperber, 1996; Tooby & Cosmides, 1992).

It is impossible to tell where these trends will lead. Darwin had hoped that his theory would eventually reveal the design features of the human mind. Neuroscience and genetics now possess powerful methods that are increasingly applied to solving psychological problems. In a more theoretical vein, Gestalt psychology, cognitivism, and, recently, the connectionist movement have followed the same path: They have bridged the gulf separating the mental, biological, and physical worlds, and have provided new languages for characterizing the mind more precisely. The mental has become a part of the landscape of natural causation, where the theory of evolution by natural selection can be brought to bear. Thus, the stage may be set for the development of a psychology that will be more aware of its own natural foundations.

CONCLUSION

Biological thinking was intimately intertwined with each of the social sciences at their respective inceptions. Much of this early influence involved borrowing images from physics and biology, and, in some cases, borrowing back ideas from social discourse that had been expropriated by the natural sciences. Yet after this promising connection among the "life sciences"—both biological and social—each discipline failed for a time to utilize evolutionary theory as it developed in the latter decades of the 19th century and the first decades of the 20th century. In sociology and anthropology, H. Spencer's ([1852]1888) metaphor about "the survival of the fittest" along with Darwin's ([1859]1964) emphasis on "natural selection," created widespread suspicion of biology when used to justify Social Darwinism and eugenics. (Interestingly, sociologists and anthropologists embraced radical equipotentiality—which promises that human wants and beliefs are arbitrary social constructions that can be easily molded by social engineers into any form determined by the rulers of a society. Yet such theories were used to justify repression and genocide by Marxist regimes in (for example) Cambodia, China, and the USSR. Why these theories were not considered equally morally suspect for the genocides they "legitimated" remains a mystery, which will have to be addressed by future historians of science.) Biology kept a foothold in anthropology via the "physical" side of the discipline, whereas Darwinian metaphors in sociology were sustained via Durkheim's influence on urban ecology and later organizational ecology. In economics, Adam Smith's borrowing back from biology of the notion of division of labor and Veblen's advocacy of evolutionary economics were lost as the application of metaphors from physics and engineering—first articulated by Smith, but given substance by Pareto (who, ironically, later abandoned such mathematical formalisms for sociology)—came increasingly to push biological metaphors and then institutional considerations out of economics in favor of a narrow focus on market dynamics and equilibrium processes. In psychology, the early adaptationist implications of James' and McDougall's work were lost, somewhat because of Darwin's emphasis on continuity, but primarily because of the rise of behaviorism.

Each discipline has now begun to entertain biological ideas. Anthropology and, relatedly, archaeology have been the most influenced under the impact of sociobiological, dual inheritance, and coevolutionary approaches. Economists have started to incorporate ideas from evolutionary biology and evolutionary psychology into their theories and models (e.g., Cosmides & Tooby, 1994; Frank, 1988; Hirshleifer, 1987; Hoffman, K. McCabe, & V. Smith, 1995; Posner, 1992; Romer, 1993; Rothschild, 1992). Sociology has, by and large, rejected sociobiology, but has expanded on the ecological model first proposed by Durkheim's adoption of Darwin's idea of natural selection. Among psychologists, there is a growing interest in evolutionary psychology, and especially in basic questions about the universal architecture of the human mind.

It is unclear what the future holds. Within the natural sciences, physics, chemistry, biology, geology, astronomy, and other disciplines peacefully coexist, without fear that one discipline will "swallow" another. But for most of the 20th century, the social sciences have not shared a similar sense of equanimity. Aside from the movements discussed above, these disciplines have regarded biology (and one another) with a certain degree of paranoia. This trend may not continue, however. One possibility is that the various social sciences will adopt some biological ideas and reject others, in a piecemeal way, invoking evolution (and psychology) only when it is required to solve a specific problem within the discipline. Another possibility is that psychologists will fully incorporate evolutionary concepts into their work, recognize the relevance of research from the other social sciences and, as a result, develop an ever more detailed map of the evolved architecture of the mind. If so, then models of this evolved cognitive architecture may assume increasing importance in economics, sociology, and anthropology which, after all, make many assumptions about human nature and human decision-making. In this possible future, the various disciplines within the biological and behavioral sciences will work together, in a mutually reinforcing way. We cannot, however, rule out a very different scenario: one in which the traditional rejection of such a synthesis prevails in the social sciences, and biological ideas are either ignored, or applied in a purely methaphorical way.

2

SHIFTING BOUNDARIES BETWEEN THE BIOLOGICAL AND THE SOCIAL: THE SOCIAL AND POLITICAL CONTEXTS

Peter Weingart
University of Bielefeld
Bielefeld, Germany

Sabine Maasen
Max Planck Institute for Psychological Research
Munich, Germany

Ullica Segerstråle
Illinois Institute of Technology
Chicago

Most of the agitation over and resentment against sociobiology is triggered by the conviction that the biological explanation of human behavior, and thus of cultural facts, is, at best, a category mistake and, at worst, represents the ideological sin of "biologizing." In fact, the emotional intensity of the debate can only be explained by strong value commitments apparently underlying the positions taken. The debate over sociobiology and, more generally, the legitimate or illegitimate use of biological categories in social science discourse is evidently as much a political as a scientific one.

To regard the "biologization" of social facts as illegitimate, first of all, presupposes that a distinction between the "natural" and the "social" is available, and, second, that violating this distinction is injurious. The differentiation between "natural" and "social" phenomena and the establishment of "social facts" as an independent subject matter of a scholarly discipline dates back to roughly the turn of the century, when sociology became recognized as a separate subject of teaching. (To limit the account by this criterion is justified on the grounds that only afterward could the issue of "right" and "wrong" concepts arise. This is not to deny, of course, that notions of nature and society existed long before.) Altogether, the differentiation of biology and sociology is an extended process, and closer examination reveals the interplay and transfer of concepts and models used to describe nature and society.

The negative connotation evoked by biological concepts that describe and explain social phenomena is even more recent. Although "evolutionism" and Darwinism, in particular, were originally associated with social progress, and therefore hailed by the political Left, the negative evaluation of Social Darwinism and its association with reactionary politics began to be established in the 1930s, when the combination of a crude Social Darwinism and racist theories served to justify antisemitic and eugenic measures. This was particularly true in Germany where it culminated in the Holocaust. In his 1945 *Social Darwinism in American Thought*, American historian Richard Hofstadter was perhaps the first author to make a point of the conclusion drawn from this experience: that biological ideas "are utterly useless in attempting to understand society," and that "the life of man in society, while it is incidentally a biological fact, has characteristics which are not reducible to biology and must be explained in the distinctive terms of a cultural analysis" (Hofstadter, 1945, p. 176).

Since then, that historical experience is taken to be proof of the connection between attempts at "biologizing" man and society on the one hand, and a specific sociopolitical context on the other. However, equating biological arguments with conservative and/or reactionary politics rests on the assumption that the former are used to legitimize the latter, or on the equally nebulous assumption that biological arguments can only thrive, or are brought about, in such contexts. Although this may have been the case at a particular time in history, the link between reactionary politics and biological concepts and models in social thought cannot be generalized in this way.

The following analyses in the spirit of a (historical) sociology of knowledge and discourse, respectively, aim to show that the boundaries drawn between such seemingly obvious categories of the "natural" and the "social" are by no means fixed, objective, and unequivocal. Rather, it can be shown that they shift in the course of history and are dependent on the context of values and the development of political and scientific discourse.

To prevent a misunderstanding that this perspective seems to initiate, two points must be addressed explicitly. It is possible to show that scientific knowledge is always associated with social and political values, and that this relationship is ambiguous and subject to constant change. But from the vantage point of such an analysis, it is not possible to take sides at the end for the "better science." The decision that science (or scientific knowledge) is superior ("true") to that which is considered "ideological" ("false") is a product of an ongoing discourse—of a constant rearrangement of social interpretations and applications. Even when knowledge seems to be fully institutionalized, it is never eternally fixed. To look at the debates over where the boundary between the "natural" and the "social" are to be drawn requires the analyst to remain one step removed.

The first part (with the focus on Germany) traces the history of what used to be called *social biology*. This history explains, to a large degree, when and why certain value judgments—such as Hofstadter's—have become associated with efforts to apply biological categories to society and social phenomena, and how these have shifted over time. The analysis is extended (with the focus on the United States) to tracing reactions to modern sociobiology in a climate pervaded by post-World War II environmentalism. An examination of the positions taken in the "sociobiology debate" questions the contention that there is a direct link among scientists' scientific views, political convictions, and the social consequences of their theories.

The second part consists of a case study of female sexuality that refocuses the argument. Just as there is no one-to-one relationship between scientific positions and political convictions, so there is none between scientific positions and the social values attached to them. By revealing different disciplinary interpretations of female orgasm in different social contexts, the analysis demonstrates how a "biological" phenomenon—sexuality—is disavowed, constituted, and explained, depending on how disciplinary boundaries are drawn and social roles and values are designed.

FROM "SOCIAL BIOLOGY" TO "SOCIOBIOLOGY"

Peter Weingart and Ullica Segerstråle

A. Designs of a "Social Biology"—1860–1945

Ambivalence of Meaning and Interpretation. Darwin is said to have been astonished by the rapid acclaim that his *Origin* found in Germany where the first translation was published (1860). However, the response of the scientific community had been more cautious than that of popularizers of scientific ideas (Kohn, 1965). The difference between scientific and popular reactions to Darwinism point to a special feature of the German context, compared with France and Britain. Politically fractured, with a liberal revolution crushed, the intellectual expectations for progress were as high as they were frustrated. The belief in science in general, and in scientific materialism, in particular, came to assume the function of a popular ideology in a highly literate society. This was documented by the large amount of popular science journals with a fairly large readership, as well as countless popular science books.

In this setting, Darwin's theory of evolution was immediately interpreted as a *Weltanschauung*—one competing with others, notably with Christianity. Haeckel, Darwin's most prolific popularizer in Germany, was only one of many authors to point out that Darwin's theory had a profound impact on the ruling *Weltanschauung,* and would affect everybody's personal, scientific, and social views (Haeckel, 1863). This does not mean that Darwin was given a uniform reading. On the contrary, his work was taken to support many positions, as Kelly (1981) noted: "Materialists, idealists, aristocrats, democrats, conservatives, liberals, and socialists, as well as protagonists of virtually every shade of religious opinion, all staked out their claims in Darwinian territory" (p. 7). But the common denominator of all these accounts was that science was the ultimate authority to which any side of the ideological spectrum could appeal.

The apparent ambiguity of Darwin's work, with respect to the interpretative interests prevailing at the time raises the question of the justification of equating a certain theory with specific political positions. Of the wide variety of interpretations given of Darwin, two will be taken as examples, one on each side of the political spectrum.

In his 1863 speech before the *Naturforscherversammlung* in Stettin, Haeckel characterized the principal conflict of his time as that between

Bible-bearing conservatives and progressive scientists. This polarization was inherently political because Protestantism was *de facto* a state religion, with the Prussian monarchy legitimating itself as "God-given." Catholicism, which played a similar role in the southern states like Bavaria and in Austria was another target. Haeckel, as well as the other most outspoken protagonists of Darwin's theory, Ludwig Büchner, Carl Vogt, and Jakob Moleschott, supported scientific materialism. Their aim was a rationalization and secularization of the prevailing Christian world view, and Darwin's theory provided a forceful scientific explanation of the world. The assumption of divine intervention in nature—of a Creator who was responsible for the creation of new species and the disappearance of old ones—was no longer necessary.

The application to humans and the crucial equation of evolution with progress were even more consequential for their impact on popular discourse. This was partly endorsed by the translation of Darwin's notion of "struggle for life" or "struggle for existence," which became *Kampf ums Dasein* in German. Combined with the translation of "perfection through the struggle of existence" as *Vervollkommnung*, Darwin's metaphor assumed a normative and value-laden meaning. Evolutionary theory was thus interpreted as a theory of progress of the human race. In this reinterpretation of Darwin's theory, the complex mechanism of selection and adaptation of competing organisms in their environment was replaced by their linear succession. "Fitness" became *Tüchtigkeit* in German, and thus assumed the meaning of an inherent, valuable quality of organisms, humans in particular. To Haeckel and the popularizers, Darwin's theory suggested that progress was a natural law (see Büchner, 1872).

The intention of this interpretation of Darwin was clearly political, designed as an attack on religion, metaphysics, and idealist philosophy. Ultimately, the fundamental reform of the dominating *Weltanschauung* announced by Haeckel was to lead to a reform of society. Therefore, it is no accident that Darwin's theory became appropriated by the progressive forces in society, foremost the Socialists. Despite Marx's own misgivings about a naturalistic and ahistorical interpretation of "economic laws," Socialist authors in Germany throughout the 1870s increasingly took recourse to Darwin, most prominent among them Karl Kautsky, Friedrich Albert Lange, and August Bebel (see Kautsky, 1879; Lange, n.d.). Few socialist theoreticians missed the opportunity to cite evolutionary rhetoric to argue for the lawlike inevitability of the downfall of capitalism and the necessity of socialism.

Perceived in this connection, Darwin's theory also induced the corresponding reactions. An incident illustrating the political implications of Darwinism was the famous Haeckel–Virchow controversy at the 1877 Congress of the Association of German Scientists and Physicians in Munich. Rudolf Virchow, in his speech "The freedom of science and the modern state," attacked Darwinism and its premature application to other subjects, insisting that the theory of descent was still an unproved hypothesis.

Virchow, a progressive in the 1848 revolution, had anticipated Bismarck's *Sozialistengesetz* of October 1878 (following an assassination attempt on the Emperor earlier that year), which prohibited all political activity of Socialists and Social Democrats and also discredited a budding social science. Virchow equating Darwinism with Socialism dealt a serious blow to Haeckel, who tried to escape its impact by insisting that if one were to assign a specific political tendency to Darwinism, it could only be an aristocratic one, by no means democratic, and least of all socialist (Haeckel, 1908). With this defensive interpretation at a time when it had become politically fatal to be attacked for, and associated with Socialism, Haeckel had opened up the second line of the reception of Darwinism—the more conservative bourgeois Social Darwinism.

Although Virchow's attack caused Haeckel's star to decline, his propagation of an "aristocratic" reading of Darwinism nevertheless slowly gained acceptance. The time between 1873–1896 has been described as a period of economic and ideological depression (Rosenberg, 1976). The enthusiasm for a "Manchester-like" liberalism in the wake of the foundation of the German Empire, supported by the establishment of large corporations with their concentration of capital, gave way to a more pessimistic outlook when the depression set in after 1873. Increasing unemployment due to productivity changes, the transition from an agrarian to an industrial society, a population growth of roughly 10 million between 1873–1895, as well as a dramatic urbanization added to the potential for sociopolitical conflict and brought about the political organization of the workers. Both the Social Democratic Party and the Free Trade Unions gained a considerable following, the dimensions of which became fully apparent only after 1890, when the ban against them (*Sozialistengesetze*) was lifted again. The lower classes had entered the political stage, and the bourgeoisie feared their impact. After the two assassination attempts on the Emperor in 1878 and Bismarck's successful attack on liberalism, the political climate became markedly more conservative. This was also the soil in which the other interpretation of Darwin's theory—Social Darwinism—could take root and flourish.

However, the shift occurred neither suddenly nor unequivocally. In fact, public interest and enthusiasm for Darwinism, as reflected in discussions in the popular science magazines, had subsided by the 1890s. The debate over the aristocratic versus the democratic or socialist character of Darwin's theory remained unresolved, as did the issue of whether society was based on a selective struggle for existence, in which the "best" survived, or whether that struggle led to degeneration and ultimate downfall. Clearly, Darwinism had become a fashion, a scientific theory that received many different and even contradictory readings, and its ubiquitous usage makes a one-to-one match with specific interests problematic. In particular, it is clear today that Social Darwinism in the stricter sense of the word never achieved mass popularity, and the widespread, but tenuous and occasional use of Darwinian terminology, especially of the "struggle"-metaphor, should not be mistaken for being Darwinism (see Bannister, 1979; Kelly, 1981; Weingart, 1995).

Biology as Social Theory.   The terminological and conceptual impact of Darwinism on popular science and the general ideological discourse is undeniable. But what about its influence on systematic social thought? Sociology as an academic discipline did not appear until 1875 in Germany. The first generation of sociologists in Germany—Caspari, Scherrer, von Lilienfeld, Schäffle, and Gumplowicz—was Darwinian in outlook. The reception of Darwin's *Descent of Man* was enthusiastic once it had been translated in 1871, and his theory of evolution was attractive to disciplines dealing with historical questions because it seemed to offer an explanatory model of change on a sound scientific basis. The young adherents of Darwinism considered sociology the "twin brother of science" (*Naturwissenschaft*), rather than part of the humanities (*Geisteswissenschaften*), because it applied the theory of evolution and "other important modern ideas from science" to the area of social science (*Sozialwissenschaft*). These early sociologists, although engaged in carving out an independent place in academia for sociology, still remained bound by the framework of biological categories (Caspari, 1873).

The most conspicuous feature of the "Darwinist sociologists" was their use of the organicist metaphor in describing society in general and the state in particular, regardless of their differences over the methodological status of the metaphor. Claims of identity between the natural and social organisms did not prevent them from insisting on the independence of sociology as a discipline, and legitimizing this insistence by referring to the unique and particular nature of human societies. Paradoxically, in contrast to their radical claims and language, the Darwinist "struggle for life" led them to identify collective behavior and the interaction of groups—emergent social structures in modern terms—as an independent subject matter of sociology.

It must be kept in mind that the transfer of categories between biology and sociology was commonplace at the time simply because no clear disciplinary delineation existed. Both the more clearly defined delineation between biology and sociology, and thus the option of a reductionist "social biology," were made possible by new developments in biology—notably advances in the theory of heredity that suggested a much more decisive role of the hereditary material and the operation of selection.

The social science (*Gesellschaftslehre*) developed by a movement of biologists, physicians, and anthropologists around the turn of the century was built on the fundamental facts and laws of biology. The movement's agenda of disciplinary development and research, although related to that of the "first generation of sociologists" who had pioneered a Darwinist sociology three decades before, differed in important respects. It was explicitly reductionist. *Social biology,* as it was called, was conceived along a continuum with race biology, in the sense that society and race were two kinds of interwoven group structures. But because the biological base of society was represented in individuals, race biology was the fundamental social science. The concept of race was now based on the modern theory of inheritance—Weismann's, Roux', de Vries', and soon also Mendel's, including its early misconceptions. It was defined in terms of heritable traits and their continuity in an immutable germ plasm. Thus, the quality of the hereditary material had to be the ultimate object of analysis, and the processes of selection became the referent for the functional analysis of social institutions. The reductionist logic apparent in this conception of a social biology led directly to an applied perspective: to race and social hygiene or, in terms more common outside Germany, *eugenics*. The "applied science" of race hygiene quickly became synonymous with social biology and thus the focal point of the reduction of social to biological analysis.

The social biologists postulated a problem—degeneration—and offered the answer in circular fashion. The belief that degeneration was, in fact, taking place was held by the Social Darwinists in opposition to

Darwin. It was combined with Weismann's theory of the "continuity of the germ plasm," which became the basis of the "hard theories of heredity" and of a radicalization of Social Darwinism in a specific direction after the turn of the century. Given the immutability of the hereditary material as postulated by Weismann, the focus was necessarily on the agents of selection. "Culture" (i.e., modern society and its institutions) was understood as counteracting or undermining the effect of natural selection, and was thus held responsible for the threatening degeneration. A theme of that time, and a typical expression of the cultural pessimism setting in shortly before the turn of the century, was the ambivalence toward the advances of modern medicine, because they only served to keep individuals alive and reproducing who, under the conditions of "natural selection," would not have survived. Part of this framework was the glorification of premodern life, which found its expression in a wide range of "back-to-nature," reform, and health movements.

Improvement of the endangered or already degenerated hereditary stock could only be achieved by the control of individual reproductive behavior and/or the reform of social institutions found to be counterselective. This logic led eugenicists to undertake a systematic analysis of the selective functions of social institutions. Thus, eugenics focused on human reproduction and its institutions, the choice of mates, and marriage proper (Schallmayer, 1918). The selection-oriented social analysis was translated into a comprehensive scheme of technocratic social reform.

Eugenics became a movement mostly within the framework of public health throughout the Western industrial countries, especially Britain, the United States, the Scandinavian countries, and Germany. This suggests that its popular and political attraction had its basis in features common to all these societies: the fear of degeneration dramatized by the new genetics and seemingly corroborated by the side effects of the transition from agrarian to industrial societies (see Kevles, 1985). For a complex set of reasons, it was only in Germany that it was carried to extreme measures, and ultimately became associated with the racist atrocities of the Third Reich. One reason is to be seen in an increasingly utilitarian discourse on health care throughout the 1920s. The progressive decline in the defense of the human rights of the handicapped, which even involved the church, must be attributed to the economic crisis in conjunction with Germany's burden of war reparations. The welfare-oriented public health system was in a state of collapse. In addition, due to the unique combination of eugenics and physical anthropology (later, in 1925, institutionalized in the

Kaiser-Wilhelm-Institut in Berlin), theories of race became an element of eugenics. Thus, the German version of race hygiene had two facets: hereditary health and racial purity.

A further factor was the symbiosis between the medical profession's striving for political influence and recognition and the Nazi party's considering race hygiene and race biology as crucial elements of its ideology. One of the leading race hygienists and geneticists in Germany at the time, Fritz Lenz, explicitly claimed an "essential relationship" between race hygiene and the "Fascist idea of the State." "While the liberal and, in essence, also the social democratic ideas of the state are based on an individualistic *Weltanschauung*, fascism does not recognize the value of the individual. Its ultimate goal is eternal life, which is perpetuated through the chain of generations, and that means the race" (Baur, E. Fischer, & Lenz, 1931, p. 415). The restructuring of a large number of institutions, the orientation of society to the principles of hereditary health and racial purity, and the need to overcome the anticipated opposition all made fascism, or at least an authoritarian state, a compelling option for selectionist eugenicists.

Ultimately, the Nazis came to power and did provide race biologists and race hygienists with the means to put their theories into social practice. Most of the grandiose eugenic schemes remained utopian. Only forced sterilization on a mass scale and state regulations of marriages, as well as indirect measures such as income tax gradations and land ownership provisions favoring large families, were actually implemented. The euthanasia program carried out in the late 1930s and the Holocaust, although not directly connected to eugenics, which was only focused exclusively on the regulation of reproduction, must nevertheless be considered an outgrowth of the "biologization" of social and health policies. The negation of the individual and the orientation to the *Volkskörper* undermined any notion of human rights, and prepared the ground for a hitherto unknown and brutal way of thinking.

Because biology as a science, and particularly the biology of race, had claimed and been granted authority of definition in social and political matters, it also became identified with the crimes committed in its name. When the Nazi regime collapsed in 1945, biology had lost any legitimacy in commenting on social phenomena, the concept of race was tabooed, and Social Darwinism became synonymous with Hitler's rule. This historical experience underlies the negative connotations attached to subsequent use of any biological argument in the context of social analysis.

Biology as Ideology? It is fairly rare in history that sociopolitical contexts change rapidly and leave the ideas that used to provide their interpretative resource literally "in the cold." Revolutions and/or the collapse of political systems with their respective ideologies do not occur very often. In the case of Nazi Germany, military defeat also led to the demise of the national socialist ideology—an important element of which had been race biology and race hygiene. The reverberations of this collapse could be felt far beyond the confines of German society and its political system. They extended to the scientific community all over the world insofar as biology was concerned.

Herman J. Muller, one of the leading American geneticists at the time, a eugenicist by conviction, and the first president of the newly founded "American Society for Human Genetics," in his presidential address analyzed the political repercussions in clear terms. *Human genetics* (as the field now came to be called) had become the punching bag of the extreme Right (fascist racists) and the extreme Left (Lysenkoism). The only way to avoid the dangers and pitfalls of racism and irrational environmentalism was, in Muller's opinion, to link human genetics closer to general genetics. The rationale of this move was to have human genetics integrated with medicine and oriented by a consensual concept of disease. The focus of human genetics, in contrast to eugenics, had to be the individual, rather than the hereditary stock, or, in modern terms, the gene pool of the population. Muller had thus announced the withdrawal of biology from any kind of social analysis.

This conscious reorientation, which was motivated explicitly by the change in the political climate, did not proceed without conflict and opposition. An illuminating incident is the history of the so-called "UNESCO-Statement of the Nature of Race and Race Differences by Physical Anthropologists and Geneticists." This initiative of a political body of the world scientific community was supposed to signal a conceptual as well as a theoretical reorientation—a shift toward the "environmental paradigm" in the explanation of human behavior. A first draft of the declaration was formulated in 1949 primarily by social scientists, although aided by critical assessment from geneticists like Muller, Huxley, Dunn, and Dobzhansky. This draft met with harsh opposition from geneticists and anthropologists, mainly because it suggested that the concept of "race" should be replaced by that of "ethnic groups," that genetic differences should not be considered an essential factor in determining the cultural achievements of different peoples, and that personality and character should be viewed as raceless. Two years later, a second attempt at formulating a more consensual declaration was made by including a larger number of geneticists and physical anthropologists. The ensuing discussions among them reflected their inability (i.e., primarily on the side of the anthropologists) to dissociate themselves from the morphological race concept. The declaration never achieved its original purpose of condemning the scientific (biological) legitimation of racism because, instead of the political consensus it was supposed to demonstrate, it only illustrated the intellectual diversity and political backwardness of the scientists (Provine, 1973).

Nevertheless, the declaration signaled the politically motivated departure from the race concept, which was supported by developments from within science. The advent of molecular biology, and with it the insight into a hitherto unknown complexity of genes and hereditary traits, rendered the comparatively crude classification of races absurd. American geneticists Leslie C. Dunn and Theodosius Dobzhansky paved the way for a perspective informed by population genetics, much more in line with "modern" (i.e., democratic) values: Stressing the (genetic) diversity within a race, ather than the racial averages, they defined *races* as "populations which differ in the frequencies of some gene or genes" (Dunn & Dobzhansky, 1946, 1952). Races could now only be seen as reproductive communities whose delimitation grew increasingly difficult as mobility increased. The focus on the scope of differences being larger than the similarities undermined any evaluations associated with specific racial traits. Dunn and Dobzhansky also represented a new understanding of heredity itself, according to which only those traits that were vital in all environments of the species were genetically fixed like blood groups), whereas those that were advantageous in different environments varied accordingly (e.g., skin color). Although their views had not yet become the consensus of the scientific community at the time, they entered into the UNESCO-Declaration and ultimately prevailed.

The Environmentalist Paradigm. There is an explicit connection between the UNESCO declaration and the events in Germany under the rule of the Nazis. It is also noteworthy that an international organization acted with a political declaration to counter the political abuse of science, phrasing it in terms of a scientific problem. Not surprisingly, this was pointed out by German anthropologists against whom the declaration was directed in the first place (Weingart, Kroll, & Bayertz, 1988).

Although the UNESCO statement marked the explicit declaration of environmentalism as the politically and intellectually sanctioned approach in opposition to biological determinism, this shift was prepared much earlier in the United States. In contrast to Germany, the political system in the United States remained stable throughout the "era of fascism" in Europe, and the flirtation with eugenics took place in a different political context. Thus, unlike Germany's radicalization of "biological determinism" in the wider sense, in the United States a variety of political factors prevented a similar development. Degler (1991) focused on the shift that occurred in the general atmosphere in the late 1920s. He noted the growing social influence of the immigrants and the Northern urban blacks after the Great Migration, two groups who together formed the social basis for Roosevelt's presidency in 1932. He also argued, following Samelson (1978) and Weiss (1979), that the Great Depression of the early 1930s made it harder to support any idea of an innate relationship between economic status and biological fitness—a popular Social Darwinist argument at the time. Also, by the 1920s, social scientists, as well as people in general, had come to realize that the earlier Americanization movement was unsuccessful, and started accepting cultural pluralism as the model for accommodating ethnic and racial differences in the population. Finally, a direct reason for the turn to environmentalism in academia was the change in the social scientists' own ethnic backgrounds (Cravens, 1978; Degler, 1991; Samelson, 1978).

In addition to these internal changes within the United States, news from abroad affected the academic climate. During the 1930s, the support for the eugenics movement in the United States, which had been strong earlier in the century, dwindled rapidly under the impression of reports of escalating Nazi sterilization practices. In 1938, the American Anthropological Association took an unusual action and passed a unanimous resolution denouncing "racism" (Degler, 1991). (At that time, the term *race* was broader than today, encompassing what we now call *ethnic* or *cultural group*.) As a result of the new intellectual climate, during the 1930s and 1940s, the use of terms like *heredity* and *instinct* largely disappeared from the social sciences, and there was a dramatic decline in the number of articles on racial and sex differences (Degler, 1991).

However, the reasons for the shift toward environmentalism in American social scientific thought were not only social and political. There were also scientific reasons for "the retreat of scientific racism" during the 1920s and 1930s (Barkan, 1992; for a criticism of Barkan's notion of "scientific racism," see Segerstråle, 1993). The biological paradigm, once predominant, was now in decline among social scientists. It had become apparent that genetics was more complicated than earlier assumed. For instance, assumptions about a deterioration of the genetic potential in a population due to race-crossing could not be scientifically supported any longer. In biology, the dichotomy of genes versus environment had been replaced with a conception of gene–environment interaction. Some have argued that the relatively swift transition from hereditarianism to environmentalism in the 1930s was due, to a large extent, to the efforts of the anthropologists Franz Boas and his students Ruth Benedict, Margaret Mead, and others, who were actively emphasizing culture over biology (Barkan, 1992; Degler, 1991).

With the UNESCO declaration, the climate in society and academia had "officially" shifted in favor of environmental explanations, and was to remain so for the next generation of scholars. During the next two decades, there were developments both in the political and scientific arenas. In the 1960s, the student and Civil Rights Movements, and a series of social policy measures such as the famous Head Start program, fueled the hope that social progress could be achieved through changing the social environment, although it soon became apparent that this was more difficult than anticipated. In 1972, some data were finally available to support the environmentalist position regarding biological differences among human populations, also corroborating the views originally advanced by Dunn and Dobzhansky in connection with the UNESCO statement. Based on research on the distribution of human blood factors, some researchers concluded that most of human biological differences are between individuals of the same population (i.e., geographic group or race; Lewontin, 1972, 1974b). This led most biologists to the conclusion that race was not a biologically meaningful concept. The obvious political significance of these research results was that they could now be used to undermine any biological justification for racial discrimination. The environmentalist paradigm had triumphed with the help of biological data.

However, in a social and academic climate with a taboo on biological explanations, these relatively new findings in biology and their social implications had not yet been assimilated as part of the prevailing cultural belief. This means that nonbiologists may not have been aware of recent developments in biology and genetics, but still thought in old-fashioned ways about "nature versus nurture," instead of gene–environment interaction, and about immutable racial types, instead of populations with large amounts of variation among their individuals. This informational lag among the public may explain why, at the beginning of the sociobiology controversy, emotions were stirred up to such an extent. It could be argued that what was attacked was not sociobiology, but "sociobiology," as stereotyped by the critics and feeding on earlier biological conceptions.

B. The Political Context of Sociobiology

The Sociobiology Controversy: New Biology and Old Politics. For reasons shown in the previous historical account, any new theory dealing with biological aspects of human behavior almost inevitably becomes a bid both in a scientific and a political game. From this, a paradoxical situation arises: The new theory's ability to prove itself on its scientific merits, its claim to representing the most recent developments within biology, is undermined by its perceived political connotations, which derive their force from outdated biological beliefs. This is well demonstrated in the sociobiology controversy emerging in 1975 around E. O. Wilson's *Sociobiology: The New Synthesis* (see also Segerstråle, 1983, 1986).

Wilson's book came out in the summer of 1975. The first reviews, chiefly by biologists, were very appreciative. Wilson had spent about 5 years trying to put together the latest theories and empirical studies about animal social behavior (the project was heralded in E. O. Wilson, 1971a, 1971b). However, in this book, Wilson did not limit himself to the evolution of animal behavior, but, in addition, in the first and last chapter, explicitly discussed human sociobiology. According to him, the main group he wanted to provoke were the social scientists, who he thought were being "unscientific" in their refusal to consider biological dimensions in their explanations. He did not anticipate political objections from the Left (E. O. Wilson, 1978, 1994; Lumsden & E. O. Wilson, 1983). But he may have ignored or underestimated the prehistory of a "social biology" with which his program would become associated.

Wilson's book had the effect of a red flag for those among the American intelligentsia (including many biologists), who were convinced that humans are predominantly cultural beings. In the fall of 1975, a group of

Wilson's own colleagues from Harvard and others in the Boston area launched a hostile attack on him in the form of a letter in *The New York Review of Books* (E. Allen et al., 1975). They saw Wilson's extension of sociobiology to humans as an example of the old "biological determinism," which they connected to Social Darwinism, Nazism, and racism. They said that his aim was to prevent social reform by claiming evidence for a fixed human nature, suspiciously similar to the status quo in present American society. The aspect that caught the general public's attention was that among the cosigners of this letter were a couple of Wilson's closest colleagues from Harvard, biologists Richard Lewontin and Stephen J. Gould. The critical campaign initially launched by the letter writers, called "The Sociobiology Study Group," continued despite protests from Wilson as to his real motives (see Sociobiology Study Group of Science for the People, 1976; E. O. Wilson, 1976). Meanwhile, the academic community became polarized in pro- and anti-Wilson positions, and *Wilson* and *sociobiology* soon became ugly words for many who implicitly trusted the critics' analysis.

The critics' political goal was to fight "biological determinists" by proving the latters' claims to be scientifically false, outdated, and politically dangerous. Participating in this movement were, among others, the groups *Science for the People* in the United States and their sister organization in the United Kingdom, consisting of biologists, medical researchers, psychologists, and anthropologists, and also academics from fields unrelated to biology, such as physics and chemistry. The biological determinists, or *reductionists* as the critics termed them, were (and still are) academics working on various kinds of biological aspects of human or animal behavior, such as IQ research, behavioral genetics, and sociobiology. In fact, the sociobiology debate "inherited" many of its leading critics from the earlier IQ controversy around Arthur Jensen (see Jensen, 1969), starting in 1969 and continuing in the 1970s.

This is significant, because one of the leading "antiracist" activists in the campaign against Jensen, Richard Lewontin, had been brought to Harvard from the University of Chicago by Edward Wilson himself only a year before the controversy. Lewontin's role as a political activist at the time may clarify why sociobiology became his next natural target.

Already at Chicago, Lewontin had taken on himself to reveal "racist" research. In 1973, he was one of the signers of a petition published as an advertisement in the *New York Times* (October 28, 1973), urging a stop to "racist" research. (This advertisement carried over 1,000 signatures.)

But at the same time, Lewontin had contributed research that could be used to dismiss suggestions, such as the one by Arthur Jensen, that there may be a genetic basis for cognitive differences between different racial groups. In the 1960s, Lewontin discovered that most genetic variations cross group boundaries, and in 1972 he found that the same was true for humans, at least for blood group data.

In February 1975, in a NOVA program on Public Television, Lewontin attacked earlier and contemporary scientists for "lying" about genetic differences while posing as experts. He also warned the public against a new racism raging in academia, and told them to watch out for "experts" attempting to legitimize the status quo (see Lewontin, 1975). This explains why Wilson's book, *Sociobiology,* appearing in the summer of 1975, was an obvious candidate for a critical examination of political messages and racist implications.

There were some problems in making *Sociobiology* fit Lewontin's antiracist scheme. Not only was there no overt racism in *Sociobiology,* but Wilson emphasized population genetics and explicitly quoted Lewontin's 1972 article dealing with blood group data, adding, "There is no *a priori* reason for supposing that this sample of genes possesses a distribution much different from those of other, less accessible systems affecting behavior" (E. O. Wilson, 1975, p. 550). In an interview with the *Havard Crimson* in December 1975, Lewontin responded, "Sociobiology is not a racist doctrine, but any kind of genetic determinism can and does feed other kinds, including the belief that some races are superior to others" (*Harvard Crimson,* December 3rd, 1975). In his eyes, this was reason enough to stop sociobiology.

In this case, it is relevant to know that Lewontin's mentor was the eminent Russian-American geneticist, Theodosius Dobzhansky. For Dobzhansky, "population thinking" was both a scientific and moral/political issue. Increased knowledge of individual genetic differences would help individuals and society maximize their potential (e.g., Dobzhansky, 1968, 1974). However, Lewontin adopted only part of his thinking: the opposition to typological thinking and group averages in science, and the opposition to racism in society. What he did not accept was the necessary counterpart to this view: the stress on individual genetic differences. Presumably, one reason for this was precisely the ease with which the "innocent layman" and academics alike might still be caught in typological thinking, or, like Jensen, feel free to (erroneously) extrapolate from individual to group differences. In fact, the prime targets of Lewontin's attacks as a critic have been exactly those scientists who have explicitly voiced Dobzhansky-style beliefs about the social value of identifying individual, genetically based talent (e.g., B. D. Davis, 1975, 1985).

Because Lewontin is only one, albeit prominent, spokesman within the scientific community, representing one of two major factions of this debate, it is necessary to look beyond personal biographies. We need to address more fundamental, systematic differences between the sociobiologists and their critics. These concern particularly their respective views of "good science" and the proper social role of the scientist.

C. Conflicting Views About "Good Science"

In both the IQ and sociobiology controversies in their American setting one can perceive a polarization of the academic community into two main camps, across disciplines. Typical of the first camp is a prediction-oriented, operational or model-building approach, combined with a positivist belief in the inherent morality of science and a communicative interest in reporting scientific progress to the laymen. This view happens to coincide with the traditional approach of naturalistically oriented evolutionary biologists. Among the typical features of the opposing camp are a cognitive commitment to the search for an underlying reality, a belief in scientific experiments as representing the best science, and a critical attitude toward statements of members of the first camp, resulting in a search for "hidden agendas." At the same time, this is typical of a newer breed of reductionistically trained biologists (and other scientists). Thus, within the biological community, there is an opposition between "communicative naturalists" and "critical experimentalists."

These two general epistemological orientations seem to be connected to two different scientific and moral/political socialization processes: traditional "positivist" scientists, believing in the just and proper functioning of the democratic process, and the 1960s' radical generation who support a general conspiracy theory and suspect manipulation by those holding power. The political aim of the latter is to prevent the power brokers from abusing science for political purposes. Thus, these two types of scientists could be characterized as "planters" who want to produce useful knowledge, and "weeders" who want to weed out "bad" knowledge from the beginning by attacking "bad scientists."

There is an additional cognitive dimension underlying both approaches: an unproblematic coupling of scientific and moral concerns.

For the first group of scientists, scientific knowledge is objective, and thus unconnected to its social origin or social use. For the second group, "bad science" is ideologically motivated, and therefore lends itself to social abuse, whereas "good science" is/does not. The logic here is that if dangerous consequences can be inferred from a theory, then it "must" be ideologically motivated, as well as bad or old-fashioned, scientifically speaking (for a closer discussion, see Segerstråle, 1992).

Consequently, the plausibility arguments presented by sociobiologists were subjected to immediate scrutiny for social implications, and these became equated with the "moral error" of particular scientists. At the same time as sociobiologists were presumed to be "bad," both scientifically and morally/politically, the critics were creating their own "good" antiagenda, systematically connecting scientific to political concerns. One suggestion was to develop an "emancipatory" science (Rose, 1982a, 1982b), which would simultaneously be scientifically and politically acceptable, as well as superior to the prevailing reductionist paradigm. Levins and Lewontin's (1985) ambitions to develop a "total" Marxist world view in their *The Dialectical Biologist* implied an additional attempt to merge science and political activism. Both "good science" and weeding out "bad science" now became political activities.

Again, there was no one-to-one match between scientific and political convictions. Some activists among the scientists did not consider it necessary or even useful to get involved in the sociobiology controversy at all. Salvador Luria, a molecular biologist at MIT, wondered why the critics were wasting so much time and energy on a detailed criticism of Wilson. According to him, sociobiology was not even a "good" political issue, because it could not be used for a political mobilization of people at large (which the IQ controversy arguably could). Others, like George Wald, a Harvard biologist, thought that there existed many more important things for academics to deal with, such as the nuclear threat, and that sociobiology was a sheer waste of time. Finally, Noam Chomsky, the MIT linguist known for his radical views, could not be persuaded to join the anti-Wilson campaign, largely because he could not see anything wrong in Wilson's search for a general human nature (see interviews with Luria, Wald, & Chomsky; cited in Segerstråle, 1983). In other words, it is possible to be a political activist, even a Marxist, while being a traditional "reductionist" scientist at the same time.

D. Sociobiology and Conservative Politics

As is common in this kind of controversy, the critics' attack on sociobiology focused on its projected social consequences—namely, the threat of
political abuses by reactionary forces, which the theory was supposed to
invite or facilitate. As it turned out, once the controversy had been
launched, sociobiology did indeed get applause from right-wing groups.
In 1979, *The Spearhead*, a journal of the National Front in England, published an article by Richard Verrall (1979) that claimed: "Our racialist
viewpoint which sees the national family as an organic whole, within
which the individual fulfills his wider purpose of contributing to its
strength and survival, is endorsed by the sociobiologists" (cited in Beckwith, 1981/1982, p. 316). In France, *La Nouvelle Droite* quoted Jensen
and later moved on to using sociobiological arguments to promote their
view of hereditary barriers between individuals and races (Beckwith,
1981/1982). Alain de Benoist, editor of *Nouvelle Ecole*, was said to be
particularly attracted to sociobiology as a new way to address the central
issues of the traditional Right, which had been discredited by their association with Nazism. According to one observer, the journal's rosters
"read like a high-school reunion of old reactionaries and fascists" (Sheehan, 1980; for further documentation, see Beckwith, 1981/1982; Montagu, 1980).

The critics saw the employment of sociobiology to back up various
right-wing claims as proof of the correctness of their analysis. In 1981
the leading British opponent to sociobiology, Steven Rose, went as far as
writing a letter to *Nature*, urging certain named sociobiologists to actively distance themselves from being quoted by right-wing groups, lest
people would believe that these scientists in fact *approved* of such uses
of their theories (see replies from Dawkins, 1981; Maynard Smith, 1981;
E. O. Wilson, 1981).

In a related type of argument, often used to support the former, the
allegation of "bad" science is linked to political bias. More specifically, it
is shown that conservative or reactionary political positions were, at the
time, justified with scientific theories and/or evidence that later on turned
out to be wrong. Such proof, then, serves to delegitimize the political positions in question. Thus, in this sense, "bad" scientists, such as craniolo-
gists, are denounced for having committed the "moral" error of drawing
erroneous conclusions (see, e.g., Gould, 1981). Apart from the questionable equation of "correct" science with the morally and politically good,

the argument also implies that only "bad" science gets politically abused. However, even a superficial look into history reveals that such a comforting delineation does not hold water. The danger of exaggerated claims about the political or moral relevance of science pertains to all of science (see Weingart, 1988). The criticism of political ideology would have to be based on other than scientific grounds.

Two objections must be raised against the critics' overall argumentative strategy. First, the "use" of a theory to support certain ideological positions is not identical to an "inherently" ideological nature of a theory. For example, it is neither logically necessary nor historically true that a "hereditarian" position is associated with conservatism and an "environmentalist" one with progressive thought. Many hereditarians were actually socialist reformers. Examples are, among others, the left-wing biologists in Britain in the 1930s (see e.g., Werskey, 1978) and the early eugenicists in Germany and the Soviet Union (see Graham, 1977). In his response to his critics, E. O. Wilson (1975b) brought up the interest of such left-wing intellectuals as Noam Chomsky and Herbert Marcuse in the biological foundations of human nature. From the latters' point of view, there are in fact good political reasons for arguing for a relatively fixed human nature, because postulating an endlessly malleable human nature would legitimize any oppressive social regime (Chomsky, 1975; Marcuse, 1955). Also R. D. Masters (1982) pointed out that it is a mistake to automatically identify sociobiology with conservative political thought. In his view, sociobiological thinking and its central idea of inclusive fitness theory is clearly part of the individualist tradition in Western thought, but this tradition may be used for either conservative or progressive purposes. According to R. D. Masters (1982), the reason that sociobiology has been treated as a politically conservative ideology when applied to humans is that the critics have confounded two parallel distinctions in the Western theoretical tradition: on the one hand, the distinction between individualistic theories of the cost–benefit or social contract type and systemic theories, and, on the other hand, the distinction between the political Right and Left. Indeed, it is ignored that many systemic theories have been conservative (e.g., Durkheim) and many individualistic theories progressive (e.g., Rousseau).

Going on to the question of the political orientation of modern sociobiologists, it turns out that the alleged connection between right-wing political interests and sociobiology, however suggestive and politically useful, is not widely supported in practice. In fact, as van den Berghe (1981) pointed out some time ago, one might as well make the opposite case politically:

> Actually, a review of the politics of leading sociobiologists would lend more credence to the contention that sociobiology is a Communist conspiracy: J.B.S. Haldane, who is generally credited for having first hit on the notion of kin selection, a theoretical cornerstone of sociobiology, was a leading member of the British Communist Party; so was John Maynard Smith. E.O. Wilson and most other leading sociobiologists are left-of-center liberals or social democrats. "Racist" Trivers is even married to a Jamaican and is heavily involved in radical black politics (p. 406).

It should, then, be considered an empirical question of where exactly a specific "biological determinist" stands politically. It is not enough to subject statements or theories to a scrutiny aimed at uncovering hidden ideological assumptions.

The emergence and reception of sociobiology has been associated with the rising conservatism in the 1970s and the rise of biological determinist thought (e.g., E. Allen et al., 1975; Alper, Beckwith, & L. F. Miller, 1978). According to Lewontin, Rose, and Kamin (1984), "the renaissance of interest in IQ, genetics, and race, the invention of a sociobiological theory of human nature, and the explicit linkage of social violence with brain disorders" (p. 22) have all been given direct impetus by social events in the early 1970s.

It is true that the appearance of E. O. Wilson's (1975) *Sociobiology* and Dawkins' (1976) *The Selfish Gene* roughly coincides with a conservative tide which led eventually to Reaganomics and Thatcherism. But what is the connection between the background motivation for a scientific publication and the particular political climate at the time? Wilson's book was 5 years in the making and was started in the late 1960s—if anything a time of student radicalism and the Civil Rights Movement. Furthermore, this book clearly reflects internal developments within the field of evolutionary biology—in fact, it is an overview of new biological theory and empirical studies during the preceding 20 years. This is also true of Dawkins' book.

A more promising question is whether a connection can be established between the conservative mood and the popularity of Wilson's book. The most that could probably be said is that, in the conservative climate of that period, sociobiological ideas may have attracted more attention among scientists (both pro and con) and the public than had the political climate been different. The attention paid to particular topics in science by the media is a fairly reliable indicator of their fit with the political climate; this connection is largely constructed by the media, not just reported.

It may appear today that the ideological function of biology has come to an end simply because modern genetics is taken to be a truth consonant with the values of a multicultural world, in which the peaceful coexistence of all human beings is governed by their mutual respect and recognition of their equality and dignity. This should not obscure the fact that biology is still taken to support political judgments and values when, for example, recent results of genetic research are taken as proof of the monocentric origin of the human species and, thus, as a delegitimation of any hierarchy of human races (Cavalli-Sforza, 1992; Cavalli-Sforza, Menozzi, & Piazza, 1994). It is a more benevolent and moderate "biologization," and certainly a more restrained one, compared with that of the 19th and early 20th centuries. But it is still a scientific argument mobilized in favor of (or against, as the case may be) a political one. Thus, it demonstrates the continued reflection of sociopolitical values in scientific concepts and theories. The past experience with the ideological uses of biology was catastrophic. It serves as a reference for today's assessment of the ideological function of biology. Perhaps today's experience will serve as a more positive example in the future.

FEMALE ORGANISMS' ORGASMS: THE SOCIAL AND BIOLOGICAL CONSTITUTION OF A "NATURAL" PHENOMENON

Sabine Maasen

For decades, the issue of female orgasm has attracted the attention of several disciplines: psychoanalysis, sexology, and sociobiology. While arguing about the "true nature" of female orgasm by way of discipline-specific reasoning, the different approaches also rely on and produce social views of gender-specific sexualities. *Prima facie*, the female orgasm is a physiological response. However, this particular response is the subject of discussion within and among different scientific disciplines. A major reason for this multidisciplinary interest and dispute about female orgasm is its inextricable linkage to questions about its social significance (i.e., about female gender roles).

The focus of this discussion is on the genealogy of modern sociobiological concepts of female orgasm. Not only are they conceptually influenced by their predecessors, but they are also embedded in a social context providing them with pretheoretic assumptions regarding gender-specific sexual norms. The uncertainty of what may be conceived of as a scientifically and socially "correct" concept of female orgasm is shown in recent attempts to combine psychological, sexological, and sociobiological thinking, as well as in debates among feminists about the most emancipatory way to conceptualize female orgasm. The result that developmental and adaptationist accounts within evolutionary biology are claimed to account for both "conservative" and "progressive" views of female orgasm reveals what has been shown in the preceding: There is no one-to-one correlation between political convictions and scientific assumptions.

"Unlike the unicorn, which is specially interesting precisely because it does not exist, the female orgasm definitely exists and yet inspires interest, debate, polemics, ideology, technical manuals, and scientific and popular literature solely because it is so often absent" (Symons, 1979, p. 86). This observation correctly characterizes the present state of discussion on the "nature of the female orgasm." However, looking back at the course the debate has taken since the end of the last century, it becomes clear that, at one time, the "nature of the female orgasm" was ascribed the status of a unicorn. Victorian society had adhered to the ideal of the passionless woman. Only in the 1920s was the female sexual desire (within marriage) acknowledged as something valuable, and its absence considered a medical problem—called *frigidity*. Frigidity became the object of a great variety of therapeutic interventions, which eventually became widely popular in the 1970s. The end of the 1980s saw the appearance of yet another form of sexual therapy proceeding in an entirely novel direction: It rests on a sociobiological interpretation of the phenomenon. This account redirects the analysis of female orgasm toward its evolutionary and genetic foundations and its consequences.

"In the transition from ape to human, female sexuality was put into the service of securing paternal investment. To enable females to bond with one single male, the natural impulse to mate with any healthy, powerful male had to be curbed... This meant that inhibitions had to be developed" (Glantz & Pearce, 1989, p. 126). Such inhibitions, once evolved, enable the organism to delay and modify acts that formerly must have been "instinctive," and hence beyond control. Presumably, in the hunting and gathering environment, the ability *not* to respond allowed the human female to direct her sexuality as to ensure paternal investment. According to this line of reasoning, the occurrence of orgasm in a woman is a signal indicating a mate who is willing to care for his offspring. This mechanism thus enhanced a female's reproductive success (see Glantz & Pearce, 1989).

In our current environment, however—namely, modern Western society—this inhibitory reaction turns out to be too strong, and thus is regarded as "dysfunctional"; frigidity is an example of a "mismatch between normal genes and a changed environment" (Glantz & Pearce, 1989, p. 28). Within the framework of this evolutionarily founded, psychological construct, the absence of female orgasm is analyzed as a genetically rooted, although now anachronistic, mode of reaction. Thus, within psychotherapy, it assumes the status of a symptom with a new meaning: Frigidity indicates the psychological inability to bond, which is phylogenetically evolved. Thus, it is in need of more sophisticated treatment (see Glantz & Pearce, 1989).

In this approach, Glantz and Pearce combined two discursive treatments of the female orgasm: the therapeutic/medicalizing discourse initiated by Freud (1905) and the sociobiological discourse revitalized by the debate conducted by Gould (1987) and Alcock (1987). Both discourses have, in their own way, endeavored to explain the "nature" of the sexual: The therapeutic discourse analyzes sexual practices in terms of the analytic difference between *normal* and *abnormal*, whereas the sociobiological discourse looks at them in terms of the analytic difference between *adaptive* and *nonadaptive*. These different analytic frames of reference make both discourses seem mutually exclusive.

Nevertheless, the two discourses show some parallels: Just as the therapeutic discourse considers "biological" aspects, such as anatomy and physiology, so, too, the sociobiological discourse takes into account "psychological dispositions." The primary link between the discourses, however, is their common presupposed framework, which, following Laqueur, can be called the "Two-Sex Model" (i.e., two genders/two bodies). Having emerged in the 18th century, the notion of two genders also demanded biological explanations. This became especially relevant with respect to (gender-specific) sexuality: The female orgasm was now assigned a place within the field of a specifically female physiology; sexual organs were differentiated by special terminology, such as "vulva." Moreover, women were assigned their own, if ambivalent, sexual character (passionless/hypersexual). All this was "part of a grand effort to discover the anatomical and physiological characteristics that distinguished men from women. Orgasm became a player in the game of sexual differences" (Laqueur, 1990, p. 150).

The psychoanalytic and sociobiological conceptions of the female orgasm represent two further moves in this "game." The sexology of the second generation represents yet a further contribution: Only within the theories developed by Kinsey and others has the orgasm become a "natural unit" of sexological research and intervention.

In all these diverse conceptions, the nature of the female orgasm has become a symbol of the social norms of sexual differentiation. At the same time, changing social climates elicits new (inter)disciplinary concepts, such as the following:

- The psychoanalytically informed discourse supports a patriarchal order of the sexes. The model of heterosexual, genital penetration, in conjunction with the ideal of vaginal orgasm, generates the social role of the reproduction-oriented woman.
- The sexological discourse favors a model of sexual democracy in marriage; the ideal of a couple's shared orgasm signifies the differentiation of the sexual and reproductive functions of female sexuality. Orgasm becomes a clearly definable unit of therapeutic intervention; "frigidity" becomes established as a specifically female dysfunction.
- The sociobiological discourse has to confront a set of split norms: The therapeutically articulated norm of sexual equality and the social norms of sexual differentiation have found expression in a controversy that debates the "adaptedness" of the female orgasm: Whether female orgasm is adaptive also says something about the sexual and social significance of this phenomenon. Feminist critique is also divided on this issue.

These discursive contributions, which are dealt with shortly, continuously produce and shape, from various discipline-specific angles, the nature of female orgasm, and thereby rely on, and constitute, the social order of the genders. A permanent rearrangement of the relationship between a woman's sexuality and reproduction characterizes the genealogy of this discourse. The various contributions have constituted the female orgasm as a psychological, biological, and/or social "problem." Each of them defines, although slightly differently, what biological aspects are relevant for an explanation of female orgasm, and how they should be interrelated with psychological and social factors.

A. Psychoanalysis: Freud

In his essay on transformations of puberty, Freud (1905) claims that the "leading erotogenic zone in female children is located at the clitoris"— which is, as he pointed out, "homologous to the masculine genital zone of the glans penis" (p. 121). After recognizing the phenomenon and locating it anatomically, he assumed a further transformation in female sexual development to be necessary. According to Freud, "mature" female sexuality is dictated by a transfer from clitoral to vaginal orgasm. However, in the normal course of events, the clitoris retains a function: The task, namely, of transmitting the excitation to the adjacent female sexual parts, "just as pine shavings can be kindled in order to set a log of harder wood on fire" (Freud; cited in Gould, 1987a, p. 18).

How could Freud, being an expert in neurology and having access to available medical knowledge, have arrived at such a conception of female sexual development, Laqueur (1990) asked, mentioning a number of English, French, and German manuals of the 19th century that present elaborate descriptions of the topic. Moreover, Laqueur noted that the abundance of specialized nerve endings in the clitoris and the relative insignificance of the vagina had been known in outline for hundreds of years.

As for the scientific peculiarity of the Freudian conception, two complementary answers are given. One answer focuses on the disciplinary autonomization of psychoanalysis vis-à-vis biology. According to J. Mitchell (1989), for instance, Freud strictly rejected "the notion that psychology corresponds in a one-to-one relationship with biology" (p. 354). Why? This is referred to by the second answer. Laqueur highlighted the underlying social assumptions that guided Freud's reasoning. Namely, according to Laqueur, Freud's postulate of a sexual asymmetry of the sexes can only be explained by the fact that he linked it with widely held views of the social asymmetry of the sexes. According to these views, women were expected to be passionless spouses. However, this role did not align with the female sexual biology: The clitoris' easy responsiveness to touch makes it difficult to domesticate it for reproductive, heterosexual intercourse (see Laqueur, 1990). This situation required a framework where passion was deviant, and hence where there was no difference between a woman's sexual disposition and her gender role. To achieve this, Freud made use of the biological approaches of his time, but eventually went beyond them, constituting a psychobiology of sexual development that, for both sexes, runs parallel at first, but then becomes differentiated.

In the various developmental stages of human sexuality, named by Freud as the *oral*, *anal*, and *genital* phases, the individual favors certain objects and practices of sexual pleasure. In a "normal" sexual development, all partial instincts are suppressed by way of "organic repressions" in favor of one single form of sexuality characterized by Freud as "mature" (i.e., heterosexual, genital, and reproductive). According to Sulloway (1982), the universality of Freud's developmental model of human sexuality can be said to be a consequence of its phylogenetic foundation, "providing these phases with their regularity, their independence from culture" (p. 209). In particular, Freud adopted the "fundamental biogenetic law" by E. Haeckel and other late 19th-century thinkers, enlarging on a special aspect: He advanced that, by implication, the developing child recapitulates the sexual history of the race, too (see Sulloway, 1982).

However, this developmental dynamic only refers to the period of sexual development shared by both sexes. Except for the "fact" that female sexual development seems to require a further thrust of repression, Freud offered no phylogenetic explanations, but did emphasize psychoanalytic interpretations as opposed to possible biological ones: The repression of clitoral sexuality renders women demure, which, in turn, serves as a stimulus to men's libido, increasing its activity (see Laqueur, 1990).

Additionally, this conception is paralleled by anatomical reinterpretations. Until the 19th century, woman was understood as man inverted: In particular, the vagina was regarded as a penis (see Laqueur, 1990). What was emphasized by Freud is no less than what Laqueur called the epistemological transformation of the "One-Sex Model" into the "Two-Sex Model." The model that views woman as a social and sexual variant of man is replaced by one in which woman becomes a social and sexual contrast to man. For this, "natural symbols" were required: an anatomical interpretation that conceptualized the clitoris as a specifically male, leading erotogenic zone, and the vagina as a specifically female one.

Anatomy, Physiology, and Biogenetics.   Apparently none of the biological approaches, in the form that Freud might have been acquainted with, was deemed sufficiently by him to make plausible the difference in a woman's sexual development as he perceived it. Rather, it is the socially founded notion of two genders that informs the psychoanalytic interpretation of the sex difference which, in turn, claims additional legitimation through the authority of biology. More precisely, the psychological interpretation is backed by a biologism dating back to the 18th century, which postulates two biological genders with distinctive organs and physiologies; by an evolutionism that ensures the adaptation of the genitalia to heterosexual intercourse (Lamarckianism); and by a biogenetic foundation (Haeckel) that safeguards the independence of cultural characteristics. Yet with respect to the development of female sexuality, Freud's psychoanalytic discourse goes beyond these biological approaches by proposing a psychobiology that grants these presumed developmental processes a psychological explanation. In this way, Freud's conception of the vaginal orgasm constitutes a contribution to the generation of the reproduction-oriented woman. Yet there is a problematic side to female sexuality fixed on reproduction: The "passionless" woman threatens the continuity of marriage (i.e., the only legitimate framework provided for heterosexual, genital, and generative sexuality).

B. Sexology: van de Velde, Kinsey, Masters, and Johnson

The sexual reform of the 1920s can be regarded as a solution to the problem of female sexual desire—but only within marriage. In fact, the Victorian ideal of the passionless woman is now resigned to the clinical diagnosis of frigidity (see Lützen, 1990). Its counterpart (i.e., the issue of female sexual desire) is discussed within a new frame: the preservation of marriage. The most influential proponent of the sexual reform in the German-speaking countries, Theodor Hendrik van de Velde, demanded an eroticization of marriage as a precondition for its stability; the erotic ideal was the "shared orgasm." Thereby, he abolished a crucial difference that had placed women in one of two exclusive social categories: "frivolous persons" who knew the pleasures of love, or "respectable spouses" who acknowledged the duty of reproduction (see Kohlhagen, 1992).

Accepting both desire and reproduction within the institution of marriage, Kinsey (1953) then explained the two roles of sexual physiology by an evolutionary process. The fact that a woman's desire seemed to be highest when she was least likely to conceive showed him that natural selection had affected a radical separation of sexual and reproductive functions in humans (see Robinson, 1977). Moreover, Kinsey denied that menopause led to any diminution in female sexual response.

Against this background, Kinsey shifted the discussion of the female orgasm away from the topic of its reproductive purpose toward the question of the anatomy of sexual response. Pointing at the homologous origins of the structures of the two sexes, Kinsey claimed that the clitoris was the primary center of sexual stimulation in a woman. Kinsey advanced a critique not only of an erroneous theory (i.e., Freud's notion of vaginal orgasm), but also of the popular, although now frustrating, practice of sexual therapy that did not succeed in "this biological impossibility" of transferring "clitoral responses" to "vaginal responses" (Kinsey, 1953).

In the 1960s and 1970s, Masters and Johnson asserted that every female orgasm, whether the source of stimulation be "superficial" (clitoral) or "deep" (vaginal), involves the same empirically verifiable occurrence—namely, the development of a so-called "orgasmic platform" (e.g., W. Masters & V. Johnson, 1966) and its pleasurable resolution in contractions. Thus, Masters and Johnson did away with the clitoral–vaginal distinction, but introduced different *loci* of sexual stimulation that result in identical orgasmic experiences. If vaginal stimulation in conjunction with heterosexual genital intercourse was preferred by some women, the reasons were mainly psychological—leaving aside the aspect of reproduction. By this, they emphasized the difference between the physiological and psychological ability to achieve orgasm (i.e., the psychological acceptance of sexuality in general; see W. Masters & V. Johnson, 1966).

As a result of these sexological findings, the focus of attention now shifted to orgasm as a "natural unit" of sex research and sex therapy. Sex research made use of recording instruments that "proved" women have orgasms (as well as nonhuman female primates; see Haraway, 1989). Sex therapy established the norm of an "ideal orgasm" that led to a sharp increase in the number of men and women with "dysfunctions." The new norm caused them to look at any deviations as "problems" in need of treatment, and caused sexologists to explore the phenomenon in further detail. Thereby, sexology has come to look on itself as "orgasmology" (Béjin, 1986). Parallel to the sexological accentuation, however, a medicalizing discourse that runs in the opposite direction survived: The maturity of vaginal orgasm was taught in mainstream gynecological textbooks to generations of medical students and physicians into the 1970s, and physicians offered women the ability to have orgasms by "reconstructing the vagina to make the clitoris more accessible to direct penile stimulation" (see Bleier, 1984, pp. 172ff).

Sex research and sex therapy, and even traditional sexual medicine have consolidated the view that women have a "right" to have orgasms. At the same time, however, new approaches emerge that again create the impression that the female orgasm is an especially problematic phenomenon—problematic not only in the sense of psychosexual anomaly or dysfunction; but problematic also in terms of biological functionality. When a flood of sex manuals and guides began to offer help (to couples) on how to achieve sexual fulfillment, and when feminism began to discuss multiple orgasms in women (Sherfey, 1972), as well as aspects of "New Motherhood;" sociobiology appeared on the scene, proposing to reopen the debate on the human (sexual) behavior repertoire—this time from an evolutionary perspective.

C. Sociobiology: Gould, Symons, Alcock

The evolution-oriented interest focuses on the "adaptedness" of female orgasm (i.e., it is considered a trait that has become fixed because it conferred a greater reproductive advantage to those individuals who possessed it in the past than to nonpossessors). Among sociobiologists, this question has found expression in a scientific controversy about the most appropriate account of female orgasm: either the developmental account (Gould, Symons, Lloyd), in which clitoral orgasm is explained by a direct selection for the male trait, the female one being a necessary concomitant; or an adaptationist one (Alcock, Morris, Hrdy), which argues for a direct selection for the adaptedness of the female trait (see S. D. Mitchell, 1992). The developmental reformulation undertaken by Gould and sharply criticized by Alcock promptly instigates one more episode in a heated debate: Critics inside (Caulfield, 1985; Hrdy, 1981) and outside the biological disciplines (Geertz, 1980) perceive an implicit question about the sexual and social significance of female orgasm.

For the "developmental league," and based on Elizabeth A. Lloyd's research and analysis, Gould (1987a) first identified the location of the female orgasm as the clitoris, and then joined Kinsey's "homological reasoning": "Males and females are not separate entities, shaped independently by natural selection. Rather the two sexes are variants upon a single ground plan, elaborated in later embryology. The clitoris has to be regarded as the homologue of the penis, it is the same organ endowed with the same anatomical organization and capacity of response (Gould, 1987a, p. 16). In his conclusion, Gould followed Symons (1979) who

stated that available evidence does not "warrant the conclusion that female orgasm is an adaptation. Orgasm is most parsimoniously interpreted
as a potential *all* female mammals possess" (p. 89; italics added).

Alcock (1987) disagreed. In his opinion, female orgasm, although
different in pattern and timing from male orgasm, *is* an adaptive trait.
Yet, according to him, criteria may exist for the reproductive success that
differ on a gender-specific level. A male's reproductive success is often
correlated with the frequency of copulations, whereas a female's reproductive success seems linked with increasing the probability of having
children who receive paternal care (see Alcock, 1987). Considered from
this point of view, if females reach orgasm more often with partners who
offer parental care to their children than with explicitly nonparental partners, as well as with partners who care about them enough to attend to
their sexual enjoyment, then the response can be used as an indicator for
future fitness. Thus, orgasm serves as a kind of "paternity control" with
respect to sexual partners (see Alcock, 1987).

Similar to Freud, the sociobiological discourse also addresses the
clitoris and vagina, but they are placed in a different argumentative context. In the Freudian conception, the question is about the immature or
mature *Leitzone* of sexual desire, thereby eventually combining female
desire and reproduction, whereas the sociobiological discourse identifies
clitoris and vagina as organs serving distinct tasks: either sexual desire *or*
reproduction. However, against the background of a rigid functionalist
program, this discourse, too, faces a dilemma: If evolution arises from a
struggle among organisms for differential reproductive success, sexual
pleasure must have evolved as a stimulus for sexual response. Why is it,
then, that for women the site of orgasm is divorced from that of intercourse (see Gould, 1987a)?

This phenomenon is disquieting for the vast majority of evolutionary
biologists, as confirmed by research done by Lloyd (1993). After a closer
examination of 13 studies on the evolution of human female orgasm,
Lloyd found that 12 of them assume female orgasm to confer "a *direct
selective* advantage on its possessors" (p. 143). The crucial ingredient in
these adaptationist theories is the notion of a "pair-bond," according to
which female orgasm evolved "because it gave the female a reward and
motivation to engage in frequent intercourse, which is itself adaptive, because it helps cement the pair-bond" (Lloyd, 1993, p. 144).

Variants of this view have been proposed by Morris (1967), Eibl-
Eibesfeldt (1975), Beach (1974), and others. All these contributions start

from the assumption "that orgasm is an adaptation unique to the human female and thus is to be explained by selective forces operating exclusively in the human lineage" (Symons, 1979, p. 75). Another set of theories assumed orgasm to be common (and adaptive) among nonhuman females as well (Sherfey, 1972).

Looking at both the developmental and adaptationist accounts from a philosophical perspective, S. D. Mitchell (1992) concluded that Gould and Alcock "accept the potential relevance of a plurality of causal processes including adaptation and development, [but] they disagree about which particular combination of forces is responsible for the causal history of clitoral orgasm" (p. 143). By disentangling the different explanatory strategies of developmental and adaptationist accounts, respectively, S. D. Mitchell also revealed that the issue of female orgasm has become what may be called an "accidental battleground" for this debate. The reason for this can be found in the social significance of the issue: Scientific explanations of female orgasm deal with more than just a physiological response. Rather, as feminists started to argue in the 1970s, there are implicit social assumptions contained in both adaptationist and developmental accounts. But the feminist response is divided: One camp of critics puts up an adaptationist counterconception (Hrdy), whereas the other celebrates the final separation of female sexuality and reproduction (Lloyd). Whether they opt for adaptationist or developmental theories, they do so for the sake of saving the social and sexual significance of the female orgasm.

D. The Feminist Critique: Hrdy, Lloyd

One type of criticism was raised by Hrdy. Hrdy (1981) made her conception of female orgasm part of a female-centered view within adaptationist reasoning: Important ingredients of her evolutionary account are "sexual selection," "anisogamy," as well as "competition among assertive, dominance-oriented females" as central principles of primate social life. According to her "manipulation hypothesis," orgasm in female primates favors a tendency (of the females) to "mate with a number of males in order to confuse information available to males about paternity and thereby extract investment in, or tolerance for, their infants from different males" (Hrdy, 1988, pp. 128ff, see also Hrdy, 1981, p. 174). The evolutionary point of having a clitoris and a "situation-dependent, concealed ovulation" (Hrdy, 1988, p. 187) is a matter of giving females a competitive advantage vis-à-vis male physical power. Unlike traditional interpretations, this thesis assumes that individual females ardently seek to mate more than once or twice, even when they are not ovulating or are actually pregnant. Female orgasm in the feminist perspective appears as the privileged sign of female agency (see Haraway, 1989). The name of the game is strategic genetic investment.

This kind of feminist critique elicits feminist critique: Haraway disapproved of Hrdy's concept because females remain committed to reproduction. However, as Haraway pointed out, the discourse in which Hrdy's claim is embedded is not a maternalistic one, but a discourse on female sexual efficiency. For instance, female mammals can now be observed to exhibit all kinds of competitive and cooperative relationships to enhance their reproductive (i.e., sexual and economic) success. However, the notion of "female agency," through such means as orgasmic sexual assertiveness, assigns female orgasm to the extensive series of proximate moves in the grand ultimate game of genetic investment. Thus, Hrdy "leaves intact a deep (re)productionist ethnophilosophy translated into a technostrategic language of universal investment games" (Haraway, 1989, p. 366).

Another type of critisicm (i.e., developmental) is raised by Lloyd. She argued that most observations, data collections, and theories are affected by background assumptions of the scientists (see Lloyd, 1993). The tacit adaptationist assumption is that of a very tight link between sex and reproduction. Studies of both nonhuman female primates and human females provide evidence for this assumption.

With respect to nonhuman primates, Lloyd referred to studies that claim a hormonal determination of sexual behavior, the estrus being operationally defined as the period in "which the female is willing to participate in sex." This view yields misleading results, such as the occurrence of estrus being usually overestimated. Moreover, one cannot possibly ask whether estrus and sexual interest are independent events. Most convincing, however, have been studies of female homosexual, and therefore nonreproductive, activity, which testified most clearly to the independence of hormonal status and sexuality (see Lloyd, 1993).

The same, if often implicit, equation of sexual and reproductive behavior is found in studies dealing with human females. The aforementioned "pair-bond theories" assume that intercourse reliably leads to orgasm in females. However, available clinical cross-cultural studies demonstrate that this is not the case. Around 90% of women experience orgasm, but 30% never do so during intercourse, and only 20%–35% always have orgasms during masturbation. Lloyd (1993) concluded, "If orgasm is an adaptation which is a reward for engaging in frequent intercourse, it does not seem to work very well" (p. 144).

Physiological data and homo- and heterosexual patterns of behavior in humans as well as nonhuman primates all indicate that a model according to which all basic aspects can be examined in terms of reproduction cannot be correct. Instead, Lloyd (1993) proposed to conceive of sexuality "as an autonomous set of functions and activities, which are only partially explained in terms of reproductive functions" (p. 140). According to Lloyd, the developmental view yields explanations about women's sexuality that are consistent with both accepted clinical conclusions and evolutionary theory. Thus, Lloyd's account, making use of biological arguments, leaves space for nonreproductive elements of female sexuality.

E. Social and Biological Significance of Female Organisms' Orgasms

The female orgasm continues to be caught up in a "reproductive circle": Even after the sexologists of this century have separated the sexual functions from the reproductive functions of female sexuality, the sociobiological discourse reunites them by introducing the question of female sexual desire into the adaptationist game for reproductive success: In some versions, this trait serves as a motivation to engage in frequent intercourse, which in turn helps to stabilize the pair-bond. In its feminist version, sexual pleasure and concealed ovulation are conceived of as an active stake of the women participating in this game. Nonadaptationist approaches are still a minority issue. Similarly, the views are divided on which approaches constitute the (sexually and socially) more emancipated ones. Hrdy equated the adaptiveness of a trait and its social significance, and hence regarded only an adaptationist account of female orgasm as emancipatory, whereas Lloyd spoke for the opposite.

The notion of female orgasm is a joint venture of disciplinary discourses and social norms of gender differentiation. On the one hand, social "facts" (i.e., two genders) and cultural values (i.e., the primacy of motherhood, emancipation) deeply influence disciplinary and interdisciplinary accounts of female orgasm: What is regarded as biological, sociological, and/or psychological evidence is subject to continuous debate. On the other hand, scientific concepts deeply influence everyday notions of female orgasm, providing them with the dignity of scientific authority.

From a naturalist perspective, this process might be conceived of as a highly sophisticated way to disorder a "natural" phenomenon. From a constructivist point of view, this process is a sophisticated way to produce and change the order of things. The genealogy of the discourse on female orgasm has revealed that the frontiers between the "biological" and "cultural" have been constantly reassessed. Therefore, it is almost certain that the nature of female orgasm, once constituted as a "problem"—psychological, biological, social—will continue to inspire interest and debate for some time.

FINAL CONSIDERATIONS

The historical analysis of the changing contexts of biological theorizing about human society, as well as the study of the pervasiveness of social presumptions in biological discourses, reveal a compelling fact: Political convictions and social values and assumptions are an inexorable part of scientific thought, and, likewise, scientific discourses can have an equally strong influence on them. This unavoidable mutual influence appears in different degrees of intentionality and awareness. With the notion of hierarchically structured genders, sociobiologists seem to have, largely unwillingly, transferred particular social models to their evolutionary thinking. By contrast, race biologists deliberately legitimized a hierarchy of races when making use of evolutionary concepts like the "survival of the fittest." As far as the reception of scientific theories in public discourses is concerned, an unreflected use of individual concepts and disregard of context is probably the rule.

Although the mutual influences of biological theorizing and social discourse are inevitable, they nevertheless make for no more than a nondeterministic coupling. This renders any attempt to derive the political function of a (biological) theory from its content a dubious project. Conversely, biological (and sociobiological) theories cannot be linked to certain political convictions and/or social values. This contingent relationship between social values and biological theorizing held true for evolutionary and hereditarian explanations at the beginning of the century, which were used for conservative and progressive policy recommendations alike, and for adaptationist explanations in our time, which are both welcomed and rejected in the name of the progressive goals of an influential social movement—feminism. The politically motivated criticism of "biologizing" is justifiable on the basis of historical experiences (e.g., its role in Nazi ideology), but it cannot be justified by inherent logical connections.

Evolutionary theorists, in particular, cannot deny the influence of political convictions and social values on their speculative reconstructions of the past, which consequently give guidance and orientation to their contemporaries. Thus, by invoking the past, the present constitutes the inescapable context of interpretation. Nevertheless, the explanatory strategy of these theories differs. On the one hand, there are paleoanthropological theories that trace the roots of the modern intelligent and civilized human being (see Landau, 1984). In these theories, the protagonist, a hominid, "starts from humble origins on a journey in which he will be both tested by environmental stresses (savannah, predators, etc.) and by his own weaknesses (bipedalism, lack of biological armaments) and gifted by powerful agents (intelligence, technical innovations, social cooperation) until he is able to transform himself into a truly human hominid, the hero's final triumph which always ends the story" (Fedigan, 1992, p. 120).

On the other hand, the reference to the distant past has also informed numerous variants of cultural pessimism, with a clear normative message to present-day societies. The glorified state of nature; the salutary, although cruel, operation of natural selection; the adaptedness of human behavior and the human mind and, conversely, its maladaptedness to modern culture; and the inherent inability of the human brain to cope with the consequences of its own creations are recurring topics in evolutionary accounts that have informed public debates about political, scientific, and technical advances as much as they have drawn criticism from more modernist quarters.

There can be no doubt that the different evolutionary narratives reflect the social and political values of the society or societies in which they are situated, as does the particular state of research. The Spartans or Germanic tribes, the Goths and the Vikings, convey images of "Nordic" superiority and the presumed ideals of national character around the turn of the century in the same way as "Lucy" is taken today as proof provided by nature of the common origin of all human races, thus demonstrating the illegitimacy of any hierarchical ordering.

However, unlike Hofstadter, the studies presented in this chapter do not claim that biological ideas 'are utterly useless in attempting to understand society' (see Hofstadter, 1945). Rather, they draw attention to the different political and social assumptions underlying scientific reasoning in general, as well as to the usage of biological concepts in particular—be this homological or analogical. Therefore, scientists who try to explain the present state of human sociality by referring to the evolutionary past should, at the very least, be aware of the political and social sensitivities of their time and the possible interpretations of their theories.

3

THE WHYS AND HOWS OF INTERDISCIPLINARITY

Sandra D. Mitchell
*University of California
San Diego*

Lorraine Daston
*Max Planck Institute for the
History of Science
Berlin, Germany*

Gerd Gigerenzer
*Max Planck Institute for
Psychological Research
Munich, Germany*

Neven Sesardic
*Miyazaki International College
Miyazaki, Japan*

Peter B. Sloep
*Open Universiteit Heerlen
The Netherlands*

Can we imagine an intellectual relationship between the biological and social sciences, which is one of neither reduction nor isolation, but of sharing the scientific study of humans, simultaneously conceived as organisms and as social, enculturated beings? This chapter is about the philosophical and methodological reasons for posing the biological question to the social sciences, in light of a new understanding of what interdisciplinary scientific work means. A special concern in this chapter is to show that the ontological and methodological barriers thought to separate the biological and social sciences are often the products of a crude caricature of the interactions between scientific disciplines. Interdisciplinary human science without either reductionism or isolationism is possible.

The first section surveys the philosophical grounds for embracing a scientific pluralism. What are the grounds for thinking that the various forms of reductions are either possible or desirable? Philosophers have recently been skeptical of the unification of the sciences, conceived of as the reduction of all scientific knowledge to a few fundamental laws of physics. Why might we expect a deeper and broader understanding to emerge from taking more than one approach to the same subject matter? There are several reasons: The world may split more or less cleanly into levels of organization, different idealizations capture different aspects of the phenomena, and the advantages of a cognitive division of labor are clear. All these reasons suggest that an isolation of disciplines would be unproductive. Normally, one expects full understanding of a given domain of phenomena to emerge only when perspectives are integrated. Several examples taken from the recent literature on evolution and culture clarify both the motivation for, and the nature of, the integration.

The second section examines three specific strategies of integration: What theoretical, conceptual, and methodological bridges span the biological and social sciences? Our examples are the transfer of metaphors and models between the biological and social sciences, the attempts to construct a common language as viewed by proponents and opponents of anthropomorphic description, and the shared techniques of statistical inference that connect disciplinary realms. In none of these cases are the integrative strategies uncontroversial, and our analyses are often critical of current practices. However, all three offer successful examples of integrating the approaches and findings of the biological and social sciences, which are neither reductive nor isolationist.

We seek to address the doubts of the thoughtful critic who wonders, *in principle,* what grounds there might be for optimism about a new start in the troubled relations between the biological and social sciences. We cannot seek to shoulder the whole burden of encouragement: The proof of the scientific pudding is results, not programmatic enthusiasm. We do hope to dispel some worries by outlining why interdisciplinarity is, in this case, both desirable and possible, what kind of interdisciplinary work suits this case, and how we should and should not go about doing it.

UNITY OF SCIENCE

A. Global Unity

Sandra D. Mitchell

Whenever it is suggested that the theories and methods characterizing one scientific discipline have contributions to make to the solution of problems found in separate disciplines, the fear of expropriation arises.

The source of this fear is a specific and widespread, but outdated, conception of the unity of science as entailing reduction of all sciences to physics, and prohibiting disciplinary autonomy or pluralism. The section describes and defends a framework of integrative pluralism that makes room for the plurality of theories and methods used in generating integrated explanations.

Two approaches might be taken to interdisciplinarity. Disciplines are both social and cognitive enterprises. They are constituted by the domain of objects studied, a language to describe those objects, a central set of problems, the methods used to solve those problems, and the theories employed to explain and predict phenomena within their purview. In addition, they have social, institutional, and historical dimensions that identify individuals and schools within a given discipline (and its subdisciplinary divisions), as well as institutions that reward success and certify competence (including academic departments, journals and funding agencies; see Whitley, 1984) Although the historical, social, and institutional factors play important roles for the nature, possibility, and success of interdisciplinary research (D. T. Campbell, 1969), this chapter focuses primarily on the cognitive dimensions.

Within our scope, there are still many types of interactions connecting biology and the social sciences—ranging from the direct application of biological theories to problems traditionally in the domain of anthropology or sociology, to the borrowing or sharing of methodological tools, to the recognition of the significance of empirical results and explanations in one domain for the solutions of problems in the other, to the transfer of more abstract models with significant modification and development in application to human culture. In short, there is much and varied cross-disciplinary traffic. But do these interactions provide a source merely for inspiration, or is there something more to interdisciplinary research?

There are a variety of stances one might take in response to these questions, which depend, in part, on the way scientific disciplines are constituted. The following considers the type of unity or integration that applies when one construes science as a collection of theories and observation statements, as structured by disciplines focused on both different domains of objects or levels of organization, and inquiries into different questions and their respective answers. We distinguish between global (see Diagram 3.1) and local unifications, and argue in favor of one variety of local unification—namely, integrative pluralism.

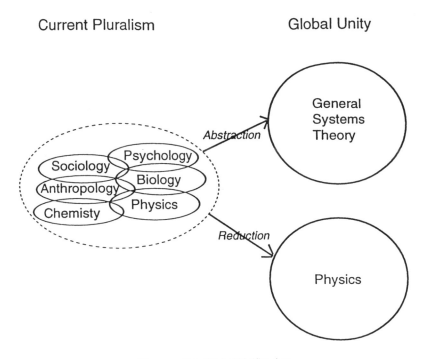

Diagram 3.1: Global Unification

We start by observing the fact of pluralism. A glimpse of the current scientific theories and explanations of human culture reveals diversity both within and between separate disciplines. There is a plurality of theories, models, and conceptual schemata from biology, psychology, anthropology, and other sciences that is brought to bear in explaining human cultural phenomena. Nevertheless, the common sense view and the premise of modern science is that we study one world, which, although available to multiple conceptualizations, does not warrant inconsistent claims. This assumption explains the conflicts that arise between alternative theories and explanations, and provides an intuitive appeal for some form of integration or unification of beliefs about our world. How can we make sense of both the fact of current pluralism and one-world metaphysics?

General systems theory, most generally identified with Bertalanffy (1975) takes as fundamental to all objects under scientific study the mathematical relationships describing the structure of systems. Although presently scientists might divide among numerous disciplines (the fact of pluralism), their activities would be united by describing each separate domain (e.g., physical systems, biological-ecological complexes, firms in an economy) as instances of a single set of abstract mathematical theories describing the behavior of complex systems in general (the goal of general systems theory). Although the theories of the various disciplines would have a certain autonomy with respect to their individual descriptive languages, general laws of systematic relations would be seen as isomorphic across these discourses. Yet even if one were to grant that all systems (e.g., human social groups, social insect colonies, and genomic regulatory systems) can be described in terms of some set of generalized differential equations, this would hardly constitute grounds for a content-rich unity. It is the way that a generalized system gets particularized in the various instances of its use that captures what is distinctive of a given system (Berlinski, 1976; Hempel, 1951). So the "general" in general systems theory amounts to the general-purpose nature or flexibility of mathematics as a descriptive tool. Because even this has its limits (see p. 142, this volume), one can be sure that general systems theory cannot replace the explanatory projects of the different disciplines. Thus, the fact of pluralism is not a temporary embarrassment to the aim of global unity of science, but rather represents a necessary and desirable division of cognitive labor.

A more modest strategy of exploring homologous structures across disciplinary domains, or of using knowledge of formal relations derived in one discipline in application to another, is not to be dismissed. However, any projected global unity that minimized the relevant autonomy of the various disciplines would be misplaced. The attempts to generate the general, unified systems theory since Bertalanffy's 1975 call to arms has shown no diminution in the plurality of theories and explanations, and no *in principle* argument can guarantee such global success.

By far the most common path to global unity has been through reduction. On this view, the ultimate and global unity of science is thus constituted by the transformation of the current body of scientific statements, which includes theories in distinct languages of many disciplines (the fact of pluralism) into a set of fundamental laws governing the behavior of fundamental elements and expressed in a single, formal language—namely, that of physics (the goal of reduction). Strategies toward achieving ultimate reduction may promote pair-wise reductions from higher to lower levels.

B. Reductionism and Supervenience

Neven Sesardic

The philosophical debate about reductionism has a curious recent history. Within less than 40 years (from the mid-1930s to the end of the 1960s), philosophers of science have in succession defended and, indeed, taken seriously the following claims on the issue: (a) that reductionism is *a priori* true, (b) that it is contingently true, (c) that it is contingently false, and (d) that it is a priori false. Of these, (a) is now completely abandoned, (b) is moribund, (c) is presently a dominant view, and (d) is an influential and controversial position (see D. Davidson, 1970), but largely restricted to the philosophy of psychology.

The a priori truth of reduction is the ambitious, purely linguistic reduction advocated by logical positivists. Science was to be unified by translating the content of all "higher" sciences (sociology, psychology, biology) into physical language. This project has failed. A given theory can be reduced to another one only if there is a close match between fundamental concepts of the two disciplines. This is Ernest Nagel's (1961) "condition of connectability." However, advocates of reduction came to recognize that the link between the concepts, if it obtains at all, has to be contingent, rather than analytic, and established through empirical discovery, rather than through "meaning postulates." The argument that reduction is contingently true, however, encounters a formidable difficulty in satisfying the connectability condition: There are strong general grounds for not expecting property-to-property correspondence across different sciences. Put differently, things that are similar from the point of view of Theory T_1 need not, and as a rule will not, be similar from the point of view of Theory T_2. But if taxonomies of two theories are so disconnected, the talk of reduction does not seem to make much sense. Psychological "pains" may not correspond to a simple category of neurophysiological patterns. Why is this so?

The so-called argument from multiple realization has been used extensively to establish the contingent falsity of reduction in different contexts (biology vs. chemistry, psychology vs. neurophysiology, sociology vs. psychology, economics vs. physics, etc.). According to this argument, any property of the "higher" theory is likely to be instantiated in so many different ways at the level of the "basic" theory that the resulting disjunctive and gerrymandered predicates will cease to represent natural kinds. Natural kinds are understood as classifications of real properties in the world. Hence, terms that refer to natural kinds can appear in scientific laws and function in explanations. The property of having a particular molecular structure is taken to represent a kind (e.g., gold) and explain other associated properties, whereas having the properties of being shiny, yellow, and malleable are not thought to designate a natural kind. (The words *higher* and *basic* are used here in a neutral sense: The first refers to the theory whose reduction is being considered, and the second to the would-be reducing theory.) For example, there may be useful relations to be discovered about optimal foraging behaviors in general (see chap. 1). Instantiations of these patterns may be found in insects, birds, humans and other mammals. Clearly, the proximate mechanisms controlling the various behaviors are diverse, including chemical, visual, and rational modalities that do not easily map onto a physical kind of classification.

Problems do not disappear once one decides to dismiss reductionism as a simplistic and, in the end, untenable, philosophical position. Antireductionism has serious metaphysical and epistemological difficulties of its own. First, although rejecting thoroughgoing reductionism, a number of authors seem to want to preserve the idea that higher level facts are dependent on the lower level facts. Even after renouncing the hope of reducing, say, psychology to neurophysiology, one might still wish to assert that, if relevant neurophysiological facts are fixed, psychological facts are thereby also determined. The same holds for the relation between biological facts and physicochemical facts, and between properties of social wholes and psychological facts. Some philosophers follow this view all the way to a form of physicalism by insisting that all sciences are ultimately anchored in physics; their view is epitomized in the slogan, "No difference without physical difference."

A weak form of reductionism is sought by appeals to the relation of asymmetric dependence or, technically, "supervenience." Roughly, a family of Properties A is said to supervene on another family of Properties B only if it is impossible for two things to differ with respect to Properties A without also differing with respect to Properties B. The task of conceptually sharpening this preliminary definition has proved to be exceptionally delicate. Analytical attempts to make precise the shared intuition of this dependence relation led to the proliferation of incompatible definitions of *supervenience*. Worse still, most of these definitions (or all, as some think) failed by being too strong and entailing reductionism, or by being too weak to convey the meaning of intended ontological dependence (for an overview article, see Kim, 1990a).

Despite the success or failure to defend asymmetrical dependence, if so desired, the antireductionist would still face two other major difficulties; one having to do with explanation, and the other having to do with causality.

1. Explanatory Autonomy?

First, there is the problem of "the division of explanatory labor." For the reductionist, this was a nonproblem because of the belief that all properties of a "higher" science were always just a subset of the properties of the more basic science; in fact, all explanatory work was done with the conceptual resources of the basic discipline. Many antireductionists are prone to oppose this view by a contrary claim of the complete explanatory autonomy of higher theories with respect to the lower level ones. Relying on the essential incongruity of different taxonomies, they tend to argue that a question raised within a given conceptual framework can always be relevantly and satisfactorily answered without leaving that same framework. This would mean not just that higher sciences have no reason to fear preemption by more fundamental disciplines, but, furthermore, that they could afford not to care at all about what happens at the more fundamental level. This isolationist overreaction to the threat of reductionism is not viable. Cases will exist when two levels of explanation are insulated from one another due to our temporary ignorance of how to integrate them, but such examples do not support the strong philosophical claim for explanatory autonomy. (For an argument to this effect, concerning the relation of psychology and neurophysiology, see Kalke, 1969; H. A. Simon, 1970.)

There is evidence, too, that taxonomies of different levels are not always mutually independent. An antireductionism that required total disconnection between levels would be too strong. Concepts of higher sciences have occasionally been modified and redefined to adapt them to more basic categories. A simple illustration is the way chemistry handed over to physics the sovereignty over its fundamental concept, "chemical element." Elements are defined by the number of protons in the nucleus; as a consequence, it happens, somewhat paradoxically, that isotopes of the same chemical element differ in their chemical properties. Building on sporadic examples of this kind, and above all on the hope that similar instances will be massively forthcoming in the near future, some philosophers are trying to breathe fresh life into reductionism. Particularly in the area of psychology, these philosophers are prophesying the transformation beyond recognition of its conceptual apparatus with the advance of knowledge about underlying brain processes, and that "mature" psychology will eventually become indistinguishable from neurophysiology (see Churchland, 1986). Such a sweeping optimism concerning the approaching fusion of higher sciences with their *antidisciplines* (the term for lower sciences in E. O. Wilson, 1978) lacks support and, to a great extent, remains a mere article of faith. If the declaration of full explanatory autonomy of the higher sciences was seen as an overreaction to reductionism, the contrary firm belief that higher theories will be "cannibalized" by the more fundamental ones may in turn be regarded as an overreaction to the previous overreaction. In the present context, steering away from the extremes appears to be the only justifiable course.

2. The Specter of Causal Inertness

Taking up the problem of causality, what first attracts notice is that it pulls in the opposite direction from the explanation issue. Most regard higher sciences as indispensable for the task of giving explanations. Explanation being interest-relative, it sounds plausible to argue that, when the event to be explained is stated in terms of a given theory, any attempt to explain it by switching to a deeper-level vocabulary must end up by answering a different question, or by "changing the subject" (D. Davidson, 1970). The concept of causality is different. Causal relations are detached from any pragmatic component: They obtain independently of one's interests, descriptions, and beliefs. With causality, we cannot so easily resort to the strategy that worked nicely with explanation—by making the analogous "division of causal labor" among various sciences and having pluralistic peace.

In fact, arguments have recently been produced for the view that all causal labor is actually done at the most fundamental, physical level, and that, consequently, the possession of other (biological, psychological, etc.) properties can have no causal impact whatsoever. The skepticism about the causal efficacy of "higher" properties flows from their being construed as dispositions with multiple physical realizability. To take a biological example, relatively greater fitness in an environment is the cause of greater reproductive success. Suppose fitness under given circumstances is increased by either being darker or by being stronger than one's conspecifics. Arguably then, the enhanced reproductive success of some organisms is not caused by their fitness (the property of being darker or stronger), but by their being darker or being stronger. The basic idea is that multiply realizable properties are disjunctive properties, and that disjunctive properties are inappropriate candidates for causal roles. A suggestion that a combination of causally efficacious properties could be causally efficacious would strike some philosophers as akin to the joke of Richard Feynman, who once said to his audience: "The thing that holds you in your seats is a combination of gravity and politeness" (Feynman, 1985, p. 4). There is no scientific theory (i.e., physical etiquette?) investigating the causal powers of such a property.

Another argument to the same effect starts from two plausible principles; (a) the materialistic rejection of substance dualism, and (b) the causal closedness of physics (the belief that any physical event is exhaustively causally determined by the physical properties of its causes). On this basis, it is then inferred that there simply no causal work remains to be done by other properties.

Alternative solutions to the problem of causal inertness have been proposed (see Jackson & Pettit, 1990; Kim, 1990b; Le Pore & Loewer, 1987; Sober, 1984), but at the present stage of discussion, these issues remain highly controversial. Reviving reductionism may be a dead option, but the antireductionists have serious philosophical problems on their hands as well.

3. Five Interfield Dilemmas: A Recapitulation

To structure this fairly condensed discussion of reductionism and autonomy, Table 3.1 is offered as an overview of the different standpoints discussed here. The strongest antireductionist position is substance dualism (or perhaps substance pluralism). This position claims that the higher and the lower sciences are divided by an ontological barrier, and that they deal with completely different spheres of reality. It is in this way that mind was separated from brain in Cartesian dualism, life from nonlife in the élan vital theories, social wholes from psychological facts in the radical versions of methodological holism, and so forth. Substance dualism is a historically important view, but plays no role in the contemporary debate. A weak version of substance monism (*token physicalism*, in the philosophical jargon) is widely accepted.

A subtler form of dualism (*property dualism*) is a more serious contender. For instance, even after conceding that all psychological events are neurophysiological events, some still deny that psychological properties are (only a subset of) neurophysiological properties. The strength of this move is best seen by comparing it with its contrary—property monism. Property monism is, in fact, equivalent to reductionism (i.e., the view that, despite the lower and higher disciplines having different sets of predicates, they both denote only one kind of properties—those of the lower discipline), and this view is highly implausible for the already adduced reasons. Today, everyone is aware that it is non sequitur to argue directly for property monism from the strong case for substance monism; thus the recognized implausibility of substance dualism is no argument against property dualism. In short, whereas the truth of substance dualism does lead to property dualism, the truth of substance monism implies nothing about the ontology of properties.

TABLE 3.1

Five Interfield Dilemmas

Substance	Property	Interproperty Relationship	Explanation	Causality
Dualism	Dualism	Supervenience	Autonomy	Inertness
Monism	Monism	Independence	Nonautonomy	Efficacy

The further question about interproperty relationship makes sense only under the assumption that there are two families of properties (property dualism). The philosophical scene is dominated here by the search for the supervenience relation. Of course, there are skeptics who think that the appeal to supervenience is "obscurantist in the extreme" (Schiffer, 1987, p. 154). Still others regard it as an attempt to have one's cake (to be openly antireductionist) and to eat it too (to preserve, nevertheless, the pet reductionist claim about the ontological primacy of physics). But the sheer bulk of work done on this topic across different theoretical fields (biology, psychology, sociology, ethics) testifies that such a pessimistic attitude may be premature.

The explanatory dilemma autonomy vs. nonautonomy is the most central question of all five. It is "semiconnected" to the issue of property ontology. That is, property monism (reductionism) entails nonautonomy: The existence of only one kind of property, that of the lower discipline, implies that the whole explanatory work is done "from below," regardless of whether we are aware of it. But the similar inference from property dualism (antireductionism) to explanatory autonomy does not go through. The fact that different conceptual resources cannot be amalgamated into one whole does not mean that they cannot be fruitfully combined. Needless to say, the tendency toward making higher disciplines explanatorily autonomous and insulated from the lower level approaches is not based solely on the invalid inferential move from property dualism. Among factors motivating the isolationist attitude are reasons like the inertia of disciplinary compartmentalization, the fear of one's own field of study being appropriated by "intruders" from other sciences, and perhaps also the pure uneasiness about having to come to terms with fundamentally different theoretical approaches. These are sociological excuses, not philosophical reasons. Isolationist explanatory pluralism could legitimately result from genuine difficulties involved in a project of integrating different explanatory strategies.

Finally, the issue of causality raises a puzzling two-pronged argument that the further away one's explanatory account is from the physical level, the more distant is one from the truly operative causal features of the situation. Social sciences would fare worst under this picture because their categories would be at several removes from the uniquely causally efficacious physical properties. In the 1950s and the 1960s, philosophers would hardly worry about this: From the neo-Wittgensteinian perspective, dominant at the time, in social science there was no place for causal explanation (see chap. 1). In contrast to the natural sciences, the task of explanation was regarded here as limited to making actions intelligible in the light of agent's reasons, and any use of causal idioms in the context of humanities was regularly dismissed as a crude methodological mistake. However, the situation has dramatically changed. The arguments for the noncausal stance crumbled under criticism, and the search for causal mechanisms has become a standard aim in social science research. Therefore, the alleged causal inertness of nonphysical properties remains an unresolved philosophical problem.

C. Alternatives to Global Unity

Sandra D. Mitchell

Given the philosophical and practical problems associated with global unity through systems theory or reduction, one may ask, what are the alternatives? When global unity is rejected and pluralism is embraced, does that mean that we must adopt an isolationist policy, or is there some other form of local integration that can be defended? The fact that diversity exists within the many disciplines studying human culture cannot be denied. But why is this the case? There seem to be two major sources for pluralism: (a) the division of domains of objects into levels of organization, and (b) the variation in problem areas or levels of analysis. Each of these forms of pluralism is considered in turn.

1. Levels of Organization

One way in which different approaches to the study of nature are divided, and hence disciplinary boundaries constructed, is with respect to the objects of study. The ordering of "levels of organization" (Diagram 3.2) has had a long and varied history. For example, one hierarchical framework construes each lower level system as constituting the parts of the next higher: cell, organ, organism, group, organization, society, and supranational system (J. G. Miller, 1978), or, alternatively, elementary particles, atom, molecule, macromolecule, cell, tissue, organ, organism, population, community, earth's surface, planet, star system, galaxy, and universe (Bonner, 1969; Salthe, 1985). A scientific discipline can then be delimited by explanatory theories directed at the causal interactions within a given level of organization (see Wimsatt, 1987). A hierarchical ontological ordering, combined with a monistic metaphysics might seem to imply reduction to the more "basic" objects. Yet as was argued, this is not a necessary conclusion. Even without reifying the levels and invoking some kind of metaphysical dualism (or even pluralism), the autonomy of current investigations of objects at the different levels can be defended (Dupré, 1983).

Grounds for defending autonomy can be found in viewing the objects at each level of organization as abstractions or idealizations. For example, predator–prey or parasite–host theories explain population-level interactions and identify abstract individuals in terms of their role in those interactions. The theories are then used to explain actual interactions between concrete individuals, such as particular lynxes and hares or malaria viruses and humans. Yet the abstract individual identified by its functional role in the population models does not map identically onto the concrete individuals described at the next level down (i.e., the individual organisms; a lynx is truly described at the same time as a predator and perhaps a prey in an ecosystem, an individual of a certain rank in the social hierarchy of a kin group, as well as a mammalian organism, a homeostatic endotherm, and other things).

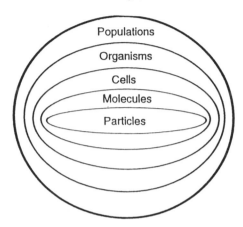

Diagram 3.2: Levels of Organization

Actual, complex events or concrete individuals—the constituents of the one-world ontology—are, at the same time, instances of objects of abstract theories concerned with different levels of organization. For example, the event of, say, a marriage may be described by abstracting out the cultural roles expressed (outmarriage or cousin marriage, etc.), or seen as a biological occurrence of pair bonding between individual organisms, a physiological event with hormonal and other biochemical features, as well as a physical event of interacting particles. Reductionism requires replacing the higher level abstractions with lower level ones. However, the abstractions that constitute objects at the different levels are not isomorphic across levels. The weaker relationship of supervenience might describe properties of different levels. But this weak form of physical reductionism does not entail disciplinary imperialism as a strategy. Thus, the fact that cultural roles are filled by individual organisms that house biochemical processes constituted by physical particle interactions does not entail reductionism and its consequent unity, but rather what might be called the *disunity of science* (Fodor, 1974; see also Dupré, 1983, 1993). The objects of scientific study are better thought of as complex and diverse, rather than inclusive sets nested neatly in some hierarchical ordering. Granting the disunity of theoretical objects, what now of explanation? How are theories of, say, population phenomena (like evolving gene frequencies) and individual phenomena (like embryological development or cognitive processing) brought together?

2. Levels of Analysis

The relations among the numerous theories found in the current plurality are not of a piece. Some may offer conflicting explanations of a given set of phenomena (like the wave and particle theories of light in the 19th century, or preformationist vs. epigenetic theories of embryogenesis), whereas others seem to be compatible alternatives directed at either different levels of organization or addressing different questions about a single domain. The implications for interdisciplinarity of each of these situations are investigated next.

Competitive Pluralism. Endorsing pluralism of competing hypotheses has been defended as both a spur to theoretical development and a rational response to our inability to judge the future fruitfulness of present theories. The former argument suggests that potentially problematic areas for a given hypothesis are more readily identified if there is competition with alternative views. Given the assumption that science develops by solving problems, competition is seen as a means to more quickly eliminating inferior approaches and substituting superior ones. The second argument acknowledges that it is impossible to infer future relative or absolute success from the current performance of competing theories. Thus, it is rational for the scientific community as a whole to support the maintenance and development of multiple alternative theories that have some probability of future success (Beatty, 1987; Kitcher, 1991). Any fallibilist with respect to scientific truth must accept this sort of pluralism. In either case, endorsing pluralism in the form of competition between incompatible explanations has the ultimate goal of resolving conflict by the adoption of one of the competitors and the elimination of the other.

Compatible Pluralisms. A different sort of pluralism—that between compatible alternatives—does not recommend resolution of alternatives to a single theory. Recently, within biology, one such view has been defended. This approach appeals to distinct "levels of analysis" as making room for multiple hypotheses. A plurality of compatible solutions to independent problems are thought to be generated as answers to distinct questions about the domain of study. Each of the various questions posed identifies an autonomous level of research, rather than the source of a rival theory. In 1988, Sherman revived Mayr's (1974) distinction between proximate, or "how," questions and ultimate, or "why," questions, as well as Tinbergen's (1963) elaboration of the categories into four distinct "levels of analysis" (see S. D. Mitchell, 1990): evolutionary origins, functional consequences (the two "why" questions), ontogenetic proces-

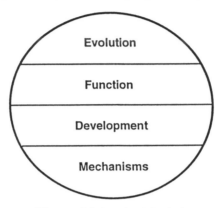

Diagram 3.3: Levels of Analysis

ses, and mechanisms (the two "how" questions). Sherman further divided questions of mechanisms into those that target physiology and those that target cognition. For example, biologists concerned with the behavior of nest parasitism by cuckoos might approach this phenomenon with four different questions. Those concerned with evolutionary origins would investigate why this behavior arose in the lineage of cuckoos when it did, those with functional concerns would ask what current consequences the trait has on reproductive success, queries about ontogenetic processes would aim to explain how the behavior comes to be expressed in the life cycle of the cuckoo when it does, and those interested in mechanisms would detail the environmental triggers and hormonal or cognitive mechanisms that then issue in the behavior. Different questions invoke different explanatory schemata. Sherman (1988) claimed: "Every hypothesis in biology is subsumed within this framework; competition between alternatives appropriately occurs within and not among levels" (p. 616). Thus, answers to questions at the different levels represent compatible components of a pluralistic, multidimensional body of knowledge.

Granting that this describes current pluralistic practice, the question remains as to what relations should connect these autonomous enterprises. One reading of this type of compatibilism leads to an isolationist stance with respect to the separate analysis (i.e., not only do explanations at different levels not compete, but there is no suggestion for their integration).

The problem with the isolationist picture of compatible pluralism is that it presupposes explanatory closure and a narrowness in scope of scientific investigation, which precludes the type of fruitful interactions between disciplines and subdisciplines that has characterized much of the history of science. Even when the unlikely situation occurs—that a scientist is narrowly concerned with only one level of analysis—it is a mistake to think that the answers to other questions have no bearing on the investigation at that level. As was argued earlier, there may be causal dependence (symmetrical or asymmetrical) or causal interaction between processes described by the different analyses. If so, remaining within a single level will fail to provide understanding for the questions addressed *at that very level*. For example, evolutionary psychology maintains that cognitive mechanisms have evolved in the same manner as anatomical features (i.e., they are the result of natural selection operating during our evolutionary past). If this is so, then asking only for current functions of human behaviors may lead one to incorrectly describe the proximate psychological mechanisms responsible. Thus, although the relationship between analyses of different causal processes, or different levels of analysis, is not one of direct competition, neither is it of justified ignorance or isolation. Instead, it is suggested that an integrative model provides a more promising framework in which to promote interdisciplinarity.

Integrative Pluralism. Answers to scientific questions attempt to specify the causal mechanisms that are responsible for the puzzling phenomena. For example, one might ask why all cultures have some form of incest taboo, or why a specific society employs a polygamous marriage pattern and another does not. One answer might be to show how people come to adopt a given belief about appropriate marriage partners, detailing perhaps the religious and institutional context structuring socialization, or by appeal to the social transmission of ideas—showing how, given the preceding beliefs or context, the frequencies of different beliefs or behaviors, and the impact of these on transmission patterns, the subsequent set of beliefs would result. These types of approaches specify the mechanisms responsible for enculturation.

One also might ask for the evolutionary explanation of the presence of certain social patterns or beliefs. Here one might describe the effect of various beliefs on the genetic reproductive fitness of people adopting them in specified environmental situations. This might be offered to explain why, say, one population is polygamous and another monogamous, given the different fitness consequences for the behavioral patterns in their respective environments. Such an account appeals to natural selection as the cause of the presence of a given pattern and the cultural variations observed. These theories might plausibly stand on their own and offer complete explanations of the phenomena, if the world was such that situations of simple, singular causal processes, rather than complex, interacting causal processes were predominant.

Instead, it is often methodologically useful to see how far one explanatory schema can go toward explaining a complex event, and then querying what other mechanisms might account for the remaining, unexplained variation. Although differences in explanatory strategies should be recognized as not necessarily competing, and the autonomy of the theoretical models acknowledged (because each abstracts away the operation of the other causal forces), we suggest that a locally integrative, rather than an either global-unity or isolationist, pluralism is the appropriate strategy to adopt. To see this, one must first distinguish between the theoretical models that specify the causal interactions invoked, and the application of such models to the explanation of a specific case.

The answers to different questions appeal to distinct abstract models of causal processes, as well as specify their application to concrete instances. Fundamental scientific laws used in explanations of concrete phenomena have *ceteris paribus* clauses (Cartwright, 1980). Namely, they describe what is to be expected in idealized situations, when only one of a set of potential causal factors is operating (i.e., when nothing else is interfering). All simple models also suffer by design from this type of unrealism. If one accepts that multiple causal factors can, and often do, interact in the production and maintenance of human cultural practices, that the real cases are complex, without the *ceteris paribus* proviso, the laws would be literally false. With the proviso, however, such models do not directly account for many, if any, real cases. That is, although abstract models describe the effects of the operation of a single causal process, our world does not normally approximate the ideal worlds that the models directly represent. The concrete explanatory situations on which we bring the abstract models to bear are messy, perhaps unique products of historical contingencies and interacting, multiple causal factors. In this sense, the simplified, abstract, theoretical models developed in science are literally false (see Wimsatt, 1987). This does not make them undesirable or useless (see Richerson & Boyd, 1987). Indeed, simplification allows models to be mathematically and empirically tractable for increasing precision of assumptions, crisper testability, and allowing counterintuitive results to be generated. The robust convergence of results of a variety of simple models is evidence that the result does capture a feature found in the complex world.

Nevertheless, the pragmatic virtues of simplicity are most frequently bought at the cost of realism in explanation (Levins, 1966). Although it is possible that a single causal process may completely determine a particular event, given the complexity and diversity of human cultural phenomena, simple models are more likely to capture partial causes. In this situation, individually more complete models may be developed, if there are means to replace the false assumptions in the model by more realistic descriptions (e.g., in models of language acquisition or measures of genetic fitness). At the most concrete level in generating an explanation, a model may introduce all of the relevant features that uniquely characterize a given event (e.g., the ecological conditions of a particular lake). However, the cost here is that of generality. A full-scale map of a town would express the greatest realism, yet it would be as useless for finding city hall as would a map that represented the town as a single point. So, too, all that is true in a concrete model of Clear Lake will likely not apply directly to a neighboring lake. It is by distinguishing the idealized models from their applications that one can identify the location and scope of integration.

In short, isolationist pluralism employs levels of analysis framework to endorse a strategy of limiting interactions among various theories offering explanations in a given domain. Although some scientists may restrict their interests to a specific level only, this is not necessarily the case. Pluralism better describes the causal models that, by modeling the contribution of individual causes, necessarily abstract away the operation of other compounding factors. By so doing, they can make no incompatible claim about the operation of the ignored causes. Once this structure of causal models is recognized, one may understand why competitive interactions arise within a level (e.g., how best to measure fitness in determining the current function of a cultural trait).

However, the model must be distinguished from its application. In application, one can immediately see that causal models that provide answers at different levels are indeed related. Thus, although pluralism is to be defended, it is not the pluralism of questions and the consequent independence of answers, but rather a pluralism of models of causal processes that may describe contributing factors in a given explanatory situation. This is not to recommend an "anything goes" pluralism. Not all explanations are equally good. Hence, to defend a strategy of pluralism for causal models and criticism of explanatory applications of those models requires a further account of how idealized models are to be integrated into explaining concrete, nonideal cases.

Integrating Models. As a preliminary investigation, three types of integration are considered: (a) mechanical rules, (b) global and local unifications, and (c) explanatory, concrete integration.

(a) *Mechanical rules and relative importance questions.*   Vector addition in physics is an example of a general method for quantitatively combining the effects of independent forces of, say, gravity and electromagnetism on the motion of a body. It has been argued that this type of integration may be adequate to predicting and explaining the joint effects of mutation and selection on gene frequencies (Wright, 1969; see also Sober, 1987). However, the approach does not work for all cases, but only when selection, drift, and migration are weak forces, and mutation and selection act in sequence, and hence do not interact in nonlinear ways. Such mechanical methods may apply in relatively limited cases, and hence do not offer general algorithms for integrating models of different causes. Especially in the case of cultural or sociological processes (like learning) and biological causes (like natural selection), it is likely that the causes do not operate serially, but rather interact.

   This view is currently reflected in the arguments of the coevolutionists who reject the completeness of either purely biological explanations or purely cultural ones (see chap. 10). Furthermore, the causal interactions may not yield a situation where each force always contributes to the joint effect in the same way, be it statistically additive or quantitatively expressed, and that a single mathematical function would apply. A common currency in which to measure the effects of contributing causal processes seems to be a minimal condition for using such mechanical algorithms. For these reasons, it seems that this mode of integration is not widely applicable.

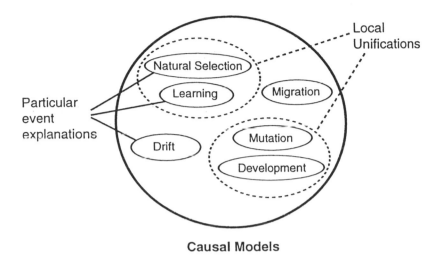

Causal Models

Diagram 3.4. Integrative Pluralism

(b) *Global and local unifications.*   Some have counseled the strategy of
    increasing the realism of the assumptions made in the abstract theo-
    ries that model specific causal processes (Burian, 1986; Richerson &
    Boyd, 1987). The aim of this type of integration appears to be the de-
    velopment of local or nongrandiose models, rather than a grand uni-
    fied theory, in which all aspects of the complex processes are repre-
    sented. The latter types of global unifications might be accomplished
    by reducing one field to the other, or by developing a new "interfield"
    theory that replaces both prior schemata (Darden & Maull; 1977, e.g.,
    of biochemistry or general systems theory). Arguments against global
    unity have already been presented. However, there is no *prima facie*
    reason to reject the aim of more modest integrative models.
        Though diversity and variation seem to work against the combi-
    nation of generality and realism in a single model, attempts to pro-
    duce such local integrations will aid in discovering inconsistencies
    among the constituents and further the ability to generate successful
    explanations. Cosmides and Tooby's (1987) insistence that sociologi-
    cal theories directly take into account more evolutionarily sophisti-
    cated models of human cognition (rather than the general processing
    mechanism, or *tabula rasa,* models that are implicit) can be seen as a
    step toward local theoretical unification. There are reasons to be pes-

simistic about global unity, because there do not appear to be univocal rules governing the nature of sociocultural constraints on biological processes or vice versa (Durham, 1991). Although at times such constraints may limit or enhance the operation of natural selection by proscribing or promoting certain types of genetic variation (by infanticide of twins, or prohibitions on marriage partners), at other times biological causes act to modify cultural forces. Nevertheless, more local unification of models and theories is to be encouraged.

(c) *Explanatory, concrete integration.*   Another locus of integration is in the explanation of concrete phenomena (what one might take as the most local approach). This constitutes a piecemeal strategy for integration. The plurality of models is recognized, as well as the nonindependence of at least some of the contributions to complex combinations. At the same time, it acknowledges the singularity of the particular combination of causal processes responsible for any given phenomenon.

Using a piecemeal approach means admitting that the general explanatory strategies appealing to specific causal processes make simplifying assumptions, which are literally false in describing an actual causal history. One expects neither the actual processes in need of explanation to directly reflect the content of the models, nor that the theoretical models will be modified to incorporate the details of all potential causal factors in a general framework. Rather, the actual configuration of complex processes resulting from biological and sociological causal mechanisms will be determined on a case to-case basis.

Global unification of social science and biology via reduction or replacement by a general theory is neither the necessary outcome nor the desired goal of the investigation of the impact of biological theories, explanations, and data on social science. However, complete autonomy and oblivious isolation of the individual disciplines are not defensible. Integrative pluralism, which recognizes the different objects abstractly constituted by different theories and the different questions one can address to a complex phenomenon, allows compatible pluralism at the level of theoretical modeling, encourages local unification of theoretical models, and demands interaction and integration into the explanation of concrete events.

The view of science presented endorses a plurality of strategies for engaging in interdisciplinary interaction. No single theoretical framework, no simple algorithm, will suffice. All depends on the situation at hand, the mix of models to be unified, the facts to be explained, the interests of the research community, and so on. We turn now to some of the means and obstacles to achieving the type of interdisciplinarity counseled by integrative pluralism. The following section considers how concepts and models are metaphorically transferred between scientific domains, how anthropomorphism has fared in discussions of relations between biology and human culture, and how statistical tools in their transportation between disciplines carry theoretical content.

INTEGRATIVE STRATEGIES

A. The Metaphorical Transfer of Models

Peter B. Sloep

A discussion of the metaphorical transfer of models is actually akin to the more general case of the metaphorical transfer of concepts. Indeed, although lack of space prevents us from developing the point any further, an increasingly more influential view of theories and models—the so-called "semantic" view of theories—views entire models as single predicates, be it extremely complex, set theoretical ones (for an overview, see Thompson, 1989; see also Doucet & Sloep, 1991, Lloyd, 1988). So, just as the concept of "being blue" is a predicate, so is the concept of "being a Newtonian particle system" or "being a Mendelian inheritance system." However, because models tend to be complex, we first take a look at the simpler case of the metaphorical transfer of simple concepts. In doing so, we introduce some terminology that allows us to more easily grasp the "mechanics" of the process of metaphorical transfer. For ease of exposition, we use a familiar example, although from a historical point of view it is less than accurate to portray it as a case metaphorical transfer.

Transfer of Concepts: Selection. The example discussed here is the well-documented case of—in the words of Robert Young—"the analogy [Darwin made] from the artificial selection of breeders to a natural mechanism" (Young, 1971, p. 455). The natural mechanism at stake is of course natural selection.

For many years, Darwin studied artificial selection as practiced by human breeders (and by himself, too) to find a mechanism by which species could be modified. An example discussed by Darwin is the increase in the number of tail feathers of a particular breed of pigeons. This increase is brought about by intentionally selecting pigeons with the largest number of feathers and allowing them, and only them, to procreate. By repeating this selection process generation after generation, a variety of pigeon (the fantail) is bred that "has thirty or even forty tail feathers, instead of twelve or fourteen, the normal number in all members of the great pigeon family" (Darwin, 1859, p. 21).

Darwin likened this selection process by human breeders to a process of selection performed by "nature":

> [A]ny variation, however slight and from whatever cause proceeding, if it be in any degree profitable to an individual of any species, in its infinitely complex relations to other organic beings and external nature, will tend to the preservation of that individual, and will generally be inherited by its offspring. The offspring, also, will thus have a better chance of surviving, for, of the many individuals of any species which are periodically born, but a small number can survive. I have called this principle, by which each slight variation, if useful, is preserved, by the term Natural Selection, in order to mark its relation to man's power of selection. (Darwin, 1859, p. 61)

Put in more modern terms, if some organism with a particular suite of heritable characteristics leaves more offspring in its lifetime than its conspecifics (for whatever reason, it might be better at avoiding being eaten by predators or herbivores, it might be more efficient in digesting its food, etc.), then, given the availability of only limited resources, it will increase its proportional representation in the next generation of the population. To the undiscriminating observer, it looks as if someone intentionally selected this organism. Just as fantails arise because of the breeders' efforts, natural species are so wonderfully adapted to their environment because of some natural selective agent.

We have here a transfer of the notion of selection by breeders (in modern terms, *artificial selection*) to selection by some natural agent (what Darwin called *natural selection*). If we take a somewhat detached look at the prior example, the following can be seen to have occurred. A particular concept (artificial selection), which is a familiar concept in a particular domain of discourse (the language of human breeders), got transferred by Darwin to another domain (at the time called *natural his-*

tory). Darwin introduced a new term—Natural Selection—to distinguish it from "man's power of selection" (artificial selection).

It is of crucial importance to notice that the term *selection* in "natural selection" is used in a metaphorical sense. It could not have been used in a literal sense because there is no intentionally selecting agent involved. Darwin used it because the result of the natural process that takes place looks as if some intentional agent has been at work.

Clearly, the use of the selection metaphor somehow helped Darwin formulate his new theory. The interesting question is how it did help him. The answer does not lay a claim on historical accuracy; rather, it is a rendering of what happened in the light of the particular theoretical perspective we entertain and believe to be revealing and instructive in cases as this.

In all likelihood, Darwin's own rationale for developing the analogy seems to have been that it put him on a sure footing with the ideas of both Herschel and Whewell, two leading philosophers of science in his days. In line with their ideas, Darwin believed that, by drawing the analogy between both types of selection, he was gaining evidential support for his natural selection thesis. Apart from that, for someone who was spreading a controversial message, it was certainly a wise tactic to secure the support of Herschel and Whewell (see Ruse, 1979, pp. 166–180, for a lengthy discussion of Darwin's motives).

We can also look at the prior example with the help of three notions introduced by Hesse (1974): positive, negative, and neutral analogy. These notions are used because they are helpful in elucidating the point we want to make. Hesse's accompanying analysis, in particular more recent versions of it (see Hesse, 1974, 1986) is much richer than our elementary use of her classification suggests. Notice that artificial and natural selection share particular features. The most crucial one is that differential survival and reproduction occur (i.e., in going from the parental to the filial generation, some organisms have increased their relative representation in the population). In the case of artificial selection, the choices human breeders make are responsible for this. In natural selection, "nature" chooses (i.e., checks on increases in numbers, competition between species, climate, etc. cause differential survival and reproduction, or, in present day terms, all act as selective agents). Hesse referred to such similarities as *positive analogies*. Positive analogies are important because they provide the *prima facie* reasons for using the selection metaphor. Metaphorical transfer of concepts without a positive analogy between the original concept and its metaphorical counterpart—if such a notion is at all conceivable—is senseless.

But natural selection and artificial selection also differ. Our use of the phraseology "it looks as if someone selected them" was intentional. Although the proto-fantails were hand-picked by their breeders, in natural populations selection results from natural processes in the struggle for existence. Here we have a difference or negative analogy, as Hesse called it: a human selecting agent vs. natural processes. Negative analogies are as essential an ingredient of metaphorical transfer as positive analogies. A metaphor without them would cease to be a metaphor (i.e., an explicitly nonliteral referring term); it would be the "real thing" (i.e. a literal referring term), and one would end up with an identity relation rather than an analogy. At the same time, negative analogies embody the limitations of a metaphor; as such, they flag a warning sign. If negative analogies are not recognized for what they are, mistaken inferences may follow. A case in point would be to attribute the intentionality of a human breeder to a natural selection process: Natural processes cannot have purposes.

Although positive and negative analogies point to the initial plausibility and limitations of a metaphor, respectively, the rationale for the use of metaphors is the existence of what Hesse called *neutral analogies*. (This discussion completely ignores metaphor use for pedagogical reasons, although interesting connections exist; see J. Martin & Harré, 1982.) The class of neutral analogies is potentially composed of both negative and positive analogies. However, it is not yet know where a particular analogy under consideration will end up. To be more precise, suppose we have at our disposition a stock of features that characterize a concept in its literal usage (i.e., before transfer) and we investigate what happens to these features when the concept gets transferred. We then ask ourselves whether, after transfer, a particular feature of the concept used literally will belong to the negative or the positive analogy. Viewed this way, the neutral analogy marks the value of the metaphorical use of concepts because it holds the premise for conceptual innovation of the domain of discourse to which the metaphor is applied. To give an example, although one may admit that natural processes do not have purposes, it is conceivable that the process of evolution proceeds toward a particular goal (e.g., increased complexity). The (neutrally) analogical feature, then, is that both processes are directed. Darwin wavered between rejecting increased complexity as a goal of evolution (his original position) and accepting it (his later position; Benton, 1987; Ruse, 1988, 1993). The point here is not that evolution is goal-directed, but that the artificial selection metaphor prompts one to ask this question.

Transfer of Models: Cultural Inheritance. This admittedly sketchy account of how metaphors perform their function in the conceptualization of new and unfamiliar fields of science we will now extend to the metaphorical transfer of models. For brevity's sake, a model is considered to consist of a coherent and structured system of concepts that is about a particular physical system. Hence, a model is always considered to be an abstraction from nature, although not necessarily a formal (mathematical) one. This discussion begins by examining Boyd and Richerson's (1985) claim that, "social learning and cultural transmission can be modeled as a system of inheritance" (p. 430). Put differently, models used to understand the transmission of genes (genetic inheritance) can be used to conceptualize processes of cultural transmission or cultural inheritance. This section focuses on the transfer of a particular model that is easy to grasp, and yet conveys the essentials

TABLE 3.2

Transmission Rule for a Dichotomous Trait in a Population of Haploid, Sexual Organisms (adapted from Boyd & Richerson, 1983, table 3.5)

Possible Couples of Parents		Probability That a Child has Genotype	
Male	Female	a	b
a	a	1	0
a	b	1/2	1/2
b	a	1/2	1/2
b	b	0	1

Note. On each line the two right-most columns give the probability that a child of two parents with the characters specified in the two left-most columns has either genotype a or b.

Consider a genetic inheritance model that describes how the occurrence (frequency) of a particular dichotomous trait (a trait that may occur in two different states—a and b) changes from generation to generation in a population of haploid sexual organisms (each individual has either character a or b). Although the idea of a haploid sexual organism may seem odd, such organisms actually exist (a fungus like Neurospora is a well-known example). The oddity may vanish once one realizes that human gametes, the entities that engage in reproduction, are haploid too; the difference is that, with humans, the most conspicuous life form is diploid, whereas with fungi it is haploid. The advantage in the present context of using haploid sexual reproduction is that one may ignore complications like genetic dominance and its cognates. To keep track of changes in gene frequencies, we need to describe how children inherit characters from their parents (i.e., a transmission rule is needed). Table 3.2 gives such a rule. The table specifies the probability of a particular kind of offspring for every possible couple of parents.

Assuming (among other things) an initial frequency of p individuals with character a, equal reproductive success for a individuals and b individuals, and random mating of parents (e.g., a individuals have no particular preference for a or b individuals, one can show that the frequency p does not change from generation to generation (we do not perform the necessary algebraic manipulations, which can be found in any introductory text on the subject; basically, one sums the probability of a offspring weighted by the frequency of a couple over all possible couples). Because we are dealing with a dichotomous trait, it suffices to keep track only of the frequency p of individuals with trait a. The frequency of individuals with trait b will be $1-p$ and also remains unchanged. This result—and generalizations of it—is known as the Hardy–Weinberg law. Its importance is that it specifies a baseline: If character frequencies change, there must be something causing it (see Sober, 1984).

Boyd and Richerson (1985) transferred this model from the domain of genetical inheritance, where it originated, to that of cultural inheritance. Their reason for doing so was their wish to arrive at a cultural transmission model. Before discussing the latter model, one should ask what reasons Boyd and Richerson had to consider for such a transfer: What were the positive analogies that supported transfer? They provided a number of them. In their own words, their starting point was the realization that, "the cultural continuity of groups is due to inheritance of beliefs and values, and is not merely a result of the effects of individual learning and correlated environments" (p. 32).

Rather, the continuity ensues from a transmission process; it results because knowledge is transmitted (through social learning) from parents, peers, and others to relatively naive individuals. This observation grounds the analogy between the two kinds of inheritance systems. In both, there is an "exemplar" (biological parent or cultural "parent"; we avoid their term *model* because it would be confusing in the current context) and an "imitator" (biological offspring or cultural "offspring"), and in both, "information" (genes or knowledge) is stably transmitted (i.e., few errors are made). Moreover, the number of exemplars is small compared with the size of the population (two parents or the few people one is influenced by, and the focus of attention—the imitator—is one individual at a time ("child" or "pupil"), although to calculate population effects, one averages over them (in biological and cultural evolution). Finally, there is an information complex (genome or cultural repertoire) being transmitted. This complex acts as an organized whole, in that genes/pieces of knowledge may affect each other.

Of course, there are also negative analogies to be reckoned with. In genetic inheritance models only two parents are possible, whereas in the cultural case it is obvious that one's biological parents as well as other persons in that generation may act as exemplars (e.g., one's teachers). Also, cultural transmission other than age-vertical (i.e., from parents to children) is likely to occur as children pick up many habits from their peers. But there is more: cultural mating differs from genetic mating; generation length in genetic inheritance is fixed, it is variable in cultural inheritance; genetic offspring receive the genetic information in one fell swoop, in cultural inheritance knowledge is transmitted over a long period of time in bits and pieces to individuals that become culturally more sophisticated over time (because of this difference, order of transmission may matter); in cultural inheritance phenotypic characters are acquired directly by phenotypic copying, in genetic inheritance indirectly through the genes (although one could argue that in phenotypic copying the route is also indirect as it runs through the brain; but even so, it would be indirect in a different sense). Although the list could be continued almost at will, it already amply illustrates that the transfer of genetic inheritance models to the cultural domain is a genuine case of analogical transfer with limitations and dangers.

Stepping down again from the philosophical metalevel to that of the actual science, what does the cultural equivalent of the genetic inheritance model announced earlier look like? To avoid undue complications, it also assumes a dichotomous trait (see Table 3.3). However, to add some realism, three exemplars instead of two are considered. Therefore, the required transmission rule should also be adapted. (A further disanalogy is that probabilities A_1, A_2, and A_3 need not be all identical [i.e., 1/3]; the only requirement is that they sum to 1.)

TABLE 3.3

Transmission Rule for the Vertical Transmission of a Dichotomous Cultural Trait in a Population of Naive Individuals That Are Influenced by Three Exemplars (adapted from Boyd & Richerson, 1985, table 3.6).

Cultural Variant Characterizing the Exemplar			Probability That Naive Individual Acquires a Particular Cultural Variant	
1	2	3	c	d
c	c	c	1	0
c	c	d	$A_1 + A_2$	A_3
c	d	c	$A_1 + A_3$	A_2
d	c	c	$A_2 + A_3$	A_1
d	d	c	A_3	$A_1 + A_2$
d	c	d	A_2	$A_1 + A_3$
c	d	d	A_1	$A_2 + A_3$
d	d	d	0	1

Note. On each line the two right-most columns give the probability that an imitator influenced by three exemplars with the behaviors specified in the three left-most columns has either cultural trait *c* or *d*. Weights A_1, A_2, and A_3 describe how important the exemplars of different social roles are in transmission.

The interesting question (one of the neutral analogies) to be investigated is whether, like the Hardy–Weinberg law states for traits *a* and *b* in the genetic case, the frequencies of traits *c* and *d* also remain stable in the absence of outside forces. Algebraic manipulations similar to the ones required in the genetic case show exactly that to be the case. It is clear that the value of an approach like Boyd and Richerson's lies in obtaining this kind of result. The transfer of a genetic model to the cultural domain allows one to easily arrive at a conclusion hitherto unknown.

The genetic model has more neutral analogies to offer. As already indicated, deviations from the frequency expected on the Hardy–Weinberg law should be sought in the operation of various disturbing forces. In genetics, one distinguishes the force of mutation. Applied to the model, this would mean that, with probability μ_a, *a* is allowed to change into *b* and also that, with probability μ_b, *b* is allowed to change back into *a*. (Note that this particular notion of mutation excludes true novelty. Including novelty would be mathematically intractable.) Given these conditions, a given initial frequency p of a will change until it reaches an equilibrium

$$\hat{p} = \frac{\mu_b}{\mu_a + \mu_b} .$$

The cultural analogon of mutation would be the less-than-faithful imitating of exemplar behavior by cultural offspring. Not surprisingly, given error rates $(_c$ and $(_d$ the equilibrium frequency

$$\hat{p} = \frac{\mu_d}{\mu_c + \mu_d} .$$

Yet another example is the equivalent of genetic drift. Genetic transmission, like cultural transmission, is described in terms of probabilities. In genetic transmission, the frequency of a trait may "drift" away considerably from the expected value if the population has a small size. Every next generation should then be treated as a sample from a statistical population· The smaller the sample, the larger the expected deviation. In cultural transmission, one would expect similar drift effects—cultural drift—to occur.

But not all forces in cultural transmission have analogs in genetic transmission. A particularly striking example is what Boyd and Richerson dubbed "Lamarckian inheritance." In cultural transmission, it may occur that a cultural parent in his or her own lifetime adopts a particular habit after rational consideration or trial and error, rather than through imitation of others. There is nothing in a cultural inheritance system that stands in the way of transmitting such information. In a genetic inheritance system, however, this kind of inheritance would amount to a Lamarckian view. Despite some dissenting voices, this view has been broadly rejected in genetics.

Summary.   The upshot of the prior discussion is that models, much like simple concepts, may be transferred from one domain of scientific discourse to another. In both cases, perceived positive analogies are the primary reason for considering transfer at all, negative analogies point to issues to be cautious about, and neutral analogies are the sought source of new hypotheses awaiting to be pursued. Thus, the metaphorical transfer of models is a fruitful and decidedly nonreductive means of interdisciplinary, integrative interaction.

B. Anthropomorphism

Lorraine Daston

Some common descriptive language for human and nonhuman species seems a prerequisite for comparing the phenomena and theories of the biological and social sciences. Yet for historical and substantive reasons, extending the language for the human species has been controversial on theoretical, methodological, and moral grounds. Anthropomorphism has counted as a scientific sin since the 17th century (and as a theological sin long before that; see Fritsch, 1943; Heinrich, 1986; Marmorstein, 1937). It is also one of the most common reproaches hurled at those who seek a rapprochement between the study of the behavior, social organization, and cognition of humans and that of other organisms. The uses and abuses of anthropomorphism are a staple theme of the methodological reflections in recent works on primatology, as well as in ethological studies of more remotely related species such as ducks, snakes, or social insects (Ristau, 1991). Thoughtful critics question the scientific accuracy and political propriety of terms like "duck rape", "ant slavery," or even "baboon intentionality." Equally thoughtful respondents argue that evolutionary theory justifies the use of empathy and analogies, at least when the species in question shares the greater part of our own evolutionary history, or that, even when it does not, the heuristic gains of such analogies outweigh the methodological and political risks. No one who works at the intersection of biology and the social sciences can afford to ignore this issue. This section clarifies the meaning and scientific desirability of anthropomorphism by addressing the following issues: relationships between anthropomorphism and anthropocentrism, varieties of anthropomorphism, and arguments for and against the selective use of anthropomorphism.

Anthropomorphism vs. Anthropocentrism. *Anthropomorphism* means the attribution of human traits to a nonhuman entity, animate or inanimate; *anthropocentrism* means privileging human viewpoints and desires above all others. Many judge both terms to be scientific felonies, and deem them to be as closely allied as "breaking" and "entering" are in the police ledger. Is our current brand of antianthropomorphism indissolubly linked to antianthropocentrism? Should we ban both from science for the same reason—that they violate the ideal of aperspectival objectivity, which insists that scientists should strive to abandon all merely particular viewpoints, be they of class, nationality, gender, epoch, or even species, in favor of what the philosopher T. Nagel (1986) has called "the view from nowhere?"

It is possible to detach anthropomorphism and anthropocentrism. All four combinations of pro/anti attitudes toward anthropomorphism and anthropocentrism can be exemplified by cases in the history of science. Medieval and Renaissance natural historians were simultaneously proanthropomorphism and proanthropocentrism; 17th-century mechanical philosophers were antianthropomorphism, but proanthropocentrism; Darwin and many other 19th-century evolutionary thinkers were proanthropomorphism and antianthropocentrism; most late 20th-century thinkers declare themselves to be antianthropomorphism and antianthropocentrism (see Table 3.4). Background assumptions dictate whether, for example, proanthropocentrism will lead to proanthropomorphism. Combining the two is common enough, as in the case of medieval natural historians who argued that God supplied abundant examples of virtue in the animal world—the chastity of the camel, the altruism of the stork—so that even the illiterate could receive instruction by observation. Rejecting one but embracing the other is also possible, as in the case of the 17th-century Cartesians who argued that because God and man enjoyed a monopoly on activity, material objects (including animals) could not have desires, goals, or even feelings. If the background assumptions for holding what might otherwise be taken to be the same positions differ, the meaning of the positions themselves often differ as well. For example, the proanthropomorphism of the medieval bestiaries and that of Darwin are separated by more than just a gulf of centuries.

TABLE 3.4

Anthropomorphism versus Anthropocentrism

	Proanthropocentrism	Antianthropocentrism
Proanthropomorphism	Medieval and Renaissance bestiaries	Darwin's theory of the evolution of the emotions and moral sense
Antianthropomorphism	17th-century mechanical philosophy	20th-century philosophy of science

The point about such historical thought experiments is that antian-thropocentrism alone cannot suffice to justify the taboo against anthropomorphism. We must take care to distinguish the two, as well as our grounds for holding or rejecting each. Our current grounds for rejecting anthropomorphism in science have a complex relationship to anthropocentrism, which exhibits different aspects in different disciplines. Physicists, chemists, or astronomers reject anthropomorphism because of an ontological view about the kinds of entities that can be reasonably thought to think, feel, exhibit intentionality, and so on, and because of a methodological view about the theoretical forms best suited to the goals of, inter alia, prediction, intelligible explanation, and coherence with other theories. These ontological and methodological views are often intertwined, because intelligibility of an explanation depends crucially on the kind of entity or process to be explained. If one believes that planets are animated by angelic intelligences, for example, it makes sense to invoke final causes to explain their motions.

In the modern physical sciences, anthropocentrism becomes the explanation for regrettable instances of anthropomorphism, and the moral and intellectual grounds for censuring anthropomorphism. Here, anthropocentrism simultaneously implies childish vanity, which makes man the measure of all things, and an impoverished scientific imagination which imprisons the scientist within the narrow confines of human experience. Anthropomorphism is not only an ontological and methodological mistake; the anthropocentrism that underlies it is also read as evidence of character flaws and/or dullness.

The situation in biology differs because the modern discipline does not permit distinctions in kind between humans and other organisms. Evolutionary theory posits phylogenetic continuities and adaptive convergences among species that must have left some traces in the way organisms look and act. As a rule of thumb the closer the phylogenetic kinship of any two species, the more substantial their resemblances. Empirically, it may turn out that two species closely related by phylogeny differ significantly on this or that dimension of structure or behavior, or that selection has created similarities among distant species. But the Darwinian presumption favors incremental changes, which sum up to dramatic ruptures only over eons and taxa.

Thus, in biology, the charge of anthropomorphism often cuts against that of anthropocentrism, as Darwin's own case clearly shows. To maintain that humans differed radically from other primate species in moral sense and intelligence was, in his opinion, simply an unreasonable and arrogant insistence on the prerogatives and privileges of our own species (Durant, 1985). On this view, a deliberate strategy of anthropomorphism—interpreting, for example, the dance of bees in terms of "symbolic communication" (Griffin, 1976) or the grunts of vervet monkeys in terms of higher order intentionality (Cheney & Seyfarth, 1990; Dennett, 1988)—may be intended to counteract that aspect of anthropocentrism that stems from species vanity. Here, theoretically grounded (just *how* well grounded needs to be debated on a case-by-case basis) anthropomorphism combats, rather than derives from, morally objectionable anthropocentrism.

However, the intellectual reproach to anthropocentrism—that our own peculiar species experience constricts our ability to imagine other, more scientifically satisfactory possibilities—remains an objection to anthropomorphism even in biology. Because close phylogenetic ties justify only a presumption of similarity, simple projection of human traits onto other species could often be misleading. A symmetric strategy of balancing anthropomorphism with zoomorphism (i.e., reinterpreting human conduct and mental life in terms of other species) might in principle correct this bias, but in practice hits the same obstacle that drove researchers to anthropomorphic projections in the first place. It would require a superhuman imagination to transcend the categories and language that shape our species' own inner life.

Anthropomorphisms in the Plural. Given that all possible combinations of pro- and antianthropomorphism and pro- and antianthropocentrism have actually been instantiated in the history of science, and that the charge of anthropocentrism can, at least in biology, be further dissected into a moral and an intellectual reproach, it is clear that our wholesale way of talking about these practices in science must be refined. In the context of interactions between the biological and social sciences, it makes sense to distinguish at least three practices that are all commonly bundled together as anthropomorphism: empathic anthropomorphism, default anthropomorphism, and heuristic anthropomorphism.

The impulse behind empathic anthropomorphism is psychological; its justification is both theoretical and moral. The theoretical justification is evolutionary, and usually (although not always) cast in terms of phylogenetic proximity. For example, primatologist de Waal (1989) has defended a restricted version of empathic anthropomorphism:

Obviously this more empathic approach to animal behavior is hard to apply to slugs, frogs, or butterflies, but since my research is devoted entirely to monkeys and apes, I believe in its value ... Provided that it is based on intimate knowledge and translated into testable hypotheses, anthropomorphism is a very useful step toward understanding a psychology similar to and almost as complex as ours. (p. 25)

The moral justification is both antianthropocentric—it would be the height of arrogance to reserve consciousness, purposefulness, moral sense, intelligence, and so on, for our own species—and empathic, based on the sentiment that at least some other species have a social and mental life recognizable to our own. The empathic response to other species is moral and emotional, in that it often leads to the extension of personhood and the rights thereof to these species. Thus, in view of Darwin's marked empathic anthropomorphism, especially with respect to dogs (see, e.g., Darwin, cited in Barrett, 1985; Darwin, [1872]1965, [1871]1981), it is not surprising that he supported British antivivisection legislation, although this position meant he was at odds with much of the professional scientific community (French, 1975; Ritvo, 1987). Conversely, moralists who argue for animal rights often invoke some form of empathic anthropomorphism (P. Singer, 1976). Although some students of animal behavior try to differentiate between the theoretical and moral justifications of empathic anthropomorphism (Griffin, 1984), in practice they are difficult to disentangle, because empathy is both a method and a moral sentiment.

Critics of empathic anthropomorphism contend that it (a) suffers from the vices of default anthropomorphism, and (b) indulges in sentimental fantasies about other species (Zuckerman, 1991). Ever since C. L. Morgan's (1884) trenchant critique of Romanes' (1883) claims for consciousness and choice on behalf of animal minds as irredeemably anecdotal and unjustifiably anthropomorphic (see also R. J. Richards, 1987), many ethologists and comparative psychologists have adapted Morgan's canon as their motto: "In no case may we interpret an action as the outcome of the exercise of a higher psychical faculty, if it can be interpreted as the outcome of one which stands lower in the psychological scale" (C. L. Morgan, 1895, p. 53). Hence, stances on method, psychological theory, and empathic anthropomorphism are strongly correlated: Those who cultivate empathic anthropomorphism also tend to countenance single incident, "anecdotal" evidence and embrace cognitive models; those who reject empathic anthropomorphism tend to insist on statistical protocols, laboratory experiments, and behaviorist explanations. (It should be noted that this correlation is by no means a necessary one. It is possible to find anecdotes cast in scrupulously behaviorist language [e.g., Kummer, cited in Whiten & Byrne, 1988], and statistical analyses conducted in terms of frankly anthropomorphic categories [e.g., Silk, 1992].) This correlation begets some confusion, because the legitimacy of empathic anthropomorphism is seldom debated alone, but rather as part of controversies over the explanatory adequacy of behaviorism or the methodological propriety of aggregating anecdotes (Griffin, 1976, 1984; Whiten & Byrne, 1988).

By contrast, default anthropomorphism is employed as a spontaneous descriptive style, rather than as a chosen strategy. In its most sophisticated form, default anthropomorphism has been defended on the grounds of convenience and clarity: "If a biologist may not use the common words, he will be forced to invent a whole new set of jargon terms for nonhuman societies, an unfortunate direction since there are too many jargon words in any science as it is" (Bonner, 1980, p. 10). In its crassest form, it is presented, without any defense, as a transparent description: "It sounds like a neutral enough, nonsubjective observation. But it is not. Did [Diane] Fossey see the gorilla 'spying' the vine? How could she have recognised that she had 'spied' it, except on the basis of her subsequent behaviour interpreted as an act of tactical deception?" (Humphrey, 1988, p. 258). Sophisticated or crass versions of default anthropomorphism can usually be distinguished by examining whether explicit arguments are presented in justification of the frankly human terms of description.

The crass version has been frequently and fiercely criticized. *Vulgar anthropomorphism* is philosopher Philip Kitcher's label for the crass or unreflective assimilation of the behavior of nonhuman species to that of humans on the basis of "superficial similarity." Especially when the behaviors in question concern the politically volatile areas of sex and power, he and others worry about the vicious circle that is closed when the behavior of nonhumans is glibly described in terms of that of humans and then put forward as an evolutionary argument that the human behavior in question is "natural": "The claim about humans is magic—a rabbit pulled out of a well-prepared hat" (Kitcher, 1985, p. 185; see also Haraway, 1989). However, it should be pointed out that a reprehensible, vulgar anthropomorphism cannot work by itself—its "magical" efficacy depends on several other dubious, tacit assumptions. First, it is assumed that what holds for the behavior of one species (ducks, ants, chimpanzees, etc.) will hold for all, in particular for humans. Second, it is assumed that what is "natural" is also inevitable and/or desirable for human societies. Without these further missteps in reasoning, anthropomorphism, no matter how vulgar, would hardly pose political problems.

Other critics emphasize theoretical objections to default anthropomorphism, in both its sophisticated and crass forms, contending that it seriously distorts our understanding of the behavior of nonhuman species, whatever its implications, real or alleged, might be for human behavior (S. D. Mitchell, 1990). In this vein, primatologist Hans Kummer has complained of the premature extension of cognitively "demanding" explanations to primate behavior: "in doing so we simply project our everyday percepts for human behavior .... By forestalling detailed research it deprives us of the opportunity to discover the fascinating social Umwelten and Innenwelten in which other species live" (Kummer, Dasser, & Hoyningen-Huene, 1990, p. 93). Here, even the sophisticated version of default anthropomorphism stands condemned, for convenience and clarity may mask the quite alien truth of the matter.

Heuristic anthropomorphism defends the application of terms coined for human behavior to other species on the grounds of structural similarities. These need not always conform to phylogenetic lineages: The argument is that similar adaptive problems often find similar "solutions"—an argument that, in principle, supports all kinds of inter-species analogies, not just anthropomorphic ones between humans and nonhumans. For example, pair-bonding may be regularly correlated with territoriality, in songbirds as well as antelopes (P. J. Jarman & M. V. Jarman, 1973; Tompa, 1962). Heuristic anthropomorphism, when pursued as an explicit strategy, is a straightforward example of the use of analogy in scientific hypothesizing, and demands the usual care in distinguishing positive, negative, and neutral correspondences between the two domains under comparison, as argued earlier. In the special case of heuristic anthropomorphism, care must be taken to distinguish the empirical and conceptual attractions of an analogy from the covertly anthropocentric attractions of mere familiarity.

Evaluating Anthropomorphism. For biologists and social scientists to participate in interdisciplinary interaction, it must, in principle, be possible to compare observations and theories on the behavior and social organization of humans and nonhumans—without prejudging the question of significant similarities by loading the language of description. It has long been clear that certain forms of anthropomorphism—the crass versions of default anthropomorphism—will prejudge the issue. Nevertheless, a blanket ban on all anthropomorphism has precisely the same preemptive effect. We have every reason to believe that the question of similarity requires finely differentiated answers, both with respect to various species and various behaviors: Sometimes anthropomorphic language is justified and sometimes it is not.

Therefore, it behooves researchers to differentiate correspondingly in their discussions of anthropomorphism as a method, distinguishing between anthropocentrism and anthropomorphism, and attending to which form of the latter is at issue in any given case. The polarization of methods that often sharpens the debate over anthropomorphism in the study of animal behavior should be recognized as contingent rather than necessary. Existing analogies, be they positive, negative, or neutral, are conclusions drawn from empirical investigation. For example, although behaviorist explanations may ward off the crass kind of default anthropomorphism, the cognitive explanations advanced by some ethologists are not necessarily condemned to such crassness.

Similarly, although experimental or statistical protocols may scotch the sentimentalized version of empathic anthropomorphism, not all anecdotal evidence reeks of the Victorian favorite-pet story. Given the thickly moralizing tone of many debates over anthropomorphism, it should also be borne in mind that even the sins of anthropomorphism are multifarious: It may be an intellectual sin against scientific objectivity, a moral sin against species humility, or a political sin against the possibility of social reform. Whether these sins are single or compound, venial or cardinal, must be judged according to context. This can be generalized to a rule—namely, that there is no hard-and-fast rule of how to separate the anthropomorphic dross from the anthropomorphic gold, and that arguments as to what kind of anthropomorphism may be justified by what kind of evidence must be judged on a case-by-case basis, considering the positive, negative, and neutral analogies that may be contained therein.

Yet some may despair of the possibility of escaping undesirable forms of anthropomorphism. They are pessimistic about the possibilities of climbing out of our own conceptual skins and creating alternatives to our own psychological and social categories. In other words, they fear that we may have reached the outermost limits of aperspectival objectivity. There are, however, reasons for hope: Historians and anthropologists sometimes succeed in understanding societies remote from our own in time and space; moreover, the history of science bears witness to the slow, halting construction of a nonanthropomorphic language in the physical sciences since the 17th century. There exist at least precedents for shedding both social and psychological forms of subjectivity—precedents that demonstrate that the achievement of aperspectival objectivity demands an extraordinary power of imagination. To achieve this for the minds and societies of other species, if minds and societies there be, taxes the scientific imagination still further, but perhaps not beyond all possibility.

TOOLS

Gerd Gigerenzer

What biology and the social sciences uncontroversially share are certain analytical tools. Scientific tools, such as statistical techniques, are vehicles of interdisciplinarity, as are theories. However, controversies tend to focus on the transfer of theories from the biological to the social domain and vice versa, rather than on the invasion and conquest by tools. Debates about reductionism, pluralism, and metaphorical transfer witness this preference. After all, the prevailing view of scientific tools is that they are theoretically neutral—impartial and objective instruments for evaluating theories, not partisans in theoretical disputes. We argue here for a fresh look at the role of tools. Tools are not theoretically inert. Rather, they share most of the problems of theoretical transfers, and should no longer be taken as uncontroversial.

Historically, methods often were developed for a specific subject, and only slowly freed themselves from specific contents. When the British polymath, Francis Galton, invented a method to measure how much offspring deviated from their parent stock, he launched the analysis of correlations; when Charles Spearman designed his two-factor theory of intelligence, he launched factor analysis; Fisher's analysis of variance (ANOVA) started out in agriculture and eugenics, and so on (see Gigerenzer et al., 1989). Most of these ended up as all-purpose methods. One consequence of this liberation is the widespread fiction that methods are essentially undiluted positive analogies.

We argue that methods carry theoretical assumptions that need close examination for negative analogies, as with any interdisciplinary transfer. For instance, factor analysis and multiple linear regression can only "see" the linear relationships in the world, and the correlation coefficient is like an observer that ignores differences in means and variances in the two variables correlated. Thus, these methods are strictly limited tools—they let us clearly see some aspects of the world, and are mute on others.

Analytical tools have a double function: They are means of generating and processing data to evaluate theories about some domain, and they also shape our theorizing about the domain. Our topic is the potential of ubiquitous analytical tools for shaping theories and research programs, and to generate tool-laden theories. Although this section draws the reader's attention to this double function of tools, it is not intended as a blanket critique of tool-laden theories. Critique only applies to the naive use of tools (i.e., using techniques without realizing in what way they shape the theoretical questions; Lewontin, 1974a). The following illustrates this issue with one of the most frequently used methods in the social and biological sciences—the ANOVA.

A. Analysis of Variance

ANOVA was developed by Ronald A. Fisher and first applied to the examination of the yield of 12 potato varieties under six conditions of manure (Fisher & Mackenzie, 1923). From agriculture, ANOVA spread through biology and the social sciences (but not through molecular biology and the physical sciences). In several disciplines, ANOVA and related inferential techniques became institutionalized after World War II as the *sine qua non* of scientific method. For instance, by 1970, about 70% of the articles in major psychology journals used ANOVA for drawing inferences from data to hypothesis (Edgington, 1974). As we shall see, fields like human behavior genetics would look completely different without ANOVA.

What is ANOVA? What follows is a brief sketch of the two-factorial case (for more, see Fisher, 1935; Wahlsten, 1990). Many studies attempt to understand the causes of individual differences in some trait (such as height, intelligence, aggression). Two classes of causes are commonly distinguished; heredity (H) and environment (E). ANOVA is based on a simple causal model, $\underline{T} = \underline{H} + \underline{E} + \underline{M}$, where $\underline{M}$ is measurement error. Using simplifying assumptions (e.g., that there errors are independent of the levels of H and E, and that all covariances are zero), the model is:

$$\text{Var}(T) = \text{Var}(H) + \text{Var}(E) + \text{Var}(HE) + \text{Var}(M).$$

In words, the variance in the trait (the individual differences) is the sum of the variance in heredity, environment, interaction, and measurement error. Based on this model, ANOVA decomposes any set of empirical measurements T, obtained in a H x E design with various levels of H and E, into these four variances.

B. Tool-Laden Research Programs

What questions can a two-factorial ANOVA answer? Whether main effects (genotype and environment) and interaction are significant, and if so, how much variance is "explained" by each of these sources. This is called the *ANOVA problematic*, and is indeed the research program of human behavior genetics. Relative contribution and possible interaction are the objects of investigation. The relative contribution Var(H)/Var(T) is known as the heritability coefficient (h2) in the broad sense. In laboratory animal studies, heredity can be experimentally manipulated (through selective breeding), as can the environment, and heritability coefficients can be calculated based on an experimental design. However, in human behavior genetics, experimentally controlled mating and environments are not ethically possible. Thus studies rely, among others, on comparisons between identical and fraternal twins, reared together and apart. The human behavior literature is filled with heritability coefficients, from coefficients around .8 for the inheritance of intelligence (IQ) to around .3 for the "heritability" of various features of a child's family environment, such as expressiveness and achievement (Plomin & Bergeman, 1991). However, statisticians (e.g., Kempthorne, 1990) have repeatedly argued that such heritability coefficients for species that cannot be experimentally manipulated are meaningless and should be ignored.

One goal of the biological and social sciences is to give a causal account of nature. What can ANOVA contribute to that goal? Consider this simplest case: How can two supposed causes, heredity (H) and environment (E), produce some trait T? Models for how these causes combine include additive combinations (T = H + E), multiplicative combinations (T = H x E), threshold models (e.g., E only has an effect on T if H has a value above or below a certain threshold), and various polynomial combinations (such as in the law of falling bodies). With three variables, this number increases, including multiplicative combination (such as Hull's,

1952, theory of reaction potential) and distributive combination (such as Spence's, 1956, theory of reaction potential).

Note that the ANOVA problematic is different from the general question guiding causal analysis. A causal analysis investigates *how* several variables act together in a temporal sequence. In contrast, the ANOVA problematic, aims to measure relative importance, and silently *assumes* one particular causal model: additivity. Thus, the ANOVA problematic presupposes a causal model, rather than asking what kind of causal model it is. ANOVA estimates additive causal contributions; but when the causes are not additively combined, the meaning of the resulting estimated relative contributions is unclear, and the tool it not the right tool for the job.

How is the empirical adequacy of the ANOVA presuppositions (i.e., whether the additive causal model holds) decided? There have been two kinds of answers; general evaluations and empirical tests for specific phenomena. Concerning the first, many critics have argued that additivity of nature and nurture is highly unrealistic: "Obviously, there will always be some interaction; we need only think about 'some village Hampden, some mute inglorious Milton, some Cromwell' of Gray's Elegy, or a Beethoven born in a slum" (Kempthorne, 1990, p. 138). Fisher (1951) warned of the coefficient of heritability as "one of those unfortunate shortcuts which have emerged in biometry for lack of a more thorough analysis of the data" (p. 217). Let us now take a closer look at the empirical test.

There is a routine empirical test of the crucial additivity assumption: whether the interaction H×E is significant. If two factors are truly additive, then the interaction should not be significant. Conversely, nonsignificance of interaction is usually (and often mistakenly) taken as evidence for additivity of genetic and environmental factors. Plomin and Bergeman (1991), for instance, argued that, with few exceptions, they have not yet found such interactions. These tests of interaction are performed by ANOVA.

Here we can see the double function of this tool: A research program is suggested *and* tested by the same tool. The ANOVA problematic is posed, while ANOVA is used to decide whether in the light of data, the problematic is meaningful. There is a serious problem, however: ANOVA tests of interaction often have only low statistical power (J. Cohen, 1977). The power of a test of interaction is the probability of finding a significant interaction, if there really is one. For instance, for a 5×5 (genotype x environment) design, a median effect size, a conventional

5% significance level, and 10 subjects in each of the 25 groups, the
power of an interaction test is only .14 (Wahlsten, 1990). In other words,
if there is nonadditivity, the ANOVA test nevertheless produces a non-
significant result in 86% of such cases. By contrast, if there is additivity,
the ANOVA test produces a significant result in only 5% of the cases—
from the same design. That is, the rate of one error (inferring additivity
although there is non-additivity) is 86%, whereas the rate of the other
possible error (inferring nonadditivity although there is additivity) is only
5%. Despite such unequal chances, researchers have concluded from
nonsignificance that additivity holds although the chances of making an
erroneous inference are strikingly higher in this case. Therefore, if there
is an interaction in this situation, researchers would be better off basing
their conclusions on the tossing of a coin than on an ANOVA test of interaction, whereas they have a good chance of finding additive effects if
they do exist. Because calculations of power are rarely made—an omis-
sion consistent with how ANOVA is taught in many textbooks, and with
Fisher's own doctrine—there is a risk of importing a theoretical distortion
with every use of ANOVA.

C. Additive Causes and Relative Importance Questions

Tool-laden research programs and the use of ANOVA to test the
ANOVA problematic are not restricted to human behavior genetics or
animal behavior genetics. For example, causal attribution theory (Kelley,
1967), postulates that the mind attributes a cause to an effect in the same
way as behavioral scientists now do—namely, by (unconsciously) cal-
culating an ANOVA. ANOVA provides the framework for understanding the mind and, at the same time, the tool to test predictions of this
framework in the laboratory. Here are some more examples: Additivity of
components of variance has been proposed as a definition of the units of
selection (Lloyd, 1989). Questions of the relative importance of various
factors as determined by ANOVA's have become the research program
for many subdisciplines in the biological and social sciences (Lloyd,
1989). Since the 1960s, traditional personality psychology has been
revolutionized by the ANOVA question: How much in the variability of a
behavior can be explained by the variability in traits, how much by the
variability in situations, and how much by interaction? (For more
examples of where relative importance questions replace causal analysis,
see Gigerenzer & Murray, 1987).

D. Null Models

ANOVA is a special instance of a larger class of techniques for hypothesis testing, which Fisher (1935) called *null hypothesis testing*. For instance, the hypothesis of no interaction is a null hypothesis. Null hypothesis tests are asymmetric tests. Only the null hypothesis is statistically specified, the alternative (e.g., interaction) is not. Partly as a result of this, the null has a different status than the alternative: Unless disproved, the researcher sticks with the null hypothesis of "chance" or "no causal effect." In ecology as well as evolutionary biology, the Fisherian message of the importance and primacy of null hypotheses has been used to argue that null models, postulating random mechanisms, have a special epistemological status compared with causal or adaptationist models (e.g., Strong, 1980).

For instance, modern community ecology has shown that the average species:genus ratios for plants and animals are smaller in isolated communities (e.g., islands) than in large ones (e.g., mainland). This puzzling fact was originally explained by extinction caused by competitive exclusion, which most likely occurs within restricted areas, from where it is hard to escape. This interspecific competition hypothesis was challenged by a random colonization hypothesis postulating that the smaller species:genus ratio can be explained by a random sampling model. Small random samples from large populations will have lower species:genus ratios, independent of competition. The debate is not about the fact itself, but the proper explanation. Both hypotheses fit the extant data equally well. Then the argument was offered that the random colonization hypothesis, just like random drift, is a null hypothesis, whereas the intraspecific competition hypothesis, just like selection or migration, is not. Furthermore, it was argued that, unless the null hypothesis can be rejected, the alternative hypothesis cannot be accepted, just as in the typical use of ANOVA. Strong (1980) claimed that null hypotheses "have logical primacy," and Simberloff (1983) claimed they are more parsimonious.

This example illustrates how specific features of null hypothesis testing have turned into (or at least have been used to support) the logical primacy of certain kinds of theoretical explanations. Note that other tools, such as Neyman-Pearson hypothesis testing, would *not* have suggested such an idea. In contrast to Fisher's ANOVA, Neyman-Pearson statistics starts with two symmetric statistical hypotheses (instead of one null), which are treated as equal. Thus, no hypothesis enjoys logical primacy.

Thus far, we have presented examples of how an analytical tool shapes theoretical arguments. But it is not only the mathematics of a tool (e.g., the additive model), but also its practical use that can shape theoretical arguments (Gigerenzer, 1991). The argument that null models have logical primacy is an example. It is based on the widespread but conceptually confused practice of null hypothesis testing in the biological and social sciences, and not, as suggested by Strong (1980), on Fisher's theory of null hypothesis testing. In practice, the null ("chance") is understood to oppose an alternative causal hypothesis ("causal effect"), as is the case when the random colonization hypothesis confronts the interspecific competition hypothesis (Sloep, 1993). However, in statistical theory, the null is opposed to another statistical hypothesis, and both must be distinguished from the level of causal hypotheses. In the logical primacy argument, these two levels are confounded, as they often are in practice (Gigerenzer, 1993). A null hypothesis does not imply the absence of a cause; an alternative (statistical) hypothesis is always a "chance" hypothesis, just as the null is, only with different parameters. Thus, it is not Fisher's null hypothesis testing, as claimed by Strong (1980), but the actual practice of doing null hypothesis testing that is the mistaken basis of the argument.

E. Methodological Pluralism

Analytical tools can shape theoretical questions and research programs. They are not neutral general-purpose tools. Although this section concentrated on ANOVA because it has been so widely used in the biological and social sciences, we could have chosen Pearson correlations or other tools to make the same point about unreflected usage. What lesson is to be drawn? First, let us realize that tools are theoretically active. This means that we willy-nilly make theoretical choices when we use a tool, and we should be aware of those. Second, when a tool is used in a discipline in a mechanical and mindless way, we should beware of the consequences for individual theories and whole research programs. For instance, only if the mechanical use of ANOVA is abandoned can the goal of partitioning variance among mutually exclusive and additive causes be added by serious attempts to understand how the causes—genetic and environmental—actually interact. Finally, methodological pluralism follows as a necessary consequence if we choose tools by depending on the theoretical models they carry with them, rather than by habit.

One pressure selecting against methodological pluralism is the old idealization of tools as neutral and objective. It is often understood that there can only be one "objective" tool, not two or more. Null hypothesis testing is a good example.

Sociobiologists, animal researchers, experimental psychologists, and several other groups of biologists and social scientists perform a mechanical ritual of null hypothesis testing, without taking account of the plurality of tools developed after Fisher published his famous Design of Experiments in 1935 (Gigerenzer & Murray, 1987). Institutionalization of a particular statistical tool seems to provide objectivity in fields that strive for certification as genuine science. The price that has been paid for this illusion of objectivity by means of mechanical tool use is that the tool-ladenness of theories is being overlooked. In a Trojan-horse fashion, tools can be smuggled in and become entrenched in whole theoretical frameworks. Despite their different reputations, tools and analogies exhibit almost the same set of dangers and opportunities in an interdisciplinary context.

The danger is not that they are doing it, but that we take no notice, being blinded by habit or by the anxiety that surrounds the teaching and use of statistics in both the biological and social sciences (Gigerenzer, 1993). Anxiety and neglect of theoretical assumptions built into tools have a common root: Both stem from a superficial or faulty grasp of the statistical concepts underlying them, due to cookbook-style teaching and mechanical use of computerized "packages." Only when researchers truly understand their tools will they be able to use them intelligently and without fear.

CONCLUSION

This chapter attempted to quiet the fears of disciplinary imperialism that arise when the idea of biology and social science integration is broached. Rather than succumb to the monolithic philosophical frameworks of global unification, we have counseled pluralism. But the pluralism advocated here is not an uncritical isolationism. Instead, we have promoted integrative pluralism—a view acknowledging the partial autonomy of theories, concepts, models, and methodological tools, while requiring active, reflective, and piecemeal integration of the contributions of many disciplines and approaches in explaining the complex phenomena of human culture.

ACKNOWLEDGMENT

This chapter is a product of intense and fruitful interdisciplinary interactions. During 1991-1992, while in residence in Bielefeld, the authors met regularly forming a seminar to discuss the problems and promises of interdisciplinarity. An outline for the chapter was negotiated and sections were drafted by the individual authors indicated. Multiple versions were subjected to critical and constructive review by the group. The final text reflects much of this interdisciplinary effort. We thank the ZiF for the opportunity to collaborate.

PART II

HOMOLOGIES

INTRODUCTION: THE VALUE AND LIMITATIONS OF HOMOLOGIES FROM BIOLOGY IN THE STUDY OF CULTURE

One reason for utilizing biology to understand humans is the fact of human natural origins. Humans evolved from apes. Our epigenetic development follows patterns similar to other vertebrates. In our ecological interactions with other species and the physical environment, we face challenges of survival and reproduction much like any other organism. Thus, scientific inquiry based on a homological line of reasoning always has ready justifications. Reconstructions of our phylogenetic past serve the understanding of our current morphological design, as well as psychological and behavioral dispositions. Comparative analyses elucidate which features we share with other species and which combinations of traits are different, in particular with respect to ecologically similar species. Information like this can illuminate biological foundations (i.e., constraints and conditions, of human culture).

Social scientists, although not denying that human beings are organisms after all, still have difficulties in seriously considering the implications of this approach. While not ignoring it completely or abandoning it, for fear of political abuse or scientific reductionism (see General Introduction, chaps. 2 and 3), they elude direct consideration by pointing to a division of scientific labor: The biological sciences address questions that treat humans as a species among other living creatures, whereas social scientists ask questions that treat humans as unique cultural beings.

Because human beings are both just another species and a particularly highly developed one, an isolationist stance of scientific division of labor is unwarranted. No doubt the sophistication of human cultural capacity is impressive and requires special attention—a task the social sciences like anthropology, sociology, and psychology fulfill. However, rather than reifying the division of the world into the "Natural" and the "Cultural," the biological and the social sciences need to cooperate to grasp the complexity of human cultural phenomena. Indeed, issues such as the evolution of social intelligence, language, nonverbal communication, and human social institutions, or the ecology of human behavior, call for interdisciplinary interaction. Each of the features involved (e.g., the capacity

151

for speech or rule-governed behavior) has some parallels in other organisms, but the combination and degree of exaggeration of these features indicates that the ways in which humans are unique are crucial to the explanations of their behavior.

Thus far, interdisciplinary cooperation *strictu sensu* (i.e., the search for compatible accounts of human cultural phenomena from different disciplines) is the exception. Mutual ignorance, at worst, and analogical transfer of biological concepts, at best, still dominate the situation. Attempts to explore human cultural phenomena that transgress the boundary of a single social or biological discipline are rare. Thus, recent evolutionary theory from sociobiology and population genetics attracted attention because of their various claims to answer questions relating to the development of human culture, social behavior, the development of social institutions, and their transformation. Within the social sciences, such attempts reflect a minority position at best and passionate rejection at worst. Apart from anthropology and psychology, there are only a few sociologists who seriously consider human biological design to play a constitutive role in the current designs of human societies.

Homologically based studies seek to discover basic similarities to other species, as well as the phylogenetic roots of our capacity for culture. Facing the "homological challenge," the social scientist meets with archaeological or paleoanthropological studies, which suggest that the abilities and limitations that our morphology, behavorial, or psychological dispositions impose may be remnants of ancestral adaptations—features designed for other environments. Also, ethological studies commonly reveal morphological traits and behavioral dispositions that testify to the fact that basic dispositions for sociality (see chap. 6), communication, and "intelligent" behavior (see chap. 4) are far more widespread than previously thought. The capacity for communication, either by mimic and gestures or speech signals, does not categorically separate humans from all other species (see chap. 5). Some institutions characteristic of human societies—the family, economic division of labor, and communication—are found in various forms in other animal societies. Do similar environmental challenges shape such institutions in humans and nonhumans (see chap. 7)?

It is these kinds of similarities to other organisms and their social life that support an evolutionary conception of human uniqueness, as in Foley's (1987) argument advanced in *Another Unique Species*. His point was to emphasize that all species are unique, and that the concepts and methods of ecology and evolution are designed to shed light on biotic diversity. The contributors to Part II, like Foley, use theory from evolutionary ecology to understand the evolution, proximate biological underpinnings, and ecological consequences of unique human features.

There are a number of excellent reasons to expect that treating humans as another unique species is a research program worthy of pursuit (see Beatty, 1987, for a discussion of "worthy of pursuit"). The most important of these are:

1. *Behavioral continuities.* Human biology, in many respects, is obviously quite conservative; "animal models" are important to biomedical research for this reason, despite the unique elements of our anatomy and physiology. Much human behavior shows unmistakable signs of being similarly conservative, as Darwin ([1872]1965) argued in his *Expression of Emotion in Man and Animals.* Chapters 5 and 6 discuss a number of examples in the realm of nonverbal communication and basic elements of our social "instincts." Where continuity is strong, functional interpretations based rather directly on nonhuman animal models have a sound foundation, as is quite plausibly the case for incest/inbreeding avoidance, for instance.

2. *Behavioral phylogeny.* Many other aspects of our behavior have indeed been modified in the course of our evolution. As usual, however, evolutionary processes have built on existing adaptations to create new ones, so that we have to understand the current human behavior or behavioral capacity in terms of the constraints of evolutionary history. Chapter 4 investigates the widely mooted social intelligence hypothesis for the phylogeny of advanced cognitive abilities in primates. The discussion of nonverbal behavior in chapter 5 and that of evolutionary sociology in chapter 6 draw on phylogenetic analysis to understand the origins and current function of derived, unique aspects of human behavior. There are historical footprints on even our most strikingly unique features—as on the anatomy of bipedalism, to pick a less controversial example than behavior.

3. *Proximal mechanisms of derived behavior.* Our unique behavior is subserved by anatomical and neurophysiological mechanisms. Language is an important example. It is interesting to understand just how the unique human ability to speak is organized at the biological level (chap. 5). Chomsky's (1959) innatist theories of grammar have long attracted attention, and recent work strengthens the argument

that innate cognitive "organs" like linguistic capacities must have a-risen as adaptations (see chap. 6). The workings of these mechanisms and their evolutionary origins are interesting, interrelated sets of questions. Among other things, we cannot understand the constraints on and opportunities open to unique features like language and other aspects of culture until we understand their biological basis. The exact nature of innate constraints on cultural behavior is still subject to great uncertainty even in the case of language, but the case for a simple *tabula rasa* or hierarchical model is quite weak. Attempts to restrict biology to a distinctly peripheral role in explaining human behavior using such constructs are probably doomed. More likely, biological, cultural, and environmental will turn out to be intimately intertwined.

4. *Adaptive behavior.* Human behavioral variation is often adaptive in the biological sense of favoring survival and reproduction. A long tradition of functionalism in the social sciences appeals to the intuition that variation in human sociocultural institutions is adaptive. The huge range of environments to which people have managed to spread and their oft-dominant role in those environments suggests that the functionalist intuition has to be substantially correct. What biology brings to the table is a precise definition of adaptation drawn from evolutionary theory, and a considerable number of specific models predicting how people should forage, choose their mates, compose their families, and the like, drawn from evolutionary ecology (chap. 7). Mechanisms of phenotypic flexibility—learning, intelligence, culturally acquired techniques—allow humans to solve an unprecedentedly diverse array of adaptive problems. It is likely that mechanisms of phenotypic flexibility first arose because they were usually successful at solving adaptive problems, such as foraging nearoptimally on a wide variety of resources in a wide variety of environments. It may be, as the Darwinian psychologists argue (chap. 6), that much behavior in the complex societies of the Holocene is maladaptive because it is based on psychological mechanisms adapted to Pleistocene past. However, humans have prospered wonderfully in the Holocene, suggesting that the adaptationist program will work more often than not across the full range of societies studied by anthropologists and sociologists.

It should be evident that the "humans-as-another-unique-species" perspective does not deny the unique course of human evolution. Even the most dedicated homologist holds that the differences that evolved in humans have at least some significance beyond reproductive isolation from related species and a slight shift in ecological relationships that commonly accompany speciation. Such modest but significant differences between sister species probably characterized chimpanzees and australopithecines 4 or 5 million years ago. Modern human behavior includes differences vis-à-vis all other animals of much greater magnitude and theoretical significance.

Part II investigates the aspects of human culture and social organization that present fundamental challenges to the "another-unique-species" approach. Cultural evolution arguably introduces new evolutionary mechanisms that are not part of the standard biologists' tool kit. Human societies arguably have emergent systemic properties not present in other animal societies. For that matter, again arguably, nonhuman social and ecological systems contain phenomena that are not well explained by the adaptationist program. Notwithstanding such possibilities, at the bare minimum sound adaptationist hypotheses are essential benchmarks against which to compare other explanations.

Phylogenetic reconstruction and comparisons across species are of special importance to social science studies of basic human institutions, and do not necessarily compete with each other. The emergence of the family, group structures, or psychological dispositions may be linked to insights regarding the issue of "cultural universals." With respect to the incest taboo, for example, anthropological findings and evolutionary studies on the phylogenetic roots of this particular behavioral pattern, which today appears to be a psychological reluctance to mate with close relatives, may complement each other.

Human distinctiveness reconsidered in the light of phylogenetic reconstructions and comparisons across species reveals that current human cultural settings are, indeed, affected by our biological design. Available evidence compels us to assume that human culture is due to both biological and (if ever more prevailing) cultural forces. Yet our aim is not to draw new borderlines between the biological and the social. Rather, we want to avoid conceptions that regard biology as the "substrate" acted on by human sociality as a result of which human culture emerges. In our view, any satisfactory scientific explanation inseparably comprises social and biological elements. This holds both for homological and analogical approaches.

The approaches that reflect this view are those of gene–culture coevolution. They largely agree on the assumption that there is a connection between biological and cultural mechanisms of change. They differ as to the kind of linkage between them (i.e., whether the transmission of cultural properties is related to biological reproduction, or whether cultural evolution can run counter to the fitness maximization). In a sense, the range of coevolutionary approaches extends from those claiming a homological relationship between biological and cultural phenomena (R. D. Alexander, 1979) to those postulating patterns of cultural change that proceed analogously to evolutionary mechanisms, but are independent as to fitness maximization (Cavalli-Sforza & Feldman, 1981). In the first case, cultural phenomena are yet another tool to serve the purpose of fitness enhancement; in the latter case, this would be but an accidental result.

Part III explores some of the promises and achievements of the coevolutionary approaches. Prior to a closer examination of the different efforts to grasp the intricate relationship between biological and social elements in the evolution of human culture, however, Part II lays the foundation by giving an overview of homologically oriented studies.

4

THE SOCIAL INTELLIGENCE
HYPOTHESIS

Hans Kummer
University of Zurich
Switzerland

Lorraine Daston
Max Planck Institute for
the History of Science
Berlin, Germany

Gerd Gigerenzer
Max Planck Institute for
Psychological Research
Munich, Germany

Joan B. Silk
University of California
Los Angeles

Intelligence is part of culture. It developed culture's material underpinnings and rationalizes cultural norms. Although it was once thought to be a unitary capacity that served equally well in all contexts, more recent research in child psychology (e.g., R. Gelman, 1990) and animal ethology has shown that much of intelligence is powerful only in certain domains of the environment for which it was evolved. Species and even contexts have their own intelligences. If this is true, the student of culture should begin to wonder in which section of reality our ancestral primate intelligence was originally designed because it might still bear traces of that origin.

In various forms, Jolly (1966), Humphrey (1976), Chance and A. P. Mead (1953), and Byrne and Whiten (1988) have proposed the hypothesis that the natural intelligence of primates, including humans, originated in the social domain. We primates primarily would be not intelligent tool users or ecologists, but clever social strategists.

WORKING DEFINITION OF PRIMATE INTELLIGENCE

By *intelligence* we mean the observed ability to cope with complex situations, in a more or less specific domain, by flexible responses designed to meet the subject's changing goals, regardless of how this ability was acquired (because this has not been determined in the available field studies of primate social behavior). By *complex situations* we mean those that are: (a) rich in combinatorial possibilities, (b) variable in the sense that its objects undergo regular change, and/or (c) unpredictable in the sense of sudden changes that cannot be easily extrapolated. By *flexible responses* we mean the ability to match behavior to a wide range of specific situations. More intelligence is required if entities that compose a situation are many, diverse, changing, fast, and/or multiplex in their relations. The intelligent subject must be capable of flexibly forming and reforming categories—of not only generalizing, but of returning to the level of exemplars to re-generalize them into new categories.

This is the general definition that seems to conform to the term used by the authors of the social intelligence hypothesis. For both research and debate, operational definitions of specific intelligences are clearly more useful.

A. Structure of the Hypothesis

The social intelligence hypothesis (SIH) can be divided into several sub-hypotheses:

1. The social environment of a group-living species is objectively more complex than its ecological environment (Humphrey, 1976; cited in Byrne & Whiten, 1988). However, not every species perceives and acts on that complexity. For example, the members of a termite colony vary individually, but they do not generally seem to recognize and exploit this variation; their societies are anonymous. Throughout this chapter, the objective complexity of an environment (the *Umgebung*) should be carefully distinguished from the complexity with which an animal copes (its *Umwelt*).

2. Primates were selected for social intelligence before they became intelligent in other domains (Byrne & Whiten, 1992). This implies that either their social intelligence is qualitatively different from ecologi-

cal (i.e., nonsocial) intelligence, or—if it is not—it is only triggered by, and applied to, conspecifics (see Fig. 4.1).

3. Such an evolutionary head start for social intelligence, if it is not merely accidental, must have been caused by preadaptations and/or selective pressures that were specific to the early representatives of the primate order. If they were also present in related taxa, these should have been selected for a similar social intelligence. In the evidence presented for this aspect of the hypothesis, selective pressures for sociality, per se, and for a particular form of intelligence designed to manage sociality have not always been clearly distinguished.

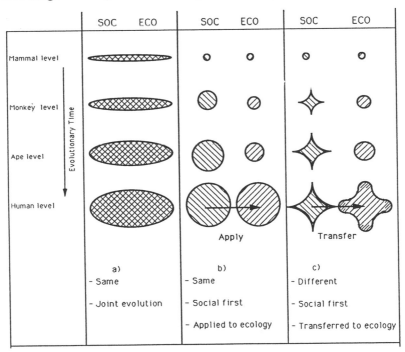

Fig. 4.1   Some simple versions of the SIH (columns). It shows the power (size of symbols) and the domain-specific structure (shape of symbols) of intelligences on the phylogenetic branches of mammals, monkeys, apes, and humans: (a) a null hypothesis: Social (soc) and ecological (eco) intelligence are not separated by domain and evolve under selection by both environments; (b) intelligence is not domain-specific in structure, but is used more often in the social context where it is primarily selected; it is then applied to eco as well; (c) early selection in social contexts produces a domain-specific social intelligence, which is eventually transferred to eco problems.

4. Specifically, social modes of intelligence have transferred to and influenced modes of ecological intelligence.

Because intelligence does not correlate with the degree of sociality
across the animal kingdom, SIH is not a trivial claim. It postulates that
primates evolved a special kind of sociality that exploits and selects for
intelligent assessment of, and action on, social relationships. This kind is
supposedly not found among most other mammals, and certainly not
among the highly social bees and ants, although the latter exceed primates with respect to group size, division of labor, and care among group
members. Therefore, one has to search for selective pressures that promote intelligent sociality, not just sociality as such. Selective pressures
for the latter have been explored by Wrangham (1980) and van Schajk
(1983).

SIH has become rather popular despite of its present vagueness. This
chapter attempts to critically examine its components and the preliminary
evidence mustered so far in its favor.

IS THE SOCIAL ENVIRONMENT MORE
COMPLEX THAN THE ECOLOGICAL ONE?

The principal argument advanced for distinguishing social from ecological intelligence is that (a) intelligence is specialized to domains, and (b)
the social and ecological domains differ fundamentally. Proponents of
the social intelligence hypothesis contend that the social environment
among primates is more complex than their ecological environment because social partners do not just act; they react and interact in unpredictable ways (Humphrey, 1976). In contrast, so the argument continues, the
ecoogical domain is comparatively stable, governed by regularities and
uniformities that must, to be sure, be mastered by "accumulated learning," but not by "creative intelligence."

Is it true that social interactions are "more complex" than interactions
with the extrasocial world? Several terms must be clarified before attempting to answer this question. First, although the terms *nature*, *objects*, and *technology* are often used interchangeably (because all are nonsocial) in discussions of the SIH they are by no means synonymous. Not
all natural processes (e.g., prevailing wind patterns or riverbed floodings)
can be classed as manipulable "objects," the raw materials of technology.
Second, there are some entities that straddle the social/ecological bound-

ary: For example, do predator–prey interactions count as ecological or social (Jolly, 1966; cited in Byrne & Whiten, 1988)?

There is some reason to doubt the blanket claim that social conditions are more complex than ecological ones. Complexity could mean: (a) many possible combinations and permutations of elements; (b) a great diversity of individuals and/or kinds; (c) variability in the sense of regular change in things, organisms, or events; and/or (d) unpredictability in the sense of irregular change. The various formulations of the SIH appeal, at one time or another, to all of these sources of complexity, but most emphasize the unpredictability of social interactions. The assumption, at least to Western humans, that the natural world is more predictable, and therefore less complex, seems to be based on a common, but nevertheless distorted, reading of the history of science and technology. This reading assumes success in explaining, predicting, and controlling natural phenomena to depend on the existence of all-encompassing and unexceptioned regularities. Yet the epoch-making theories in the natural sciences owe their extraordinary success, in large part, to idealizations, which delete much of the complexity that encumbers any individual case in favor of an abstract, preferably mathematical model (Wimsatt, 1987). So, for example, Galileo explained the motion of falling bodies by studiously ignoring air currents, surface area, viscosity of the medium, and the myriad other factors making any actual case of free fall unpredictable, and by concentrating solely on the idealized, fictional case of uniform acceleration in a vacuum (Koyré, 1968).

Two features of scientific idealizations bear on the question of the relative complexity of the ecological and social domains. First, picking out a regularity is not enough; the successful theory is one that isolates a strong regularity that swamps the multiple sources of complexity. Whether such strong regularities exist in a given domain of phenomena is an open question, and not one that necessarily respects the natural–social divide. Game theoretic models of certain social interactions may be more accurate predictors than probabilistic models of certain physical disequilibrium processes. When Kummer (1975) excluded historical antecedents, gelada baboons established social structures of unusual regularity. Second, even if one is lucky and brilliant enough to find a strong regularity, and to construct an idealized theory around it, this does not imply that the theory alone can predict the behavior of an actual individual case to any tolerable degree of accuracy, even in physics (Cartwright, 1983). The accuracy required in practical situations, as opposed to scientific explanations, will almost always account for some of the complexity that it is the triumph of the idealized theory to exclude.

Because the welfare of all organisms depends, first and foremost, on the actual case at hand, rather than the idealized case of theory, the genuine regularities revealed by theory may not apply at the relevant level. At the level of practice, inanimate objects and physical processes may be at least as significantly unpredictable as the social behavior of conspecifics. Just how unpredictable and how significantly so depends on the organism's environment. For example, organisms that depend mostly on the positions and apparent motions of the fixed stars will have a simpler time of it than organisms that depend on water eddies. Therefore, it seems premature to claim that social interactions are more complex than ecological ones: Whether this holds true for any given primate species is a question that must be investigated in its particulars. On the surface, ecological processes in the habitat can be quite as complex and unpredictable, according to the number of their elements and the distance and delays between causally connected events.

If primates were more intelligent socially than otherwise, they could be so not because the social environment was by itself more complex, but because they coped more intelligently with it than with predators and plants. Otherwise, the objective complexity of the reacting and interacting conspecific should have selected intelligence in most social animals, not just in primates. The next step is to assess the special ways in which primates cope with their conspecifics.

THE NATURE AND PRIMACY OF SOCIAL INTELLIGENCE IN PRIMATES

This section characterizes what we consider special traits of primate sociality. It then inquires whether these characters could have been formative in the development of an intelligent sociality.

A. Special Characters of Primate Sociality

The following is a list of character traits of primate sociality:

1. Tropical primates mate and give birth throughout the year. Other mammals adjust their group types to the mating versus nonmating

season, whereas many primates adjust their diverse and often incompatible social motivations to one permanent group type. They can rapidly switch between motivations.

2. In many other group-living mammals, subordinate males live apart from the females in all-male groups or alone; when in a group, they do not mate. In many primate species, males of inferior fighting power do not leave the group, but behaviorally submit to dominant males and await their chance for copulation. They adjust their behavior to exactly where the receptive female and male competitors are and what they do. Perhaps, then, primates can subordinate their own motivations to circumstances better than other mammals.

3. In certain polyadic interactions, a monkey can simultaneously sexually appease a powerful ally and threaten her opponent (Kummer, 1967); she can simultaneously have otherwise incompatible motivations by separating them according to partner.

4. Primates living in large groups assess at least the dominance status, the reproductive state, and the behavioral tendencies of others with respect to themselves (e.g., Strum, 1987). Some perceive and honor a special ecological skill in a group member (Stammbach, 1988). They select, guard, and defend valuable partners, and improve their inclinations toward them (e.g., by courtship; Kummer, 1978). In principle, a social partner is capable of both attack and support, and animals have evolved social techniques to change their partners' motivations in favor of the latter. The "reconciliations" that primates seek after a conflict with a group member (e.g., de Waal, 1989) are an example of such cultivation of relationships; they can reestablish the mutual tolerance of their former opponents (Cords, 1992). All these abilities are also known of other mammals, with the possible exception of recognizing skills in others and of reconciliation. Primates may be special only in that they do not cultivate one relationship at a time (e.g., a mate), but have many diverse relationships with many partners within the same hour, remembering which stage of the relationship they have reached with each of them (Kummer, 1975; Smuts, 1985).

5. In their complex polyadic interactions, primates simultaneously interact with several partners and exploit the variety of power, aggressive tendencies, and relationships to their advantage (Harcourt & de Waal, 1992), thereby changing from one role to another (e.g., from being the victim of an aggression to fighting back with an ally recruited in

the meantime). Thus, primates seem to process information on the interaction of several different social objects at great speed. But again, the complexity of the interactions is no proof that all their details are perceived or intended by the participants.

6. Ungulates and carnivores that form individualized groups typically include only one adult male and only one kinship group of females. In contrast, the primate species which lend particular support to the SIH include up to 10 adult males that compete for females, and several female kin groups that can compete for food. Crucial in this is that each male or kin group can ally with some competitors against others. They form changing coalitions within the group, and therefore can *choose* their allies, which selection should cause them to do with great care.

According to this list, primates may excel beyond other mammals in the versatility of social motivations according to situations, and in using their knowledge of individual relationships during polyadic interactions. However, one should remember, that the database on primates is both larger and more oriented to social behavior than that on other mammals.

B. Are Primates More Intelligent in the Social Than in Other Domains?

Individuation of Group Members.   Animals perform in complex ways without our type of intelligence: They navigate, build hives, and interact in large, structured societies by assumedly unintelligent behavioral mechanisms and by learning. Why would primate social behavior be a "Machiavellian" (Byrne & Whiten, 1988) game that is not or cannot be played by instinct? One answer is particularly likely. Primates may have begun to exploit the individual differences among their companions more than did other mammals, and far more than they exploited such differences among individual food plants or predators. Arguments in favor of this hypothesis are: (a) the opportunity for changing coalitions in multimale and multikin groups should strongly select for such a capacity; (b) the versatility of social motivations, although not itself intelligent, appears to have evolved for interacting in such a social network; and (c) individuality cannot be handled by instinct because each individual is a phylogenetic novelty.

The predators of primates also come as individuals, and there is no reason to assume that these vary less than primates. They are goal-seeking and sometimes deceptive like members of one's own species. A primate should benefit from knowing their idiosyncrasies. We do not know whether they really do, but we do not expect a high degree of individuation for several reasons. An individual predator or prey is met too rarely to learn much about him. Most of its motivational states are irrelevant to the primate in the first place. It is enough to recognize whether the predator is in a hunting motivation. There is also no cooperative relationship with a predator or prey, and therefore no submission, reconciliation, and coalition that would benefit from individuation.

Treating group members as individuals may be the foundation of primate social intelligence, but by itself does not require intelligence; more file space is sufficient. Whereas a primate keeps a file of response profiles of each group member in each of its motivations, it may keep a single file applicable to all members of a predator or food species.

Combinatorial Prediction and Action.   If there is a particular primate social intelligence, it may have originated as an ability to differentiate and influence phylogenetically novel objects that differ minimally, but critically, and the ability to cope with and even arrange constellations among them.

Proponents of the SIH agree that its core is the combinatorial prediction and action in polyadic encounters. A subject does this more easily if it knows the relationships among others. It is probable that some nonhuman primates know about dominance and kin relationships among other group members. Dasser (1988) showed that long-tailed macaques have an abstract concept of the mother–child relationship that is independent of the child's age and size. Cheney and Seyfarth (1990) claimed that solving problems of transitive inference is a skill that monkeys "use daily in assessing other individuals' dominance ranks" (p. 258). However, because a group member can potentially observe every dyad in his or her group, no inference is required.

It is still unknown how much of the combinatorial complexity emerging from individuation is actually exploited. Social intelligences should be explored by experimentation on specific abilities (e.g., what a monkey or ape learns from observing interactions among two others and then uses for dealing with them).

Combinatorial treatment is conspicuously lacking in the encounters of primates with prey and predators. Even in the cooperative hunting of monkeys by chimpanzees (C. Boesch & H. Boesch, 1989;Goodall, 1986), where the hunting tactics include different roles, the chimpanzees predict combined actions of their fellow hunters, but apparently not of the prey. Most correlations among ecological events in the habitat are presumably too weak, and the events too widely separated in space and time, to be used for combinatorial predictions by nonhuman primates. The ecosystem is most likely too complex to be the primary object of their intelligence—and of ours.

Physical and Social Tools. We are better equipped to assess problems and skills in the domain of tools than in a gathering life because humans use variants of all the tool techniques so far observed in nonhuman primates. On the surface, monkeys clearly appear more skillful in the use of social than of technical tools. They select and appease dominant allies and instigate them to attack opponents at an early age, but the use of a stick to poke or hit, or of a stone to throw or crush, is rare in the wild (Hauser, 1988). Among the great apes, only chimpanzees show a more balanced performance in the two domains: They recruit allies, but also harvest termites with sticks and crack nuts with stone hammers, to name just a few (C. Boesch & H. Boesch, 1990). Technical tool use appeared later in primate phylogeny than social tool use. Is this because their social intelligence is greater?

We have analyzed a social and a nonsocial tool technique to compare their complexity. In "protected threat" (Kummer, 1967), a baboon (the agent) induces a dominant member (the tool) to attack a third one (the target): It threatens target, simultaneously appeases tool, and maneuvers to prevent target from doing likewise. The nonsocial technique is chimpanzees cracking hard nuts on a root anvil by hitting them with a suitable stone (C. Boesch & H. Boesch, 1983). Protected threat was mastered by baboons at puberty; chimpanzees are adult before they are accomplished hammerers. The value of such a comparison across genera is highly problematic, but the analysis led to a question worth pursuing. It suggested that hammering is not objectively more complex than protected threat. The latter is easier because it is composed of elements that are effective by themselves, whereas the elements of hammering are effective only in the finished combination. It is not greater intelligence that produces the social stratagem, but the possibility of a gradual development that is rewarding at every stage.

Theory of Mind. Humans evolved an ability to impute mental states to themselves and to another organism. They have a "theory of mind" (Premack & Woodruff, 1978). To represent what another perceives, wants, or knows without confounding it with one's own mental states is plausibly the most purely social way of thinking. Byrne and Whiten (1990) collected a corpus of observations, mainly from the field, from many primatologists and primate species—scenes that suggest that one monkey or ape deceived another. They defined *tactical deception* as "acts from the normal repertoire of the agent, deployed such that another individual is likely to misinterpret what the acts signify, to the advantage of the agent" (p. 3). This definition leaves open whether the deceiver used a theory of mind. Clearly, the most records came from chimpanzees, followed by baboons (Byrne & Whiten, 1992). By their criteria, the authors inferred that both groups had in some scenes attributed knowledge or perception to their victims, and many field workers share this compelling impression (e.g., Jolly, 1988). De Waal (1982) reported episodes among chimpanzees that seemed to leave no other explanation than the attribution of mental states; for example, a male with a wounded hand limped only when he was in view of the male who had bitten him.

Unfortunately, such observations can always be explained as prediction from learned conditionalities of acutely observed behavior (Heyes, 1993). Humans infer mental states of others largely by observing their behavior. Why should we assume that a baboon also translates his or her knowledge about behavior into theories about mental states instead of using it directly? Humans do the latter with respect to complex machinery. The only substantial experimental evidence for a theory of mind in non-humans, however, is the classical study by Premack and Woodruff (1978), which suggests that a chimpanzee attributed intentions to humans. So far, tests on monkeys have been negative and unconvincing as to method (Heyes, 1993); their assessment of complex polyadic interactions may be steered by percepts of specific behavioral sequences that a human would interpret as intentions, such as chasing or sneaking up (Dasser, Ulbaek, & Premack, 1989; Kummer, Dasser, & Hoyningen-Huene, 1990). Such hypothetical percepts would have predated the dichotomy between causal and intentional interpretations in phylogeny. The actual processes by which animals assess the impending behavior of conspecifics may not follow the dichotomy of "mere" associative learning versus attribution of mental states, and may not even have been imagined so far.

SELECTIVE PRESSURES

A. Selective Pressures in Primates

The SIH demands that one identify selective pressures that favored an intelligent sociality in primates, but were not present in, say, carnivores.

The Social Group as a Polytechnic School. Humphrey (1976) suggested that primates critically depend on a wide factual knowledge of technique and habitat, and that the individual can acquire it only by learning from the group. According to Humphrey, that acquisition does not require great intelligence, but the maintenance of a society that can protect slow learners and transmit knowledge does.

There are several reasons to question the validity of this general argument. First, it is not clear why primates need to master sophisticated technical skills to prosper in their natural environment. A variety of other animals occupy the same habitat, but do not seem to require such skills. Second, primates do not seem to be exceptional in their formal knowledge and technical skills under natural conditions. Monkeys make relatively limited use of tools in the wild, and only chimpanzees select and modify natural objects for use as tools (Essock-Vitale & Seyfarth, 1987). Third, since Humphrey's article was originally published, we have become much more cautious about the conclusion that pimates acquire much of their behavior through social learning (i.e., by imitation or teaching). Well-documented examples of imitation and teaching are scarce (Galef, 1988; Visalberghi & Fragaszy, 1990).

Continuous Sexual Competition. Chance and A. P. Mead (1953; cited in Byrne & Whiten, 1988) first pointed out, that because of the year-round reproduction of tropical primates, one or more females are sexually receptive for most of the time. Subordinate group males are under frequent conflict between approaching an estrous female and avoiding more dominant males trying to monopolize the female. Therefore, male behavior should be under strong selection for the ability to withstand conflict and to continuously equilibrate their position in space.

Chance and A. P. Mead related this generalized ability to the enlargement of the neocortex in the primate order. This remains a plausible idea, although it is not quite evident why sexual competition scattered over the year should exert greater selective pressure than the intense competition during a concentrated mating season. It is the ability of subordinate males to live so close to the dominant male that seems both a cause and a consequence of selection for equilibration. It is not clear why other mammal orders did not respond to the same selective pressure.

B. Selective Pressures in Other Taxa

In principle, there is no reason that the general logic of the SIH should be applied only to primates. One of the thorniest problems of the hypothesis lies in determining whether the observed association between social complexity and cognitive characteristics is a product of a causal relationship between these variables, as the hypothesis suggests, or whether both features arise as a result of other, presently unidentified factors (Dunbar, 1992; Harcourt & de Waal, 1992). If it were possible to demonstrate that social complexity and cognitive abilities are correlated in a number of diverse taxonomic groups, our confidence in the general validity of the social intelligence hypothesis would be strengthened.

Studies of the toothed whales, including dolphins, provide support for the SIH, in that this group includes species that are both socially complex and intelligent (Connor, Smolker, & A. F. Richards, 1992; Herman, 1980). They display considerable variation in the size, stability, and degree of cohesion of social groups. Dolphins living in inland waters are largely solitary. Other dolphin species form large and stable groups that frequently divide into smaller subgroups based on age, gender, reproductive status, and kinship. In some species, groups sometimes merge into feeding aggregations that number hundreds of individuals. Pilot and killer whales form stable and cohesive groups of approximately 40 individuals. Some species seem to rival primates in their degree of social complexity (Connor, Smolker, & A. F. Richards, 1992; Wells, Scott, & Irvine, 1987).

Like primates, dolphins and whales are generally thought to be highly intelligent. Laboratory experiments have shown that bottle-nosed dolphins have a well-developed auditory memory system, representational ability, capacity for rule-governed behavior, and imitative and observational learning abilities (Herman, 1980). The brains of some dolphin species are relatively larger than those of any of the nonhuman primates (Connor, Smolker, & A. F. Richards, 1992), and the cetaceans as a group are more highly encephalized than any taxon besides the primates (Eisenberg, 1981; Macphail, 1982).

Bottle-nosed dolphins form social groups in which individuals associate in temporary parties that vary in size and composition, much like those of chimpanzees. Near Australia, males form regular and exclusive associations with one or two other males in nonagonistic contexts, and these pairs or triplets collectively herd females (Connor, Smolker, & A. F. Richards, 1992). Pairs or triplets also preferentially associate with certain other pairs or triplets. The relationships among these units are sometimes cooperative, as they may jointly attempt to appropriate females from other males and may recruit support from one another in such efforts. This is similar to the changing coalitions among macaque kinship groups. Connor, Smolker, and A. F. Richards (1992) argued that multifaceted social bonds among (sub-)groups do not exist in any primate except humans.

TRACES OF SOCIAL INTELLIGENCE IN ECOLOGICAL INTELLIGENCE

A. In Nonhuman Primates

Within his version of the SIH, Humphrey (1976) suggested that humans are predisposed "to try to fit nonsocial material into a social mold" (p. 312). Our ecological intelligence would maintain characteristics of its social origin.

A transfer of social ways of thinking to nonsocial material could be expected even in nonhuman primate species if: (a) social intelligence were domain-specific, (b) if its application to some nonsocial problems were profitable, (c) if selection pressure on solving the respective social problem had been stronger than on solving the nonsocial problem, and (d) if the social module were accessible to nonsocial stimuli and action patterns. For example, a social technique, evolved because it was beneficial at every step, could have transferred to a nonsocial task where only finished performance succeeded. We know of no nonsocial tasks sufficiently similar to a social one where this would be conceivable.

Whether a theory of mind exists in nonhumans is too uncertain to then consider further its transfer to nonsocial objects. Therefore, the remaining sections of this chapter are restricted to humans. They (a) flesh out the theory of mind concept with human examples, (b) explore Humphrey's idea of its transfer to the nonsocial, and (c) differentiate the fundamental tenet of the SIH—that social intelligence differs from that used in other domains.

B. Theories of Mind in Humans

Leslie (1987a) suggested that theories of mind are "metarepresentations" that try to capture other organisms' representations of states of the world. How do we know that a chimpanzee, a child, or an adult actually has a theory of mind? The debate on this issue cannot be reviewed here (see Carey & R. Gelman, 1991; Perner, 1991), but some findings with infants and children that illustrate how theories of mind have been inferred from experiments are considered.

The available evidence indicates that a common sense theory of mind emerges during preschool years in normal children, including moral development (Wimmer, Gruber & Perner, 1984), understanding the consequences of false belief (Wimmer & Perner, 1983) and the consequences of ignorance (Baron-Cohen, Leslie, & Frith, 1985). Pretense in play is an early feature of a child's theory of mind (e.g., "pretend that these three objects are mama, papa, and me"); according to Leslie (1987b), it emerges in normal children roughly between 18 and 24 months of age. In the third year, children tend to acquire and use cognitive terms such as *think, know, remember, pretend, dream, believe,* and *wonder* (Bretherton & Beeghly, 1982). By 4 years of age, children are capable of perspective change (i.e., switching between metarepresentations of different people).

For instance, Perner, Leekam, and Wimmer (1987) showed 3-year-old children a confectionery packet well known to British children. When asked what it contained, the children answered "Smarties." To their dismay, they were shown that the box contained a pencil. Despite that they could remember this, when asked what a friend would think when he saw the box, nearly half of the children were unable to predict the false belief that they had suffered and answered, instead, "a pencil." Most 4- and 5-year-olds, however, seem to be capable of switching perspectives and inferring the consequences of a false belief. Several experiments have used the following scenario. There is a box and a basket. Someone hides a piece of chocolate in the box and walks out of the room. Someone else, unknown to the hider, transfers the chocolate from the box to the basket.

The hider returns, and the child is asked where the hider will look for the chocolate. Younger children tend to point to the basket (where the object really is), whereas 4-year-olds and older children point to the box, switching to the hider's perspective (Baron-Cohen, Leslie, & Frith, 1985; Wimmer & Perner, 1983).

Childhood autism has been linked to the defects in the theories of mind of the autistic children. For instance, clinically normal 4-and-a-half-year-olds and children diagnosed as autistic (mean age = 12 years; mean IQ = 82) were given the Wimmer–Perner test. The success rate for the normal children was 85%; for a control group of Down's syndrome children (mean age 11 years, mean IQ = 64) the success rate was 86%. By contrast, 80% of the autistic children failed.

C. Evidence of Traces of Social Intelligence from the History of Science

Our almost irresistible tendency to widen the circle of anthropomorphism to embrace not only species that share a large part of human evolutionary history, but also inanimate objects like chemical elements or even artifacts like television sets, suggests that we are more comfortable conceiving the natural world in social terms than vice versa. Some proponents of the SIH argue that this anthropomorphic tendency points to the social origins of human intelligence—origins that still constrain our thinking even in areas in which we deem anthropomorphism to be out of place. For example, Humphrey (1976; cited in Byrne & Whiten, 1988) noted that high-energy physicists speak of "families" of elementary particles endowed with "strangeness" and "charm," and adduced the mingling of science with mysticism or "magical systems of interpretation" as strong evidence for the inherently social nature and, by implication, social origins of all human intelligence.

At least two words of caution about the interpretation of such "irrational" elements in the modern natural sciences are in order here. First, these sciences are highly elaborated systems of thought, and therefore should not be conflated with the intuitive, informal ways of thinking that may be natural to humans (Efron & Fisch, 1991). The anthropomorphic terminology of *strangeness* and *charm* corresponds to thickly mathematized properties of elementary particles which defy common sense intuitions. Indeed, it is just because these properties so baffled intuition that physicists felt licensed to christen them so whimsically. The best way to get at unvarnished intelligence in science is probably not through its public formulations, which have been pressed through the sieve of argumentative forms and tabus refined over centuries and instilled by intense professional socialization, but rather through the informal, private conversations of scientists (Atran, 1990; Traweek, 1988). Perhaps still more direct evidence about the essentials of untutored human intelligence would come from subjects who are genuinely untutored, not just unbuttoned (e.g. child development studies).

Second, just because a thought system such as religion or magic is not scientific by modern criteria does not mean that it reveals more about the nature of unadulterated human intelligence. Science is not the only highly elaborated intellectual structure that humans have produced; historians and cultural anthropologists have shown by numerous examples how magical systems may easily rival scientific theories in diversity and baroque conceptual intricacy (Thorndike, 1941). Therefore, it would be overly hasty to adduce the anthropomorphism of some religions (of course, others have been at least as vehemently antianthropomorphic as modern science) or magical systems as evidence for the intrinsically social nature of human intelligence, for the same reasons it would be risky to do so for anthropomorphism in public science. All three are refined, artificial—not raw, natural—products of the human intellect. These reservations do not refute the transfer version of the SIH, but they militate for a closer, more differentiated look at the evidence for traces of social intelligence in human ecological intelligence.

D. What Kind of Social Intelligence?

One problem in evaluating the evidence for or against the SIH is that the meaning of *intelligence* is notoriously vague. The concept of intelligence as a unified, general ability was invented only recently, in the mid-19th century, by Herbert Spencer, Hippolyte Taine, and Francis Galton, among others (Daston, 1992). But the meaning of intelligence has not remained stable. For instance, Binet and T. Simon (1914) distinguished tests of instruction (reading, arithmetic, spelling) from tests of intelligence. Their tests of intelligence included questions about social skills, social interactions, morals, and other forms of what is now called *social intelligence* (e.g., "Why should one judge a person by his acts rather than by his words?"). Only slowly did the social and moral come to be seen as different from the technical and abstract; in contemporary psychology, the borders are still in flux.

Because the meaning of terms like *social* and *technical intelligence*, as well as their relations, are far from being clear, it is better to talk about specific abilities. This section deals with a prototypical, nonsocial reasoning task in human psychology—namely, a task of logical thinking—and the thesis that the human mind uses a specific kind of social intelligence to understand that task.

The Idea of a General-Purpose, Content-Independent Intelligence. Psychology has a long tradition of studying reasoning, judgment, and decision as the application of formal, content-independent rules. Examples are the rules of propositional logic and Bayesian statistics. This research stands in a still longer philosophical tradition, which assumes that the laws of logic and probability are the laws of intelligent reasoning. In contrast, the SIH assumes that there are (at least) two kinds of intelligences: social and nonsocial. If there is anything that can be properly called nonsocial intelligence, logical reasoning is a good candidate.

Here is an example of how logical reasoning has been studied in experimental psychology. In 1966, Peter Wason introduced what later became known as the *4-card problem* (or selection task): A subject is given a conditional of the form "if P then Q." The task is to select information that could falsify the conditional. For instance, four cards are laid on a table. Each card has a letter on one side and a number on the other side. The rule is, "If there is a vowel on one side, then there is an even number on the other side." Only the face-up sides of the four cards can be seen, and these read A, B, 3, and 4. Your task is to indicate those card(s) and only those cards that you need to turn over to find out if the rule has been violated.

In an avalanche of studies performed in many countries, most subjects chose A and 4, and many others chose A only (e.g., Griggs & Cox, 1982). However, if subjects reasoned according to propositional logic, then their answer should differ from the common response. A conditional of the type "if P then Q" is logically inconsistent only with "P and not Q." Thus, subjects should chose the "P" and the "not Q" cards, which correspond to the "A" and "3" cards in our example. However, only a few subjects did so (typically around 10%). These stable results were taken by many to shatter the century-old conviction that the human mind actually reasons by logic. But if humans were not reasoning by formal logic, how did they reason?

Social Contracts: Reciprocal Altruism. This question turned out to be a hard nut to crack. Specifically, the psychology of reasoning has been little concerned with questions of content (e.g., What makes humans reason differently about alphanumerical rules and postal rules?). Rather, most work has focused on general-purpose, content-independent processes and structures (e.g., How do humans reason about conditionals?), just as Skinner's behaviorism sought general-purpose, content-independent laws of operant conditioning that hold irrespective of the nature of the stimulus and response.

What could a content-dependent or domain-specific account look like? In 1989, Leda Cosmides proposed a domain-specific and evolutionary view of reasoning: If the conditional in the 4-card problem is a social contract, then humans reason about this conditional, using a specific kind of social intelligence that she termed a *social contract schema. Domain-specific* means that Cosmides' social contract (SC) theory explains reasoning in one content domain: social contracts. A social contract has the structure, "if you take the benefit, then you pay the costs (or meet the requirement)."

In brief, the evolutionary part of SC theory is: Humans spent more than 99% of their species history as Pleistocene hunter–gatherers. For hunter–gatherers, social contracts (i.e., cooperation between two or more individuals for mutual benefit) were necessary for survival. But cooperation (reciprocal altruism) cannot evolve in the first place unless one can detect cheaters (Trivers, 1971). Consequently, a set of reasoning procedures that allows one to detect cheaters efficiently—a cheater-detection algorithm—would have been selected. Such a Darwinian algorithm would focus attention on any person who has accepted the benefit (did he or she pay the cost?) and on any person who has not paid the cost (did he or she take the benefit?).

Therefore, Cosmides argued, if a conditional is identified as a social contract (via its cost–benefit structure), then a cheater-detection algorithm is activated that searches for information of the kind "benefit taken and costs not paid," rather than for logical violations of the kind "P and not Q." This should hold even in laboratory experiments designed to test logical reasoning. In a series of experiments, Cosmides (1989) indeed demonstrated that, if a rule were identified as a social contract, most subjects chose the "benefit taken" and the "cost not paid" cards, and the interindividual variation in judgments found when (the same) rules were not identified as social contracts largely disappeared. This result held independently of whether the social contracts were familiar or unfamiliar to the subjects.

Despite this empirical support, the idea that reasoning might be domain-specific, and that (at least) one of those domains involves the action of an evolutionarily selected social intelligence (cheater detection), stirred up a violent controversy in cognitive psychology (e.g., Cheng & Holyoak, 1989; Cosmides & Tooby, 1992; Pollard, 1990). One conjecture was that, in most of Cosmides' tests, the "benefit taken" and "cost not paid" cards that indicated cheater detection coincided with the "P" and "not Q" cards, indicating logical reasoning. Thus, Cosmides might have just found an ingenious method to facilitate logical reasoning: Social contracts "somehow" facilitate logical reasoning, but there is no need to invoke cheater detection, so the argument went.

Gigerenzer and Hug (1992) found a way to play the prediction of the cheater-detection algorithm against that of propositional logic. They extended the tests of a social contract schema by including, among others, the perspective of the person or party engaged in an interaction. If reasoning is based on a Machiavellian social intelligence, then it is designed not to detect cheating per se, but rather to prevent one from being cheated by someone else (and not necessarily vice versa). Gigerenzer and Hug introduced social contracts in which both parties could cheat. An example was, "If a previous employee gets a pension from a firm, then that person must have worked for the firm for at least 10 years." The four cards read: "got a pension," "did not get a pension," "worked 10 years for the firm," "worked 8 years for the firm." Subjects were told that each card provides information about one previous employee. The task was to indicate those card(s) that one needs to turn over to find out if the rule had been violated. One group of subjects was cued into the perspective of the employee; a second group was cued into the perspective of the employer.

What counts as being a victim of cheating depends on one's perspective. Therefore, if subjects' reasoning is directed toward cheater detection, those who have been cued into the perspective of the employee should choose the "did not get a pension" and the "worked 10 years for the firm" cards, whereas those cued into the perspective of the employer should choose the "did get a pension" and the "worked 8 years for the firm" cards. What counts as logical reasoning, however, is aperspectival.

The logical term "P and not Q" corresponds, independent of the perspective, to the "did get a pension" and the "worked 8 years for the firm" cards.

Thus, the perspective change experiment results in competing predictions: If reasoning is based on a cheater-detection algorithm, then subjects in the two perspectives should choose two different pairs of cards, as specified before. If reasoning is based on propositional logic, and if reasoning about social contracts somehow facilitates logical reasoning, then subjects should choose the same pair of cards, independent of their perspective. Gigerenzer and Hug (1992) showed that their subjects' reasoning followed—in this example, as well as in similar examples—the prediction of the cheater-detection algorithm, and not that of logical reasoning.

Domain-Specificity and the Nature of Social Intelligence. These results demonstrate how a specific kind of social intelligence is used by humans to solve reasoning problems that were originally meant by experimenters to test logical reasoning. But they can do more: They may suggest ways to think about social intelligence.

Whiten and Byrne (1988) asked several questions about what they termed *Machiavellian intelligence* and what Humphrey and others have called *social intelligence*. We comment on the first two of these questions.

First, what is social intelligence? One answer would be: Social intelligence is a general-purpose ability, just as Francis Galton's "natural ability" or Charles Spearman's g-factor were supposed to be. The alternative would be that social intelligence is of several kinds, each designed for solving important adaptive problems. The domain-specific approach described here represents the latter view: The mind has available a limited repertoire of schemata of social interaction, such as social contracts, threats and warnings, and an inference mechanism that maps concrete situations onto these schemata. Once a schema has been activated, attention is distributed in a characteristic way. For instance, if a social contract schema is activated, attention focuses on information that can detect cheaters. This view does not assume that there is a one-dimensional measure of "more-or-less" of social intelligence. Rather, there are several aspects of which one can have more or less (Gigerenzer, 1997).

Second, is social intelligence qualitatively different from, or more sophisticated than, technical intelligence? The domain-specific view implies "yes" to the first part of Whiten and Byrne's second question. Not only are social and technical intelligences qualitatively different, but so are the various social intelligences. For instance, devoting attention to cheater detection is of little use in most social and technical domains, except in social contracts. However, the second part of this question appears rather metaphysical. If there is no single measure of "more-or-less" of social intelligence, then there seems to be, *a fortiori,* no simple way to decide whether social intelligence is more sophisticated than technical intelligence. Is it more sophisticated to invent the wheel or to outwit six competitors for a mate? The domain-specific approach to human reasoning shows the importance of making the concept of intelligence more specific to design testable versions of the SIH.

CONCLUSIONS

The following list summarizes the conclusions drawn in this chapter:

1. The assumption that the social environment is more complex than the ecological environment is not convincing. If primates are socially more intelligent than others, it is because they cope with conspecifics intelligently.

2. Many primate and some dolphin species have evolved societies in which several competing units can play a game of changing coalitions. Such a game could have selected the following characters of primate sociality: A differential perception and treatment of group members as individuals beyond the level of individuation given to extraspecifics; the observed versatility of diverse social motivations in polyadic interactions; and acute observation and learning of others' behavior to the point where old-world primates, notably chimpanzees and baboons, succeeded in tactical deception. Some or all of the latter may operate without theory of mind in monkeys.

3. Theory of mind, the attribution of mental states to another, is the most characteristic content of social intelligence. It has been plausibly demonstrated in a chimpanzee, but not yet in monkeys. The selective pressures that caused the shift from reading behavior to mind reading are unknown, but the new kinds of cooperative techniques that emerged at about the same time may be connected with it: Chimpanzees, but not monkeys, show moderate degrees of sharing. Hu-

mans develop division of labor and reliably meet after separation. Reciprocal altruism, which leads a marginal existence among animals, flourishes in humans. These activities may profit from, or even depend on, theory of mind.

4. The use of "social tools" appeared earlier than that of technical tools in primate phylogeny. A specific social intelligence might account for this, but the postulate is unnecessary in at least one case: Social tool use is composed of elements that are effective by themselves and permit gradual learning. This is not true for some technical tools, where incipient techniques are useless.

5. The specific selective pressures that would have led primates to evolve an intelligent sociality are still obscure. The occurrence of both high intelligence and complex social systems with changing coalitions among toothed whales agrees with the SIH.

6. The idea that the pioneering social intelligence was later transferred and applied to nonsocial problems and left its traces in the way they were solved is not substantiated in nonhumans, and needs a more differentiated look in humans.

7. Research on reasoning in humans shows that the concept of a "social" intelligence may be too broad, and that natural intelligences may be specialized for narrower domains within the social. Experimental research on such specific capacities on both humans and nonhumans seems the surest way toward the testing of the SIH, if it addresses abilities that have been found relevant in the field. Comparative field studies of primates and other mammals would be useful.

5

THE SOCIAL AND BIOLOGICAL FOUNDATIONS OF HUMAN COMMUNICATION

Alexandra M. Maryanski
University of California
Riverside

Peter Molnár
Semmelweis University Medical School
Budapest, Hungary

Ullica Segerstråle
Illinois Institute of Technology
Chicago

Boris M. Velichkovsky
Dresden University of Technology
Dresden, Germany

Language has traditionally been seen as the characteristic that sets humans and animals apart—a view that also has been strongly reflected in the social sciences. Different aspects of language have been intensely studied within a variety of academic fields, and have given rise to quite a few scholarly debates. Although research on human language has a long tradition, nonverbal communication—the study of communication through other channels than the spoken language—is a relatively new field, with researchers in many different disciplines, partly overlapping those of language research. Thus, it is not surprising that many of the same academic controversies that appeared in relation to language have also emerged with regard to nonverbal communication.

At least two biological givens—the "hard-wiredness" of the human capacity for language and the importance of nonverbal communication for the development of human sociality—seem to have been largely accepted by social scientists, although in general they have been weary of biological explanations of social and cultural phenomena. Indeed, the suggestions provided by earlier biological theories have typically been mostly speculative and not intrinsically more convincing than sociocultural explanations. Today, it is possible to do sophisticated neurophysiological and psychophysiological studies of human communication, linking insights derived from these to concepts from evolutionary biology, psychology, and behavioral research. What emerges is an increasingly complex picture of our ability to communicate as simultaneously biologically and socioculturally influenced, with a few capacities apparently more biologically "hard-wired" than others, and therefore probably crucial as communicational building blocks (especially the capacity for language, emotional communication, face recognition, and imitation).

As often happens in academia, many of the earlier controversies within both language and nonverbal communication research have later been resolved in ways that incorporate both warring sides. Current experimental results at the neurophysiological level point to the soundness of such a synthesis, and particularly to the need to take both culture and biology into account when discussing human communication. In the light of available experimental evidence, purely sociocultural theories now seem increasingly untenable.

Also, the dividing line between human and animal communication appears less clear-cut than before. On the one hand, the importance of nonverbal communication for human social life is now receiving growing recognition, and language experts continue turning to preverbal communication for clues to the infant's linguistic development. On the other hand, there is accumulating evidence of symbolic or protosymbolic communication in animals, although the extent to which this is indeed the case still remains controversial. Although students of human and animal communication are now bringing together their insights into nonverbal behavior, there is a renewed interest in the unique linguistic capacities of humans and the use of a variety of forefront scientific methods in research on human language.

The purpose of this chapter is to outline a comprehensive framework for the study of the basic nature of all dimensions of human communication, with particular emphasis on nonverbal communication as a crucial link between culture and biology. Hence, the discussion in this chapter is conducted at several different levels: from evolutionary considerations of nonverbal communication and language, to developmental, physiological, neurophysiological, and functional aspects of communication—at each point addressing the inextricable interrelationship between the social and biological foundations of human communication.

The two sections in this chapter are devoted to nonverbal communication and language communication, respectively. They also include central insights from two ZiF conferences on these topics. These conferences were arranged during the year of the group project to provide a forum for interdisciplinary exchange between forefront researchers from a wide variety of academic fields. Both of these conferences have been edited as books, and exist as sister volumes to the present volume. We refer the reader to *Nonverbal communication: Where nature meets culture* (Segerstråle & Molnár, 1997) and *Communicating meaning: The evolution and development of language* (Velichkovsky & Rumbaugh, 1996).

BIOLOGY WITH A HUMAN FACE: NONVERBAL COMMUNICATION AND SOCIAL INTERACTION

Ullica Segerstråle and Peter Molnar

1. Nonverbal Communication: Culture or Biology?

Nonverbal communication seems ideally suited to address the problem of the relationship between culture and biology. As a field, it is inherently multidisciplinary, connecting a number of different research paradigms (e.g., ethology, anthropology, linguistics, sociology, psychiatry, social psychology, comparative psychology, developmental psychology, psychophysiology, and neurophysiology). Nonverbal communication research is conducted in regard to a multitude of channels in both humans and animals. In humans, it typically deals with facial expressions, gaze, nonverbal vocal expressions, postures, gestures, and spatial distance. However, despite that nonverbal communication is obviously an important everyday phenomenon—there have been estimates that up to two thirds of human behavior in dyadic interaction is nonverbal (Birdwhistell; cited in Knapp, 1978)—nonverbal communication has been largely ignored in the social sciences. The social sciences have typically emphasized the human capacity for language while being suspicious of biology. The most notable exception is the symbolic interactionist school in sociology, represented by George Herbert Mead, who introduced the notion of a "conversation of gestures" to explain the origin of the social Self (G. H. Mead, 1934). Since then, the role of nonverbal communication has been recognized within the traditions of microsociology (Collins, 1975, 1981; Goffman, 1959, 1972; Scheff, 1990; J. H. Turner, 1997) and ethnomethodology (Garfinkel, 1967). (Not surprisingly, the de facto ethological roots of naturalistic sociological approaches, such as Goffman's, have not been touted.)

Another reason for the relative invisibility of nonverbal communication within the social sciences is the particular history of this type of research, originating in fields removed from the core of the social sciences. Early nonverbal communication research resulted from a collaboration between structural linguists, psychiatrists, and anthropologists inspired by the new developments in information theory and cybernetics, starting in the mid-1950s. This approach, "context analysis," was concerned with how interactions are organized, based on the behavioral repertoires that participants in any given communication community regularly draw on (behavioral practices related to language, gesture, orientation, posture, and spacing). Here, direct parallels were drawn to anthropological linguistics in the Sapir–Whorf tradition (Sapir, 1949; Whorf, 1956). Communication was seen as a continuous multichannel process, where acts as such did not have intrinsic meaning, but were to be analyzed in terms of the significance they have in the overall structure of interaction (Kendon, 1990).

Famous products of this "structural" tradition were, among others, the development of kinesics, the study of movement (Birdwhistell, 1970); proxemics, the study of distances (Hall, 1959, 1966); and detailed work on the organization of interaction in psychotherapy sessions (Scheflen, 1973). Other important research dealt with interaction synchrony (Kendon, 1973), *self-synchrony* (i.e., how gestures tend to accompany speech; Condon & Ogston, 1966), and turn-taking in conversations (Duncan, 1972). Although the time-consuming kinesics notation developed by Birdwhistell seems now to have been abandoned, there has recently been interest in detailed studies of posture (see e.g., Bull, 1987; Frey & von Cranach, 1973; Heller, 1997). The importance of simultaneous multichannel communication is further reflected in the whole notion of paralanguage—the idea of qualification of a verbal message with the help of nonverbal communication, such as pitch of voice, facial expressions, gestures, or postures (Trager, 1958).

One of the central concepts inspiring the "structural" research tradition is the notion of *feedback*. In human interaction, this means continuous monitoring of the communication flow between interactants based on the multichannel cues picked up. An interesting consequence of this back-and-forth signaling is that a sender's message, while being sent, may be continuously modified based on the instantaneous feedback he or she obtains from the receiver. In fact, later psychophysiological research bears out the truth of this notion: Humans seem indeed to be genetically disposed for acting both as senders and receivers at the same time (Dimberg, 1997).

It is interesting to compare this development with another school of thought in nonverbal communication, coming largely from ethology, experimental psychology, and psychophysiology. That school is not looking for principles for the organization of behavior in human communication, but instead for evidence of human behavioral universals. This school is represented by students of human ethology (Eibl-Eibesfeldt, 1975, 1989; Schiefenhövel, 1997), those searching for universal facial expressions of emotion (Ekman, 1973; Ekman & R. Davidson, 1994; Ekman & Friesen, 1969, 1975, 1978; Ekman & Keltner, 1997; Izard, 1977; Zajonc, 1980), and researchers in the psychophysiology of the human face (Dimberg, 1982, 1996; Öhman & Dimberg, 1978). This line of research has its ultimate roots in Darwin's ([1872]1965) famous *The Expression of The Emotions in Man and Animals* (e.g., Ekman, 1973).

Until recently, the academic climate has been polarized between "nature" and "nurture." Nonverbal communication has been no exception. This is well reflected in a book such as Knapp's (1978) *Nonverbal Communication*. Knapp took great care to present the evidence, pro and con, of the existence of human universals in nonverbal communication in an even-handed way. On the one hand, he discussed the pioneering kinesics research of Ray Birdwhistell, who, in the tradition of linguistic anthropology, insisted on the total determination of nonverbal behavior by culture or language group. On the other hand, Knapp presented research supporting the idea of a biological basis for nonverbal behavior: primatological studies indicating homologies between primate and human facial expressions (Chevalier-Skolnikoff, 1973; van Hooff, 1972), human ethological research on facial expressions of blind and deaf children (Eibl-Eibesfeldt, 1973) and cultural universals (Eibl-Eibesfeldt, 1972), and cross-cultural research on facial expressions using the standardized FACS (Facial Action Coding System) photograph-recognition method (Ekman & Friesen, 1978).

In the 1990s, it is no longer possible to postulate a simple either—or situation when it comes to culture and biology. Additional evidence has accumulated to tip the balance in favor of the biological foundations of nonverbal behavior—or, more correctly, an answer which inseparably involves both culture and biology. New research comes from many fields—above all on facial expressions of emotions, led by Ekman and his collaborators (Ekman & R. Davidson, 1994; Ekman & Keltner, 1997; Levenson, Ekman, & Heider, 1992), but also on cognition, whereby the original Sapir–Whorf thesis of linguistic relativism (i.e., that our language determines our categories of thought) is becoming increasingly untenable (e.g., Bornstein, 1977, 1996; Harnad, 1997).

As Ekman and Keltner have pointed out, the earlier conception of alternative cultural and biological explanations of nonverbal behavior was based on mistaken assumptions: Earlier researchers did not make the crucial distinction between voluntary and involuntary expression of emotion, nor consider the possibility that culture could "order" persons to mask their true emotions (Ekman & Keltner, 1997). However, other useful distinctions *were* made, such as a differentiation between emblems (nonverbal gestures which can be translated into words), illustrators (movements which accompany spoken language), affect displays, regulators (movements which regulate the conversation flow), and adaptors (habitual behaviors not intended for communication; Ekman & Friesen, 1969). To adequately answer the question of the biological foundations of nonverbal communication, a broader repertoire of methods in different disciplines, including psychophysiological and neurophysiological research, would have to be employed.

2. New Findings in Nonverbal Communication and Emotions

An obvious starting point for any effort to integrate biology and the social sciences is to recognize the coexistence and equal relevance of different types of research in behavior. The best argument in this respect is probably Tinbergen's (1963) famous "Four Questions." Tinbergen pointed out that "why" questions concerning behavior can be legitimately asked at four different levels: phylogenetic, ontogenetic, physiological, and functional (see chap. 3). Applying this to nonverbal communication, one might talk about the evolutionary preparedness of senders and receivers, the ontogenetic development of interpersonal communication skills, the physiological concomitants of various types of nonverbal interactions, and the social function of a particular message. But one might also simply choose to see the four questions as representing four different aspects of the same problem. In this case, one would not be looking for four separate answers to the Four Questions, but instead for one complex interdisciplinary answer involving a plurality of levels in biology, which may, in turn, be related to insights from the social sciences. This was the rationale for organizing an interdisciplinary conference on nonverbal communication at ZiF as part of the general group project.

The intellectual goals of the conference "Nonverbal Communication and the Genesis of Culture (March 4–6, 1992) were manifold. The topic of nonverbal communication concretely demonstrates the reality of the *interaction* between biology and culture (see Hinde, 1987; Reynolds, 1980). This appeared particularly important in the light of the furor raised over the early sociobiological attempts to persuade social scientists about the virtues of biology (see E. O. Wilson, 1975; for sociological reactions at the time, see Wiegele, 1979; for anthropological ones, see Leach, 1981; Sahlins, 1976). Also, the "cognitive revolution's" overemphasis on the linguistic capabilities of humans made it seem worthwhile to reestablish a central role of emotion as a guide for cognition (e.g., Plutchik, 1984). Finally, it seemed that important answers to questions about human language, too, would be found at the preverbal or nonverbal level.

The ZiF conference brought leading students of nonverbal interaction from different disciplines and traditions together in the same forum. It soon became clear that there is now a great complementarity of perspectives, or even a slow but steady convergence among various fields of nonverbal research. On the one hand, there is increasing interdisciplinary agreement that some aspects of human nonverbal communication are indeed relatively "hard-wired," whereas other aspects are more amenable to cultural influences. On the other hand, there is mounting evidence for voluntary or strategical control of emotional expressions in animal communication, as well as for rudimentary aspects of symbolic communication. This opens up exciting possibilities for more unified efforts among students from research fields which were earlier separated.

It seems that the much-debated question of human universals can be usefully approached by concentrating on human predispositions to nonverbal communication, rather than on the manifestations of particular behavioral universals across cultures. An important piece of evidence here comes from psychophysiological studies demonstrating the "prewiring" of facial display and reception of emotions in young infants (Dimberg, 1997; Öhman & Dimberg, 1978). In young infants, studies continue demonstrating an innate fear reaction to negative faces (Dimberg, 1997), whose physiological concomitants are similar to other well-known fear reactions (e.g., to snakes; Öhman, 1986; Sackett, 1966).

Meanwhile, the newest research on cross-cultural universals in facial expressions of emotions shows a connection of facial display also with physiology (as measured by galvanic skin response or heart rate) and with regional activity of the brain. Significantly, the same physiological effect (or brain activity) is also achieved when research subjects are instructed to put together a facial expression muscle by muscle (Ekman & R. Davidson, 1994; Ekman & Keltner, 1997; Ekman, Levenson, & Friesen, 1983; Levenson, Ekman, & Heider, 1992). There is also a new counterargument against those who argue for a purely cultural or personal control of emotions. Research shows that humans have a limited capacity to successfully mask their emotions: The external eye muscle involved in the so-called "Duchenne smile" is *not* under voluntary control, which makes it possible for an observer to distinguish genuine from false smiles (Ekman, 1985; Ekman & Friesen, 1982; Ekman & Keltner, 1997). In response to those who feel that the research on universal emotions has focused too much on those basic emotions that can reliably be identified in the face (e.g., happiness, sadness, surprise, fear, anger, and disgust), there are now studies of universals that also involve body movement, particularly a tell-tale movement sequence indicating embarrassment (Ekman & Keltner, 1997; Keltner, 1995).

Further evidence that the dispositions to interpersonal interaction in different nonverbal channels (face, voice, touch, etc.) are relatively hardwired comes from research on grooming behavior (Suomi, 1997). Grooming is ubiquitous both in animals and humans, but may recently have become "repressed" or institutionalized by culture (as manifested by the hairdresser and barber professions; Schiefenhövel, 1997). To the list of universally routinized gestures collected over the years by the Eibl-Eibesfeldt school of human ethology (e.g., the famous eyebrow flash, a greeting that also indicates surprise or fear), two new candidates have now been added: the "nose wrinkle" as a gesture for slight social distancing and the "disgust face" as a strong signal of social repulsion (Schiefenhövel, 1997). This line of reasoning explains the human capacity for cross-cultural understanding as grounded in our common anatomical-emotional history.

Another set of studies is devoted to the development of these interactional skills in ontogeny and the importance of the social context. Ever since H. F. Harlow's (1959) famous monkey experiments, in which infant monkeys preferred a terry-cloth "mother" to a milk-providing wire "mother" and Bowlby's (1969) studies of attachment and loss, the hard-wiredness of the mother–infant bond (i.e., our basic predisposition to affective sociality) has been clear (see Suomi, 1997). Further detailed studies of early mother–infant bonding show the role of nonverbal communication in the development of the infant's social skills, particularly through the infant's increasing realization of the social meaning of the smile (K. Schneider, 1997). Here, a new realization is the important guiding role of parents in turning the "biological" infant into a "cultural" being (Papoušek & Papoušek, 1997). Developmental research on monkeys also shows the continued role of the parent as a trainer of the infant's social capabilities. A dramatic example of how a nurturing environment may overcome a genetic handicap is the case of congenitally shy infant monkeys. Under the care of a nurturing foster mother, monkeys with such a shyness trait may in fact turn into superior social performers (Suomi, 1997).

In humans, this early bonding also apparently helps prepare the way for the infant's later language development. Studies have shown that neonates not only "lock into" the gaze of their mothers, but also move rhythmically to the sounds of the mother's voice (Brazelton, Koslowski, & Main, 1974; Condon & Sander, 1974; H. Papoušek & M. Papoušek, 1997; Trevarthen, 1977). It even seems that, at a very early stage, infants learn to distinguish the sounds of their mother tongue from the sounds of other languages (Kuhl, K. A. Williams, & Lacerda, 1992).

The function of nonverbal communication was addressed by several participants. It has already been forcefully argued (e.g., Marler, 1984) that it is a mistake to believe that human messages are cognitive and intentional, whereas animal signals are expressive and involuntary. Now, ingenious naturalistic and laboratory experiments with tape recorders and video cameras have further strengthened the thesis that animal signals may in fact function as rudimentary symbolic communication systems. In vervet monkeys, the alarm calls corresponding to threats from eagles, leopards, and snakes are all context-sensitive (Cheney & Seyfarth, 1990; Marler & Evans, 1997). Just as the meaning of words becomes more specified during the course of semantic development in children, vervet monkeys first show a generalized responsiveness to moving aerial stimuli, which is then sharpened by experience to correspond to one eagle species among many. Animal alarm calls are also subject to an "audience effect"—they are not made if there is no obvious recipient (Marler & Evans, 1997). (A similar audience effect was documented in the smiles of young children: In task-oriented situations, the social structure of the situation has an influence on whether the expressive or communicative function of the smile will dominate; K. Schneider, 1997.)

Although human ethologists tend to draw parallels between nonverbal behavior in humans and primates, other researchers warn that we cannot automatically assume homology between facial expressions when comparing primate and human facial displays (Preuschoft & van Hooff, 1997). Although phylogenetically human smiling and laughter can be seen as modifications of the primate "bared-teeth" and "open-mouth" displays, primates often use "smiling" and "laughter" *instrumentally* in communication (e.g., as appeasement strategies). A new, intriguing "power asymmetry hypothesis" suggests that despotic societies require a clear distinction between displays for submission and friendliness, whereas in egalitarian societies the distinction can be blurred (Preuschoft & van Hooff, 1997).

Finally, both nonverbal communication and spoken language might be explained as evolutionary adaptation of early hominids to particular ecological conditions. According to this reasoning, the sensory modalities typical of primates evolved in an arboreal zone, but were later modified during adaptation to an open-country zone. After bipedalism had opened up the vocal tract, speech emerged in an evolutionary process, which also brought vocal sounds under volitional, cortical control. These later got connected up with a cultural tradition involving symbols (Maryanski, 1997).

3. Nonverbal Communication and the Social Sciences

What can be said about the relevance of the findings concerning the nonverbal communication of emotions to the understanding of human interaction? For many emotions, there seems to exist a connection among display, mimicking, and physiological response (Ekman & R. Davidson, 1994; Ekman & Keltner, 1997; Suomi, 1997; for mimicking as an inborn response, see, among others, T. M. Field, Woodson, Greenberg, & D. Cohen, 1982; McDougall, 1908; Meltzoff, 1985). Thus, it is not surprising to find veritable "epidemies" of nonverbal behavior, such as yawning or laughing (Schiefenhövel, 1992). The fact that emotions are easily perceived and felt among humans gives us a basis for empathic understanding. It also supports the notion that emotions may sweep through masses of people who are in close visual or physical contact, a well-known social psychological phenomenon, and which is probably directly connected to

Durkheim's famous "conscience collective" (Durkheim [1912]1954). Insights into nonverbal communication may also contribute to refinement of now extant or future models involving the transmission of culture, where imitation is taken to be ubiquitous sign of cultural inheritance (Boyd & Richerson, 1985; Durham, 1990, 1992).

It seems that we can easily detect nonverbal signs of deception or even embarrassment (Ekman, 1985; Ekman & Keltner, 1997; Keltner, 1995). Why is this important? One suggestion is that the capacity for the detection of lying, and thereby finding out the truth about other people's verbal statements about commitment or cooperation, is basic to the evolution of cooperation (Frank, 1997). Perhaps it is because we are used to congruence between channels that we are particularly sensitive to incongruence between the verbal and nonverbal ones and between stated and felt commitment. Further light must be thrown on this ability of the brain to cross-check information within itself by recent research in neuroscience—particularly the idea of the "triune brain" (MacLean, 1990), where more ancient parts of the brain (the mammalian limbic system regulating emotions and the Reptile complex connected to fight-or-flight behavior) are in constant communication with the neocortex.

So far, we have been trying to show how the more biologically oriented tradition within nonverbal communication may be relevant to the social sciences. However, representatives of the cultural tradition in nonverbal research pointed out that nonverbal expression and body language form only a small part of the broad repertoire that humans have for communicating emotion, status, and power. Meanwhile, culture may affect biology in the sense that posture (and backache) is a product of interaction between anatomy and the work requirements for particular classes or groups in particular cultures (Heller, 1997). Culture-specific emotional attitudes may be transmitted by childrearing practices. In this way, they may influence personality development and produce a particular "national character" (e.g., the "idle hands and absent eyes" of the Sebei; Goldschmidt, 1997). Finally, we are reminded once again of the radical conventionality of cultural symbols. For instance, the code of silence in medieval monasteries shows how ostensibly "obvious" gestures and signs may have quite unexpected meanings. As to the social conventions typical of an epoch, interesting information can be derived from studying postures and gestures in medieval pictures (Nitschke, 1997).

Thus, despite the seemingly increasing convergence between nature and nurture in nonverbal communication studies, the battle for an interactional approach is not yet won. Recently, there has been a resurgence of the militant cultural perspective, this time under the heading of "the social construction of emotions" (e.g., Harré, 1986). The argument here is that people learn to label a state of general physiological arousal based on categories obtained from their culture. The often-invoked scientific backup for this is Schachter and J. Singer's (1962) famous, but disputed, article concerning situational influences on the labeling of emotions. To its structure, the social constructivist claim about emotions appears quite similar to the previous linguistic relativistic thesis of the cultural determination of our categories of thought, except that here we are dealing with emotions rather than cognitions.

In response to this, the universalist—or rather, interactionist—may point to the earlier mentioned research showing that not all facial movements are under voluntary control (Ekman & Keltner, 1997). Interestingly, one of the most adamant current spokesmen *against* the social construction of emotions has been the sociologist Theodore Kemper—a leading figure in the new field of "sociology of emotions" (Kemper, 1978, 1981, 1987, 1990; examples of constructivists are Hochschild, 1979, Shott, 1979). In support of his position, he has quoted physiological data (studies of epinephrine/norepinephrine levels, serotonin and activity patterns in the nervous system). In this process, Kemper has tended to fall into sociological reductionism: According to his approach, all basic emotions can be classified and organized along the two social axial dimensions of status (affiliation) and power (coercion; for a similar argument, see Collins, 1975, 1981).

Scheff (1990), in turn, tried to connect social norms to our (internally experienced and outwardly detectable) feelings of pride and shame when we obey or disobey social rules (for a similar view, see Goldschmidt, 1990). J. H. Turner (1997) again gave a comprehensive overview of the possible social functions of emotions and nonverbal communication. He suggested, among other things, that the development of emotional communication in humans was a necessary prerequisite for social bonding among asocial hominids (see Maryanski & J. H. Turner, 1992). Perhaps the best route for combating exaggerated claims of the social construction of emotions may be to point to the close interrelation between cognition and emotion (see Plutchik, 1984). To the extent one is willing to accept the reality of cognitive biases in human reasoning (Cosmides & Tooby, 1987; Nisbett & Ross, 1980; Tooby & Cosmides, 1990b; Tversky

& Kahneman, 1974) it seems but a step to accept the existence of basic emotional biases as well.

At its most elementary level, nonverbal communication may be seen as an interactive process driven by the twin human predispositions to emotionality and sociality, both of which directly relate to the communication capacity of the human face. So far, research has shown the great speed with which the mother–infant bond is formed through newborns' preferential tracking of facelike stimuli (e.g., M. H. Johnson, Dziurawiec, Ellis, & Morton, 1991), and our very rapid encoding and decoding capacity regarding facial emotional messages (Dimberg, 1997). Thus, the clue to human communication may be found in the face, which seems surprisingly hard-wired for nonverbal communication. There is an area of the brain specifically devoted to facial recognition (Geschwind, 1979), and presumably also specific "face neurons" for facial recognition in the human neocortex. Such neurons have been recently reported for facial recognition in monkeys (Perrett, Rolls, & Caan, 1982; Weiss, 1988; Young & Yamane, 1992) and sheep (Kendrick & Baldwin, 1987).

Thus, although we have discussed the importance of development and culture in regard to nonverbal communication, face recognition may be one of the few hard-wired biological predispositions that we have. Face-recognition as a generic ability in humans also appears quite compatible with such neural network theories of the human mind as Edelman's (1992; see also Sacks, 1993).

The excitement of current research into nonverbal communication reinforces our belief that this is a strategical site for addressing the multilevel interaction between biology and culture in an interdisciplinary way. We hope that soon many more social scientists will overcome their fear that biology necessarily equals reductionism, and will, rather, come to see the biology involved in this kind of interaction-oriented research as "biology with a human face."

BIOLOGICAL AND CULTURAL PARAMETERS OF LANGUAGE: SOME NEW STRATEGIES AND A COLLISION OF PARADIGMS

Alexandra M. Maryanski and Boris M. Velichkovsky

1. A Historical Overview of Language-Origin Theories

Leading on from nonverbal to verbal communication, few topics have fired the imagination of scholars more than speculation on the origins of language. In 1863, Thomas Huxley wrote that, "the question of questions for mankind—the problem which underlies all others is the ascertainment of the place which man occupies in nature and of his relations to the universe of things" (p. 45) More than a century later, the standing of *Homo sapiens* in the "natural scheme of things" is still controversial, especially with regard to whether language is species-specific to humans.

This engrossment with the genesis of language has resulted in the publication of over 12,000 essays on this topic. At the start, *glottogenesis* was viewed as a "gift of the gods," with theological speculation on Adam and Eve and the language they spoke in paradise. By the 17th century, language was viewed as a "product of the intellect," with metaphysical explanations on how humans invented language by virtue of their superior intellect and social need to communicate (Hewes, 1975, 1977). In the 19th century, under the tutelage of Darwinian scholars, language was seen as a "product of selection" along with other components of human culture. For much of the 19th century, language research focused on two theoretical approaches: (a) the historical reconstruction of extinct languages through comparative philology on language families, and, (b) the evolutionary reconstruction of language through knowledge of primitive languages.

In the historical approach, comparative research on extinct languages emphasized that modern Indo-European languages were descendant "daughters" from an ancient mother language. Through a comparative analysis of language families, scholars were able to reconstruct past languages with the intention of recovering the original protolanguage. In the second evolutionary approach, primitive cultures and their contents (which included language) were seen as living representatives of earlier stages of evolutionary development, through which modern European cultures had already passed. All known languages were pigeonholed according to assigned evolutionary stages, with the belief that a "stage-one" protolanguage would eventually be discovered in remote linguistic communities. However, when past and present languages were all found to be linguistically complete, the classic stage-model approach to language was cast aside; with continued criticism, dialogue on the origins of language was banned in most academic circles.

2. Current Theories on the Biological Foundations of Language

The 1950s marked a revival of interest in the genesis of language. Currently, the evolutionary approach to language is guided by three broad and overlapping research questions: (a) What are the biological foundations of language? (b) When and why did human's language evolve? (c) What, if any, properties are unique to humans for the acquisition and use of language? These questions are examined in turn.

What are the Biological Foundations of Language?   Although all modern theories conceptualize language in an evolutionary framework—indeed, even the most conservative scholars recognize that language has biologically evolved components (e.g., apparatus used in the articulation of speech)—the trend has been toward separating the language facility into two distinct parts: (a) research on the evolution of crucial properties and capacities necessary for language, and (b) research on the structure and use of human language as a completed form. A focus on the phylogenetic aspects of language includes such topics as the cerebral organization of language (e.g., whether language processors are localized around "core regions," or dispersed along complex and overlapping networks), the cognitive processing equipment of language (e.g., whether language utilizes a general processor or a domain-specific language modular), and the origins of language (i.e., whether language was sprung as an "emergent property" through cerebral activation, or was fashioned from components that were "built up" in a stair-step fashion).

In contrast, a focus on human language as a completed system includes such topics as the ontological development of language (e.g., what is the relationship between language and ontology/maturation), the sociological development of language (e.g., what social and environmental variables activate phonological organization and performance), the many topics involved in historical linguistics; the structure of sign language with comparisons between lexical signs and oral representations, and the acquisition of second or multiple languages (for discussions, see Bachman & Albert, 1991; Maryanski & J. H. Turner, 1992; Newmeyer, 1984; Poizner, Bellugi, & Klima, 1990; Steklis & Erwin, 1988).

When and Why Did Humans Evolve Language?   According to the fossil record, the first hominids (i.e., australopithecines) appeared in Africa around 5 million years ago. The compelling linguistic dispute with regard to early hominids turns on which sense modality first fostered language-based communication. Proponents of "the visual-gestural" hypothesis argue that early hominids first used visual hand signs to communicate. Only later in hominid evolution did the auditory sense become the modality for symbolic communication, possibly because of altered environmental conditions and the adaptive advantages of speech over signs. Support for this hypothesis comes from research on visual signing apes. In contrast, proponents of the "vocal-auditory" hypothesis contend that sound symbols were first and foremost, arguing that, early in hominid evolution, bipedalism opened up the vocal tract, which, given time and the right selection pressures for development, eventually evolved into full-blown propositional speech.

Evidence to support the vocal-auditory hypothesis begins with the earliest Homo, *Homo habilis* (1.5–2 million years ago) who is successfully followed by *Homo erectus* (1.6 million years ago). Essentially, proponents point to the significant increase in the brain size of *habilis* over the small-brained australopithecines. Additionally, they suggest that the brain of early Homo is developed in Broca's area (for the serial programming of speech sounds) and in Wernicke's area (for speech comprehension). This suggests an early Homo ability for a repertoire of voluntary vocalizations. However, proponents of the auditory modality hypothesis are still divided on the question of *which Homo* was capable of producing a full repertoire of vocal sounds for full-blown human speech (for discussions, see Arensburg et al., 1990; Duchin, 1990; Fleagle, 1988; Foley, 1984; Hewes, 1975; P. Lieberman, 1984; Tobias, 1985, 1987).

What, if Any, Properties Are Unique to Humans for the Acquisition and Use of Language?   When language is equated with speech production, it is unique to humans. But when language is viewed as a particular kind of cognitive capacity, there is considerable controversy— indeed acrimony—among scholars. In many respects, this controversy is difficult to resolve, no matter what kind of evidence is brought to bear, because there is still no clear, agreed on definition of what language is. For this controversy, two basic language arguments can be discerned:

(a) language is unique to humans and marks a major cognitive "discontinuity" with nonhuman primates; and (b) language is a quality that varies in degree among higher primates (especially hominoids) and marks a point of cognitive "continuity" among human and nonhuman primates. Let us begin with the four main lines of argument in the "discontinuity" position.

In the discontinuity position, proponents argue that there are major vocal discontinuities between human and nonhuman primates: Vocalizations in nonhuman primates express only emotions (Darwin's original argument), vocalizations in nonhuman primates are not concerned with the naming of objects (a crucial dimension of speech), and vocalizations in nonhuman primates only occasionally carry a precise message to others. Moreover, proponents argue that many neurological discontinuities separate nonhuman primates. For example, primate vocalizations originate in limbic tissue for emotionally based calls, whereas human vocalizations originate in neocortical tissue for voluntary based sounds. Proponents also question ape acquisition and use of representational symbol systems: Apes are said to learn symbols only because important rewards, such as food, water, freedom from the cage, and so on, are associated with certain symbols. Additionally, apes are symbol users only because trainers will accept no alternative type of response (i.e., apes are not "dumb," they are just not natural language users). Apes demonstrate few instances of real grammar, and do not create independent and novel sentences that move beyond the simple process of associative learning, where only certain combinations are rewarded.

Proponents of the discontinuity position contend that humans alone are genetically predisposed to language, revealing a biologically triggered sequence. This sequence includes such factors as the spontaneous emergence of language for normal children, the existence of a "critical period" for language acquisition, and the further development of language capacities with biological maturation. Some language scholars even contend that only human children are born with such attributes as (a) a "language acquisition device," which allows for the learning of grammar rules that underlie a native language; (b) an "evaluation procedure," which enables children to "choose" the correct set of rules that best fit the primary linguistic data; and (c) a number of "language universals," which give human children "wired-in" knowledge about all native languages (for discussions, see Chomsky, 1986; Fodor, Bever, & Garrett, 1974; Lenneberg, 1967; Sebeok & Umiker-Sebeok, 1980; Terrace, 1985).

In the continuity position, proponents argue that humans' capacity for language is shared with our hominoid relatives. Two lines of research support the continuity position: First, there is a large literature on the linguistic competence of apes when symbolic codes are channeled through the visual and haptic modalities. After efforts to teach speech to apes were abandoned, researchers found that apes were able to use visual-gestural symbols to denote objects, order them grammatically, and "talk" to humans through sign language (Ameslan) or artificial languages (computer buttons or manipulation of plastic disks). Proponents aver that whatever cognitive abilities make language possible, they are not unique to humans, but underscore the evolutionary continuity of primates, especially hominoids.

In general, African pongids are able to perform the following cognitive functions: (a) they can learn large vocabularies of arbitrary symbols and use them to represent objects, actions, and relationships; (b) they can use these symbols spontaneously in conversations that communicate with humans and each other; (c) they can learn simple grammar rules about how to string symbols together; and (d) they can use existing symbols to construct appropriate "new words" to coordinate their activities and announce or comment on their intended actions. Recent findings also document the unprompted learning of visual-gestural symbols by bonobo chimpanzees *(Pan paniscus)*, simply by offhand exposure to a linguistic environment. Bonobos can also cognize, but not produce, English speech sounds at the level of normal 2½- to 3-year-old human children. Additionally, comparative research on sign language usage in young deaf children and African pongids reveals that both apes and deaf children have similar developmental states, such as using the same sign order and semantic relations at the earliest stages of "language."

Second, a substantial literature now exists on higher primate neurological processes. Once language is no longer cast as human speech, but as a cognitive capacity, inquiry into similarities and differences in ape and human neurobiology becomes appropriate. Recent studies have documented that African apes have elaborated skills for both intra- and inter-cortical tasks, while bonobo chimpanzees have skills for a symbol-to-symbol transfer (auditory-word to a visual-sign transfer; Savage-Rumbaugh et al., 1993). A capacity for such associations is now viewed as a precondition for language.

Experimental work has also detailed the evolutionary continuities in ape cortical structures in motor and sensory zones, and in augmented "supramodal processing" areas for higher cortical functions. Further, because ape and human brains are built according to the same plan, human cortical language sites are homologous in cytoarchitecture with ape brains. This suggests that, at the most basic level, apes and humans share some "hard-wiring" in the brain. Additionally, bonobo auditory fields for the processing of phonemes would seem to parallel human serial processing in ways that enable both hominoids to comprehend spoken words and sentences. Thus, those in the continuity camp contend that, whereas humans possess greater neurological capacities for full-blown adult language, this does not negate that apes possess the same neurological capacities, but in a more modest form (for discussions, see Gardner, Gardner, & Cantfort, 1989; Maryanski & J. H. Turner, 1992; Savage-Rumbaugh et al., 1993; Steklis & Erwin, 1988).

Bridging the Dichotomy of the Continuity–Discontinuity Position. The ZiF special conference on the biological foundations of language proceeded on the assumption that a comparison of possible stages of language evolution from a phylogenetic, ontogenetic, and sociogenetic perspective could bridge the prior dichotomy as to whether language is unique to humans. This interdisciplinary strategy led to the tentative proposal that the influence of biological or cultural factors during various stages of hominid linguistic evolution may have varied dramatically. Four basic mechanisms were proposed as underlying the evolution of language in humans: (a) vocal sounds (Bornstein, Lieberman, Maryanski), (b) cognitive capacities (Deacon, Harnad, Sperber, Maryanski), (c) an enlarged brain (Deacon, Friederici), and (d) changing social structures (Bechtel, Dolgopolsky, Scheerer).

There was some agreement that the segment of human evolution leading to full-blown language function was not a monotonous, unidirectional progression. Rather, the four main mechanisms of linguistic evolution buttressed each other and built up a structure of coevolutionary relationships. Language probably evolved in successive stages over time, with each progressive change linked to anatomical expansion of new areas of the brain, which, in turn, generated new modes of cognition and communication. Additionally, this process initiated a wave of "downstream" changes in the functional specialization of older neurophysiological structures (Bornstein, Deacon, Friederici). On the evolutionary time scale, human language appeared so quickly because it was mostly concocted from older parts that had originally evolved for purposes other than vocal communication. This probably accounts for why so little quantitative genetic change was necessary to make such a qualitative difference in human evolution.

In turn, new forms of social organization came forth to reinforce and further develop the internal mechanisms of processing language. Perhaps this is why sophisticated linguistic performances can be shown even in specific cultural environments, in young children with relatively underdeveloped brain functions (Abrahamsen, Bornstein), in patients with lesions of traditional language centers (Friederici, Velichkovsky), as well as in nonhuman primates (Maryanski, Rumbaugh).

In some higher primates, according to a commonly accepted view, the sequencing and comprehension mechanisms were already developed for the planning and monitoring of actions, respectively. Only the articulatory apparatus, and perhaps a specialized grammatical ordering, had to be added (Lieberman). In laboratory conditions, chimpanzees (*Pan paniscus* and—to a lesser degree—*Pan troglodytes*) can demonstrate not only functional use of lexical semantics, as well as a kind of protosyntax, which is reflected in the specific ordering of linguistic items (Rumbaugh). However, even in human ontogenesis, the development of an autonomous grammar can last for the first 10 years or more (Friederici).

As a whole, recent research now seems to be backing away from the strict polarization discussed earlier with regard to the continuity–discontinuity language camps. The focus of discussion at the conference was mostly on the continuity of biological mechanisms of language evolution and the discontinuity of cultural "scaffolding," which enables fast functional reorganization of biological mechanisms. Unfortunately, research on origins and development of language cannot be easily integrated into research generated by the discontinuity camp as long as their mainstream definition of language is limited to viewing language as a closed formal system for syntactic manipulations (Fodor, Chomsky).

Future conference topics should refer to issues such as the genesis of language, the interface of genes and culture, as well as the Homo that first acquired full speech functions. It is with interdisciplinary strategies as outlined earlier that questions relating to the origin of language and speech, as well as to the biological and cultural factors involved, might find answers that, rather than reifying the distinction between the natural and the cultural, disclose their intricate, if always changing, relationship.

6

EVOLUTIONARY THEORY AND HUMAN SOCIAL INSTITUTIONS: PSYCHOLOGICAL FOUNDATIONS

Nancy W. Thornhill
University of Southern California
Los Angeles

Alexandra M. Maryanski
University of California
Riverside

John Tooby
University of California
Santa Barbara

Leda Cosmides
University of California
Santa Barbara

Peter Meyer
University of Augsburg
Augsburg, Germany

Jonathan H. Turner
University of California
Riverside

The standard rationale for the social sciences being separate disciplines from biology rests on the assertion that human social behavior is uniquely complex. Anthropologists and sociologists often argue that human institutions managing the reproductive, productive, and symbolic features of human social life bear only remote connections to the phenomena of evolutionary biology. Proponents of more interdisciplinary views assert that at the very least, biology underpins sociocultural systems. Human behavior is implemented by human brains and bodies, to which evolutionary considerations add the fact that humans must have evolved from an ape–human common ancestor relatively recently.

For other animals, evolutionists interested in behavior have made immense strides, sparked by Hamilton's (1964) famous papers on inclusive fitness showing how selectionist theory could account for one of the most important general features of animal social organization—the importance of kinship as a principle of social organization. Since the important article of R. D. Alexander (1974) and E. O. Wilson's (1975) perhaps unintentionally incendiary last chapter, many evolutionists have used the new tools to explain human behavior. In other animals, complex societies appear to be rooted fairly directly in psychological mechanisms that cause cooperation, coordination, and division of labor. The advanced insect colonies may indeed have self-organizing properties, but behavioral biologists have gone far without seeing much need for a nearly autonomous institutional account of the form commonly advocated by social scientists.

Of course, even the most extreme proponents of the institutional approach recognize that humans are biological organisms that evolved. They merely find this relatively uninteresting. Taking comfort from an earlier generation of evolutionary biologists like Dobzhansky (1968), they conceive of human social institutions as an emergent superorganic system little constrained or limited by the organic substratum. Dobzhansky's theoretical statement of this problem is brief and tries to have it both ways: "In producing the genetic basis for culture, biological evolution has transcended itself—it has produced the superorganic" (p. 18); "Yet the superorganic has not annulled the organic" (p. 19). The first quote concludes one paragraph, and the second is the topic sentence of the next. This chapter outlines how evolutionary thinkers have approached the task of getting beyond the lofty, but vague, rhetoric of Dobzhansky's day to more specific questions and analyses about how evolved individual psychology generates and/or is generated by social institutions.

Modern Darwinians interested in human behavior agree that a much richer and more interesting interpenetration of biological and sociocultural accounts is becoming possible, as much as we disagree about just what form that interpenetration should take. One tack is to suppose that human societies are less different than other animal societies than we might think. Perhaps human institutions can be accounted for in terms of individually evolved psychological predispositions, plus a relatively simple and transparent set of rules for the self-organization of such individuals into complex social systems. This approach is the Darwinian version of "methodological individualism," which has animated attempts to apply economists' models based on individual rationality to explaining social institutions (Coleman, 1991). The complementarity of the evolutionists' and economists' approaches was noted by Hirshleifer (1977). Many evolutionary psychologists are interested in replacing the economist's excessively idealized, selfish rationalist with a human psychology that actually evolved while retaining the individualist focus. Other authors assume that "superorganic" socio-cultural institutions are real and more or less limited to humans; they ask how individual level psychological processes constrain or are constrained by human social systems. No matter how spectacularly novel human institutions are, they certainly cannot exist without human minds, and must have been built up over many millennia as human minds, which have an evolved architecture, interacted.

The first section of this chapter sets out the standard sociological and anthropological account of human institutions as persistent, emergent, dynamic entities. Maryanski and J. H. Turner argues in this section that the evolution of human societies is affected by "Spencerian Selection"— the systematic, institutionalized creative search for solutions to felt problems. This process is more like development of an individual (by analogy with learning) than evolution of a population by natural selection.

Darwinians may either try to sweep away or build to this account, or something in between. In any case, interdisciplinary dialogue with the disciplines of sociology and anthropology is currently structured by the historical tension between macro (institutional) and micro (individualist) explanations, which have been one of the main axes of theoretical dispute in these sciences since their emergence. From the point of view of most practitioners in these disciplines, the question is how evolutionary accounts contribute to these traditional debates.

In the second section, the evolutionary individualist position of contemporary evolutionary psychologists is outlined by N. Thornhill, Tooby, and Cosmides. The argument is that human social behavior is underpinned by many highly specialized information-processing systems—mental organs that guide behavior in adaptive directions, or at least did so in the environments of the past in which these innate mechanisms evolved. Evolutionary psychologists of this persuasion think that there are alternative explanations for sociocultural institutions of the form described by Maryanski and J. H. Turner in the first section.

For example, what seem to be "superorganic" institutions may be a rather direct outcome of the interaction of mental organs with variable environments that evoke particular seemingly transmitted cultural responses. The apparent history may be illusory, however; individual responses to environment may be much more important. If so, large-scale, patterned social behavior must arise from relatively transparent self-assembly of a population of adapted minds, much as in the nonhuman animal case. An example is incest avoidance, which seems to be a product of a specific innate propensity to avoid mating with individuals of one's own household (the Westermarck hypothesis). The institution of nonincestuous marriage and the rather elaborate taboos and prescriptions that surround it may derive directly from the mental organ, rather than from traditional, transmitted cultural institutions.

Social scientists of the traditional school are sometimes inclined to dismiss this hypothesis out of hand. They do so at their peril, as is clear from the two intellectual roots of evolutionary psychology. The Darwinian part is obvious, and evolutionary theory is a powerful set of tools. Not quite so obvious is the relationship to Noam Chomsky's innatist theory of language, and especially to the synthesis of innatist and evolutionary theories in Pinker's (1991, 1994) theory of the language "instinct." The basic rules of grammar may be innate mental modules of great power. Children deprived of a fully functional language—because they are reared in a community where a crude pigin is the only shared medium of communication among adults—may use their fully functioning access to the language instinct to elevate a pigin to a grammatically rich creole in one generation (Bickerton, 1981). So, too, other social "instincts" might allow people to reconstruct other features of social life if a catastrophe like enslavement broke the seemingly necessary chains of cultural transmission. In principle, Chomsky's (1965) revolutionary impact on linguistics could reasonably be replicated for any domain where traditional culture has been invoked to explain human behavior. A quite radical alternative to the traditional view of institutions is thus possible.

Maryanski's use of phylogenetic analysis introduces another analytical technique from evolutionary biology. Darwinian processes depend on descent with modification. At each step in the evolution of a lineage, evolutionary processes make marginal, usually adaptive, changes in populations. The evidences of the haphazard, historically contingent process by which natural selection operates was one of the most important contributions to the downfall of supernatural creation hypotheses in the 19th century. An all-wise "Designer" would not have left clumsy traces of contingent history in his or her work, such as the myriad of anatomical details that Huxley (1863) used to demontrate our kinship with the apes. History generates the constraints and opportunities that channel evolution down certain paths, but not others, in any given lineage. Behavior is no less reflective of phylogeny than anatomy, as Darwin ([1872]1965) showed in his *The Expression of Emotions in Man and Animals.*

Because the human scale of social organization arose only once, but was very successful once achieved, historical constraints on and opportunities for our evolution are likely to have been quite important. Maryanski's reconstruction of the last common hominoid ancestor leads her to the at first surprising conclusion that its social organization was built on weaker ties and much more fluid social structure than monkeys and some later apes. On this system, it was possible for selection to elaborate a social structure with strong ties between males and females (marriage), reinforced by our highly unusual sexual division of labor. Because most social primates have strong intergenerational bonds, especially among females (more rarely males), it is hard to see how divergences in the human direction could start without a hominoid ancestor with weak social bonds.

The continued relatively weak, fluid ties of humans, the pair-bonded family aside, meant that social institutions not directly rooted in biology could flourish, allowing institutional elaboration based on, but not specifically determined by, biology. The point is that the relationship between biology and sociocultural institutions is not uninteresting just because it might have allowed "emergent" sociocultural institutions to arise. Quite the contrary, if such strange things do exist, it is all the more interesting to know how on earth such a capacity could arise, given that it must have been adaptive at each step from there to here.

It is also interesting how psychology and institutions interact in the day-to-day life of individuals, as they must even if the institutional level is emergent in some strong sense.

The last section of the chapter proposes a general model of how human emotions regulate the relationship between the biological and institutional imperatives of social life. The organic and institutional levels of behavioral determinants have to be linked in "real time," not just in the deep past of evolutionary history. The human affect system plays this mediating role according to Meyer's hypothesis. Important elements of the emotions are purely biological, in the sense that they are the product of neurotransmitters. Biological imperatives like hunger, fear, and lust feed into affect. At the same time, the institutionalized social environment also generates and manipulates emotions, often by using dramatic rituals that have quite direct and easily understood effects on the biological basis of emotions.

Everyday human life is played out on the arena of emotions where biological and institutional forces interact quite directly and intimately. Once again, incest and the incest taboo are illustrations. Would not such taboos be entirely redundant unless they were required to supplement, modify, or regulate the apparently innate tendency to avoid inbreeding anyway?

Meyer's message is clear: If institutional imperatives are not derived directly from biology, then a good description of the way biological and institutional forces are integrated in human psychology is essential. Once again, our common aim is to replace formulas of a generation ago, like Sahlins' (1976a,b) and Dobzhansky's with concrete, empirically testable models of human social cognition.

A SOCIOLOGICAL VIEW OF INSTITUTIONS

Alexandra M. Maryanski and Jonathan Turner

One of the most often used, yet elusive, concepts in sociology and social science is that of "institution." As the traditional subject matter of sociology and anthropology, institutions constitute the core of social organization, although their central place in social science theory allows for multiple meanings and definitions (e.g., Ogburn & Nimkoff, 1959; Parsons [1935]1990; J. H. Turner, 1972). Yet most social scientists refer to economic, political, religious, and other institutions as if they had precise meanings.

Despite the disagreement, however, there is a clear convergence of meaning that is important to bear in mind in view of new efforts by evolutionary psychology, sociobiology, and biologically oriented sociologists to explain institutional dynamics in terms of evolutionary models and the prescriptions offered by them. A first element of all sociological conceptualizations of institutions is that they are composed of systems of normative rules. The emphasis here is on *systems* of rules. An institution is not defined by a single rule, such as an incest or marriage rule, but by these rules in conjunction with other rules, thus constituting a system of rights, duties, and obligations.

A second feature of institutions is that they are constituted, in part, by values or standards of right, wrong, good, and bad. This value-laden character of institutions operates at several levels. At the normative level, institutional norms carry a moral and imperative quality; for the individual actor, institutional activity is affective and emotional because it is guided by internalized moral codes that are used for self-evaluation, as well as for the evaluation of others—a theme developed at greater length in the last section of this chapter.

Third, institutions are composed of networks of status positions in which individuals are incumbent and to which normative and value elements are attached (Maryanski, 1987). These networks of positions are organized into diverse types of corporate units (e.g., groups, bureaucracies, etc.), which are, in turn, interconnected. These interconnected sets of corporate units are devoted to resolving specific adaptation problems confronting a population (e.g., production, reproduction, regulation, distribution, anxiety reduction, health, etc.). This gives each institution a distinct character (e.g., economic, kinship, political, religious, medical, etc.). From a sociological viewpoint, any one institution is "embedded" within other institutions (Granovetter, 1985). Explanations for the operation of one institution must include analyses of the direct, indirect, and reverse causal effects with other institutions. From this perspective, the dynamics of institutions constitute complexes of emergent causal effects.

A final feature of institutions is that they persist over time by virtue of: (a) transmission processes in which new generations of actors are socialized into the values and normative elements of institutions, and (b) inertia tendencies of all structures, stemming from the interconnections among networks of status positions and the corporate units organizing these positions, preventing any individual from having direct impact on them.

These features may be combined into this definition of *institutions:* networks of value-laden and normatively regulated activity in status positions, organized into diverse types of corporate units, focused on specific sets of adaptation problems encountered by a population, and persisting by virtue of transmission and structural inertia. Although definitions in the social sciences vary somewhat, they converge on these basic elements.

Much more problematic than these definitional issues is an explanatory question, which constitutes the core of this chapter: How are the emergence, persistence, and dynamics of an institution, or part thereof, best explained? In essence, such a question addresses the central issue of any social science (i.e., that of sociocultural change).

Explanations of why institutions emerge and how they operate have always been problematic and controversial in sociology. There are several lines of contention: (a) Are explanations to be micro and explain institutions in terms of simpler, consistent processes and mechanisms, or are these explanations to be macro and account for institutions in terms of societal and population-level forces? (b) Are explanations to focus on the "ultimate causes" of the first institutions—usually conceived to be kinship, economy, and religion—or are these explanations to examine the causal interplay of forces in more proximate, historical, or contemporary cases? (c) Are explanations to be historical and descriptive, or are they to be nomothetic and explain institutions in terms of basic and universal forces?

Sociology and anthropology have developed explanations with respect to all of these options, whereas recent psychologically and biologically oriented explanations of institutions have been primarily micro and nomothetic. Although these more recent approaches stand in contrast to what has been the dominant approach in both sociology and anthropology—macrolevel functionalism and developmentalism—they offer new perspectives and strategies to explain social institutions. In the following sections, three new approaches are presented: evolutionary sociology, evolutionary psychology, and a biosociological explanation of institutions.

1. Institutions in Sociology

In virtually all explanations of institutions within sociology, there is a functional argument: Institutions emerge and persist because they resolve some problem of survival and adaptation faced by a population; that is, institutions exist to meet survival needs and requisites—a line of argument fraught with logical problems (see J. H. Turner, 1991). Nonetheless, sociologists have consistently employed, if only implicitly, the notion of requisites to define or explain institutions. For example, H. Spencer (1874–1896 [1898]) saw institutions emerging and evolving to meet three basic needs: operation (i.e., production and reproduction), distribution (e.g., movement of materials, people, and information), and regulation (e.g., use of power for coordination and control). Later, Durkheim ([1893]1933) asserted that institutions develop to satisfy one major requisite—the need for integration—because solving Hobbesian conflicts between individuals greatly improves human life.

Among anthropologists, Radcliffe-Brown (1935, 1952) echoed Durkheim's argument, whereas Malinowski (1944) took a more Spencerian position by developing an important and still relevant distinction between biologically based and derived needs. Indeed, Malinowski listed sets of biological needs necessary for biological maintenance (or what he termed *vital sequences*) and implicitly asserts that these vital sequences were the first impetus to the creation of institutions. But he quickly added that, as institutional structures and systems of symbols (i.e., culture) are created, they generate new, derived needs not related to their biological origins. For Malinowski, there are four basic derived needs at the social system level: production or economic needs, reproduction or educational needs, authority or political needs, and social control needs. At the cultural system level, there are three basic derived needs: information needed for adjustment to an environment, symbols needed for providing a sense of control over destiny or chance, and symbols needed to create a communal rhythm in daily routines.

Subsequent generations of functionalists all sought to develop similar lists of "societal needs" and then use these to explain the existence of institutions in terms of how they meet each need on the list (e.g., Aberle et al., 1950). Parsons' (1978) four functions paradigm for all "action systems" (behavioral organism, personality, social systems, and culture) is perhaps the most famous of these efforts. Luhmann's (1982) emphasis on needs "to reduce complexity" is yet another recent example of explanations of institutional structures in terms of needs.

In all of these functional explanations, there is an implicit selectionist model, but it is not a model of Darwinian individual selection. The non-Darwinian argument is this: Biological needs for maintenance of the social organism first generated selection pressures for the creation of institutions; those populations of individuals that did not create institutions like kinship, economy, and religion failed to survive; and once institutional structures exist and are in place, new selection pressures for additional institutional structures emerge as a population grows in size, or confronts problems of adjustment within and between institutions and other social structures. In this argument, selection does not necessarily involve competition among alternatives, but the opposite: Selection is for new sociocultural arrangements where none or few exist, or where existing institutions are inadequate for the task of maintaining a population in an environment. Just whether such selection pressures for new kinds of sociocultural arrangements actually generate these arrangements is a matter of luck, chance, rational choice, creative energy, diffusion, or some other nongenetic process. J. H. Turner (1995, 1997) termed such selection *functional selection* or, in deference to the first sociologist to employ this logic, *Spencerian selection*.

Functional or Spencerian selection can, of course, operate concurrently with Darwinian selection. Indeed, Durkheim ([1893]1933) explicitly borrowed from Darwin the notion of density and competition, but he took the idea in a more Spencerian direction, asserting implicitly that Darwinian selection can create the conditions for functional selection. As Durkheim argued, population growth and ecological concentration increase density and set into motion competition for resources, which lead to the specialization of the population into a division of labor (as opposed to speciation in biology) that is regulated by new types of symbol systems. The second part of this argument is heavily Spencerian because density and competition increase a search for new alternatives, rather than a selection among preexisting alternatives in a genotype or cultural inventory.

2. Macrolevel Development

The functional selection arguments have always been linked to developmental analyses of institutions. These analyses emphasize that long-term historical trends move toward ever greater differentiation among institutions and more complex mechanisms for integrating diverse institutions. The driving force behind such differentiation is a combination of increasing population size, diffusion from more advanced populations, environmental exigencies (sociocultural as well as biophysical), and internal sociocultural imperatives, such as technological development and structural/cultural constraints. These forces represent a combination of selection among existing or available sociocultural alternatives and selection for new cultural alternatives.

Typically, these developmental analyses—which, it should be noted, are normally called *sociocultural evolution* by sociologists (see chap. 1)—trace sequences of institutional differentiation, beginning with (a) the separation of kinship, economy, and religion, and then (b) moving through the emergence of new institutions such as the polity, law, education, science, and medicine. During this 'evolutionary' or developmental process, the organizational units structuring networks of positions, and the values and norms regulating these networks, become distinctive for each institution, posing new problems of integration.

These kinds of scenarios are highly descriptive, and they usually posit a driving force, such as technology, (G. Lenski, 1966; L. A. White, 1949), population growth (Boserup, 1981; H. Spencer, 1874-96), and new integrative processes (Parsons, 1966, 1971). Yet, beneath the surface description of how a driving force increases institutional complexity is a selection argument. Sometimes, it is more Darwinian, emphasizing conflict and competition over scarce resources within and between populations, whereas at other times, it is Spencerian, stressing searches for new institutional systems in the face of potentially disintegrative pressures and problems.

3. New Microlevel Alternatives to Macro-Level

The theoretical turn in sociology to microlevel explanations of institutions is decidedly dominated by rational choice theories (Lindenberg, 1990). Indeed, the same game theoretic models that some biologists have borrowed are used here. Rational choice theorists begin by attacking functional explanations as unable to explain why institutions are created in the first place, and why actors are willing to participate in them once they exist. Even if they acknowledge that the implicit selection arguments in functional analysis do offer an explanation of why institutions emerge and persist, rational choice theorists would be unsatisfied because, ultimately, their goal is to explain institutions in terms of some elementary, constitutive principle of the behavior of individual actors who will become incumbents in the positions of institutional systems that they create. These principles assume utility-maximizing actors (the sociological equivalent of fitness-maximizing individuals and "selfish genes") and then ask the question: Why would rational and selfish actors create systems of value-laden norms in restrictive corporate units? Do not such cultural systems and organizational units impose costs and reduce options for utilities?

The answers to these questions can become complex, but the general idea is quite simple: Under certain conditions, it is rational to construct restrictive norms and organizational units as a means to reduce "negative externalities" (utility-depriving consequences), and thereby increase utility-maximizing payoffs. The vocabularies differ somewhat, depending on whether one begins with the "free-rider" problem (Olson, 1965) or the "prisoner's dilemma," but the explanations are eventually the same. For the free-rider problem, the issue is how to limit the rational tendency of actors to consume a jointly produced good without contributing to its production—a tactic that will eventually impose negative externalities on all because the joint good will be decreasingly available for consumption and because of those who continue to produce the joint good in the face of rampant free-riding will incur high costs for a problematic payoff. This dilemma is great when the joint good is highly valuable, when its production must be undertaken collectively, and when actors are dependent on a particular kind of organizational unit for its production. The prisoner's dilemma is a problem of cooperation. Here, when individuals act to maximize their own payoff, this jointly issues in lower individual payoffs than a cooperative strategy. The solution for both is for rational, utility-maximizing actors to create norms (both proscriptive and prescriptive), monitoring procedures, and sanctioning systems in organizational units (Coleman, 1991; Hechter, 1987; Heckathorn, 1988). Thus, the emergence and persistence of institutions are to be explained as a response by rational and selfish actors to problems like free-riding or prisoner's dilemma in the production and distribution of joint goods necessary for the survival of the species, as well as the organization of ever more complex social systems.

Rational choice theories locate the mechanism for the maintenance and evolution of social institutions in the decision making of individuals. The individualist stance is familiar to evolutionary thinking, though counter to traditional macro-level perspectives in sociology. Evolutionary psychologists are prepared to go a step further than classic rational choice theorists, substituting a theory of a complex evolved human psychology for the stylized rational actor. It is to this challenge to the conventional view that we now turn.

INTRODUCTION TO EVOLUTIONARY PSYCHOLOGY

Nancy W. Thornhill, John Tooby, and Leda Cosmides

Darwin was the first evolutionary psychologist. His phylogenetic analysis focused on the facial and postural expressions of human emotions (Darwin, [1872]1965). He showed that expressions of human emotions had homologues in certain nonhuman mammals, demonstrating that there was descent with modification by selection in the context of the morphological, physiological, and psychic mechanisms underlying emotional expression. Darwin's ([1871]1874) study of human psychology involved speculations about the kinds of selective forces that produced certain psychological adaptations.

The most significant recent developments in evolutionary theory pertain to the clarification of the evolution of social behavior. Major advances are found in Hamilton's (1964) hypothesis that altruism involving benefits conferred on relatives other than offspring (nonparental nepotism) will evolve in a straightforward fashion, when the concept of individual fitness is more inclusive, including not only the production and aiding of offspring, but also the individual's influence on the survival and reproduction of genetic relatives other than offspring. G. C. Williams (1966; see also R. D. Alexander & Borgia, 1978; Dawkins, 1976; Lewontin, 1970) argued that individual selection, and not group selection, is responsible for adaptations. The evolution of reciprocal altruism was illuminated by Trivers (1971), R. D. Alexander (1979, 1987), and Axelrod and Hamilton (1981). The evolution of parent–offspring interactions was placed in an evolutionary theoretical perspective by R. D. Alexander (1974) and Trivers (1974). Important extensions of Darwin's ([1871] 1874) evolutionary theory of sexual interactions were provided by Bateman (1948), G. Parker (1970), and Trivers (1972).

The emphasis during the period of synthesis—the 1970s—was on behavior, not underlying psychological mechanisms. It simply was assumed that psychological adaptations exist that would cause humans to pursue the proximate rewards and avoid the proximate punishments that historically affected inclusive fitness of individuals. The first major treatment of human psychological adaptations appeared at the close of the 1970s. In *The Evolution of Human Sexuality*, Symons (1979) focused on evolved sex differences in emotional adaptations.

From these beginnings emerged the field of Darwinian psychology, as it is called by Symons (1987), or evolutionary psychology (Cosmides & Tooby, 1987; Daly & M. Wilson, 1988). The foundation of this field is the study of the mental mechanisms that generate behavior, using the theory of evolution by natural selection to develop hypotheses about their design. According to this view, behavior in the present is generated by information-processing mechanisms that exist because they solved adaptive problems in the past—in the ancestral environments in which the human line evolved. Thus, a necessary (although not sufficient) component of any explanation of social behavior is a description of the design of the computational machinery that generates it. The goal of evolutionary psychologists is to map the evolved architecture of the human mind, which, they argue, is composed of a large number of functionally specialized information-processing devices: cognitive adaptations. The proposed domain-specificity of these devices is what separates evolutionary psychology from studies of human social evolution which implicitly assumes that "fitness-maximization" is a mentally (although not consciously) represented goal, the mind being composed of domain general mechanisms that "figures out" fitness-maximizing behavior in any environment—even evolutionarily novel ones (see Borgerhoff Mulder et al., chap. 7, this volume).

1. Adaptationist Logic

There remains some skepticism about the application of adaptationism to the study of human behavior and feelings and the mental adaptations that cause them (e.g., Scarr's, 1989, view of evolutionary psychology; but see Crawford, M. Smith, & Krebs, 1990). To prevent unnecessary disputes, it seems appropriate here to discuss some potential confusions.

The goal of Darwin's theory was to explain phenotypic design: Why do the beaks of finchs differ from one species to the next? Why do animals expend energy attracting mates that could be spent on survival? Why are human facial expressions of emotion similar to those found in other primates? The evolutionary process he outlined has two components: chance and natural selection. Natural selection is the only component of the evolutionary process that can introduce complex functional organization in to a species' phenotype (Dawkins, 1986; G. C. Williams, 1966).

At a certain level of abstraction, every species has a universal, species-typical, evolved architecture. For example, one can open any page of the medical textbook, *Gray's Anatomy*, and find this evolved architecture described down to the minutest detail—not only do we all have a heart, two lungs, a stomach, intestines, and so on, but the book describes human anatomy down to the particulars of nerve connections. This is not to say that there is no biochemical individuality: No two stomachs are exactly alike—they vary a bit in quantitative properties, such as size, shape, and how much HCl they produce. But all humans have stomachs, and they all have the same basic functional design—each stomach is attached at one end to an esophagus and at the other to the small intestine, each secretes the same chemicals necessary for digestion, and so on. Presumably, the same is true of the brain and, hence, of the evolved architecture of our cognitive programs—of the information-processing mechanisms that generate behavior. Evolutionary psychology seeks to characterize the universal, species-typical architecture of these mechanisms.

In evolutionary biology, there are several different levels of explanation that are complementary and mutually compatible. Misunderstandings sometimes arise when people hear evolutionary explanations because they think an explanation at one level precludes or invalidates explanations at another.

The function of the brain is to generate behavior that is sensitively contingent on information from an organism's environment. Therefore, it is an information-processing device. It is important to know the physical structure of a cognitive device and the information-processing programs realized by that structure. There is, however, another level of explanation—a functional level. In evolved systems, form follows function. The physical structure is there because it embodies a set of programs; the programs are there because they solved a particular problem in the past. This functional level of explanation is essential for understanding how natural selection designs organisms.

An organism's phenotypic structure can be thought of as a collection of "design features"—micromachines, such as the functional components of the eye or liver. Over evolutionary time, new design features are added or discarded from the species' design because of their consequences. A design feature will cause its own spread over generations if it has the consequence of solving adaptive problems: cross-generationally recurrent problems whose solution promotes reproduction, such as detecting predators or detoxifying poisons. If a more sensitive retina, which appeared in one or a few individuals by chance mutation, allows predators to be detected more quickly, individuals who have the more sensitive retina will produce offspring at a higher rate than those who lack it. By promoting the reproduction of its bearers, the more sensitive retina thereby promotes its own spread over the generations, until it eventually replaces the earlier model retina and becomes a universal feature of that species' design.

Hence, natural selection is a feedback process that "chooses" among alternative designs on the basis of how well they function. It is a hill-climbing process, in which a design feature that solves an adaptive problem well can be outcompeted by a new design feature that solves it better. This process has produced exquisitely engineered biological machines—the vertebrate eye, photosynthetic pigments, efficient foraging algorithms, color constancy systems—whose performance is unrivaled by any machine yet designed by humans.

By selecting designs on the basis of how well they solve adaptive problems, this process engineers a tight fit between a device's function of and its structure. To understand this causal relationship, biologists had to develop a theoretical vocabulary that distinguishes between structure and function. In evolutionary biology, explanations that appeal to the structure of a device are sometimes called "proximate" explanations. When applied to psychology, these would include explanations that focus on genetic, biochemical, physiological, developmental, cognitive, social, and all other immediate causes of behavior. The functional level is sometimes called an "ultimate" or "distal" explanation because it refers to causes that operated over evolutionary time.

An organism's phenotype can be partitioned into (a) adaptations, which are present because they were selected for; (b) by-products, which are present because they are causally coupled to traits that were selected for (e.g., the whiteness of bone); and (c) noise, which was injected by the stochastic components of evolution. Like other machines, only narrowly defined aspects of organisms fit together into functional systems: Most ways of describing the system will not capture its functional properties. Unfortunately, some have misrepresented the well-supported claim that selection creates functional organization as the obviously false claim that all traits of organisms are funtional—something no sensible evolutionary biologist would ever maintain. Furthermore, not all behavior engaged in by organisms is adaptive. A taste for sweet may have been adaptive in ancestral environments, where vitamin-rich fruit was scarce, but it can generate maladaptive behavior in a modern environment flush with fast-food restaurants. Moreover, once an information-processing mechanism exists, it can be deployed in activities that are unrelated to its original function—because we have evolved learning mechanisms that cause language acquisition, we can learn to write. But these learning mechanisms were not selected for *because* they caused writing.

Adaptations are problem-solving machines, and can be identified using the same standards of evidence that one would use to recognize a human-made machine: design evidence. One can identify a machine as a TV rather than a stove by finding evidence of complex functional design: showing, for example, that it has many coordinated design features (antennaes, cathode ray tubes, etc.) that are complexly specialized for transducing TV waves and transforming them into a color bit map (a configuration that is unlikely to have risen by chance alone), whereas it has virtually no design features that would make it good at cooking food. Complex functional design is the hallmark of adaptive machines as well. One can identify an aspect of the phenotype as an adaptation by showing that (a) it has many design features that are complexly specialized for solving an adaptive problem, (b) these phenotypic properties are unlikely to have arisen by chance alone, and (c) they are not better explained as the by-product of mechanisms designed to solve some alternative adaptive problem.

To understand what complex adaptations "look like," it helps to consider a standard example—the vertebrate eye and its associated neural circuitry (for its role in understanding adaptations, see Pinker & Bloom, 1990). The eye consists of an exquisitely organized arrangement of cells, structures, and processes, such as (a) a transparent protective outer coating that bends light, the cornea; (b) an opening, the pupil, through which light enters; (c) an iris, which is a muscle that surrounds the pupil and constrictus or dilates the aperture, regulating the amount of light entering the eye; (d) a lens, which is both transparent and flexible, and whose curvature and thickness can be adjusted to bring objects of varying distances into focus; (e) the retina, a light-sensitive surface that lies in the focal plane of the lens: This multilayered neural tissue lining the inside back of the eyeball is, in effect, a piece of the brain that migrated to the eye during fetal development; (f) classes of specialized cells (rods and cones) in the retina that transform sampled properties of ambient light through selective photochemical reactions into electrochemical impulses; (g) the activation by these electrochemical impulses of neighboring bipolar cells, which, in turn, feed signals into neighboring ganglion cells, whose axons converge to form the optic nerve; (h) the optic nerve, which carries these signals out of the eye and to the lateral geniculate bodies in the brain; and (i) the routing of these signals to the visual cortex, into a series of retinotopic maps and other neural circuits, where they are further analyzed by a formidable array of information-processing mechanisms that also constitute crucial parts of the visual system.

The eye is by no means a unique case. For example, immunologists have traced out a similar, immensely articulated architecture of complexly interrelated defenses (the blood, monocytes, histocytes, free macrophages, T lymphocytes, B lymphocytes, spleen, thymus, and so on). In fact, virtually every organ that has been examined so far betrays a complex functionality unmatched as yet by any system engineered by humans. More than a century of research and observation confirms that selection builds into organisms a complex functional organization of an eyelike precision and quality.

Theories of adaptive function can guide investigations of phenotypic design. Those who study species from an adaptationist perspective adopt the stance of an engineer. For example, in discussing sonar in bats, Dawkins (1986) proceeded as follows: "I shall begin by posing a problem that the living machine faces, then I shall consider possible solutions to the problem that a sensible engineer might consider; I shall finally come to the solution that nature has actually adopted" (pp. 21–22). Engineers figure out what problems they want to solve, and then design machines that are capable of solving these problems in an efficient manner. Evolutionary biologists figure out what adaptive problems a given species encountered during its evolutionary history, and then ask themselves, "What would a machine capable of solving these problems well under ancestral conditions look like?" Against this background, they empirically explore the design features of the evolved machines that, taken together, comprise an organism. Of course, definitions of adaptive problems do not uniquely specify the design of the mechanisms that solve them. Because there are often multiple ways to achieve any solution, empirical studies are needed to decide "which nature has actually adopted." But the more precisely one can define an adaptive information-processing problem—the "goal" of processing—the more clearly one can see what a mechanism capable of producing that solution would have to look like. This research strategy has dominated the study of vision, for example, so that it is now commonplace to think of the visual system as a collection of functionally integrated computational devices, each specialized for solving a different problem in scene analysis (e.g., judging depth, detecting motion, analyzing shape from shading, etc.; Marr, 1982; Ramachandran, 1990).

The species-typical organization of the psychology and physiology of modern humans has an evolutionary explanation and an evolutionarily patterned architecture. At its core, the discovery of the design of human psychology and physiology is a problem in reverse engineering: We have working exemplars of the design in front of us, but we need to organize our sea of observations of these exemplars into a map of the causal structure that accounts for the behavior of the system. Although the psychological architectures of organisms are infused with complex functional organization, this is not always easy to see. (Indeed, although many social and biological scientists are willing to concede that the body is full of the most intricately functional machinery, heavily organized by natural selection, they remain skeptical that the same is true of the mind.) For the purpose of discovering, analyzing, and describing the functional organization of our evolved psychological structure, the information-processing language of cognitive science is, perhaps, the most useful (Cosmides & Tooby, 1987; Symons, 1979; Tooby & Cosmides, 1992). It has several advantages over behavioral categorization systems and/or the causal language of neuroscience.

First, the evolutionary function of the brain is the adaptive regulation of behavior and physiology on the basis of information derived from the body and the environment. How an organism processes information determines how it will behave; how it behaves can have an enormous impact on its reproduction, and therefore on the reproduction of the design features of which it is composed. Therefore, it is meaningful to ask what kind of *cognitive* design features would have constituted good solutions to adaptive information-processing problems that persisted over many generations. Evolutionary biology, paleoanthropology, hunter–gatherer studies, and so on supply definitions of the recurrent adaptive problems humans faced during their evolution, and investigates the information-processing mechanisms that evolved to solve them. Natural selection responds to differences in function, and therefore has less to say about neural implementations: If two neural structures create the same information–behavior relationship at the same cost, then natural selection will not be able to "see" them.

Second, information-processing mechanisms are complex adaptations, and there are strong theoretical reasons why the genetic basis of any complex adaptation needs to be universal. These arise from constraints on organismic design imposed by the exigencies of sexual recombination (Tooby & Cosmides, 1990b).

Third, genes and the environment jointly interact to produce our neural circuits, and these circuits process information—they are cognitive programs. But it is our cognitive programs that cause our behavior. Moreover, these programs generate behavior on the basis of *information* that they extract from the environment and from other parts of the body. If the informational input is changed, the behavior will often change. So when people with the same cognitive programs are exposed to different kinds of information, this will cause their cognitive programs to generate different representations about the world—different knowledge—and this will lead them to behave in different ways. For this reason, one expects to find very few *behaviors* that are universal across cultures, even though all people have basically the same cognitive programs.

To capture evolved functional organization, one needs a language that can describe what is invariant across individuals and generations. This process of description is key: choosing the wrong descriptive categories can make everything about an organism appear variable and transitory, and, therefore, immune to scientific explanation. By contrast, well-chosen categories can bring out the hidden organization that reappears from individual to individual, and that, consequently, allows psychological phenomena to be described both economically and precisely.

2. Evolutionary Biology and Cognitive Psychology

Theories about selection pressures operating in ancestral environments place important constraints on—and often define—what can count as an adaptive function. Indeed, many theories of adaptive function define what would count as adaptive *information processing*. Consider, for example, Hamilton's (1964) rule, which describes the selection pressures operating on mechanisms that generate behaviors that have a reproductive impact on an organism and its kin. The rule defines (in part) what counts as biologically successful outcomes in these kinds of situations. These outcomes often cannot be reached unless specific information is obtained and processed by the organism.

In the simplest case of two individuals, a mechanism that produces acts of assistance has an evolutionary advantage over alternative mechanisms, if it reliably causes Individual i to help Relative j whenever $C_i < r_{ij}B_j$. In this equation, $C_i = cost$ to i of rendering an act of assistance, measured in terms of foregone reproduction. B_j = benefit to j of receiving that act of assistance, measured in terms of enhanced reproduction, and r_{ij} = the probability that a randomly sampled gene will be present at the same locus in the relative due to joint inheritance from a common ancestor.

Other things being equal, the more closely psychological mechanisms reliably produce behavior that conforms to Hamilton's rule, the more strongly they will be selected for. Under many ecological conditions, this selection pressure defines an information-processing problem that organisms will be selected to evolve mechanisms to solve.

Using this description of an adaptive problem as a starting point, one can immediately begin to define the cognitive subtasks that would have to be addressed by any set of mechanisms capable of producing behavior that conforms to this rule. For example, what information-processing mechanisms evolved to reliably identify relatives? What criteria and procedures do they embody—for example, do these mechanisms define an individual as a sibling if that individual was nursed by the same female who nursed you? What kind of information is processed to estimate r_{ij}, the degree of relatedness? Under ancestral conditions, did siblings and cousins co-reside, such that one might expect the evolution of mechanisms that discriminate between the two? After all, $r_{i\,full\,sib} = 4r_{i\,first\,cousin}$. What kind of mechanisms would be capable of estimating the magnitudes of the consequences of specific actions for one's own and for others' reproduction? How are these various pieces of information combined to produce behavior that conforms to Hamilton's rule?

First, this example shows how knowledge drawn from evolutionary biology can be used to discover functional organization in our psychological architecture that was previously unknown.

Second, the example illustrates that one can easily use the definition of an adaptive problem to generate hypotheses about the design features of information-processing mechanisms, even when these mechanisms are designed to produce social behavior. It allows one to break the adaptive problem down into cognitive subtasks, such as kin recognition and cost–benefit estimation, in the same way that knowing that the adaptive function of the visual system is scene analysis allows one to identify subtasks such as depth perception and color constancy.

Third, the example shows how knowing the ancestral conditions under which a species evolved can suggest hypotheses about design features of the cognitive adaptations that solve the problem. For example, co-residence is a reliable cue of sibship in some species, but other cues would have to be picked up and processed in a species in which siblings and cousins co-reside.

Fourth, Hamilton's rule provides a standard of good design for this particular problem. Such standards are an essential tool for cognitive scientists, enabling the latter to identify whether a hypothesized mechanism is capable of solving the adaptive problem in question, and to decide whether that mechanism would do a better job under ancestral conditions than alternative designs. Thus, it is possible to apply the powerful methods of learnability analysis outside of psycholinguistics (i.e., to adaptive problems involving social behavior).

Fifth, this example illustrates how insights from evolutionary biology can bring functional organization into clear focus at the cognitive level, but not at the neurobiological level. Hamilton's rule immediately suggests hypotheses about the functional organization of mechanisms described in information-processing terms, but it tells one very little about the neurobiology that implements these mechanisms—it cannot be straightforwardly related to hypotheses about brain chemistry or neuroanatomy. Once one knows the properties of the cognitive mechanisms that solve this adaptive problem, however, it should be far easier to discover the structure of the neural mechanisms that implement them.

The intellectual payoff of coupling theories of adaptive function to the methods and descriptive language of cognitive science is potentially enormous. By homing in on the right categories—ultimately, adaptationist categories—an immensely intricate, functionally organized, species-typical architecture can appear.

The Design of Psychological Mechanisms.   The evolved mesh between the information-processing design of human psychological adaptations, their developmentally relevant environments, and the stably recurring structure of humans and their environments is pivotal to understanding how an evolutionary psychological approach to culture differs from traditional social science approaches. For traditional anthropologists, cultures vary from place to place, and there is nothing privileged about a conceptual framework that captures underlying patterns of cross-cultural uniformity, compared to the infinite class of perspectives by which human thought and behavior appear everywhere different (Geertz, 1973, 1983; see Brown, 1991, for a critique of this view). Nevertheless, from the "point of view" of natural selection, such uniformities are indeed privileged, and for a very simple reason. However variable cultures and habitats may have been during human evolution, selection would have sifted human social and cultural life (as well as everything else) for obvious or subtle statistical and structural regularities, building psychological adaptations that exploited some subset of these regularities to solve adaptive problems. (One of the problems that had to be solved using regularities was the problem of learning "culture" itself.)

Thus, Geertz's starting point—that humans have evolved to use culture—is obviously true. But the next step in his logic—that humans do not have general cultures, only particular ones, and so evolved to realize themselves only through cultural particularity—is the error of naive realism. No instance of anything is intrinsically (much less exclusively) either "general" or "particular"—these are simply different levels at which any system of categorization encounters the same world. Selection operated across ancestral hominid populations according to what were, in effect, systems of categorization—screening cross-cultural variability for any recurrent relationships that were relevant to the solution of adaptive problems.

Thus, the issue is this: During the Pleistocene, were there any statistical and structural uniformities to human life from culture to culture, and habitat to habitat, that could have been used by species-typical problem-solving machinery for the adaptive regulation of behavior and physiology? Anthropological orthodoxy to the contrary, human life is full of structure that recurs from culture to culture. (Or, if one prefers, there are innumerable frames of reference within which meaningful cross-cultural uniformities appear, and many of these statistical uniformities and structural regularities could potentially have been used to solve adaptive problems.) Exactly which regularities are, in fact, part of the developmentally relevant environment that is used by our universal architectures is a matter to be empirically determined on a mechanism-by-mechanism, case-by-case basis. Adults have children; humans have a species-typical body form; humans have characteristic emotions; humans move through a life history cued by observable body changes; humans come in two sexes; they eat food and are motivated to seek it when they lack it; humans are born and eventually die; they are related through sexual reproduction and through chains of descent; they turn their eyes toward objects and events that tend to be informative about adaptively consequential issues; they often compete, contend, or fight over limited social or subsistance resources; they express fear and avoidance of danger; they preferentially associate with mates, children, and other kin; they create and maintain enduring, mutually beneficial individual relationships with nonrelatives; they speak; they create and participate in coalitions; they desire, plan, deceive, love, gaze, envy, get ill, have sex, play, can be injured, are satiated; and so forth. Our immensely elaborate species-typical, physiological, and psychological architectures not only constitute regularities in themselves, but also impose within and across cultures all kinds of regularities on human life, as do the common features of the environments we inhabit (see Brown, 1991, for an important exploration of the kinds and significance of human universals).

Human developmental mechanisms have been born into one cultural environment or another hundreds of billions of times, so the only truly long-term, cumulatively directional effects of selection on human design would have been left by the statistical commonality that exists across cultures and habitats. Embedded in the programming structure of our minds are, in effect, a set of assumptions about the nature of the human world we will meet during our lives. So (speaking metaphorically), we arrive in the world expecting, Geertzian fashion, to meet some particular culture about whose specifically differentiated pecularities we can know nothing in advance. We also arrive expecting to meet, in one and the same embodiment, the general human culture as well—that is, recognizably human life manifesting a wide array of forms and relations common across cultures during our evolution (or at least some set out of the superset). Thus, human architectures are "pre-equipped" (i.e., they reliably develop) specialized mechanisms that "know" many things about humans, social relations, emotions and facial expressions, the meaning of situations to others, the underlying organization of contingent social actions (such as threats and exchanges), language, motivation, and so on.

Domain-Specific Psychology.   Evolutionary psychologists have argued that one can expect the evolved architecture of the mind to contain a number of computational mechanisms that are domain-specific and functionally specialized. This view of the mind is crucial to understanding how an evolutionary psychological approach to culture and the development of social institutions differs from other approaches.

Psychologists have long known that the human mind contains circuits that are specialized for different modes of perception, such as vision and hearing. But until recently, it was thought that perception and language were the only domains for which one would find cognitive processes that are specialized (e.g., Fodor, 1983). Other cognitive functions—learning, reasoning, decision making—were thought to be accomplished by circuits that are very general-purpose: jacks-of-all-trades, but masters of none. Prime candidates were "rational" algorithms: ones that implement formal methods for inductive and deductive reasoning, such as Bayes' rule or the propositional calculus. "General intelligence"—a hypothetical faculty composed of simple reasoning circuits that are few in number, content-independent, and general purpose—was thought to be the engine that generates solutions to reasoning problems. The flexibility of human reasoning—that is, our ability to solve many different kinds of reasoning problems—was thought to be evidence for the generality of the circuits that generate it.

An evolutionary perspective suggests otherwise (Tooby & Cosmides, 1992). Biological machines are calibrated to the environments in which they evolved, and they embody information about the stably recurring properties of these ancestral worlds. (For example, human color constancy mechanisms are calibrated to natural changes in terrestrial illumination; as a result, grass looks green at both high noon and sunset, even though the spectral properties of the light it reflects have changed dramatically.) Rational algorithms do not, because they are content-independent. Bayes' rule, for example, can be applied indiscriminately to medical diagnosis, card games, hunting success, or any other subject matter. It contains no domain-specific knowledge, so it cannot support inferences that would apply to mate choice, for example, but not to hunting.

Evolved problem-solvers, however, are equipped with crib sheets: They come to a problem already "knowing" a lot about it. For example, a newborn's brain has response systems that "expect" faces to be present in the environment: Babies less than 10 minutes old turn their eyes and head in response to facelike patterns, but not to scrambled versions of the same pattern with identical spatial frequencies (M. H. Johnson & Morton, 1991). Infants make strong ontological assumptions about how the world works and what kinds of things it contains, even at 2½ months (the point at which they can see well enough to be tested). They assume, for example, that it will contain rigid objects that are continuous in space and time, and they have preferred ways of parsing the world into separate objects (e.g., Baillargeon, 1986; Spelke, 1990). Ignoring shape, color, and texture, they treat any surface that is cohesive, bounded, and moves as a unit as a single object. When one solid object appears to pass through another, these infants are surprised. Yet a system with no privileged hypotheses—a truly "open-minded" system—would be undisturbed by such displays. In watching objects interact, babies less than a year old distinguish causal events from non causal ones that have similar spatio-temporal properties; they distinguish objects that move only when acted on from ones that are capable of self-generated motion (the inanimate–animate distinction); they assume that the self-propelled movement of animate objects is caused by invisible internal states—goals and intentions—whose presence must be inferred, because internal states cannot be seen (Baron-Cohen, 1995; Leslie, 1988, 1994). Toddlers have a well-developed "mind-reading" system that uses eye direction and movement to infer what other people want, know, and believe (Baron-Cohen, 1995). (When this system is impaired, as in autism, the child cannot infer what others believe.) When an adult utters a wordlike sound while pointing to a novel object, toddlers assume the word refers to the *whole* object, rather than one of its parts (Markman, 1989).

Without these privileged hypotheses—about faces, objects, physical causality, other minds, word meanings, and so on—a developing child could learn very little about his or her environment. For example, a child with autism who has a normal IQ and intact perceptual systems is, nevertheless, unable to make simple inferences about mental states. Children with Williams syndrome are profoundly retarded and have difficulty learning even simple spatial tasks, yet they are good at inferring other people's mental states. Some of their reasoning mechanisms are damaged, but their mind-reading system is intact.

Different problems require different crib sheets. For example, knowledge about intentions, beliefs, and desires, which allows one to infer the behavior of persons, is misleading if applied to inanimate objects. Two machines are better than one when the crib sheet that helps solve problems in one domain is misleading in another. This suggests that many evolved computational mechanisms will be domain-specific: They will be activated in some domains, but not others. Some of these will embody rational methods, but others will have special purpose inference procedures that respond not to logical form, but to content types—procedures that work well within the stable ecological structure of a particular domain, even though they might lead to false or contradictory inferences if they were activated outside of that domain.

The more crib sheets a system has, the more problems it can solve. A brain equipped with a multiplicity of specialized inference engines will be able to generate sophisticated behavior that is sensitively tuned to its environment. In this view, the flexibility and power often attributed to content-independent algorithms is illusory. All else equal, a content-rich system will be able to infer more than a content-poor one.

Machines limited to executing Bayes' rule, *modus ponens*, and other "rational" procedures derived from mathematics or logic are computationally weak compared with the system outlined earlier. The theories of rationality they embody are "environment-free"—they were designed to produce valid inferences in *all* domains. They can be applied to a wide variety of domains, however, only because they lack any information that would be helpful in one domain, but not in another. Having no crib sheets, there is little they can deduce about a domain; having no privileged hypotheses, there is little they can induce before their operation is hijacked by combinatorial explosion. The difference between domain-specific and domain-independent methods is akin to the difference between experts and novices: Experts can solve problems faster and more efficiently than novices because they already know a lot about the problem domain.

At the turn of the century, W. James (1890) argued that human behavior is more flexibly intelligent than that of other animals because we have *more* "instincts" than they do not fewer. But precisely because these instincts work so well—because they process information so effortlessly and automatically—we tend to be blind to their existence. His view, which was ignored for much of the 20th century, is being vindicated today. There is now evidence for the existence of circuits that are specialized for reasoning about objects, physical causality, number, the biological world, the beliefs and motivations of other individuals, and social interactions (for a review, see Hirschfeld & S. Gelman, 1994). The learning mechanisms that govern the acquisition of language are different from those that govern the acquisition of food aversions, and both of these are different from the learning mechanisms that govern the acquisition of snake phobias (Garcia, 1990; Pinker, 1994; Cook, Hodes, & Lang, 1986).

"Instincts" are often thought of as the polar opposite of "reasoning" and "learning." Nonhuman animals are widely believed to act through "instinct," whereas humans "gave up instincts" to become "the rational animal." But these reasoning circuits and learning circuits have the following five properties: (a) they are complexly structured for solving a specific type of adaptive problem, (b) they reliably develop in all normal human beings, (c) they develop without any conscious effort and in the absence of any formal instruction, (d) they are applied without any conscious awareness of their underlying logic, and (e) they are distinct from more general abilities to process information or behave intelligently. In other words, they have all the hallmarks of what one usually thinks of as an "instinct" (Pinker, 1994). In fact, one can think of these specialized computational systems as *reasoning instincts* and *learning instincts*. They make certain kinds of inferences as easy, effortless, and "natural" to us as humans as spinning a web is to a spider or dead-reckoning is to a desert ant.

This suggests that human reasoning is flexible and effective because it is generated by a large collection of separate devices, each specialized to solve a different type of problem. On this view, the circuits that govern human reasoning and learning can solve such a wide variety of problems for the same reason a Swiss Army knife can: Instead of a "single blade" turned equally to all tasks, the human mind contains a wide variety of specialized tools (e.g., Pinker, 1994; Sherry & Schacter, 1987; Tooby & Cosmides, 1992).

Some of the most important adaptive problems our hunter–gatherer ancestors had to solve involved navigating the social world, and some of the best work in evolutionary biology is devoted to analyzing constraints on the evolution of mechanisms that solve these problems. Many of the adaptive problems posed by hunter–gatherer social life are characterized by strict evolvability constraints, which could only be satisfied by cognitive programs that are specialized for reasoning about the social world (Tooby & Cosmides, 1992). Such analyses suggest that our evolved mental architecture should contain a large and intricate "faculty" of social cognition. A small, but growing community of cognitive scientists have been investigating this faculty (e.g., Baron-Cohen, 1995; Cosmides & Tooby, 1992, 1994; Fiske, 1991; Jackendoff, 1992; Leslie, 1988, 1994). Their research suggests that the evolved architecture of the human mind contains a number of social inference modules—computational mechanisms that are specialized for reasoning about different aspects of the social world. These include a "theory of mind" mechanism (Baron-Cohen, 1995; Leslie, 1987), an eye-direction detector (Baron-Cohen & Cross, 1992; Baron-Cohen, 1994), social contract algorithms (Cosmides, 1989; Cosmides & Tooby, 1987, 1992); mechanisms for interpreting threats (Tooby & Cosmides, 1989b), mechanisms governing mate choice (Symons, 1979; D. M. Buss, 1994), sexual jealousy (M. Wilson & Daly, 1992), parenting (Fernald, 1992; Mann, 1992), and a wide variety of other social domains (for a partial review, see Barkow, Cosmides, & Tooby, 1992).

Many social domains are associated with "hot cognition": emotional reactions. Ever since Darwin (1871, 1872), emotions have been seen as the product of the evolutionary process and usually, although not always, as functional adaptations (e.g., see Arnold, 1960, 1968; Chance, 1980; Daly, M. Wilson, & Weghorst, 1982; Eibl-Eibesfeldt, 1975; Ekman, 1982; Fridja, 1986; Hamburg, 1968; Izard, 1977; Otte, 1974; Plutchik, 1984; N. Thornhill, 1996; N. Thornhill & R. Thornhill, 1987; Tomkins, 1962, 1963; Tooby & Cosmides, 1990a). Functional or not, emotions collectively provide a dense and pervasive network of domain-specific phenomena that has consistently resisted assimilation to any traditional psychological or anthropological theory. Early examples, from the heyday of learning theory, include the Harlows' (1959) demonstration that an infant's love for its mother is not a conditioned response to food rewards, and Garcia and Koelling's (1966) work showing that equipotential models of classical conditioning could not explain the acquisition of food aversions, with their attendant feelings of disgust (Garcia, 1990). The behaviorist hope that motivated behavior could be explained by a short list of drives, rewards, or reinforcers has not panned out.

In contrast to their reputation as crude and indiscriminate responses, on closer scrutiny, each emotion appears to be an intricately structured, information-sensitive regulatory adaptation. In fact, emotions appear to be designed to solve a certain category of regulatory problems that inevitably emerge in a mind full of disparate, functionally specialized mechanisms: the problem of coordinating the menagerie of mechanisms with each other and with the situation they are facing (Tooby, 1985; Tooby & Cosmides, 1990a).

Daly and M. Wilson (1988), for example, have been exploring the evolved complexity and functional subtlety of human motivational systems, especially those that regulate parental care, spousal relations, sexual jealousy, sexual proprietariness, and risk taking (see also Daly, M. Wilson, & Weghorst, 1982; M. Wilson & Daly, 1992). By using behavioral phenomena such as violence and homicide as dependent measures, they have been able to investigate how the operation of these systems is affected by factors such as gender, age, kinship, reproductive value, number of children, and other situational variables (see also Mann, 1992). Similarly, in the areas of human mate choice and sexuality, research has shown that the construct of a "sex drive" is completely inadequate for coping with the structured richness of the situational factors processed by the sexual psychologies of men and women across cultures (e.g., D. M. Buss, 1993; Sadalla, Kenrick, & Vershure, 1987; Symons, 1979; Townsend, 1987). These studies indicate that prior theories of motivation are too simple to account for the phenomena they seek to explain. They will have to be replaced with theories positing a far more elaborate motivational architecture, equipped with an extensive set of evolved information-processing algorithms. These will be sensitive to a long list of cues and dimensions—ones that were reliably correlated with evolutionarily-recurrent situations that had large fitness consequences in ancestral environments.

Research generated by a theory positing a more elaborate motivational architecture indicates that the human mind contains evolved emotional and motivational mechanisms that are specifically targeted to address adaptive problems involved in parenting, emotional communication with infants and adults, kinship, mate choice, sexual attraction, aggression, avoidance of danger, mate guarding, effort allocation in child care, and so on. It means that humans are endowed with psychological adaptations that contain contentful structures that are are "about" their mothers, "about" their children, "about" the sexual behavior of their mates, "about" those identified by cues as kin, "about" how much to care for a sick child, and so on. The richness of their structure is underdetermined by the environment; they are not derived exclusively from either a short list of drives or from social values that vary from culture to culture in a highly contingent way.

When one's research focus is widened beyond arbitrary laboratory tasks, to include the complex performances on real-world tasks that are orchestrated by natural competences, behaviors and knowledge structures appear that are too richly patterned to have been generated by the operation of content-independent mechanisms alone (Tooby & Cosmides, 1992). Studies of this kind withstand cross-cultural scrutiny, and indicate that a great deal of the substance of social life attributed to "culture" around the world is, in fact, caused by the operation of contingently responsive domain-specific mechanisms, which infuse distinctively human patterns into the life of every culture.

Psychological Adaptations and the Generation of Culture. What does the rise of domain-specific psychology mean for theories of culture? By themselves, psychological theories do not and cannot constitute theories of culture. They only provide the foundations for theories of culture. Humans live and evolve in interacting networks that exhibit complex population-level dynamics, and so theories and analyses of population-level processes are necessary components for any full understanding of human phenomena. Nevertheless, increasing knowledge of our evolved psychological architecture places increasing constraints on admissible theories of culture. Most fundamentally, if each human embodies an evolved psychological architecture that comes richly equipped with content-imparting mechanisms, then the traditional concept of culture must be completely rethought.

Culture has been the central concept of the traditional social science models. The traditional view contends that culture is: (a) contingently variable information that is socially learned, (b) what is contentful and organized in human mental life and behavior, and (c) the sets of similarities in thought and behavior, and intergroup or cross-location differences called cultural differences. In particular, as described in the first section of this chapter, social scientists have generally assumed that what they call *social institutions* are a superorganic cultural stratum that largely controls human behavior, with evolved mechanisms playing a distinctly subordinate supporting role.

On this traditional view, evolved mechanisms are considered relatively unimportant because they are assumed to be content-free. If instead the human mind is permeated with content-rich organization that does not originate in the social world, then it can be expected to shape social interactions and the dynamics of cultural transmission in profound ways (for discussion, see Tooby & Cosmides, 1989a, 1992). To borrow an example from Sperber (1985), it is easy for us to remember the gist of the story of Little Red Riding Hood, but difficult to remember a 20-digit number; the reverse is true of a digital computer. What is attended to, what is remembered, what one will be impelled to communicate to others—these cannot help but be affected by the nature of the mind that is doing the attending, remembering, and communicating.

Nevertheless, even for those who admit that the mind has some content to impart that is not socially supplied, the distribution of within-group similarities and between-group differences remain a striking phenomenon to be explained. Such patterns were taken by many to confirm that most of the rich substance of human life was supplied by patterns of "information" derived from the external environment. (N.B. It is not clear what it means to say that "information" exists apart from an interpretive mechanism that can "read" it—i.e., apart from the structure of a mind. A CD does not contain music except insofar as there are CD players that can read it, i.e., translate its structure into sound.)

Although this conclusion may seem compelling, a thought experiment can illustrate why it is unfounded. Imagine that extraterrestrials replaced each human being on earth with a state-of-the-art CD jukebox that has thousands of songs in its repertoire. Each jukebox would be identical. Moreover, each would be equipped with a clock, an automated navigational device that measures its latitude and longitude, and a circuit that selects what song it will play on the basis of its location, the time, and the date. What the extraterrestrials would observe would be the same kind of pattern of within-group similarities and between-group differences observable among humans: In Rio, every jukebox would be playing the same song, which would be different from the song played by every jukebox in Bejing, and so on, around the world. Each jukebox's "behavior" would be clearly and complexly patterned because each would have been equipped with the same large repertoire of songs. Moreover, each jukebox's behavior would change over time because the song it would play would be a function of the date and time, as well as its location. Jukeboxes that were moved from location to location would appear to adopt the local songs, sequences, and "fashions." Yet the generation of this distinctive, culture-like pattern would involve no social learning or transmission whatsoever.

This pattern would be brought about because, like humans, the jukeboxes would share a universal, highly organized architecture that is designed to respond to inputs from the local situation (e.g., date, time, and location). Analogously, humans in groups can be expected to express, in response to local conditions, a variety of organized within-group similarities that are not caused by social learning or transmission. Of course, these generated within-group similarities will simultaneously lead to systematic differences between groups facing different conditions.

Thus, complex shared patterns that differ from group to group may be evoked by circumstances or produced by differential transmission. For this reason, the general concept of "culture" in the standard model's sense is a conflation of *evoked culture* and *transmitted culture*. Given that the mind contains many mechanisms, we expect that both transmitted and evoked factors will play complementary roles in the generation of differentiated local cultures. The operation of a richly responsive psychology, plus the ability to socially "learn," can jointly explain far more about "culture" and cultural change than either can alone.

For example, when conditions change (e.g., when a previously abundant resource becomes difficult to obtain, such that luck plays a larger role in its acquisition than skill and effort) a different set of domain-specific mechanisms may be activated, evoking a different set of attitudes and goals. These mechanisms may make certain ideas (e.g., that resources obtained by luck should be shared widely and generously) more appealing, causing them to spread quickly by transmission, and certain other ideas (e.g., that individuals should share resources just within the nuclear family) unappealing, causing them to disappear just as quickly (e.g., Kaplan & K. Hill, 1985). In contrast, the "do what your parents did" concept of culture is not a principle that can easily explain why cultural elements change, where new ones come from, why they spread, or why certain complex patterns (e.g., pastoralist commonalities) recur in widely separated cultures. Darwinian students of cultural evolution (see chap. 9) recognize this need for an evolved, culture-evoking psychology by entering psychological terms into their models in the form of "decision-making forces." Unfortunately, because of the neglect of the problem by most social scientists interested in culture, the empirical side of the story is in quite poor shape, depite the enormous mass of data collected by anthropologists and sociologists. With the exception of linguistics, investigations of cultural transmission that are based on empirical studies of the content-imparting properties of cognitive mechanisms have only recently begun (e.g., Boyer, 1994).

It is especially important to recognize that the environmental factors that cause contentful mental and behavioral organization to be expressed do not necessarily constitute the processes that constructed that organization. In the case of the jukebox, it would be a mistake to attribute the organized content manifested by the music to the environmental stimuli (i.e., the location, date, and time) that caused one song to be played rather than another. The stimuli did not compose the music; they merely caused it to be expressed. Similarly, our psychological architectures come equipped with evolved contentful organization, which can remain latent or vary in its expression according to procedures embodying any degree of complexity. Because our psychological architecture is complexly responsive, the practice of equating the variable with the learned is a simple nonsequitur. The claim that some phenomena are "socially constructed" merely means that the social environment provided some of the inputs used by the psychological mechanisms of the individuals involved.

In short, observations of patterns of similarities and differences do not establish that the substance of human life was generated by content-independent learning mechanisms. In any specific case, we need to map our evolved psychological architecture to know which elements (if any) are provided by transmission, which by the rest of the environment, which by the architecture, and how all these elements causally interact to produce the phenomenon in question. Admittedly, the jukebox thought experiment is an unrealistically extreme case in which a complex, functionally organized, content-sensitive architecture internalizes no transmitted informational input other than an environmental trigger. But this case is simply the mirror image of the extreme view of the human mind as a content-free architecture where everything is provided by the internalization of transmitted input.

Our central point is that, in any particular domain of human activity, the programming that gives our architecture its ability to contingently respond to the environment may or may not be designed to accept transmitted representations as input. If it does, it may mix in content derived from its own structure and process the resulting representations in complex and transformative ways. Our complex, content-specific, psychological architecture participates in the often distinct processes of generating (a) mental content, (b) local similarities and between-group differences, and (c) what is "transmitted." Indeed, it also participates in the complex process of internalizing what others are "transmitting." Of course, it is also true that environmental inputs transmitted and internalized early in development may become part of the architecture as far as subsequent behavior is concerned, as the adult phenotype "boots up." It has become a truism to say that genes do not cause development in isolation from environmental inputs. We simply insist that the mirror image is true as well. No matter how complex the information present in a culture may be, it is a functionless abstraction unless there exists a sophisticated mechanism that can interpret it.

Incest Avoidance.   Incest rules and behavior have long been among the favorite topics of the social sciences. Given the near universality of incest "taboos" across human societies, the study of incest is considered to be at the very heart of anthropological theory (Boehm, 1989; Fox, 1976, 1980; Lévi-Strauss, 1969; D. M. Schneider, 1956; L. A. White, 1948), yet little understanding of the subject has been achieved. Many of the traditional social scientific hypotheses (reviewed in Ember, 1975; Shepher, 1983) that still find favor among incest researchers (see Spain, 1987 and several commentaries therein, 1988) lead to this biologically anomalous conclusion: No matter how devastating incest may be (in terms of offspring viability and fecundity), it is the favored form of mating because of incestuous desires that originated with our remote ancestors, and that have beem maintained throughout human evolutionary history (see N. Thornhill, 1990a, for a review). This idea stems directly from theories advanced by Freud in the early part of this century. Freud's influence on the social sciences, in particular with regard to incest research, has been enormous (Boehm, 1989; Daly & M. Wilson, 1988).

Many social scientists begin their investigations of human inbreeding with the following two Freudian assumptions: First, close kin are desired as mating partners by most humans (see N. Thornhill, 1990b, for a review). "Psychoanalytic investigations have shown beyond the possibility of doubt that an *incestuous love choice* is in fact the first and regular one, and it is only later that any opposition is manifested toward it, the causes of which are not to be found in the psychology of the individual" (Freud, 1953, pp. 220f). Freud's description of the mental mechanisms underlying the avoidance of incest rests uneasily in the minds of evolutionary psychologists. The reason is that incest is a behavior that, if engaged in, seriously detracts from the reproductive potential of individuals.

Mating with close kin can have serious negative effects on fitness (see N. Thornhill, 1990b, for a review). The theory of evolution by selection suggests that individuals will not exhibit systematic inclinations to behave in ways contrary to their own reproductive advantages (e.g., by preferentially engaging in sexual liaisons with close relatives that would end in the production of defective offspring). Selection for close-kin mating avoidance seems to have produced the psychological mechanism that promotes voluntary incest avoidance in humans—the Westermarck effect (Shepher, 1971, 1983; Westermarck, 1891; Wolf & Huang, 1980). The Westermarck effect is a mechanism promoting sexual aversion toward kin; it is triggered by close, physical association between co-socialized individuals during a sensitive stage of development (N. Thornhill, 1990b).

The Westermarck effect arises from a psychological adaptation that promotes incest avoidance under appropriate circumstances. Although vague on the details, Westermarck's hypothesis for incest avoidance can be interpreted as follows: The psychological mechanism responds to specific cues in the environment (i.e., the presence of individuals who are raised together in intimate social contact) and triggers sexual repugnance and incest avoidance. This does not seem to describe the same sort of ontogeny of incest avoidance that Freud had in mind. Freud's position on incest was that it inolves intense erotic *attraction*. If so, this would mean that the mind contains mechanisms designed to *decrease* their rate of reproduction. Perhaps the environmental cues are the same as those identified for the Westermarck effect, but the psychological response is the opposite: intense sexual attraction rather than sexual repugnance. Rather than making the two theories complementary, as some have argued they are, this clearly separates Freudian and Westermarckian theories. Freud considered his theory an evolutionary one. If it is proposed as an evolutionary alternative, it must make predictions that are different from those made by other evolutionary hypotheses.

The Westermarck effect is best conceived of as a specialized mental mechanism that allows close kin to be perceived as inappropriate mating partners through the psychological affect of sexual disinterest, even repugnance. Evidence supporting the Westermarck effect was indirectly obtained through "natural experiments" in which nonrelated opposite-sex individuals were raised together in social situations mimicking sibships. One of these occurred in Israeli kibbutzim (Shepher, 1971). In this social situation, children were raised in cohorts of their age-mates. These children were not siblings, but were raised as such by women in the kibbutz who were assigned to be their nannies. Despite a strong ideology within the kibbutz to marry within one's age cohort, there were no marriages between cohort members in any age group from 1920 to 1960 (Shepher, 1983).

The second, frequently cited "natural experiment" supporting the Westermarck effect is the Taiwanese practice of *sim-pua* marriage. This is a marriage system in which a family adopts a daughter as an infant and raises her to adulthood to become the wife for their son (with whom she has been raised). The marriages are characterized by low fertility, high rates of divorce and high rates of extramarital sexual liaisons, compared with other, more conventional kinds of marriage in Taiwan (Wolf & Huang, 1980). Although *sim-pua* marriages are usually engaged in by families of lower socioeconomic status (SES), this effect holds even when one controls for SES.

The two prior studies address nonrelatives who are raised in conditions mimicking the nuclear family. Typically, over evolutionary time, individuals who were raised in close proximity were also close relatives. There are other studies that have addressed the Westermarck effect with respect to genetic and step-kin (brothers and sisters and fathers and daughters); (Lebanon: J. McCabe, 1983; Middle Eastern village: Pastner, 1986; United States: H. Parker & S. Parker, 1986), all of which support it as a mechanism promoting incest avoidance.

Incest seems to be avoided by people, even in the absence of rules regulating it. Thornhill's studies (N. Thornhill, 1987, 1990a, 1990b, 1991; N. Thornhill & R. Thornhill, 1987) have investigated many aspects of this phenomenon. For example, in a survey of 186 of the world's societies (the Standard Cross Cultural Sample—SCCS), only 44.7% were found to have rules against sexual behavior within the nuclear family. In many societies, the idea of sexual contacts occurring between fathers and daughters or brothers and sisters is considered "laughable" or "foolish," and is viewed with disbelief.

In modern, industrial societies, the majority of behaviors labeled *incest* involve steprelatives, and are likely only when the Westermarck effect is not activated. Ultimately, incest is probably avoided because of its reproductive costs, allowing selection to produce a human mind that learns voluntary incest avoidance through a mental adaptation that processes incest-specific environmental information.

What, then, are the rules supposedly aimed at regulating incest about? There is another category of behavior that is often called *incestuous*, especially by ethnographers, but also commonly in Western industrialized nations (i.e., the marriage between cousins). This kind of inbreeding is better referred to as "nonincestuous" because costs associated with it, although real, are less devastating than those associated with incest. Furthermore, these costs have not resulted in selection similar to that designing the Westermarck effect, and nonincestuous inbreeding avoidance is not a prevalent feature of human societies. On the contrary, even in the face of real (perhaps substantial) genetic costs, people nonincestously inbreed. This suggests that there may be an advantage to this behavior large enough to outweigh these costs. N. Thornhill (1990a, 1991) hypothesized that nonincestous inbreeding is engaged in by families to facilitate concentration of wealth and power within them.

This hypothesis allows many predictions about societal rules regulating the extent of nonincestuous inbreeding. It implies that rules regulating nonincestuous inbreeding should be made in response to: (a) the likelihood that wealth and power can be concentrated within lineages by inbreeding, and (b) the threat this event poses to rule makers.

One prediction is that, in highly stratified societies, the rules regulating nonincestuous inbreeding should be more extensive (i.e., number of included relatives) than in societies with little stratification. This prediction stems from the disparity in wealth and status in such societies. Under highly stratified systems (indeed, under any system of stratification), it is often in the ruler's best interest to inhibit any form of family or lineage endogamy because of the potential of a moderately wealthy family to increase wealth and power by preferential marriage of kin, thus threatening the ruler's position in society. This prediction was supported:

There is a significant positive correlation between stratification and the extension of rules regulating nonincestuous inbreeding.

A second prediction is that highly stratified societies should impose harsher punishment for infraction of nonincestuous inbreeding rules than societies with little stratification. Because rule makers in highly stratified societies are men with great power, they have increased ability to enforce rules as a result of greater control over necessary and desirable resources. Given the predictable concern for limiting family endogamy, it would be surprising if this concern were not reflected by a predictable variation in the severity of punishment. Consequences associated with rule breaking should bear a direct relation to the desire of the rule maker to control any particular behavior. Given that family endogamy can threaten the position of leaders in a society, not only should elaboration of inbreeding rules correlate positively with stratification, so should severity of punishment.

This prediction was supported: The correlation between harshness of punishment and degree of social stratification is significantly positive. Punishment for infraction of inbreeding rules ranges from none in nonstratified societies to extremely harsh in highly stratified, despotic societies.

Third, nonincestuous inbreeding rules should not apply to the rule makers in a society. More explicitly, as stratification increases, inbreeding rules should be less equitably applied. The prediction was met: In stratified societies, rulers are rarely expected to observe the marriage rules, and frequently marry their own relatives.

In summary, a central, although not exclusive, feature of any evolutionary psychological explanation for a social institution, such as incest avoidance in kinship, would be the specification of the psychological mechanisms that generate individual behavior. Many of these mechanisms are domain-specific, having evolved as adaptations to environmental challenges in our evolutionary past, such as the costs of inbreeding.

EVOLUTIONARY SOCIOLOGY

Alexandra M. Maryanski

The biology of humans potentially influences institutional structures and systems of symbols via phylogenetic history, as well as current or past adaptation. Phylogenetic constraints are certainly important on a relatively short time scale. As discussed in the previous section, adaptation is always to past environments, generating lags between adaptation and current environments. But such constraints also operate on a much longer time scale because the basic anatomy of an organism is hard to modify. Vertebrate body plans have a series of limitations and opportunities, and some structures, like the eye, are rather similar across the whole order. The constraint of having the nerves and blood vessels of the vertebrate eye maladaptively in front of, rather than behind, the light-sensing retina is an ancient constraint. Adaptation and phylogeny sometimes offer variant hypotheses, as when a phylogenetic constraint limits the quality of an adaptation. Humans can swim, but are ill adapted to it compared with a seal. However, in most cases, phylogenetic history only imposes limits on the range of adaptations "explored" by an evolving lineage. Occasionally, a constraint becomes an opportunity, and rather novel new adaptations arise in "preadapted" lineages. Humans were able to explore a cultural niche, presumably because selection had already favored in the primate a greater neurological flexibility than in other mammalian orders. What concatenation of phylogenetic constraints/opportunities gave rise to the particular derived features of social life that occur in our species?

This section offers a phylogenetic hypothesis for the evolution of social and organizational propensities in *Homo sapiens* that were inherited from hominoid ancestors. Essentially, what is postulated are some of the selection forces that modified and adjusted these propensities to the open range of the African savanna and, in turn, to a hunting and gathering subsistence mode in relatively small bands composed of nuclear family units. In performing this kind of exercise, it is possible to examine in a new light the biological basis of the first institutions—economy, kinship, and religion—and the selection pressures on subsequent institution-building as hominid social organization grew ever more complex.

This approach does not necessarily contradict the thrust of evolutionary biology, human sociobiology, or evolutionary psychology. Instead, it argues that a phylogenetic alternative that does not challenge macrolevel explanations is a more viable strategy than one involving microreductionism. The approach outlined here and expanded on elsewhere (Maryanski & J. H. Turner, 1992) supplements standard social science, macrolevel functionalism by indicating the biologically based constraints that the primate legacy has constantly placed on the development of human institutions as sociologists and anthropologists generally understand them (see the prior section on the sociological view of institutions).

1. The Primate Legacy

On the basis of earlier analyses of social relations among humans' closest relatives, the apes, a cladistic/network analysis of the organizational tendencies of the Last Common Ancestor (LCA) to humans and present-day apes can be constructed (see Maryanski, 1992; Maryanski & J. H. Turner, 1992). The technique is to (a) consider the social network patterns of the four extant apes and a sample of old world monkeys, (b) outline the regularities in social relations as a function of position on the phylogenetic tree, and, in the light of the "regularity" and "relatedness" hypotheses, (c) formulate inferences about the networks of the LCA of apes and humans (see Jeffers & Lehiste, 1979; Platnick & Cameron, 1977). The analysis leads to a striking conclusion. Like the contemporary apes phyletically closest to humans, the (LCA) evidenced a fluid organizational structure, consisting of a low level of sociality and a lack of intergenerational group continuity over time. The proximal reasons for this structure are a combination of several forces: (a) female (and also male) transfer from the natal unit at puberty, which is the opposite trend from monkeys where male transfer alone leaves females to form intergenerational matrilines; (b) shifting mating patterns that make it impossible to know paternity (with the gibbon being an exception); and (c) relatively low social bonding among most adults. These features are then associated with the dramatic decline of ape species during the Miocene, when species of monkeys suddenly proliferated and, according to the fossil record, moved into the former ape niches, perhaps because Cercopithecoid monkeys developed a competitive, dietary edge over the hominoids. Whatever the explanation, the fossil record confirms that, during the Miocene, ape niches were usurped by monkeys and that, during this replacement phase, apes were undergoing anatomical modifications for forelimb dominant locomotion and other novel skeletal features that characterize both apes and humans today (Andrews, 1981).

The compulsory movement of all remaining hominoids into a new niche must have also entailed corrective organizational changes to facilitate survival and reproductive success, which, given the anatomical changes, would point to "terminal branch feeding"—a marginal habitat with thinly distributed resources. Given the ecological marginality of this habitat, selection pressures would surely have worked against large, intergenerational groupings or stable cliques through time. Instead, if the network reconstruction of the LCA population is correct (Maryanski,

1992; Maryanski & J. H. Turner, 1992), pressures in the new adaptive zone selected for (a) a dispersal of females from mother at puberty (a rare phenomenon among primates [and mammals] in general), thereby preventing the continuance of the mother–daughter relationship known to be the core building block for monkey (and prosimian) kinship networks and for group continuity over time; and (b) behavioral tendencies toward relatively low sociality, high individualism, and autonomy, which created, at the organization level, loose and fluid social structures, compared with the monkey case.

At a point in time, however, descendent ape populations branched off from the LCA population and moved into forest zones, where selection seemingly favored the building of a few social network ties—a trend evidenced by the novel organizational structures of each contemporary ape species (see Maryanski & J. H. Turner, 1992). Still later in time, and as a consequence of drier climatic conditions, some monkeys and apes left the shrinking forests and moved to a more open, adaptive zone, where, in the face of heavy predation, selection favored a more tight-knit social structure (Maglio & Cooke, 1978; Malone, 1987). For savanna-living monkeys, structured organizational patterns could be easily achieved by building on existing tendencies to construct matrilines and hierarchies of dominance, whereas descendant apes of the LCA legacy had to surmount a biological legacy of few strong adult ties, a lack of kinship cliques that provided group continuity over time, or stable hierarchies on which to develop tighter patterns of social organization in the light of the obvious selection pressures for doing so.

If we use humans' closest relative, the chimpanzee (*Pan troglodytes*), as a feasible model of the type of hominoid on which selection for more structure was working, institutions in the hominid line would have to accommodate the phylogenetic inertia of low sociality, high individualism, female transfer from the natal unit at puberty, few strong ties between adults (save for mother–son and male sibling relationships), little stable pair-bonding between adult males and females, and father-absent child-drearing. How, then, could institutional structures be created from this fluid network base under intense selection pressures for more social structure?

2. The First Institutions: Kinship and Economy

Kinship. In the social structure of a chimplike protohominid, the social ties in place consisted of (a) strong ties between mother and young, but with female transfer away from the natal group at puberty; (b) more enduring ties between mother and son (because males remain in their natal unit); (c) enduring ties between brothers; and (d) selected "friendship" ties between male dyads (see Maryanski, 1993, for a detailed discussion). This structure poses the problem of how to build a kinship system revealing intergenerational continuity in the light of the fact that mother and son do not mate with each other, the father role does not exist, and daughters (in every extant ape species) normally leave their natal unit after puberty, which circumvents the creation of stable matrilines.

There was only one viable path in which to build stable intergenerational ties in such a social system, especially because there is already a biologically guided avoidance of mother–son "incest" and, to a lesser extent, of brother–sister "incest," and this path is to create a stable male–female relationship (Maryanski, 1993). Thus, contrary to most arguments, the "incest taboo" has deep roots in our primate heritage because mother–son sexual avoidance is evidenced among Old World higher primates in general (Pusey & Packer, 1987), although it was to be considerably elaborated on culturally, especially when lineages and clans were created in horticultural societies. However, the crucial evolutionary step was not an incest rule, but some form of "marriage rule" that bound males and females together over time, and hence established father–offspring ties that made patrilocal residence a reality. The creation of this relationship between males and females would have to overcome the genetic propensity for weak male–female ties, as well as reduce, to some extent, the promiscuity of males and females. For this to have occurred, evolutionary pressures must have been intense. Yet only in this way could stable relations between males and females, as well as birth-parents and offspring, develop. In a situation where phyletic propensities lead females to disperse at puberty, and mother–son and brother–sister to avoid each other sexually, a monkey-style matrilineal route to intergenerational kinship formation was closed off. Such a kinship institution (i.e., nuclear family units without unilinear descent) is what typifies bands of hunter–gatherers, and so stabilization of male–female mating, and not the incest taboo, was the cornerstone of the first kinship systems among hominids.

Economy. Evolving along with kinship or the system of reproduction was an institution for economic production. This system again transforms male–female behavioral and organizational patterns. As selection worked to stabilize male–female–offspring ties, it also operated to create a productive or economic division of labor between the sexes: males hunt, females gather. Correspondingly, there are divisions between the sexes in all known societies with respect to these and related household chores (Murdock, 1949). This adaptation is highly unusual. Even in bird, where male parental care is common, economic specialization of the sexes is usually modest.

Thus, the economy as an institution was first based on an economic division of labor between the sexes. This division accommodated primate-based female bonds to offspring by keeping mother close to her offspring, while enabling males (who, among most primates, are not bonded to offspring) to leave the kinship unit for a time. Only a strong marriage rule could keep this system from reverting back to the typical loose and fluid hominoid organization.

The important social innovation in the division of labor is that patterns of exchange reciprocity were created: Males exchanged their food for that gathered by females, although it would be females mostly giving males their production, because early hominid males were probably scavengers rather than hunters (Fleagle, 1988). But whatever its asymmetry, the "principle of reciprocity" found among all known hunting and gathering peoples was institutionalized out of the economic division of labor between the sexes in productive activity. It would work to reinforce bonds between males and females, who, as evolved apes, would be disposed to go their separate ways and to be only weakly connected. Thus, the principle of reciprocity was one key mechanism for overcoming the hominid predisposition toward individualism and low sociality. This principle was later to be elaborated to create more complex social institutions.

3. Institutional Elaboration and Differentiation

In contrast to applications of evolutionary reasoning, such as that developed in the previous section hypothesizing that biological factors "evoke" sociocultural phenomena, there is no assertion here that the subsequent development of human social institutions has been "guided" or "directed" by humans' primate legacy. Indeed, just the opposite has occurred: Hominid propensities for autonomy, low sociality, weak social ties, loose and low-density networks, and individualism have, if anything, been violated by the construction of "cages"—first, systems of unilineal descent with the advent of horticulture, and, later, state power and rigid stratification.

Clearly, intense evolutionary pressures—Darwinian, Spencerian, and other—from population growth and integrative problems associated with structural differentiation have driven institutional elaboration and development more than human biology. Human biology has been involved in two senses: (a) maintenance and reproduction of the species have certainly represented a constant selection pressure on institutional development, as all functionalist theories emphasize; and (b) preferences of humans for autonomy, weak ties, solidarity at only the community level (as opposed to the tight-knit group level), mobility, and individualism have perhaps exerted pressures for change in rigid, cagelike social constructions. Or, at the very least, these hominid preferences carried from the LCA have made humans highly receptive to more fluid social constructions and patterns of organization that come with high degrees of institutional differentiation, market mechanisms for distributing resources, and democratic political institutions legitimated by ideologies stressing freedom and individual rights. However, being receptive to such arrangements is a far cry from dictating these arrangements. Biological approaches that make the latter assertion are simply ignoring the powerful, emergent properties of institutional structures, whose elaboration and development are guided more by Spencerian selection than Darwinian selection because the latter created "human nature."

Evolutionary sociology emphasizes that biological models, as they are applied to the analysis of institutions and other sociocultural constructions, are analogies of processes across realms of the organic and superorganic universe for heuristic purposes. Moreover, much institutional development is driven by Spencerian selection for new structures and symbols (by agents who can think, build, adopt, copy, and instruct), rather than Darwinian selection among existing variations. Most significant, to the degree that Darwinian selection in the distant past has created organisms with biologically based behavioral propensities that circumscribe institutional development, these propensities are not domain-specific or highly restrictive in any sense of "programming" institutional elaboration. Rather, they are simply the preference of an evolved ape for relatively loose, fluid, and weak social ties as well as autonomy and freedom. The vast diversity of human social institutions and their rapid evo-

lution signal how weak the influence of the purely biological on the sociocultural must be.

ON THE ORIGINS OF HUMAN SOCIAL INSTITUTIONS:
A THREE-LEVEL MODEL

Peter Meyer

The biosociological model proposed next suggests integrating the biological and the social level via the notion of human affectivity, which, at an
epigenetic level, assumes a mediating role between the evolutionary and
cultural forces. The human emotional system is open both to inputs from
biologically mediated drives and those generated by sociocultural institutions. For example, fear of death on the battlefield regularly induces the
most dramatic examples of panic and terror, such as involuntary defeca-
tion and urination. In addition, the sight of gory death invokes intense
feelings of revulsion. Yet quite abstract motives of loyalty to a social
group drive men to battle, and loyalty to their comrades and obedience to
constituted authority keep them fighting under the most horrific circumstances. In the face of such experiences, of which combat is an extreme
but unfortunately not uncommon example, it is hard to deny the role of
biology, institutions, or the individual's emotions in managing the sometimes congruent, sometimes conflicting demands of the other two.

Modern sociological theory, as well as traditional political philosophy, have to address the Hobbesian problem of how social order is feasible in view of antagonistic tendencies of individuals. According to Durkheim (1980), sociology's answer to this problem is to suggest that, "the
major impact on man's collective existence does not originate from the
fact that something is actually in common, quite the contrary, it is common to all because it is collective, i.e. obligatory" (p. 42). It may be inferred that the nature of social facts is thoroughly normative, and that these
norms, according to Durkheim, do not emerge from any specific aspect
of their physical environment or from some aspects of their organic substratum. The only feasible source of social norms are some other norms,
such as the more embracing intellectual traditions of a given society.

As noted in the first section of this chapter, traditional sociological
accounts of the evolution of human social institutions endorse what
might be conceived of as a top–down approach. On this view, social or-

der does follow from social norms, and sociology has to be confined to the study of social norms and their social preconditions.

In contrast with this, evolutionary approaches in biology, anthropology, and psychology sometimes seem to suggest that many of the sociocultural institutions may be accounted for solely in genetic terms. These accounts endorse what might be conceived of as a bottom–up approach. On this view, social order follows from genetic dispositions that endow humans with a set of universal, highly organized, and contentful behavioral dispositions. As a result, humans, in response to local conditions, express a variety of within-group similarities that are not caused by social learning or transmission (as argued in the prior section on evolutionary psychology).

According to a biosociological approach, both views are wrong if they alone are taken to be sufficient for explaining the evolution of human social institutions. Rather, such explanations require a three-level model that integrates both biological and sociological perspectives. On the biosociological view, social institutions are conceived of as including three distinct levels: (a) genetic, (b) epigenetic, and (c) sociocultural selection. Due to some emergent properties, social institutions, like cultural units in general, develop their own mode of propagation, producing new variants either by the mechanism of Spencerian selection or those described in chapter 10, or both. However, although these processes of cultural mutations are provided with some inbuilt selective agents of their own, they are also coupled with natural selection on genes, along the lines of the coevolutionary mechanisms suggested in chapter 10. Thus, the emergent properties of cultural processes, the biological bases, as well as their feedback to natural selection should be accounted for. Taking the biosociological approach, Levels (b) and (c) cannot be understood in (exclusively) genetic terms. Nonetheless, they are regarded as intimately related to and interconnected with Level (a).

The human emotional system, situated at the epigenetic level, is introduced as the missing link between the biological and the social. Affect and emotion are part of the more embracing system of human physiology. The affective system can be understood as an organism's inbuilt program that compels it to do some things more readily than others. Divided into three categories (i.e., flight, attack, and bonding; see R. D. Masters, 1986), the affect readies human organisms to respond in any situation with adequate actions.

On this view, culture provides institutional arenas (e.g., religious ritual) where human physiology, operating through the emotional system, provides input to the social sphere, as well as accepting input from it. When sacred rituals find a lack of congruence between Levels (a) and (c), it is because the emotions generated lead to conflict, and hence to tendencies to change Level (c). Over the long run, such conflicts must have also modified the biological substratum to create the possibility of the three-level structure. The three categories of affectivity constitute a framework of proximate causations, accounting not only for individual actions, but also for what sociologists conceive of as the "emergence" of social order.

Human affectivity provides an individual with a fixed set of perceptive thresholds and dispositions, the particular meaning of which is dependent on the respective individual's ontogeny. Because the process of ontogeny presupposes some sort of social environment, the recurrence of certain patterns of interaction with children's environment will affect the development of their emotional system as they mature. For example, they will learn how to define the ingroup of those to whom a bias toward affiliation is expected, and outgroups, toward whom wariness, fear, or hate is the appropriate affective response. As a result of a similarity of environments during ontogeny, humans will usually share numerous affective-emotional evaluations, as well as cognitions. Regarding the origin of human sociality, the sharing of evaluative standards and cognitions is, of course, a foundation for the establishment of patterns of social expectations and ongoing social intercourse.

In turn, recent findings indicate that any individual who succeeds in synchronizing his or her own behaviors with that of others will be likely to increase his or her sense of well-being. McGuire and Raleigh (1986) revealed that, by synchronizing their overt behaviors, individuals show an increase in their supplies of neurotransmitters, such as serotonin, which, in turn, are directly related to indications of low stress and relaxed affect. This feedback system allows for the nonreductive hypothesis that social behavior may be influenced by both the individual's neurophysiological state, as well as some environmental factors.

Given that human affectivity is, in fact, a product of phylogeny, it should be expected that there are numerous similarities between human cultures beyond the various differences, which, undoubtedly, also exist. In fact, Murdock (1945) suggested 72 universal cultural institutions. With respect to the origin of human sociality, these similarities seem to indicate that the "obligatory force" of most social norms has not evolved accidentally. On the contrary, their obligatory power has evolved as an expression of certain sets of evolutionarily tested biological information. Due to the nature of the human system of biological information, most of it requires additional inputs of information prior to its transformation into overt behavior. Usually, this part is being played by ontogenetic learning, which, in turn, includes cultural information. Obviously, the inclusion of cultural information in individuals' minds gives rise to some emergent properties of systems of social rules, such as their "extra-mental" characteristics, emphasized by Durkheim. The well-known data on the effects of in-group and out-group classification illustrate the central mediating role played by the emotions.

According to this biosociological approach, the evolution of certain types of cultural institutions, as well as social rules, may, or even must, be tracked down to the principles of genetic replication and to the evolution of certain types of psychological dispositions.

The evolution of the incest taboo may serve as an example. How does human affectivity mediate between the phylogenetic roots of this institution and its cultural expression? A major cause for the existence of the taboo is to be found in the selective advantage of certain sexual avoidances throughout phylogeny, as was argued in the prior section on evolutionary psychology. Given the assumption that the hunter–gatherer economy prevailed for the most extended period in human history, it may be hypothesized that human affectivity has been designed for this type of social organization, with an average membership of some 10–15 individuals. Because the majority of these were usually close relatives, there must have been a means to avoid the potentially disastrous consequences of incest. According to some anthropological accounts, the evolution of an exchange pattern between neighboring social groups provided a suitable means to guard against such dangers. In the human species, these avoidances, like any other behavior, have to be mentally processed (i.e., they must be applied to individuals as well as their relations).

Regarding the relation between average size of primordial groups and affective processes, it may be suggested that, due to the necessity of incest avoidance, a psychological mechanism should be expected to have evolved. This mechanism, although providing for a preference for optimally sized groups, will neither necessarily preserve affective-emotional ties between kin nor prevent individuals from establishing intimate social relations with different sets of individuals throughout their lifetime. In other words, due to the necessities of incest avoidance, individuals must be prepared to renounce "primary intimacy" once they enter the reproductive phase and want to establish "secondary intimacy" (Bischof, 1985). Regarding the nature of affective ties among human beings, the foregoing considerations seem to suggest a thorough adaptability of such ties to the needs of the social environment. Human social evolution has tapped the genetic emotions that lead to incest avoidance to create marriage rules that link families into much larger social units in a systematic fashion. As noted in the previous section, such institutional constructions are possible because Level (a) does not completely determine Level (c). As strong as the emotions generated by Level (a) are, Level (b) cannot even develop properly in the absence of social cues. "Wild" children raised in severely deprived social environments are grossly dysfunctional. Solitary confinement is more emotionally trying than any other punishment, even for emotionally healthy adults. For example, American fliers held in solitary confinement in North Vietnam risked, and regularly suffered, life-threatening punishment for clandestine communication with their fellows.

Against this background, human affectivity may be understood as a differential energization of particular sequences of social life. The selective advantage of this mechanism becomes apparent when one sets out to account for recent findings, according to which incestuous matings are a fairly frequent type of behavior in modern society. Despite the taboo, incest does occur. Obviously, the genetic disposition alone is not sufficient for bringing about a stable psychological inhibition against incestuous matings. As opposed to this, the three-level model suggests combining of the notion of genetically programmed dispositions with the notion of ontogenetic learning. The latter may or may not stabilize the genetic dispositions. It is the lack of reliability in genetic dispositions and their phenotypic effects that explains why evolution has favored the establishment of social institutions. In that sense, culture ensures the development of behavior that has proved to be advantageous throughout phylogeny.

To identify the principles of genetic replication and the evolution of certain types of psychological dispositions is, of course, not to deny that the social rules can eventually acquire emergent properties. For example, the biological roots of the social rule of the incest taboo were developed in the evolutionary context of the small hunter-gatherer group, where inbreeding costs would be high. This established the affective disposition against sexual desire for close relatives. However, it is within specific cultural settings that this affective response is given content. Generally, the negative response is directed to genetic relatives, via the ontogeny of childrearing within genetic families, thereby specifying the object of affect. The logic of the social rule applies even to cases where the ontogenetic social environment diverges from the original evolutionary one. An adopted child, developing within a family of nongenetic relatives during the critical period, will nevertheless have the affective response with respect to the nongenetic family.

With respect to the problem of the origin of human sociality, this chapter advocates a biosociological view. Unlike in Durkheim and some of his followers, a biosociological perspective is not limited to studies of social norms, and does not refrain from asking questions about the conditions for the evolution of any particular type of social rule. On the contrary, biosociology has to raise questions about the evolutionary foundations underlying certain types of normative infrastructure.

The three-level model proposed herein suggests that human sociality is founded on various layers of biological causality, which, in turn, give rise to certain psychological dispositions favoring some types of behavior over others. It is further suggested that human sociality, in a basic sense, is built on individuals' dispositions and needs. According to Lumsden and E. O. Wilson (1983), many dispositions adhere to "epigenetic rules" (i.e., to biologically transmitted tendencies to learn or behave in one fashion rather than another). The human affectivity (Level [b]) has been shown to play a major role in mediating between the biological (Level [a]) and the social sphere (Level [c]). Once a pattern of interaction is established, certain social expectations and social norms are likely to arise. In fact, these norms may acquire emergent properties in the Durkheimian sense, but these properties could never have evolved unless the various biological layers had come into existence prior to them.

CONCLUSION

This chapter demonstrated that the traditional debates between macro- and micro-explanations of human sociality are not solved by merely invoking Darwinism as if it were a talisman that would dispel all error in the social sciences. Some evolutionary theorists are willing to double the bid of the traditional institutional approach. They argue that Darwinian theory can increase the sophistication and power of the micro approach to the point that the institutionalists must ultimately lose the hand. The position of the evolutionary psychologists is a powerful and subtle one, and it should be taken seriously. Perhaps what we perceive as institutions are evoked by evolved psychological mechanisms. However, perhaps human psychology is "designed" just to support the existence of social institutions. There are quite plausible evolutionary scenarios by which such an institution supporting human psychology could come to pass.

The spotlight is on social and cognitive psychology to conduct the appropriate experiments to tell us how people evolved to do what they actually do. Do "institutions" appear as a result of humans using an innate social grammar that is powerful enough to reinvent them with little or no help from transmitted culture? Or is the human emotional system adapted to living in groups in which culturally transmitted institutions subjected to Spencerian selection are necessary even for ordinary functioning? To our mind, these are no longer uncertain questions for which everyone can have a learned opinion, but ones setting researchable challenges to the earnest theorist and empiricist.

The challenge that remains is not to produce a further dichotomization of approaches. Rather, it is to attempt their integration to achieve a fuller understanding of the interdependence of individuality and sociality. More and more knowledge from different realms is potentially relevant, and the first step to achieve integration may, indeed, be to proceed in terms of multilevel models. It is crucial to resolve contradictions that may come to light, and even more to focus on the interrelationships of the different levels, and to specify the links among them.

This challenge remains as an open frontier for research on the emergence of institutions. It is obvious that traditional sociological theories of institutions may encounter challenges when taking into account insights gained by evolutionary theory and the new questions they raise. New theoretical and empirical work is required to address these challenges. Some of the questions to be raised are the following: Under what conditions do conflicts arise among evolved psychological mechanisms, affectivity, and current institutions, and how and at what level could they be resolved? Rather than postulating biological constraints on sociocultural developments (or vice versa), focusing on conflicts would highlight the dynamics of these developments. After all, the crucial issue between biology and the social sciences is this: How is the elaboration of social institutions beyond the biologically plausible to be explained? Both the adaptationist and the phylogenetic accounts can render plausible explanations of behavior of the early hunter-gatherer mode of existence. Since then, human society and culture have developed and reached a level of enormous complexity and diversity. Careful reconstruction of the lines of descent may, indeed, reveal the evolutionary roots of current institutions, but how are we to explain their final form? The question may also be turned around: What effect do existing social institutions have on the content and expression of evolved psychological mechanisms? The answers to these questions are also relevant to the nature of evolved psychologies. Complex societies of the Holocene are in the nature of a large-scale natural experiment imposed on the minds of Pleistocene hunter–gatherers. The details of how recent social evolution has managed to accomplish the creation of such novel societies using Pleistocene psychology should say interesting things about the nature of that psychology. At this stage of interdisciplinary work, it is appropriate to raise these questions in the hope that further development within anthropology, psychology, and sociology will take into account the insights gained by the various evolutionary perspectives.

ACKNOWLEDGMENTS

We thank the University of Bielefeld and the Center for Interdisciplinary Study (ZiF) for inviting us to participate in the research year resulting in this book. We are most grateful to ZiF support staff for myriad of services they provided to make life and work a breeze. We are most grateful to Peter Weingart and Sabine Maasen for conceiving and carrying out the project and for their unfailing friendship.

The work on this chapter was partly supported by NSF Grant BN9157-449 (John Tooby).

7

THE PLACE OF BEHAVIORAL ECOLOGICAL ANTHROPOLOGY IN EVOLUTIONARY SOCIAL SCIENCE

Monique Borgerhoff Mulder
University of California
Davis

Peter J. Richerson
University of California
Davis

Nancy W. Thornhill
University of Southern California
Los Angeles

Eckart Voland
Justus-Liebig-University Giessen
Germany

Evolutionary approaches to human behavior fall into three broad categories: behavioral ecological anthropology, evolutionary psychology, and cultural inheritance theory. All make rather different use of evolutionary theory in developing and testing hypotheses for human behavioral variability, such that considerable controversy has arisen over what is the proper study of evolutionary influences on human affairs.

Because of the wide variability in social organization among human societies, anthropology offers fertile fields for exploring evolutionarily inspired hypotheses for human diversity. Perhaps for this reason, empirical studies in behavioral ecological anthropology (also known as human behavioral ecology, sociobiology, Darwinian anthropology) have grown particularly fast over the past decade (see chap. 1, this volume; Borgerhoff Mulder, 1988a). However, the field has also attracted considerable criticism. Although much of this originates among nonevolutionary anthropologists and social scientists deeply opposed to evolutionary thinking for historical and ideological reasons (see J. H. Turner, chap. 1), particularly precise and insightful criticism comes from other evolutionarily minded social scientists (evolutionary psychologists and cultural inheritance theorists), and is the concern in this chapter. We do not broach broader debates within evolutionary theory. For example, we defend neither the selectionist orientation in this chapter nor the exclusive focus on selection at the level of the individuals (rather than of alleles or groups). To do so would detract attention away from current debates within the evolutionary social sciences. Readers are directed to chapter 10, where selectionist thinking is placed in broader scientific, philosophical, and historical contexts.

The chapter first introduces the principal theory, assumptions, and methods of behavioral ecological anthropology; provides a brief review of areas where predictions from behavioral ecological theory have been tested with human data, and summarizes one such study in more detail (the Krummhörn study of Northern Germany). The chapter refers to this German material to clarify issues for readers not familiar with the human behavioral ecological literature. The chapter then outlines the central theory, assumptions, and methods used in evolutionary psychology and cultural inheritance theory. Finally, it explores the interface of behavioral ecological anthropology with evolutionary psychology and cultural inheritance theory, focusing specifically on modes of selection, targets of selection, evidence of adaptation, evolved mechanisms and their specificity, and the problem of novel environments.

BEHAVIORAL ECOLOGICAL ANTHROPOLOGY

A. Theoretical Background

The field of human behavioral ecology has been extensively reviewed in easily accessible recent sources (Borgerhoff Mulder, 1991; Cronk, 1991; E. A. Smith, 1992). Therefore, these introductory remarks are brief. The history of evolutionary theory in anthropology is outlined in chapter 1.

Behavioral Ecological Theory.   Behavioral ecology is part of evolutionary ecology, the branch of evolutionary theory that analyzes adaptations in an ecological context. Studying behavior in relation to the ecological and social environment flourished in the 1970s, following on the innovative theoretical work of Hamilton (1964), G. C. Williams (1966), Maynard Smith (1974a,b), and Trivers (1971, 1972). These advances opened up new ways to look at an animal's behavior, particularly social behavior. In brief, individuals are viewed as facultative opportunists who assess—either consciously or not, on either the behavioral or evolutionary time scale—a wide array of environmental conditions (both social and ecological) and determine the optimal fitness-maximizing strategy, whereby they can outcompete conspecifics in terms of the numbers of genes transmitted to subsequent generations. As such, behavioral ecology relies on Darwinian theory in a homologous sense, and incorporates among its theoretical tools individual selection, inclusive fitness theory, optimization models, and game theory.

To develop models of optimal behavior, behavioral ecologists typically ignore the nature of the genetic control of phenotypic design, employing a set of simplifying assumptions—a research strategy dubbed "the phenotypic gambit" (Grafen, 1984; E. A. Smith, 1992). Among these are the assumptions that (a) natural selection can override such conflicting forces as drift, (b) sufficient genetic variation in the past has allowed evolution of the optimal phenotype, and (c) any deviations from simple Mendelian inheritance of phenotypes will not significantly affect the expected evolutionary outcome. Although disregard for the genetic control of adaptations has been criticized (Lewontin, 1979), cases where the specifics of inheritance might make a difference are thought to be rare (Grafen, 1984; Maynard Smith, 1982). The problems with this position are discussed in the section on cultural inheritance theory (below).

Although behavioral ecological anthropology is commonly differentiated from other branches of the social sciences in terms of its primary concern with evolutionary (functional *sensu;* see Tinbergen, 1963) questions, it is important to stress that proximate, ontogenetic, and phylogenetic questions are critical to an adequate evolutionary account (Boyd et al., chap. 10, this volume; N. Thornhill et al., chap. 6, this volume).

Assumptions. Behavioral ecological anthropologists adhere to what J. P. Gray (1985) termed the *weak sociobiological thesis.* Variations in behavior are considered expressions of a human genotype, essentially similar across contemporary populations, that has endowed our species with universal psychological predispositions. These are hypothesized to generate variations in response to environmental influences—variations that tend, or tended once, to be adaptive. Tooby and Cosmides (1990a) made a strong case for the position that, at the genetic or design level, adaptations will almost always be species-universal, although their expression may be limited by sex, life history stage, or circumstance. Simi-

lar assumptions underlie studies of the evolutionary significance of behavior among nonhumans.

Nevertheless, behavioral ecological anthropologists also make use of
the phenotypic gambit in their attempts to specify how different strategies
are adapted to different environmental conditions. The phenotypic gambit
fosters two deep tendencies in this approach: First, decision-making processes tend to become "black-boxed." Investigators assume that, given a
particular constellation of environmental conditions, "an actor somehow
uses (unspecified) cognitive processes, in conjunction with information
gathered by whatever (unspecified) processes, to arrive at an optimal solution" (E. A. Smith, 1992, p. 12). The limitations of this view have attracted criticism for naive adaptationism and psychological agnosticism,
as discussed later.

Second, the phenotypic gambit directs attention toward specifying
adaptations in terms of their fitness consequences, with investigators necessarily measuring these in *current* environments, whereas in fact the
mechanisms underlying behavior owe their existance to *past* selection
pressures. Thus, the most common research strategy within behavioral
ecological anthropology is to examine the fitness consequences of behavior in contemporary environments while acknowledging that the psychological apparatus—whereby adaptive behavioral responses are produced, such as emotions, basic motivations, learning, and decision-making abilities—are products of past evolutionary pressures (e.g., Irons,
1991). This entails the assumption that critical environmental features
that both affect the expression of the phenotype and mediate its fitness
consequences have been relatively stable and are still present. Where environmental conditions have changed rapidly, serious interpretational
problems can arise.

Methods. In practice, behavioral ecological investigators first develop a model, relying either on formal rules of logic and mathematics or
empirical findings among nonhumans. From these models, hypotheses
are derived that are tested against empirical evidence—the results of
specifically designed field studies in (primarily) traditional and historical
populations or quantified comparative ethnographic sources. These results are then used to evaluate, modify, or replace previous models. Although this is essentially a hypothetico-deductive approach, alternative
hypotheses cannot always be effectively dismissed, such that the methodology is often more one of plausibility than of falsification (Brandon,

1990). Studies can be placed along certain continua reflecting variability in methodological tactics, which, if depicted at this stage, may help clarify subsequent controversies discussed in this chapter.

First, sociobiological studies focus on the fitness consequences of behavior, whereas behavioral ecological studies place more emphasis on the social and ecological constraints on individuals' behavioral options (E. A. Smith, 1992). Both tactics constitute critical components of a successful evolutionary analysis.

Second, depending on the question at hand, proxy currencies for fitness are used, ranging from rates of food acquisition to estimates of an individual's proportional genetic representation in future generations. Thus, in studying prey choice among foragers, strategies are compared in terms of caloric returns (Kaplan & K. Hill, 1992). In assessing reproductive competition in contemporary society, the number of potential conceptions is estimated (Perusse, 1992a). In examining reproductive strategies in traditional and historical populations, numbers of surviving children are measured (Low, 1993). Each kind of currency constitutes a useful empirical tool while generating different kinds of methodological and interpretational problems. Such problems include: Does differential energy-harvesting efficiency translate into fitness differences? Can long-term fitness differentials be estimated from single generational studies?

Third, there is variability in the complexity with which models are developed and tested. At its simplest, descriptive predictions derived from appropriate areas of evolutionary theory are tested on single or multiple populations. Thus, drawing on theoretical expectations contingent on sex differences in parental investment in mammals, D. M. Buss (1988) predicted that men and women across human societies will differ in the characteristics they value in potential mates. Specifically, he proposed that females are preferred for their youth and chastity, and that males are preferred for their capacity to acquire resources. Qualitative expectations such as these can be made more precise by using optimality methods to generate quantitative predictions. Thus, Blurton Jones (1986) examined whether women optimize the lengths of their birth intervals so as to maximize lifetime reproductive success.

Finally, models can be rendered still more realistic (and complex) by factoring in the behavioral tactics of *other* individuals in the population through the use of game theoretical calculations. Thus, Hawkes (1990) showed that hunting game and sharing it with all the band members can be evolutionarily stable, although such resource targeting lowers the hunter's mean foraging returns. This is because everyone prefers to have good hunters in the band, and is willing to grant them certain favors. Note that at each level of complexity, the model can be made even more specific by including the ecological criteria constricting options.

B. Empirical Advances

There are as yet only loose links between the topical areas addressed by behavioral ecological anthropologists. Nevertheless, they fall into two broad classes—studies of subsistence and reproduction—and have been recently reviewed (Borgerhoff Mulder, 1991; Cronk, 1991; E. A. Smith, 1992).

Under the category of *subsistence strategies*, the main topics examined include how individuals secure access to resources, how they choose which resources to harvest, and in what kinds of social groups they cooperate for acquiring, sharing, and consuming resources. Studies have depended on data drawn primarily from foraging populations, and have tested models designed to identify the adaptive significance of territoriality and resource defense, reciprocity and reciprocal resource access, and foragers' choice of resources. Although, in many cases simple models have been successful in predicting foragers' choice of resources, the models are currently being extended to incorporate such factors as risk, micronutrient needs, mating strategies, and phenotypic differences among individuals (Kaplan & K. Hill, 1992).

In the category of *reproductive strategies*, many topics have been investigated. These include such life history issues as maturation, age of first and last reproduction, and senescence; birth spacing and offspring quantity and quality; and the ecological determinants of mating systems (Borgerhoff Mulder, 1992). Other topics include kinship (Hughes, 1988), descent systems (Hartung, 1982; N. Thornhill & R. Thornhill, 1985), and sociocultural change (Cronk, 1989). How men use economic and political power to their own reproductive purposes has been one particularly fruitful area of empirical research (Irons, 1993), as has been the question of how parents allocate resources between sons and daughters (Sieff, 1990).

We turn now to a brief outline of the main findings of one such study of reproductive strategy. This study represents strands of both the sociobiological and the behavioral ecological tradition, and measures fitness primarily in terms of numbers of surviving offspring. As yet, it tests models derived from simple logical deductions from evolutionary theory, without recourse to optimality or game theoretic considerations.

C. The Krummhörn Study

Family reconstitution of premodern rural populations can be used to examine some of the key issues in behavioral ecological anthropology. Data from 7 of 32 parishes of the northwest German coastal Krummhörn (Ostfriesland) region have been used to examine how reproductive tactics can be seen as adaptations to the ecological and social circumstances of the 18th and 19th centuries (Engel, 1990; Voland, 1990, 1995).

The Krummhörn coastal marshes were settled in early European history and, at least between the 17th and 19th centuries, experienced no noteworthy changes in population density. The population consisted mostly of Protestant reformed denominations. Subsistence was dominated by agriculture and dairy farming. Social stratification was marked. Wealthy farmers (full-time peasants) were clearly differentiated in every material and immaterial aspect of their lifestyles from the smallholders who relied primarily on medium or high-skilled trades (millers, smiths, bakers). Beneath the smallholders were the landless, supporting themselves primarily through agricultural day labor or simple rural trades.

Although inevitably there are problems with the use of historical materials (e.g., primarily the limitations of the records and the indirect nature of the evidence on socioecological conditions), the findings reviewed later contribute to an understanding of the factors that influence the mating and parental strategies of men and women in densely populated European agricultural communities. Three sets of results are briefly summarized: male reproductive strategies, female choice, and parental decisions concerning investment in sons and daughters.

Male Reproductive Strategies. Irons (1979) proposed that individuals strive for sociocultural (often economic) success as a proximate means to attain reproductive success. The simplest test of this hypothesis is to show positive correlations between reproductive success and socioeconomic status (SES), as has indeed been done for many traditional and preindustrial populations (Irons, 1993).

Historical demographic data offer a special opportunity to assess the long-term fitness consequences of single-generational reproductive outcomes. In the Krummhörn study, long-term fitness was computed as the sum of the residual reproductive values of all of the living direct descendants, with each value weighted by the coefficient of relatedness. This measure of the long-term local reproductive success of a family was positively correlated with the size of the land exploited by the family. Indeed, 100 years after the marriage, the fitness of a prosperous farming couple was almost twice as high as that of an average family. The causes of this difference lay both in the increased marital fertility of rich farmers and the improved social opportunities of their children, because the children of the rich farmers were much less likely to emigrate than those of the poorer farmers (Voland, 1990).

Female Choice. In 18th- and 19th-century Germany, the brides of wealthy farmers were several years younger than those of agricultural workers, with data from premodern Krummhörn fitting well into this general pattern. Between 1720 and 1874, the average age of a man at his first marriage was just under 30 years; this did not vary among social groups. In contrast, farmers' brides were, on average only, 24.9 years old, and a full 2.3 years younger than those of the unpropertied section of population (Voland & Engel, 1990). A simple economic explanation for this pattern—that farmers' daughters marry particularly early because they need not enter service as maidservants to save for their dowries— was rejected: Despite marked social endogamy, the economic circumstances of a woman's natal family had no significant influence on marriage age (Voland & Dunbar, 1997).

Voland and Engel (1990) proposed that the Krummhörn women were exercising a fitness-maximizing conditional strategy of partner choice. They suggested that the maxim of a woman read: "When you are young, be particularly demanding and only marry a man of high economic status. As you become older, be less exacting with respect to your partner's economic circumstances." The Krummhörn data reveal such a trend. The younger a woman married, the more likely it was to a well-situated man. Almost one third of the women under 20, but not even 10% of the women over 30, married wealthy farmers. Conversely, almost every 5th wealthy farmers married a woman under 20, but only every 25th man without real estate did so. Voland and Engel argued that if one assumes that all men prefer younger to older brides, the variation in age of Krummhörn brides arises from an age-dependent female choice rule. Clearly, male competition may also be implicated, particularly if wealthy farmers are more likely to be successful within the marriage market.

Parental Investment in Sons and Daughters. On account of the density of human settlements in the Krummhörn, there were some quite distinct patterns of social mobility in relation to sex and status. The sons of farmers tended to stay in their socioeconomic class, either as a result of marrying endogamously or remaining celibate, whereas farmers' daughters were just as likely to marry their social inferiors as they were to marry into their own class. These circumstances create a situation in which the relative advantage of raising sons and daughters varies according to parents' class, hence presenting investment trade-off decisions for parents.

A striking congruence was found by Voland, Siegelkow, and Engel (1991) between the marriage probabilities of individuals of different SES and sex and their survival probabilities as children. In particular, the survival chances of daughters born to prosperous farmers were much higher than those of their brothers—a brother–sister differential not observed in the other socioeconomic classes. Voland et al. suggested that parental manipulation may be responsible for the remarkably low survival of sons of wealthy farmers—specifically, that parents are minimizing the net costs of raising sons for whom expected reproductive potential is on average quite low, and for whom rearing costs (particularly in terms of inheritance) are high. Again, the Voland et al. study pointed to critical ecological influences on these survival differentials—in particular, the acute land shortages in the Krummhörn. Furthermore, from their study, one would predict that, in growing populations, where the economic chances of farmers' sons are less curtailed by land shortages, wealthy farmers should not show daughter preference (see e.g., Hrdy & Judge, 1993).

Summary. The power of a behavioral ecological anthropological analysis such as this lies in linking different strategies within the population to fitness consequences, as conditioned by local social and ecological conditions. The interpretations are clearly not proved, but they are plausible. Although as yet there is little comparative material with which to test the generality of these findings, qualitative observations on the ecological conditions of the Krummhörn parishes permit inferences to be made as regards the particular circumstances to which these strategies are adapted (see Voland, Dunbar, Engel, & Stephan, 1997).

OTHER EVOLUTIONARY APPROACHES

A. Evolutionary Psychology

Evolutionary psychology is distinguished from behavioral ecological anthropology in its explicit attempt to identify the psychological mechanisms generating behavior. An evolutionary anthropologist asks, "Are the parental strategies of wealthy and landless Krummhörn farmers adapted to the marital chances of their offspring?", whereas an evolutionary psychologist seeks to determine *how* such different parental solutions are reached. This entails asking questions about the evolved "design" of the psychological mechanisms underlying behavioral responses—in particular, the way in which critical features of the environment are perceived, and the role of individual ontogeny in the elicitation of such responses. Thus, evolutionary psychology is concerned with characterizing the psychological mechanisms that generate the behavior patterns studied by behavioral ecological anthropology.

A major methodological difference between the two approaches lies in the emphasis evolutionary psychologists place on reconstructing the evolutionary environments in which selection acted to produce the adaptation in question. With such a hypothesized environment in mind, commonly referred to as the "environment of evolutionary adaptedness" (Symons, 1979), evolutionary psychologists seek to develop testable hypotheses about the nature of the adaptation in question (see also Cosmides & Tooby, 1992; N. Thornhill & R. Thornhill, 1983).

Two principal methodologies are engaged, either separately or in conjunction, by evolutionary psychologists (although not exclusively by evolutionary psychologists) to define psychological adaptations. The first entails characterizing the information that the adaptive mechanisms are thought to process. Critical components of this information reflect the nature of the social and environmental problems that humans faced during their evolutionary history. For example, a major direction of current evolutionary psychological research involves characterizing the sex-specificity of psychological adaptations. Due to the typically asymmetrical contribution of the two sexes to the rearing of offspring, evolutionary game theory shows that the reproductive strategies of the two sexes often differ substantially (Maynard Smith, 1982; Trivers, 1972). Even in cases like humans, where males sometimes make substantial contributions to parental care, it is reasonable to assume that the problems faced by the sexes in the environment of evolutionary adaptedness were markedly different from one another in some domains.

The second methodology employed by evolutionary psychologists is the comparative method. Psychological adaptations are assumed to be species-typical (i.e., universal, across human minds, regardless of cultural variability). Cross-cultural, comparative studies are designed to elucidate just such universality. Thus, in their early work on infanticide, Daly and M. Wilson (1984) characterized the design of a general human infanticidal proclivity through determining statistical regularities to the specific kinds of situations in which infanticide occurs across the ethnographic record.

N. Thornhill & R. Thornhill's (1983) studies on sexual coercion have revealed the same robust pattern of regularity in aspects of sexual coercion across cultures (but see N. Thornhill, 1996). Note how these studies differ from the work of human ethologists, who search more specifically for universalities in behavioral patterns, rather than for universalities in the rules whereby behavior is elicited by varying social and environmental conditions.

B. Cultural Inheritance Theory

Cultural inheritance theory is distinguished from behavioral ecological anthropology and evolutionary psychology by its focus on the evolutionary properties of cultural inheritance. Most modern social scientists subscribe to the view that much, if not most, human behavioral variation is a result of patterns of behavior learned socially from others. Teaching, imitation, and related mechanisms (see Durham et al., chap. 9, this volume) transmit information from experienced to naive members of society in a way that is broadly analogous to genetic inheritance. Cultural evolution theorists have developed a family of Darwinian models to investigate the evolutionary properties of this socially learned variation (Boyd & Richerson, 1985; Cavalli-Sforza & Feldman, 1981; Durham, 1991).

Cultural transmission is different from genetic transmission in a number of respects. Many more than two cultural "parents" can influence naive individuals as they acquire an item of culture. Individually learned skills or ideas can subsequently be transmitted, making culture a system for the inheritance of acquired variation. People are not passive recipients of their culture, but can make decisions about which variants to adopt or abandon. As a result of such differences, the evolutionary properties of cultural systems differ markedly from those of genetic systems. A rather large conceptual, theoretical, and empirical task is to reconstruct Darwinian theory to accommodate these novel features of culture (see Boyd et al., chap. 10, this volume; Hejl et al., chap. 11, this volume).

A major topic for cultural inheritance theory has been the adaptiveness of culturally transmitted traits. Unlike most social scientists, who view culture as liberating humans from the constraints of natural selection, most of the contributors to this theory suppose that the cultural system is an adaptation that arose by natural selection. Over the last few million years of the hominid evolution, cultural capacities contributed dramatically to an anatomy (large, complex brain), life cycle (long period of juvenile socialization), and resource acquisition strategy (culturally transmitted technology), all intricately adapted to acquire and use socially learned information. It is exceedingly unlikely that such a large series of apparently integrated functional changes could have occurred except under the influence of natural selection. However, much like the work in conventional population genetics, models constructed by cultural evolution theorists have shown that dynamics of cultural evolution, and cultural coevolution with gene-based structures, do not always give rise to patterns of behavior that would be predicted from fitness-optimizing considerations alone.

In the conceptually most straightforward case, the forces derived from an adapted psychology that invents and selects cultural forms, and perhaps from natural selection on cultural variation, will cause cultural forms to conform to ordinary fitness-optimizing rules. To the extent that the assumptions of the models are empirically correct, they justify the gambit (used by behavioral ecological anthropology and evolutionary psychology) of ignoring the details of the inheritance system in estimating fitness-maximizing behavior. Among cultural inheritance theory proponents, Durham (1991) cogently argued that cultural variations are genetic fitness-enhancing in most instances.

In other models, cultural evolutionary processes make a much bigger difference. For example, Boyd and Richerson (1985) showed how the "more-than-two parents" feature of cultural transmission can lead to a situation in which group selection on cultural variation is easier to imagine than it is in the case of genetic transmission. They argued that this peculiarity of the cultural transmission system could have arisen for ordinary adaptive reasons, and then set up conditions in which advanced sociality based on cultural group selection became a major feature allowing the pattern of human organization that we see. This argument is similar to the case made for the social hymenopteran: that peculiarities of a haplo-diploid sex determination system predispose this group to the evolution of eusociality. Some kinds of apparently adaptive behaviors unique to humans, like complex societies based on cooperation among distantly (genetically) related individuals, might not be able to evolve on the basis of genetic inheritance alone, but may be quite possible where genes co-evolve with culture.

In still other models, frankly pathological traits can be carried by the cultural system. Especially where there is a rapid horizontal spread of fads and fashions, it is quite possible that selection acting on cultural variants might favor the spread of cultural subsystems that are antithetical to individual fitness.

As with the phenotypic gambit, researchers like Boyd and Richerson (1985) and A. R. Rogers (1988) have argued that future work is likely to show that the ignore-culture gambit is frequently, but not always, a useful simplification in the analysis of human behavior. At the current state of knowledge, it is not possible to be confident of the limits of the fitness-optimizing simplification in the face of the potential complexities demonstrated in the cultural inheritance models.

THEORETICAL INTERFACES

Much of the discourse over the proper study of evolutionary influences on human behavior centers on criticism exchanged among proponents of behavioral ecological anthropology, evolutionary psychology, and cultural inheritance theory. Thus, Flinn and R. D. Alexander (1982) and Daly (1982) defended behavioral ecological anthropology against cultural inheritance theory; Symons (1987) and Tooby and Cosmides (1990b) argued for the importance of studying psychology rather than behavior, while Caro and Borgerhoff Mulder (1987), Betzig (1989), and Turke (1990) argued the converse; and Durham (1991) emphasized the value of coevolutionary theory over simple sociobiological models. Repeatedly too, often in these very publications, proponents have made calls for conciliation (see Blurton Jones, 1990). The final section of this chapter has two aims: to explore, as far as possible, the areas of agreement between the three subfields; and to provide a simple guide to their differences.

The implications for future research directions are discussed in the conclusion.

A. Natural Selection and Cultural Selection

One important point of debate among evolutionary thinkers centers on the basic processes of cultural evolution, which are the analogues of drift, mutation, migration, natural selection, and sexual selection. Although contributors agree about the basic list of conceivable forces, they have different ideas about the relative importance of the various processes, and hence the substantive nature of cultural evolution. A more technical discussion of these problems is presented in chapter 9, but a basic background is required to make sense of debates among advocates of behavioral ecological anthropology, evolutionary psychology, and cultural inheritance theory positions.

The most general picture of human gene–culture evolution is of two systems of inheritance that affect human evolution, each subject to a long list of evolutionary forces. The basic list for the genetic system also applies to the cultural system. Thus, as Dawkins (1982) discussed in the context of memes, there is no reason to suppose that ordinary natural selection cannot act on culture just as it does on genes to select for memes that are efficient at replicating themselves in the next generation.

The main difference between genetic and cultural transmission is that culture is a system that includes the potential for the inheritance of acquired variation. It is also a sequential system of transmission, because many genes are already expressed as socialization starts. Thus, cultural evolution is subject to controls via human choices about the adoption and invention of cultural variants. Unfortunately, a wide variety of terms have been applied to these forces by different authors, obscuring the high level of general agreement about their basic properties and importance. Cavalli-Sforza and Feldman (1981) and Durham (1991) called them *cultural selection.*

These forces are products of human psychology. Suppose all humans have approximately the same psychology, at least at birth, but that at various times and places the environments they live in differ dramatically. A population of hunter–gatherers, moving slowly poleward from tropical latitudes, will invent and acquire by diffusion new items of technology suitable to the environments through which they pass. The culturally selective decisions to invent or adopt new techniques will partly or wholly substitute for the effects of natural selection directly on traditions of tool-making, food choice, social organization, and the like. It is important to realize that *cultural selection*, like *natural selection* for that matter, is a collective term for a number of distinct processes, some of which are not even well conceptualized, much less well explored. This fact has led to much debate among cultural inheritance theory scholars, but is of less concern here.

Most behavioral ecological anthropology and evolutionary psychology students cautiously agree with advocates of cultural inheritance theory that, at an abstract and hypothetical level, a full-dress coevolutionary scheme is at least a conceptual framework in which traditional social science claims about the importance of transmitted culture can be investigated in a Darwinian framework. However, the three positions do differ substantially in the extent to which they rely on natural and cultural selection when generating hypotheses for behavioral diversity.

A behavioral ecological anthropology proponent usually assumes that cultural selection is strong, and that the psychology guiding cultural selection uses rules of considerable generality. In the limit, one might imagine an economist's omnipotent rationalist to be this single rule: "Do whatever it takes to maximize your fitness in whatever environment you find yourself." In this case, there is no culture, of course, because omnipotence would serve as a substitute for having to learn from anyone else. This limiting caricature aside, cultural inheritance theory-inspired modeling shows that much weaker cultural selection, taking full advantage of learning economies by using imitation, can reach fitness-optimizing behaviors rapidly and efficiently, compared with a purely genetic system (see E. A. Smith & Winterhalder, 1992b). As with natural selection, what seems like weak cultural selection from the psychological perspective can be quite strong at population level. This effect is an important candidate for explaining the adaptive advantage of having culture at all, and is a highly plausible justification for expecting at least an approximation to genetic fitness optimizing in many culturally coded behaviors.

Evolutionary psychology proponents share the assumption of strong cultural selection, but are uneasy with the view that human psychology can be characterized by learning and biasing rules of sufficient generality to result in fitness-maximizing behavior in all environments. Evolutionary psychology advocates hypothesize a richly structured set of mental organs adapted to past, rather than present, environments generating the forces of cultural selection. Thus, the evolutionary psychology and behavioral ecological anthropology positions agree that cultural selection rooted in adaptive psychologies is the main cause of cultural evolution, at least in those cases where there is enough transmission relative to direct individual choice to justify the assumption of cultural transmission at all.

Cultural inheritance theory advocates imagine that the broader array of forces may, at least in some interesting cases, be important. Natural selection directly on cultural variation has the potential to generate virus-like memes. Natural selection on cultural variation at the group level may be responsible for the high levels of cooperation seen in humans. Cultural rules may generate cultural selection, and cultural rules could even impose themselves on genetic evolution via mate choice (see also Durham, 1991). Human natural history furnishes many examples of apparently maladaptive and group-functional cultural traits, lending some credence to cultural inheritance theory claims.

B. Targets of Selection

Adaptation.   An adaptation is any phenotypic feature of an organism that is designed by natural selection to solve specific problems posed by the social and ecological environment during a species' evolution (Burian, 1983; Mayr, 1983; G. C. Williams, 1966). Claims that a trait is an adaptation necessarily invoke a particular causal history—namely, that the trait evolved by natural selection because of its consequences on its bearer's fitness in past environments.

Although most evolutionary social scientists agree on this definition, at least three controversial issues have been of concern. First, can behavior be characterized as an adaptation? Second, how can one identify evolutionarily significant units as the targets of selection? Third, what constitutes appropriate evidence of an adaptation, or how can one best investigate its causal history?

Adaptation and Behavior.   There has been sharp difference in opinion over whether behavior can (R. D. Alexander, 1990; Turke, 1990), or cannot (Symons, 1989; Tooby & Cosmides, 1989c, 1990b), be viewed as an adaptation. At the heart of the controversy is the following: For a trait to be an adaptation, as defined earlier, it must be part of the recurrent design of individuals. Because behavior, at least in the everyday sense, often implies a random, unpatterned, transient thing, evolutionary psychologists have preferred to direct investigation to the more stable design features underlying behavior—specifically psychological mechanisms. However, an adaptation consists of the complete set of rules regulating the epigenetic processes between gene and phenotype, including the expression of the behavior (R. D. Alexander, 1990; Dawkins, 1982). Consequently, if there is any patterned design in the expression of behavior, behavior *is* rightfully part of the adaptation.

Thus, the claim that a behavior pattern such as polyandrous marriage is *not* an adaptation (Symons, 1989) can be countered by evidence that polyandrous marriage decisions show regularity with respect to socioeconomic causation, which indeed they do (J. H. Crook & S. J. Crook, 1988; Durham, 1991).(They are particularly likely to show regularity when they are a traditional cultural institution, as is indeed the case with polyandry in some parts of the world.) The challenge, then, to behavioral ecological anthropology is to provide sufficiently precise accounts of the regularities of behavioral phenotypes, such that these can legitimately be viewed as naturally selected features of the organism. This research program is already well advanced in the study of nonhuman behavior (J. R. Krebs & N. B. Davies, 1991), and is growing fast in human studies (E. A. Smith & Winterhalder, 1992a). In short, the issue of whether behavior is legitimately viewed as an adaptation can be empirically solved, and need not constitute an intellectual gulf between evolutionary psychologists and anthropologists.

Adaptations as Strategy Sets. However, focusing on specific behavioral traits as adaptations may be unproductive for other reasons. In humans, the pathways between genes and behavioral phenotypes are undoubtedly intricate, with behavioral outcomes depending on complex environmental influences and interactions. In such circumstances, as S. D. Mitchell (1990) pointed out, a particular behavior is expressed in a given environment because of a rule coding for that environment-behavior pairing. Hence, if there is (or was) genetic variation in this rule, the adaptation must be identified as a strategy set (a suite of responses to different conditions) or a reaction norm (Stearns, 1989; Via, 1993), not a specific behavior. Given the high probability of intricate algorithmic underpinnings of social behavior, it therefore seems most reasonable that evolutionary social scientists should focus on strategy sets as the targets of selection.

At first glance, behavioral ecological anthropologists appear to characterize adaptations rather simplistically, examining quantitative behav-

ioral traits such as number of spouses, time spent in pursuit of a prey species, proportional allocation of resources to sons and daughters, and so
on, rather than strategy sets. On closer inspection, however, it is clear that
they are describing how *variation* in these traits (e.g., the number of co-
wives that is tolerated or the amount of food that is shared) is dependent
on social and ecological features. Thus, what is really under investigation
is the decision rule generating the set of behavioral outcomes. Indeed, as
Symons (1987) noted, almost any description of behavior necessarily has
recourse to the decisions of the actor (see also Irons, 1990).

Evolutionary psychologists typically have been much more careful
than behavioral ecological anthropologists in defining adaptations as
strategy sets, at least insofar as they focus on the psychological propensities guiding decisions. Thus, in a study of infanticide, Daly and M. Wilson (1984) identified as an adaptation not the behavioral trait of infanticide, but the parental inclination to vary the love and solicitude offered a
child according to certain specified circumstances (see also R. Thornhill
& N. Thornhill, 1991).

How Does Cultural Inheritance Theory Fit In?   Cultural inheritance theory places explicit emphasis on information (rules, principles,
beliefs, etc.) as the transmissable units, and hence targets of, selection
(Weingart et al., chap. 8, this volume; Durham, 1991). Consequently, in
many cases, the research strategy of cultural inheritance theory dovetails
nicely with that of evolutionary psychology and behavioral ecological anthropology. Thus, Durham's (1991) attempt to depict the cultural principles associated with diverse marital arrangements among Tibetan serfs
entails a methodology almost indistinguishable in many aspects from that
of a behavioral ecologist (Durham, 1991; Borgerhoff Mulder & S. D.
Mitchell, 1994): to determine the principles guiding marital decisions by
comparing them in relation to such cues as number of sibs, availability of
property, and so on.

Where the cultural inheritance theory strategy differs is in the emphasis put on who does the choosing—natural selection or people, and on
how the "fitnesses" of different strategy sets are determined. Cultural inheritance theory also has a close relationship to evolutionary psychology
as regards targets of selection. The rules that appear in this theory derive,
at least in part, from psychological structures. Cultural inheritance theorists, beginning with D. T. Campbell's (1965) pioneering essay, view human psychology as adapted for the management of culture (see Lumsden

& E. O. Wilson, 1981; Pulliam & Dunford, 1980). Many cultural inheritance theory models could be interpreted as exploring the functional constraints and opportunities that apply to the evolution of a culture-manag-
ing mind.

Summary. Behavioral ecological anthropology, cultural inheritance
theory, and evolutionary psychology attempt to depict the design of an
adaptation, focusing on different, but complementary aspects of the phenotypic expression. Behavioral ecological anthropology attempts to pin-
point environmental contingencies in the real world, whereas evolutionary psychology aims at constructing the rule or decision algorithm
through experiments and questionnaires. Cultural inheritance theory investigates a further important aspect of how the rules or ideas guiding
strategy sets spread, and how these might, under some circumstances,
spread in ways antithetical to those of an organic evolutionary model,
given the different patterns of transmission of ideational units. In view of
this interrelatedness of purpose among these three approaches, studies
that attempt to build on and integrate the strengths of each field are sorely
needed.

C. Current Fitness Consequences as Evidence of Adaptation

The principal methods of studying phenotypic design are the comparative
method, study of evolutionary stable strategies, use of optimality models,
modeling of the genetic evolution of phenotypes, and studies of current
selection and differential fitness. Although most evolutionary biologists
appreciate the value of each of these methods, the importance of current
fitness differentials has been hotly debated in the field of human studies.
In fact, some of the disagreement can be reduced to an epistemological
difference in opinion with respect to what constitutes an adequate explanation for phenotypic variability. This section looks at this important issue, and then briefly discusses an associated corollary methodological
matter that has somewhat derailed the discussion.

The Contribution of Studies of Fitness. Adaptations consist of
the cumulation of phenotypes with specific designs that contributed to
positive fitness effects in the past. Hence, *current fitness* is, by definition,
irrelevant to the argument of whether a trait is an adaptation. The obvious, if somewhat trite, logic of this reasoning, and the equally obvious

fact that *past fitness* consequences of traits cannot be directly studied, have spawned a variety of different empirical approaches to the study of adaptation (Caro & Borgerhoff Mulder, 1987). Perhaps most controversially, it has also led evolutionary psychologists to conclude that "measuring reproductive differentials is at best an inefficient and ambiguous way to illuminate adaptation" (Symons, 1989, p. 131), or simply "incidental to Darwinian explanation" (Tooby & Cosmides, 1990b, p. 378).

This point was argued most forcefully by R. Thornhill (1990), who, in a direct critique of selectionist studies in biology (e.g., Clutton-Brock, 1988; Wade, 1987), proposed that the study of functional consequences of behavior provides only *indirect* evidence of adaptation because the strength of current selection on a trait varies according to numerous environmental factors. Thornhill's point rests on the fact that reproductive differentials (and selection coefficients) are specific to different environments, which is well known (e.g., Daly & M. Wilson, 1983). Therefore, the question is perhaps more fruitfully posed as follows: What is the precise significance of current reproductive differentials in the study of adaptation?

Three such roles can be specified: Studies of fitness consequences inspire hypotheses, test hypotheses, or provide explanations for adaptive design, falling along an "inspire, test, explain" continuum. In addition, studies of fitness consequences give insight into the process of natural selection in actual populations.

Loose recourse to the explanatory role, such as claims that human behavioral ecological approaches *explain* human behavioral variability, has been rightly criticized. Thus, Barkow (1989) noted that, even if correspondences between behavior and fitness can be shown in contemporary populations, these tell nothing about the nature of the human psyche, and therefore little about *how* adaptive solutions are reached. At the heart of the issue is this: A genuine explanation requires not just a demonstration of the rules of a correspondence between behavior and fitness (or norms of reaction), but a causal model explaining why these correspondences are there (Tooby & Cosmides, 1990b). The implication for behavioral ecological anthropology is that it should be more cautious in its claims to have provided an explanatory framework.

However, just because the *explanatory* role of current fitness studies is somewhat limited, this in no way means that conducting evolutionary anthropology in contemporary developing or modern populations is worthless. As many have recognized, evolutionary psychology is guided at all stages in its hypothesis development by an understanding of how selection works. The role of contemporary fitness studies as a source of inspiration is, in this respect, hardly controversial. Thus, the nature of current selection on a phenotype provides an important piece of evidence in determining an adaptation's design.

The question of whether studies of current fitness consequences test hypotheses about adaptive design is more problematic. Despite the emphasis on hypothesis testing in behavioral ecological anthropology, Darwinian hypotheses are often posed without any clear specification of the "null hypothesis" (i.e., of what is to be retained if the hypothesis is not supported). Thus, Symons (1989) was right to point out that failure to support Darwinian hypotheses does not call Darwinism into question, and that these so-called Darwinian hypotheses are not Darwinian at all. Indeed, his critique of the research reported in Betzig, Borgerhoff Mulder, and Turke's (1988) edited volume is that the hypotheses are constructed too loosely to be refutable (see Brandon, 1990).

Increasingly, however, hypotheses are being posed that can be tested, with specific predictions about how environmental cues might influence behavior in ways consistent with evolutionary theory. Thus, Kaplan and K. Hill (1985) examined a variety of hypotheses for food sharing among the Ache foragers of Paraguay by deriving and testing alternative predictions pertaining to kin selection and risk reduction. Similarly, Borgerhoff Mulder (1988b, 1995) investigated different factors that might be expected to influence how much mating effort is exhibited by different Kenyan Kipsigis men. Indeed, the goal of behavioral ecological anthropology is to test different hypotheses for the links between socioecology and behavior, with the underlying agenda of identifying the regularities in such correspondences that might constitute part of an adaptation (or strategy set). Perhaps phrased as such, the study of current fitness differentials becomes less contentious.

Problems with Studies of Fitness Differentials.   Nevertheless, there *are* difficulties with using the fitness consequences of behavior as a way to determine adaptation; these are linked to methodological problems and to the assumption of environmental stability. Although the latter issue is discussed in a subsequent section, it is argued here that the methodological difficulties associated with discerning fitness consequences have been used as an inappropriate reason by R. Thornhill (1990) and others (Symons, 1992) for altogether abandoning the study of fitness consequences.

Studies of reproductive success are not ideal for assessing the fitness value of a trait for at least two reasons (e.g., Caro & Borgerhoff Mulder, 1987). First, reproductive variance among individuals may be random with respect to transgenerationally recurring traits, such that fitness differentials say nothing about adaptive design (Clutton-Brock, 1988). Second, there is the old problem of determining whether the fitness differentials associated with a recurrent phenotypic design are indeed the consequence of this design, or of a correlated trait (Grafen, 1988). Clearly, studies of reproductive success provide a cumbersome and distal measure of the outcome of an adaptive design. It is partly because of this problem that studies in the realm of behavioral ecological anthropology should focus on various currencies, including the proximate outcomes of behavior.

However, the important point is that, although evolutionary biologists rightly recommend a cautious approach to the study of current function through analyses of reproductive success, they certainly do not claim that the study of fitness consequences is invalid for gaining insight into adaptations or the evolutionary process. In evolutionary biology, the measurement of current fitness consequences of phenotypes and genotypes is a methodological staple.

Summary. Despite some methodological problems with discerning fitness effects, studies of the fitness consequences of behavior in contemporary societies have a role to play in both inspiring evolutionary hypotheses and testing specific models of how individuals vary their behavior under different environmental conditions in a regular way.

More generally, it is important to remember that one of Darwin's chief points against creationism was the crudity and imperfection of the process of adaptations through natural selection, as opposed to God's design. Studies of such imperfections remain of central importance within biology (Endler, 1986). Therefore, the behavior of populations in environments far from selective equilibrium are likely to be especially informative as natural experiments. Both cultural inheritance theory and evolutionary psychology are concerned with this issue. For example, in conditions far from the "environment of evolutionary adaptedness," one may observe both strong actual fitness differentials within a population *and* cultural selection as a result of psychological predispositions, which does not move the population in the direction of the fitness optimum. The varying intuitions of behavioral ecological anthropologists, evolutionary psychologists, and cultural inheritance theorists about the relative import-ance and strength of these different processes need to be tested at the proximal level as a complement to the often ambigous interpretation of putative adaptations.

D. Mechanism

Behavioral ecological anthropology can be, and has rightly been, criti-cized for its mechanistic agnosticism. Anthropologists simply attribute an adaptive correspondence between behavior and environment to some kind of all-purpose fitness-maximizing machinery situated somewhere within our cognitive processing skills, either conscious or not. Thus, an-thropologists commonly comment on the fact that humans behave *as if* they were maximizing their fitness (e.g., Irons, 1979). However, as noted previously, correlations between behavior and particular environmental or social contingencies tell little about *how* adaptive solutions are reach-ed.

Emphasis on Mechanism in Evolutionary Psychology. The ab-sence of proposed mechanisms promoting adaptive behavioral ends has posed a rather serious problem in behavioral ecological anthropology. Practitioners generally rely on a bit of hand-waving vagueness when pressed on mechanism, and resort to an explanation based on selection promoting a generalized fitness-maximizing human mind. That is, the human mind is assigned a general goal (to maximize fitness).

Evolutionary psychologists are more specific about the nature of the mind. They maintain that, insofar as selection acts on mental constructs, these are honed into functionally designed mechanisms (adaptations), that deal with the peculiarities of environmental input. It is the peculiari-ties of the environmental challenge that cause the adaptations to be do-main-specific. Human social environments are tremendously complex. For evolutionary psychologists, therein lies the rationale for domain-specificity. An analogy is often employed at this juncture. Consider the vertebrate eye. It consists of dozens of extraordinarily complex, highly specific features that, together, solve an adaptive problem for the organ-ism. Moreover, none of the features was present in ancestral conditions. Selection, acting over long periods of evolutionary time, produced responses to adaptive problem after adaptive problem associated with vertebrate vision. Each adaptation was closely coordinated with the next, resulting in the precision of the modern eye. Complex problems require complex solutions, and evolutionary psychologists reject the domain-general fitness-maximizing model of the human mind for this reason. (Also see Thornhill et al., chap. 6, this volume.)

Specificity of Mechanism. Frustrated by the black-box formulation of a general-purpose fitness maximizer, evolutionary psychologists argue for predominance of domain-specific mechanisms, providing some evidence of these in, for example, the realm of social contracts (Cosmides & Tooby, 1992). To date, the debate on this issue between behavioral ecological anthropology and evolutionary psychologists has been somewhat vague, perhaps representing yet another swing of the pendulum between general and specific learning mechanisms in psychology (Perusse, 1992b). Furthermore, the social contract evidence is open to strong criticism (Cheng & Holyoak, 1989; P. S. Davies, Fetzer, & Foster, 1995). Therefore, this issue is treated briefly here, although the implications for the study of populations in highly novel circumstances are taken up in more detail later.

Clearly, instructions that sculpt an organism perfectly and instantaneously into the optimal design required by each environment encountered, inherited as a trait "be an all-purpose fitness maximizer," would at best be inefficient and most probably impossibly complex (Cosmides & Tooby, 1987). However, the categorical conclusion that general mechanisms are an impossibility (Cosmides & Tooby, 1987) seems overstated, or at least poorly specified. The use of the vertebrate eye as a prototype for all adaptations is potentially misleading.

Other, rather elegantly "designed" and highly adaptive organs are polyfunctional and flexible, including the vertebrate liver and immune system, elephant trunks, and human hands. Although mechanisms must be domain-specific to some extent if they are to be efficient, evolutionary biologists commonly adhere to some notion of a hierarchy of mechanisms that become increasingly specific with respect to processing information relevant to particular environmental domains (R. D. Alexander, 1990). This position is clearly spelled out by Barkow (1989; see also Irons, 1990). Indeed, Tooby and Cosmides (1989c) recognized that the domain-specific, special-purpose mechanisms are most probably "organized into a coevolved, highly intricate architecture." Thus, one might expect some algorithms to coordinate decisions over big things, such as how much effort to devote to reproductive, as opposed to somatic, ends, and others to process specific information relevant to particular domains, such as whether to taste a novel food source. To make any more categorical assumptions than these is premature at this stage.

In summary, although it is clear that an appropriate characterization of how the mind works is critical to any serious advances within the evolutionary social sciences, little is known so far about the distribution of specificity and generality of purpose with respect to adaptive mechanisms.

E. Problem of Novel Environments

For how much of human history (or prehistory) can one assume that the environment has remained sufficiently unchanged for appropriate behavior to be elicited and genuine functional outcomes to be observed? This question about the flexibility of human responses to novel circumstances links closely to the issue of mechanism specificity, as can be seen in the later discussion of polyandry.

Specific-Purpose Mechanisms Fail in Novel Environments. A fundamental assumption of evolutionary psychology is that the human psyche is adapted to the conditions of the Pleistocene, that it has undergone only minor modification since that time, and that it is not well adapted to contemporary conditions (e.g., Symons, 1979; Tooby & Cosmides, 1989a; 1990b). This position is based on the observation that more of human evolution took place in Pleistocene than post-Pleistocene conditions. At the heart of this assumption lies another: Because specialized mechanisms, by definition, are triggered by a limited set of cues and cannot perform in more than one domain, such mechanisms inevitably fail in environments presenting modified cues. The implication of such assumptions is that contemporary behavior cannot be an adaptation. Thus, Symons (1989) argued that Tibetan polyandrous marital decisions are not adaptations, because none of the environmental features to which polyandry is currently a response (limited estates, monasticism, and taxation) existed in the Pleistocene.

The arguments with which behavioral ecological anthropology has countered these claims are now well rehearsed (e.g., Betzig, 1989; Irons, 1990; Turke, 1990), and can be summarized as follows. First, it is questionable to what extent the critical social conditions have been altered in post-Pleistocene conditions (e.g., R. D. Alexander, 1990); the gist of this argument is that the modern world is not so different from the Pleistocene as it might at first appear. Second, behavioral ecological anthropologists stress the acute methodological problems inherent in deducing the predominant selective conditions in a period long past and (most probably) highly variable in both spatial and temporal terms (e.g., Foley, 1988, 1995). Third, in ruling out as irrelevant all studies of contemporary societies, evolutionary psychology, to some extent, precludes any test of the alternative view—the hypothesis that the human psyche operates reasonably adaptively outside of the Pleistocene (Caro & Borgerhoff Mulder, 1987; Turke, 1990). Fourth, the position of evolutionary psychologists (as that of behavioral ecological anthropology) rests on the as yet unresolved assumptions concerning mechanism specifity and/or generality.

Consciousness and Planning. How individuals cope with novel environments can be thought about in different ways. R. D. Alexander (1990) suggested that every novel circumstance elicits the control of a combination of special and general-purpose mechanisms, rendering it less than inevitable that change in the environment will throw phenotypic development off course. As an example of a domain-general mechanism affording greater flexibility to novel environments, Alexander proposed consciousness, by means of which situations not previously encountered can be contemplated and planned for. Through such scenario-building, individuals can coordinate information derived from more specific mechanisms in the development of an appropriate strategic response. In short, Alexander viewed consciousness as a general-purpose mechanism evolved to coordinate responses to novel circumstances—novelty that no doubt characterized the Pleistocene, as well as later conditions.

Counter to this, Tooby and Cosmides (1990b) argued that even consciousness and planning offer no escape from the past. They stressed that an organism's perception of current environments is so heavily constrained by machinery evolved to deal with the recurrent structures of past environments that adaptive responses to novel conditions are unlikely. Hence, they argued that humans are "adaptation executors," not fitness maximizers (Tooby & Cosmides, 1990b), envisioning rationality as trapped in history.

The Cultural Adaptation. Cultural inheritance theorists have stressed the role of culture as a device for the rapid evolution of adaptations based on cultural selection to supplement natural selection. The Pleistocene was an environment of unusually rapid, noisy change; much of human psychology, at least as regards culture management, may be a product of adaptation to environmental chaos. The range extensions of modern humans during the late Pleistocene, and our dramatic ecological success in the Holocene, are evidence of human adaptive flexibility at the expense of adaptive precision, in terms of this argument. It follows that culturally determined behavior will often be approximately fitness maximizing under quite novel and recent circumstances. Thus, behavioral ecological anthropology hypotheses are always plausible candidates to explain behavior; even when they fail, they are an essential benchmark for comparison with competing hypotheses (see Borgerhoff Mulder, 1996; Voland, Dunbar, Engel, & Stephan, 1997).

Empirical Solutions. The primary value of this debate over the impact of novel environments has been to highlight that practically nothing is known of the potentially disruptive effects of novel conditions in any domain. Thus, it is not known at what point along the path from genotype to phenotype to reproductive consequences novel environments will interfere with the expression and fitness effects of adaptations (Turke, 1990), whether these environments really are novel in significant ways, nor how well cultural adaptations compensate for the effects of even highly novel environments. Consequently, empirical research is necessary on *both* the relationships between environmental cues and phenotypic expression, the goals of behavioral ecological anthropology and evolutionary psychology, and the relationships among cues, phenotypes, and proximate fitness currencies or estimates—the specific goal of behavioral ecological anthropology. Perusse's (1992a) study showed that a man's socioeconomic status (SES) is positively correlated with an estimate of the number of his potential conceptions, but not with overall reproductive success. This represents an interesting step in the direction of studying mechanism, function, and fitness differentials concurrently. Such studies are also very much in the direction of the process-level studies necessary to make the cultural inheritance theory approach more empirical.

Summary. Returning to Symons' arguments on polyandry, with which we opened this section, it seems entirely premature to rule out Tibetan marital decisions as adaptations on the grounds that environmental features to which polyandry is currently a response (limited estates, monasticism, and taxation) did not exist in the past. In fact, the limited data available on polyandry in foraging populations (LeVine & Sangree, 1980), nonhuman mammals, and birds (Clutton-Brock, 1991) suggest that mate-sharing occurs in situations of resource shortages that are more general than taxation, so that the mechanisms underlying polyandry are somewhat more general than supposed. Nevertheless, the whole debate about novel environments raises the critical question of how the environment is perceived.

CONCLUSIONS

This chapter discussed the tenets of three distinct, yet overlapping evolutionary approaches currently marshaled to explain what humans do. Throughout the 1980s, behavioral ecological anthropology was put on the defensive by challenges from evolutionary psychologists and cultural inheritance theorists. This chapter emphasized how these three fields share enough aspects to allow them to be comfortably characterized as different, complementary solutions to the same explanatory problem. Interestingly, their different emphases on the process of natural selection reflects, to some degree, the division within evolutionary biology—between population geneticists, for whom selection is a somewhat peripheral process, and organismic biologists, who are specially interested in adaptive puzzles. In the briefest of terms, among almost all evolutionary social scientists, the study of adaptation is important. However, there is controversy over how to conduct such study, and over how much attention to give to other evolutionary processes.

Behavioral ecological anthropology and evolutionary psychology differ on which aspect of the phenotype has been targeted as the focus of selective processes, leading to a further disagreement surrounding legitimate methods of investigation. It is tempting to invoke U.S. Supreme Court Justice Hugo Black's comment given in the famous ruling on pornography: "I do not know what (an adaptation) is but I know it when I see it!" Tongue-in-cheek aside, the sentiment is in fact true. All evolutionary social scientists are empiricists of some sort. It is observation of behavior that leads to speculation about adaptation. There can be no question that behavior forms at least some integral part of adaptive design. Even if functional design is found in control mechanisms (such as psychological ones), it seems clear that the best remedy for incorrectly identified functional design is the empirical discovery that the apparent reproductive impact of an adaptation in current material environments is not as expected.

Cultural evolutionary models have often been viewed as antithetical to conventional evolutionary social science (Flinn & R. D. Alexander, 1982) because of their analogical, as opposed to homological, use of selectionist thinking. However, cultural evolutionists necessarily acknowledge the role of natural selection on human decision makers, both in the recognition of genetic constraints on learning mechanisms (Boyd & Richerson's, 1985, "natural origins" assumption; see also Durham, 1991) and in the concern with the conditions under which different kinds of decision-making processes will predominate (Boyd & Richerson, 1985, chaps. 4 and 5, this volume; Durham's comparative modes of coevolution, chap. 9, this volume). Hence, cultural inheritance theory offers an important ontogenetic component to the behavioral ecological anthropology model, and suggests a powerful explanation for the occurrence of maladaptive behavior. Clearly, both analagous and homologous uses of evolutionary theory in its application to humans are warranted.

Historians of science remind us that successful science results from productive controversy, generating progressively better answers, leading to still more productive controversy. It is important to note how closely the debates among evolutionary social scientists resemble the debates that have animated 20th-century evolutionary biologists. All evolutionary social scientists agree that human evolution is complicated, especially due to culture. The potential existence of a number of rather exotic processes, by the standard of the basic fitness-optimizing model of natural selection, is clear. Researchers disagree over which processes are likely to be most important under what circumstances.

Levels of selection, whether culture is subject to selection directly, and the relative importance of natural selection on culture relative to the various kinds of cultural selection are all at issue. In biology, progress in resolving such questions is slow due to the complexity and diversity of organic evolution. However, the synthetic framework provided by the modern synthesis has helped focus debate and make controversy productive. Contention among behavioral ecological anthropology, evolutionary psychology, and cultural inheritance theory positions is likely to prove similarly productive. As in evolutionary biology, these are problems that can be addressed by reasonably straightforward empirical and theoretical methods.

ACKNOWLEDGMENTS

We are all exceedingly thankful to the University of Bielefeld for their invitation to ZiF, to the staff of the Centre for their unfailing cooperation and assistance during our stay, and particularly to Peter Weingart for his warm welcome and friendship to us all. This chapter was written in the summer of 1992. Although it has not been extensively updated in the intervening years, we believe the fundamental arguments, and particularly the grounds for compromise between evolutionary subdisciplines that we define, stand. We also note that the latest edition of the leading volume in the study of behavioral ecology (Krebs & Davies, 1997) includes for the first time a whole section on mechanism and extensive material on phylogeny and development. Clearly, synthesis is in the air!

PART III

ANALOGIES

INTRODUCTION: THE VALUE AND LIMITATIONS OF ANALOGIES FROM BIOLOGY IN THE STUDY OF CULTURE

In what sense is society like an organism or a population of organisms? In what way is the evolution of the state from less organized collectivities like the evolution of multicellular organisms from unicellular ones? In what way is the increase in frequency of nuclear families in modern Western societies like the change in frequency of light wing coloration in populations of peppered moths? Such questions mark the promise and raise the problems of analogies between the domains of biology and the social sciences.

This section argues that analogies have offered, and continue to offer, important resources for explaining sociocultural change. In our view, analogies are not just indicators of some shared properties—a linguistic category for descriptive or pedagogical enhancement. Rather, analogies are open-ended and interactive tools for raising questions, pointing to areas of study, and developing theories (see chap. 3). This distinguishes the analogical from the homological approach. In the points of view expressed in Part II, biology is used directly to explain the behavior of one particular lineage of primates. The question of how humans evolved specific adaptations appealed to the resources of biology as biology. In addition, human culture and institutions invite the use of biological analogies because of a number of more general and abstract similarities.

Biological evolution is a historical process subject to historical "accidents" or contingencies, and the operation of selective, random, self-organizing, and transmission processes. It produces complex adaptations built over time from simpler forms. Human culture and institutions are also historically changing and complex entities dependent on the transmission of information from generation to generation. The causal processes modeled in explaining biological evolution might find analogs in the processes operating in social evolution. The advantages of an analogical strategy include the illumination not only of further similarities, but also the recognition of substantial differences between the two domains compared. The analogies drawn between biological and cultural systems do not entail the reduction or subsumption of culture to biology. Analogies offer conceptual inspiration and methodological tools in a free spirit, compelling no more rigid adherence to the sources than is really useful.

Why do biological analogies have a certain *prima facie* plausibility? First, for all our peculiarities, the functional demands of human life are similar to those of any other organism. We use rather unusual means to accomplish the ordinary biological goals of surviving and reproducing in an environment. Part II, especially chapters 6 and 7, referred to functional homologies that give explanatory power to direct extensions of evolutionary reasoning to the human case. For the analogical project, we expect that the unique means humans use to adapt to, and interact with, environments by cultural and complex structural innovations will show many positive analogies to biological processes that serve the same or similar functions. Even where negative analogies turn out dominant, and differences in the two domains mostly preclude theoretical borrowing, seriously addressing the problem, starting with the possibility of positive analogy is likely to be an extremely useful process (see chaps. 7, 8, and 9), because the comparative question of why humans are so different in some respects from other animals is itself interesting and soluble only within a common conceptual framework.

Second, explanations of human behavior are fundamentally historical. Proximally, we behave as we do mostly because that is how our predecessors behaved. Ancient societies behaved differently from contemporary ones because of historical differences, and the diversity of contemporary societies is likewise a product of history. Such historical processes bear witness to the role of historical contingencies, accidents of style or habit, which, although not necessary, are nevertheless preserved through historical transformations alongside functional convergences and parallels. In the long run, the processes of history have shaped human behavior in response to the environment and other factors. But in the short run, culture and social institutions can explain much of individual behaviors (see chaps. 8, 9, and 10).

The biologist concerned with evolution, development, and ecology confronts the same epistemological problems of explaining historical phenomena as the social scientist. By contrast, most physical science disciplines are fundamentally ahistorical, or at any rate have only recently come to take history seriously. Thus, we would expect fewer analogical borrowings from physics or chemistry than from the essentially historical discipline of evolutionary biology (see chap. 10). Of course, the historical physical sciences, like geology, do play an important role in the study of evolution, including human evolution. The evolution of nonliving systems may also be a source of analogies, although without the functional similarities to living biological and cultural systems, positive analogies are less likely.

Third, both biological and sociocultural systems are complex. They exhibit part–whole relations, growth and development, differentiation, and specialization. The *superorganism* terminology used by Spencer (1873) marks the self-conscious analogy of complex society to the biological organism. Similar terminology has been employed by ecologists to describe the systemic complexity of ecological communities. The ontogenetic processes studied by developmental biologists and ecologists may also serve as resources for generating models of social complexity. In part, complexity may be the result of the multitude of weak causes operating jointly on historically entrenched elements in producing the effects we observe. Complex systems cannot, in the end, be treated as approximating simple masspoints subject to a single force. In this respect, biological organisms as products of physical and chemical constraints, phylogenetically induced structural constraints, environmental adaptive requirements, and the like are similar to historical, structural, adaptive, complex, sociocultural systems. In addition, *self-organization*—a process by which parts structure themselves into coherent wholes with the introduction of an external goal or force—has been proposed as modeling self-replication and genomic structure (Kauffman, 1993), as well as thermal convection phenomena (Nicolis & Prigogine, 1989) and social insect organization (Page & Mitchell, 1991; Seeley, Camazine, & Sneyd, 1992; Tofts & Franks, 1992). As an analogous set of complex behaviors, human societies may also be subject to their own self-organizational processes (see chap. 11).

One of the major criticisms leveled against the human sociobiological program was that it oversimplified in subsuming cultural change under the category of strictly organic evolution. Cultural evolution is based on the behavioral, institutionally mediated, transmission of behaviors, norms, and ideas, not on genetic replicators. However, Darwinian processes are not bound by the material structure of genes. For example, natural selection operates wherever there is heritable variation affecting fitness. Of course, we must operationalize the basic components of the selection process for culture: the units of variation, the units of selection, and cultural fitness. By using habits, rituals, and ideas as units of variation and selection, and focusing on the cultural inheritance system, the exploitation of the theoretical tools of population genetics becomes possible. This allows the construction of models explicitly incorporating major differences between genes and culture, but also makes extensive use of biological concepts and methods to the extent that analogies do exist (Boyd & Richerson, 1985; Cavalli-Sforza & Feldman, 1981). A considerable body of work stresses the formal similarities between the genetic system and the cultural system, recognizing the unique features of each and advocating a coevolutionary approach—mutual effects of the two inheritance systems on each other (for a comprehensive review of such theories and a detailed presentation of a coevolutionary theory, see Durham, 1991).

The basic differences between changing cultures and changing biological populations preclude mere subsumption. It is commonly understood that new cultural practices can be produced in direct response to perceived needs, unlike the randomly generated novelty in evolutionary processes. It is sometimes supposed that this process makes sociocultural theory in terms of the Darwinian model impossible. However, Darwin himself was a proponent of "inherited habits" and found no contradiction. The Darwinian modelers of cultural evolution have used terms such as *vicarious forces*, *epigenetic rules*, and *decision-making forces* to capture the Lamarckian properties of cultural evolution that are missing in the biological analog (Boyd & Richerson, 1985; D. T. Campbell, 1965; Lumsden & E. O. Wilson, 1981). As a result of combining active decision-making processes with transmission and natural selection, cultural features change at a faster rate than genetically controlled traits. Presumably, the faster tracking of variable environments is one of the adaptive advantages of culture; a system of culture perfectly analogous to genes would have had no advantages over that system, and would never have arisen.

Even more radically, some Darwinian theorists portray the interaction of genes and culture as a coevolutionary process in which cultural evolution is generally likely to play the leading or driving role. In the case of language, for example, biology has evolved to support a cultural system: However much language evolution may have been controlled by its organic substratum, language as a cultural feature has presumably been the leading and organic capacity, the lagging, variable in the coevolving system. Language capacity is an indirect adaptation that only makes sense in an environment where language is used. As a protolanguage evolved that strained some existing general- or dual-purpose organic capacity, the increasing advantages of language would generate a selection for a more elaborate organic capacity (see chap. 5; Velichkovsky & Rumbaugh, 1996).

It is hard to imagine the opposite scenario because, for the organic capacity to lead, it would have to be primarily an adapation to something else, with language being the passive by-product. The specificity of at least parts of the anatomical support for language makes this implausible. Indeed, it is often assumed that massive cultural capacities are the fundamental adaptation and main derived feature that distinguish humans from other primates. On this argument, most of our distinctive organic traits, like large brain size, are presumably a direct result of the potential inherent in cultural evolution. Proximally organic capacities may control cultural evolution, but ultimately the dynamics of cultural evolution control what capacities arise. At least the coevolutionary concept forces us to keep track of evolutionary dynamics of both parts of the system and think carefully about how they are related (see chap. 9).

Part of the promise of the analogical project for the social sciences lies in its potential to break the deadlock of theories of sociocultural change. These theories are the cornerstone of sociology and anthropology, as well as the other social sciences. Despite their central role and the plethora of attempts to arrive at a satisfactory level of sophistication, no such state has been achieved. All major theoretical programs in sociology, such as Spencerian evolutionism, Durkheim's theory of social differentiation, and Parsonian functionalism and its conflict theoretical derivatives, have met with criticism for their implicit or explicit progressivism, and their inability to account for processes of revolution, devolution, and disintegration. Responses to these shortcomings in the form of "primary factor" theories, such as Marx's class conflict, Weber's rationalization, Ogburn and Ellul's technological change, and Bell and Touraine's transition to postcapitalism, have shed light on particular areas of change (political, scientific, technological, social structural), and have provided insights of rich detail into partial processes of change. But they suffer from their assumptions of single factor and unidirectional causality. In particular, the transition from micro- to macrolevel processes remains largely unaccounted for (J. C. Alexander et al., 1987). Only recently has the unsatisfactory state of theoretical development in sociology with respect to the problem of social change, initiated renewed attempts on the level of general theory that respond to the issue of the micro–macro divide:

rational choice theory, theories of self-organization, and evolutionary theory.

Evolutionary theories of cultural change built by analogy with Darwinian theories of biology may prove to play a central role in the explanation of social change. To whatever extent human social behavior results from norms, habits, skills, world views, and similar culturally transmitted traditions and institutions, social change requires a theory of evolution. The incentive to clarify the processes and mechanisms of social development and change is high. In addition, there are many grounds on which the prima facie analogies between biological and sociocultural objects can be drawn. Thus, analogical projects are apt. A more detailed exploration of similarities and dissimilarities requires one to look more closely at the biological models available and their applicability in the social sciences. This strategy has already yielded important theoretical and empirical results.

WHAT KINDS OF ANALOGIES DOES BIOLOGY OFFER?

The dynamic processes that influence biological systems are rather diverse. A preliminary classification yields four mechanisms for change.

1. *Developmental processes.* Classically, developmental biologists study the dynamics of cell differentiation, tissue, growth, and organ growth in the embryo. Cognitive scientists have concentrated on behavioral development, both in the sense of anatomical maturation and learning, and other developmental responses to variable environments. Self-organization, which in general includes replication and feedback processes, also focuses on part–whole relationships. The units of analysis are individual and subindividual, and the time scale is one generation.

2. *Strategic interaction processes.* Individuals must make dynamic adjustments to each other's behavior (e.g., finding a place in a dominance hierarchy). Members of the same social group, conspecifics and other competitors, as well as predators and prey may all play "games" with each other. In some solitary species, these dynamics may be relatively simple and even unimportant. In social species, they are typically highly complex and important. For example, market mechanisms can create large-scale, complex games that dynamically integrate entire societies. The units of attention in biologists' studies of

game dynamics are individuals and small groups, and the time scales are a matter of hours to a generation.

3. *Ecological processes*. Populations grow, compete, prey on one another, extend their ranges, or go locally extinct. Collections of species on the landscape (ecologists' "communities") can change rather dramatically due to these processes. Typical units of analysis are species populations, and the time scales of interest are a few to many generations.

4. *Evolutionary processes*. The modern synthetic theory of organic evolution, based on combining Darwin's theory of evolution by natural selection (based on an analogy with human selection of plant and animal varieties) with the genetic theory of inheritance ("inheritance" is another analogy to a human social institution), describes this complex of dynamic biological processes. Due to the diversity and complexity of organisms, evolutionary biologists have produced a large and still rapidly growing body of theoretical and experimental work on Darwinian topics. The core of the discipline focuses on the evolution of gene frequencies or quantitative characters in terms of sexually reproducing populations subject to selection, mutation, and drift; but the variations on these themes are numerous. Units of analysis range from genes to populations, and the time scales are from a few to many generations.

In addition to biological dynamics, changes in the physical environment, such as climate change, play an important role in biotic change. The dynamics of the physical environment are no doubt important in processes of cultural change, but we doubt that much analogical borrowing from these fields will be helpful, at least compared with biology.

This conceptual taxonomy of dynamic processes is for convenience only, and is not meant to imply that processes that fall in different categories in the rather arbitrary scheme do not interact. In fact, every realistic example of cultural and organic evolution is a complex system of interacting dynamic processes. Epigenetic inheritance systems, such as the cultural system or the biological ones described by Jablonka (chap. 11), lead to a mixture of Darwinian and developmental dynamics. In the case of culture, the normally developmental process of individual learning is coupled with an inheritance system via socialization, and the cultural tradition is subject to the analog of Darwinian dynamics in biology. The analytical distinctions are meant to help clarify thinking about these processes, not to compartmentalize them and obscure interactions.

It is interesting to note that the biologists' taxonomy of processes differs from that common in the social sciences. Social scientists are inclined to think that a distinction between individual level and group or population level processes provides a more intuitive scheme than the one we use. The biologist's processes link levels. Delevopment is about how genes and cells mature into integrated individuals. Game dynamics is about how individual decisions are scaled up to produce aggregate outcomes (Coleman, 1991). Darwinian dynamics consider the interaction of genes, chromosomes, individuals, subpopulations, populations, and species, although classical studies would only consider two at a time for practical purposes. Ecological dynamics consider individuals, populations, multispecies assemblages, landscape level interactions among communities, and the globe as a whole, although, again, practical constraints limit any one study. Geophysical studies are typically multiunit.

In all four types of dynamics, it is common to postulate links between levels, as well as downward causation from larger scale units to smaller ones. For example, in ecology, population density commonly affects individual behavior, and vice versa. One of the useful things that analogies sometimes put on the table is a cross-cutting view of the nature of the process. From the natural scientists' point of view, the debates between methodological individualism and collectivism, and the erection of a seemingly intractable dichotomy between macro and micro explanations, seem quite artificial. This does not neccessarily mean that natural scientists have easy answers to classical social science problems. Rather, the viewing of long-standing problems with novel concepts and methods always has some promise, if any analogies at all can be found.

COMPLEXITY AND INTERACTION BETWEEN PROCESSES

The distinctions between types of biological processes are only analytical, of course. In most biological phenomena, more than one—if not all four, plus physical environmental change—are intimately involved. Suppose we are interested in the evolution of a particular species by Darwinian processes. Developmental dynamics are a critical bridge between the genes that are transmitted, and the phenotype on which selection falls.

Selective forces can certainly be generated due to individuals' places in their social system and larger ecological community, as determined by game and ecological dynamics. Geophysical processes are also a classic source of selective pressures, and driving variables for community change due to ecological processes responding to physical change. In principle, and often in fact, evolutionary change is the outcome of an interaction among all four types of processes.

Making such distinctions has been critical to scientific progress, as Falk and Jablonka illustrate in chapter 11 with respect to developmental and evolutionary processes. Late 19th-century biology had reached an impasse because the two were confounded conceptually. Important advances were made when the earlier Mendelians realized that the questions had to be separated.

Theorizing in biology did not stop with Darwin, however. There are recent and somewhat controversial issues that may provide useful insights concerning analogous reasoning in the social sciences. One is a revival of the proposal that changes in DNA can be directed, and a suggestion that, in addition to the DNA inheritance system, epigenetic inheritance systems operate at the cellular level and are important in ontogeny and evolution (Jablonka & Lamb, 1989). These developments demonstrate that the environment can simultaneously be the agent of both variation and selection, and point to the complexity of the "evolutionary game," which has to accommodate different inheritance systems and different units of variation and evolution.

There is little doubt that the environment is sometimes the inducer of specific variations, as well as the agent of selection, although there is an ongoing controversy as to the interpretation of this phenomenon (for recent criticisms and reviews, see Foster, 1992; Lenski & Mittler, 1993). The false dichotomy between nature and nurture, heredity and environment, is exposed in a particularly forceful and challenging manner. In addition to the DNA inheritance system based on the precise replication of DNA strands, there are also epigenetic inheritance systems in cells, which are of fundamental importance in multicellular organisms. These are the systems responsible for what is commonly called *cellular memory*—the persistence through cell divisions of differences in functional and structural states of cells with identical DNA. Different cell types are generated from the fertilized egg, and the various determined states are transmitted through many cell divisions (skin cells remain skin cells, kidney cells remain kidney cells, etc.), despite the absence of the stimuli that induced these characters during the development.

Some of the biochemical mechanisms responsible for the preservation of functional states are becoming increasingly well understood (see Jablonka, Lachmann, & Lamb, 1992, for a review and discussion of the various epigenetic inheritance systems); in some cases, there is evidence that epigenetic features such as chromatin marks can be transmitted between generations of individual cells. The heritable epigenetic variations often occur in response to environmental stimuli, and are often clearly directed, although nonspecific random epigenetic variations are also common and important. It is clear that *Lamarckian evolution* may prove to be more adequate and promising for modeling cultural evolution than models of conventional neo-Darwinian evolution.

These concrete proposals exemplify a point made repeatedly by Darwinians (e.g., D. T. Campbell, 1975; Dawkins, 1982). It is a mistake to identify biological models with a narrow set of standard textbook examples. Biotic systems are complex and diverse, and surprising new phenomena emerge regularly. Given the differences between humans and standard textbook biological systems, we might expect the closest analogies to human culture and social organization to appear in exceptional places, such as non-Mendelian inheritance systems and species with complex societies like those of social insects.

Aside from the vast and currently rapid advances in the understanding of biological dynamics of all kinds since Darwin, some social scientists' frustrations with biological analogies appear to stem from mistaking the method of using simple models for heuristic purposes or the claim that complex processes can actually be reduced to simple models. Much as in economics, the heuristic use of simple models as tools to study an obviously much more complex reality should not be mistaken for the claim that biological phenomena actually are simple, or that sociocultural phenomena are ontologically simple (see chap. 3).

CONVERGENT INVESTIGATIONS FROM OTHER TRADITIONS

The deductive argument of the Darwinian theory of culture is that cultural evolution is inherently a system evolving at the population level with essential similarities to organic evolution (see chaps. 8, 9, and 10). One kind of empirical support for this claim is that social scientists have independently developed research programs with close parallels to those employed by evolutionary biologists, although their application remained less formal than in biology and they did not spread beyond particular local research traditions to the extent known in biology. In fact, most of the basic methods needed for a critical empirical analysis of the processes of cultural evolution already exist in one social science subdiscipline or another. Thus, it is demonstrably practical and logically appealing to use Darwinian concepts and methods as one major set of tools to achieve a common theoretical framework for the social sciences.

We illustrate this claim with a fairly detailed discussion of one research program—sociolinguistics—and a briefer characterization of several other, equally important areas. According to sociolinguists (Wardhaugh, 1992), the key issue in language evolution is whether small-scale, interindividual variation in people's speech is theoretically significant. Classical linguists, of whom Chomsky (1975b) is a modern representative, distinguish between competence to speak a language and the performance produced by the actual language individuals. Such linguists believe that evolution of language competence, a knowledge of the essential rules of a language, is widely shared by speakers and is invariant among speakers of a given language. Individual differences in performance are taken to be minor departures from the rules defined by competence, and are of little interest to linguists. By contrast, sociolinguists hypothesize that patterned variation between speakers occurs at all levels, and that what ultimately become major changes in language originate in small variations pioneered by small groups of speakers. For sociolinguists, the distinction between competence and performance is overdrawn at best; much small-scale variation in "performance" is patterned by microdialectal "competences" that are often controlled by only a small segment of the larger speech community.

Note that this debate closely parallels Mayr's (1982) distinction between essentialism and population thinking. For classical linguists, it seems that ideal abstract rules define a language, just as many biologists before Darwin thought that essential invariant forms defined a species. For essentialists, the variation of individual specimens was just failure to conform to the essential type. On this hypothesis, the process by which new forms arise is difficult to imagine and unlikely to be observed, because somehow the whole speech community or species has to leap to the new form all at once. Indeed, classical linguists (e.g., de Saussure, 1959) argued that linguistic evolution is unobservable.

Like Darwin, sociolinguists invert essentialist logic. According to the population thinking view, small-scale variation is the raw material out of which large-scale change is gradually built by evolutionary processes. This hypothesis, if true, also makes evolutionary processes observable, because the patterns and dynamics of everyday events that affect small-scale variation in "performance" are easily observable. If it is plausible that one can account for the large-scale changes between languages (or species) by the accumulation of observable small-scale changes, a satisfactory evolutionary account is possible, even if direct observation of large-scale change is difficult.

Sociolinguists have built a strong empirical case for their populational hypothesis. Labov (1972, 1980) conducted the most promising research program in this tradition. His methods involved collecting samples of speech from a speech community by tape-recording and analyzing phonological (pronunciation, dialect) variation. For example, he studied the pronunciation of the diphthongs in words like *out* and *house* on Martha's Vineyard, an island off the coast of Massachusetts, and the patterns of use or nonuse of *r* in words like *car* in New York City.

In Labov's study on Martha's Vineyard, it was possible to use dialect survey work from the 1930s to directly verify that today's older speakers still use much the same variants they used as young people. Thus, the more extreme forms of diphthongs used by young Martha's Vineyard speakers today can confidently be attributed to a microevolution of dialect.

In cases where a dialect is "in motion," variation is typically highly patterned with regard to sociological variables, from which the causes of language change can be inferred. There are no simple generalizations about dialect microevolution. Labov (1972) listed 13 separate dynamic processes implicated in sound changes. Two of the most important primary causes of change—change from below and hypercorrection from above—can serve as examples. In the case of change from below, language is part of a complex of markers of local identity. On Martha's Vineyard, most residents earn a living by catering to the whims of tourists and wealthy summer residents from the mainland. Most people do not particularly like this social situation, and admire the lifestyle and independent ways of the few islanders that earn a living by fishing. As a by-product of admiring fishermen, islanders imitate their patterns of speech. Although it is not a conscious process, fishermen act as leaders of dialect evolution, pushing Martha's Vineyard diphthongs toward values quite different from the mainland standard dialect. Change from below is usually led by groups with a strong sense of localism, usually meaning the lower middle or upper working class; the Martha's Vineyard example is typical of this pattern. Both higher and lower classes tend to eventually follow changes led by these innovating groups.

An increase in the use of *r* in New York speech is an example of hypercorrection from above. Many New Yorkers, especially middle-class women, view the relatively *r*-less dialect of New York as undesirably lower class. In an effort to conform to prestige norms that they only imperfectly control, they tend to use even more *r* than upper class speakers actually use. Hypercorrection pushes the standard dialect toward ever greater exaggeration of the form originally perceived as marking prestige. Interestingly, in England, *r*-less speech is perceived as marking prestige, and the hypercorrection from above mechanism works in the opposite direction to that in New York.

Sociolinguistic studies provide impressive documentation of the utility of a non-essentialist, populational approach to the study of culture change and the functions of cultural variation. Studies such as Labov's have many technical weaknesses, such as relatively small sample size, that limit their utility. More important, like the studies of many field biologists, crucial elements of a truly complete study of evolutionary dynamics are missing (see Brandon, 1990, for a discussion of the sort of arduous standards an ideal study would have to meet). The transmission processes and intimate, individual level psychological processes involved in developing a dialect variant and using it are not addressed directly in most of this work. For example, it would be useful to study the details of dialect development during childhood and adolescence to directly observe the "decisions" that speakers make as they learn their dialect.

Other bodies of empirical work with strong Darwinian analogies include:

1. *Historical linguistics.* As is covered in more detail in chapter 11, the investigation of the longer run patterns of cultural evolution is well developed in the case of language. Other areas of history, for example the history of technology, involved in the reconstruction of the development of well-controlled items of culture often closely resemble similar studies in biology.

2. *Studies of the diffusion of innovations.* Rogers' (1971) classic meta-analysis of some 1,200 empirical studies of the diffusion of innovations is still a useful source of inspiration regarding mechanisms of cultural change. Most such studies describe the spread of successful technical innovations such as hybrid corn seed within a community (less frequently, the failure of an unsuccessful innovation to spread). Causal processes are inferred from the patterns generated by the patterns of spread, and from questionnaire data designed to elicit reasons for adoption or nonadoption directly. There is ample evidence that "perceived advantage" is commonly considered important in adoption decisions. There are also abundant cases in which the effects of "opinion leadership" by prestigious individuals influences the adoption or nonadoption of innovations. As with sociolinguistics, studies of the diffusion of innovations resemble evolutionary biologists' field-based studies of microevolution.

3. *Controlled studies of social learning.* Bandura and Walters (1963) and coworkers (Rosenthal & Zimmerman, 1978) pioneered the controlled laboratory study of social transmission in humans. A rather large body of work has developed in this tradition, which is the rough analogue to classical Mendelian transmission genetics in humans. As useful as this literature may be, many theoretically interesting questions have not been addressed. The focus of social learning theory has been cognitive and not populational, and the questions driven by the population level consequences of social learning have been comparatively neglected in otherwise admirable studies.

4. *Controlled laboratory studies of cultural evolution.* Jacobs and D. T. Campbell (1961) first demonstrated such a method. A small number of individuals form the initial population; as "generations" proceed in the experiment, original individuals are removed and new, naive individuals are added. Typically about three complete replacements of individuals occur in the course of an experiment. Although relatively few studies in this tradition have been conducted, some of the experiments have been quite ambitious and yielded striking results. Insko et al. (1983), who are social psychologists, attempted to test theories of the evolution of division of labor and stratification drawn from anthropology. The authors showed quite dramatic evolutionary change for their groups, and quite different results in an open trade (functionalist) versus a coercive (conflict-theoretic) experimental treatment. For example, a subjectively legitimate form of leadership arose in the

open trade case, and a conflict-ridden, classlike form arose in the coercive treatment. These studies are rather similar to "population cage" methods, which *Drosophila* population geneticists and others have used since the 1920s to investigate microevolution.

5. *Statistical analysis of large data sets.* Several research traditions in social science analyze sets of data in which some human behavior relevant to the dynamic properties of cultural evolution is studied. For example, demographers often analyze birth and death rates as functions of sociological variables. In a few cases, the cultural heritability of a trait is known well enough to estimate from such studies what some components of the "fitness" of a cultural trait might be. The best case is religious preference, where transmission is largely vertical and where conversion rates are sometimes known (e.g., Janssen & Hauser, 1981). It has been suggested that several multigeneration panel studies might be quite suitable for an evaluation of properties of cultural evolution (James Chisholm, personal communication).

6. *Animal social learning studies.* Comparative psychologists and ethologists have done a considerable amount of work on animal "protoculture" (Heyes & Galef, 1996). It is an open question how closely most well-studied examples of animal social learning resemble human culture (Laland et al., 1993; Tomasello, Krueger, & Ratner, 1993), but one day good animal models of social transmission may be added to the spectrum of methodological tools used to study human culture.

Although this list can be extended, this brief and limited survey should be sufficient to remove doubts that important parallels between biological and cultural processes exist. In principle, these analogies imply a common Darwinian science of evolution, with a considerable two-way flow of ideas between students of human peculiarities like culture and the larger science as applied mainly to the genetic system in all its complexity and diversity. Because of a history of much stronger commitment to Darwinian analysis in biology, compared with the social sciences, the flow of tools in this area will be mostly from biology to social science for some time to come. The same is not true in the realm of game dynamics, where the development of sophisticated theories of individual decision making and stategic interaction was largely in the hands of social scientists until biologists recently began to borrow these tools and apply them to animal behavior (e.g., Krebs & Davies, 1978; Maynard Smith, 1982).

CONCLUSION

The chapters in this part detail the role that rigorous analogical theorizing can play in addressing traditional problems of the social sciences. By advocating such a strategy, it is clear that we are not importing wholesale a set of models completely foreign to at least some of the scientific work already being pursued in the social sciences. Rather, the analogical approach is warranted by the argument of structural similarities between biological and sociocultural processes. It is often compatible with assumptions already employed in social science explanations, although part of the value of analogies is to challenge traditional, even cherished, perspectives. The indroduction of analogies that ultimately prove useful are bound to discomfort and anger traditionalists, and we feel no need to make a particular apology for this inevitable result. Nevertheless, we do not advocate simplistic answers to traditional social science problems that trade on shock value merely for the fun of it. We do advocate a methodology for detecting the differences between biological and social processes, and for developing and refining social evolutionary theories to explain culture and social institutions. Biology is frequently a useful starting point, source of tools, or basis for creative inspiration in this project. As indicated at the onset, analogies allow for the exploration of descriptive, dynamic, and explanatory similarities across disciplinary boundaries. Similarity is, of course, a symmetrical relationship. Hence, the fruitfulness of an analogical strategy is not limited to one direction of influence. Our approach to the analogical strategy allows for a rich network of theoretical borrowings to be possible from biology to social sciences, and from social sciences to biology.

8

UNITS OF CULTURE, TYPES OF TRANSMISSION

Peter Weingart
University of Bielefeld
Germany

Robert Boyd
University of California
Davis

William H. Durham
Stanford University
Stanford

Peter J. Richerson
University of California
Davis

Cultural heritage has a broad series of positive analogies to biological processes, but confusion due to negative analogies is quite real. The aim of this chapter is to show how exploration of positive analogies can help illuminate the study of culture without undue confusion due to dissimilarities between the two kinds of inheritance systems. Generalizing the concept of inheritance from the perspective of evolutionary biology draws attention to two elements: what is transmitted and how it is transmitted. In the classic biological case, these topics are the provinces of genetics and population genetics, respectively. Of course, there is no way to draw a clean distinction between the basic elements or units of an inheritance system and the patterns of transmission that generate population level effects, which are, in turn, the focus of the interaction of inheritance systems with environments that produce the actual forces of evolutionary change. This chapter presents taxonomies of both, and discusses their implications when applied to culture. The next chapter turns to the main processes of change.

As noted earlier, biology is a rich and complex source of analogies. The classic rough similarity between culture and the textbook diploid sexual system of genetic inheritance is the most rudimentary starting point. Biologists sometimes have to address the role of inheritance systems that are quite different from genes. For example, animals exhibit simple systems of social learning (protoculture). Many systems of reproduction besides the standard obligate-sexual diploid pattern are common. Such systems require quite different treatment than genes, and provide some interesting hints about how we might think about the more complex human systems. Human culture is also diverse. There is no guarantee that the transmission of language and skills such as archery or bicycle riding is exactly similar. What is advocated here is not a simple, formalistic application of stereotyped biological models to culture, but rather considering human culture in a broadly comparative framework, in which a great diversity of inheritance systems is a fit subject for interdisciplinary theorizing, based on a disciplined use of analogy.

UNITS OF CULTURE

William H. Durham and Peter Weingart

A. Theoretical Desiderata

The qualities required for purposes of theory construction form two sub-categories: features assumed and required by the selective retention framework, and features required by prevailing culture theory in the social sciences (see e.g., Shweder & LeVine, 1984). Taking the former first, selective retention models assume that cultures are assemblages of subunits, each of which has the requisite properties of a "replicator" (or, more specifically, an "active germ-line replicator"; see Dawkins 1982). Dawkins (1982, [1976]1989) summarized these features as *fecundity* (i.e., the capacity for successful replication among culture carriers), *longevity* (the capacity of persistence through repeated replication), and *fidelity* (the capacity for relatively accurate replication). Hull (1982) added a further useful distinction between *replicators* (entities that are copied directly) and *interactors* (entities that interact directly with environments, causing differential replication). Following Hull, this chapter distinguishes between the cultural entities (the replicators) and their human carriers (the interactors), focusing attention on the fecundity, longevity, and fidelity of the former.

Dawkins proposed these properties as general features required for any system of entities to evolve through differential replication, including cultural systems. Although they are necessary to any satisfactory unit of culture, they are also insufficient if evolutionary culture theory is to link up with other forms of culture theory in the social sciences. Therefore, we would add a number of additional theoretical desiderata to Dawkins' list.

First, a bona fide unit of culture must have conceptual or ideational reality. Such units will certainly influence specific behaviors and cultural traits through the cultural analogue of what biologists call *epigenetic processes*—processes that connect genes with their phenotypic effects. Indeed, in empirical work, units of culture may best be known or inferred from their visible, phenotypic manifestations; moreover, in many instances, they may not exist apart from behaviors and everyday practice. But this point remains: Much of culture is premises and understandings that neither inhere in, nor map isomorphically onto, behaviors (e.g., see Durham, 1991). Certain premises or understandings affect *all* behaviors exhibited by an individual or group, and certain behaviors have different meanings between groups. To reduce culture to observable behavior is to ignore its critical generative dimension—a mistake roughly tantamount to treating genes as traits and ignoring pleiotropy, dominance, and other developmental complexities of the gene–phenotype connection.

Second, and equally important, a bona fide unit of culture must have a history of social transmission. By most accounts, a history of social transmission is the defining feature of "culture": It is this that makes conceptual/ideational information "cultural." The point is not academic—because in the newly emerging subfield of "evolutionary psychology," *culture* has been defined instead as "any mental, behavioral, or material commonalities shared across individuals ... regardless of why these commonalities exist" (Tooby & Cosmides, 1992, p. 117). By this definition, something can be construed as fully "cultural" *without* any history of social transmission; it is then said to be "evoked culture." To reduce confusion, we stick with "history of social transmission" as a requisite feature of cultural units.

Third, a unit of culture must be an embedded, component part of a greater conceptual system—the "culture" from which it comes. Thus, it must exhibit the properties of what hierarchy theorists call a *holon*, embodying a "dual tendency to preserve and assert its individuality as a [quasi-independent] whole, *and* to function as an integrated part of (an existing or evolving) larger whole" (T. H. F. Allen & Starr, 1982, p. 9). In effect, units of culture are never truly independent, even if, in the name of tractability, models of culture may make that assumption. We view recognition of their place in the greater cultural system, with all the constraints and ramifications that may entail, as a required feature of a cultural unit.

To many culture theorists, the essential defining feature of culture is the meaning of "X" to its practitioners—what it "says" and "stands for," what makes it important and convincing to the locals (for two classic examples, see Geertz, 1973; L. A. White, 1949). This means that the unit of culture should incorporate culture's important symbolic dimension. According to this view, it is not enough to include within the unit simply the instruction "how to do X," where X is some phenotypic manifestation like technology or behavior. To account for the emergence of "meaning," it seems helpful to assume that the communication of mental images through language and related imitative capacities builds up structures and memory, both in individual brains and between individuals that continuously select new experience. By this, the essence of "culture" is created by the continuous flow of communication of mental images among members of communicating populations of different generations; a "social memory" is created. The "evolution" of mental images is due to the process of transmission among individuals. Here, the rule applies that the symbols must be precise enough to allow interindividual communication and flexible enough to allow variation. There must be sufficiently overlapping experiences so that meaning can be conveyed. Most important, this dissolves the spurious contradiction among individuals as "members" of a culture and "culture" as "external" to individuals. This property of cultural units is currently the most needing conceptual clarification, if the claims of symbolic anthropologists are to be modeled.

One can also make the case that an extended debate over units of cultural transmission, although important, is premature (Boyd & Richerson, 1985). This position is based on two related points: one theoretical and one empirical.

The theoretical point is that a (generically) Darwinian analysis of evolution is appropriate, given almost any kind of inheritance system, as Dawkins argued. As long as culture acts as a system that maintains heritable variation at some level or another, the population level processes that Darwinian methods are designed to model will be important. Roughly, if a character is influenced by a large number of independent genes, with small additive effects on the expression of the value of the trait expressed by individuals, inheritance approaches the kind of blending system that Darwin imagined by finite approximation. Under the influence of mutation, or perhaps some other process, variation can be maintained in such systems. In the case of culture, both discrete-valued, unit-like inheritance and purely blending quantitative models lead to perfectly consistent theories. Furthermore, other schemata of inheritance are quite possible. It is often possible to show that the outcome of evolutionary processes is not very sensitive to the exact mechanism by which heritable variation is maintained. Often quantitative character models with blending lead to the same general conclusions as discrete-valued characters.

The empirical point is that social scientists have not yet devoted much effort to the characterization of the details of how culture is socially transmitted and stored in brains. Thus, debate about the nature of the units of culture has a somewhat scholastic flavor.

Linguistics is the most advanced field in this regard, and a rather elegant theory of the linguistic category was recently proposed (Lakoff, 1987). If Lakoff and like-minded coworkers are correct, the linguistic unit is a rather ramshackle assemblage of meanings anchored by common sense prototypes, but extended metaphorically by various principles to related usages. This structure is apparently very unlike genes.

Unfortunately, essentially nothing is known about how even linguistic categories are built up during ontogeny or over evolutionary history. Surely, many individuals contribute, but little is known of the number or their roles. How much individual level variation is there? Is there more variation for recent, rarely used, or more abstract parts of the category relative to core prototypes? Are meanings inherently discrete or continuous, or is this analogy with genetics useful? How tightly linked are the submeanings of a word to each other? Do linguistic concepts come in linked multiconcept packages? The answers to such questions can be given for the basic Mendelian elements of the genomes of most types of organisms, but they are essentially unanswered for culture.

B. Units Come with Assumptions

The problem of identifying a consensual definition of *culture* is only amplified by efforts to build evolutionary models that presume to represent cultural change with some degree of generality, and thus to "capture" the most basic or widely agreed on features of culture within their arguments.

Most of the models are built as analogies to classical population genetics, and thus are built on the assumption of "interchangeable parts" in culture that are analogous to the interchangeable genes and alleles of population genetics. As a result, the main general properties of culture must be accommodated by evolutionary models, and many of those properties must also inhere in the small "pieces of culture" that make the theory work. Advocates of modeling justifiably argue that there is nothing wrong with such an approach, so long as it is understood that the provisional models bracket and perhaps even distort the "true" nature of cultural units.

A study of culture used in the literature confirms that recent models of cultural evolution automatically build in substantial assumptions about culture through the choice of units and unit-based processes that are used to represent it. Sometimes the units are only vaguely described, leaving important features to be filled in by inference or guesswork, and sometimes explicit discussion is avoided altogether. Nonetheless, substantial assumptions about culture and social organization are built into these models through overt or covert assumptions about units and unit-based processes. Willy-nilly, models of cultural evolution (including those of the authors of this chapter) that work like models in classical population genetics give rise to the following kinds of assumptions about cultural processes.

First, existing models assume that cultural evolutionary change results from the differential propagation of cultural phenomena within and between human populations (which are, in turn, assumed to be recognizably distinct and bounded entities). Other kinds of processes—like the biological reproduction of culture carriers, or the differential persistence of social institutions—are assumed to have influence only to the extent that they impinge on the differential propagation of cultural phenomena per se.

Second, existing models assume that cultural evolution can be modeled by examining change in one or a few "focal features" at a time. That is to say, current models approach cultural systems as divisible into discrete properties (variously taken as "traits," "beliefs," etc.), which are then treated as real and distinct components of the given culture. Interactions among a small number of such entities have been modeled, but not enough to qualify as the "systemic" or "holistic" approach deemed essential by other theorists. However, advocates of models hold that whenever "linkage" between small units can be made explicit it can also be modeled.

Third, most current models feature decision making—that is, repeated human choice among variable units—as an important, if not *the* important, mechanism of change. This assumption carries with it important ramifications, not fully appreciated at present, if only because powers of decision-making are far from uniformly distributed in human populations. As a result, social structure plays a pivotal role in the direction and rates of cultural change guided by decision processes. It follows that the success of decision-making models of cultural evolution will depend both on adequate identification and delineation of the social structure of decision-making, and on satisfactory definition of the "variants" available as choices to those who decide. Both are essential. Thus, there is a need for models that explicitly incorporate the social structure of decision-making, transforming the amorphous populations of genetic models into the stratified, political entities that are appropriate for culture. There is also a need for more attention to the qualities one should expect in a useful, operational "unit of culture." This chapter focuses on the second of these needs.

C. Units of Culture—A Survey and Assessment

First suggestions of "units of culture" appeared at least as early as 1945 (Herskovits, 1945), and since then some 50 different concepts have been put forward . The increase of such attempts may indicate the growing discontent with the holistic tradition of the analysis of culture, as well as the interest in applying evolutionary theory. Another trend, although much less clear in quantitative terms, is the turn to mental states (i.e., cognitive units), which occurs under the impact of the cognitive and brain sciences on anthropology (already diagnosed by Keesing [1974] over 20 years ago). To the extent that this development affects anthropology as a whole, it also reflects the discipline's turn away from sociology toward evolutionary biology.

Stuart-Fox (1986) summarized this trend in a classification of three categories of units of cultural replication: (a) cultural "traits" with a material basis, (b) behavioral units, and (c) mental aspects. The most compelling rationale to proceed to mental states is the argument that both behavioral and material aspects of culture are "phenotypic expressions of the mental aspect of culture as this is appropriated in individual minds" (Stuart-Fox, 1986, p. 73). Given the sizable body of literature on units, each of these categories comprises quite heterogeneous conceptualizations. Although it is not feasible to treat each one separately, we would slightly revise the classification.

The categories do not delineate all the proposed units (i.e., some are compounds of several categories). With these qualifications in mind, the classification can also be read as the postulated development from holistic to "atomistic" notions of culture, from a phenomenological to an analytical level of observation, although this does not hold for the actual development in time.

Artifacts.   Artifacts as units of culture are probably closest to 19th- and early 20th-century anthropology. They have also led to cross-fertilization between anthropology and history of technology, and have informed sociological/historical theories of social change (L. White, 1962). In older studies, no attempts were made to conceptualize them in the framework of evolutionary theory. In evolutionary studies, artifacts are usually connected with other items (or units) of culture, or the term (cultural) *artifact* is meant to include material objects and structures, organizations, ideas, customs, and languages (Boulding, 1978; D. H. Fischer, 1989; Pulliam & Dunford, 1980).

Taken in its pure form, the paradigmatic case of artifacts is a tool or a technology. The obvious and most fundamental problem is that technologies do not self-replicate without human intervention. This led Cavalli-Sforza and Feldman (1981) to distinguish between first-order organisms (humans) and second-order organisms (artifacts), and to postulate that Darwinian fitness of the latter is dependent on the cultural selection by the former. Clearly, this complication is reason enough to proceed from the level of artifacts to that of ideas and knowledge.

A further problem concerns the level of analysis. Technologies have to be classified on a phenomenological level; any attempts to isolate core principles or mechanisms of construction have engaged analysts in underdetermined, thus fruitless genealogies. The issues of identity, composite elements, and boundaries are far from unambiguous.

Finally, the fact that artifacts are always taken in conjunction with other items or "units" suggests that there is no support to the thesis that "cultural evolution" could be sufficiently explained in terms of the genealogy of artifacts. However, it is a matter of pragmatics to take artifacts as the unit of analysis, much like evolutionary studies of phenotypic traits in biology, simply because the artifacts are available and observable, whereas the ideas underlying them are not. The problem of observability and the risks of inferences from phenotype to "genotype" underlies the entire "units-of-culture" enterprise.

Behavior. "Behavior" as a unit of culture has been propagated in many variations, and reflects the position of anthropology between its traditional neighbor, sociology, and behavioral genetics. R. D. Alexander (1979) spoke of "traits of culture" that can be imitated, plagiarized, or taught. Durham (1976) took "practices retained as the result of socialization and teaching based upon the previous experience of others'" (p. 94) as units, Murdock (1971) spoke of "shared habits" that constitute a culture, and Kottack (1971) distinguished "sociocultural forms" that are "actual behavior patterns." Behavioral components also appear in definitions of units such as Lumsden and E. O. Wilson's (1981) "culturgens," and Pulliam and Dunford's (1980) "cultural traits."

"Behavior" as a unit of culture shares practically all of the problems that were listed for artifacts. First of all, delineating behavioral patterns is dependent on phenomenological classification which is fraught with dangers of misinterpretation given the intentionality and symbolic nature of behavior. At best, only the subset of automatic reflexes (e.g., cough, sneeze) seems to be unequivocally comparable across cultural boundaries.

Typically, the rationale for choosing behavior as a unit is the mechanism of its transmission (i.e., imitation and learning) and observability. But behavior has a mental basis, however implicit. The phenotype–genotype relationship between behavior and its mental basis cannot be assumed to be a one-to-one expression, which leads into even more severe complexities, as in genetics proper. The more meaning-laden and socially interrelated with others' behaviors, the more explicit is the mental processing that takes place.

Cognitive Units: Ideas and Mental States. Because of the derived nature of behavior and artifacts, one can discern an apparent trend toward ideational or cognitive definitions of units of culture. This trend was even preceded by a move from overt to abstract behavior; that is, to "control mechanisms—plans, recipes, rules, instructions—for the governing of behavior" (Geertz, cited in Keesing, 1974). Thus, the common denominator of ideational or cognitive units is to be seen in their role as determining behavior (i.e., their belonging to the informational paradigm).

Examples are abundant. Bajema (1978) defined *culture* as "nongenetic information about the environment that is stored, interpreted, utilized, and transmitted via the brain" (p. 48), and that establishes a direct analogy between the gene as the basic unit of information in the genetic system and the "idea" in the cultural system. Cavalli-Sforza (1971) took "a new idea" as the "equivalent of a mutant in sociocultural evolution," R. D. Masters' (1970) "verbal or cultural symbol pools" fall in this category, as do Pulliam and Dunford's (1980) "cultural traits" and Richerson and Boyd's (1978) "culture type," as the cultural message inherited by an organism from other individuals. In an attempt to draw on connectionism and Johnson-Laird's concept of mental models, Bloch (1990) pointed to the role of nonlinguistic knowledge, which, to the extent that its transmission is known at all, is learned through imitation of, and tentative participation in, practices. With this, he revived in different guise the idea of implicit or tacit knowledge.

Although there is some overlap with other definitions, these "cognitive" units can be said to be within a class, insofar as the focus of conceptualization is on an informational causation of behavior. Thus, they also include various notions of "standards," "rules," "beliefs," and so on. In some analogies, information/knowledge is taken to be the genotype and the resulting behavior the phenotype. A further attribute is that they are shared; this explains, to the extent that it exists, homogeneity of behavior. This reasoning follows the paradigm of information theory, according to which, in crude terms, the content of an information is unambiguous and leads to the same, or similar, reactions. In this context, "meaning" accrues from the fact that the information or knowledge is shared.

In essence, the definitions of ideational or cognitive units of culture represent a continuum ranging from implicit nonverbal to explicit systematic knowledge. The application of evolutionary theory to the development of knowledge is, of course, the concern of evolutionary epistemology. A selected number of problems are obvious and have been raised before. The delineation of an idea or element of knowledge is as unclear as the possibility of comparing ideas with respect to importance and descent (i.e., their interrelatedness and meaning; Hull, 1982). In particular, the informational assumption that an idea means the same or a sufficiently similar thing to everyone in different situations is questionable. This points to a substantial problem of assuming a unitlike "identity" of ideas.

Apart from these problems, a crucial issue is that of replication: During transmission, what, if anything, is truly replicated? There are several basic approaches to conceptualizing replication. One is to relate ideas to behavior in the sense of "social learning" (i.e., information acquired by teaching, or imitation leading to sufficiently stable behavioral dispositions; Boyd & Richerson, 1985). In this approach, individual behavior is the expressed "phenotype" of underlying ideational units. Social learning is the mechanism of transmission. But to distinguish "culture" (as the "mental states" of individuals) from the products of culture (i.e., behavior), is to invite a serious methodological problem: Namely, how can we infer back to mental states from a product—behavior—that always results from an interaction of mental states and environmental contingencies? It is the problem of separating out from behavior exactly what is in the head versus what is in the environment. This problem is analogous to inferring genetic causation from the observation of certain traits like intelligence, and it is also at the basis of the fundamental problem in the social sciences of relating attitudes to behavior.

Another approach becomes apparent in Dawkins' (1976) widely recognized conceptualization of a unit of culture—the "meme." Dawkins explicitly took the gene as an analogy to introduce the "meme" as the replicator that leaps from brain to brain by way of imitation, thus representing an evolutionary process far faster than genetic evolution. Examples include "tunes, ideas, catch-phrases, clothes, fashions, ways of making pots or of building arches" (Dawkins, 1976. P. 206). Dawkins' "memes" and some other, similarly defined units are characterized as mental states, implying that they are neuronally represented in the brain. Thus, replication (and selection) is somehow mediated by the structure of the brain.

The difficulty of this explanation is documented by Dawkins' inconsistency on this point. On the one hand, following Humphrey, the "meme" is seen as a "structure in the nervous systems" of individuals; on the other hand, he attributes the survival value of specific memes in the meme pool to their "great psychological appeal" (Dawkins, 1976, p. 207). The latter obviously refers to content and meaning in relation to assumed psychic dispositions, whereas the former has nothing to do with it. The implicit problem that all materialist conceptualizations of units entail is the traditional "mind–body problem."

This was fully evident when Dawkins (1976) addressed the issue of replication. The construct appears in the quote: "The idea of hell-fire is *self-perpetuating*, because of its own deep psychological impact. It has become linked with the god meme because the two reinforce each other, and assist each other's survival in the meme pool" (p. 212, italics in original). In other words, replication or self-perpetuation relies on the meaning relation to other memes (ideas), and it is, in turn, assumed to have "psychological impact." The most fundamental objection to this type of conceptualization of units of culture is that, for the explanation of replication and selection, it has to rely on, and reproduce, an argumentative structure.

A similar line of theorizing was pursued by Stuart-Fox (1986). However, the crucial term in Stuart-Fox's conceptualization is not the unit of culture, but the *individual mental culture*. Proceeding from Johnson-Laird's "mental models," Stuart-Fox introduced long-term memory as the necessary condition for the retrieval of mental models and the attribution of meaning and context to perception.

Close to that of Stuart-Fox (1989) is J. Hill's (1989) definition of *concepts* as "units of cultural replication," and Swanson's (1983) definition of *sociogenes*. A number of points in Swanson's scheme merit mention. To account for cultural and individual differences, he assumed that the sociogenes of any individual are not a reflection of the total sociogene pool, but that enough sociogenes are shared to allow individuals to be identified as members of a specific culture with the "unshared genes, in different combinations, providing each of us with an individual uniqueness" (p. 93). For Swanson, "experience of the past" operates as a selective mechanism. As he pointed out, for change to be possible, symbols must be familiar or precise enough to allow interindividual communication and flexible enough to allow variation, and there must be sufficiently overlapping experiences so that meaning can be conveyed.

None of these last authors paid much attention to problems of delineating their units nor of establishing their particulate nature as a precondition for evolution. As Hull (1982) asked, what kinds of relations bind memes together in memetic systems? How are memes and memetic systems individuated at any one time or through time? Their being analogous to genes is suggested terminologically, rather than by careful definition and empirical demonstration. These and other inconsistencies in constructing analogies point back to the question of how precise the construction of which analogy is supposed to be in the first place, or what the function of the metaphorical exercise is to be.

The previously discussed strategies are all variants of an evolutionary epistemology, insofar as they posit a tenuous role of the human brain in the replication and selection of cognitive units. The issue is whether the architecture of the brain is supposed to have a constitutive or "trivial" role (i.e., whether it structures "meaning" or simply processes content, as in the case of the function of memory). One consequence of the difficulties of linking brain structure to "meaning" has been to omit any reference to the brain altogether, and to conceptualize the ideational units in such a way that they self-propagate. In discussing Dawkins' "memes," Walton's "viral sentence," and others, Hofstadter (1983) pointed to the phenomenon of self-replication by self-reference. The self-referential logical structure of certain sentences may be taken as a formal model only. An elaborated approach using the same structure is found in Sperber's (1985) epidemiology of representations. Likewise, a related approach in sociology is that of autopoietic systems (i.e., self-replicating systems of communication that are operationally closed, and thus evolve by virtue of the recursive application of the same principle). Luhmann (1986, 1990), the chief propagator of this theory in sociology, insisted that only communication can communicate, and that only in a network of communication can action arise. This approach has the advantage that it proceeds from observable phenomena and does not have to rely on inferences about the psychology of individuals. By definition, the system of communication is analytically independent of the individuals who take part in it. Although the notion of self-referentiality in language and communication provides a particular solution to the problem of replication, it is difficult to see how the examples of "viral sentences" can have any significance for the evolution of culture other than being exemplars. Only in the elaborated form of a theory of differentiated systems of communication, as done by Luhmann, does that significance become manifest.

D. Concluding Assessment: What Is the Meaning of This?

This analysis shows that some kind of "unit of culture," with some set of built-in properties, is assumed by *all* selective retention models of cultural evolution. The unit may be vague or implicit (sometimes deliberately) or it may be well-defined and operationalized. But in all cases, the assumed unit is endowed with a number of properties that are crucial to the conceptualization of culture and cultural change. We believe that models of cultural evolution should be judged as much by what they assume about culture via the choice of units, as by their specific predictive or explanatory power.

Not one unit described in the literature has shown itself to be adequate for the task. We believe that some measure of progress has been made in the shift from artifacts and behaviors to ideas and mental states. But we also believe that some major substantive and philosophical issues remain. One of these unresolved issues—and surely one of the more important ones—is the "problem of meaning" (i.e., the problem of how to define and operationalize units of culture to allow for their full local signification, and any change in that signification across time and space). In other words, the problem is how to frame an evolutionary theory of culture that fully recognizes, incorporates, and exploits culture's symbolic dimension. Regardless of whether this is a matter of vagueness on the part of anthropologists and sociologists, as Darwinians suspect, or a deficit of their models, as social scientists believe, the problem is currently serious enough to prevent a broader reception of cultural evolutionary models within the social sciences.

Some first steps have been made on the "meaning problem" (e.g., Durham, 1991), but they remain far from adequate. If we are right, one implication is that cultural evolutionary analysis should evolve to embrace two distinguishable activities or "aspects": (a) a general and comparative aspect, addressing questions such as: *What are the units of the case? What are the (general) mechanisms of cultural change at work in this instance?;* and (b) an important specific and particularistic aspect, focusing on the local context and meanings, tending definition to the units and power to the mechanisms. Without the second aspect, as Hull (1982) pointed out, evolutionary theories of culture cannot explain very much regarding changes in the content of human conceptual systems. At best, they might describe the symbol-free diffusion of entities—such as novel phonemes or morphemes introduced into a language—that do not need preexisting interpretation for their local acceptance. For these reasons, the integration of meaning into cultural evolutionary theory is likely to be a watershed event. This is also to be understood as a challenge to the social sciences—namely, to clarify and operationalize the concept of meaning itself.

The diffusion of specific "units" (components of language, types of behavior) and possibly the evolution of the "organism" of which they are a part, can proceed without any claims made as to their being the essence of culture. It is then a matter of empirical research, if these units behave as predicted by evolutionary theory, and what effect their diffusion has on the system of reference. A number of authors (Hull, 1982; Marks & Staski, 1988) have pointed out that there is ample disagreement about "appropriate reference classes for theories of biological evolution."

How can there be a solution in the much more complex analogy to culture? The focus placed on cognitive units under the influence of the brain sciences, and the attempt to apply evolutionary theory, conceal the continuing dramatic ignorance about the brain, as well as the even more shocking lack of knowledge regarding the involvement of emotional components in human communication. A warning from history may be in order: The situation is strikingly similar to the early and ill-fated strategy of certain camps of genetics who, driven by enthusiastic speculation, identified all kinds of common sense attributes of people, especially racial ones, as "traits" whose genetic determination was postulated by them and then searched for in vain by way of inference from genealogies. The crucial task of establishing "heritability" is already a highly complex endeavor on the level of human organisms, and even more so on the level of cognitive entities. Evolutionists and anthropologists have to beware so as not to make the same mistakes as the eugenicists.

In another sense, the search for appropriate units of culture has led away from problems of analogy and toward those of homology. By drawing on the cognitive and brain sciences, new and fascinating perspectives have been opened to account for human culture—its distinction from animal societies, its apparent dual nature of being both in individuals' brains and their environment, and its dynamics. Most important, rather than contradict, they seem to supplement established knowledge in the social sciences.

TYPES OF TRANSMISSION: A TAXONOMY OF CULTURAL INHERITANCE SYSTEMS

Peter J. Richerson and Robert Boyd

A. Introduction

This section aims to use analogies from biology to help separate culture as an object for evolutionary analysis from a number of confusing "inheritances" that are unsuited to evolutionary analysis, and to understand the diversity of human cultural systems that are broadly analogous to genetic transmission. The most basic criterion for an inheritance system to evolve by Darwinian processes is that it be informational. Analytically, it is useful to think of any inherited endowment as being composed of an informational component and a material component. By definition, information exists when an energetically minor cause can have energetically major effects (Engelberg & Boyarsky, 1979).

The genetic inheritance system is an excellent example of information. In most zygotes, the energy content of the genome's DNA is a tiny proportion of the total endowment from parents, yet it is mainly responsible for the pattern of development. Because the cost of information is low, it is easy to produce copies, making fecundity possible. If the transmission system is accurate, the system will exhibit fidelity. If transmitted information remains relatively unaffected by direct environmental modification, it will exhibit longevity. The task here is to develop a basic natural history of the human inheritance systems that may or may not meet Dawkins' ([1976]1989) criteria for objects of evolutionary analysis.

The inheritance of cultural artifacts and other material resources is highly analogous to biological reproduction. All cultural transmission involves some material embodiment. Sometimes information is systematized and encoded so the transmission is rapid and inexpensive to copy, as in linguistic communication. This is a limiting case in which there is no material package of all. By contrast, a proposal of marriage accompanied by a diamond ring embodies the message in an expensive artifact.

Large material endowments (the inheritance of expensive artifacts) are common and have important effects, but by themselves are not subject to evolutionary processes. Most kinds of material endowments fail one or more of Dawkins' criteria of fecundity, longevity, and fidelity. A farm implement wears out and cannot replace itself. A farm is a piece of real estate that can persist indefinitely, but cannot reproduce. There are some interesting cases, such as livestock, that certainly coevolve with human cultures in the domestication situation. Of course, modern culture depends extensively on specialized memory aids like books and blueprints, but these are clearly information-rich extensions of the mind, and have a relatively small material component.

The material versus informational inheritance distinction is closely related to the genotype-phenotype distinction in biology, and by analogy suggests a "culturetype"-phenotype distinction in the Darwinian analysis of cultural evolution, as noted in the previous section of this chapter. A number of distinctions need to be made to rule out phenomena that are not truly cultural.

B. Important Distinctions

An informational quality is necessary for the evolution of a system of inheritance, but not sufficient to guarantee that Darwinian processes are important. Moreover, many additional details affect how evolutionary processes act to cause change. It has proved important to understand the inheritance system in quite some detail to understand many features of the evolutionary process, even when only a genetic unit of inheritance is involved, much less when more exotic informational entities like culture arc involved.

Communication Versus Inheritance. Humans and other social animals acquire a vast amount of information from each other. Some of this information is about events that are highly circumscribed in time and space. Examples include the information about a pending predator attack communicated in an alarm call, or the hot tips exchanged by investors gossiping on the trading floor. As Galef (1988) noted in his elegant dissection of varieties of animal social learning, behaviors like a yawn or the startled flight of a bird can trigger the contagious spread of the behavior. However, communication is a special and marginal category of social learning in his analysis because of the transitory effects it has on phenotype—its lack of longevity.

Simple communication is governed by short-term game and developmental processes, not evolutionary processes. The effects of any given item of information are quite ephemeral. Selection and other forces cannot build up or force down the frequency of yawning or being startled in the population by acting on particular yawns or startles as they spread through a population.

There is a continuum from purely ephemeral communications to lifelong changes of phenotype. Some relatively ephemeral changes may have an important Darwinian element to their dynamics. For example, if investors are influenced in their investment strategy by the successes and failures of their colleagues, it is easy to imagine Darwinian processes playing some role in population level behavior. During times of contraction, the overbold are removed preferentially from the pool of investors by bankruptcy, and the cautious have a disproportionate influence on the strategies of their fellows. During booms, the reverse will tend to occur. The boldness of investment strategy may be modified by individuals through experience. However, this response might be slow relative to the direct impact of events on the same individuals' economic success. Thus, a process highly analogous to natural selection may reduce the average boldness of a population of investors during an economic contraction. It is an interesting empirical question whether this process is more or less important than the developmental process by which individuals' learn new strategies to cope with the change investment environment. Probably, neither can be be neglected.

Once the Weissmannian barrier between phenotype and heritable information is breached, as it certainly is in a cultural system of inheritance, developmental processes like learning and Darwinian dynamics will begin to interpenetrate. Then the task of sorting out the positive and negative analogies becomes a serious, although not necessarily difficult, problem (see chap. 3, this volume). Consider the example of rumors. Most rumors spread briefly and then die out like simple communications. However, some rumors seem to adapt to the human mind and cultural circumstances in ways that are more Darwinian. A rumor may pass on to the status of a folk belief and persist indefinitely. Communications may be one ultimate source of new elements of culture.

It is also likely that everyday ongoing communication is a vehicle for cultural transmission. If there is a pattern of attitude or knowledge that is embedded in a series of communications, communicants may synthesize a fully cultural belief from a large sample of communications, each of which by itself is dominated by information of only ephemeral effect.

Individual Versus Social Learning. The traditional nature-nurture dichotomy is unfortunate from the point of view of applying Darwinian theory to cultural evolution because it treats both culture and individual learning as environmental effects. Ordinary individual learning is a developmental system of phenotypic flexibility. Almost all animals have at least some capacity to learn. Fewer species appear to have a capacity to acquire information from conspecifics by even rudimentary social learning, and the massive use of imitative learning may well be restricted to humans. Widely cited examples animal social learning, such as the apparent traditions of diving for mussels in the River Tiber by some populations of rats have not been verified under controlled conditions (Galef, 1988). Only when information is transmitted among individuals does an inheritance system meeting the fecundity and longevity criteria exist.

Individual and social learning can be linked to a system for the inheritance of acquired variation that has a distinct negative analogy to genes. What one person learns as an individual, others can usually imitate. The process must be far from automatic because among animals generally, individual learning is nearly universal, but social learning is rare. Lamarckian systems are easily modeled (and investigated empirically) by bringing the Darwinian and developmental elements into a common framework (e.g., Boyd & Richerson, 1985).

Social Facilitation Versus Social Transmission. This is another contrast emphasized by Galef (1988). Social support, resources, or physical protection may be required before an individual can engage in individual learning. However, such social support may not have any effect on what variant is learned, and no cultural transmission occurs although learning may be an intensely social process. Dawkins' fidelity criterion fails. This category is at least officially important in modern middle-class pedagogy, in which parents and teachers go to great lengths to provide stimulus and support for children to "think for themselves" and "learn to learn." There may be much cultural transmission occurring in such contexts, of course, especially in humans. Among animals that show much less sophisticated systems of imitation, more or less pure social facilitation of individual learning may be important. In humans, social facilitation may vary from culture to culture, and may act as a regulator of innovation rates.

Imprinting Versus Social Transmission. In imprinting, animals acquire important information necessary for species-typical behavior from parents early in life. For example, many birds take their caretakers for the species with whom they are supposed to mate. Caretakers are normally their real parents, but when humans hand-rear birds, considerable confusion ensues.

Normal imprinting carries a chain of species recognition and other species-typical behavior forward through time, and exhibits the key features of longevity, fecundity, and fidelity. However, imprinting remains a marginal category for Darwinian analysis. In the case of imprinting on species-typical behaviors, the system appears to carry no variation, and most interesting Darwinian processes are concerned with the evolutionary dynamics of heritable variation.

C. Types of Cultural Transmission

A number of systems of social learning exhibiting fidelity, fecundity, and longevity are important in humans, as well as other animal species. It is important to keep this diversity in mind because the application of analogies from biology depends on the details of how inheritance systems operate. Population geneticists insist that the details of the genetic system (haploidy versus diploidy, linkage patterns, autosomes versus sex chromosomes, etc.) play an important role in evolutionary dynamics. The same argument applies to culture. Indeed, some forms of social transmission seem as different from one another as genetic and epigenetic inheritance systems in biology. The following discussion is based on Galef's (1988) taxonomy, with extension for the human case.

1. Individual Level Social Transmission

Human or animal individuals can acquire information from other individuals. The other individuals are termed *models* in the experimental literature on human social learning (Rosenthal & Zimmerman, 1979). The acquiring individual can be influenced by one or many models, can learn once per lifetime, or update by continuously sampling the pool of models. It is this type of social learning that has been the focus of most analogical investigations applying Darwinian dynamics because the positive analogy to genes is strong (Boyd & Richerson, 1985; Cavalli-Sforza & Feldman, 1981; Pulliam & Dunford, 1980). The many simple disanalogies between patterns of cultural and genetic transmission (e.g., the possibility of having many models instead of only two parents) require considerable rethinking of evolutionary models, even assuming that only conventional evolutionary forces like mutation, migration, drift, and selection are at play on cultural variation.

At the psychological level, there appear to be several mechanisms by which variation can be passed from individual to individual by a cultural system *sensu lato*. The mechanisms vary in the cognitive processes used to replicate the representation of a model's behavior in the naive individual's mind, and in sources of reinforcement that motivate the attempt to replicate the model's behavior or stabilize it against loss.

a) Variation in Cognitive Mechanisms

Ideas communicated by a Shared Symbol System.   Humans can express ideas in language, graphs, numbers, artistic representations, and the like. The shared conventions of the symbol system, and the adaptation of the human mind to deal with symbols (see chaps. 5, 6, and 7, this volume), appear to make this pathway of transmission uniquely important in humans. A large quantity of information can be transmitted relatively rapidly by a well-organized symbol system. Even so, the time required for a child to learn the symbol system and then acquire information using it makes cultural transmission a temporally extended process that takes up a significant fraction of the human lifetime. Animals can apparently use shared codes like alarm calls to transmit some cultural information—a mechanism Galef termed *observational conditioning*.

Behavioral Variants Acquired by Direct Imitation.   Many motor skills and similar behaviors may be acquired by humans by direct observation of models and replication of their behavior unmediated by language or other symbol systems. Donald (1991) argued that the symbolic form of culture evolved from a capacity for "mimesis"—the ability to freely replicate the observed acts of others. He cited 19th-century accounts of deaf-mutes, who could acquire a near-normal repertoire of most kinds of motor and social skills without any command of language—the most important form of symbolic communication. Perhaps children are adapted to learn language by a bootstrapping process that depends substantially on direct imitation to acquire phonemes and the most basic conceptual tools to begin to decode linguistic utterances. The alternative hypothesis is that many of the rules required to deal with symbolic culture are genetically coded, as in Chomskyan linguistics (see chaps. 5 and 6, this volume).

Behavior Acquired by Stimulus Enhancement.   The best attested examples of animal social transmission involve this cognitively rudimentary mechanism. The presence of conspecifics in the environment often makes certain cues more salient than others. In the well-studied laboratory system of social acquisition of food preferences in rats, the smell of food on a nestmate's breath, scent marking around food sources, trail making, and the like direct the learner's attention to some features of the environment and away from others. If the feeding behavior that occurs in these locations is rewarding, the naive rat will tend to replicate the feeding behavior of nestmates. We suppose that humans also learn behaviors incidentally as a result of social enhancement of cues, although to our knowledge there are no well-studied examples. For example, neophyte hunters may follow the trails of more experienced hunters and learn some bits of hunting technique as a by-product of traveling to one place rather than another.

Behavior Acquired by Match to Sample.   In some cases, naive individuals may learn to match the behavior of models by some sort of conditioning regime. The result of such conditioning is called *matched dependent behavior* by psychologists. A hungry youngster that observes and mimics the behavior of a foraging adult is likely to be reinforced for the mimicry by acquiring food. The acquisition of a behavior in this way is, in the simplest cases, hardly different than the case of stimulus enhancement, except that the behavior of the animal, rather than some cue-like smell, is the discriminative stimulus for the behavior.

b) Variation in Sources of Reinforcement

Once a bit of information is acquired, it is liable to be treated as a simple communication and become rapidly lost. To acquire sufficient longevity to have ongoing phenotypic effects and a chance to be transmitted, the item must be stabilized in the brain of the social learner. Three classes of reinforcers can accomplish this.

Environmental Reinforcement. In simple cases, the environment may reward socially transmitted behavior directly, as is typically assumed to be the case in animals using the stimulus enhancement or match to sample cognitive modes. Of course, environmental reinforcement could be required to "fix" behaviors in which essential information was transmitted by cognitively complex forms of social transmission as well.

Social Reinforcement. Models may not be passive in the transmission process. They may actively participate through some form of teaching. The simplest form of teaching would be a socially imposed operant conditioning regime designed to replicate the reinforcer's behavior. In more complex cases, imitation or symbolic communication may be used along with social reinforcement. Teaching is obviously important in humans, although how important relative to other, less deliberate forms of social transmission is not so clear. The importance of teaching in other species is more controversial (Caro & Hauser, 1992; Galef, 1988). It is also possible that powerful individuals use reinforcement to inculcate behaviors in naive individuals that are in the interest of the powerful (Durham, 1991).

Internal Reinforcement. In the case of behaviors that routinely need to be acquired culturally, naive individuals may find the replication of modeled behavior reinforcing independent of environmental or social reinforcement. The eminent student of human social learning, Albert

Bandura (1986) reviewed evidence that internal attentional and motivational features of the social transmission process are crucial to human cultural transmission. People attend to models, covertly rehearse observed behavior, and replicate behavior, all in advance of any environmental or social reinforcement. Sometimes no reinforcement is ever forthcoming or is very subtle, yet behaviors persist. Sometimes punishment actually improves the acquisition of punished behaviors through its effect on attention (Nuttin, 1975), pointing out the complex interaction between internal rewards and external reinforcement in the cognitively complex case of human social learning. In a species adapted to acquire a large cultural repertoire, internal reinforcement practically has to be the dominant motivation for acquisition. It seems hard to believe that much of an individual's vast set of cultural items, could ever have been subject to environmental or social tests of much complexity. People are adapted to acquire many cultural items, either for the pleasure of doing so or because attentional processes make it impossible not to learn what one notices.

2. Collective Level Cultural Transmission.

Following Durkheim, many sociologists insist that it is social institutions, not individuals, that should be the focus of analysis (see chaps. 6 and 11, this volume). This raises an issue for the application of Darwinian analogies if what is meant is that somehow the analysis can dispense with an account of individuals (or similar units). However, the individualism of a typical Darwinian analysis is partly a product of the real biological importance of individuals in many systems, and the ease of counting and experimenting with them. Evolutionary biologists are quite prepared to be skeptical of the fundamental importance of any particular unit in particular cases (e.g., L. W. Buss, 1987; Dawkins, 1982).

This section is concerned with a particular piece of the broader problem of supraindividual units. Are there any examples in which the evolving information is not transmitted from individual to individual and does not exist in individuals' heads, but is carried at the supraindividual level? Human societies are remarkable for having at least the appearance of supraindividual level teleology/teleonomy. Such purposive entities as firms, tribes, states, and the like may emerge from a combination of group selection, ecological dynamics, and developmental dynamics, while still retaining the ordinary human individual as the only agent of cultural transmission. However, perhaps there are other modes of transmission not entirely dependent on, or reducible to, individual transmission.

Nelson and Winter (1982) conducted the most sophisticated investigation of this problem. Their theory of economic evolution focused on the firm as the main unit of account and the firm's routines as the analogue of its "memory" and "genes." They were reacting to the extreme individualism of typical economic analysis, in which it seems trivial for one firm to imitate the behavior of others if that is desirable. Nelson and Winter argued that, empirically, firm routines are quite stable even in the face of changing environments, and that even successful routines are hard to imitate. Thus, firms with a successful routine can typically grow quite large by replicating the routine before the innovations or imitations of other firms reduce the advantage. The question is what creates the reality of organizations, and does the transmission of information at the organization level play a key role in this reality? Nelson and Winter offered a number of interesting arguments.

Much Information is in Individual Heads.   A vast amount of the necessary information to run a firm is in individual heads. However, if it were all there, then it would seem possible to replicate a successful firm's technique simply by hiring the appropriately skilled individuals. To the extent that firm routines are not easily replicable, other sources of information must be important.

Some Information is in Artifacts.   Some of the information required to operate an organization is stored in the physical arrangement of settlements, trails, factory floors, offices, and the like. In literate societies, substantial amounts may be stored in files, manuals, databases, and similar media. The organization may collectively own information resources as in a legally defined trade secret, patent or copyright, and informal equivalents. Firms can share or reproduce such information for the use of a subsidiary or new division, but even massive recruitment of individuals may not suffice to replicate information of this type in an outside organization.

Some Information Is in Solutions to Games with Multiple Evolutionarily Stable Strategies.   Some features relevant to the functioning of an organization may be properties of collective interaction. The operation of a firm may depend on the solution to complex games of coordination, contest, mutualism, and reciprocity (Boyd & Richerson, 1990). In these situations, evolutionarily stable strategies tend to multiply and withi-group processes tend to stabilize whatever strategy among many becomes common. There may be many possible routines for solving the "political" problems of a firm. The sheer complexity of the solution to many interlocking problems dispersed through a large organization means that no individual knows more than a few pieces of the whole solution. From the individual point of view, it often makes sense to conform to the prevailing evolutionarily stable strategies in the organization, which are a feature of the organization, not any given individual.

It is perhaps easiest to see the potential for transmission at the group level if one considers an extreme case in which individuals learn the solution to a game of coordination by trial and error, rather than ordinary cultural transmission. As a naive individual interacts with other members of an organization, he or she is rewarded when he or she conforms to the prevailing solution to the game and punished when he or she attempts uncommon strategies (which might seem quite reasonable, and in fact be superior solutions, if they were common). A property of the organization will impose itself on individuals in this way. The solution will be transmitted to the future even in the complete absence of individual level culture.

Some Information Is Managed by Institutions of Command and Control. Many organizations are formally organized to manage personnel, make collective decisions, and deploy resources. General goals exist, and institutions of leadership and public participation may exist to implement them. In the case of complex societies, constitutions, codes of law, administrative regulations, policy and procedure manuals, and the like formalize and store this information externally (see Hejl, chap. 11, this volume; Maryanksi & Turner, chap. 6, this volume). Even if individuals understand these institutions and can replicate them, as functional entities they require assembling a whole organization to put them into action.

An individual entrepreneur might replicate an organization on his or her own knowledge, but the new firm as a growing concern often finds the founder quite dispensable. To the extent that an organization is a teleological or teleonomic entity, there is an organizational phenotype. Boards of directors and similar institutions make and enforce decisions, including decisions that change the organizational culture. With a complex division of labor, the problem arises that it may require many types of specialized individual knowledge to replicate a firm; many founding individuals are thus required to replicate the knowledge. If externally obtained knowledge is crucial, an organization can be replicated only if it acquires copies of such information. If such solutions are not in any one individual's head, it may require a functioning fraction of the organization to replicate it. Such replications will not occur by individual level activity alone, but must be organized by institutions of command and control.

The nearest parallel in biology to a human organization is perhaps a complex, modular, multispecies symbiosis that reproduces mainly by budding or some other form of asexual reproduction. Such organisms are not uncommon (L. W. Buss, 1987), but they have not been the focus of much theoretical attention. It seems certain that a large fraction of organizational routines are transmitted from individual to individual by the various forms of cultural transmission outlined earlier. However, it will not do to neglect the possibility of transmission at the institutional level. If such transmission is important, it may permit the evolution of organizations and institutions that are substantially beyond the control of individual psychological predispositions (see Meyer, chap. 6, this volume).

CONCLUSION

The examination of cultural analogies to units and systems of transmission in biology leads to important questions, if not easy answers. In this chapter, a basic exploration of the analogy between genes and other biological phenomena and human culture clearly demonstrates the poverty of any attempt to draw one-for-one parallels between culture and genes, especially to the simple textbook genetics that are often imagined to be the only analogical tool available.

What is much more promising is to consider human culture in a broadly comparative mode. There are actually a large variety of units of inheritance and patterns of information transmission that are at least partly understood. Limited textbook simplifications do not do justice to the variety within either biological systems or human culture. Arguing to reject all use of analogy in theorizing about human culture—because the most "advanced" human system, language-based symbols, is rather different than diploid genetics—ignores the lessons that might be gained by the broader comparative approach.

In such a comparative framework, human cultural systems do seem to find a natural place. For example, Dawkins' (1989 [1976]) criteria of fecundity, fidelity, and longevity are useful concepts with which to address a variety of nongenetic systems of inheritance. The animal behaviorists' distinction between communication and social learning is similarly fundamental. As different as human cultural systems are from biological ones, the basic dimensions of analysis developed for biological systems are a good starting point for the analysis of culture.

The comparative approach is not aimed at wholesale substitution of biological concepts for those derived from the social sciences. Rather, it is meant to illustrate an important general theme of this book. Analogies are tools to understand complex, diverse phenomena. Where positive analogies occur, they have much to contribute by exchanges among disciplines. One contribution is to provide nuts-and-bolts methods and models (see chap. 9, this volume). A more conceptual contribution has been emphasized here.

Viewing human culture through the lens of biological concepts of inheritance startles and provokes the imagination. In some cases, we have reached the conclusion that such images are mere distortions, and that traditional social scientific approaches have little to learn from biologists. In other cases, the biologists' view asks new questions and adds interesting twists to old ones. What are the units of cultural variation, if indeed they are unitlike? Is the nature of the unit variable from subsystem to subsystem? Whatever the nature and variety of units, how are they replicated in new individuals (or organizations)? Biology is privileged in the interdisciplinary analogical project only because, for historical reasons, knowledge of one particular, although important, inheritance system— that based on DNA—has outpaced all others. The biologists offer exceedingly useful, ready-made tools, although ones that will necessarily be modified not only for the study of human culture, but also of animal social learning, epigenetic inheritance, and any other inheritance systems we happen to discover.

9

MODELS AND FORCES OF CULTURAL EVOLUTION

William H. Durham
Stanford University
Stanford

Robert Boyd
University of California
Los Angeles

Peter J. Richerson
University of California
Davis

Whereas the previous chapter dealt with units of cultural transmission and mechanisms of preservation and propagation, the goal of this chapter is to summarize and critique leading efforts to build and test models of cultural evolution. The first section focuses on processes of transformation in cultural evolution, and offers a kind of status report on the construction of models. The second section discusses two cases to which the models of cultural evolution have been applied. These demonstrate the explanatory power of evolutionary analogies.

PROCESSES AFFECTING CULTURAL EVOLUTION

William H. Durham

In 1965, D. T. Campbell proposed a general theoretical framework for modeling the processes of cultural evolution. The framework outlined a promising "analogy between natural selection in biological evolution and the selective propagation of cultural forms" (see D. T. Campbell, 1965, p. 26), but went largely unnoticed until the advent of the sociobiology debate in the mid-1970s. That debate spawned renewed interest in the topic of cultural evolution, and in the idea that human populations are possessed of *two* evolving inheritance systems: genes and culture (see Keller, 1915; Waddington, 1961). The challenge became how to put Campbell's suggestions into practice: how to devise and test an analogous "variation-and-selective-retention" model for cultural evolution.

The task has many facets. D. T. Campbell (1965) initially identified three basic requirements for a "selective retention" model of cultural evolution: "1. The occurrence of variations: heterogeneous, haphazard, 'blind,' 'chance,' 'random,' but in any event variable. 2. Consistent selective systems: selective elimination, selective propagation, selective retention, of certain types of variants. 3. A mechanism for the preservation, duplication, or propagation of the positively selected variants" (p. 27).

As he put it, "If there are representatives of these three requirements" within cultural systems, then an analogous "socio-cultural 'evolutionary' process... is inevitable" (p. 27). Therefore, it should be possible to develop models of cultural change that are roughly analogous to the quantitative formulations of population genetics (such as directional and balancing selection, density-dependent selection, sexual selection, etc.).

Today, the requirements are known by slightly different names. For example, Campbell's "selective systems" might now be called "processes of transformation." Also, one might well augment the number of requirements by one or two, as was arguably implicit in Campbell's formulation anyway, and thus include: (a) operational units of cultural transmission (i.e., subsets of a culture's ideational content that are taught and learned as coherent wholes), and (b) sources of relative isolation between cultures (i.e., sources of relative impediment to social transmission, without which there might well be cultural evolution, but of only a single global culture).

But the basic idea is still the same as Campbell set forth back in 1965. In principle, one can build models of cultural change that are analogous to population genetics models provided that one can satisfactorily identify each of these components within human cultural systems, and then faithfully represent their properties and effects within iterative arguments, qualitative and/or quantitative.

A. Processes of Transformation

As Campbell realized in 1965, "the potential selective systems [of cultural evolution] are so numerous and so intertwined, and the selective criteria so difficult to specify, that quite respectable intellectual grounds are provided for a denial of the existence of a socio-cultural evolutionary process" (p. 29). Nevertheless, he went on to propose a set of six mechanisms: "the selective survival of complete social organizations," "selective diffusion or borrowing between social groups," "selective propagation of temporal variations," "selective imitation of interindividual variations," "selective promotion to leadership and educational roles," and "rational selection" (i.e., deliberate, self-conscious decision-making).

Today, the list of candidate mechanisms has grown considerably, but consensus is also growing about which ones are the most salient and general. Table 9.1 compares three recent inventories of the "forces" of cultural evolution. The table differentiates two different categories of forces—namely "nonconveyance forces" (such as diffusion, innovation, and copy error), which cause cultural evolution through the repeated introduction of variation into cultural systems, and "conveyance forces," which cause cultural evolution through the differential transmission of variants among human carriers. But the table also shows that there is substantial convergence among models, at least those heavily influenced by population genetics (for alternative approaches, see Dawkins, 1993; Delius, 1989; Loprcato, 1984; Marks & Staski, 1988; Schmookler, 1984). Because most models today emphasize conveyance forces, the discussion here focuses on Category B.

The conveyance forces in the models of Cavalli-Sforza and Feldman (1981), Boyd and Richerson (1985), and Durham (1991) boil down to three main kinds of forces: (a) "transmission forces," in which structured regularities in the social situation of transmission confer a social context advantage on certain variants; (b) "natural selection," in which the life history consequences of different cultural variants produce a "cultural parenting" advantage for some of them ("cultural parenting" refers to success as a transmitter of culture); and (c) "decision-making forces," in which some form of evaluative judgment is responsible for giving a preference advantage to certain variants. These different kinds of advantage, singly and in combination, are regarded by their proponents as the major causes of cultural transformation within human populations.

Transmission Forces. Consider first the transmission forces, a group of mechanisms championed by the "cultural transmission model" of Cavalli-Sforza and Feldman (1981). These mechanisms depend on dif-

Table 9.1

A Comparison of Transformational Processes in Three Recent Models of
Cultural Evolution

	Transformational Processes		
Category	Model by Cavalli-Sforza & Feldman (1981)	Model by Boyd & Richerson (1985)	Model by Durham (1991)
A. Nonconveyance forces	Mutation Purposive Random	Cultural mutation NS* Accidental	Innovation/synthesis Deliberate Random
	Migration Cultural Demic	NS Diffusion Migration	Introductions Diffusion Migration
	Cultural drift	Drift	Cultural drift
B. Conveyance forces	Transmission Vertical Horizontal Oblique	Guided variation	Transmission forces Differential modeling Role selection
	Natural selection (*sensu strictu*)	Natural selection (*sensu latu*)	Natural selection (*sensu strictu*)
	Cultural selection	Biased transmis- sion Direct Indirect Frequency- dependent	Cultural selection Primary value Secondary value Imposition Choice

*"NS" means "not specific.

Note. In this table, natural selection *sensu strictu* refers to "consequences at the level of Darwinian fitness" (after Cavalli-Sforza & Feldman, 1981, p. 351); natural selection *sensu latu* means differential success as a transmitter of culture (after Boyd & Richerson 1985, p. 175).

ferences in the social situation of cultural transmission (i.e., on differences in who transmits cultural information to whom). Cavalli-Sforza and Feldman explored three different modes of cultural transmission: vertical (meaning parent–offspring), horizontal (among peers), and oblique (beween generations, but not parent–offspring), and many different ratios of teachers to learners, such as many–one, one–one, and one–many. Quantitative models of the spread of particular traits (their choice for the unit of culture) by different mechanisms bring Cavalli-Sforza and Feldman to the conclusions that "the mode of transmission is of great importance in determining the rate of change of trait frequencies in populations," and "a scale of transmission mechanisms, graduated by the ratio of number of teachers to number of people taught, is useful in predicting qualitatively the rate of evolution and the chance of [cultural] polymorphism" (Cavalli-Sforza & Feldman, 1981, pp. 356ff; *polymorphism* refers to the simultaneous existence, at substantial frequency, of two or more cultural variants in a population). Accordingly, they found that "the greater the contribution from earlier generations (e.g., via parental, oblique, and grandparental transmission), the slower the rate of cultural evolution" (Cavalli-Sforza & Feldman, 1981, p. 353). They argued that this theoretical expectation, among others, is supported by the relative cultural conservatism that has been documented for certain hunting–gathering societies (e.g., the long-term persistence of their technology and subsistence techniques; see also Hewlett & Cavalli-Sforza, 1986).

Natural Selection. Consider next the natural selection of cultural variation, which is one of the forces modeled by Boyd and Richerson (1985) in their book *Culture and the Evolutionary Process.* For Boyd and Richerson, natural selection operates in a cultural context whenever "individuals characterized by different variants of [a] culturally transmitted trait have different probabilities of becoming cultural parents," and are thus passing the trait along to naive individuals (Boyd & Richerson, 1985, p. 175). They implied that there are two ways to achieve differential "cultural parenting." First, natural selection will operate when two or more alternative traits in the same environment "merely have differential effects on the life chances of the individuals that perform them" (Boyd & Richerson, 1985, p. 175). In such a situation, one of the variants will gain ascendancy via the classical Darwinian mechanism of differential survival and/or reproduction (coupled with parent–offspring cultural transmission). It will be selectively preserved by virtue of its survival and reproduction advantage.

A second route to differential parenting is the one that D. T. Campbell (1965) called "selective promotion to leadership and educational roles" (p. 31). As Boyd and Richerson noted, this route requires that "a system of social learning and a pattern of social life [makes] some individuals more likely to be models than others" (Boyd & Richerson, 1985, p. 175). In this case, natural selection will favor Trait X whenever (a) there is competition for social roles that are influential in cultural transmission, and (b) carriers of Trait X more often attain those roles than do carriers of other variants (see Boyd & Richerson, 1985). Boyd and Richerson suggested that the demographic transition may offer a suitable example. If belief in delayed marriage and limited family size makes individuals sufficiently more likely to become successful teachers and managers in a given population, and if these roles are sufficiently important in cultural transmission, then beliefs promoting reduced fertility will tend to spread through the population.

Decision Making Forces.   The third type of conveyance force depends on the value-driven decisions of human beings. There is reasonable agreement on the nature and effects of this kind of force, but there remain some differences in its conceptualization. To Boyd and Richerson (1985), this process is known as "biased transmission" of three different kinds. First, there is direct bias, in which "people may adopt some cultural variants rather than others based on their judgments about the properties of the variants themselves" (Richerson & Boyd, 1985, p. 10). Boyd and Richerson suggested that Anglo-American food preferences may be an example of direct bias. Second, there is frequency-dependent bias, which occurs whenever "a naive individual uses the frequency of a variant among his models to evaluate the merit of the variant" (Richard & Boyd, 1985, p. 206). As an example of frequency-dependent bias, Boyd and Richerson cited work by social psychologists showing that people tend to adopt majority opinions, even when their own experience is contrary. Finally, there is indirect bias whenever "naive individuals prefer some models over others based on an indicator trait and [then] use such preferences to determine the attractiveness of that model for other characters" (Boyd & Richerson, 1985, p. 243). Boyd and Richerson offered the example of dialect evolution on Martha's Vineyard as a case in point: Local residents' "admiration of the fishermen's independent ways and [their] scornful distaste for visitors leads to the inadvertent copying of the fishermen's dialect" (Boyd & Richerson, 1985, p. 247). In recursive mathematical models, Boyd and Richerson explored the evolutionary implications of these three forms of biased transmission.

Cavalli-Sforza and Feldman (1981) and Durham (1991) used the *cultural selection* to refer to the same kinds of processes (also Rindos, 1985, 1986), but they subdivided and categorized component mechanisms in a different way. For instance, Durham (1991) distinguished four intergraded forms of cultural selection using two (presumably) orthogonal axes. First, there is a "decision axis" that ranges from relatively autonomous choice at one end—wherein existing cultural variants are differentially propagated by the elective judgments of decision makers—to rigid, socially constrained imposition at the other—wherein selection is preempted by decision makers who are able to foist off their (often selfish) choices on other, less powerful members of the population. All points in between correspond to value-guided human decisions; the distinguishing feature is simply the relative freedom of choice of those who bear the selected variant(s). This axis allows Durham's framework to take existing social structure (i.e., the existing political and economic relationships among individuals and groups in a population) into account, eliminating the air of "radical individualism" that has plagued other models, although it does not explicitly provide for interactive changes through time in that structure.

Second, Durham posited an "evaluation axis," orthogonal to the decision axis, which measures the relative importance of two kinds of values. Durham's scheme distinguishes primary values, which require no input from social transmission (i.e., they are viewed as developing within individuals from the ontogenetic interplay of nature and nurture), from secondary values, which individuals acquire through social transmission. Thus, the evaluation axis runs from decisions in which primary values are the most important to decisions in which secondary values predominate. Durham argued that these intergraded forms of cultural selection warrant conceptual distinction because the direction and rates of cultural evolution can be vastly different among them. He further hypothesized that cultural selection guided predominantly by secondary values—so-called "secondary value selection"—is the main, but not exclusive, means of cultural evolutionary change.

According to Durham (1992), fitting examples of each of these forms of cultural selection can be found in the literature on the cultural evolution of incest taboos (i.e., of the rules prohibiting sexual activity among kin). Cultural selection directed by primary values—called "primary value selection"—is the main force sustaining incest taboos in the arguments of Westermarck ([1891]1922) and his supporters today. In Westermarck's theory, a psychological aversion to sex (a *primary value* in Durham's terminology) develops between males and females who have been reared in close association from an early age, and this aversion generates moral disapproval of sex with kin. The taboo itself then "expresses the general feelings of community and punishes acts that shock them" (Westermarck, [1891]1922, p. 204); it is shaped and sustained by the aversion that most people feel.

In contrast, Burton's (1973) "folk theory" of incest prohibition—or its extension into "optimal outbreeding theory" (Durham, 1991)—is an example of secondary value selection. In Burton's theory, people observe the harmful genetic effects of inbreeding when it occurs, and attribute them to the displeasure of some powerful local deity. The belief that a fruitful union is divinely sanctioned (a *secondary value* in Durham's terminology because the concept of divinity requires social transmission) compels the choices that shape and sustain the prohibition (e.g., Durham, 1991).

To turn to the second, "decision axis" of cultural selection, both the Westermarck and Burton theories posit that taboo variants are selectively retained through choice (i.e., relatively unconstrained decision making). A contrasting view, in which incest prohibitions are defined and sustained through the imposition of powerful rulers, is given by N. Thornhill (1991; see also chap. 6, this volume). Thornhill claimed that incest rules are imposed to promote the specific reproductive interests of those who rule. The argument underscores that the various forms of cultural selection (choice, imposition, etc.) warrant distinction because they direct cultural evolution in different directions.

B. Cultural Evolution in Relation to Genetic Fitness

One reason that processes of transformation are central to models of cultural evolution is that they predict certain kinds of relationships between genetic and cultural change. The remainder of this chapter focuses on those predicted relationships, and specifically on the relationships between the direction of genetic and cultural change. This focus is of special interest because of the "leash argument"—the argument (first given by E. O. Wilson 1978) that "the genes hold culture on a leash," which constrains the directions and rates of its change.

Because "the genes" evolve subject to genetic selection—a process preserving those genetic variants that promote effective design for survival and reproduction—measures of "reproductive success" and "genetic fitness" are useful for comparing genetic and cultural change. If the "leash" is short (and the cultural dog at the end is small or well behaved), the cultural variants selectively retained by mechanisms of cultural evolution should confer genetic fitness in almost all cases. If the leash is long (or the cultural dog is large and ill behaved), cultural evolution will be self-guiding to an appreciable degree, and the selected cultural variants may affect genetic fitness much more commonly.

As explained, the models outlined earlier all imply that the question of the length of the leash and the size and obedience of the dog are the paramount, unsolved problems. They suggest that processes of cultural transformation can and do cause maladaptations—that is, phenotypic properties conferring a relative loss of genetic fitness for their cultural carriers. Further, as is seen in the examples, there is no reason why the *leash* metaphor cannot be reversed. Sometimes culture may drive genetic evolution instead of being controlled by it. In the process, the coevolution of genes and culture may produce novel culture-based adaptations that could never arise by selection acting on genes alone.

Enhancement. We begin with a look at the ways in which cultural mechanisms can cause enhancement—that is, ways in which cultural mechanisms can favor cultural variants that enhance the genetic fitness of those who bear them. Two categories of conveyance forces described previously are obvious candidates. The "natural selection of cultural variation" is one: Many (but certainly not all) of the phenotypic effects of cultural variants that have given them a "cultural parenting" advantage will also give them a genetic parenting advantage. The connection is particularly straightforward in cases where the cultural parenting advantage of a given variant stems from its beneficial effect on the fertility and/or survivorship of its bearers.

For example, consider the case of traditional maize processing techniques in the New World as described by Katz, Hediger, and Valleroy (1974; see also Katz, 1982). These researchers found that most American-indian populations who heavily depended on maize as a dietary staple also had an alkali processing technique, such as presoaking or cooking maize with lime, ashes or lye. By enhancing the balance of essential amino acids, and by freeing otherwise unavailable niacin (thereby preventing pellagra), the alkali treatment know-how could well enjoy a cultural parenting advantage through its actual survival and reproduction advantage (coupled with parent–offspring social transmission). Although it is far from clear that this technique evolved to cultural prominence in this way, that is certainly one possibility. When contemporary populations are asked, they generally articulate no advantage to the custom beyond simply softening the tough outer layer of the kernel.

By the same token, cultural selection can also be a powerful force for enhancement, particularly where there is an ample degree of choice among variants. This follows from the reasonable supposition that the outcome of choice is governed by evolved values, primary and/or secondary, and these values will often—but again not always—promote the adoption of adaptively advantageous variants.

Consider first the primary values. As argued by Pugh (1977) and Durham (1991), the human decision system evolved its primary values precisely because their net effect was generally adaptive in the environments of human prehistory. In a real sense, they evolved as operational surrogates for the criterion that genetic selection metaphorically "employs" in making its "selections"—namely, genetic fitness. As surrogates, they are far from perfect in carrying out this evolutionary mandate. Still, they are an important source of bias in favor of fitness-promoting cultural variants. Moreover, normal ontogeny guarantees them a privileged "residential" status within the human decision system. Barring some unusual intervention in the nervous system, all decisions are subject to their input, regardless of whether that input governs the outcome.

Viewed in this light, "secondary" values may also be seen as surrogates or extensions of primary values. Secondary values evolve culturally in an environment (namely, the minds of human beings) that is intrinsically populated with primary values. They are relentlessly subject to primary value feedback—the long reach of the leash—and are perpetually vulnerable to being edited or deleted. Given time and freedom of choice among cultural carriers, one might expect there to emerge a general, if imperfect, congruence between the evaluations returned by the primary and secondary values (and between them and genetic fitness). Calling this the *principle of congruence,* Durham (1991) argued that, "for most of the last two million years, the average net effect of secondary values has been to promote decisions that enhanced the reproductive fitnesses of those who guided" (p. 448) the cultural evolutionary process.

One possible example of enhancement by secondary value selection has already been mentioned—namely, the role of secondary values (e.g., the pleasure and displeasure of the deity) in Burton's theory for the evolution of incest taboos. Another interesting candidate is offered by our own Western scientific method: The evaluative criteria that statisticians call *critical values* (e.g., $p < 0.05$, or $p < 0.01$) are certainly socially transmitted conventions, and they are often crucial to the selective retention (or elimination) of alternative hypotheses, including some of major consequence to human survival and reproduction.

The point, then, is that cultural selection *can* be a powerful force for enhancement. However, it must also be emphasized that enhancement is not an inevitable outcome of decision-making forces. As emphasized by Cavalli-Sforza and Feldman (1981), decisions are often preempted altogether by greater forces in social life. Secondary values can hardly cause enhancement when these other forces "destroy or minimize the amount of variability in cultural traits, and lead to the adoption of trait values not by choice but by default" (p. 63). But even when decision making is possible, it may also be ineffective, as Boyd and Richerson (1985) emphasized because people can be completely unaware of the consequences of their choices. Decision making may also be ineffective at producing enhancement because even routine choices can have unintended consequences; what may begin as a clever fitness-promoting endeavor can wind up bringing death and devastation (for provocative examples, see Farvar & Milton, 1972).

Opposition. As interesting as enhancement may be, it is far less important and provocative than is opposition—a second mode of relationship implied by evolutionary models of culture. The reason is that, in opposition, the "leash" is ineffective: Opposition exists when the variants favored by cultural processes have the net effect of reducing the genetic fitnesses of their carriers. In such circumstances, cultural evolution proceeds in a direction counter to that expected in genetic evolution guided by Darwinian natural selection. Therefore, it becomes important to ask, which of the various mechanisms or forces of cultural evolution are capable of causing opposition, particularly sustained, long-term opposition?

As surprising as it might at first seem, the models considered here suggest that virtually all of the main contenders—transmission forces, natural selection of cultural variation, and decision forces—can and do cause opposition in the course of human affairs, but they do so in different ways. Consider first natural selection: A clear case may be made for opposition any time that success at being a teacher or model for certain beliefs (i.e., success at "cultural parenting") competes with success at biological parenting. As intuition suggests and models confirm, a cultural variant that makes its carriers devoted teachers could well be successful at social transmission, despite its causing a reduction of genetic fitness.

Richerson and Boyd (1984) provided a provocative example: They suggested that religious celibacy could evolve to cultural prominence in a population through differential cultural parenting if, "by avoiding the costs of bearing or supporting children, celibates could devote more resources to spreading their beliefs by nonparental transmission" (p. 434; see also Dawkins, 1976; Ball, 1984). The idea is plausible and worthy of further exploration; certainly it should be tested against other contending explanations for traditions of celibacy (see e.g., Boone, 1986; Goody, 1983).

In the meantime, however, it does seem to assume that (a) celibacy is positively valued within the population, such that some individuals choose that option when it is energetically presented to them (which then raises pertinent questions about the primary and secondary values in the population); (b) potential followers can be misled or "brainwashed" into compliance, perhaps because the special effort at cultural parenting is able to block or override the normal feedback of prevalent primary and secondary values; or (c) someone has the ability to preempt the adopters decision-making process, and thus to impose the outcome. Parallel issues can be raised about the cultural parenting pathway to opposition in other contexts (such as the demographic transition example mentioned earlier). Still, theoretical models imply that natural selection is among the forces that give the leash good length.

Turning now to decision-making forces, consider the following hypotheses from Durham (1991): "first, that most cases of opposition [in the ethnographic record], especially enduring opposition, are socially imposed; and second, that opposition can also occur through selection by choice but only because of the imperfect nature of the human decision system" (p. 371). Of these two routes to opposition, Durham inferred causal priority on the part of imposition because "the persistence of [reproductively] suboptimal variants is specifically motivated by the interests of an outside individual or group for whom there generally *are* benefits. At least in principle, imposed opposition is indefinitely sustainable" (italics in original), (Durham 1991, p. 371).

As examples of imposed opposition, Durham (1991) cited the implementation and persistence of land laws in El Salvador (which reduced to poverty much of the indigenous population while benefiting a small group of entrepreneurial elites), the manipulation of the incest prohibition by the Catholic Church prior to the Reformation (according to the analysis by Goody, 1983), and the impositions of parents among the thongpa stratum of Tibetan serfs, which was a contributory force in the maintenance of Tibetan Lamaistic tradition—the latter being an example of what R. D. Alexander (1974) called *parental manipulation*. In each case, resources and/or reproductive opportunity were effectively stripped from the affected population for a period of at least three or four generations. In the case of El Salvador, however, it is not clear that the imposed restrictions translated into a net loss of genetic fitness because, by Durham's own account, the growth rate of the affected population has been among the world's highest (see Durham, 1979). In contrast, opposition by choice is held to be

> generally a transient side effect of various imperfections in [the human] decision system, four of which are particularly important [as follows]:
>
> 1. *Value blockage.* Though normally strong and effective, secondary values can be weakened or blocked altogether through such means as brainwashing ... or addiction to chemical substances.
>
> 2. *Value displacement.* Even when effective, secondary values can actively favor maladaptive [i.e., fitness-reducing] variants when they are used in novel social-ecological contexts (value disequilibrium); when they are transferred from an appropriate domain of choice to an inappropriate one (value generalization); or when, for whatever reason, one or more are temporarily singled out and given undue weighting (value reification).
>
> 3. *Consequence imperception.* Even where secondary values are not blocked or displaced, they can still be ineffective if people do not perceive at least some of the deleterious consequences of a given choice that causes opposition.
>
> 4. *Cause imperception.* Finally, even where people do perceive some of the deleterious consequences of their actions, they may fail to link those consequences to one or more [cultural beliefs] that they have the power to change by their own choice. (Durham, 1991, pp. 371–372)

As a result of these four kinds of imperfection, singly or in combination, the human decision system is prevented from doing what Durham (1991), Pugh (1977), and others argued it evolved to do—namely, to produce choices equivalent to those that genetic selection would have favored under parallel circumstances.

A fascinating case of opposition by choice has been described among the Fore peoples of the eastern highlands of New Guinea (Alpers, 1992; Durham, 1991; Gajdusek, 1977; Glasse, 1967; Lindenbaum, 1979; see also Goodfield, 1985). It concerns endocannibalism (the consumption of flesh from deceased kin or co-residents), a cultural novelty introduced to the Fore peoples via diffusion from the north during the first decade or two of this century. Although endocannibalism may well have had adaptive consequences at the start (by offsetting the declining supply of wild game), it wound up causing an epidemic of the lethal nerve degeneration disease, *kuru*, which, in less than 30 years, killed thousands of Fore, mostly women and children (who had handled diseased flesh).

Many lessons have been gleaned from this tragedy, and among them is the message that choice can produce devastating levels of opposition. In terms of the typology of imperfections introduced earlier, value blockage and consequence imperception cannot be blamed for the opposition. The Fore were acutely aware of the devastation of *kuru,* and struggled mightily to understand and eradicate its cause. However, they were hindered in this effort by value displacement and cause imperception. The long and variable latency of the disease hid its connection with endocannibalism from both the Fore and Western observers for many years. All the while, the Fore actively valued the practice: With tragic irony, endocannibalism was believed to speed the return of a fallen warrior's spirit to the pool of "life force" for his lineage, which was believed vital for community defense.

Boyd and Richerson (1985) offered two provocative models for the cultural evolution of maladaptive features, each of which incorporates various imperfections of the human decision system. The first of these models is a runaway process that can occur under certain conditions of cultural change through indirect bias (see Boyd & Richerson, 1985). The process can be illustrated with a hypothetical scenario for the evolution of a cultural tradition of growing yams of exaggerated proportion, such as are featured in periodic yam feasts on the Micronesian Island of Ponape:

> Suppose that at some earlier time Ponapeans did not devote any special effort to growing large yams. It seems reasonable that under such conditions more skillful or industrious farmers might have tended to bring larger yams to feasts and thus that the size of a man's yams would provide a useful indicator trait for all kinds of skills and beliefs associated with farming. By imitating [these men], naive individuals

could increase the chance that they would acquire the cultural variants they needed to be successful farmers... [and thus] the beliefs or practices that lead to larger yams would increase. Individuals with a stronger tendency to admire large yams will be more likely to acquire these beliefs. This will cause the two traits to be correlated—and therefore when the practices that lead to large yams increase, so too will the admiration for the ability to grow large yams. (Boyd & Richerson, 1985, pp. 269ff)

Consequently, the larger the yams, the more large yams are admired, and this positive feedback quickly produces grotesque, potentially maladaptive, extremes. Boyd and Richerson (1985) suggested that tattooing in Polynesia provides a second example. More generally, they argued that human prestige systems commonly show signs of exaggerations that are hard to explain on fitness grounds.

The second model is still more interesting because it involves an intergroup selection process—a topic that has long been controversial in the study of genetic evolution. The model outlines a way in which group functional behaviors requiring individual sacrifice can evolve through the proliferation of such groups, provided that some form of biased transmission (e.g., frequency-dependent bias) operates to maintain differences between groups:

Consider a large population subdivided into many smaller, partially isolated groups. Suppose that biased cultural transmission maintains cultural differences among these groups despite frequent contact... and that these cultural differences affect the welfare of the group. For example, groups [with more restrictive food taboos] may tend to harvest game [at or below] the maximum sustainable yield, while groups [with less restrictive taboos] over exploit their game resources [and thereby suffer nutritionally]. Further suppose that social groups are occasionally disrupted and their members dispersed to other local groups [at a rate that varies inversely with] the overall welfare of the group ... Thus, according to our hypothetical example, groups with less restrictive food taboos will, on average, be more likely to be broken up and dispersed. Finally, suppose that as some groups decline and disappear, other groups grow and eventually divide [at a rate which increases] with the overall welfare of the group. Thus, the growing, dividing groups will tend to have more restrictive food taboos [and thus the group-functional] behavior will tend to spread as a result of selection among groups. (Soltis, Boyd, & Richerson, 1994, pp. 475)

The key to the mechanism is the assumption that the value or values directing biased transmission (e.g., "adopt the majority preference" in the case of frequency-dependent bias) override more selfish values that may favor a different action with respect to the food supply. In effect, the model requires a special form of value generalization: Individuals must follow the majority preference despite their own hunger. Where true, opposition is then created by cultural group selection.

EMPIRICAL STUDIES

Peter Richerson and Robert Boyd

A. Introduction

To date, the use of Darwinian ideas to study cultural evolution has been mostly a conceptual and theoretical exercise. The empirical science lags. In the introduction to this part, we reviewed partial analogs of micro-evolutionary studies that have developed independently in a number of social science subdisciplines. There seems to be no special impediment to applying microevolutionary tools to culture. In this chapter, Durham introduces a different empirical problem. How do we test the general, large-scale prediction of the many hypotheses that can be derived from the theory? Micro tests of assumptions and mathematical tests of logic play roles, but they cannot alone answer such broad questions such as, how tight are the various genetic leashes? To understand these, we have to appeal to the evidence of the large-scale and long-term results of genetic and cultural coevolution.

Social scientists are used to providing an interpretation of historical trajectories and current social institutions. Indeed, the conceit would seem to be that an interpretation can be given for any historical trajectory or any current social practice. Social scientists and historians seem compelled by tradition to tell stories about their data. Although there is nothing wrong with such storytelling in principle, it is intrinsically a weak method of critically examining theoretical principles (D. T. Campbell, 1965; McNeill, 1986). The problem is the very great complexity of human history and human societies. For any given institution, much less for the many necessary to make a viable society, perhaps most or all of the processes described in Part I have affected its evolution. Detailed evidence is usually lacking. In this event, almost any internally consistent set of categories will furnish a vocabulary that seems to account reasonably well for the case at hand. Marxism, functionalism, methodological individualism, and many other schemata can be made to work equally well (or rather equally badly because rival interpretation schemata have harsh critiques of each other). This "cyclical and repetitive opposition" is a major embarrassment to the social sciences (Sahlins, 1976). Various forms of Darwinism can easily be used as interpretive frameworks in just this traditional fashion (Betzig, 1989; Darlington, 1969).

The macro evidence is useful to test theory, if it is handled with a great deal of methodological care. Somehow, the intrinsic complexity of the cases has to be finessed. In fact, most are likely to remain irremediably muddy and useless. The basic trick is to expose the variation due to processes of interest against the background complexity. One approach is to discover cases that are unusually simple, so that confounding variables can be eliminated. A second is to collect data from many examples and analyze them in a comparative framework, controlling for confounding variables statistically. Both approaches provide a chance of exposure of the processes implied by the interpretation to clear logical or empirical challenge. We have used this strategy in a limited number of cases to test the applicability of Darwinian theory to cultural evolution. Two examples arc reviewed later (see also Boyd & Richerson, 1985; Durham, 1991).

Often the criterion of simplicity is best met in cases where an unusual pattern is evident. If we notice a large deviation from what the simple version of a theory predicts, or a rare phenomenon that departs from the common run of cases, it is often because a single variable operating under unusual constraints is responsible for the effect. Such cases form natural experiments, in which it is practical to infer the main causes operating with relatively high confidence. In more typical cases, multiple causes are frequently mixed together in a most confusing manner, each contributing only a small amount to the variation observed. Truly heroic effort would be needed to reach a satisfactorily critical explanation. For example, as noted earlier, we usually expect behavior to be adaptive, or reasonably close to adaptive, due to a complex mixture of genetic, cultural, and individual processes. All of the evolutionary hypotheses reviewed in this book predict that adaptation will be common (but natural theology did too). Thus, ordinary cases of apparently adaptive behavior are hardly useful at all to test theory. The specific processes that generate adaptations are only dimly revealed except in special cases.

B. Lactose Malabsorption Example

Durham (1991) illustrates how the careful analysis of a strategically selected simple case, supplemented by the comparative method, can yield
useful progress. It is a basic assumption of the Darwinian theory of culture that long-lived cultural traditions should cause a coevolutionary response on the part of genes, as well as vice versa. Genetic evolution
should be driven by culture as much as vice versa. This general picture of
the evolution of culture is quite different from a theory that ties culture
closely to a genetic leash. If the coevolutionary picture is correct, cultural
processes may have acted to create the environment under which primary
values and other basic psychological attributes of humans evolved as adaptations. This hypothesis, however plausible in principle, is difficult to
test. Much of this coevolution presumably occurred in the remote past, so
that genetic adaptation to the cultural environment is complete, leaving
little genetic variation relevant to the coevolutionary process to observe.

However, we might hope to catch a few such events in progress in
contemporary populations. Showing in one simple case that cultural evolution can drive genetic responses does not prove much all by itself. However, it does provide an illustration of a process in action. Multiplying
such examples and introducing other sorts of evidence gradually build a
case for the importance of a particular type of explanation. In evolutionary biology, in the face of similar levels of complexity, even the case for
the basic importance of natural selection has been built in a piecemeal
fashion over more than a century since Darwin's work, and the one perfect study does not yet exist (Brandon, 1990).

The case of adult lactose malabsorption is perhaps the most convincing example yet worked out of culture-driven genetic change, although
there are a number of other promising cases in the realm of food and disease, due to the relative recency with which human populations have adopted agriculture and soared to high densities (Stinson, 1992). If the cultural revolution initiated by the origin of food production a few thousand
years ago can be shown to have caused a few significant changes in human genes, it is more likely that more massive changes accompanied the
even more fundamental developments in cultural capacities over the past
2 million years.

The case is relatively simple in the way a cultural innovation (dairying) affected a human genetic polymorphism for adult lactose absorption/
malabsorption. The genetic system is composed of a single locus with

two alleles, adult absorption dominant. Data relevant to the hypotheses described later have been collected on 60 ethnographically varied human populations, permitting a solid comparative analysis. Because the genetic system is so simple and the comparative data relatively ample, a close interpretive analysis of this strategically selected case yields considerable insight into the processes of gene–culture coevolution. A more complex genetic system with limited comparative data would almost certainly entangle the analysis of too many complexities to be useful.

In most of the world's human populations, as in most mammals, adults lose the ability to absorb lactose, the main sugar in milk. Lactose malabsorption, in turn, causes gastric distress in most malabsorbers who attempt to drink milk or other lactose-rich dairy products. In Northern European populations and among a few African groups, most adults retain the ability to absorb lactose. All of the groups in which high frequencies of adults retain the ability absorb lactose have a long tradition of dairying. This fact led Simoons (1969) and McCracken (1971) to propose that a history of dairying had led to a selection pressure for adult lactose absorption. Some European and African populations have a tradition of dairying that reaches back to the so-called "secondary products revolution," when many processing techniques were added to the basic agricultural tool kit. These innovations date to ca. 6,000–8,000 years ago, leaving enough time for relatively weak selection for adult absorption to raise frequencies to observed levels (Bodmer & Cavalli-Sforza, 1976). It is important to note that the initial steps of dairying can take place even when absorbers are in low frequency. Many malabsorbers can come to tolerate fresh milk, it might be an important supplemental food for children who still absorb, and various processing techniques can be used to reduce the lactose content of dairy products.

A complicating factor for the Simoons–McCracken hypothesis is that many populations with an apparently long history of dairying still have low frequencies of adult lactose absorption. These populations are concentrated in the Middle East and Southern Europe, where archaeological records indicate stock raising was first developed. Adults in this region typically consume milk in processed forms that are low in lactose (e.g., yogurt and related products from which lactose is removed by a lactic acid fermentation).

Durham (1991) reviewed evidence that suggests that adult absorption of lactose was favored in northern European dairying populations because of the effect of lactose in promoting the absorption of calcium ion in the gut. In low-latitude populations, the photosynthesis of vitamin D by UV light in the skin provides the standard human mechanism for enhancing calcium absorption. Northern Europe is historically a region plagued by diseases associated with poor absorption due to low photosynthesis rates of vitamin D, due, in turn, to low exposure to UV under cloudy, high-latitude conditions. Agricultural populations with low consumption of animal products rich in vitamin D are especially likely to suffer from vitamin D deficiency. Thus, high-latitude hunters and gatherers (e.g., Eskimo, Lapps) have low frequencies of adult absorption, and also have diets rich in vitamin D. Adult absorption is highest in groups like Danes, Swedes, Germans, and French, which have a history of (a) mass diets heavily dependent on a mixture of grains and dairy products, (b) relatively low levels of consumption of vitamin D rich animal products, and (c) living in low UV environments.

The high frequency of adult lactose absorption among tropical pastoralists heavily dependent on milk requires a separate explanation under this hypothesis. Presumably, such people find the drinking of fluid milk especially important for reasons unrelated to calcium absorption, such as a substitute for water in hot, arid conditions, or because a need for frequent movement, combined with a lack of draft animals, makes the production, storage, and transport of processed milk products cumbersome.

Perhaps the most interesting feature of the adult lactose absorption case is that it illustrates how cultural evolution can lead to the creation of a new adaptation, in which the genetic part of the response lags behind. Once we understand that cultural evolution is a fully dynamic process, it no longer seems quite safe to neglect the details of cultural evolution and adopt the phenotypic gambit or similar simplifying strategies, as R. D. Alexander (1979) laid the groundwork for and some of his followers have adopted (e.g., Betzig, 1989).

C. Human Cooperation

As noted by Cronin (1991), evolutionary biologists gain confidence in the mechanism of natural selection as much from the failures of the adaptation prediction as from its successes. Cooperation is an excellent example. Evolutionary theory predicts that most cases of cooperation in nature are likely to result from kin selection or reciprocity, rather than from group selection, although large-scale cooperation is often a major adaptive advantage. This expectation is borne out by the commonness with which cooperation is based on kinship, and the dramatic ecological success of the few lineages that manage to use this mechanism to achieve large-scale cooperation. As Hölldobler and E. O. Wilson (1990) noted, ants, bees, wasps, termites, and naked mole rats provide a number of independent inventions of eusociality via kin selection for worker sterility, and eusocial species are among the most widespread and abundant insects, despite being only a tiny handful of all insect species. If group selection were a generally feasible mechanism, cooperation in large groups would presumably not be restricted to the few odd creatures whose biology predisposes them to large-scale cooperation via kin selection.

Cooperation is the dog that usually does not bark according to evolutionary theory. When it does, as in the fascinating cases of the social insects, the conformance of the cases to the few kinds of exceptions predicted by the theory gives us added confidence in the routine power of natural selection to prevent cooperative adaptations that require group selection.

The theory of natural selection predicts other specific kinds of limitations to a naive panadaptationism. Sex ratio is one example. A 1:1 sex ratio is usually not ecologically adaptive (far fewer males would do), but is rather dictated by the fact that departures toward a more adaptive ratio have the effect of making males fitter that females. Thus, a genetic factor increasing the chance that an individual will become a male when males are less common than females will be favored, and natural selection will favor an ecologically inefficient sex ratio under most, but not all, circumstances (Charnov, 1982).

Human cooperation is a special case within a special case. Like the eusocial insects, we apparently owe our ecological dominance to our ultrasociality. The importance of the phenomenon dictates that attention be paid to it, even if large methodological difficulties make a definitive answer difficult. Like our dependence on culture, the human ability to form large cooperative groups with an extensive division of labor is a major distinctive feature of our behavior. We are drawn to understand such phenomena, and cannot neglect them merely because they are methodologically challenging.

Can such studies avoid the pitfalls of interpretationalism? First, note that any pattern of behavior that is unique to humans, or of which we are an unusual exemplar, has the marks of a potential natural experiment, if we express the problem in a comparative mode. As for the general problem of the multiple possible causes of ordinary adaptations, the reasons that humans differ in some respects from other animals may be relatively easy to understand compared with the reasons that, in other ways, we are not so unusual. Unusual features are often due to the extreme operation of one or a few causes that can be picked from the usual morass. Second, the important part of the natural experiment strategy is to maximize the vulnerability of processes used in interpretation to challenges on the basis of logical cogency and empirical verisimilitude, rather than to construct the investigation to avoid such exposure, as interpretationalist programs do. In fundamentally important cases like human cooperation, we should employ a suite of tools to build a set of hypotheses and then a long-term strategy for investigation. Rather than just "explain" human cooperation as a large-scale adaptive peculiarity of humans, we should try to list the kinds of theoretical and small-scale empirical claims that are consistent with any proposed explanation of the case.

Richerson and Boyd (1987) characterized this strategy for attacking the major questions of human evolution and behavior as building "plausibility arguments." In the case of complex questions like the evolutionary explanation of human cooperation, it is vain to hope for success by posing a small set of mutually exclusive hypotheses and then seeking a single or small set of definitive test(s). However, it is still possible to make progress within the standard fallibilist, hypothetico-deductive framework. The trick is to use a mixture of theoretical and empirical arguments to build logically coherent candidate explanations for the phenomena. In the end, the component building blocks of the several competing plausibility arguments may end up being rearranged, replaced, or combined for a synthetic answer. This is a version of the disciplined pluralism advocated in chapter 3.

Boyd and Richerson (1985; Richerson & Boyd, 1989; see also Soltis, Boyd, & Richerson, 1991) developed a plausibility argument that might explain human cooperation deriving from the dynamics of gene–culture coevolution. The basic idea is that group selection may be much easier when the variation on which it acts is cultural rather than genetic. They conceive of this analysis as a plausible alternative or complement to more conventional explanations of human altruism derived directly from considerations of selection acting on genes, such as those given by Hamilton (1975) or R. D. Alexander (1987). The argument in outline is as follows.

Human patterns of cooperation do not fit comfortably into those of any known animal model. Human populations are often highly cooperative, as illustrated by such phenomena as cooperation in warfare, and can be described as ultrasocial. However, other ultrasocial animals, such as the social bees, wasps, ants, and termites, are based on kin selection favoring reproductive suppression of the workers that provide benefits to the colony, or similar mechanisms. The cooperation found in other vertebrates, including other primates, is much more limited than in the human case, and can be easily explained by the now-classical mechanisms of kin selection and reciprocity. Although it is not a closed issue that some form of reciprocity (R. D. Alexander, 1987) or kin selection (van den Berghe, 1981) could provide part of the explanation of human cooperation, the basic comparative natural history of humans in the context of the broader animal kingdom suggests an unusual causal mechanism. At the very least, the basic empirical facts do not discourage a search for an unusual or unique explanation for human altruism.

Humans are apparently unique in their massive dependence on culturally transmitted information. Certainly, there is ample evidence that humans can easily acquire behaviors and rules by social learning, and that even our closest relatives like chimpanzees are highly limited in this regard (Tomasello, 1996). Our apparently unique dependence on culture is, *prima facie*, a plausible place to search for an explanation for our apparently unique pattern of cooperation.

The cultural transmission system has a number of potentially important features that may make group selection on cultural variation easier than in the genetic case. Following G. C. Williams (1966), most evolutionary biologists believe that the potential for group selection in organic evolution is theoretically implausible as well as empirically unnecessary. Subsequent theoretical work has shown that variation between groups is hard to maintain in the face of selection and migration. However, the deductive, theoretical part of this argument does not follow for some plausible patterns of cultural transmission. For example, a conformity effect will strongly protect between-group variation and potentiate group selection on cultural variation. If people use a rule like!'when in Rome do as the Romans do" when acquiring culture, migrants from one community to another will have little effect on their host communities. Technically, cultural variation can be subject to a positive frequency-dependent form of biased transmission (primary or secondary values selection) that overcomes the main theoretical flaw in typical group selection explanations, by easily maintaining ample variation between groups on which group selection might work. With a genetic system of inheritance with only one or two parents, individuals simply do not have the information to use frequency in the population to affect their genetic makeup, even if such a decision were biologically feasible.

There is some weak empirical evidence that people do use conformist rules when imitating others, although this is one of the many questions about how cultural transmission processes work that is practically unstudied. There is stronger empirical evidence that many of the population level requirements of the conformity/group selection model are met in simple human societies. For example, conformity will not maintain much heritable variation between groups if new groups following extinctions are formed of random recruits from the larger population. But between-group variation is easily maintained if new group formation is affected by splitting of old groups.

Unlike genetic group selection, cultural group selection under conformist transmission does not require the physical extinction of people, but merely the dispersal of individuals from losing groups. The evidence developed by Soltis (Soltis, Boyd, & Richerson, 1994) on the population level patterns of group extinction and new-group formation from unacculturated Highland New Guinea suggests that group extinction could be powerful enough to have a substantial role in long-term cultural evolution. Moreover, rates of evolution by group selection in the New Guinea case also seem to be low enough to account for the observed levels of variation among cultural groups and imperfections in cooperative adaptations.

Patterns of altruism are consistent with the prediction that people are most likely to cooperate with people with whom they are co-socialized in some culturally defined group, as any cultural group selection hypothesis requires. The durability of ethnicity as a locus of cooperation and political organization is an example. In modern complex societies, it is common to emphasize co-socialization of individuals, especially when high levels of cooperation are required. Military training typically involves the building of *esprit de corps* through deliberate inculcation of pseudo- or quasiethnic symbolic cultural systems. For example, in experimental studies, where people are asked to play a prisoner's dilemma game in the laboratory, indicators of belonging to a common group substantially increase rates of cooperation.

Although the cultural variation in cooperation patterns is substantial, there is also some evidence that genetically coded, psychological traits may have coevolved with an environment of cultural group selection. At the level of comparative natural history, humans seem "docile" and predisposed to cooperate (H. A. Simon, 1990). Notwithstanding strong patterns of cooperation within, but not between, cultural ingroups, variation at the individual level is extreme and altruistic acts are easily displaced to "inappropriate" targets (i.e., pets).

Recent detailed studies of the psychology of human altruism suggest that, once a feeling of empathy with another is triggered, people are motivated to help by a genuinely altruistic desire, not merely some form of egoism, such as a desire to avoid unpleasant sights and sounds. Batson (1991) created a number of experimental manipulations in which subjects whose empathy was aroused by the suffering of another either could or could not anonymously escape without helping the victim. The provision of anonymous escape did not decrease rates of helping in his experiments. He argued that his results are sufficient to reject current versions of psychological explanations of altruistic acts as being covertly self-interested in one way or another.

In the simpler and more accessible example of adult lactose absorption, we have already seen how cultural evolution can cause a coevolutionary response on the part of genes. By extrapolation, such a culture-led evolutionary process, acting over a longer period of human evolutionary history, could easily have led to a fundamental reworking of human psychological dispositions.

Our plausibility argument for cultural group selection is a modernization and elaboration of Darwin's ([1871]1874) proposal that intergroup competition aided by "inherited habit" led to the rise of the special "moral and intellectual faculties" of humans. Through a long history of coevolution, humans are plausibly genetically adapted to live in an environment of culturally defined groups that have been subject to group selection. We claim that competing arguments have a much more difficult time accounting for the apparent absence of the human pattern of cooperation among other animals, and the great variety of apparently culturally shaped forms of cooperation, notwithstanding virtual ubiquity of some elements of cooperation in human adaptive complexes.

Each point of the argument rests on a theoretical model, experimental result, or empirical observation, some of them fairly sound, others currently quite soft. Some challenges to the argument would force revision, and others might invite wholesale skepticism. Still, a successful explanation will almost certainly have to have some of the general features of the cultural group selection argument. For example, a successful explanation must account for the differences between humans and other animals (especially other primates), for the generality of cooperative adaptations in humans, and yet for the diversity and historical trajectory of increasing scales of cooperation among human communities.

This argument should be compared with other accounts, especially those given by evolutionary biologists, who stress more individualistic explanations of human behavior. For example, the indirect reciprocity argument of Alexander seems only partially cogent on theoretical grounds (Boyd & Richerson, 1988, 1989, 1992b), but it is easy to imagine that there is a synergistic interaction between indirect reciprocity and cultural group selection. A substantial amount of additional work is clearly required to refine both of these arguments.

D. The Challenge of Empirical Cases

There are three basic challenges to the adequacy of any evolutionary theory. First, the theory must be cogent. Making this test is the task of the formal theorist using (usually) mathematical models. The second is the conformity of the theory to micro evidence about the details of the postulated process. Such evidence comes from controlled experimental investigations or comparative studies that use some variant of the natural experiment approach. Third, one can attempt to account for the actual events of specific evolutionary events. None of the three kinds of challenges has any sort of privileged warrant for deciding important issues. For the complex issues involved in human gene–culture coevolution, any account must meet all three challenges simultaneously. Perhaps the most important message derived from the cases is how hard it is to make any sense at all of most real examples. This should not be surprising. Organic and cultural evolution are massive tangles of complex processes operating in a historically contingent world. Usually most of the critical data are missing and unobtainable at reasonable cost with existing techniques. Making even a few cases theoretically useful requires patience, caution, methodological ingenuity, and luck. The blithe interpretationalism so common in the social sciences, which assumes that there is a current set of explanatory principles that can satisfactorily account for virtually any case brought under examination, is exceedingly naive.

CONCLUSION

William H. Durham, Robert Boyd, and Peter J. Richerson

The models and forces discussed in this chapter lead toward one conclusion that is perhaps more important than the others. The work reviewed in this chapter strongly suggests a considerable symmetry of influence between the way that genes influence phenotypes, the way that culture influences phenotypes, and the way that they jointly produce phenotypes. By showing that the cultural system of information inheritance has its own peculiar mechanisms of transformation, and that, as a result of these mechanisms, cultural change can either enhance or oppose the direction of genetic evolution, a strong case has been made for the dual-inheritance view of human evolution. Put differently, the models and forces described earlier all imply that Lumsden and E. O. Wilson's (1981) idea of a "leash" between genetics and culture is an excellent metaphor if we consider its full implications. We have all seen large, poorly trained dogs on a tight leash dragging their owners through the streets. Many of us have seen unleashed dogs working in sophisticated harmony with human hunters and herders. Is the leash loose or tight? If it is tight, who is dragging whom about? Or is it mainly a matter of mutualistic teamwork? Does the answer depend on time, place, and other particulars, or are some relationships much more common than others? We cannot give convincing responses to such questions, but we can certainly pose them much more pointedly than did Campbell in his path-breaking essay over 30 years ago.

10

ARE CULTURAL PHYLOGENIES POSSIBLE?

Robert Boyd
University of California
Los Angeles

Monique Borgerhoff Mulder
University of California
Davis

William H. Durham
Stanford University
Stanford

Peter J. Richerson
University of California
Davis

Biology and the social sciences share an interest in phylogeny. Biologists know that living species are descended from past species, and use the pattern of similarities among living species to reconstruct the history of phylogenetic branching. Social scientists know that the beliefs, values, practices, and artifacts that characterize contemporary societies are descended from past societies, and some social science disciplines (e.g., linguistics and cross-cultural anthropology) have made use of observed similarities to reconstruct cultural histories. Darwin appreciated that his theory of descent with modification had many similarities of pattern and process to the already well-developed field of historical linguistics. In many other areas of social science, however, phylogenetic reconstruction has not played a central role.

Phylogenetic reconstruction plays three important roles in biology. First, it provides the basis for the classification. Entities descended from a common ancestor share novel, or derived, characters inherited from that ancestor. Therefore, it is possible to group them into hierarchically organized series of groups-species, genus, family, order, and so on in the biological case.

Second, knowledge of phylogeny often allows inferences about history. The knowledge that humans are more closely related to chimpanzees and gorillas than to orangutans provides evidence that the human lineage arose in Africa. Phylogenetic reconstructions based on the characters of extant species or cultures often allow us to reconstruct the history in the absence of a historical, archaeological, or fossil record. In practice, the history of many biological and cultural groups is so poorly known that only by combining phylogenetic and historical or archaeological information can reliable reconstructions be obtained.

Third, entities descended from a common ancestor share features that may constrain the pathways that more recent evolution has followed. For example, selection for terrestrial locomotion may lead to quadrupedal locomotion in a small monkey that runs along the tops of branches, but to bipedal locomotion in a large arboreal ape that swings below branches (Foley, 1987). The latter pattern allows the hand to specialize in manipulative tasks, and, on many accounts, is why the ape, but not the monkey lineage, eventually was able to produce a cultural species.

The importance of *descent* is the crux of some of the deepest controversies of all the historical sciences. Some social scientists and biologists (e.g., Boyd & Richerson, 1992a; Hallpike, 1986; Sahlins, 1976) have argued that history strongly constrains adaptation and, as a result, strictly limits adaptive interpretations of current behavior. As Francis Galton taught both biologists and social scientists in the 19th century, to account for the effects of common ancestry, the study of adaptation or function requires that patterns of descent be known. Our inability to provide appropriate roles for history and function is a chronic source of controversy.

If the analogy is real, an interdisciplinary exchange of concepts and tools could pay great dividends. In particular, social scientists may be particularly interested in the near-revolutionary developments in systematics (Ridley, 1986) and comparative methods (Harvey & Pagel, 1991) developed by evolutionary biologists in the last two decades.

The purpose of this chapter is to examine the role of descent in culture evolution theory. We believe that the critical question is whether human cultures, or parts of them, are isolated from one another to the same degree as biological entities like species and genes. Cultures are frequently characterized by sharp ingroup–outgroup boundaries (LeVine & D. T. Campbell, 1972) that may function to limit the flow of ideas from one population to another (Boyd & Richerson, 1987). However, there are also many examples of the diffusion of cultural traits across such boundaries (E. M. Rogers, 1983). Are the isolating processes sufficiently strong to provide at least a core of important cultural traits that are sufficiently protected from diffusion so that phylogenetic analysis is possible? If so, concepts and methods from biological systematics can be used to reconstruct the history of cultures. If not, human cultures are more like subspecies or local populations linked by gene flow than like reproductively isolated species. In this case, it may be useful to make separate phylogenies for each subunit of culture that is substantially protected from diffusion, in much the same way that modern molecular procedures are used to reconstruct the phylogeny of subgenomic units, especially individual genes. It may also be that there are no cultural units with sufficient coherence, and therefore that phylogenetic methods are useless.

We begin by reviewing the notions of descent used in evolutionary biology. Biologists have been making use of the concept of descent ever since Darwin, and they have developed a sophisticated appreciation for the concept and its problems that may be helpful in the human case. The complexity and diversity of biological systems of inheritance is wondrous to those brought up on the simple Mendelism of 20 years ago (Jablonka, chap. 11, this volume). Although it is likely that the process of cultural descent with modification is different from the analogous process in organic evolution, we believe that much can be learned from a biologist's century of hard work. We then consider data from the social sciences that indicate the extent to which cultures form bounded wholes, analogous to species. Finally, we consider how the descent concepts, partly borrowed from biology, might be used to tackle important questions in the social sciences.

DESCENT IN ORGANIC EVOLUTION

In biology, two different entities exhibit the clear patterns of descent with modification. The most familiar example is the species. The collection of individuals who make up a species during any generation are descended, and perhaps slightly modified, from the collection of individuals who made up the species during the previous generation. When a new species is formed, it is by the splitting of an existing species. Then each of the daughter species is descended from the single ancestral species that gave rise to them.

Much the same holds for genes one by one. Because genes result from the copying of DNA, every gene is descended from the gene that provided its template. Modified genes arise from existing genes by mutation, recombination, and gene conversion at a given locus. A genetic locus can give rise to another locus by duplicating itself on the chromosome, after which the daughter locus begins independent evolution. The relationships among genes is not simply the relationships among the species that carry them (although this is often the case). We can keep track of the relationship of genes *within* a single species (e.g., various forms of hemoglobin within human populations). It is also possible to speak of relationships among genes that are inconsistent with relationships among species. For example, genes for globin molecules in vertebrates and certain plants seem to share a more recent common ancestor than the genes in vertebrates and arthropods, as surprising as this seems at first blush (Jeffreys et al., 1983).

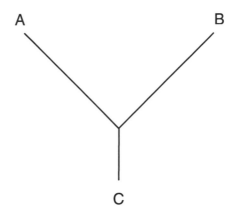

Fig. 10.1.   A hypothetical phylogeny in which Species *B* and *C* are descended from Species *A*.

Descent relationships are often represented using branching diagrams like that shown in Fig. 10.1. The diagram conveys the idea that both *B* and *C* are descended from an Ancestor *A*. (Sytematists use similar branching diagrams called cladograms to represent patterns of similarity without reference to time, or ancestor-descendant relationships; statistical clustering algorithms create treelike dendrograms also without any pretense to representing ancestor–descendant relationships. Tree diagrams are used here to represent phylogeny.) The same diagram is used to represent the relationship among different kinds of things. For biologists *A*, *B*, and *C* may represent species or genes. Social scientists use similar diagrams to express the relationship among languages, or other aspects of culture, often with the explicit intention of representing a phylogeny. What, if anything, does the descent of genes and species have in common? Can these commonalities provide some help in analyzing the descent of cultures, languages, and technologies?

A. The Descent of Genes

To answer this question, let us begin with the simpler case—the descent relationship among genes. If we ignore for a moment the possibility of recombination, every gene is a copy of another gene. Of course, that gene was the copy of yet another gene, and so on. Thus, if we pick any two genes, A and B, we can, in principle, trace back through a series of copies until we find a gene, C, that served as a template for both. We say that Genes A and B are descended from C. If mutations have occurred, A or B may be different from C and each other. As long as mutations are rare and the gene includes enough bases, then genes that share more derived mutations are more likely to be related. Taxonomists use this fact to reconstruct the branching pattern among genes sampled from living species. Notice that there is nothing in the discussion that specifies that C, A, and B have to belong to the same (or different) species. The same argument would hold regardless of whether A and B are genes found within a single species, or among distantly related species (e.g., humans and bean plants).

B. Units with Reticulated Phylogenies

Recombination—the shuffling of chromosomes of the genes along a chromosome and the sequence within a gene—complicates matters because it leads to what cladists call *reticulated phylogenies*. Fig. 10.2 shows the lineages of three genes. Recombination has occurred within the gene three times. After each recombination event, each of the daughter genes is a copy of part of each of the two parents. The daughter genes are no longer descended from the parental genes in the same way that they were in the absence of recombination. They are no longer almost exact copies of the parents, rather, they are partial copies of both parents. Further recombination events create yet more complicated patterns of relationship. After some time, every copy of the gene is related to a large number of other genes in some complicated way that utterly obscures descent. Recombination within a gene is rare, but recombination within chromosomes between different genes is quite common. Deep phylogenies can be reconstructed for genes, but only shallow ones for chromosomes.

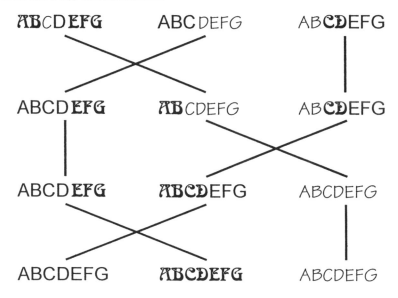

Fig. 10.2.   Recombination leads to complicated patterns of descent. Each string of letters represents a segment of the chromosome. Each generation each gene is replicated, sometimes with recombination. After four generations, each chromosome is partly descended from all three of the original chromosomes.

Gene flow (migration) among subpopulations of a species has a similar effect. Any given local group will have acquired genes from many different local groups in the past. Even if most subpopulations are created by the subdivision of a single parental population, a relatively small rate of individual level migration between subpopulations will carry genes evolved in one daughter subpopulation to its sisters. Fairly shortly, descent at the subpopulation level will be impossible to detect. Thus, there is a large range of genetic units ranging in size from roughly small chromosome segments to the subspecies for which phylogenetic analysis is usually impossible.

Some large gene collections, such as mitochondrial genomes, are protected from recombination because they are transmitted asexually. Mitochondrial phylogenies of some depth can be constructed, although they illustrate another process that eliminates phylogenetic information in the long run. Mitochondria are subject to high mutation rates. In a matter of a few million years, every descendant pair of mitochondrial genes will have independently mutated more than once, and the traces of descent will be lost. Conservative genes like the cytochrome genes have slow rates of evolution, and can be used to reconstruct phylogenetic relationships reaching back to near the origin of life, but these are exceptional. More typically, deep phylogenetic reconstructions based on less faithful structures are quite controversial even when we can be almost certain that recombination and migration have not confused the picture.

C. The Descent of Species

Species and higher taxa are the classic focus of phylogenetic analysis in biology. Linnean systematists formalized the common observation that the organic world comes in readily observable clusters. Species and higher taxa seem to be separated by distinctive gaps that do not occur within species or among many other natural objects. Darwin's theory of descent with modification gave a theoretical underpinning to the trees of relationships that Linnaeus had enshrined in a hierarchical classification system, although Darwin had little to say about the species-isolating mechanisms that enforce the gaps between species. His followers have made up for this deficiency; the issue of speciation is a major topic in modern evolutionary biology.

In the basic picture constructed by architects (e.g., like Ernst Mayr) of the mid-century neo-Darwinian synthesis, species are created when a barrier to gene flow evolves to isolate two sets of populations. Once isolated, the evolution of the two new species is independent, and slowly changes accumulate due to natural selection, genetic drift, mutation, and so forth. There may be some evolutionary differentiation within a population due to selection or drift. But interbreeding among populations unites a species, whereas absolute speciating barriers definitively separate them from other species. Over the long run, species become different enough to be classified as new genera, families, orders, and so on, up Linnaeus' hierarchy. In the classic picture, complete isolation and the slow accumulation of differences allow for the reconstruction of relationships of descent by splitting over great time depths.

The basic picture provides a clear causal explanation of the temporal and spatial coherence of species. Advocates of the biological species concept hold that only when this picture applies do we have species, properly speaking. However, there are several lines of evidence that suggest that the absence of gene flow is neither necessary nor sufficient for the existence of coherent species in the sense of lumpy entities that show clear evidence of descent. Species can maintain their coherence without gene flow within the species, and species boundaries may be maintained despite gene flow between species.

Some species have maintained species typical phenotypes, including the ability to form fertile hybrids despite long periods without any gene flow. For example, the checkerspot butterfly is found in scattered populations throughout California. Members of different populations are very similar morphologically and are all classified as members of the species *Euphydryas editha.* However, careful study has shown that there is virtually no gene flow among widely separated populations (Ehrlich & Raven, 1969). There are also many examples (Levinton, 1988) of cryptic "sibling" species that are long isolated, but have evolved no detectable morphological differences. Some taxonomists claim that it is no more difficult to detect species in asexual organisms than it is in sexual organisms (e.g., Mishler & Brandon, 1987), despite the fact that there is no gene flow to unite asexual populations.

Some species persist despite substantial gene flow (Barton & Hewitt, 1989). A hybrid zone can exist between what seem to be good species, and often a few genes have clearly leaked across the boundary from one species to another. It would seem as if such species must either be formerly geographically isolated subspecies that will hybridize away, or incipient species that will eventually evolve an isolating barrier. In fact, active hybrid zones between rather distinct species sometimes persist for long periods of time. Selection can apparently maintain the coherence of species both without any help from gene flow and in the face of substantial amounts of it.

Things are not always so neat. In bacteria, genes are frequently transmitted horizontally among lineages (Eberhardt, 1990). Bacterial DNA exists in two distinct forms: Most of the DNA is contained in a large chromosome, but about 1% is contained in small loops of DNA called *plasmids*. The two forms of DNA are transmitted differently. For the most part, the chromosomal DNA is transmitted vertically. When bacteria divide, the chromosomal DNA is duplicated, and each daughter cell contains a copy. In contrast, plasmid DNA is transmitted horizontally from one bacteria to another during conjugation. Moreover, bacteria that are classified as belonging to different genera or families according to their chromosomal DNA readily conjugate and exchange plasmid DNA. As a result, genes carried on plasmids may jump from one lineage to another quite distant one. It is not certain that two types of DNA are completely separate. Sometimes plasmid DNA may be incorporated into the chromosome, although if this occurs it is probably quite rare (Eberhardt, 1990). In the case of bacteria, there are really two sets of phylogenies: one for the chromosomal DNA and one for the mitochondrial. Relationships between these phylogenies break down rapidly because of the horizontal transmission of plasmids across chromosomal lineages.

The opposite situation occurs with the lineages of hosts and parasites and predators in many animals and plants. For example, ectoparasites like lice and fleas are often isolated within their hosts, so that host and parasite phylogenies are similar despite there being no transfer between host and parasite genomes.

THE COMMON PROPERTIES OF GENES AND SPECIES

Genes and species are units at quite different levels of organization. For them, but not units between them on the scale of organization, deep phylogenies can usually be constructed. The reason is a pair of similarities. First, both units are replicated with great fidelity and change slowly due to ongoing evolution. Second, when daughter genes and species change, these changes are not effectively shared with sister lineages by mixing or any other form of communication. For systems with high rates of change, like mitochondrial genomes, deeper descent is obscured because recently evolved differences completely obliterate the ancient similarities that are necessary to detect descent. In the case of units like chromosomes and local populations with high rates of mixing, descent is generally untraceable because descent-derived differences are erased as rapidly as they arise.

Genealogy is by itself not enough to generate much descent. There is a hierarchy of genealogical entities in biology: genes, chromosomes, individuals, populations, species, and communities. These are genealogical entities because they are all descendants of other entities at the same level. In the face of rapid mixing or evolution (or both), genealogy alone cannot preserve detectable patterns of descent, at least not for long. Note that patterns of descent are a matter of time scale. If we are interested in relationships only over a few splittings of daughter entities, these may be detectable in the face of considerable mixing and high rates of evolution.

If we want to know relationships traceable many splits ago, the criteria are more demanding.

RECONSTRUCTING CULTURAL PHYLOGENIES

Can we apply these ideas from biology to the analysis of human culture? As was seen in the previous two chapters, Darwinian models of cultural evolution hold that culture is information transmitted from individual to individual by imitation, teaching, and other forms of social learning. Various processes cause the pool of cultural variants that characterize a population's change through time.

This view of culture and cultural evolution implies the existence of a hierarchy of genealogical entities analogous to the genealogical hierarchy of organic evolution. We do not know what is the smallest unit of cultural inheritance because we do not know in detail how culture is stored in brains. Nevertheless, scholars have proposed histories of quite small elements: particular words, particular innovations, elements of folk stories, and components of ritual practice. Such small elements are linked together in larger, culturally transmitted entities: systems of morphology, myth, technology, and religion. Such medium-scale units are collected together into "subcultures" and "cultures" that characterize human groups of different scales: kin group, village, ethnic group, nation, and so forth. Cultural subunits sometimes cross-cut one another in complex ways, as when religion or occupation cross-cuts ethnicity (much like bacterial chromosomes and plasmids).

A. Four Hypotheses

Reconstructing cultural phylogenies is possible to the extent that there are genealogical entities that have sufficient coherence, relative to the amount of mixing and independent evolution among entities, to create recognizable history. There is a continuum of possible views about what units in the hierarchy of cultural descent satisfy these desiderata. It is useful to identify four regions along this continuum.

1. Cultures as Species

Cultures are isolated from one another and/or are tightly integrated. They contain within them powerful sources of isolation (ethnocentric discrimination against strangers) or coherence (such as organizing systems of thought that act as biases against ideas one by one, rather than strangers as whole individuals). Both mechanisms could cause cultures to act as single entities or "individuals" in the course of cultural evolution (see e.g., Marks & Staski, 1988). By one mechanism or another, there is little cross-cultural borrowing of any significance. New cultures are formed completely by the fissioning of populations and subsequent divergence. In this case, whole cultures are analogous to species or mitochondrial genomes. Biological methods of systematics can be applied almost intact, and deep cultural phylogenics are relatively easy to infer for at least the bulk of a people's culture.

2. Cultures with Hierarchically Integrated Systems

Although cross-cultural borrowing may be frequent for many peripheral components, a conservative "core tradition" in each culture is rarely affected by diffusion from other groups. New core traditions mainly arise by the fissioning of populations and subsequent divergence of daughter cultures. Isolation and integration protect the core from the effects of diffusion, although peripheral elements are much more heavily subject to cross-cultural borrowing. In this case, core traditions are analogous to the bacterial chromosomes and the peripheral components to plasmids. Biological methods of systematics can be modified to deal with cross-cultural borrowing. Reasonably deep core-cultural phylogenies can still be inferred, but this requires disentangling the effects of borrowing by distinguishing core and peripheral elements, and especially by methods to identify elements that "introgressed" into the core.

3. Cultures as Assemblages of Many Coherent Units.

Cultures could be quite ephemeral assemblages of small units, but the latter may have limited mixing and slow evolution. Culture may have no species, but it might have genes, plasmids, and mitochondria. Different domains may have different patterns of inheritance and different evolutionary histories. The components may be fairly large, plasmid, or mitochondrionlike, such as language, or small, solitary memes, such as the idea of using a magnetized needle to point north. Any given culture is an assemblage of many such units acquired from diverse sources. Methods of phylogeny can be applied independently to each domain. The essential problem is to determine the boundaries of the domains and establish that they are stable in time and space.

4. Cultures as Collections of Ephemeral Entities

There are no observable units of culture that are sufficiently coherent for phylogeny reconstruction to be useful. Observable aspects of culture could be the result of units that are beneath the resolution of current methods to observe. The forms of Acheulean hand axes are so similar that they cannot be used to infer anything about descent among their makers. Perhaps there were really many traditional ways to reach this apparently uniform end result. If we knew the details, we could reconstruct cultural phylogenies of hand ax making. There may be observable differences, but if they are the product of many recombining elements that cannot be observed, there is no information that would allow us to construct a phylogeny of the bits. Alternatively, if cultural evolution is sufficiently rapid, behavior may reflect such recent history that all phylogeny is lost. The "jukebox" culture, in which cultures are rapidly modeled and remodeled to serve current adaptive purposes, would have this effect due to functional convergence rapidly destroying any trace of history.

There are two issues at stake. First, when using the term *descent*, what do we mean? Proponents of the view that whole cultures are like species use *descent* to describe cultural replication of complex coherent groups by the mechanism of group fission or budding, whereas those who believe that only components of culture cohere would use descent to describe ancestor–descendant relationships resulting from any pattern of culture preserving the footprints of its history. We shall try to be clear in our own usages, but this is a merely terminological issue to which we devote no further space. Second, what is the world like? This is a much more interesting question, to which we devote the rest of the chapter. At one end of the continuum, all of the elements that make up a culture cohere and resist recombination. Cultures as a whole are analogous to species. At the other end, the observed elements of culture are the result of memes diffused or invented on a time scale too short for phylogenetic reconstruction. What is culture really like?

B. Mechanisms

There are several general mechanisms that might cause longevity and coherence in cultural units so that descent can be determined.

1. Longevity of Historical Traces

As in the case of genes, the phylogenetic process of cultural transmission provides some level of historical continuity. As with genes, the deepest phylogenies are possible when culture changes slowly and is not subject to functional convergence. Slow evolution will occur when people either cannot, or have no reason to, invent new forms. Surprisingly simple bits of culture are often apparently too obscure to reinvent, and all known modern exemplars derive from a single invention. Needham (1988) gave many plausible examples of Chinese technology that subsequently diffused to the rest of Eurasia (e.g., the magnetic compass). Nonetheless, in the long run, functional convergence seems to be the rule for technology. A long tradition in the social sciences, including the classic cultural ecology of Steward (1955) and modern evolutionary anthropology, it trades on the reality of substantial convergent evolution in human cultures. As in the biological case, the best elements for historical analysis are those that are functionally arbitrary and symbolic. Language and other symbolically meaningful, but nonfunctional, variations are often used as indices of descent, much as functionally neutral flower form is used in plant systematics. Flowers are a plant's way of communicating with pollinators, so the analogy with language is real.

The next subsection describes some mechanisms that may prevent mixing between coherent elements. Similar mechanisms may act to slow the rate of evolution if internal innovations or innovators are perceived as strange, either because of a poor internal fit or because they arouse suspicions of heresy or deviance on the part of innovators.

2. Processes That Give Rise to Coherence

What general processes could give cultural elements an enduring coherence, leaving aside the size of cohering units and their relation to one another? In the symbolic and interpretive anthropology literature, the "glue" has been attributed to the "meaning" that inheres in culture. Meaningful cultural information provides a convincing and compelling *Weltanschauung* for its bearers. Meaningful components help organize and make sense of other parts of the cultural system and natural world. They also legitimize and justify the system in the minds of its bearers. For this reason, meaningful components have variously been called "root paradigms" (V. Turner, 1977), "ultimate sacred postulates" (Rappaport, 1979), "core principles" (Hallpike, 1986), and the like. Because it is critically important to a people's understanding of the world and its place within it, they often have a special, even sacred, status. The notion of meaning is often linked to the idea of cultural holism. There is no logical reason for this limitation, and the idea may apply to cores or much smaller units. Subcultural units as small as the individual social scientific disciplines, street gangs, and clans often appear to have well-articulated systems of meaning.

The special status of meaningful elements could provide coherence in several ways. First, the internal logic of a coherent block of culture may discriminate against intrusive elements. Diffused elements may be known to individuals, but the mismatch of meanings between whole cultures or subcultures entails that "foreign" values and ideas be misunderstood, disliked, and neglected. The mismatch may be between foreign elements, but also between domains within a single culture (e.g., gender marked identities or even sets of subsistence skills; see chap. 9, this volume, for details of mechanisms).

Second, meaningful culture often involves markers of group identity that are especially salient to the definitions of ingroup and outgroup. Contexts where coherent units of meaning-rich culture are available for acquisition from foreigners are likely to involve marked ritual observances or ceremony that mobilize ethnocentric sentiments more thoroughly than mundane contacts like trade, in which symbolically less marked elements may diffuse readily. Ethnocentrism can provide an effective isolating barrier to diffusion of cultural elements in theory and apparently in practice (Boyd & Richerson, 1987) at the whole-culture level. Class, caste, gender, occupation, and even hobby groups are symbolically marked within some societies. Within bounded groups, however large they may be, intermarriage, diffusion, and other mixing processes create cultural uniformity, but there are sharp differences among them. In terms of chapter 9, this is a form of indirect bias.

Third, to the extent that what coheres in culture is a symbolic system of organizing meanings, rather than the meanings themselves, it is protected from ordinary adaptive evolutionary pressures. In language at least, the symbol system is so rich and flexible that quite novel new meanings can be coded with the existing system; only linguistically trivial changes in lexicons were needed to adapt modern languages to the industrial revolution.

Finally, elements may cohere because certain combinations are adaptive and favored by natural selection or derivative adaptive decision-making rules. Adaptive forces may simply discriminate so strongly against recombinants that coherence is maintained despite massive mixing, as seems to be the case in certain hybrid boundaries in the biological case (Barton & Hewitt, 1989). A related sort of selective "glue" could come from the multiplicity of evolutionarily stable strategies that seem to exist in social systems (see chap. 8, this volume). Perhaps the stability of coherent features comes from the failure of new or foreign social practice to fit into actual arrangements, rather than from inconsistencies at the cognitive/affective meaning level. The symbolic or ideological level may follow the social, rather than dictate it.

Rushforth and Chisholm (1991) gave a possible example in their discussion of Athapaskan "structures of communicative social interaction." According to these investigators, a core "framework of meaning and moral responsibility" has persisted among Bearlake Athapaskan of northern Canada with "extraordinarily little change" across many generations and hundreds of years (Rushforth & Chisholm, 1991, p. 64). Moreover, remarkably similar beliefs and values—urging industriousness, generosity, autonomy, and restraint—have been documented among more than 30 other Athapaskan-speaking peoples across three geographically discontinuous clusters in Canada and Alaska, the Pacific Northwest, and the American Southwest.

A deeply rooted family of social norms such as these might directly underpin social institutions. The norms that underpin social interactions are good candidates to be maintained as a coherent block because they are part of local evolutionarily stable strategies. In game theory, at least, it is easy to imagine locally and evolutionarily stable strategies for complex social institutions that are impossible to change at the margin by either diffusion or within-lineage change because small movements away from current practice are disadvantageous.

Would the multiple evolutionarily stable strategies (ESS) explanation account for the remarkable cultural persistence of Athapaskan norms? Focusing on the Bearlake version, Rushforth and Chisholm (1991) suggested that, "The Bearlake interpretive scheme has persisted because of the historically stable composition of the [social interaction] strategies it informs" (p. 119). They argued that Bearlakers pursue goals in daily life that are defined and valued by their interpretive framework of beliefs and values. The interactions that follow generate regular rewards or "payoffs" that encourage individuals to convey certain intentions to others. But the actions that convey these intentions are precisely those defined by the framework. In short, the framework persists as "an unintended consequence of the strategic behavior of individuals operating in their own interests" (Rushforth & Chisholm, 1991, p. 121).

Sometimes coherent traditions are "acquired" by imposition by an invading, dominant culture, or assimilation to an attractive one. Even in this case, little admixture from the competing coherent structure of the adopting culture need result from its transfer from one biological population to another, as in the imposition of a common Greco-Roman urban civilization on a host of "barbarian" peoples in Ancient Europe and Western Asia. Note that individual people can move readily without disturbing the integrity of the coherent elements, as the assimilation of many immigrant people to at least aspects of Anglo-American culture over the last two centuries testifies. Nevertheless, replication by transfer to a new biological population is arguably normally accompanied by much mixing of old and new, and the fission of one population into two daughters probably conserves coherence more effectively. Similarly, high rates of immigration need not necessarily result in high rates of erosion of coherence, but cultural diffusion does seem likely to be stimulated by immigration in typical cases.

C. Evidence

1. The Descent of Cultures as Wholes

Commentators such as Marks and Staski (1988) sometimes imply that they defend this position. According to McNeill (1986), historians such as Toynbee imply a position as extreme as this end of our continuum, although without any specific defense. McNeill's own magisterial *Rise of the West* was written to demonstrate how it was not possible to write a world history without acknowledging the exchange of ideas among major culture areas, much less within them. Holistic arguments, ultimately deriving from Wittgensteinian philosophy, once enjoyed great appeal in history and many branches of the social sciences, and echoes remain. For example, in linguistics, de Saussure (1959) is often cited as a proponent of extreme systemicity in language, and even today some linguists espouse this view (Wardhaugh, 1992). The limitations of such arguments have long been recognized by philosophers, and more recently by social scientists, as described in chapters 2 and 3 (this volume). As is argued there, there is such overwhelming evidence for substantial diffusion and rapid evolution in many components of culture that it is unlikely that any tenable empirical defense of a completely holistic cultures-as-species position can be offered.

2. The Descent of Core Traditions

The hierarchical hypothesis of large-scale cultural coherence rooted in a core tradition is a point along the continuum that warrants closer examination. Like Alternatives 1 and 3, it assumes that culture is an ideational system (i.e., it consists of widely shared ideas, values, and beliefs that shape behavior in local human populations; the named cultures of anthropologists). In this model, cultures are viewed as hierarchically integrated systems, each with its own internal gradient of coherence. At one extreme in the gradient are the "core" components of a culture—those ideational phenomena that constitute its basic conceptual and interpretive framework, and influence many aspects of social life. At the other are peripheral elements that change rapidly and/or are widely shared by diffusion. On this hypothesis, the processes of coherence generate one main, central core unit. But this central unit does not equally organize all elements of culture. There may be many other smaller elements that are only lightly or not at all influenced by the core.

Core Versus Periphery. Regardless of whether the core gets its coherence from meaning, protection, diffusion, structured social interaction, or from all these sources, the key assertion of this model is that core components exhibit a remarkable resilience in the course of cultural history. The core "sticks together" as a cohesive bundle even through repeated episodes of culture birth, giving rise to a set of descendant branches that then share the same "tradition." As Vansina (1990) argued based on his case study, such traditions are based upon

> the fundamental continuity of a concrete set of basic cognitive patterns and concepts.... [The] continuity concerns basic choices which, once made, are never again put into question... These fundamental acquisitions then act as a touchstone for proposed innovations, whether from

within or without. The tradition accepts, rejects, or molds borrowings to fit. It transforms even its dominant institutions while leaving its principles unquestioned. (Vansina, 1990, p. 258)

Despite these numerous sources of cohesion, the hierarchical hypothesis holds that many "peripheral" components exist that are only loosely tied to the core framework. These diffuse freely and readily, as in the well-studied case of technical innovations (E. M. Rogers, 1983). Peripheral components may include ideational elements that make sense on their own and can be socially transmitted without a lot of supplementary cultural information. Such components are assumed to play little or no organizational role within the broader ideational system, and they must be relatively easy to learn. Such components are expected to be highly "contagious," rather like Dawkins' (1993) viruses of the mind.

New forms will be adopted quickly, simply, and smoothly, particularly if there is some perceived functional advantage and low cost. In this instance, change is quick and easy: Different components come and go as independent interchangeable parts. They are likely to spread horizontally among cultures, regardless of whether those cultures are related historically by branching. For this reason, their phylogenies will have the vine-like appearance mentioned earlier. Kroeber (1948) gave a long list of well-known examples (e.g., days of the week, tobacco, printing, paper, gunpowder, etc.). Unlike the descent-of-wholes hypothesis, the hierarchical hypothesis recognizes that cores are not as completely isolated as good biological species. Kroeber's "tree of culture" implies that cultural descent is like a rain forest canopy tree—one whose crown is a tangle of branches (related by birth) and vines (related by diffusion). For some substantial period of time, one can easily distinguish what grows as branches from what grows as vines with more care, even in a thick, old tangle. Eventually, however, over the course of thousands of years, vines will proliferate and come to obscure the branches. At the same time, processes of coherence will integrate elements with separate histories. Old vines will coalesce to form a solid trunk—much like the strangler fig that starts out as a viny parasite of a tree, but gradually forms a solid trunk about its host, which then dies.

The hierarchical model also acknowledges the rapidity of cultural evolution, compared with the biological case. The evidence of a history of common descent will gradually disappear in independent lineages. Barth (1987) gave a detailed account of the rapid evolution of the core tradition of the Mountain Ok of New Guinea due to a mutationlike process. The case is probably unusual because the core traditions are transmitted in rare secret rituals that create high "mutation" rates via forgetting. But even in the absence of diffusion, evidence of common ancestry in sister cultures will degrade on the millennial time scale (compared with hundreds of millions of years, in the case of sister species of mammals). We know from the massive convergence of agricultural technology and state-level social institutions in the pre-Colombian New and Old Worlds that cultural evolution can produce spectacular adaptive change on the time scale of a few thousand years. We can almost be certain that Old–New World similarities were independently derived convergences, but only because we have the evidence of hundreds of cultures on both branches to help distinguish the vines. Notoriously, careless historians that ignore the massively redundant evidence have no trouble "finding" false descent relationships between Old and New World cultures (e.g., Heyerdhal, 1950).

The Practice of Constructing Core-Cultural Phylogenies. The hierarchical hypothesis is supported to the extent that it can be shown that a large complex of core traits has a common pattern of descent. The core traditions in question must be related through a sequence of population fissionings (allowing for the odd core transfer). The existence of only one deep element, such as language, cannot be used alone to infer the existence of a full core of shared traditions among cultures related by language only. Because language phylogenies can be traced to considerable depth using conservative aspects of vocabulary and phonology, language trees are the usual starting point for attempting to trace out the descent patterns of larger core units. Related traditions can then be used as a basis for reconstructing a fuller culture history, including the "proto-tradition" out of which they evolved (see Aberle, 1984, 1987). Sometimes genetic relatedness of the populations involved provides supplementary evidence, given that full core replication by processes other than fission of a parent culture is unusual. However, if diffusion and rapid evolution swamped all traces of relationship by birth, anthropology could not speak of branches, only vines, and Hypothesis 3 would be supported.

The work of Rushforth and Chisholm on Athapaskan similarities illustrates the method. Linguistic evidence indicates that Athapaskans are part of a second wave of Native Americans that arrive from Asia a few thousand years after the migration that contributed most known pre-Columbian populations. At contact, the Athapaskan language family was spoken by people in quite isolated clusters in Canada, California, and the Southwest (the southwestern group includes the famous Apache and Navajo). According to their analysis, the evidence suggests that a core of meaning related to social behavior coheres with language, and that all are "cognate," (i.e., related historically by culture birth; Rushforth & Chisholm, 1991).

First, the authors implied that the pertinent beliefs and values in Athapaskan populations are distinct from those of the surrounding populations belonging to other language groups (although it is also true that the differences are not thoroughly documented in their presentation). Second, similarity by diffusion can be ruled out because of the highly discontinuous geographical clustering of the carrier populations. Third, independent origins are highly improbable (Rushforth & Chisholm, 1991), even if each cluster of populations is taken as a whole.

Rushforth and Chisholm concluded that the pertinent beliefs and values are all "genetically" related, having "originated in, and developed from, a common, ancestral cultural tradition that existed among Proto-Athapaskan or, perhaps, even among [the ancestral] NaDene peoples" (Rushforth & Chisholm, 1991, p. 71). As they put it, "simplicity strongly argues" that "this cultural framework originated once, early in Proto-Athapaskan or NaDene history and has persisted (perhaps with some modifications) in different groups after migrations separated them from contact with each other" (Rushforth & Chisholm, 1991, p. 78).

The work of Indo-Europeanists to reconstruct the descent of societies speaking this family of languages is the most ambitious attempt yet made to reconstruct a pattern of descent for a core. According to some Indo-Europeanists like George Dumézil and Marija Gimbutas, the Indo-Europeans are the bearers of a core tradition consisting of language elements, myths, and a distinctive tripartite pattern of social organization that had its origin in a particular culture of steppe horse nomads. Gimbutas' reconstructed "Kurgans" lived about 6,500 years ago between the Black and Caspian Seas. Her Kurgan proposal is widely respected, but also widely criticized; a reconstruction of such breadth and depth tests the margins of the hierarchical hypothesis (Mallory, 1989).

Shared core traditions have been proposed for people in a number of different regions of the world, each with time horizons dating back at least a few thousand years. Recently reviewed in Durham (1992), these include the oft-cited case of cultural similarity among Polynesian Islanders (see especially Kirch, 1986; Kirch & Green, 1987; see critical review in Terrell, 1986), the Athapaskan (Rushforth & Chisholm, 1991) and Indo-European traditions mentioned earlier (e.g., Gamkrelidze & Ivanov, 1990; Hallpike, 1986; but see Mallory, 1989), Mayans (Vogt, 1964), Tibetans (Durham, 1991), and Tupi speakers among native South Americans (Durham & Nassif, 1991). Although one could always argue that the Polynesian case is exceptional because of the inherent isolation of its populations, plausible examples of enduring shared traditions among cultures related by birth have now been proposed for a diverse array of continental populations as well.

Consider Vansina's (1990) recent comprehensive study of political tradition in equatorial Africa. Through a controlled comparison of some 200 distinct societies in the basin of the Zaire river and its tributaries, Vansina concluded that these "widely differing societies arose out of [a] single ancestral tradition"(p. 191) by way of 3,000–4,000 years of historical transformations. As reconstructed by Vansina, the original ancestral tradition came into the region with the immigration of western Bantu-speaking farmers. They brought with them a single distinct pattern of social organization based on fragile temporary alliances into House [capital H in original], village, and district, and a common ideology and world view to go with it (see Vansina, 1990).

From this common baseline, Vansina argued, through successive splits, migrations, and expansions, "widely differing societies arose out of the single ancestral tradition by major transformations" (p. 191). The variation included, for example, two kinds of segmentary lineage societies, four kinds of associations, and five kinds of chiefdoms or kingdoms. All the while, "the principles and fundamental options inherited [at birth] from the ancestral tradition remained a gyroscope in the voyage through time: they determined what was perceivable and imaginable as change" (Vansina, 1990, p. 195).

Vansina made it clear that outside influences—"the new habitants, the autochthons [indigenous hunter-gatherers in the region], the non-Bantu, the eastern Bantu farmers with their different legacies—each influenced the development of this ancestral tradition differently from place to place" (Vansina 1990, p. 69). Yet as he repeatedly showed, change "was not mainly induced by outside influences. In all these cases [for example, in the inner Zaire basin] a chain of reactions fed continuous internal innovations. Outside innovations were accepted only insofar as they made sense in terms of existing structures" (p. 126). Even in regions where external influences played a relatively heavy role, the internal sovereignty of distinct polities meant that "internal dynamics always remain deter-mining" (Vansina, 1990, p. 192). Even with the establishment of Atlantic trade after 1480 and the attendant challenges of slave raiding and more, "the tradition was not defeated. It adapted. It invented new structures. [N]o foreign ideals or basic concepts were accepted and not even much of a dent was made in the aspirations of individuals" (pp. 236f). Inherited at birth in each equatorial society, the tradition lived on for hundreds of years more, only to be destroyed by European conquest between 1880 and 1920.

Why Core Homology Matters.   Vansina's study illustrates a key proposition of the hierarchical model. Even in continental areas with high contact between peoples, one can still trace "the historical course of a single tradition" (Vansina, 1990, p. 261). But there is a second important implication as well: Reconstructing the histories of peoples without writ-ten records requires that one distinguish between homologies (similarities produced by culture birth), analogies (similarities produced by conver-gence or parallel change), and synologies (similarities produced by diffu-sion or borrowing). The reason, as Vansina noted, is that the reconstruc-tion of past cultures requires that one "seeks out homologies first" (p. 261). Only by identifying genuine cultural homologies can one estab-lish the nature of the initial ideational system that was later transformed by historical processes. To the extent that hypothesis 2 (see pp. 364, 365) proves valid, it offers a useful tool that societies with no written records can use to gain access to their own histories.

3. The Descent of Small Cultural Components

On this hypothesis, there is no central core culture that deserves special attention in phylogenetic analysis. Rather, there are multiple "cores" and sometimes quite small units whose descent can be usefully traced. To characterize a narrow region on the continuum of possible hypotheses, we suppose that even the biggest deeply coherent blocks of culture are fairly small.

Definition.   The components are collections of memes that are transmitted as units with little recombination and slow change, and there-fore their phylogenies can be reliably reconstructed to some depth. (As for the hierarchical hypothesis, how much recombination and change is tolerable depends on the time scale—deeper phylogenies require more coherent units and slower rates of evolution.) On this hypothesis, different components diffuse and recombine at a rapid rate, compared with the rates of elements within components, so that corelike complexes of components will have shallower phylogenies than their smaller constituent components.

The processes that provide "glue" for the hierarchical core hypothesis also explain the coherence within these smaller units. The amendments needed are only quantitative. If the scope of integration provided by internal processes is limited, and if ethnocentric barriers to diffusion are weak or shifting in kinds of components is protected, recombination between large blocks of memes will be high, although the same processes may protect many small sets of coherent memes. In practice, the units have to be large enough to have significant internal complexity, or their actual documented history has to be good. Otherwise, the amount of information available for descent reconstruction is limited. Thus, before the advent of modern molecular techniques, the functionally similar genes in various bacteria had a pattern of descent, but the traces of history needed to reconstruct the pattern were absent. When genes can be sequenced, a vastly greater array of data is available by reading the DNA strands directly. Strings of functionally irrelevant, highly improbable similarities and differences in the strands can now be used to construct phylogenies where classical biologists despaired.

Is there any theoretical reason to expect smaller, rather than larger, coherent units in the cultural case? The fact that different cultural variants can be acquired from different people during different parts of the life cycle makes genealogical processes less effective at maintaining coherence than the analogous processes in the case of genetic evolution. We all have many cultural parents, with the attendant potential for independent samples of culture from many sources. At the same time, mixing could be less effective within small units because one can learn some things from one person or a small group of closely related mentors, and other things from a quite different set of mentors. This may lead to small, but coherent, subcultures within a larger culture complex. For example, the culture of science is fairly coherent and coexists within the same society as the culture of rock climbers, but people from each of these partial cultures may share the partial culture of the English language. (Of course, to some extent, science, rock climbing, and English are international institutions, and provide avenues of communication among the cultures that play host to them.) On this argument, maintaining cultural coherence over large units faces a considerable mechanical obstacle due to the hyperrecombinatorial nature of the cultural transmission system.

If one focuses on one special unit, such as those few features of language that cohere over long time scales, one may indeed find a few correlated units of other types that persist in having a pattern of descent in common with the language features, merely as a matter of chance. From one attempt at deep reconstruction to another, different pseudocore elements will be discovered.

The linguistic characters used by historical linguists (basic lexicon, phonological rules) provide good examples of what is meant by a cultural component. Linguists can reconstruct a phylogeny for a basic lexicon and phonological rules that tells us the pattern of relationships among variants of this character. For example, we know that the basic lexicon and phonological rules that characterize English and German share a more recent ancestor than either does with French. In other words, we believe that we can trace back the sizable complex of memes that underlie the English basic lexicon and phonology through a series of ancestor–descendant pairs to a point where the same people speak a language that has phonological rules and a basic lexicon that also forms the ancestor of German.

Examples of Coherence of Small Units and Recombination Among Them.   A clear example of how sets of memes exhibit considerable coherence when borrowed between groups can be seen in the adoption of the "age organization" principle by Bantu peoples in Central and Eastern Africa (LeVine & Sangree, 1962). Age sets are an institution in which children born within a few years of one another are simultaneously initiated into a group of adolescents of nearly the same age (boys and girls into different sets). After initiation, a given age set is a corporate organization that is formally charged with a series of roles in succession (warrior, married man, elder, etc.), with formal graduation from role to role of the whole set.

The Tiriki (an offshoot of the Abaluhyia Bantu), for example, currently have an age organization almost identical to that of their Nilotic neighbors, the Terik, while remaining distinctively Abaluhyia in language and culture. This situation arose as a result of intense political turmoil in the mid-18th century, when the Terik offered asylum to refugee segments of Abaluhyia lineages on condition that their men folk would become incorporated into the Terik warrior groups. At this time, the Tiriki warriors accepted the full set of initiation rituals for their sons (circumcision and seclusion), and adopted the seven named age-set system. In addition, the grades of warrior, retired warrior, judicial elder, and ritual elder emerged as the principal corporate units of political significance at the local level, and the Nilotic ideology of bravery and prowess in battle became predominant. Indeed, there is some evidence that the Tiriki became a distinct group within the Abaluhyia as a result of their adoption of Terik customs, as is indeed suggested by their name. Interestingly, the practice of female circumcision was viewed with disfavor by the Tiriki, such that they never adopted this trait. In short, this example shows how a number of cultural elements can be borrowed as a package, although not indiscriminately so, and the packages are often smallish.

Linguistics also provides many good examples. Important components of the language spoken by a group of people often have a different evolutionary history than do the basic lexicon and phonology of the same language. A substantial fraction of the words in the English lexicon (but not in the basic lexicon) share more recent common ancestors with words in French than with German. This is also true of English syntax, SVO like French, not SOV like most Germanic languages. It is even true of aspects of English phonology. For example, English speakers distinguish veal and feel, apparently as a result of the influence of Norman loan words. Thus, we can identify coherent cultural entities, words, and syntactical and phonological rules that are longer lived than the larger complex called the English language, and whose ancestry can be traced back through independent series of ancestor–descendant relationships. Thomason and T. Kaufman (1991) provided numerous other examples, including the Ma'a language spoken in northern Tanzania, which, despite classification as a Nilotic language, has a basic lexicon related to Cushitic languages and a grammar related to Bantu languages. (We return to the problems that this example raises for the practice of linguistic classification later.)

Less formal data suggest that important social organizational rules and values are often decoupled rather rapidly from descent, as can be reckoned by the user of a basic lexicon and phonology. In Central and East Africa, for example, cyclical and linear age sets, alternating generation classes, genital mutilation of males and females, warrior organizations, and many other associated practices are common among people whose basic lexicons are categorized as Nilotic, Cushitic, and Bantu. Although it was once thought that these customs were essentially of Cushitic origin, it is now clear from Ehret's (1971) linguistic analyses and voluminous ethnographic sources that different customs associated with the recruitment, function, and ritual validity of age organizations have been repeatedly borrowed between protolinguistic units over the last 5,000 years, reflecting periods of proximity, expansion, and dependence. The resulting situation is one of a thorough intertwining of social organization and language.

In some cases, the distribution of cultural traits appears to represent functional convergences, as in the case of the Tiriki, who adopted age sets and male circumcision in response to the turbulent militaristic conditions of the times. In other cases, there is evidence of a decoupling of apparently nonfunctional details. Thus, the Bantu Gusii conduct male and female genital mutilation, but apparently have never organized their men into age sets (LeVine & Sangree, 1962); the Datoga dropped the 5–8 cycling age-set system of their proto-southern Nilotic ancestors for noncycling generation classes (Ehret, 1971). The Bantu Kuria provide a particularly revealing example of this complexity (Tobisson, 1986). Men belong to age sets almost indistinguishable in name from those of the southern Nilotes, but are recruited on entirely different principles (father's set membership, rather than circumcision cohort). However, the Kuria have important military units; these are based on circumcision, but are organized quite differently from those of the Nilotes, and are quite unrelated to the age-set system that among the Kuria bears Nilotic names. The inescapable conclusion to be drawn from these complex observations is that the phylogeny of language and other cultural characters are often distinct.

Religious practices provide many further examples: the spread of the Sun Dance on the Great Plains, the spread of Islam from Western to Central and Eastern Asia and Northern Africa, millenarian movements in Melanesia, and so on. Ethnographic details are sometimes available for such borrowings, and the motives involved do not seem to be such as to enforce much coherence. For example, Sierra Leonean Creoles first adopted freemasonry in the late 1940s. The reason seems to have been that exclusive occupation of elite political roles had long served Creoles with an integrative community symbolic system. When Creoles lost power to the large majority of tribal peoples without a slave background, this symbol system was lost. Freemasonry happened to be an available substitute, and quickly became very important (A. K. Cohen, 1974). Of course, national and imperial powers sometimes maintain symbolic units over wide areas for impressive periods of time. Habsburg's success in defending

Catholicism and expelling Protestantism and Islam from their dominions during the life of the Austro-Hungarian Empire is a famous example. However, the need to exercise a large measure of brute force to succeed in such an enterprise is perhaps testimony to the long-run weakness of large-scale coherence.

There also may be rather well-bounded subcultures within a language group (as defined by a basic lexicon), as in the Indian caste system or the class, occupational, and religious subunits of many other state-level agricultural societies. Here, some memes are confined to some subset of the group—the castes, the guild, and so on. These subgroups may be marked by boundaries that are rather impervious to the flow of at least some kinds of memes. This phenomenon reaches its extreme in contemporary societies like the United States, where a diverse array of specialized subcultures of many types exists.

These subgroups may be far more enduring than the "cultures" to which they bear a somewhat temporary allegiance. For example, East Africanists often question the attribution of any time depth to the ethnic units currently residing in the area. This is not simply a consequence of European colonialist policy. Thus, Waller (1986) painted a picture of the 19th-century and earlier ephemeral political associations of clans with different linguistic and cultural backgrounds, linked through diverse patterns of intermarriage, trade, expansion, and dependency. These flexible and highly inclusive concepts of group identity are seen as an adaptation to heterogeneous and somewhat unpredictable environmental conditions (i.e., circumstances by no means unique to East Africa). Knauft (1985) told a similar story about the Gebusi and their neighbors, the Bedamini, in the Fly River area of Papua New Guinea. According to this picture, there would be frequent recombination of memes due to temporary association of peoples who exchange memes while in contact.

Comparison of Core and Small Units Hypotheses. Whether such examples are more representative than those given by supporters of the core hypothesis is an important, but unanswered, question. The little anthropological work done is not capable of answering this question. There are a few studies, but they are indecisive. Jorgensen's (1967, 1980) studies of the Salish and larger scale analysis of the Indians of western North America are examples of the kind of comprehensive cultural analysis that might deliver. However, his methods are based on measures of overall similarity and difference, and do not constitute proper analyses of descent. Biological systematists argue that the only evidence for membership in a given branch of a descent tree is given by characters that are shared by that branch alone, but not more ancient or more recent similarities, much less similarities acquired by convergence.

Even in the case of language, "wave" models of linguistic evolution have long contended with "genetic" analyses based on strict criteria of descent (Jorgensen, 1980; Mallory, 1989; Renfrew, 1987). Many features of Indo-European languages seem easier to account for, if we assume that the whole family was in contact throughout most of its history, and that innovative features tended to diffuse from multiple centers to neighboring languages. Treelike models of relationship can certainly be constructed for data that are substantially influenced by wavelike processes (e.g., with clustering algorithms). Just because a tree diagram explains much of the variation in a set of data, it does not guarantee that the descent hypothesis is correct. It would be quite interesting to see the modern "cladistic" methods of biological systematists formally applied to such cultural descent problems. At least part of the solution to the debate between proponents of hierarchical core and small units hypotheses will rest on the application of sharper methodological tools, and biologists have something to offer.

4. The Descent of Memes

The boundary of the small units hypothesis toward the small end of the continuum is not well defined. It also possible that, aside from core vocabulary and phonology, there are few multimeme cultural units that are well protected from diffusion. It could be that each of the cultural things we observe is affected by many memes, that these memes readily diffuse from one socially or linguistically defined group to another, and that memes that affect different cultural components readily recombine. For example, a religious system might be affected by many different memes: beliefs about causation, beliefs about the role of men and women, beliefs about disease, and so on. This system could diffuse from one group to another, and then some of the memes could recombine with other aspects of the culture. Beliefs about the roles of men and women that came with the new religious system might then recombine with preexisting beliefs about subsistence practices, generating new, observable subsistence variants. If we could actually measure the memes that characterize different human groups, this case would be much like the previous one, except we would reconstruct the phylogenies of memes largely instead of whole cultural components.

5. Descent Analysis: Impossible or Uninteresting?

There are several situations in which descent analysis regarding culture is impossible. If we observe phenotype, and not the mental representations that are stored and transmitted, we cannot directly measure memes. The fact that many memes affect any given observable cultural attribute makes it difficult to trace the path of recombining memes, and reconstructing phylogenies is likely to be impossible. If the actual units to which descent might apply are as small or smaller than our practically observable units, descent is impossible to trace simply because there is not enough information available to separate common descent from other hypotheses, such as independent origins. A quantitative character subject to blending inheritance is an extreme example.

In some cases, methodological improvements may increase resolution. Comparative ethnographic data with age sets scored as present/absent, or as a quantitative variable on political importance, would not contain enough detail to reconstruct much history in East Africa. A richer data set offers more possibilities, as we have seen.

The existence of coherent cultures will depend on the rate of diffusion and independent evolution. If the rate of diffusion among cultures for most characters is high, then there will be no cultural unit larger than some small atomistic unit of which to track the descent. Between the time that a newly formed group buds off its parent, and the time it creates buds itself, many new traits will have entered the group from outside. If the rate of evolution is high, the trace of history also vanishes. High rates of random evolution, especially simple characters with few observable states, will eventually result in so many random "hits" that descendant characters will have occupied all states fairly recently. Similar simple artistic motifs are found in many cultures, perhaps because artists frequently rediscover and abandon them. Functional convergence presents similar problems. Around the world, tropical horticulturalists often live in small-scale societies that are murderously hostile to their neighbors. This commonality is presumably a by-product of the population densities and level of political organization supportable in wet tropical climates, but not due to common ancestry.

Even when descent analysis is possible, it may be uninteresting. The few components that resist diffusion—basic lexicon and so on—will be descended from the grandparental group (defined in terms of basic lexicon), but most components will not be descendants of components in that same grandparental group. Put another way, a culture is nothing more than its most elementary components. Each component may well be traceable back to a grandparental society. But if we consider a neighboring society, they may share particular grandparents for particular traits at random. Phylogenetic analysis could still be conducted for an element-by-element case, and this might be of interest or utility for some special cases. However, one important use of phylogeny is to make manageable the overwhelming complexity of populations and cultures. With no coherence, the analysis of descent could promise nothing in this regard.

PARTIAL PHYLOGENIES AND THE STUDY OF ADAPTATION

Good phylogenies are crucial for the proper study of adaptation using the comparative method. Comparative studies attempt to determine the function of various attributes by looking for predicted correlations among societies. For example, N. Thornhill (1991) hypothesized that inbreeding avoidance rules function to preserve capital in powerful families. To test this hypothesis, she collected data on inbreeding rules and social stratification, predicting (accurately) that the degree of elaboration of rules would positively correlate with the degree of social stratification.

Similar studies utilizing correlations among species are widely used in comparative biology. A key problem in such comparative studies is determining the extent to which different societies (or species) are independent data points. In comparative biology, only independently derived associations are counted as separate data points. Thus, if an innovation arises and then the lineage speciates, preserving the innovation in both daughter species, the daughter species should be counted as a single data point. The first step in the proper exercise of the comparative method is phylogenetic reconstruction (Harvey & Pagel, 1991). In cross-cultural anthropology, this problem is referred to as "Galton's problem." Scholars working in this discipline attempt to select their samples so as to include only unrelated cultures or correct for diffusion by using statistical methods (Burton & D. R. White, 1987) .

Adaptations acquired by diffusion from other groups are related by descent to the adaptations in those groups. If one analogizes with the practice in biology, such adaptations would not be counted as independent cases because the adaptation in the borrowing group is *not* an innovation. However, to the extent that diffusion represents the goal-driven choices of individuals in the borrowing group (or some other potentially adaptation-producing process), the borrowed trait *is* independent. If it had not been an adaptation, it would not have been adopted. This problem is particularly acute given that the rate of diffusion of new cultural adaptations through biased transmission is likely to be much higher than the rate of innovation. If this is so, most groups will adapt by borrowing, and it is unreasonably conservative to disregard these cases.

The relationship between the Sun Dance and the buffalo hunting ecology of the Great Plains people illustrates this difficulty. A summer ceremonial called the sun dance characterized all the Great Plains buffalo hunting people. One might hypothesize that such a ceremony is related to the fission–fusion social organization that characterized the buffalo hunting ecology of those people. But does one count this as one case, or several? It is likely that this ceremony originated with the Crow and diffused to other tribes, so the various versions of the ceremony are not independent inventions. However, each group did adopt the ceremony perhaps because it served the hypothesized need. Moreover, it could be that, in the absence of diffusion, each group would have independently developed a summer ceremonial, but did not because the rate of adaptation by diffusion is faster than independent invention (Oliver, 1962).

On a longer temporal and spatial scale, the problem is also well illustrated by basic technical innovations like agriculture or iron working. The number of independent inventions of these techniques were few indeed— fewer even than the number of language-based descent groups that have subsequently adopted them. It seems absurd to say that we cannot really decide whether iron working is adaptive because all examples of iron-working technology are derived from a single common ancestor in Asia Minor about 3,400 years ago. Regardless of our answer of how many cases of iron working to count for purposes of estimating its adaptive value, it seems clear that language-based descent groups are largely irrelevant to solving this problem. We say "largely irrelevant" because it does seem that an association of an important adaptive innovation with a linguistic unit sometimes lasts long enough to carry the language area great distances, as with iron working and the Bantu expansion in Africa in the last millennium B.C. and the first millennium A.D. (Ehret, 1982); the use of abundant, but low-quality, plant resources and the spread of Numic languages in the American Great Basin (Bettinger & Baumhoff, 1982); and the domestication of the horse, invention of wheeled transport, and spread of Indo-European (Mallory, 1989). Note that such associations tend to persist only for a millennium or so, although the expansion of the innovating group is tending to preserve the association.

CONCLUSION

It seems that, as regards most meme complexes, specific cultures are more like local populations within a species than like species. The whole human species is united by complex flows of ideas from one culture to another. This has always been so, although the geographical isolation of the New World, Australia, and a few other areas from each other and Eurasia may have substantially isolated large blocks of cultures on multi-millennial time scales. On smaller time and space scales, other mechanisms of isolation and coherence do generate some patterns of descent that are traceable for a few millennia.

The use of descent analysis for cultural units has a long, but controversial, history. Many authors claim a degree of success in reconstructing the history of descent of fairly large cultural units fairly far into the past. The most interesting outstanding question is the size and time scale of coherent units of culture. Do single cores in an interrelated complex have real histories that reach back five millennia or more? There seems to be no doubt that many small units have descent relationships that can be reliably inferred for this depth, but the upper size/time limit is not well defined by current methods. There is an ill-explored neutral analogy worth further work here. The cladistic revolution in systematic biology has sharpened concepts and built new tools for phylogenetic analysis. Might they be used, despite the problem of high diffusion rates among cultures compared with species, to help advance the resolution of genetic versus wave explanations of culture history?

11

COMPLEX SYSTEMS: MULTILEVEL AND MULTIPROCESS APPROACHES

Peter M. Hejl
University of Siegen
Germany

Hubert Hendrichs
University of Bielefeld
Germany

Raphael Falk
The Hebrew University
of Jerusalem, Israel

Eva Jablonka
Tel Aviv University
Israel

The aim of this chapter is to (a) contribute to a systemic view of biological and social entities, and (b) complement the focus on intergenerational transmission by a view of transmission as a process both between and within systems. Systems are composite entities with their own internal dynamics. In contradistinction to positions of some sociobiologists, we suggest that it is profitable to maintain a multilevel approach with respect to both the organism and its subunits and to societies and their subunits, and that one must also look at multilevel processes. This includes relations between different levels, inheritance, and the regulatory systems that operate at each level.

For a long time, the relations between the organism and its parts and the society and its parts were considered to be analogical: Biologists found it helpful to think about organisms as a kind of society (Canguilhem, 1970), just as social scientists used what they knew about organisms and ecological systems to conceptualize societies. Today, after more than a century of intensive debates on epistemological and theoretical issues, we are more aware of the constitutive impact that analogies have on the formation of concepts, and hence on our perception of the phenomena to which concepts refer. This should impose on us extreme care in the unavoidable disposition to use such analogies.

Concepts and available methods (Gigerenzer, 1991) strongly influence the constitution of the objects of a discipline. This holds for biology, as well as the social sciences. In both fields, scientists have great difficulties in finding a satisfying way to understand and analyze composite entities. Moreover, the "composite unity problem" is closely linked to the old and unfortunate debate on the relation between nature and culture. This topic functions as a problem area for each of the disciplines concerned, as well as a common field of interest for both. One way to conceptualize the problem is to reformulate it as an alternative to the dichotomy of reductionism versus holism. Within biology, the issue is presented by some today as the problem of the adequacy of neo-Darwinian explanations and their relation to evolutionary and developmental change in complex organisms (Gould & Lewontin, 1979; G. Roth & Wake, 1989). In sociology, the topic recently gained new prominence under the heading "Micro–Macro Problem" (J. C. Alexander, Giesen, Münch, & Smelser, 1987). What is at stake in both disciplines is the explanation of how composite entities function, how they persist and/or reproduce, how they change, and to what degree this change is influenced from inside or outside their border. In today's discussions, analogical aspects are pushed back in favor of more causal analyses, although the use of analogies is apparently unavoidable (Falk, 1993).

For any multilevel approach, epistemological considerations and interests in causal analysis have an implication that is often more sensed than clearly perceived: For methodological reasons, each level can be conceptualized in a way that gives it a relative independence. This independence is not given by the phenomenon, but by the causal models (see chap. 3, this volume). Scientists decide on appropriate levels in the light of theoretical and empirical considerations. For example, we may ask how individual animals in a group change behavior under conditions of increasing stress, without looking at the animals' genomes, or how the productivity of a research group is affected by the amount of informal contacts between group members, without looking at the affiliations that group members might have outside the group.

Of course, depending on the questions asked, these aspects might become important and, accordingly, may have to be included. Multilevel approaches try to do this by conceptualizing levels in a way that allows the identification and analysis of the impact different levels have on each other. The multilevel approach is compatible with the "integrative pluralism" described in chapter 3: Systems have components and an organization (on both, see chaps. 2, 4, this volume); consequently, one aspect of our understanding of the features of systems is from their internal dynamics, whereas another aspect is understood by their relations with external processes.

It is because of this causal relation between "higher" and "lower" levels that the perspective adopted here cannot be subsumed under the traditional alternatives of reductionism versus holism. Reductionists start with the assumption that there exists some "basic" level, the properties of which acquire importance, because phenomena at "higher" levels may be derived entirely from the behavior of the entities at the "basic" level, whereas these entities are thought to be independent of any influence from "above." We wish to maintain that not only is there no evidence for the existence of a "natural basic level," but also that it is not necessary to assume one.

What is "basic" depends ultimately on the question one asks and on the explanatory depth one agrees on as "adequate." Moreover, it is the mutual interaction of the "higher" and "lower" levels that allowed the development/evolution of multicellular organisms (L. W. Buss, 1987). Of course, without such interlevel interactions, there would be no lasting sociocultural entities either. The problem of the reductionist conviction with respect to different distinguishable levels is its assumption that the properties of the components of the "lower" level are exhaustively defined by their behavior as separate entities, so that the emergence of properties that characterize systems cannot be explained. By contrast, holists start on the assumption that properties of systems may "emerge" at a "higher" level without clearly defining *emergence*. These "emergent properties" are then taken to determine the behavior of the system's components that constitute the "lower" levels. The problem of "strong" holism is that it does not suggest a path of how to *explain* emergent properties.

If we regard science as an enterprise of explanation based on rational arguments and experience, no "in principle" unexplainable phenomena should be used. Therefore, the position of a holism that accepts unexplainable emergent properties discredits nonreductionist thinking. However, there is no rational argument why some properties both at the "lower" and "higher" levels should not "emerge" only from interactions. To cite just one example, it can be shown with respect to social systems that emergent properties can be explained as resulting from the interaction of components, which leads to the formation of a system-specific organization of interactions and of various knowledge repertoires (Hejl, 1993).

If composite entities are conceptualized as systems within a multi-level approach (i.e., one that assumes interactions [causal relations] between levels), they may be considered as generating their behavior by themselves. To the extent that systems change as a result of such processes, these changes are necessarily and in a nontrivial way self-organizing. However triggered, if the processes are not destructive, they modify either the behavior of components or they influence the organization of the system as a whole (which, in turn, implies the modification of components). This is what seems to happen during ontogenetic development—for example, in synaptogenesis (W. Singer, 1986), where self-organizing, spontaneously generated processes of brain development are modulated by the organism's experiences in its environment.

The following three sections analyze some specific problems that surface when the systemic view of organisms and social entities is taken seriously. Consequently, the arguments are not "against" specific positions, but rather try to put them in a richer context. When it is argued that phenotypes result from the interaction of genotypes and environment, and that phenotypes may be inherited, the importance of genes is not denied. In the same way, when it is shown that mammals develop individual consciousness as well as group-specific mentalities, it is not to say that there are no genotypic influences in the formation of that behavior. Finally, when it is shown that the meaning of a message depends on the receiving system, it is not indicated that the string of entities that make up the message does not matter. Both simplistic reductionism and strong holism are replaced by an integrated approach to explain multilevel and multiprocess phenomena.

INHERITANCE: TRANSMISSION AND DEVELOPMENT

Raphael Falk and Eva Jablonka

In the beginning of the 20th century, the study of heredity was in a state of fertile ambiguity. There were many hypotheses about the nature of heredity, and many definitions of *heredity*. Mendelian genetics appeared on the stage, but it was not immediately widely accepted as a comprehensive theory of heredity, particularly by embryologists and physiologists.

Sapp (1987) noted some enlightening definitions of leading biologists from that period:

1. "The nucleus cannot operate without a cytoplasmic field in which its peculiar powers may come into play but this field is created and moulded by itself. Both are necessary to *development*; the nucleus alone suffices for the *inheritance* of specific possibilities of development." (Italics original), (E. B. Wilson, 1896, p. 327)

2. "Heredity is the law which accounts for the change of types between parents and offspring, i.e., the progression from racial towards parent type." (Pearson, 1900, p. 474)

3. "Indeed, heredity is not a peculiar or unique principle for it is only similarity of growth and differentiation in successive generations. ... The causes of heredity are [thus] reduced to the causes of successive differentiations of development, and the mechanism of heredity is merely the mechanism of differentiation." (Conklin, 1908, p. 90)

4. "Heredity may be then defined as *the presence of identical genes in ancestors and descendants.*" (Italics original) (Johannsen, 1911, p. 159)

5. "Heredity is not a nuclear phenomenon, nor a cytoplasmic phenomenon; it remains in its entirety, a cellular phenomenon." (Guyénot, 1924, p. 289)

6. "For the embryologist the word heredity takes on a very broad meaning; heredity is the totality of the developmental potentialities in the fertilized egg; it is the ensemble of the causes which make the egg produce, when in adequate environmental conditions, following a succession of well-defined processes, a new organism having all the characters of the species to which it belongs." (Brachet 1935, p. 3)

This collection of definitions and references to heredity reveals the problems that the relationship between transmission and development posed for these biologists. Some of them, notably E. B. Wilson, solved this problem by neatly differentiating between development and heredity—development was not inherited, only nuclear instructions for development were inherited. Contrarily, Conklin and Brachet identified heredity with development. Others tried to identify and localize the material units of transmission; Guyénot claimed that there is transmission and inheritance of both nuclear and cytoplasmic components, and many agreed that transmission and development cannot be separated into distinct compartments, and talked about cellular inheritance. Pearson avoided these problems by treating inheritance as a statistical regularity in pedigrees and populations.

It is obvious that there was no clear distinction between what is now called *genes* and *gene expression*. However, the different approaches to heredity could be differentiated by their focus, or lack of focus, on the developmental process. According to Delage and Goldsmith's (1912) book, *The theories of evolution*, there were two equally valid approaches to the study of heredity. The first approach was developmental, best represented by theories such as Weismann's theory, and posed the following problem: "by what physiological processes does an organism become, in the course of its development, similar to the organisms from which it descended?" (Delage & Goldsmith, 1912, p. 176). The second approach was concerned with transmission, represented by the theories of Galton and Mendel: "We may set aside the phenomena arising in the fertilized ovum and in the various tissues and take the resemblance which arises from them as granted, let our observations bear upon this resemblance, its various stages and its variations in the course of several generations" (Delage & Goldsmith, 1912, p. 176). It took quite a long time to disentangle the "confusion of the problem concerned with sorting out of the hereditary materials (the genes) to the eggs and sperms, with the problems concerning the subsequent actions of these genes in the development of the embryo" (T. H. Morgan, 1917, p. 514).

Eventually, Mendelian genetics became the dominant approach to heredity, and was accepted as relevant for the transmission of developmental traits. In a Mendelian system, if we have a heterozygous *Aa* (where *A* is dominant to *a)*, *a* is present but not expressed; in a homozygous *aa*, *a* is expressed. In both cases, *a* is transmitted without being changed—expression does not influence transmission. Indeed, classical Mendelian genetics is the theory and the set of methods introduced by Gregor Mendel and his followers; it is used to analyze the biological inheritance of determinants of traits in sexually reproducing organisms. The mechanisms that regulate transmission of the Mendelian gene are not influenced by the gene's expression or the development of the organism that this gene inhabits, nor is the gene's mode of transmission affected by the environment. The Mendelian gene was conceived as a factor that is stable in heredity and not much influenced by the environment.

Indeed, the types of characters first studied by Mendel and his successors showed relatively little sensitivity to the normal range of environmental conditions. It was just this insensitivity of Mendelian traits that allowed them to be followed precisely in the progeny in consecutive generations. However, it is a striking fact that most characters are greatly influenced by the environment, and that fact had to be reconciled with Mendelism. This reconciliation was conceptualized by Johannsen at the beginning of the century, when he introduced his categorical and clear distinction between genotype and phenotype.

In the early years of this century, Johannsen published a series of articles that were of fundamental importance in the development of genetics. Johannsen suggested that the concept of *heredity* in its biological context had to be redefined. According to him, biological heredity is not the transmission of characters (e.g., the transmission of products of human culture); rather, it is the transmission of potentialities for the building of characters (e.g., the transmission of ideas which generate cultural products). Johannsen distinguished between *heredity*, a biological concept referring to the passing on of developmental instructions, and *transmission*, a common sense concept based on human practices such as the transmission of property, which refers to the physical transmission of personal qualities. The actual way that a character is constructed depends on the potentialities—which he called *genotype*—and on the conditions in which these potentialities are realized. He defined the end product of the interaction between environment and genotype—the actual appearance of the organism—as the *phenotype*. The unit of biological heredity, the Mendelian factor that Johannsen named *gene*, was not a material model of the phenotype, but a unit of information (Johannsen, 1911).

Johannsen's distinction between genotype and phenotype was based on his own work on pure lines of beans, and fitted the patterns of inheritance of Mendelian genes. In a given pure line, all individuals are of the same genotype, although their phenotypes may differ. Johannsen claimed that selection in pure lines has no hereditary influence. The heritable genotype remains unaltered by the environment, although its material realization may well be altered. Hence, the phenotypic variations in pure lines are not inherited. In modern terms, we may say that the development, or the unfolding of the genotypic program, occurs in the real world, in a certain environment that shapes the end product, the phenotype. It is the program, not the phenotype, that is inherited.

The distinction that Johannsen made between a genotypic and an environmental component, which combine to form a phenotype, paradoxically supported the belief that there are "genetic traits," and that the genotypic component of a trait can be clearly delimited. It was believed that the genotypic component has a meaning of its own even without its interaction with the environment. This simple-minded belief led to many unfortunate conceptions of genetic determinism, such as eugenics (Falk, 1990). It resurfaced more recently in the debate on human sociobiology (see chap. 2, this volume).

If the expression of human social phenotypes (such as languages, or forms of social teaching) is as context-dependent and highly variable as it seems, it is not clear what exactly biology can say about the genetic and evolutionary basis of human sociality, except wonder at its plasticity. However, if the range of phenotypes were restricted, genetics and evolutionary biology might have been able to enlighten us more as to the constraints imposed by genetics on our social practices. But phenotypic invariance could be problematic. The genetic basis of a genus-specific trait may be different in species of the genus, and may have resulted from different selection pressures—either on the same or different inheritance systems.

The common practice of geneticists, when they consider the "inheritance of a trait" (rather than the transmission of a gene), is to talk about the heritability of this trait. Heritability expresses the proportion of the genetic component in the phenotypic variance of a character of a population in a certain environment. *Heritability* in the broad sense is defined as:

$$Vg/(Ve+Vg) = Vg/Vp$$

where Vg is the genotypic variance and Ve is the environmental variance. $Vg + Ve = Vp$, which is the phenotypic variance. Because the interaction between Vg and Ve is usually not simply additive, Vp cannot be simply identified as another term in the formula. Thus, as a measure of a correlation, heritability is an environment-dependent variable as much as a genetic variable (Falk, 1990).

Two phenomena complicate the analysis of the genetic basis of traits—plasticity and canalization. Plasticity allows the same genotype to have many different phenotypic manifestations in different environments. For example, in a pure line of plants, all of the same genotype, individuals may differ in height because of variable growth conditions. However, canalization ensures that different genotypes will produce an invariant phenotype. For example, despite genotypic variations, the developmental paths of organisms produce a typical species-specific morphology, which is secured by the regulatory homeostatic interactions between gene products that mask and compensate for deviations.

Both canalization and plasticity uncouple the genotype and phenotype to the extent that they may not even be isomorphic. Plastic traits have very low heritability (Ve is large), whereas canalized traits have very high heritability (Ve is small). Yet canalization also makes the evolutionary interpretation of invariant traits difficult because of its significant interactive component. If different genotypes produce the same phenotype under varying environmental conditions, we are in the paradoxical situation that the phenotype of the canalized trait, which presumably has high heritability, has a different genetic basis in different systems, and may have evolved under different conditions. Highly invariant, canalized traits may be the consequence of strong developmental constraints, as well as of systematic stabilizing selection (see Fig. 11.1).

The relative genetic and environmental bases of specific social traits in humans is largely unknown and is likely to be different in different societies. What is generally accepted is that many human social practices are variable and context-dependent. Specific languages, habits, rituals, and so on are of interest to anthropologists and sociologists. These context-dependent behaviors can be transmitted by imitation and teaching within a culture via the cultural inheritance system. This broad plasticity seems invariant among cultures. There is probably canalization of the ability to display plastic behaviors.

But what exactly is canalized? Some students (Donald, 1991) of human behavior argue that general cognitive strategies—certain general laws of self-organization—are strongly canalized, and that domain-specific psychological mechanisms are the result of self-organization during ontogeny. The emphasis of these scientists is not on specific adaptive scenarios, but rather on certain initial conditions (which may have been directly or indirectly selected, or may have resulted from random genetic drift) and the dynamic self-organizing properties of the cognitive system. According to this view, the genotypic specifications are mainly a constraint on specific information processing mechanisms, rather than a direct determinant. Other scientists argue that there are *many* domain-specific, information-processing, psychological mechanisms that are all separately canalized, each with a specific evolutionary history and a specific genotypic basis (Cosmides & Tooby, 1987). The emphasis here is on specific adaptations and on less global canalization and systemic organization. According to this conception, the genotypic basis specifies be-

haviors much more closely. The debate between these two points of view
is ongoing, and there is no clear resolution at present.

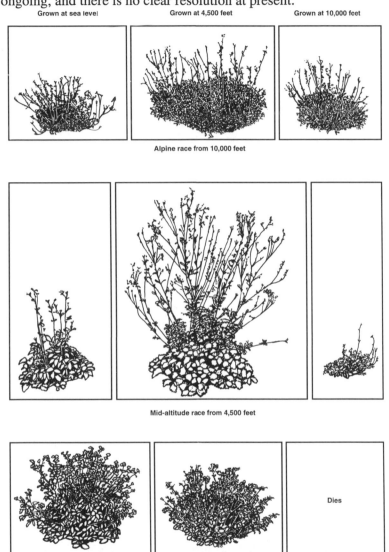

Fig. 11.1.   Three different races of *Potentilla glandulosa* grown in different environments. The differences among the plants in the same vertical column are genotypic
and are due to adaptation of their ancestors to different altitudes. The differences
among the plants in the same horizontal row represent responses of the same genotype to different environments (Clausen, Keck, & Hiesey, 1940).

The problem with the elucidation of the genetic basis of cognitive and social behavior in humans is threefold. First, we have to assign the behavioral variations in which we are interested to their proper level of analysis (i.e., decide to what extent they belong to the plastic, culturally inherited repertoire of behaviors, or to the underlying invariant pattern). Second, we have to resolve the question of the level at which canalization occurs—the specific or the global. Third, because plasticity and canalization may have opposing effects on the measurement of heritability, special care has to be taken when harnessing genetic methodologies to evaluate the genetic basis of human social behavior, except in a rather trivial sense (e.g., "everything, including social practices, has a genetic basis"). However, even if we accept that the relationship between genotype and phenotype is complex, we still remain in the realm of a conceptual distinction (albeit unresolvable) between instructions and their implementations; we still remain within the confines of the belief that, however it is specified, the genotype, not the phenotype, is transmitted between generations. The metaphor of *information* captures this belief— genetic information is passed on from generation to generation, not the implementation of this information.

The full power of the distinction between genotype and phenotype, and its implications for genetics and evolution, became manifest after the discovery of DNA and the establishment of the "central dogma" of molecular biology: The dogma that the flow of information in biological systems is unidirectional—from DNA to RNA to proteins, but not from proteins to DNA. The "central dogma" identified DNA with the genotype, and the protein with the phenotype. DNA is conceived as a pure string of instructions, and the gene as a unit of information, where the environment can only accidentally alter the instructions carried in the DNA. However, the protein (and the higher systems constructed by DNA instructions) are highly sensitive to the environment. But because the protein is not the hereditary unit, modifications in protein structure and function could not lead to their inheritance. Phenotypes are not directly inherited in biological systems.

Dawkins (1986) emphasized this distinction between instruction and implementation by focusing on the relationship between DNA and development. Because there is no one-to-one correspondence between genes and characters, when a character is modified by the environment, its description cannot be fed back into the gene. Dawkins suggested that the genotype is like a recipe for a cake: a set of complex instructions for carrying out a process.

> "Baking powder" does not correspond to any particular part of the cake: its influence affects the rising, and hence the final shape, of the whole cake. If "baking powder" is deleted and replaced by "flour", the cake will not rise. ... There will be a reliable, identifiable difference between cakes baked according to the original version and the "mutated" versions of the recipe, even though there is no particular "bit" of any cake that corresponds to the words in question. This is a good analogy for what happens when a gene mutates. (Dawkins, 1986, p. 297)

There are two major assumptions in Dawkins' *recipe/cake* metaphor, and more generally, in the identification of DNA with genotype/instruction/recipe, and the processes of development with phenotype/implementation/cake. The first assumption is that the DNA is a passive information carrier, not a response system; the second is that DNA is the one and only carrier of heritable biological information. There is accumulating evidence that these two major assumptions are unwarranted. Contrary to the cake analogy, in living systems the recipe for the next cake is generated by the cake.

Intensive studies in recent years of the specificity of DNA–protein interactions indicate that the DNA and its structure are not only "genotype" (i.e., information carriers), but also "phenotype" (i.e., responsive to developmental and environmental signals, amenable to adaptive evolutionary changes; see review by Borst & Greaves, 1987). Well-known examples of regulatory genotypic responses are the rearrangements of the immunoglobulin genes during the development of the immune system, the amplification of the chorion genes in the follicle cells surrounding the developing egg of *Drosophila*, and specific changes in the DNA of flax plants in response to growth conditions. In the latter case, the environmentally induced alteration in DNA content is transmitted to progeny (Cullis, 1984). In bacteria, the recent discussions of "directed mutations" have rekindled interest in the origin of mutations and their relationship with the environment (see Symonds, 1991, for a popular review). Using Dawkins' metaphor, a specific change in the environment may cause a corresponding specific, and sometimes adaptive, change in the recipe.

The DNA system is not the only inheritance system. Cultural inheritance is of great importance in the evolution of civilization; through it, behavioral and social phenotypes are transmitted. Furthermore, additional inheritance systems are operating at the biological, cellular level. In addition to the DNA inheritance system, there are also epigenetic inheritance systems that can, and do, directly transmit phenotypes (Jablonka & Lamb, 1989). In a multicellular organism, different cell lineages (which have the same DNA) are functionally differentiated and maintain their differentiated state through many cell divisions, in the absence of the stimuli that initiated these different states. The epigenetic inheritance systems responsible for this type of epigenctic "cellular memory" can also generate variations in the germ line, some of which can be transmitted to descendants (Jablonka, Lachmann, & Lamb, 1992). Returning to the *recipe/cake* metaphor, this means that a particular interpretation of the recipe, and even the cake itself, may be inherited.

These findings and arguments arc relevant to the problem of the relationship between inheritance and development. The existence and operation of the epigenetic inheritance systems show that the processes of evolution by natural selection may operate at different levels of individuality (genes, cells, organisms, groups), as well as on different types of hereditary variations—not only DNA variations, but also epigenetic variations. Because epigenetic inheritance systems function as inheritance and response systems, epigenetic, developmental variations can become environmentally responsive hereditary systems. Thus, development is inherited in a direct sense. At the biological level, we are returning to the broader definitions of heredity that emerged at the beginning of the century. But we can now give these definitions a more precise interpretation, suggest molecular mechanisms, and point out limitations.

In the introduction of his book on the history of heredity, François Jacob (1970) explained that living beings are special because they can retain and transmit past information.

> The two turning points in evolution—first the emergence of life, later the emergence of thought and language—each corresponds to the appearance of a mechanism of memory, that of heredity and that of the mind. There are certain analogies between the two systems: both were selected for accumulating and transmitting past experience, and in both, the recorded information is maintained only as far as it is reproduced at each generation. However, the two systems differ with respect to their nature and to the logic of their performance. The flexibility of mental memory makes it particularly apt for the transmission of acquired characters. The rigidity of genetic memory prevents such transmission. (Jacob, 1970, pp. 2–3)

Human social practices depend on the operation of cultural transmission—that much is granted by all. If we want to understand the biological and evolutionary bases of human practices, we must, contrary to Jacob, take into account *two* additional types of inheritance systems: the DNA system and the epigenetic inheritance systems. The epigenetic inheritance systems occupy a middle position between the DNA system, as perceived by Jacob, and the cultural system—they are not as rigid as the classical DNA system, nor as flexible as the cultural inheritance system. The consideration of epigenetic inheritance systems and the recent insights concerning the responsiveness of the genome (DNA) introduce an additional level of analysis into the discussions of biological and cultural inheritance and evolution. Their effects blur the distinction between heredity and development, and make the relationship between them richer and more dynamic as one would expect from the perspective of a multilevel and multiprocess approach.

ON THE DEVELOPMENT OF PSYCHOSOCIAL INDIVIDUALITIES IN GROUP-LIVING MAMMALS

Hubert Hendrichs

Social groups of animals can be understood as systems that comprise different levels and processes. As specific environments, social systems provide their members with a basal orientation. At the same time, social systems define and constrain their members' potentialities of perception, action, and mental development. Only in their specific social environment can individual animals adapt to their social and ecological situations.

The ultimate function of individual traits in the sociobiologist's view is the maximization of reproductive fitness. But this function—proximately specified by processes of feeding, avoiding predators, gaining copulations, and raising young—can only be fulfilled in the specific environments of individuals. Many other proximate mechanisms and functions are important, such as gaining attachments and orientations, maintaining control, and developing mental adaptations and coping tactics. The mental and cognitive structures used in these performances integrate inherited dispositions and ontogenetically acquired individual realizations. These structures relate each animal in an individual way to its social and physical environments. The resulting social system can, within

limits, become independent of the individual animals involved, and contributes to the specific developments of their psychosocial individual-
ities.

Individuality in this sense implies different perceptions, sensibilities,
reactions, and orientations in the different animals of the same social
system. At the same time, shared knowledge and a common "language"
are required to allow communication of intentions and successful cooperation. In the following, it is argued that some aspects of mammalian individuality and intentionality (the term is used in a broad sense, not restricted to conscious intentionality, but including unconscious, goal-directed efforts as well) need to be taken into account when investigating
the behavior of mammals, and that these are indispensable for an adequate understanding of their psychosocial reactions.

Individual Psychosocial Structures. In vertebrates, as well as in
insects, the nervous system includes neurons that develop in interaction
with specific anatomical environments (see Campos-Ortega & Hartcn-
stein, 1985; Falk & Jablonka, this chapter). As was argued earlier, the results of such developments are not completely determined genetically.
The same holds for the formation of the organization of vertebrate social
systems and, interacting with them, for the psychosocial mental organization that characterizes individual members. However, there is an important difference: The environment in which the insect nervous system
develops (i.e., the organism) is largely controlled by genetic programs,
whereas the environment in which the psychosocial development of
mammals occurs does not have such a control. The structures and qualities of this environment are generated by mechanisms less directly controlled by genetic programs. For example, the physiological reactions occurring in a state of fear are inherited, whereas the causes of fear may be
learned (see Sluckin, 1979). Behavioral elements, like the forms of
motor actions, may be inherited, whereas the activations of such actions
are learned. A signal can be transmitted and processed by inherited mechanisms, whereas its evaluation, its meaning, and the way it can be used
have to be learned.

The following questions have to be answered concerning the development in domains that are not directly genetically determined. Are individual qualities accidental (i.e., acquired by the organism during ontogeny without essentially contributing to species-specific functions)? Or
do these acquired individual qualities contribute to the animal's ontoge-

netic development? The answers to these questions obviously depend on the type of quality and organism considered. In organisms whose development is largely determined genetically, the individual qualities that do not result from genetic dispositions are predominantly accidental. In organisms whose psychosocial individuality is developed and structured in an area left open by genetic programs, these individual qualities may not be merely accidental, but of fundamental importance to the functional performance of these organisms. This is especially the case in humans, but the boundary between accidental and structural in the acquired individuality is not one between animal and humans. In both animal and humans, inherited, accidentally, and sociostructurally acquired individual qualities are found in various combinations. The evolutionary development of new levels of organization can lead to changes in the units of evolution and selection (L. W. Buss, 1987; Jablonka, 1994).

The mammalian psychosocial individuality is constructed in an area left open by genetic dispositions (see Hendrichs, 1992, 1996). The focus here is not on individually developed traits, such as the animal's preferences and aversions, but on the network connecting these acquired traits in one, relatively stable structure. Specific mental properties—like preferences and aversions or attachments and relations developed by the individual animal in interacting with its specific social environment—are essential for the control of its motivational and arousal states. They become connected in a specific way, providing the animal with an individual structure. This structure is of paramount importance to the integration of the animal's functional subsystems as well as for its orientation in its environment. Various individual mental properties develop and stabilize in a specific relation to each other—an imprinting type of relationship in a specific state of connectedness. The result is a stabilized individual mentality.

In two packs of wolves or wild dogs, prey preference may differ. When the same preference occurs, the coordination of predation may be achieved in different ways. In some packs, the animals assemble for the hunt with a great deal of agonistic behavior—growling, snarling, and snapping at each other—and they show a similar behavior after the hunt, at the prey. However, during the hunt, there are no visible agonistics, and the procedure is efficiently carried through. In other packs, there is no growling or snarling before or after the hunt; rather, the animals remain friendly toward each other in all phases. Imagine it to be possible to transfer some cubs from one pack to another and let them develop prey preference and become "snarlers" or "nonsnarlers," different from the behavior in their original pack. They would have to develop an individual structure quite different from that of their original litter mates, and they would retain this individual structure even after being brought back to their original pack.

Individually Oriented Intentionality. What characterizes the intentionality, or steering control, of an organism with such an individual psychosocial structure? This structure was produced during the animal's ontogenetic development in an environment influenced by socioculturally transmitted qualities. It was constructed in a type of organism whose steering control had phylogenetically developed away from the domain tightly controlled by genetic dispositions.

Mayr (1974) distinguished three types of control of directed processes: teleomatic, teleonomic, and teleological. Teleomatic processes reach their equilibrium and end states by means of mechanochemical properties. For example, an apple will fall off a tree and roll down a slope until the mechanical properties of the process reach a state of balance. Processes of self-organization and homeostatic processes are teleomatic as long as they result merely from mechanochemical properties of the components and are not controlled by additional programs. By contrast, teleonomic processes are directed toward a goal by specific programs, developed either phylogenetically by natural selection or ontogenetically by experience or social tradition. These types of feedback programs do not, in the biologist's view, require consciousness or a representation of the goal by the acting system. These two are different from teleological processes that are usually understood as requiring a more or less conscious intentionality of a subject, and are therefore generally considered to be of little importance to the biology of nonhuman organisms. Mental processes in higher mammals can be combinations of two or three of these types. Some processes can occur without any *awareness* (the term is used for low levels of consciousness as possibly reached by higher mammals; see Griffin, 1981), or they can be accompanied partly or fully by different levels of awareness.

In mammals, an important type of sociomental process occurs that might be considered as an intermediate form between teleonomic and the teleological types. It is controlled neither by evolved or developed feedback programs, nor by conscious intentionality. Such processes occur in situations of environmental or motivational changes. In such situations, new decisions have to be generated in a specific orientation—decisions concerning the actual behavior and its possible implications for achieving potential aims. Such decisions, which efficiently interrelate situation, orientation, and goal achievement, can be produced unguided by either previously fixed programs or awareness. These inventive decisions require a specific orientation of the animal, which is more stable than the changeable situation and the possible goals. Therefore, one could call these processes "goal-directed in an orientation" or of "oriented intentionality." They may, as a successful invention, become memorized and incorporated in the program of the animal, closing some part of the area left open by its previous programs. At the same time, they may open it up further, allowing for new inventions. In higher mammals, the open part in the steering of intentionality, the mental space not controlled by established programs, generally does not become fully closed in ontogeny. It may even be widened considerably in the direction of an elementary form of consciousness.

Consider a case of three female wolves of the same litter: Their dominance relations are clear, and they live together in a relatively small enclosure of a zoo. When the two dominant animals are active, the movements of the lowest ranking female are mostly restricted to a specific part of the enclosure; when the two dominant animals are resting, this female sometimes moves into the area that she does not usually enter; she moves cautiously, alert, and tense, keeping her attention on the two dominant animals. If one of these so much as raises her head, the low-ranking female withdraws with two or three big leaps. But if the two others show no "offense," she moves on, intensely attentive, approaching a bone with some residue of meat, sniffing at it from a small distance, but not touching it, moving on to a marking spot of the two dominant animals, sniffing it without marking it itself, always remaining attentive toward the resting dominant animals. When the two dominant females have still not shown any "offense," she relaxes and, to some extent, begins to show some signs of well-being, but still keeps her attention on the two resting animals. She finally returns to her area, displaying behavior that distinctly indicates well-being.

This is one of the relatively few ways in which this individual, strongly constrained in her actions by the other animals, can generate a feeling of well-being. This regular performance has been described in a simplified manner. The details always vary, and the evaluation of events by the wolf appear to change by the hour, motivation and attention changing with the events of the day. The dominant wolves recognize this behavior and are generally not disturbed by it. Yet on some days they are and do not tolerate it.

What are the motivations and intentions of this animal during her excursion into "forbidden territory"? What is driving her? Which are the goals of her actions? How did this behavior develop? To what extent is it inherited, to what extent learned? Such questions are difficult to investigate. But with experience and patience, it can be done, and the questions sometimes can be partly answered. The main goal of the behavior described for the wolf is not to reach the bone with its residue of meat, inspect the marking spot of the dominant animals, explore the rarely used space, or prevent the dominant animals from getting up. All these constitute goals and points of orientation for the low-ranking female wolf, but they are not the central goals of her action. Her main aim is comprised of the following tendencies: to explore the boundaries of her social existence, to build up the intensity required for that kind of enterprise, and to make use of a natural potential, the activation of which includes physiological and emotional reactions, resulting in a state of well-being. This low-ranking female wolf uses inherited qualities in a specific connection developed by it, exploring the possibilities of her specific situation and aiming at the fullest possible realization of well-being. The specific strategy was not provided by the inherited program. Its development required a number of decisions in the area left open by genetic programs. Its becoming part of the animal's program did not require any form of conscious intentionality. The actual carrying-out of the described behavior does not require consciousness, but decisions unguided by any program.

Intentionality and Awareness. Although social actions of mammals often look similar to the observer, they can be intentional or nonintentional to various degrees (i.e., they may be accompanied by different states of awareness). These differences may reflect changes in the quality of the control of the behavioral patterns involved and in their functional significance. For example, a low-ranking individual may seek the proximity and protection of a dominant individual, thereby escaping the threat or aggression of an animal less dominant than the one approached. A dominant individual may end a confrontation or fight between two subdominant animals. Such behavior may "just happen" without any intention or awareness on the part of the animals involved, or it can be learned and intentionally employed by one or more of the interacting animals. It can even be recognized and "understood" by other individuals "observing" the event. This can be inferred from the subsequent actions of these animals, including their intentional movements. These behaviors enable the experienced observer to follow such processes of orientation and decision in the observed individuals.

Seeking proximity and protection of older, more dominant animals occurs in most mammalian taxa, including marsupials. In lower mammals, such behavior rarely includes learned intentional components and is probably not combined with states of awareness. In higher ungulate-type mammals, such as the various species of pigs, cattle, and horses, learned intentional components, and elementary forms of awareness occasionally occur and can be documented. In higher carnivores, elephants, and higher primates, they regularly occur and, to varying extents, can become part of the control system, integrating the motivational components of the organism.

The attention of a mammal is only rarely restricted to one specific object or one functional or motivational context. In various stages of intensity, its attention generally covers several areas simultaneously. Thus, it is able to choose several impulses from many, and to respond to the combination of these selected impulses in a way that fits the possibilities provided by its program. In such a case, it can sometimes choose its action, although possibly not the form in which it is carried out. A mammal can even attribute specific significance and meaning to structures and events in its environment. As a result, these objects or occurrences can become a source of security or fear, of excitement or tension. In attributing such qualities to specific parts of its environment, the mammal can show signs of what, in humans, are called imagination, invention, and creativity.

In the steering of an organism's behavior, physiological, emotional, cognitive, and social processes have to be combined and integrated. These processes are operated by different mechanisms in different environments; they are differently organized and controlled. A fright reaction can change an animal at all the levels influencing its control: physiological, motivational, mental, and social. Therefore, it is misleading to conceive of a mammal as mainly controlled by its cortex. The older brain structures play an important role, and the rest of the nervous system, including its autonomous parts, is also involved. Physiological, emotional, motivational, cognitive, and psychosocial conflicts and tensions have to be resolved by the animal. Decisions concerning possible and optimal action patterns have to be taken. In the process of acting, the patterns must be maintained with some independence from the further development of the original situation with its specific constellation of incentives. The resulting behavior and the process leading to its realization can be either inherited or acquired. In many cases, the behavior shown is inherited while the program for its implementation is not. The maintenance of such a process can be achieved by adhering tenaciously to the decisions taken on entering the process, such as an attack or a chase, warding off all further influences, or by an intentional maintenance in a specific orientation, balancing influences from various domains.

The tendencies of a mammal leading to intentional, goal-directed actions and enterprises may primarily result from its effort to master the integration of various competing and interacting motivations into one distinct action, and to accomplish this integration effectively. In this process, a number of "decisions" become necessary in relation to the actual possibilities of a successful integration in a common orientation. To carry through, and thereby achieve, an effective action, specific states of arousal and "aggressive" determination are often required to maintain the various decisions thus combined in a specific goal orientation. In situations of intense conflict—not panic—when processes of intentionality and awareness reinforce each other, higher mammals can invent new solutions to their actual problems. In these situations, higher mammals may, for brief moments, be able to generate states approaching consciousness. Thus, the processes operating in a social animal's actions in a specific situation may include genetically determined, acquired, and newly generated responses. Although these last processes fall short of the highest level of conscious thought, they are nevertheless goal-directed and informed by the social structure in which an individual animal develops and lives.

COMMUNICATION AND SOCIAL SYSTEMS: EVOLUTIONARY AND DEVELOPMENTAL ASPECTS

Peter M. Hejl

With the formation of absolutist states during the 17th and 18th centuries in continental Europe and their slow development toward a more democratic self-government, law became the preferred instrument for regulating society and the state. At the same time, law changed its character. Until well into modern times, laws were taken as given, describing more or less unchangeable relations among groups or members of a society. Traditional laws were legitimate because they were old and unchanged. Consequently, new rulers had to proclaim that they would respect traditional rights and defend (not make) law. The will of rulers became a source of legality only when they had accumulated enough authority to substitute themselves for the legalizing power of tradition. The resulting "positive" or "regulatory" law (see Teubner, 1984) was conceptualized as the transference of the legislator's will to administrators and, especially, judges. Legal positivism assumes that the codified will of the legislator—the text of law—is able to determine the behavior of those who have to apply it. When more and more members of the bourgeoisie entered the slowly growing state administration and the judicial system, around the turn from the 18th to the 19th century, the legal character of what they did "in the name of law" soon became problematic. With growing codification and positivization of law, how could one be sure that those who had to apply these laws would do so in the spirit of the legislator?

Under the growing impact of scientific thinking, the problem soon gained a methodological dimension. For example, in 1807 the German jurist J. H. Zirkler published a collection of essays in which he maintained that one has to abandon the idea "that the law thinks and speaks for us" (cited in Ogorek, 1986, p. 80) so that one had just to apply it. Therefore, there was a clear recognition of the inadequacy of the positivist concept of law. Contrary to the claim of judicial positivism, Zirkler rejected the idea that the text of laws could (to use a modern term) *program* the judicial behavior of judges to the extent that they would become mere automatons that executed the legislator's intentions.

Zirkler was only one voice in a wider debate that took place during the early 19th century—a time when there was still hope to substantially advance toward a more democratic system in Germany. With the defeat of the democrats in 1848, a period began that saw, together with industrialization, the integration of the German bourgeoisie into the power centers of German society. As a consequence, the former conflict between the liberal and reform-oriented administrators/jurists and those forces that struggled for continued supremacy of the German princes lost its importance. As a result, the pendulum swung back to stronger emphasis on the application of law. Today's jurists tend to see the law more as a limitation to interpretational freedom (Herzog, 1988).

One of the interesting points in the history of law and the role of judges under Roman Law was that the arguments against the concept of the text of law as a conveyor between the legislator and the judges were never invalidated. To resume this point in another terminology: Early judicial positivists conceived of written law as a program, whereas subsequent discussions and experience clarified that this program always has to be executed by judges who have personal views, belong to the social system of justice, and so on. Although this relation between the text of law and what judges do in the courts was, and still is, often described as an "interpretation," both practitioners and philosophers of law have known since the early 19th century that this is a euphemism.

To speak of an "interpretation" makes sense only if it is possible to access directly (in a noninterpretative way) what is interpreted (the program, or the meaning of law). Unfortunately, we have direct access to only the text, not to its meaning. Thus, legislators and judges are confronted with a situation where there is consensus about the material basis of law, the text, but where its meaning exists exclusively as more or less varying interpretations of interpretations. Hence, there is a complex feedback relationship between the program and its application, or between the legislators and the judges as components of the judicial system. It is because these relationships have changed that the conflict between legislators and judges has lost its explosive character, although the question of the lawfulness of judicial decisions in a strict sense is still unsolved.

The problematic relation among the legislator, the text of law, and the judges is just one example of how difficult it is to communicate successfully. If we look at communication as a process in which there is "transmission," we might use it as a general example to discuss the relations between biological and cultural inheritance with respect to the concepts of evolution and development.

Of course, it was not accidental that the context of Roman Law had to be underlined. The problem of the application of law is, to a certain degree, typical of a judicial system based on codified law. Moreover, the meaning of *law* differs between the Anglo-American and the Continental traditions. In the Anglo-American context, with its emphasis on case law, *law* is nearer to the notion of *rights*, whereas in Continental countries, under Roman influence, one tends to think more of *general norms*.

This echoes the division between individualism and collectivism in social thinking. Hence, *rights*, in a natural rights tradition, are those that the individual can claim against others, and especially against the state; whereas *norms,* in the Continental tradition, are taken more as regulations with which individuals have to comply.

The claim here is that there exists a structural and functional similarity among (a) the application of law, (b) communication, (c) cultural heritage, and (d) biological inheritance. It is argued that the construction of these processes as "transmissions" tends to divert our attention from important aspects. As the case of the positivistic concept of "law as a program" demonstrates, the concept of transmission neglects the systems in which communication, cultural heritage, or biological inheritance take place. Moreover, as systems differentiate, these processes become distributed throughout the systems, and there seems to be a growing amount of local adaptations to conditions within them.

Although the theory of information developed by Shannon (see Shannon & Weaver, 1949) is of little utility for the explanation of communication outside the technical domain for which it was conceived (Köck, 1987), it has the great advantage of posing the problem in a clear way (see Fig. 11.2).

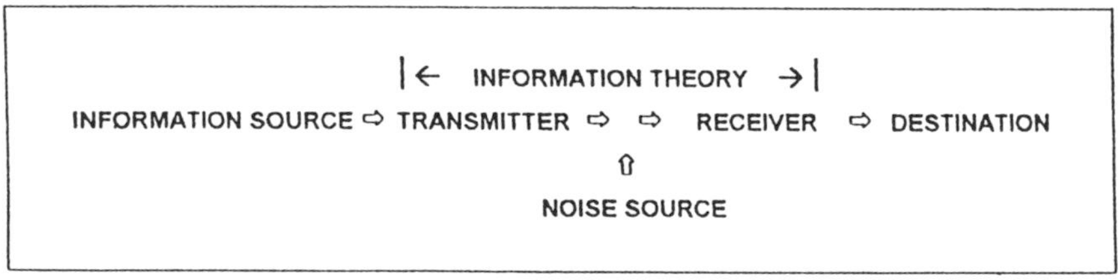

| ← INFORMATION THEORY → |

INFORMATION SOURCE ⇨ TRANSMITTER ⇨   ⇨ RECEIVER ⇨ DESTINATION

⇧

NOISE SOURCE

Fig. 11.2 Communication and information theory

Weaver (1949) explained the different steps:

> The *information source* selects a desired *message* out of a set of possible messages. The *transmitter* changes the *message* into the *signal* which is actually sent over the *communication channel* from the transmitter to the *receiver*. The *receiver* is a sort of inverse transmitter, changing the transmitted signal back into a message, and handing this message on to the destination. When I talk to you, my brain is the information source, yours the destination; my vocal system is the transmitter, and your ear and the associated eighth nerve is the receiver. In the process of being transmitted, it is unfortunately charac-

teristic that certain things are added to the signal which were not intended by the information source. These changes are called *noise* (pp. 6ff; italics original).

The authors then turned to a more detailed discussion, starting with the basic notion of *information*: "The word *information*, in this theory, is used in a special sense that must not be confused with its ordinary usage. In particular, *information must not be confused with meaning"* (Weaver, 1949, p. 8, italics added). That Shannon called his theory of signal transmission "theory of information" is probably one of the most confusing terminological decisions in recent history of science. As the quote clarifies, Shannon and Weaver were not unaware of the problem. But the original text, although quite explicit on this issue, was apparently not read very often, or at least not by those who confused the transmission of signals with the production of meaning. Shannon and Weaver's schema and their explanations clearly show that they concentrated on the process of signal transfer. Although indispensable for any type of communication, signal transfer should not be mistaken as meaning transfer. The core problem of any theory of communication is certainly the meaning of *meaning*. In the humanities and social sciences, the term is sometimes used in a way that lacks the required and possible clarity. To avoid mystification, *meaning* is identified for the present purpose with *effect* (see Hejl, 1992a; Putnam, 1988). The meaning of whatever is transmitted is then taken to be the effect it has on the receiver.

If one wants to explain a particular effect, one has to look at all stages of its production. Of course, the first stage is the transformation of what an information source wants to communicate into a sequence of transmittable physical entities: sounds, graphical, or other units that serve in a more or less fuzzy way as symbols. In the social domain of humans, the most important symbols belong to verbal language, although we have a large repertoire of nonverbal means of communication as well (see chap. 5, this volume). If we take symbols to be physical entities that stand for experiential units, it is clear that, because we evolved in a relatively uniform social and physical world, we use similar cognitive mechanisms. As a result, there is a large domain of experiences we share and hence symbolize in a corresponding way.

Nevertheless, a distinction is required between the physical units needed for transmission and symbolizing and the experienced entities. This difference is made clear in Magritte's famous painting; he paints a pipe under which he wrote: "Ceci n'est pas une pipe." Speech or text, to name two devices, are just a basis for, or a condition of, communication (a *Kommunikatbase*; Schmidt, 1980). Without such a basis, communication above a rather low level of differentiation (compared with human communication) would not occur. The experiential or cognitive units the hearer or reader of a message associates with the signal sequence he or she receives depend, to a large extent, on his or her experience.

This is not to say that in normal communication this takes place in a conscious way. On the contrary, it happens automatically and unconsciously. Because the hearer of a message associates it with what is known about the topic identified by the hearer, the latter draws on corresponding experience and knowledge of how to handle the situation. It is this identification of a sequence of signals with behavioral and/or cognitive experiences and corresponding competencies that make up the meaning of a communication: It triggers behavioral or cognitive processes that have been formed as a result of our past experience. Insofar as communication partners use the same biologically and socially evolved perceptual and cognitive mechanisms and live in the same culture (and hence dispose of shared experiences), they select signal sequences that the hearer will associate to experiences akin to those the speaker had in mind. The more this is the case, the more successful is communication.

Consequently, human communication might be described in the following way: A speaker assumes that he or she shares with a partner a set of syntactic rules and sign sequences that designate various experiences and activities. The hearer, although sharing this assumption, unavoidably uses as his or her frame of reference experiences and activities that differ to a certain extent from those of the speaker. Consequently, intended and produced meaning of a communication differ less the more similar the experiences of the communication partners are. Because communication requires signals as physical representations of meaning, the successful "transfer of meaning" is a process that presupposes a common evolutionary and/or ontogenetic history (see Hendrichs, this chapter). Signals cannot do more than specify a fuzzy set of meanings for the listener. Which one will become effective depends on his or her experience. Although based on a long coevolution of the biological and social aspects of human nature (Durham, 1991), this experience is mostly a social experience. Because it shapes this experience to an important degree, the systemic character of society has to be taken into account.

How do multilevel, multiprocess approaches allow us to conceptualize social similarities and differences? To conceptualize societies as systems is a theoretical decision. It assumes that we can distinguish social entities from a mere set of unrelated individuals and their activities. This theoretical decision will have to be justified, at least to a certain degree. Certainly, here is not the place to reopen the controversy of how to conceptualize societies. Moreover, in recent years, this debate has led to a certain convergence of formerly incompatible positions (J. C. Alexander, Giesen, Münch, & Smelser, 1987). The point to emphasize is the belief that, whatever speculation about the origins of sociality we prefer, the result of its evolution was the formation of composite social entities—social systems.

Human social units started some million years ago with families (however these might be defined; see Jones, R. Martin, & Pilbeam, 1994). During the last centuries, social units turned into nation states, with millions of only socioculturally related members. Today's societies even seem to "move" on various roads toward a world society. As the works of Cavalli-Sforza, Piazza, Menozzi, and Mountain (1988) and Cann (1988) show, there is good evidence to assume that world population originated in a single population in one site in Africa and spread slowly around the globe. As a result, if one wants to explain differences and similarities between today's cultures, there are several interacting processes to take into account. "Descent with modification" in the Darwinian sense no doubt played a role in shaping the differences between humans in various parts of the world. Migratory movements that carried knowledge of all kinds to distant places contributed to this shaping. There are the specific opportunities that different environments offer, and the slowly growing pressure from population growth.

Population growth is a factor of social change that has been known for a long time. At least since Malthus, it has been a frightening specter as well. Although unlimited birth rates might bring us near the earth's carrying capacity, it is difficult to deny that most of today's culture is part of the response our ancestors "found" or "invented" to cope with the need to coordinate growth of resources with growth of population. Of course, the answers were the formation of stable societies that could integrate more and more members due to a growing functional differentiation, first at the level of individual members and then at that of social subsystems. The first step in this direction was the transition from a gatherer and hunter subsistence mode to that of agriculture—the "Neolithic revolution." It allowed a much greater population to be sustained, and hence a greater density of social interactions. A fact some evolutionary anthropologists and psychologists (e.g., Tooby & Cosmides, 1992) do not take into account enough is that the time span of human evolution prior to this change has to be calculated in hundreds of thousands of years, whereas since the Neolithic era changes had only some 10,000 years to evolve. Although too short for much evolutionary change at the biological level, at least if we assume the traditionally proposed mechanisms of random variation and selection by the environment, it is during this extremely short time that most of human culture and knowledge was produced (hence, it seems reasonable to look at these rapid evolutionary developments as changes parallel to those the model of 'punctuated equilibrium' proposes). Of course, such changes may also have affected some of the givens of the biological evolutionary scenario as coevolutionary theory shows (chap. 9, this volume; but see L. W. Buss, 1987).

Starting already with the situation in groups of higher mammals (Hendrichs, this chapter) and primate groups (see chap. 4, this volume), and continuing with early human societies, the social group became the most important environment for human evolution. Formed by nothing but individuals, it evolved into a more and more differentiated entity analytically distinguishable from its individual members. Because of the stabilities, societies develop in different respects, their members have to adapt to life under these conditions. The importance of society as the primary environment constraining both further biological and social evolution for humans expands with increasing differentiation. This is even more so in societies where production and redistribution reach a level at which the contact with the natural environment as a source for securing food and shelter gets practically lost and/or becomes technically unproblematic. As a result, the natural environment loses its former importance as selector for cognitive and/or behavioral capacities. In this respect, it is more and more replaced (although never completely) first by other humans and then by the composite entities they form (i.e., societies or social systems).

If we agree to define *development* as the changes that transform a composite entity as a whole and take place at the level of the components of that entity and their interactions, then societies develop. In this general sense, development does not imply any "goal" or "state" analogous to that of becoming "grown up" or "mature," which is typical of the everyday usage, for example when one speaks of a child's development.

Development does not exclude environmental effects on the developmental path. As understood here, development is by no means taken as being incompatible with *evolution*. But its occurrence signals most often an increase in complexity. This happened at the biological level, at least with the formation of multicellular organisms, and again at the nonbiological level, when societies appeared that were integrated through culture. When this occurred, older evolutionary mechanisms were complemented and partly replaced by new mechanisms. Thus, in modern societies, *success* is increasingly defined in a way totally unrelated to biological reproductive success, although people have become aware that the "old" problem of survival reappears as the imperatives of peace and preservation of the environment.

The evolutionary formation of societies as units was the precondition for their internal *development*. Social differentiation occurred in a situation of shrinking resources due to a growing population. But as Durkheim (1986) already pointed out in his discussion of Spencer's sociology, such a situation would have led to generalized warfare if there had not been already established bonds of an emotional nature to prevent such a destructive course (hence the advantage of communicating emotions nonverbally; Dimberg, 1988, 1990; Ekman & Keltner, 1997). Due to these emotional bonds, interpersonal confidence could be extended to nonfamily members of the group, which, in turn, could now be formed. On this basis, a more developed sociality could evolve together with its behavioral correlate—the waiting for reciprocation of a donor of some goods or help (Cosmides & Tooby, 1992).

When social differentiation progressed beyond the rudimentary level it attained in gatherer–hunter bands, this took place under the constraint of an agricultural subsistence economy. Given the necessities of agricultural production, one can venture to say that the tripartite functional social differentiation (priests, warriors, workers) which Oexle (1988) showed for the European Middle Ages and Dumézil (1958) considered to be a particularity of Indo-European culture, is mostly an expression of differentiation under the agrarian constraint, and as such is universal (A. Nitschke, 1992, personal communication). On the basis of this apparently fundamental division of labor, further differentiations, and integrations of functions took place according to local and historical contingencies. Disregarding these details, there are, as Durkheim already hypothesized, some important effects of differentiation: Social organization plays a greater role, society's members individualize, and communication becomes more difficult.

If *societies* is defined as sets of individuals who share a certain amount of knowledge about the world and about themselves, and who interact and communicate with respect to this knowledge, their overall pattern of interactions becomes a crucial variable. This pattern of interactions may be called the *organization* of a social system (Hejl, 1990, 1992a). It has two main properties: autonomization and selectivity.

Being a pattern produced by a majority of participants in a given society, the organization is relatively independent, or autonomized. This means that the cognitive and behavioral patterns that form the organization of a society are not modified if a small number of members (or a greater number of powerless members) of a society modify their interactions. The reason is simply that the other members just continue to interact as before, given that they either ignore changes taking place "somewhere" in the network, or that any greater change of interaction patterns and their cognitive prerequisites are highly difficult to manage. As interaction patterns, the organization of a society can be analytically isolated and analyzed. It "exists," at least partly, in the form of traditions, the established division of labor, or institutions (e.g., in those called "states"). In later stages of social development, the organization is, in addition, stabilized through norms and norm-enforcing agencies. When differentiation leads to the formation of social subsystems, they are not only autonomized with respect to their individual members, but also with respect to the surrounding system.

As societies grow and differentiate, not everyone can continue to interact with everyone else. Therefore, the selection of interaction partners becomes a matter of choice, and hence integrated in the various internal differentiations. All types of social organization—the system of Hindu castes, the medieval rank system, the organization of a firm, as well as scientific disciplines—establish who are the preferred or obligatory interaction partners. This selectivity works in two directions. It excludes actors and actions as irrelevant with respect to the system. This is the establishment of a border. But the selectivity also connects those of its constituent components that shall interact. Therefore, the selectivity of a system derives its distinction from its environment and makes it a composite unity with functionally related parts. As a result, autonomy and selectivity make the organization a distinguishable characteristic of a social unity, as well as a "factor" needed to explain the behavior of that society or group (Boudon, 1980; Coleman, 1987; Fuchs, 1992).

The selectivity of the organization in weakly differentiated societies is not much developed, whereas it increases with population growth and a growing number of social subsystems. As a result, the experiences of the individual members of differentiated societies differ to a certain extent. Therefore, if there are no power elite and/or cultural convictions that impose social uniformity, the individuals will have to adopt decisions and accept responsibilities that, at an earlier stage, were located at the social level. They become increasingly conscious of their new freedom and the opportunities and risks it offers. This is what is meant by *individualization*. As can be shown, there is a feedback relation between individualization and organizational change that leads to modifications at both levels. This can be understood in a nonmetaphorical way as social self-organization (Hejl, 1992b).

Social differentiation and individualization modify the conditions under which communication is successful. The more experiences differ, the more difficult it becomes to produce the intended meaning. Societies have reacted to this in various ways. A growing abstraction of communication is one response. It shifts the "decision" of what is meant during communication from the social level to the newly formed individuals. Another solution consists, of course, in the reduction of communicative interactions down to a level where merely requests are put forward that are answered with proposals of solutions: The confidence in the specialist replaces direct understanding (and requires various social mechanisms to regulate and legitimate this process). Finally, we have a reaction to communication problems from differentiation that have become important during the last decades—namely, further differentiation. Its main expression is the formation of specialists and specialized social systems for communication. This started with the early scribes and developed into modern education and culture leading up to today's mass communication industry.

Maintenance, elaboration, and transmission of culture have to rely on communication. It is in this context that we have to ask: How does the process of cultural heritage function in a differentiated society? First, some specification of what is meant by *culture*. The term is used here to refer to ideational entities (Boyd & Richerson, 1985; Durham, 1990) that form repertoires of knowledge items. Some subsets of these ideational entities (concepts, representations, or *Vorstellungen*) might be seen by some social actors as conceptual systems (e.g., the concepts that make up a paradigm). To distinguish cultural from actual knowledge, needed for example in the everyday functioning of social systems or in technical contexts, cultural knowledge is taken to be of a higher degree of generality. Examples are the knowledge of general regulations of a national law system, a materialist view of natural processes, aesthetic criteria, manners, or, of growing importance in highly differentiated societies, knowledge of decision-producing institutions.

As mentioned earlier, the generality of cultural concepts is linked to the process of generalization resulting from differentiation. But there is an important difference between societies depending on their degrees of differentiation: The more differentiated societies are, the more cultural knowledge is produced and used in specific social subsystems. This can easily be shown with respect to politics, the economy, science, law, art, and so on.

It is at this point that the systemic character of societies again becomes important, especially their capacities for self-organization and self-regulation. The more differentiation and individualization progress, the more the part of common knowledge shrinks for the benefit of particular or subsystemic knowledge. As differentiation necessarily includes the autonomization of the resulting individuals/subsystems, one finds in parallel to their formation the appearance of general norms, and hence of norms that *have* to be interpreted according to the specific conditions under which they are "applied." These norms regulate—often via specialized subsystems, such as the judicial system—the interplay of the system's components (individuals/subsystems), and ensure that their capacities to function are not unduly restricted (otherwise advantages dependent on differentiation are lost). These external regulations (with respect to social subsystems) have to work within functional constraints proper for social systems.

There are at least two classes of constraints. The first results from the characteristic of a given system. Construed around some goal or interest, and including accepted knowledge of how to achieve this goal, every social system defines a specific class of events as relevant and dismisses the usually much larger "rest" as irrelevant. The second is due to the functioning of communication. There is a rather narrow margin for individual deviations that members of social systems accept. In contradistinction to the situation in differentiated societies, cooperation and communication in specialized subsystems can be highly efficient due to minimal differences between the members of the system (even if they disagree on everything else). Therefore, deviation quickly leads to irrelevance or incomprehensibility. Social subsystems are integrated into a selective overall organization that provides them with required inputs (potential members, material resources, recognition). At the same time, they function in an unavoidably conservative manner.

As a result, any event that affects a social system—be it the change of an economic indicator, the replacement of a leading politician by his or her opponent, an invention, or a natural catastrophe—differs in its meaning according to the social subsystem in which it is perceived. What is transmitted in singular reports or utterances is not meaning, but a fuzzy set of possibilities to construct meaning according to the criteria of relevance the receiving individuals take from the social subsystems in which they operate. Therefore, the finally constructed meaning of a communication is the result of the cognitive processes of the individuals involved and the history of the network(s) in which they act. In this sense, it seems nearly impossible to determine, in a general way, the degree to which a specific meaning results either from the selection the sender operated when he or she decided which word sequence to use, or from the process of meaning construction on the receiver's side.

Some additional remarks on the example used at the beginning might function as a résumé. If the text of law does not transport the meaning the legislator has in mind, why is there not much more variance between different "applications," as one would expect?

As recent research shows (see Hejl, n.d.; Pfeiffer & Oswald, 1989), the same offenses are in fact punished rather differently, even under identical laws. This is valid for several countries with different traditions of national law, hence apparently characteristic of the actual functioning of numerous judicial systems. Because these differences in the "application" of law are usually unknown within societies, they are not detrimental to the indispensable confidence in the judicial system. But this does not explain why the factual production of law in the judicial process does not generate a much greater and intolerable amount of divergence between different judges or courts.

To compensate for the effects of meaning construction in differentiated social systems, much more efficient mechanisms were developed, as the German example shows. It was not "justice" in an emphatic sense that was at stake in the controversy between jurists and the political authorities at the beginning of the last century. The main topic, barely hidden, was the degree of autonomy that the state—at that time, the German kings and princes—would grant to the judicial system. From a political point of view, the issue was one of power—namely, the competition for influence on societal affairs between the king and the nobility at one side, and the developing bourgeoisie on the other, whose members defined themselves more and more as citizens. For them, the establishment of a judicial system bound to "obey only the law" was a major means to limit royal interventions. Seen from a macrosociological angle, the main issue was the functional autonomy of the judicial system.

Given the existing distribution of power during the post-napoleonic period of restoration, it became clear during the debate that autonomization would be achieved only if the legislators were convinced that they could effectively regulate the judicial system. Moreover, the problem became politically less important due to a number of changes that had produced the required (picture of a) law-applying justice. The most important are: (a) the diminished emphasis on a strict application because of a growing insight into the impossibility of any "exhaustive" codification, (b) the establishment of stricter procedural regulations, (c) the creation of a career for professional judges comprising a long and carefully organized course of study and preparatory period, (d) the establishment and perfection of the system of courts of appeal, (e) a growing reference to collections of judgments in judicial decision making, (f) a certain circulation of higher judges between judicial and ministerial positions, and (g) cooperation with jurists in legislation (Ogorek, 1986).

As a result, judicial systems in modern societies (e.g., Germany) possess considerable autonomy. Due to processes of standardization controlled by jurists, judges settle disputes and punish crimes on the basis of laws they helped to formulate, and whose definite meaning is defined by the Federal Court of Justice or its equivalent. In this sense, the judicial system can serve as a paradigm both of the functioning of a big social subsystem and of its interactions with its environment. On the other side, the political system appoints holders of higher judicial offices and employs jurists in many positions, in this way using their system-specific knowledge for legislative and related purposes. Because it is the judicial system that decides, via the appeal courts and the federal court on the applicabilities of a given law, there is, by definition, no contradiction between the former and the legislator.

Hence, the texts of law "transmitted" to the judicial system determine their effects only within the functional possibilities of the judicial system. They are produced during its development as an autonomized composite entity. This holds for the effect of any communication or program transmitted to an autonomized system to regulate its behavior. If, in the case of the political system, politicians are unsatisfied with a given regulation, they have to either legislate in such a way that the judicial system adopts their views or to change the system's top officials. As every experienced politician knows, it is not enough to vote for a law without asking what cognitive construction it will trigger within the judicial system.

Of course, the autonomization of judicial systems in the tradition of Roman Law is just one example for the point I want to make. It shows the highly complex systemic preconditions required for intersystemic communication to function *as if* it consisted of a simple "transmission of meaning."

SUMMARY

Although the preceding subchapters have addressed such seemingly disparate topics as the relation between phenotypes and genotypes and the subject of inheritance systems, the formation of individualized minds in mammals, and the functioning of communication in differentiated societies, there is an important convergence of the contributions. This becomes more prominent, especially in an interdisciplinary context, if the problem is transferred to a higher level of generality.

The striking parallel among all three contributions is the critique of the abstract concept of "transmission." At all of the levels discussed, the idea of "pure" transmission is criticized. From a historical point of view, the concept of transmittable properties can be traced back to Judeo-Christian convictions that there exists some immutable essence, be it invariant (material) properties or some unchangeable (scientific or religious) knowledge. We find this idea at the basis of the (fundamentalist) belief that religious texts contain a literal meaning, the transport of which is unequivocal. It is even more strongly present in the concept of the "Holy Scriptures," where, if these are taken "literally," the material and ideational aspects are combined just as in the idea that the (material) gene embodies its meaning.

This oversimplified idea of transmission has been at the core of convictions, such as that the phenotype is determined by the genotype (Falk

& Jablonka), that the behavior of mammals exclusively expresses their attempt to maximize reproductive success (Hendrichs), or that the message transports its meaning as stipulated by cultural traditions leading to the concept of "positivistic jurisprudence" (Hejl). Because all applications of the concept of transmission use the same conceptual apparatus, it is not surprising to find the striking parallel as outlined earlier—between "phenotype" and "genotype" on one side, and "written law" and "judicial decisions" on the other.

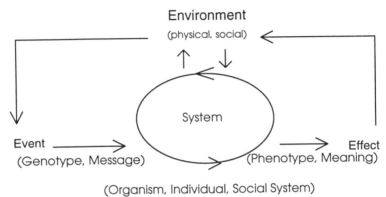

Fig. 11.3. Transmission in complex systems

"Transmission" along this line of thinking takes place either from one generation to the next, or among members of the same generation. This unacceptable view of transmission starts with the assumption that "something" is transmitted without being modified, and that all transmission channels can be reduced to one channel. Proponents of such a concept of transmission, although they admit that transmission might go in various directions (Cavalli-Sforza & Feldman, 1981) or be "biased" (Richerson & Boyd, 1989), insist on the basic theoretical idea that a more or less complete transport takes place from one point in time and space to another. (This is, of course, not to deny the heuristic and methodological importance of hypothesis testing through mathematical modeling that the trait concept encourages, as Boyd and Richerson rightly underlined.)

In contradistinction to this approach, the authors of this chapter underline that the result of what is called *transmission* has to be seen as ensuing from a more complex (Konold & Falk, 1992; Schwegler & G. Roth, 1992) process. Its basic structure is described in Fig. 11.3.

The process may be described as starting with a (communicative or regulatory) "event" that has some definite properties, be it the set of genes that make up a genotype or the symbol sequence of a message. This "event" triggers sequences of interactions in a (more or less complex) system. They lead to modifications of the system, be it processes of growth and differentiation or changes in the states of some of the system's components or subsystems, as during phases of arousal in animals or during fluctuations of economic or political activities in societies. Clearly enough, the processes triggered by the starting "event" depend in their course on the event itself. Because it is specific, it only affects those components of the system that are sensitive to the specificity of the event.

Nevertheless, dependence does not mean determination in a straightforward sense. As the triggered process takes place within a system, it is influenced by the system via interactions with other components. Moreover, the system exists in, and interacts with, a physical environment, or with an environment that consists of systems belonging to the same class of systems (a social environment). These interactions produce a continuous stream of all kinds of events that modify components and, thereby, internal interactions of the participating systems. As a consequence, any process takes place under a more or less significant influence from the environment.

But one has to be aware that a specific interaction that takes place within highly differentiated systems with many components (which, moreover, show different behaviors) is often so constrained by the obligatory secondary, tertiary, and further-down interactions with other components that the result is a "conservatism from complexity." Such a stability appears not so much at the level of the components as at that of the system's behavior. There it may take the form of conservationism or, by contrast, that of continuous, driftlike change. It is the complexity of the interplay between what takes place within the system and what is imposed on it from outside that does not allow more than a partial analysis (Schwegler & G. Roth, 1992). Yet all authors of the subchapters agree that it is in this interplay that we have to look for explanations of the variety of the effects that a communicative or regulatory event may have. It is here that one has to look for explanations of processes that appear at the genetic level as plasticity or canalization of phenotypic traits (Falk & Jablonka), or at the behavioral level as the phenomena of both the invariance and the high modifiability of behavioral sequences (Hendrichs).

Only if mechanisms that secure near invariance evolved could the system be spared of disintegration. But within this imperative, the sheer "conservatism from complexity" does not prevent change altogether. One should expect variations due to (a) accidental events; (b) internal adaptations or drifts, claimed to be "structurally required" changes (Hendrichs), like those learning processes that more complex organisms and social systems have to perform; and (c) adaptive changes triggered by repeated influences from the environment, whether they are epigenetic (Jablonka & Lamb, 1989) or genetic by nature. Finally, there are at least two types of environmental modifications that result from the functioning of systems (indicated by the arrows from *Effect* to *Environment* and *Event*).

Like all changes in the environment, these modified environments give rise to modified events for the systems concerned. First, if we take the environment of a system as the set of events that may modify the system, changes of the system that are quite misleadingly called *preadaptive,* have to be seen as "specifying": They specify a modified environment as "possible" for the system. Second, there are numerous straightforward examples of environmental changes due to the functioning of systems. When photosynthesis started some billion years ago, the environment became enriched with oxygen. Hence, aerobic energy utilization was introduced into the living world by the action of living cells on the atmosphere. Exactly the same holds in the social domain. The effects of "inventing" culture, scripture, institutions, law, science, technology, and so on have been changes in human's physical and social environments. In all these cases, it can be said that systems produced, modified, or selected environments that, in turn, had a selective influence on systems. The relation between systems and their environment is a coevolutionary one (Durham, 1991).

From this short résumé of the critique of the transmission concept, some other equally important consequences have to be drawn. If we look at the multilevel systemic context in which inheritance systems operate, reductionism loses its basis. At the same time, the analytical character of the neat, but at best discipline-specific, heuristic distinction between system and environment becomes clear: The environment of genes consists of organisms, that of organisms consists of social systems or the physical surroundings, and that of social systems consists of the genetic constraints of past evolutionary history. Once the analytical character of these distinctions is accepted, the fundamental opposition between evolution and development becomes obsolete. If evolution is seen as a process that results mainly from the interaction between a system and its environment, whereas development happens "inside" systems, then the contributions of this chapter suggest that evolutionary forces are modulated by systemic, developmental, dynamics and requirements, as demonstrated by the integration of physical, social, and psychic needs and action repertoires into what characterizes the individual mind of mammals, including humans (individualization has to be seen both as a biological and social phenomenon). Developmental processes also can be seen as motivating and integrating evolutionary mechanisms. Here, biological and social differentiation are interesting examples. As can be shown with respect to the autonomization of judicial systems (Hejl), emergent subsystems expand and become stabilized in competition with other subsystems. During this process, variants appear, occupy the scene, and eventually lose their importance. The ultimately successful solution will have to be adapted to the requirements of those subsystems with which the new subsystem interacts. As this takes place within a self-organizing network, there are numerous local processes of competition, variation, and selection/adaptation that make up the system's development.

An approach that emphasizes the importance of multiple inheritance systems—which may have different properties, each particularly significant at a particular level of organization—is necessary to achieve greater understanding of evolution and development.

REFERENCES

A

Aberle, D. F. (1984). The language family as a field for historical reconstruction. *Journal of Anthropological Research, 40,* 129–136.

Aberle, D. F. (1987). Distinguished lecture: What kind of science is anthropology? *American Anthropologist, 89,* 551–566.

Aberle, D. F., Cohen, A. K., Davis, A. K., Levy, M. J., & Sutton, F. Y. (1950). The functional requisites of society. *Ethics, LX,* 100–111.

Alchian, A. A. (1950). Uncertainty, evolution and economic theory. *Journal of Political Economy, 58,* 221–222.

Alcock, J. (1987). Ardent adaptationist. *Natural History, 96,* 4.

Aldenderfer, M. (1993). Ritual, hierarchy and change in foraging societies. *Journal of Anthropological Archaeology, 12,* 1–40.

Alexander, J. C., Giesen, B., Münch, R., & Smelser, N. J. (Eds.). (1987). *The micro–macro link.* Los Angeles, CA: University of California Press.

Alexander, R. D. (1974). The evolution of social behavior. *Annual Review of Ecology and Systematics, 5,* 325–328.

Alexander, R. D. (1977). Natural selection and the analysis of human sociality. In C. E. Goulden (Ed.), *Changing scenes in natural sciences* (pp. 283–337). Philadelphia, PA: Philadelphia Academy of Natural Sciences.

Alexander, R. D. (1979). *Darwinism and human affairs.* Seattle, WA: University of Washington Press.

Alexander, R. D. (1987). *The biology of moral systems.* New York: Aldine de Gruyter.

Alexander, R. D. (1990). Epigenetic rules and Darwinian algorithms. *Ethology and Sociobiology, 11,* 241–303.

Alexander, R. D., & Borgia, G. (1978). Group selection, altruism, and the levels of organization of life. *Annual Review of Ecology and Systematics, 9,* 449–479.

Allen, E. et al. (1975). Letter. *The New York Review of Books,* November, 13, (pp. 43–44).

Allen, T. F. H., & Starr, T. B. (1982). *Hierarchy: Perspectives for ecological complexity.* Chicago: University of Chicago Press.

Alper, J., Beckwith, J., & Miller, L. F. (1978). Sociobiology is a political issue. In A. L. Caplan (Ed.), *The sociobiology debate.* New York: Harper & Row.

Alpers, M. P. (1992). Kuru. In R. D. Attenborough & M. P. Alpers (Eds.), *Human population biology in Papua New Guinea* (pp. 312–334). Oxford, England: Clarendon.

Andrews, P. (1981). Species diversity and diet in monkeys and apes during the miocene. In C. B. Stringer (Ed.), *Aspects of human evolution* (pp. 25–61). London: Taylor & Francis.

Arbib, M. A., & Hesse, M. B. (1986). *The construction of reality.* Cambridge, England: Cambridge Univesity Press.

Arensburg, B., Schepartz, L. A., Tillier, A. M., Vandermeersch, B., & Rak, Y. (1990). A reappraisal of the anatomical basis for speech in middle paleolithic hominids. *American Journal of Physical Anthropology, 83,* 137–146.

Arnold, M. B. (1960). *Emotion and personality.* New York: Columbia University Press.

Arnold, M. B. (1968). *The nature of emotion.* London: Penguin Books.

Atran, S. (1990). *The Cognitive foundations of natural history.* New York: Cambridge University Press.

Axelrod, R. (1984). *The evolution of cooperation.* New York: Basic Books.

Axelrod, R., & Hamilton, W. D. (1981). The evolution of cooperation. *Science, 211,* 1390–1396.

B

Bachman, D., & Albert, M. (1991). *The cerebral organization of biological aspects* (Vol. 3). New York: Cambridge University Press.

Bachofen, J. J. (1861). *Das Mutterrecht [The maternal right].* Basel: Benno Schwabe.

Baillargeon, R. (1986). Representing the existence and location of hidden objects: Object permanence in 6- and 8-month old infants. *Cognition, 23,* 21–41.

Bajema, C. J. (1979). Differential transmission of genetic and cultural information about the environment: A cybernetic view of genetic and cultural evolution in animal species. In R. J. Meier, C. M. Otten, & F. Abdel-Hameed (Eds.), *Evolutionary models and studies in human diversity* (pp. 47–61). The Hague, Netherlands: Mouton.

Ball, J. A. (1984). Memes as replicators. *Ethology and Sociobiology, 5,* 145–161.

Bandura, A. (1986). *Social foundations of thought and action: A social cognitive theory.* Englewood Cliffs, NJ: Prentice-Hall.

Bandura, A., & Walters, R. (1963). *Social learning and personality development.* New York: Holt, Rinehart & Winston.

Bannister, R. C. (1979). *Social Darwinism, science, and myth in Anglo-American social thought.* Philadelphia: Temple University Press.

Barkan, E. (1992). *The retreat of scientific racism: Changing concepts of race in Britain and the United States between the World Wars.* Cambridge, England: Cambridge University Press.

Barkow, J. H. (1989). *Darwin, sex, and status: Biological approaches to mind and culture.* Toronto, Canada: University of Toronto Press.

Barkow, J. H., Cosmides, L., & Tooby, J. (1992). *The adapted mind: Evolutionary psychology and the generation of culture.* Oxford, England: Oxford University Press.

Barnes, H. E. (1925). Representative biological theories of society. *Sociological Review, 18,* 120–130, 182–194, 294–300.

Baron-Cohen, S. (1994). How to build a baby that can read minds: Cognitive mechanisms in mindreading. *Cahiers de Psychologie Cognitive, 13,* 513–552.

Baron-Cohen, S. (1995). *Mindblindness: An essay on autism and theory of mind.* Cambridge, MA: MIT Press.

Baron-Cohen, S., Leslie, A. M., & Frith, U. (1985). Does the autistic child have a "theory of mind"? *Cognition, 21,* 37–46.

Baron-Cohen, S., & Cross, P. (1992). Reading the eyes: Evidence for the role of perception in the deveolopment of the theory of mind. *Mind and Languag, 6,* 160–180.

Barrett, R. M. (Ed.) (1985). *Charles Darwin's notebooks: 1836–1844.* Cambridge, UK: Cambridge University Press.

Barth, F. (1967). The study of social change. *American Anthropologist, 69,* 661–669.

Barth, F. (1987). *Cosmologies in the making: A generative approach to cultural variation in inner New Guinea.* Cambridge, England: Cambridge University Press.

Barton, N. H., & Hewitt, G. M. (1989). Adaptation, speciation, and hybrid zones. *Nature, 341,* 497–502.

Bateman, A. J. (1948). Intra–sexual selection in Drosophila. *Heredity, 2,* 349–386.

Bateson, P. P. G., & Hinde, R. A. (1976). *Growing points in ethology.* Cambridge, England: Cambridge University Press.

Batson, C. D. (1991). *The altruism question: Toward a social–psychological answer.* Hillsdale, NJ: Lawrence Erlbaum Associates.

Baur, E., Fischer, E., & Lenz, F. (1931). *Grundriß der menschlichen Erblichkeitslehre und Rassenhygiene, 2: Menschliche Auslese und Rassenhygiene (Eugenik).* München: J. F. Lehmanns.

Beach, F. A. (1974). Human sexuality and evolution. In W. Montagna & W. A. Sadler (Eds.), *Reproductive behavior* (pp. 333–365). New York: Plenum.

Beatty, J, (1987). Natural selection and the null hypothesis. In J. Dupré (Ed.), *The latest on the best: Essays on evolution and optimality* (pp. 53–76). Cambridge, MA: MIT Press.

Becker, G. S. (1976). Altruism, egoism, and genetic fitness: Economics and sociobiology. *Journal of Economic Literature, 14* (2), 917–926.

Beckwith, J. (1981/1982). The political use of sociobiology in the United States and Europe. *The Philosophical Forum, 13,* 311–321.

Béjin, A. (1986). Niedergang der Psychoanalytiker, Aufstieg der Sexologen (The psychoanalysts' fall, sexologists' rise). In Ph. Ariès, A. Béjin, & M. Foucault (Eds.), *Die Masken des Begehrens und die Metamorphosen der Sinnlichkeit. Zur Geschichte der Sexualität im Abendland (Masks of desire and the metamorphoses of sensuality. On the history of sexuality in the Occident).* Frankfurt a. Main: Fischer.

Benton, M. J. (1987). Progress and competition in macroevolution. *Biological Revue, 62,* 305–338.

van den Berghe, P. L. (1973). *Age and sex in human societies: A biosocial perspective.* Belmont, CA: Wordsworth.

van den Berghe, P. L. (1977/1978). Bridging the paradigms. *Society, 15,* 42–49.

van den Berghe, P. L. (1980). Sociobiology: Several views. *BioScience, 31,* 406.

van den Berghe, P. L. (1981). *The ethnic phenomenon.* New York: Elsevier.

van den Berghe, P. L. (1986). Skin color preference, sexual dimorphism, and sexual selection. *Ethnic and Racial Studies 9*(1), 87–113.

Berlinski, D. (1976). *On systems analysis: An essay concerning the limitations of some mathematical models in the social, political, and biological sciences.* Cambridge, MA: MIT Press.

Bernstein, N. A. (1947). On the construction of movements. Moscow: Medgiz (in Russian).

Berry, B. J. L., & Kasarda, J. D. (1977). *Contemporary urban ecology.* New York: Macmillan.

von Bertalanffy, L. (1975). *Perspectives on general systems theory.* New York: Braziller.

Bettinger, R. L. (1991). *Hunter–gatherers: Archaeological and evolutionary theory.* New York: Plenum Press.

Bettinger, R. L., & Baumhoff, M. A. (1982). The numic spread: Great Basin cultures in competition. *American Antiquities, 27,* 485–503.

Betzig, L. L. (1989). Rethinking human ethology. *Ethology and Sociobiology, 10,* 315–324.

Betzig, L. L., Borgerhoff Mulder, M., & Turke, P. W. (Eds.) (1988). *Human reproductive behaviour: A Darwinian perspective.* Cambridge, England: Cambridge University Press.

Bickerton, D. (1981). *Roots of language.* Ann Arbor, MI: Karoma

Binet, A., & Simon, T. (1914). *Mentally defective children,* London: E. Arnold.

Birdwhistell, R. (1970). *Kinesics and context.* Philadelphia, PA: University of Pennsylvania Press.

Bischof, N. (1985). *Das Rätsel Ödipus [The Oedipal myth].* München, Zürich: Piper.

Blaffer Hrdy, S. (1981). *The woman that never evolved.* Cambridge, MA: Harvard University Press.

Blaffer Hrdy, S. (1988). Empathy, polyandry, and the myth of the coy female. In R. Bleier (Ed.), *Feminist approaches to science* (pp. 118–146). New York: Pergamon.

Bleier, R. (1984). *Science and gender. A critique of biology and its theories on women.* New York: Pergamon.

Bloch, M. (1991). Language, anthropology and cognitive science. *Man, 26,* 183–198.

Blurton Jones, N. G. (1986). Bushman birth spacing: A test for optimal interbirth intervals. *Ethology and Sociobiology, 7,* 91–105.

Blurton Jones, N. G. (1990). Three sensible paradigms for research on evolution and human behavior. *Ethology and Sociobiology, 11,* 353–359.

Boakes, R. A. (1984). *From Darwin to behaviorism: Psychology and the minds of animals.* London: Cambridge University Press.

Boas, F. (1911). *The mind of primitive man.* New York: Macmillan.

Boden, M. A. (1979). *Jean Piaget.* New York: The Viking Press.

Bodmer, W. F., & Cavalli-Sforza, L. L. (1976). *Genetics, evolution, and man.* San Francisco: Freeman

Boehm, C. (1989). Ambivalence and compromise in human nature. *American Anthropologist, 91,* 921–939.

Boesch, C., & Boesch, H. (1983). Optimisation of nut–cracking with natural hammers by wild chimpanzees. *Behaviour, 83,* 265–286.

Boesch, C., & Boesch, H. (1989). Hunting behaviour of wild chimpanzees in the Taï National Park. *American Journal of Physical Anthropology, 78,* 547–573.

Boesch, C., & Boesch, H. (1990). Tool use and tool making in wild chimpanzees. *Folia Primatologica, 54*(1–2), 86–99.

Bonner, J. T. (1969). *The scale of nature.* New York: Pegasus.

Bonner, J. T. (1980). *The evolution of culture in animals.* Princeton, NJ: Princeton University Press.

Boone, J. L. (1986). Parental investment and elite family structure in preindustrial states. A case study of Late Medieval–Early Modern Portuguese geneologies. *American Anthropologist, 88,* 859–878.

Borgerhoff Mulder, M. (1987). Adaptation and evolutionary approaches to anthropology. *Man, 22,* 25–41.

Borgerhoff Mulder, M, (1988a). Behavioural ecology of traditional societies. *Trends in Ecology and Evolution, 3,* 260–264.

Borgerhoff Mulder, M. (1988b). Kipsigis bridewealth payments. In L. Betzig, M. Borgerhoff Mulder, & P. Turke (Eds.), *Human reproductive behaviour: A Darwinian perspective* (pp. 65–82). Cambridge, England: Cambridge University Press.

Borgerhoff Mulder, M. (1991). Human behavioural ecology. In J. R. Krebs & N. B. Davies (Eds.), *Behavioural ecology* (pp. 69–68). Oxford, England: Blackwell.

Borgerhoff Mulder, M. (1992). Reproductive decisions. In E. A. Smith & B. Winterhalder (Eds.), *Evolutionary ecology and human behavior* (pp. 339–374). New York: Aldine de Gruyter.

Borgerhoff Mulder, M. (1995). Bridewealth and its correlates: Quantifying changes over time. *Current Anthropology, 36,* 573–603.

Borgerhoff Mulder, M. (1996). Responses to environmental novelty: Changes in men's marriage strategies in a rural Kenyan community. In W. G. Runciman, J. Maynard Smith, & R. I. M. Dunbar (Eds.), *Evolution of social behaviour patterns in primates and man* (pp. 203–222). London: British Academy Press.

Borgerhoff Mulder, M., & Mitchell, S. D. (1994). Rough waters between genes and culture: An anthropological and philosophical view on coevolution. *Biology and Philosophy, 9,* 471–487.

Bornstein, M. H. (1976). Infants' recognition memory for hue. *Developmental Psychology, 12,* 185–191.

Bornstein, M. H. (1996). Origins of communication in infancy. In B. M. Velichkovsky & D. M. Rumbaugh (Eds.), *Communicating meaning: The evolution and development of language* (pp. 139–172). Mahwah, NJ: Lawrence Erlbaum Associates.

Borst, P., & Greaves, D. R. (1987). Programmed gene rearrangements altering gene expression. *Science, 235,* 658–667.

Boserup, E. (1981). *Population and technological change.* Chicago: University of Chicago Press.

Boudon, R. (1980). *Die Logik des gesellschaftlichen Handelns. Eine Einführung in die soziologische Arbeitsweise (The logic of social acting. An introduction to sociological method).* Neuwied, Darmstadt, Germany: Luchterhand.

Boulding, K. (1978). Sociobiology or biosociology? *Society, 15*, 28–34.

Bowlby, J. (1969). *Attachment and loss*. New York: Basic Books.

Boyd, R., & Richerson, P. J. (1980). Sociobiology, culture, and economic theory. *Journal of Economic Behavior and Organization, 1*(1), 97–121.

Boyd, R., & Richerson, P. J. (1985). *Culture and the evolutionary process*. Chicago, IL: University of Chicago Press.

Boyd, R., & Richerson, P. J. (1987). The evolution of ethnic markers. *Cultural Anthropology, 2*, 65–79.

Boyd, R., & Richerson, P. J. (1988). Reciprocity in sizeable groups. *Journal of Theoretical Biology, 132*, 331–356.

Boyd, R., & Richerson, P. J. (1989). The evolution of indirect reciprocity. *Social Networks, 11*, 213–236.

Boyd, R., & Richerson, P. J. (1990). Group selection among alternative stable strategies. *Journal of Theoretical Biology, 145*, 331–342.

Boyd, R., & Richerson, P. J. (1992a). How microevolutionary processes give rise to history. In M. H. Nitecki & D. V. Nitecki (Eds.), *History and evolution* (pp. 179–209). Albany, NY: State University of New York Press.

Boyd, R., & Richerson, P. J. (1992b). Punishment allows the evolution of cooperation (or anything else) in sizeable groups. *Ethology and Sociobiology, 13*, 171–195.

Boyer, P. (1994). *The naturalness of religious ideas*. Berkeley: University of California Press.

Brachet, A. (1935). *Traité d'embryologie des vertébrés [Treatise on the embryology of vertebrates]*. Brussels: Masson.

Brandon, R. (1990). *Adaptation and environment*. Princeton, NJ: Princeton University Press.

Braun, D. P. (1991). Are there cross–cultural regularities in tribal social practices. In S. A. Gregg (Ed.), *Between bands and states* (pp. 423–444). Carbondale: Southern Illinois University Press.

Brazelton, B. T., Koslowski, B., & Main, M. (1974). The origins of reciprocity: The early mother–infant interaction. In M. Lewis & L. A. Rosenblum (Eds.), *Origins of behavior: Vol. I. The effect of the infant on its caregiver* (pp.). New York: Wiley.

Breland, K., & Breland, S. (1961). The misbehavior of organisms. *American Psychologist, 16*, 681–684.

Bretherton, I., & Beeghly, M. (1982). Talking about internal states: The acquisition of an explicit theory of mind. *Developmental Psychology, 18*, 906–921.

Brown, D. F. (1991). *Human universals*. New York: McGraw–Hill.

Brunton, R. (1989). The cultural instability of egalitarian societies. *Man, 24*, 673–682.

Büchner, L. (1872). *Sechs Vorlesungen über die Darwinsche Theorie [Six lectures on Darwin's theory]*. Leipzig.

Bull, P. E. (1987). *Posture and gesture*. New York: Pergamon.

Burgess, E. W. (1925). The growth of the city: An introduction to a research project. In R. Park, E. Burgess, & R. J. McKenzie (Eds.), *The city* (pp. 47–62). Chicago: University of Chicago Press.

Burian, R. M. (1981–1982). Human sociobiology and genetic determinism. *The Philosophical Forum XIII(2–3)*, 43–65.

Burian, R. M. (1983). Adaptation. In M. Grene (Ed.), *Dimensions of Darwinism* (pp. 287–314). Cambridge, England: Cambridge University Press.

Burian, R. M. (1986). On integrating the study of evolution and development: Comments on Kauffman and Wimsatt. In W. Bechtel (Ed.), *Integrating scientific disciplines* (pp. 209–228). Dordrecht, Holland: Martinus Nijhoff.

Burton, R. V. (1973). Folk theory and the incest taboo. *Ethos, 1*, 504–516.

Burton, M. L., & White, D. R. (1987). Cross cultural surveys today. *Annual Review of Anthropology, 16*, 143–160.

Buss, D. M. (1988). Sex differences in human mate preferences: Evolutionary hypothesis testing in 37 cultures. *Behavioral and Brain Sciences, 12,* 1–49.

Buss, D. M. (1993). Sexual strategies theory: An evolutionary perspective on human mating. *Psychological Review, 100,* 204–232.

Buss, D. M. (1994). *The evolution of desire.* New York: Basic Books.

Buss, L. W. (1987). *The evolution of individuality.* Princeton, NJ: Princeton University Press.

Byrne, R. W., & Whiten, A. (Eds.). (1988). *Machiavellian intelligence. Social expertise and the evolution of intellect in monkeys, apes, and humans.* Oxford, England: Oxford University Press.

Byrne, R. W., & Whiten, A. (1990). Tactical deception in primates: The 1990 database. *Primate Report, 27,* 1–101.

Byrne, R, W., & Whiten, A. (1992). Cognitive evolution in primates: Evidence from tactical deception. *Man, 27,* 609–627.

C

Campbell, D. T. (1965). Variation and selective retention in cultural evolution. In H. R. Barringer, G. I. Blanksten, & R. W. Mack (Eds.), *Social change in developing areas: A reinterpretation of evolutionary theory* (pp. 19–49). Cambridge, MA: Schenkman.

Campbell, D. T. (1969). Ethnocentrism of disciplines and the fish-scale model of omniscience. In M. Sherif & C. W. Sherif (Eds.), *Interdisciplinary relationships in the social sciences* (pp. 328–348). Chicago: Aldine de Gruyter.

Campbell, D. T. (1975). On the conflicts between biological and social evolution and between psychology and moral tradition. *American Psychologist, 30,* 1103–1126.

Campos-Ortega, J. A., & Hartenstein, V. (1985). *The embryonic development of Drosophila melanogaster.* New York: Springer.

Canguilhem, G. (1970). *Etudes d'histoire et de philosophie des sciences [Studies on the history and philosophy of the sciences].* Paris: Librairie Philosophique J. Vrin.

Cann, R. L. (1988). DNA and the human origins. *Annual Review of Anthropology, 17,* 127–143.

Caplan, A. L. (Ed.). (1978). *The sociobiological debate: Readings on ethical and scientific issues.* New York: Harper & Row.

Carey, S., & Gelman, R. (Eds.). (1991). *The epigenesis of mind.* Hillsdale, NJ: Lawrence Erlbaum Associates.

Caro, T. M., & Borgerhoff Mulder, M. (1987). The problem of adaptation in the study of human behaviour. *Ethology and Sociobiology, 8,* 61–72.

Caro, T. M., & Hauser, M. D. (1992). Is there teaching in nonhuman animals? *Quarterly Review of Biology, 67,* 151–174.

Carrithers, M. (1990). Is anthropology art or science? *Current Anthropology, 31,* 263–282.

Carroll, G. R. (1984). Organizational ecology. *Annual Review of Sociology, 10,* 71–93.

Cartwright, N. (1980). The truth doesn't explain much. *American Philosophical Quarterly, 17,* 159–163.

Cartwright, N. (1983). *How the laws of physics lie.* Oxford, England: Oxford University Press.

Caspari, O. (1873). *Die Urgeschichte der Menschheit [Primeval history of manhood].* Leipzig: Brockhaus.

Caulfield, M. D. (1985). Sexuality in human evolution: What is natural in sex? *Feminist Studies,* 11(2), 343–363.

Cavalli-Sforza, L. L. (1971). Similarities and dissimilarities of sociocultural and biological evolution. In F. R. Hodson, D. G. Kendall, & P. Tautu (Eds.), *Mathematics in the archaeological and historical sciences* (pp. 535–541). Edinburgh: Edinburgh University Press.

Cavalli-Sforza, L. L. (1992, February 7). Interview. *Nouvel Observateur.*

Cavalli-Sforza, L. L., & Bodmer, W. F. (1971). *The genetics of human populations.* San Francisco: Freeman.

Cavalli-Sforza, L. L., & Feldman, M. W. (1981). *Cultural transmission and evolution: A quantitative approach.* Princeton, NJ: Princeton University Press.

Cavalli-Sforza, L. L., Piazza, A., Menozzi, P., & Mountain, J. (1988). Reconstruction of human evolution: Bringing together genetic, archaelogical, and linguistic data. *Proceedings of the National Academy of Sciences, 85*(15), 6002–6006.

Cavalli-Sforza, L. L., Menozzi, P., & Piazza, A. (1994). *History and geography of human genes.* Princeton: Princeton University Press.

Chagnon, N. A., & Burgos, P. (1979). Kin selection and conflict. In N. A. Chagnon & W. Irons (Eds.), *Evolutionary biology and human social behavior* (pp. 213–237). North Scituate, MA: Duxbury.

Chagnon, N. A., & Hames, R. B. (1979). Protein deficiency and tribal warfare in Amazonia: New data. *Science, 203,* 910–913.

Chagnon, N. A., & Irons, W. (Eds.) (1979). *Evolutionary biology and human social behavior.* North Scituate, MA: Duxbury.

Chance, M. R. A. (1980). An ethological assessment of emotion. In R. Plutchik & H. Kellerman (Eds.), *Emotion: Theory, research, and experience* (pp. 81–111). New York: Academic Press.

Chance, M. R. A., & Mead, A. P. (1953). Social behavior and primate evolution. Symposia of the society for experimental biology. *Evolution, 7,* 395–439.

Charnov, E. L. (1982). *The theory of sex allocation.* Princeton, NJ: Princeton University Press.

Cheney, D. L., & Seyfarth, R. M. (1990). *How monkeys see the world: Inside the mind of another species.* Chicago: Chicago University Press.

Cheng, P. W., & Holyoak, K. J. (1989). On the natural selection of reasoning theories. *Cognition, 31,* 187–276.

Chevalier-Skolnikoff, S. (1973). Facial expressions of emotions in non–human primates. In P. Ekman (Ed.), *Darwin and facial expression* (pp. 11–89). New York: Academic Press.

Chomsky, N. (1959). Review of "Verbal behavior" by B. F. Skinner. *Language, 35,* 26–58.

Chomsky, N. (1965). *Aspects of the theory of syntax.* Cambridge, MA: MIT Press.

Chomsky, N. (1975a). *Reflections on language.* New York: Pantheon.

Chomsky, N. (1975b). *The logical structure of linguistic theory.* New York: Plenum.

Chomsky, N. (1980). *Rules and representations.* New York: Columbia University Press.

Chomsky, N. (1986). *Knowledge of language: Its nature, origin and use.* New York: Praeger.

Churchland, P. S. (1986). *Neurophilosophy.* Cambridge, MA: MIT Press.

Clutton-Brock, T. H. (1988). Reproductive success. In T. H. Clutton-Brock (Ed.), *Reproductive success. Studies of individual variation in contrasting breeding systems* (pp. 472–485). Chicago: University of Chicago Press.

Clutton-Brock, T. H. (1991). *The evolution of parental care.* Princeton, NJ: University of Princeton Press.

Clutton-Brock, T. H., & Harvey, P. H. (1979). Comparison and adaptation. *Proceedings of the Royal Society of London, B, 205,* 547–565.

Cohen, A. (1974). *Two-dimensional man.* Berkeley: University of California Press.

Cohen, J. (1977). *Statistical power analysis for the behavioral sciences* (2nd ed.). New York: Academic Press.

Coleman, J. S. (1987). Microfoundations and macrosocial behavior. In J. C. Alexander, B. Giesen, R. Münch, & N. J. Smelser (Eds.), *The micro–macro link* (pp. 153–173). Los Angeles, CA: University of California Press,.

Coleman, J. S. (1991). *Foundations of social theory.* Cambridge, MA: Harvard University Press.

Collins, R. (1975). *Conflict sociology.* New York: Academic Press.

Collins, R. (1981). On the micro-foundations of macro-sociology. *American Journal of Sociology, 86,* 984–1014.

Comte, A. (1830–42). *The course of positive philosophy.* London: Bell.

Condon, W. S., & Ogston, W. D. (1966). Sound film analysis of normal and pathological behavior patterns. *Journal of Nervous and Mental Disease, 143,* 338–347.

Condon, W. S., & Sander, L. W. (1974). Neonate movement is synchronized with adult speech: Interactional participation and language acquisition. *Science, 183,* 99–101.

Conklin, E. G. (1908). The mechanism of heredity. *Science, 27,* 89–99.

Connor, R. C., Smolker, R. A., & Richards, A. F. (1992). Dolphin alliances and coalitions. In A. H. Harcourt & F. M. B. de Waal (Eds.), *Coalitions and alliances in humans and other animals* (pp. 415–443). Oxford, England: Oxford University Press.

Cook, E., Hodes, R., & Lang, P. (1986). Preparedness and phobia: Effects of stimulus content on human visceral conditioning. *Journal of Abnormal Psychology, 95,* 195–207.

Cords, M. (1992). Post–conflict reunions and reconciliation in long–tailed macaques. *Animal Behaviour, 44,* 57–61.

Cosmides, L. (1979). *Good genes and bad environment: The fall of hormic psychology.* (unpublished manuscript).

Cosmides, L. (1989). The logic of social exchange: Has natural selection shaped how humans reason? Studies with the Wason selection task. *Cognition, 31,* 187–276.

Cosmides, L., & Tooby, J. (1987). From evolution to behavior: Evolutionary psychology as the missing link. In J. Dupré (Ed.), *The latest on the best: Essays on evolution and optimality* (pp.277–306). Cambridge, MA: MIT Press.

Cosmides, L., & Tooby, J. (1989). Evolutionary psychology and the generation of culture, Part II. Case study: A computational theory of social exchange. *Ethology & Sociobiology, 10,* 51–97.

Cosmides, L., & Tooby, J. (1992). Cognitive adaptations for social exchange. In J. H. Barkow, L. Cosmides, & J. Tooby (Eds.), *The adapted mind: Evolutionary psychology and the generation of culture* (pp. 163–228). New York: Oxford University Press.

Cosmides, L., & Tooby, J. (1994a). Better than rational: Evolutionary psychology and the invisible hand. *American Economic Review, 84,* 327–332.

Cosmides, L., & Tooby, J. (1994b). Beyond intuition and instinct blindness: towards an evolutionary rigorous cognitive science. *Cognition, 50,* 41–77.

Cravens, H. (1978). *The triumph of evolution.* Baltimore: Johns Hopkins University Press.

Crawford, C., Smith, M., & Krebs, C. (Eds.) (1990). *Psychology and sociobiology: Ideas, issues, and applications.* Hillsdale, NJ: Lawrence Erlbaum Associates.

Cronin, H. (1991*). The ant and the peacock: Altruism and sexual selection from Darwin to today.* Cambridge, England: Press Syndicate of the University of Cambridge.

Cronk, L. (1989). Low socioeconomic status and female-biased parental investment: The Mukogodo example. *American Anthropologist, 91,* 414–429.

Cronk, L. (1991). Human behavioral ecology. *Annual Review of Anthropology, 20,* 25–53.

Crook, J. H., & Crook, S. J. (1988). Tibetan polyandry: Problems of adapatation and fitness. In L. L. Betzig, M. Borgerhoff Mulder, & P. Turke (Eds.), *Human reproductive behaviour: A Darwinian perspective* (pp. 97–114). Cambridge, England: Cambridge University Press.

Cullis, C. A. (1984). Environmentally induced DNA changes. In J. W. Pollard (Ed.), *Evolutionary theory: Paths into the future* (pp. 203–216). New York: Wiley.

D

Daly, M. (1982). Some caveats about cultural transmission models. *Human Ecology, 10,* 401–408.

Daly, M., & Wilson, M. (1983). *Sex, evolution and behavior.* Boston, MA: Willard Grant Press .

Daly, M., & Wilson, M. (1984). A sociobiological analysis of human infanticide. In F. Hausfater & S. B. Hrdy (Eds.), *Infanticide: Comparative and evolutionary perspectives* (pp. 487–502). New York: Aldine de Gruyter.

Daly, M., & Wilson, M. (1988). *Homicide.* New York: Aldine de Gruyter.

Daly, M., Wilson, M., & Weghorst, S. J. (1982). Male sexual jealousy. *Ethology and Sociobiology, 3,* 11–27.

Darden, L., & Maull, N. (1977). Interfield theories. *Philosophy of Science, 44,* 43–64.

Darlington, C. D. (1969). *The evolution of man and society.* London: Allen & Unwin.

Darwin, C. (1859). *On the origin of species by means of natural selection, or the preservation of favoured races in the struggle for life.* London: John Murray.

Darwin, C. (1880). *The descent of man.* New York: Appleton-Century-Crofts (original work published in 1871).

Darwin, C. (1964). *On the origin of species.* Cambridge, MA: Harvard University Press (original work published in 1859).

Darwin, C. (1965). *The expression of the emotions in man and animals.* Chicago: University of Chicago Press (original work published in 1872).

Darwin, C. (1874). *The descent of man, and selection in relation to sex.* London: John Murray (original work published in 1871).

Darwin, C. (1981). *The descent of man, and selection in relation to sex.* London: John Murray (original work published in 1871).

Dasser, V. (1988). A social concept in Java monkeys. *Animal Behaviour, 36,* 225–230.

Dasser, V., Ulbaek, I., & Premack, D. (1989). The perception of intention. *Science, 243,* 365–367.

Daston, L. (1992). The naturalized female intellect. *Science in Context, 5,* 209–235.

Davidson, D. (1970). Mental events. In L. Foster & J. W. Swanson (Eds.), *Experience and theory* (pp. 79–101). Amherst, MA: The University of Massachusetts Press.

Davies, P. S., Fetzer, J. H., & Foster, T. R. (1995). Logical reasoning and domain specificity: A critique of the social exchange theory of reasoning. *Biology and Philosophy, 10,* 1–37.

Davis, B. D. (1975). Social determinism and behavioral genetics. *Science, 26,* 189.

Davis, B. D. (1985). *Storm over biology: Essays on science, sentiment, and public policy.* Buffalo, NY: Prometheus Books.

Dawkins, R. (1981). Selfish genes in race or politics. *Nature 289,* 528.

Dawkins, R. (1982). *The extended phenotype.* Oxford, England: Freeman.

Dawkins, R. (1986). *The blind watchmaker.* New York: Norton.

Dawkins, R. (1989 [1976]). *The selfish gene.* Oxford, England: Oxford University Press.

Dawkins, R. (1993). Viruses of the mind. In B. Dahlbom (Ed.), *Dennett and his critics. Demystifying the mind.* Oxford, England: Blackwell.

Deacon, T. W. (1992). Brain–language coevolution. In J. A. Howkins & M. Gell-Mann (Eds.), *The evolution of human languages* (pp. 76–91). Reading, MA: Addison-Wesley.

Degler, C. N. (1991). *In search of human nature: The decline and revival of Darwinism in American social thought.* Oxford, England: Oxford University Press.

Delage, Y., & Goldsmith, M. (1912). *The theories of evolution.* London: Palmer.

Delius, J. D. (1989). Of mind memes and brain bugs: A natural history of culture. In W. A. Koch (Ed.), *The nature of culture* (pp. 26–79). Bochum, Germany: Studienverlag Dr. Norbert Brockmeyer.

Dennett, D. C. (1988). The intentional stance in theory and practice. In R. W. Byrne & A. Whiten (Eds.), *Machiavellian intelligence. Social expertise and the evolution of intellect in monkeys, apes, and humans* (pp. 180–202). Oxford, England: Oxford University Press.

Descartes, R. (1977). *The essential writings.* New York: Harper & Row.

Dimberg, U. (1982). Facial reactions to facial expressions. *Psychophysiologie, 19,* 643–647.

Dimberg, U. (1988). Facial expressions and emotional reactions: A psychobiological analysis of human social behaviour. In H. L. Wagner (Ed.), *Social psychophysiology and emotion: Theory and clinical applications* (pp. 131–150). Chichester, England: Wiley.

Dimberg, U. (1990). Facial electromyography and emotional reactions. *Psychophysiology, 27,* 481–494.

Dimberg, U. (1997) Psychophysiological Reactions to Facial Expressions. In U. Segerstråle & P. Molnár (Eds.), *Nonverbal communication: Where nature meets culture* (pp. 47–60). Mahwah, NJ: Lawrence Erlbaum Associates.

Dobzhansky, T. (1968, February). On genetics and politics. *Social Education,* 142–146.

Dobzhansky, T. (1974). Is genetic diversity compatible with human equality? *Social Biology, 20*(3), 280–288.

Donald, M. (1991). *Origins of the modern mind: Three stages in the evolution of culture and cognition.* Cambridge, MA: Harvard University Press.

Doucet, P., & Sloep, P. B. (1992). *Mathematical modeling in the life sciences.* Chichester, England: Ellis Horwood.

Duchin, L. (1990). The evolution of articulate speech: Comparative anatomy of the oral cavity in pan and homo. *Journal of Human Evolution,* 687–697.

Dumézil, G. (1958). *L'idéologie tripartite des Indo-Européens [The tripartite ideology of the Indo-Europeans].* Brussels, Belgium: Latomus.

Dunbar, R. I. M. (1992). Neocortex size as a constraint on group size in primates. *Journal of Human Evolution, 22*(4/5), 469–493.

Duncan, S. (1972). Some signals and rules for turn–taking in conversations. *Journal of Experimental Social Psychology, 10,* 234–247.

Dunlap, K. (1919). Are there any instincts? *Journal of Abnormal and Social Psychology, 14,* 307–311.

Dunlap, K. (1922). The identity of instinct and habit. *Journal of Philosophy, 19,* 85–94.

Dunn, L. C., & Dobzhansky, T. (1946, 1952). *Heredity, race and society.* New York: New American Library.

Dunnell, R. C. (1980). Evolutionary theory and archaeology. *Advances in archaeological method and theory, 3,* 35–99.

Dupré, J. (1983). The disunity of science. *Mind, 92,* 321–346.

Dupré, J. (1991). Reflections on biology and culture. In J. J . Sheehan & M. Sosna (Eds.), *The boundaries of humanity: Humans, animals, machines* (pp. 125–131). Los Angeles, CA: University of California Press.

Dupré, J. (1993). *The disorder of things: Metaphysical Foundations of the Disunity of Science.* Cambridge, MA: Harvard University Press.

Durant, J. (1985). The ascent of nature in Darwin's descent of man. In D. Kohn (Ed.), *The Darwinian heritage* (pp. 283–306). Princeton, NJ: Princeton University Press.

Durham, W. H. (1976). The adaptive significance of cultural behavior. *Human Ecology, 4*(2), 89–121.

Durham, W. H. (1979). *Scarcity and survival in Central America: Ecological origins of the Soccer War.* Stanford, CA: Stanford University Press.

Durham, W. H. (1982). Interactions of genetic and cultural evolution: Models and examples. *Human Ecology, 11,* 289–323.

Durham, W. H. (1990). Advances in evolutionary culture theory. *Annual Review of Anthropology, 19,* 187–210.

Durham, W. H. (1991). *Coevolution: Genes, culture, and human diversity.* Stanford: Stanford University Press.

Durham, W. H. (1992). Applications of evolutionary culture theory. *Annual Review of Anthropology, 21,* 331–356.

Durham, W. H., & Nassif, R. C. (1991, September). *Managing the competition: A Tupi adaptation in Amazonia.* Presented at UNESCO Conference Food and Nutrition in the Tropical Forest, Paris.

Durkheim, E. (1933). *The division of labor in society.* New York: Macmillan. (Original work published in 1893)

Durkheim, E. (1954). *The elementary forms of religious life* (J. Swain, Trans.). Glencoe, IL: The Free Press. (Original work published in 1912)

Durkheim, E. (1980). *Die Regeln der soziologischen Methode [The rules of sociological method].* Neuwied/Darmstadt, Germany: Luchterhand. (Original work published in 1895)Durkheim, E. (1986). *De la division du travail social. Etude sur l'organisation des sociétés supérieures [On the division of social work. Study on the organization of superior societies].* Paris: Presses Universitaires de France.

E

Eberhardt, W. G. (1990). Evolution in bacterial plasmids and levels of selection. *Quarterly Review of Biology, 65,* 3–22.

Edelman, G. (1992). *Bright air, brilliant fire: On the matter of the mind.* New York: Basic Books.

Edgington, E. S. (1974). A new tabulation of statistical procedures used in APA journals. *American Psychologist, 29,* 25–26.

Efron, N. J., & Fisch, M. (1991). Science naturalized, science denatured: An evaluation of Ron Giere's cognitivist approach to explaining science. *History and Philosophy of the Life Science, 13,* 187–221.

Ehret, C. (1971). *Southern Nilotic history: Linguistic approaches to the study of the past.* Evanston, IL: Northwestern University Press.

Ehret, C. (1982). Linguistic inferences about early Bantu history. In C. Ehret & M. Posnansky (Eds.), *Archaeological and linguistic reconstruction of African history* (pp. 57–65). Berkeley: University of California Press.

Ehrlich, P., & Raven, P. (1969). Differentiation of populations. *Science, 165,* 1228–1232.

Eibl-Eibesfeldt, I. (1970). *Ethology: The biology of behavior.* New York: Holt, Rinehart & Winston.

Eibl-Eibesfeldt, I. (1972). Similarities and differences between cultures in expressive movements. In R. A. Hinde (Ed.), *Nonverbal communication* (pp. 297–314). Cambridge, MA: Cambridge University Press.

Eibl-Eibesfeldt, I. (1973). The expressive behavior of the deaf-and-blind born. In M. von Cranach & I. Vine (Eds.), *Social communication and movement* (pp. 163–194). London: Academic Press.

Eibl-Eibesfeldt, I. (1975). *Ethology. The biology of behavior.* New York: Holt, Rinehart & Winston.

Eibl-Eibesfeldt, I. (1989). *Human ethology.* New York: Aldine de Gruyter.

Eisenberg, J. F. (1981). *The mammalian radiations.* Chicago: University of Chicago Press.

Ekman, P. (Ed.). (1973). *Darwin and facial expression.* New York: Academic Press.

Ekman, P. (1982). *Emotion in the human face.* Cambridge, England: Cambridge University Press.

Ekman, P. (1985). *Telling lies: Clues to deceit in the marketplace, marriage, and politics.* New York: Norton.

Ekman, P., & Davidson, R. (Eds.). (1994). *The nature of emotion.* New York: Oxford University Press.

Ekman, P., & Friesen, W. V. (1969). The repertoire of non–verbal behaviour: Categories, origins, usage and coding. *Semiotica, 1,* 49–98.

Ekman, P., & Friesen, W. V. (1975). *Unmasking the face: A guide to recognising emotions from facial clues.* Englewood Cliffs, NJ: Prentice-Hall.

Ekman, P., & Friesen, W. V. (1978). *Facial action coding system: A technique for the measurement of facial movement.* Palo Alto, CA: Consulting Psychologists Press.

Ekman, P., & Friesen, W. V. (1982). Felt, false and miserable smiles. *Journal of Nonverbal Behavior, 6,* 238–252.

Ekman, P., Friesen, W. V., & Ellsworth, P. (1978). *Facial action coding system.* Palo Alto, CA: Consulting Psychologists Press.

Ekman, P., & Keltner, D. (1997). Universal facial expressions of emotion: An old controversy and new findings. In U. Segerstråle & P. Molnár (Eds.), *Nonverbal communication: Where nature meets culture* (pp. 27–46). Mahwah, NJ: Lawrence Erlbaum Associates.

Ekman, P., Levenson, R. W., & Friesen, W. V. (1983). Autonomic nervous system activity distinguishes among emotions. *Science, 221,* 1208–1210.

Elster, J. (1983). *Explaining technical change.* Cambridge, England: Cambridge University Press.

Elster, J. (1986). *Rational choice.* New York: New York University Press.

Ember, M. (1975). On the origin and extension of the incest taboo. *Behavior Science Research, 10,* 249–281.

Endler, J. A. (1986). *Natural selection in the wild.* Princeton, NJ: Princeton University Press.

Engel, C. (1990). *Reproduktionsstrategien im sozioökonomischen Kontext – Eine evolutionsbiologische Interpretation sozialgruppenspezifischer demographischer Muster in einer historischen Population (Krummhörn, Ostfriesland im 18. Und 19. Jahrhundert) [Reproductive strategies in socio-ecological context – An evolutionary interpretation of social group specific demographic patterns in an historical population (Krummhörn, Ostriesland, 18th and 19th centuries)].* PhD-thesis, University of Göttingen, Germany.

Engelberg, J., & Boyarsky, L. L. (1979). The noncybernetic nature of ecosystems. *American Naturalist, 144,* 317–324.

Ereshefsky, M. (Ed.). (1992). *The units of evolutions: Essays on the nature of species.* Cambridge, MA: MIT Press.

Essock-Vitale, S., & Seyfarth, R. M. (1987). Intelligence and social cognition. In B. B. Smuts, D. L. Cheney, R. M. Seyfarth, R. W. Wrangham, & T. T. Struhsaker. (Eds.), *Primate societies* (pp. 452–461). Chicago: University of Chicago Press.

F

Falk, R. (1990). Between beanbag genetics and natural selection. *Biology and Philosophy, 5,* 313–325.

Falk, R. (1993). Evolutionary epistemology: What phenotype is selected and which genotype evolves? *Biology and Philosophy, 8,* 153–172.

Farah, M. J. (1993). Neuropsychological inference with an interactive brain: A critique of the "locality assumption." *Behavioral and Brain Sciences, 17,* 43–60.

Farah, M. J., Wilson, K., Drain, H., & Tanaka, J. (1995). The inverted face inversion effect in prosopagnosia: Evidence for mandatory, face-specific perceptual mechanisms. *Vision Research, 35,* 2089–2093.

Farvar, M. T., & Milton, J. P. (1972). *The careless technology: Ecology and international development.* Garden City, NY: The Natural History Press.

Fedigan, L. M. (1992). The changing role of women in models of human evolution. In G. Kirkup & L. Smith Keller (Eds.), *Inventing women. Science, technology, and gender* (pp. 103–122). Cambridge, England: The Open University: Polity Press.

Fernald, A. (1992). Human maternal vocalizations to infants as biologically relevant signals: An evolutionary perspective. In J. Barkow, L. Cosmides, & J. Tooby (Eds.), *The adapted mind: Evolutionary psychology and the generation of culture* (pp. 19–136). New York: Oxford University Press.

Feynman, R. (1985). *QED. The strange theory of light and matter.* New York: Penguin.

Field, G. C. (1921). Faculty psychology and instinct psychology. *Mind, 30,* 257–270.

Field, T. M., Woodson, R., Greenberg, R., & Cohen, D. (1982). Discrimination and imitation of facial expressions by neonates. *Science, 218,* 179–181.

Fischer, D. H. (1989). *Albion's seed: Four British folkways in America.* New York: Oxford University Press.

Fisher, R. A. (1930). *The genetical theory of natural selection.* Oxford, England: Clarendon.

Fisher, R. A. (1935). *The design of experiments.* Edinburgh: Oliver & Boyd.

Fisher, R. A. (1951). Limits to intensive production in animals. *British Agricultural Bulletin, 4,* 217–218.

Fisher, R. A., & Mackenzie, W. A. (1923). Studies in crop variation: II. The manurial responses of different potato varieties. *Journal of Agricultural Science, 13,* 311–320.

Fiske, A. P. (1991). *Structures of social life: The four elementary forms of human relations.* New York. The Free Press.

Fleagle, J. (1988). *Primate adaptation and evolution.* New York: Academic Press.

Flinn, M. V., & Alexander, V. D. (1982). Culture theory: The developing synthesis from biology. *Human Ecology, 10,* 383–400.

Fodor, J. A. (1983). *The modularity of mind: An essay on faculty psychology.* Cambridge, MA: MIT Press.

Fodor, J. A. (1974). Special sciences. *Syntheses, 28,* 97–115.

Fodor, J. A., Bever, T. G., & Garrett, M. F. (1974). *The psychology of language: An introduction to psycholinguistics and generative grammar.* New York: McGraw-Hill.

Foley, R. (1984). *Hominid evolution and community ecology.* London: Academic Press.

Foley, R. (1987). *Another unique species: Patterns in human evolutionary ecology.* New York: Wiley and Longman.

Foley, R. (1988). Hominids, humans and hunter-gatherers: An evolutionary perspective. In T. Ingold, D. Riches, & J. Woodburn (Eds.), *Hunters and gatherers:I. History, evolution and social change* (pp. 207–221). Oxford, England: Berg.

Foley, R. (1995). The adaptive legacy of human evolution. *Evolutionary Anthropology, 4,* 194–203.

Foster, P. L., & Cairns, J. (1992). Mechanisms of directed mutation. *Genetics, 131,* 783–789.

Fox, R. (1976). *Kinhsip and marriage.* New York: Penguin.

Fox, R. (1980). *The red lamp of incest.* New York: Dutton.

Frank, R. (1988). *Passions within reason: The strategic role of the emotions.* New York: Norton.

Frank, R. (1997). Nonverbal communication and the emergence of moral sentiments. In U. Segerstråle & P. Molnár (Eds.), *Nonverbal communication: Where nature meets culture* (pp. 275–292). Mahwah, NJ: Lawrence Erlbaum Associates.

Freese, L. (1994). The song of sociobiology. *Sociological Perspectives, 37,* 337–374.

French, R. D. (1975). *Antivivisection and medical science in Victorian society.* Princeton, NJ: Princeton University Press.

Freud, S. (1905). *Drei Abhandlungen zur Sexualtheorie [Three treatise on the theory of sex].* Gesammelte Werke, Bd. V. Frankfurt/Main, Germany: Fischer.

Freud, S. (1953/1972). *A general introduction to psychoanalysis by Sigmund Freud* (authorized Engl. translation of the rev. ed. by J. Riviere). New York: Pocket Books.

Frey, S., & von Cranach, M. (1973). A method for the assessment of body movement variability. In M. von Cranach & I. Vine (Eds.), *Social communication and movement* (pp. 389–418). London: Academic Press.

Fridlund, A. (1992). Darwin's anti-Darwinism in the expression of the emotions in man and animals. *International Review of Emotion, 2* 117–137.

Friedman, M. (1953). The methodology of positive economics. In M. Friedman (Ed.), *Essays in positive economics* (pp. 3–43). Chicago: University of Chicago Press.

Frijda, N. H. (1986). *The emotions.* London: Cambridge University Press.

Frisbie, P. W., & Kasarda, J. D. (1988). Spatial processes. In N. J. Smelser (Ed.), *Handbook of sociology* (pp. 629–666). Newbury Park, CA: Sage.

Fritsch, C. T. (1943). *The anti–anthropomorphism of the Greek Pentateuch.* Princeton, NJ: Princeton University Press.

Fuchs, S. (1992). *The professional quest for truth. A social theory of science and knowledge.* Albany, NY: State University of New York Press.

G

Gajdusek, D. C. (1977). Unconventional viruses and the origin and disappearance of *kuru. Science, 197*, 943–960.

Galef, B. G., Jr. (1988). Imitation in animals: History, definitions and interpretation of the data from the psychological laboratory. In T. Zentall & B. G. Galef, Jr. (Eds.), *Social learning* (pp. 3–28). Hillsdale, NJ: Lawrence Erlbaum Associates.

Gallistel, C. R. (1990). *The organization of learning.* Cambridge, MA: MIT Press.

Gamkrelidze, T. V., & Ivanov, V. V. (1990). The early history of Indo–European languages. *Scientific American, 262*(3), 110–116.

Garcia, J. (1990). Learning without memory. *Journal of Cognitive Neuroscience, 2,* 287–305.

Garcia, J., & Koelling, R. A. (1966). The relation of cue to consequence in avoidance learning. *Psychonomic Science, 4,* 123–124.

Gardner, R., Gardner, B., & Cantfort, T. (1989). *Teaching language to chimpanzees.* Albany: State University of New York Press.

Garfinkel, A. (1967). *Studies in ethnomethodology.* Englewood Cliffs, NJ: Prentice-Hall.

Geertz, C. (1973). *The interpretation of cultures.* New York: Basic Books.

Geertz, C. (1980, January). Sociosexology. *New York Review of Books, 24,* 3–4.

Geertz, C. (1983). *Local knowledge: Further essays in interpretative anthropology.* New York: Basic Books.

Gelman, R. (1990). First principles organize attention to and learning about relevant data: Number and the animate–inanimate distinction as examples. *Cognitive Science, 14,* 79–106.

Geschwind, N. (1979). Specialization in the human brain. *Scientific American, 241,* 180–201.

Gibson, J. J. (1979). *The ecological approach to visual perception.* Boston, MA: Houghton-Mifflin.

Giesen, B. (1980). *Makrosoziologie–Eine evolutionstheoretische Einführung (Macrosociology—An introduction to evolutionary theory).* Hamburg, Germany: Hoffmann und Campe.

Giesen, B. (1991). *Die Entdinglichung des Sozialen. Eine evolutionstheoretische Perspektive auf die Postmoderne [The de-materialization of the social. An evolutionary perspective on post modernity] .* Frankfurt/Main, Germany: Suhrkamp.

Gigerenzer, G. (1991). From tools to theories. A heuristic of discovery in cognitive psychology. *Psychological Review, 98*(2), 254–267.

Gigerenzer, G. (1993). The superego, the ego, and the id in statistical reasoning. In G. Keren & C. Lewis (Eds.), *A handbook for data analysis in the behavioral sciences: Methodological issues* (pp. 311–339). Hillsdale, NJ: Lawrence Erlbaum Associates.

Gigerenzer, G. (1997). The modularity of social intelligence. In A. Whiten & R. W. Byrne (Eds.), *Machiavellian intelligence II.* Cambridge, UK: Cambridge University Press. (In press)

Gigerenzer, G., & Hug, K. (1992). Domain–specific reasoning: Social contracts, cheating and perspective change. *Cognition, 43,* 127–171.

Gigerenzer, G., & Murray, D. J. (1987). *Cognition as intuitive statistics.* Hillsdale, NJ: Lawrence Erlbaum Associates.

Gigerenzer, G., Swijtink, Z., Porter, T., Daston, L., Beatty, J., & Krüger, L. (1989). *The empire of chance: How probability changed science and everyday life.* Cambridge, England: Cambridge University Press.

Glance, N. S., & Huberman, B. A. (1993). *Organisational fluidity and sustainable cooperation.* Unpublished manuscript.

Glantz, K., & Pearce, J. (1989). *Exiles from Eden. Psychotherapy from an evolutionary perspective.* New York: Norton.

Glasse, R. M. (1967). Cannibalism in the kuru region of New Guinea. *Transactions of the New York Academy of Sciences, 29,* 748–754.

Goffman, E. (1959). *The presentation of self in everyday life.* New York: Penguin.

Goffman, E. (1972). *Relations in public.* New York: Harper Colophon Books.

Goldschmidt, W. (1990). *The human career: The self in the symbolic world.* Cambridge, MA: Blackwell.

Goldschmidt, W. (1997) Nonverbal communication and culture. In U. Segerstråle & P. Molnár (Eds.), *Nonverbal communication: Where nature meets culture* (pp. 229–243). Mahwah, NJ: Lawrence Erlbaum Associates.

Goodall, J. (1986). *The chimpanzee of Gombe. Patterns of behaviour.* Cambridge, MA: Harvard University Press.

Goodfield, J. (1985). *Quest for the killers.* New York: Hill & Wang.

Goody, J. (1983). *The development of the family and marriage in Europe.* Cambridge, England: Cambridge University Press.

Gould, S. J. (1981). *The mismeasure of man.* New York: W. W. Norton.

Gould, S. J. (1987a). Freudian slip. *Natural History, 2,* 14–21.

Gould, S. J. (1987b). Stephen Jay Gould replies. *Natural History, 96,* 4–6.

Gould, S. J. (1991). Exaptation: A crucial tool for evolutionary psychology. *Journal of Social Issues, 47,* 43–65.

Gould, S. J., & Lewontin, R. C. (1979). The spandrels of San Marco and the Panglossian paradigm: A critique of the adaptationist programme. *Proceedings of the Royal Society London, B, 205,* 581–598.

Grafen, A. (1984/1991). Natural selection, kin selection and group selection. In J. R. Krebs & N. B. Davies (Eds.), *Behavioural ecology: An evolutionary approach* (pp. 62–84). Sunderland, MA: Sinauer Associates.

Grafen, A. (1988). On the uses of data on lifetime reproductive success. In T. H. Clutton-Brock (Ed.), *Reproductive success: Studies of individual variation in contrasting breeding systems* (pp. 454–471). Chicago: University of Chicago Press.

Graham, L. R. (1977). Political ideology and genetic theory: Russia and Germany in the 1920s. *Hastings Center Report, 7,* 30–39.

Granovetter, M. (1985). Economic action and social structure: The problem of embeddedness. *American Sociological Review, 91,* 481–510.

Gray, H., & H. V. Carter (1971). *Gray's Anatomy.* New York: Mosby-Yearbook Inc.

Gray, J. P. (1985). *Primate sociobiology.* New Haven, CN: HRAF Press.

Griffin, D. R. (1981). *The question of animal awareness: Evolutionary continuity of mental experience.* New York: Rockefeller University Press.

Griffin, D. R. (1984). *Animal thinking.* Cambridge, MA: Harvard University Press.

Griggs, R. A., & Cox, J. R. (1982). The elusive thematic–materials effect in Wason's selection task, *British Journal of Psychology, 73,* 407–420.

Gumplowicz, L. (1875). *Rasse und Staat. Eine Untersuchung über das Gesetz der Staatenbildung [Race and state. An investigation of the law of formation of the state].* Wien: Mauz.

Guyénot, E. (1924). *L'hérédité [Heredity].* Paris: Doin.

H

Haeckel, E. (1863). Über die Entwicklungstheorie Darwins (On Darwin's theory of evolution). In H. Schmidt (Ed.), *Gemeinverständliche Werke (Popular works), Bd. 5* (pp. 3–32). Berlin: Kroener.

Haeckel, E. (1908). *Freie Wissenschaft und freie Lehre. Eine Entgegnung auf Rudolf Virchows Münchener Rede über "Die Freiheit der Wissenschaft im modernen Staat" [Free science and free teaching. A response to Rudolf Virchow's Munich address on "The freedom of science in the modern state].* Leipzig: Kroener.

Hall, E. T. (1959). *The silent language.* New York: Fawcett.

Hall, E, T. (1966). *The hidden dimension.* New York: Doubleday.

Hallpike, C. (1986). *The principles of social evolution.* Oxford, England: Clarendon.

Hamburg, D. A. (1968). Emotions in the perspective of human evolution. In S. L. Washburn & P. C. Jay (Eds.), *Perspectives on human evolution* (pp. 246–257). New York: Holt, Rinehart & Winston.

Hamilton, W. D. (1963). The evolution of altruistic behavior. *American Naturalist, 9,* 354–356.

Hamilton, W. D. (1964). The genetical evolution of social behaviour. *Journal of Theoretical Biology, 7,* 1–52.

Hamilton, W. D. (1975). Innate socioaptitude of man: An approach from evolutionary genetics. In R. Fox (Ed.), *Biosocial anthropology* (pp. 133–155). London: Malaby.

Hannan, M. T., & Freeman, J. (1977). The population ecology of organizations. *American Journal of Sociology, 82,* 929–64.

Hannan, M. T., & Freeman, J. (1987). The ecology of organizational founding: American Labor Unions, 1836–1985. *American Journal of Sociology, 92,* 910–943.

Hannan, M. T., & Freeman, J. (1988). The ecology of organizational mortality: American Labor Unions, 1836–1985. *American Journal of Sociology, 94,* 25–52.

Hannan, M. T., & Freeman, J. (1989). *Organizational ecology.* Cambridge, MA: Harvard University Press.

Haraway, D. (1989). *Primate visions: Gender, race, and nature in the world of modern science.* London: Routlege & Kegan Paul.

Harcourt, A. H., & de Waal, F. M. B. (1992). *Coalitions and alliances in humans and other animals.* Oxford, England: Oxford University Press.

Harlow, H. F. (1959). Love in infant monkeys. *Scientific American, 20,* 2–8.

Harlow, H. F., & Harlow, H. K. (1962). Social deprivation in monkeys. *American Scientist, 7,* 1–11.

Harnad, S. (1996). The origins of words: A psychophysical hypothesis. In B. M. Velichkovsky & D. M. Rumbaugh (Eds.), *Communicating meaning: The evolution and development of language* (pp. 27–44). Mahwah , NJ: Lawrence Erlbaum Associates.

Harpending, H., Rogers A. R., & Draper, P. (1987). Human sociobiology. *Yearbook of Physical Anthropology, 30,* 127–150.

Harré, R. (Ed.). (1986). *The social construction of emotions.* Oxford, England: Blackwell.

Harris, C., & Ullman, E. (1945). The nature of cities. *The Annals of the American Academy of Political and Social Sciences, 242,* 7–17.

Harris, M. (1979). *The rise of anthropological theory.* New York: Crowell.

Hartung, J. (1982). Polygyny and inheritance of wealth. *Current Anthropology, 23*, 1–12.

Harvey, P. H., & Pagel, M. P. (1991). *The comparative method in biology.* Oxford, England: Oxford University Press.

Hauser, M. D. (1988). Invention and social transmission: A case study with wild vervet monkeys. In R. W. Byrne & A. Whiten (Eds.), *Machiavellian intelligence: Social expertise and the evolution of intellect in monkeys, apes and humans* (pp. 327–344). Oxford, England: Oxford University Press,.

Hawkes K. (1990). Why do men hunt? Benefits for risky choices. In E. A. Cashdan (Ed.), *Risk and uncertainty in tribal and peasant economies* (pp. 145–166). Boulder, CO: Westview.

Hawley, A. H. (1944). Ecology and human ecology. *Social Forces, 27*, 398–405.

Hawley, A. H. (1950). *Human ecology.* New York: Ronald.

Hawley, A. H. (1971). *Urban society: An ecological approach.* New York: Ronald.

Hawley, A. H. (1973). Ecology and population. *Science,* 1196–1201.

Hawley, A. H. (1978). Cumulative change in theory and history. *American Sociological Review, 43*, 787–797.

Hawley, A. H. (1981). Human ecology: Persistence and change. *The American Behavioral Scientist, 24*, 423–444.

Hawley, A. H. (1986). *Human ecology: A theoretical essay.* Chicago: University of Chicago Press.

Hayek, F. A. (1982). *Law, legislation, liberty* (E–volume combined edn). London: Routledge & Kegan Paul.

Hayek, F. A. (1988). *The fatal conceit: The errors of socialism, Collected Works of F. A. Hayek* (Vol. 1). London: Routledge & Kegan Paul.

Hebb, D. O. (1949). *Organization of behavior.* New York: Wiley.

Hechter, M. (1987). *Principles of group solidarity.* Berkeley, CA: University of California Press.

Heckathorn, D. (1988). Collective sanctions and the emergence of prisoner's dilemma norms. *American Journal of Sociology, 94*, 535–562.

Heinrich, K. (1986). *Anthropomorphe: Zum Problem des Anthropomorphismus in der Religionsphilosophie [Anthropomorphies: On the problem of anthropomorphy in the philosophy of religion].* Basel: Stroemfeld, Roter Stern.

Hejl, P. M. (1990). Self-regulation in social systems. In W. Krohn, G. Küppers, & H. Nowotny (Eds.), *Selforganization—Portrait of a scientific revolution* (pp. 114–127). London: Kluwer Academic Publisher.

Hejl, P. M. (1992a). Die zwei Seiten der Eigengesetzlichkeit. Zur Konstruktion natürlicher Sozialsysteme und zum Problem ihrer Regelung [The two faces of autonomy. On the construction of natural social systems and their regulation]. In S. J. Schmidt (Ed.), *Kognition und Gesellschaft. Der Diskurs des Radikalen Konstruktivismus 2 [Cognition and Society. The discourse of radical constructivism 2]* (pp. 167–213). Frankfurt a.M.: Suhrkamp.

Hejl, P. M. (1992b). Selbstorganisation und Emergenz in sozialen Systemen [Self-organization and emergence in social systems]. In W. Krohn & G. Küppers (Eds.), *Emergenz. Die Entstehung von Ordnung, Organisation und Bedeutung [Emergence. The formation of order, organization, and meaning]* (pp. 269–292). Frankfurt a.M.: Suhrkamp.

Hejl, P. M. (1993). Culture as a network of socially constructed realities. In D. Fokkema & A. Rigney (Eds.), *Trends in cultural participation since the middle ages* (pp. 227–250). Amsterdam, Philadelphia: J. Benjamins.

Hejl, P. M. (n.d.). *Autonomie und Kontrolle [Autonomy and control].* (In preparation)

Heller, M. (1997) Posture as an interface between biology and culture. In U. Segerstråle & P. Molnár (Eds.), *Nonverbal communication: Where nature meets culture* (pp. 245–262). Mahwah, NJ: Lawrence Erlbaum Associates.

Hempel, C. G. (1951). General systems theory: A new approach to unity of science, 2. *Human Biolology, 23*, 313.

Hendrichs, H. (1992). Die individuelle Selbstgestaltung von Umwelt und Wohlbefinden bei Säugetieren [Individual shaping of environment and well-being in mammals. In W. Niegel & P. Molzberger (Eds.), *Aspekte der Selbstorganisation [Aspects of selforganization]* (pp. 27–40). Berlin: Springer.

Hendrichs, H. (1996). The complexity of social and mental structures in non-human mammals. In E. L. Khalil & K. W. Boulding (Eds.), *Evolution, order, and complexity* (pp. 104–121). London: Routledge.

Herman, L. M. (1980). Cognitive characteristics of dolphins. In L. M. Herman (Ed.), *Cetacean behavior: Mechanisms and functions* (pp. 363–429). New York: Wiley.

Herrnstein, R. J. (1977). The evolution of behaviorism. *American Psychologist, 32*, 593–603.

Herskovits, M. J. (1945). The process of cultural change. In R. Linton (Ed.), *The science of man in the World Crisis*. New York: Columbia University Press.

Herzog, R. (1988). Rechtsfortbildung durch Richterrecht in der Bundesrepublik Deutschland [The development of law through judicial decisions]. In *Das Recht in einer freiheitlichen Industriegesellschaft* (Veröffentlichung der Walter-Raymond-Stiftung, Vol. 26) (pp. 21–34). Köln, Germany: Bachem.

Hesse, M. B. (1966). *Models and analogies in science*. Notre Dame, IN: University of Notre Dame Press.

Hesse, M. B. (1974). *The structure of scientific inference*. London: Macmillan.

Hesse, M. B. (1986). Theories, family resemblances and analogy. In D. H. Helman (Ed.), *Analogical reasoning* (pp. 317–340). Dordrecht: Kluwer.

Hewes, G. (1975). *Language origins: A bibliography* (2 volumes). The Hague: Mouton.

Hewes, G. (1977). Language origin theories. In D. M. Rumbaugh (Ed.), *Language learning by a chimpanzee* (pp. 3–53). New York: Academic Press.

Hewlett, B. S., & Cavalli-Sforza, L. L. (1986). Cultural transmission among Aka pygmies. *American Anthropologist, 88*(4), 922–934.

Heyerdhal, T. (1950). *Kon–tiki: Across the Pacific by raft*. New York: Garden City Books.

Heyes, C. M. (1993). Anecdotes, training, trapping and triangulation: Do animals attribute mental states? *Animal Behaviour, 46*, 177–188.

Heyes, C. M., & Galef Jr., B. G. (1996). *Social learning in animals: The roots of culture*. San Diego, CA: Academic Press.

Hill, J. (1989). Concepts as units of cultural replication. *Journal of Social and Biological Structures, 12*, 343–355.

Hinde, R. A. (1987). *Individuals, relationships and culture: Links between ethology and the social sciences*. Cambridge, England: Cambridge University Press.

Hinton, G. E., & Shallice, T. (1991). Lesioning an attractor network: Investigation of acquired dyslexia. *Psychological Review, 98*, 74–95.

Hirschfeld, L. (1996). *Race in the making: Cognition, culture, and the child's construction of human kinds*. Cambridge, MA: MIT Press.

Hirschfeld, L., & Gelman, S. (Eds.). (1994). *Mapping the Mind: Domain specificity in cognition and culture*. New York: Cambridge University Press.

Hirshleifer, J. (1977). Economics from a biological viewpoint. *Journal of Law and Economics, 20*(1), 1–52.

Hirshleifer, J. (1987). On the emotions as guarantors of threats and promises. In J. Dupré (Ed.), *The latest on the best: Essays on evolution and optimality* (pp. 307–326). Cambridge, MA: MIT Press.

Hochschild, A. (1979). Emotion work, feeling rules and social structure. *American Journal of Sociology, 85*, 551–575.

Hodgson, G. M. (1993a). The Mecca of Alfred Marshall. *The Economic Journal, 103*, 406–415.

Hodgson, G. M. (1993b). *Economics and evolution: Bringing life back into economics.* Cambridge, England: Polity Press.

Hodos, W. & Campbell, C. B. G. (1969). Scala naturae: Why there is no theory in comparative psychology. *Psychological Review, 76*, 337–350.

Hoffman, E., McCabe, K., & Smith, V. (1995). Behavioral foundations of reciprocity: Experimental economics and evolutionary psychology. *Economic Science Laboratory, University of Arizona.*

Hofstadter, R. (1945). *Social Darwinism in American thought 1860–1915.* Philadelphia: University of Pennsylvania Press.

Hofstadter, R. (1955). *Social Darwinism in American thought, rev. ed.* Boston, MA: Beacon Press.

Hofstadter, R. (1983). Metamagical themas. *Scientific American, 248*, 14–22.

Hölldobler, B., & Wilson, E. O. (1990), *The ants.* Cambridge, MA: Harvard University Press.

van Hooff, J. A. R. A. M. (1972). A comparative approach to the phylogeny of laughter and smiling. In R. A. Hinde (Ed.), *Nonverbal communication* (pp. 209–241). Cambridge, England: Cambridge University Press.

Horgan, J. (1993). Eugenics revisited. *Scientific American, 268*, 92–100.

Hoyt, H. (1939). *The structure and growth of residential neighborhoods in American cities.* Washington, DC: U.S. Government Printing Office.

Hrdy (Blaffer Hrdy), S. (1981). *The woman that never evolved.* Cambridge, MA, London: Harvard University Press.

Hrdy, S. (1988). Empathy, polyandry, and the myth of the coy female. In R. Bleier (Ed.), *Feminist approaches to science* (pp. 118–146). New York: Pergamon Press.

Hrdy, S., & Judge, D. S. (1993). Darwin and the puzzle of primogeniture. *Human Nature, 4*, 1–45.

Hughes, A. L. (1988). *Evolution and human kinship.* Oxford, England: Oxford University Press.

Hughlings-Jackson, J. J. In J. Taylor (Ed.) (1959). *Selected writings of John Hughlings-Jackson* (pp. 5–73). New York: Basic Books.

Hull, D. L. (1952). *A behavior system.* New Haven: Yale University Press.

Hull, D. L. (1965). The effect of essentialism on taxonomy: 2000 years of statis. *British Journal for Philosophy of Science, 15*, 314–326.

Hull, D. L. (1982). The naked meme. In H. C. Plotkin (Ed.), *Learning, development and culture* (pp. 273–327). London: Wiley.

Humphrey, N. K. (1988). Lies, damned lies and anecdotal evidence. *Behavioral and Brain Sciences, 2*, 257–258.

Humphrey, N. K. (1976). The social function of intellect. In P. P. G. Bateson & R. A. Hinde (Eds.), *Growing points in ethology* (pp. 303–317). Cambridge, England: Cambridge University Press.

Huxley, T. H. (1863). *Evidence to man's place in nature.* London: William & Norgate.

Huxley, T. H. (1920). On the relations of man to the lower animals. In A.L. Kroeber & T. T. Waterman (Eds.), *Source book in anthropology* (pp. 45–70). Berkeley: University of California Press. (Original work published in 1863)

I

Insko, C. A., Gilmore, R., Drenan, S., Lipsitz, A., Moehle, D., & Tribart, J. (1983). Trade versus expropriation in open groups: A comparison of two types of social power. *Journal of Personality and Social Psychology, 44*, 977–999.

Irons, W. (1979). Cultural and biological success. In N. A. Chagnon & W. Irons (Eds.), *Evolutionary biology and human social behavior: An anthropological perspective* (pp. 257–272). Boston: Duxbury.

Irons, W. (1990). Let's make our perspective broader rather than narrower. *Ethology and Sociobiology, 11*, 361–374.

Irons, W. (1991). Anthropology. In M. Maxwell (Ed.), *The sociobiological imagination* (pp. 79–100). New York: SUNY Press.

Irons, W. (1993). *The cultural and reproductive success hypothesis: A synthesis of empirical tests.* Paper presented at the annual meetings of the American Anthropological Association, Washington, DC.

Izard, C. E. (1977). *Human emotions.* New York: Plenum.

J

Jablonka, E. (1994). Inheritance systems and the evolution of new levels of individuality. *Journal of Theoretical Biology, 170*, 301–309.

Jablonka, E., & Lamb, M. J. (1989). The inheritance of acquired epigenetic variations. *Journal of Theoretical Biology, 139*, 69–83.

Jablonka, E., Lachmann, M., & Lamb, M. J. (1992). Evidence, mechanisms and models for the inheritance of acquired characters. *Journal of Theoretical Biology, 158*, 245–268.

Jackendoff, R. (1992). *Languages of the mind.* Cambridge, MA: MIT Press.

Jackson, F., & Pettit, P. (1990). Program explanation: A general perspective. *Analysis, 50*, 107–117.

Jacob, F. (1970). *The logic of life.* London: Allen Lane.

Jacob, F. (1989). *The possible and the actual.* New York: Penguin.

Jacobs, R. C., & Campbell, D. T. (1961). The perpetuation of an arbitrary tradition through several generations of laboratory microculture. *Journal of Abnormal and Social Psychology, 62*, 649–658.

Jacobs, R. C., Jordan, M., & Barto, A. (1990). Task decomposition through competition in a modular connectionist architecture: The what and where in vision tasks. *COINS Technical Report, Volume 90–27.*

James, W. (1890). *The principles of psychology.* New York: Holt, Rinehart & Winston.

Jarman, P. J., & Jarman, M. V. (1973). Social behaviour, population structure and reproductive potential in impala. *East African Wildlife, 11*, 329–338.

Janssen, S. G., & Hauser, R. M. (1981). Religion, socialization, and fertility. *Demography, 18*, 511–528.

Jeffers, R., & Lehiste, I. (1979). *Principles and methods for historical linguistics.* Cambridge, MA: MIT Press.

Jeffreys, A. J., Harris, S., Barrie, P. A., Wood, D., Blanchetot, A., & Adams, S. (1983). Evolution of gene families: The globin genes. In J. S. Bendall (Ed.), *Evolution from molecules to men* (pp. 175–196). Cambridge, England: University of Cambridge Press.

Jensen, A. R. (1969). How much can we boost IQ and scholastic achievement? *Harvard Educational Review, 39*, 1–123.

Jepsen, G., Mayr, E., & Simpson, G. G. (Eds.). (1963). *Genetics, paleontology and evolution.* New York: Atheneum.

Johannsen, W. (1911). The genotype conception of heredity. *The American Naturalist, 45*, 129–159.

Johnson, G. A. (1982). Organisational structure and scalar stress. In C. Renfrew, M. Rowlands, & B. Segraves (Eds.), *Theory and explanation in archaeology* pp. 389–421). New York: Academic Press.

Johnson, M. H., Dziurawiec, S., Ellis, H., & Morton, J. (1991). Newborns' preferential tracking of face-stimuli and its subsequent decline. *Cognition, 40*, 1–19.

Johnson, M. H., & Morton, J. (1991). *Biology and cognitive development: The case of face recognition.* Oxford, England: Blackwell.

Jolly, A. (1966). Lemur social behaviour and primate intelligence. *Science, 153,* 501–506.

Jolly, A. (1988). The evolution of purpose. In R. W. Byrne & A. Whiten (Eds.), *Machiavellian intelligence: Social expertise and the evolution of intellect in monkeys, apes and humans* (pp. 363–378). Oxford, England: Oxford University Press.

Jones, S., Martin, R., & Pilbeam, D. (Eds.). (1994). *The Cambridge encyclopedia of human evolution.* Cambridge, England: Cambridge University Press.

Jorgensen, J. G. (1967). *Salish language and culture* (Vol. 3). Bloomington, IN: Indiana University Language Science Monographs.

Jorgensen, J. G. (1980). *Western Indians: Comparative environments, languages, and cultures of 172 Western American Indian tribes.* San Francisco: Freeman.

K

Kalke W. (1969). What is wrong with Fodor and Putnam's functionalism. *Nous, 3,* 83–94.

Kaplan, H., & Hill, K. (1985). Food sharing among Ache foragers: Tests of explanatory hypotheses. *Current Anthropology, 26,* 223–245.

Kaplan, H., & Hill, K. (1992). The evolutionary ecology of food acquisition. In E. A. Smith & B. Winterhalder (Eds.), *Evolutionary ecology and human behavior* (pp. 167–201). New York: Aldine de Gruyter.

Katz, S. H. (1982). Food, behavior, and biocultural evolution. In L. Barker (Ed.), *The psychobiology of human food selection* (pp. 171–188). Westport, CT: Avi Publishing Co.

Katz, S. H., Hediger, M. L., & Valleroy, L. A. (1974). Traditional maize processing techniques in the New World. *Science, 184,* 765–773.

Kauffman, S. (1993). *The origins of order.* Oxford, England: Oxford University Press.

Kautsky, K. (1879, April). Darwinismus und Sozialismus [Darwinism and socialism]. *Der Sozialist* (Wien), *34.*

Keesing, R. (1974). Theories of culture. *Annual Review of Anthropology, 3,* 73–97.

Keller, A. G. (1915). *Societal evolution: A study of the evolutionary basis of the science of society.* New York: Macmillan.

Kelley, H. H. (1967). Attribution theory in social psychology. In D. Levine (Ed.), *Nebraska symposium on motivation* (Vol. 15) (pp. 192–238). Lincoln: University of Nebraska Press.

Kelly, A. (1981). *The descent of Darwin, The popularization of Darwinism in Germany, 1860–1914.* University of North Carolina Press: Chapel Hill.

Keltner, D. (1995). The signs of appeasement: Evidence for the distinct displays of embarrassment, amusement, and shame. *Journal of Personality and Social Psychology, 68,* 441–454.

Kemper, T. D. (1978). *A social interactional theory of emotions.* New York: Wiley.

Kemper, T. D. (1981). Social constructivist and positivist approaches to the sociology of emotions. *American Journal of Sociology, 87,* 336–362.

Kemper, T. D. (1987). How many emotions are there? Wedding the social and the autonomic components. *The American Journal of Sociology, 93,* 263–289.

Kemper, T. D. (1990). *Research agendas in the sociology of emotions.* Albany, NY: SUNY Press.

Kempthorne, O. (1990). How does one apply statistical analysis to our understanding of the development of human relationships. *Behavioral and Brain Sciences, 13,* 138–139.

Kendon, A. (1973). The role of visible behaviour in the organization of face-to-face interaction. In M. von Cranach & I. Vine (Eds.), *Social communication and movement: Studies of interaction and expression in man and chimpanzee* (pp. 29–74). New York: Academic Press.

Kendon, A. (1990). *Conducting interaction.* Cambridge, England: Cambridge University Press.

Kendrick, K., & Baldwin, B. (1987). Cells in temporal cortex of conscious sheep can respond preferentially to sight of faces. *Science, 236,* 448–450.

Kevles, D. (1985). *In the name of eugenics.* Berkeley: University of California Press.

Kim, J. (1990a). Supervenience as a philosophical concept. *Metaphilosophy, 21,* 1–27.

Kim, J. (1990b). Explanatory exclusion and the problem of mental causation. In E. Villanueva (Ed.), *Information, semantics and epistemology.* Oxford, England: Blackwell.

Kinsey, A. (1953). *Sexual behavior in the human female.* Philadelphia: Saunders.

Kirch, P. V. (1986). *The evolution of the Polynesian chiefdoms.* Cambridge, MA: Cambridge University Press.

Kirch, P. V., & Green, R. C. (1987). History, phylogeny, and evolution in Polynesia, *Current Anthropology, 28*(4), 431–456.

Kitcher, P. (1985). *Vaulting ambition: Sociobiology and the quest for human nature.* Cambridge, MA: MIT Press.

Kitcher, P. (1991). The division of cognitive labor. *The Journal of Philosophy, 87,* 5–22.

Klineberg, O. (1935). *Racial differences.* New York: Harper & Bros.

Knapp, M. L. (1978). *Nonverbal communication in human interaction.* New York: Holt, Rinehart & Winston.

Knauft, B. (1985). *Good company and violence: Sorcery and social action in a lowland New Guinea society.* Berkeley: University of California Press.

Köck, W. K. (1987). Kognition – Semantik – Kommunikation [Cognition – semantic communication]. In S. J. Schmidt (Ed.), *Der Diskurs des Radikalen Konstruktivismus [The discourse on radical constructivism]* (pp. 340–373). Frankfurt a.M.: Suhrkamp.

Köhler, W. (1947). *Gestalt psychology: An introduction to new concepts in modern psychology.* New York: Liveright.

Koffka, K. (1935). *Principles of Gestalt psychology.* London: Routledge & Kegan Paul.

Kohler, T. A., & van West, C. R. (1995). *The calculus of self-interest in the development of cooperation: Sociopolitical development and risk among the Northern Anasazi.* In J. A. Tainter & B. B. Tainter (Eds.), *Evolving complexity and environmental risk in the prehistoric Southwest* (Proceedings of the Santa Fe Institute 24) (pp. 119–137). Reading, MA: Addison-Wesley.

Kohlhagen, N. (1992). *Tabubrecher. Von Frauen und Männern, die unsere Sexualität erforschten [Taboo breaker. On women and men who investigated sexuality].* Hamburg: Luchterhand.

Kohn, D. (1965). *The Darwinian heritage.* Princeton, NJ: Princeton University Press.

Kolb, B., & Whishaw, I. Q. (1990). *Fundamentals of human neuropsychology.* New York: Freeman.

Konner, M. (1991). Human nature and culture: Biology and the residue of uniqueness. In J. J. Sheehan & M. Sosna (Eds.), *The boundaries of humanity: Humans, animals, machines* (pp. 103–124). Berkeley: University of California Press.

Konold, C., & Falk, Ruma. (1992). Encoding difficulty: A psychological basis for "misperceptions" of randomness. *Proceedings of the Sixteenth Annual Meeting of the International Group for the Psychology of Mathematics Education, 2,* 9–16.

Kottack, C. P. (1971). Cultural adaptation, kinship and descent in Madagascar. *Southwestern Journal of Anthropology, 27,* 129–147.

Koyré, A. (1968). *Metaphysics and measurement. Essays in the scientific revolution.* Cambridge, MA: Harvard University Press.

Krebs, J. R, & Davies, N. B. (Eds.) (1978). *Behavioural ecology.* 1st edition. Oxford, England: Blackwell.

Krebs, J. R, & Davies, N. B (1991). *Behavioural ecology.* 2nd edition. Oxford, England: Blackwell.

Krebs, J. R, & Davies, N. B (1997). *Behavioural ecology.* 4th edition. Oxford, England: Blackwell.

Krementsov, N. L., & Todes, D. P. (1991). On metaphors, animals, and us. *Journal of Social Issues, 47,* 67–81.

Kroeber, A. L. (1948). *Anthropology.* New York: Harcourt Brace.

Kuhl, P. K., Williams, K. A., & Lacerda, F. (1992). Linguistic experience alters phonetic perception in infants by 6 months of age. *Science, 255,* 606–608.

Kummer, H. (1967). Tripartite relations in Hamadryas baboons. In S. Altmann (Ed.), *Social communication among primates* (pp. 63–71). Chicago: University of Chicago Press.

Kummer, H. (1975). Rules of dyad and group formation among captive Gelada baboons. In S. Kondo, M. Kawai, A. Ehara, & S. Kawamura (Eds.), *Proceedings of the Symposia of the Fifth Congress of the International Primatological Society* (pp. 129–159). Tokio: Japan Science Press.

Kummer, H. (1978). The value of social relationship to nonhuman primates. *Social Science Information, 17,* 687–705.

Kummer, H., Dasser, V, & Hoyningen-Huene, P. (1990). Exploring primate cognition: Some critical remarks. *Behaviour, 112,* 84–98.

Kuo, Z. Y. (1921). Giving up instincts in psychology. *Journal of Philosophy, 18,* 645–664.

L

Labov, W. (1972). *Sociolinguistic patterns.* Philadelphia: University of Pennsylvania Press.

Labov, W. (Ed.). (1980). *Locating language in time and space.* New York: Academic Press.

Lakatos, I. (1971). Falsificationism and the methodology of scientific research programmes. In I. Lakatos & A. Musgrave (Eds.), *Criticism and the growth of knowledge* (pp. 91–195), Cambridge, England: Cambridge University Press.

Lakoff, G. (1987). *Women, fire, and dangerous things: What categories reveal about the mind.* Chicago: University of Chicago Press.

Laland, K. N., Richerson, P. J., & Boyd, R. (1993). Animal social learning: Toward a new theoretical approach. *Perspectives in Ethology, 10,* 249–277.

Landau, M. (1984). Human evolution as narrative. *American Scientist, 72,* 262–268.

Lande, R. (1976). The maintenance of genetic variability by mutation in a polygenic character with linked loci. *Genetic Research, 26,* 221–235.

Lange, F. A. (no year). *Die Arbeiterfrage [The labor question].* Leipzig.

Laqueur, T. (1990). *Making sex. Body and gender from the Greeks to Freud.* Cambridge, MA: Harvard University Press.

Lashley, K. S. (1963). *Brain mechanisms and intelligence.* New York: Dover.

Leach, E. (1981). Sociobiology and anthropology: Wedding or rape? *Nature, 291,* 267–268.

Lee, R. B. (1992). Art, science or politics? The crisis in hunter–gatherer studies. *American Anthropologist, 94,* 31–54.

Lenneberg, E. (1967). *Biological foundations of language.* New York: Wiley.

Lenski, G. (1966). *Power and privilege.* New York: McGraw-Hill.

Lenski, G., Lenski, J., & Nolan, P. (1991). *Human societies: An introduction to macrosociology.* New York: McGraw-Hill.

Lenski, R. E., & Mittler, J. E. (1993). The directed mutation controversy and Neo-Darwinism. *Science, 259,* 188–193.

Le Pore, E., & Loewer, B. (1987). Mind matters. *Journal of Philosophy, 84,* 630–642.

Leslie, A. M. (1987a). Pretense and representation: The origins of "theory of mind." *Psychological Review, 94,* 412–426.

Leslie, A. M. (1987b). Children's understanding of the mental world. In R. L. Gregory (Ed.), *The Oxford companion to the mind* (pp. 139–142). Oxford, England: Oxford University Press.

Leslie, A. M. (1988). Some implications of pretense for the development of theories of mind. In J. W. Astington, P. L. Harris, & D. R. Olson (Eds.), *Developing theories of mind* (pp. 19–46). New York: Cambridge University Press.

Leslie, A. M. (1994). ToMM, ToBy and agency: Core architecture and domain specificity. In L. Hirschfeld & S. Gelman (Eds.), *Mapping the Mind: Domain specificity in cognition and culture* (pp. 119–148). New York: Cambridge University Press.

Levenson, R. W., Ekman, P., & Heider, K. (1992). Emotion and autonomic nervous system activity in the Minangkabau of West Sumatra. *Journal of Personality and Social Psychology, 62*, 972–988.

Lévi-Strauss, C. (1969). *The elementary structures of kinship* (J. H. Bell, J. R. von Sturmer, & R. Needham, trans.). Boston, MA: Beacon.

LeVine, R. A., & Campbell, D. T (1972). *Ethnocentrism: Theories of conflict, ethnic attitudes, and group behavior.* New York: Wiley.

LeVine, R. A, & Sangree, W. H. (1962). The diffusion of age–group organization in East Africa: A controlled comparison. *Africa, 32*, 97–110.

LeVine, R. A., & Sangree, W. H. (1980). Conclusion: Asian and African systems of polyandry. *Journal of Comparative Family Studies, 7*, 385–410.

Levins, R. (1966). The strategy of model building in population biology. *American Scientist, 54*, 321–431.

Levins, R., & Lewontin, R. C. (1985). *The dialectical biologist.* Cambridge, MA: Harvard University Press.

Levinton, J. (1988). *Genetics, paleontology, and macroevolution.* Cambridge: Cambridge University Press.

Lewontin, R. C. (1970). The units of selection. *Annual Review of Ecology and Systematics, 1*, 1–18.

Lewontin, R. C. (1972). The apportionment of human diversity. *Evolutionary Biology, 6*, 381–398.

Lewontin, R. C. (1974a). The analysis of variance and the analysis of causes. *American Journal of Human Genetics, 26*, 400–411.

Lewontin, R. C. (1974b). *The genetic basis of evolutionary change.* New York: Columbia University Press.

Lewontin, R. C. (1975). *Transcript of the NOVA program, WGBH Boston, #211.* Transmission by PBS, February 2.

Lewontin, R. C. (1979). Sociobiology as an adaptationist paradigm. *Behavioral Sciences, 24*, 1–10.

Lewontin, R. C., Rose, S., & Kamin, L. (1984). *Not in our genes.* New York: Pantheon.

Lieberman, L. (1989). A discipline divided: Acceptance of human sociobiological concepts in anthropology. *Current Anthropology, 30*, 676–682.

Lieberman, P. (1984). *The biology and evolution of language.* Cambridge, MA: Harvard University Press.

Lilienfeld, P. (1873–1881). *Gedanken über die Socialwissenschaft [Thoughts on social science].* Mitau: E. Behre.

Lilienfeld, P. (1898). *Zur Vertheidigung der Organischen Methode in der Sociologie [On the defense of organic method in sociology].* Berlin: Reimer.

Lindenbaum, S. (1979). *Kuru sorcery: Disease and danger in the New Guinea Highlands.* Palo Alto, CA: Mayfield.

Lindenberg, S. (1990). Homo socio-economics: The emergence of a general model of man in the social sciences. *Journal of Institutional and Theoretical Economics, 146*, 727–748.

Lloyd, E. A. (1988). *The structure and confirmation of evolutionary theory.* New York: Greenwood.

Lloyd, E. A. (1989). A structural approach to defining units of selection. *Philosophy of Science, 56,* 395–418.

Lloyd, E. A. (1993). Pre-theoretical assumptions in evolutionary explanations of female sexuality. *Philosophical Studies, 69,* 139–153.

Lockard, R. (1971). Reflections on the fall of comparative psychology: Is there a message for us all? *American Psychologist, 26–32.*

Lockhart, R. S., & Craik, F. I. M. (1991). Levels of processing: A retrospective commentary on a framework for memory research. *Canadian Journal of Psychology, 44,* 87–112.

Lopreato, J. (1984). *Human nature and biocultural evolution.* Boston, MA: Allen & Unwin.

Lorenz, K. (1965). *Evolution and the modification of behavior.* Chicago: University of Chicago Press.

Low, B. S. (1993). Ecological demography: A synthetic focus in evolutionary anthropology. *Evolutionary Anthropology, 1,* 177–187.

Luhmann, N. (1982). *The differentiation of society.* New York: Columbia University Press.

Luhmann, N. (1986). *Was ist Kommunikation? [What is communication?].* Presentation at the symposium "Lebende Systeme—Konstruktion und Veränderung von Wirklichkeiten und ihre Relevanz für die systemische Therapie". Heidelberg, GermanyLuhmann, N. (1990). *Die Wissenschaft der Gesellschaft [The science of society].* Frankfurt a.M.: Suhrkamp.

Lumsden, C. J., & Wilson, E. O. (1981). *Genes, mind, and culture: The coevolutionary process.* Cambridge, MA: Harvard University Press.

Lumsden, C. J., & Wilson, E. O. (1983). *Promethean fire. Reflections of the origins of mind.* Cambridge, MA: Harvard University Press.

Luria, A. R. (1932). *The nature of human conflicts.* New York: Liveright.

Luria, A. R. (1970). The functional organization of the brain. *Scientific American, 222,* 66–78.

Luria, A. R. (1980). *Higher cortical functions in man.* New York: Basic Books.

Lützen, K. (1990). *Was das Herz begehrt. Liebe und Freundschaft zwischen Frauen [All you wish for. Love and friendship among women].* Hamburg: Kabel.

M

Mace, W. M., & James, J. (1977). James J. Gibson's strategy for perceiving. In R. Shaw & J. Bransford (Eds.), *Perceiving, acting, and knowing* (pp. 62–89). Hillsdale, NJ: Lawrence Erlbaum Associates.

MacLean, P. D. (1990). *The triune brain in evolution.* New York: Plenum.

Macphail, E. M. (1982). *Brain and intelligence in vertebrates.* Oxford, England: Clarendon.

Macphail, E. M. (1987). The comparative psychology of intelligence. *Behavioral and Brain Sciences, 10,* 645–689.

Maglio, V., & Cooke, H. B. S. (1978). *Evolution of African mammals.* Cambridge, MA: University of Harvard Press.

Maine, H. (1861). *Ancient law.* London: John Murray.

Malinowski, B. (1944). *A scientific theory of culture.* Chapel Hill: University of North Carolina Press.

Mallory, J. P. (1989). *In search of the Indo–Europeans: Language, myth, and archaeology.* London: Thames & Hudson.

Malone, D. (1987). Mechanisms of hominoid dispersal in miocene East Africa. *Journal of Human Evolution, 16,* 469–481.

Malthus, T. R. (1798). *An essay on the principle of population, as it affects the future improvement of society, with remarks on the speculations of Mr. Goodwin, M. Condorcet, and other writers.* London: Johnson.

Mandeville, B. (1970). *The fable of the bees, edited with an introduction by P. Harth from the first complete edition of 1724*. New York: Penguin.

Mann, J. (1992). Nurturance or negligence. Maternal psychology and behavioral preference among pre–born twins. In J. Barkow, L. Cosmides, & J. Tooby (Eds.), *The adapted mind* (pp. 347–398). New York: Oxford University Press.

Marcuse, H. (1955). *Eros and civilization*. Boston: Beacon.

Markman, E. M. (1989). *Categorization and naming in children: Problems of induction*. Cabridge, MA: MIT Press.

Marks, J., & Staski, E. (1988). Individuals and the evolution of biological and cultural systems. *Human Evolution, 3, 3,* 147–161.

Marler, P. (1984). Animal communication: Affect or cognition?. In K. R. Scherer & P. Ekman (Eds.), *Approaches to emotion* (pp. 345–365). Hillsdale, NJ: Erlbaum.

Marler, P. (1991). The instinct to learn. In S. Carey & R. Gelman (Eds.), *The epigenesis of mind* (pp. 221–231). Hillsdale, NJ: Lawrence Erlbaum Associates.

Marler, P., & Evans, C. S. (1997). Communication signals of animals: Contributions of emotion and reference. In U. Segerstråle & P. Molnár (Eds.), *Nonverbal communication: Where nature meets culture* (pp. 151–170). Mahwah, NJ: Lawrence Erlbaum Associates.

Marmorstein, A. (1937). *The old rabbinic doctrine of God: II. Essays in anthropomorphism*. Oxford, England: Oxford University Press.

Marr, D. (1982). *Vision: A computational investigation into the human representation and processing of visual information*. San Francisco: Freeman.

Marshall, A. (1890). *Principles of economics*. London: Macmillan.

Marshall, J. C. (1981). Cognition and the crossroads. *Nature, 289,* 613–614.

Martin, J., & Harré, R. (1982). Metaphors in science. In D. S. Miall (Ed.), *Metaphor: Problems and perspectives* (pp. 89–106). Sussex, NJ: Harvester Press, Humanities Press.

Maryanski, A. M. (1987). African ape social structure: Is there strength in weak ties. *Social Networks, 9,* 191–215.

Maryanski, A. M. (1992). The last ancestor: An ecological network model on the origins of human sociality. In *Advances in human ecology* (Vol. 1, pp. 1–32). Greenwich, CT: JAI.

Maryanski, A. M. (1993). The elementary forms of the first proto-human society: An ecological/social network approach. In *Advances in human ecology* (Vol. 2, pp. 215–241). Greenwich, CT: JAI.

Maryanski, A. M. (1994). The pursuit of human nature in sociobiology and evolutionary sociology. *Sociological Perspectives, 37,* 375–389.

Maryanski, A. M. (1996). Was speech an evolutionary afterthought? In B. M. Velichkovsky & D. M. Rumbaugh (Eds.), *Communicating meaning: The evolution and development of language* (pp. 79–102). Mahwah, NJ: Lawrence Erlbaum Associates.

Maryanski, A. M. (1997) Primate communication and the ecology of a language niche. In U. Segerstråle & P. Molnár (Eds.), *Nonverbal communication: Where nature meets culture* (pp. 191–209). Mahwah, NJ: Lawrence Erlbaum Associates.

Maryanski, A. M., & Turner, J. H. (1991). Biological functionalism. In J. H. Turner (Ed.), *The structure of sociological theory* (pp. 152–178). Belmont, CA: Wadsworth.

Maryanski, A. M., & Turner, J. H. (1992). *The social cage: Human nature and the evolution of society*. Stanford, CA: Stanford University Press.

Masters, R. D. (1970). Genes, language and evolution. *Semiotica, 2,* 29–320, 311.

Masters, R. D. (1982). Is sociobiology reactionary? The political implications of inclusive–fitness theory. *Quarterly Review of Biology, 57,* 275–292.

Masters, R. D. (1986). Ostracism, voice and exit: The biology of social participation. In M. Gruter & R. D. Masters (Eds.), *Ostracism: A social and biological phenomenon. Ethology and Sociobiology, 7, 3/4,* 231–247. New York: Elsevier.

Masters, W., & Johnson, V. (1966). *Human sexual response*. London: Churchill.

Maynard Smith, J. (1974a). *Models in ecology*. Cambridge, England: Cambridge University Press.

Maynard Smith, J. (1974b). The theory of games and the evolution of animal conflicts. *Journal of Theoretical Biology, 47,* 209–221.

Maynard Smith, J. (1978). Optimization theory in evolution. *Annual Review of Ecology and Systematics, 9,* 31–56.

Maynard Smith, J. (1981). Genes and race. *Nature, 289,* 742.

Maynard Smith, J. (1982). *Evolution and the theory of games*. Cambridge, England: Cambridge University Press.

Maynard Smith, J. (1985, September 26). The birth of sociobiology. *New Scientist,* pp. 48–50.

Maynard Smith, J. (1990, 27 September). Triumphs of Colonialism. *New York Review of Books,* 36–37.

Mayr, E. (1942). *Systematics and the origin of species from the viewpoint of a zoologist*. New York: Columbia University Press.

Mayr, E. (1959). Typological versus population thinking. In *Evolution and anthropology: A centennial appraisal* (pp. 409–412). Washington, DC: Anthropological Society of Washington.

Mayr, E. (1974). Teleological and teleonomic: A new analysis. *Boston Studies in the Philosophy of Science, 14,* 91–117.

Mayr, E. (1982). *The growth of biological thought: Diversity, evolution, and inheritance*. Cambridge, MA: Harvard University Press.

Mayr, E. (1983). How to carry out the adaptationist program? *American Naturalist, 121,* 324–334.

McCabe, J. (1983). FBD marriage: Further support for the Westermarck hypothesis of the incest taboo? *American Anthropologist, 85,* 50–69.

McClelland, J. L., Rumelhart, D. E., & The PDP Research Group. (1986). *Parallel distributed processing: Explorations in the microstructure of cognition* (Vols. 1 & 2). Cambridge, MA: MIT Press.

McCracken, R. D. (1971). Lactase deficiency: An example of dietary evolution. *Current Anthropology, 12,* 479–517.

McDougall, W. (1908). *Introduction to social psychology*. London: Methuen.

McGuire, M. T., & Raleigh, M. (1986). Animal analogues of ostracism: A social and biological phenomenon. In M. Gruter & R. D. Masters (Eds.), *Ostracism: A social and biological phenomenon. Ethology and Sociobiology, 7,* 3/4, 53–67. New York: Elsevier.

McKenzie, R. (1933). *The metropolitan community*. New York: McGraw-Hill.

McNeill, W. H. (1986). *Myth, history, and other essays*. Chicago: University of Chicago Press.

McPherson, J. M. (1981). A dynamic model of voluntary affiliation. *Social Forces, 59,* 705–728.

McPherson, J. M. (1983). An ecology of affiliation, *American Sociological Review, 48,* 519–532.

McPherson, J. M. (1990). Evolution in communities of voluntary organizations. In J. H. Singh (Ed.), *Organizational evolution* (pp. 224–245). Newbury Park, CA: Sage.

Mead, G. H. (1934). *Mind, self and society*. Chicago: University of Chicago Press.

Meltzoff, A. N. (1985). The roots of social and cognitive development: Models of man's original nature. In T. M. Field & N. Fox (Eds.), *Social perception in infants* (pp. 1–30). Norwood, NJ: Ablex.

Meyer, P. (1987). Universale Muster sozialen Verhaltens: Wie entstehen aus genetischer Variabilität strukturell ähnliche Lösungen? [Universal patterns of social behavior: How do similar structures arrive from genetic variability?] *HOMO, 38,* 3/4, 133–144.

Meyer, P. (1989). On human universals: Their origin and operation in the light of evolutionary biology. In W. A. Koch (Ed.), *The nature of culture* (pp. 192–215). Bochum, Germany: Studienverlag Dr. N. Brockmeyer.

Miller, J. G. (1978). *Living systems.* New York: McGraw-Hill.

Mishler, B., & Brandon, R. (1987). Individuality, pluralism, and the species concept. *Biology and Philosophy, 2,* 397–414.

Mitchell, J. (1989). On Freud and the distinction between the sexes. In L. Spurling (Ed.), *Sigmund Freud. Critical assessment: Volume II. The theory and practice of psychoanalysis* (pp. 352–360). London: Routledge & Kegan Paul.

Mitchell, S. D. (1987). Competing units of selection? A case of symbiosis. *Philosophy of Science, 54,* 351–367.

Mitchell, S. D. (1989). The causal background for functional explanations. *International Studies in the Philosophy of Science, 3,* 213–230.

Mitchell, S. D. (1990). Units of behavior in evolutionary explanations. In M. Bekoff & D. Jamieson (Eds.), *Interpretation and explanation in the study of animal behavior.* Boulder: Westview Press.

Mitchell, S. D. (1992). On pluralism and competition in evolutionary explanations. *American Zoologist, 32,* 135–144 .

Montagu A. (Ed.). (1980). *Sociobiology examined.* Oxford, England: Oxford University Press.

Morgan, C. L. (1884). Instinct. *Nature, 29,* 370–374.

Morgan, C. L. (1895). *An introduction to comparative psychology.* London: Walter Scott.

Morgan, L. H. (1877). *Ancient society.* London: Macmillan.

Morgan, T. H. (1917). The theory of the gene. *The American Naturalist, 51,* 513–544.

Morris, D. (1967). *The naked ape.* New York: Dell.

Murdock, G. P. (1945). The common denominator of cultures. In R. Linton (Ed.), *The science of man in the world crisis* (pp. 123–142). New York: Columbia University Press.

Murdock, G. P. (1949). *Social structure.* New York: Macmillan.

Murdock, G. P. (1971). How culture changes. In H. C. Shapiro (Ed.), *Man, culture and society* (p. 331). New York: Oxford University Press.

N

Nagel, E. (1961). *The structure of science.* New York: Harcourt Brace.

Nagel, T. (1986). *The view from nowhere.* Oxford, England: Oxford University Press.

Needham, J. (1988). *Science and civilization in China.* Cambridge, England: Cambridge University Press.

Neisser, U. (1967). *Cognitive psychology.* New York: Appleton-Century-Crofts.

Nelson, R., & Winter, S. G. (1982). *An evolutionary theory of economic change.* Cambridge, MA: Belknap Press of Harvard University Press.

von Neumann, J., & Morgenstern, O. (1944). *The theory of games and economic behavior.* Princeton, NJ: Princeton University Press.

Newmeyer, F. (Ed.). (1988). *Linguistic theory: Foundations* (Vol. 1). New York: Cambridge University Press.

Nicolis, G., & Prigogine, I. (1989). *Exploring complexity: An introduction.* New York: Freeman.

Nisbett, R. A. (1969). *Social change and history.* New York: Oxford University Press.

Nisbett, R. A., & Ross, L. (1980). *Human inference: strategies and shortcomings of social judgment.* Englewood Cliffs, NJ: Prentice-Hall.

Nitschke, A. (1997) Sign languages and gestures in Medieval Europe: monasteries, courts of justice, and society. In U. Segerstråle & P. Molnár (Eds.), *Nonverbal communication: Where nature meets culture* (pp. 263–274). Mahwah, NJ: Lawrence Erlbaum Associates.

Nuttin, J. M. (1975). *The illusion of attitude change.* London: Academic Press.

O

O'Brien, M., & Holland, T. D. (1992). The role of adaptation in archaeological explanation. *American Antiquity, 57*, 36–59.

Odum, E. P. (1959). *Fundamentals of ecology.* London: Saunders.

Oexle, O. G. (1988). Die funktionale Dreiteilung als Deutungsschema der sozialen Wirklichkeit in der ständischen Gesellschaft des Mittelalters (The functional tripartition as a explanatory scheme of social reality in the medieval social order). In W. Schulze (Ed.), *Ständische Gesellschaft und soziale Mobilität (Social order and social mobility)* (Schriften des Historischen Kollegs, Kolloquien 12) (pp. 19–51). München: Oldenburg.

Ogburn, W., & Nimkoff, M. (1959). *A handbook of sociology.* London: Routledge & Kegan Paul.

Ogorek, R. (1986). *Richterkönig oder Subsumtionsautomat? Zur Justiztheorie im 19. Jahrhundert (The judge as a king or as an automaton of subsumtion? On 19th century legal theory).* Frankfurt a.M.: Klostermann.

Öhman, A. (1986). Face the beast and fear the face: Animal and racial fears as prototypes for evolutionary analyses for emotion. *Psychophysiology, 23*, 123–145.

Öhman, A., & Dimberg, U. (1978). Facial expressions as conditioned stimuli for electrodermal response: A case study of "preparedness." *Journal of Personality and Social Psychology, 36*, 1251–1258.

Oliver, S. (1962). Ecology and cultural continuity as contributing factors to social organization of the Plains Indians. *University of California Publications in Archaeology and Ethnology, 48*, 1–90.

Olson, M. (1965). *The logic of collective action.* Cambridge, MA: Harvard University Press.

Orlove, B. S. (1980). Ecological anthropology. *Annual Review of Anthropology, 9*, 235–273.

Otte, D. (1974). Effects and functions in the evolution of signaling systems. *Annual Review of Ecology and Systematics, 5*, 385–417.

P

Page, R., E., & Mitchell, S. D. (1991). Self-organization and adaptation in insect societies. In N. A. Fine, M. Forbes, & L. Wessels (Eds.), *PSA 1990, Vol. 2*, 289–298. East Lansing, MI: Philosophy of Science Association.

Papoušek, H., & Papoušek, M. (1997) Preverbal communication in humans and the genesis of culture. In U. Segerstråle & P. Molnár (Eds.), *Nonverbal communication: Where nature meets culture* (pp. 87–107). Mahwah, NJ: Lawrence Erlbaum Associates.

Park, R. E. (1916). The city: Suggestions for the investigation of human behavior in an urban environment. *American Journal of Sociology, 20*, 577–612.

Park, R. E. (1936). Human ecology. *American Journal of Sociology, 42*, 1–15.

Park, R. E., & Burgess, E. W. (1925). *The city.* Chicago: University of Chicago Press.

Parker, G. A. (1970). Sperm competition and its evolutionary consequences in the insects. *Biological Review, 45*, 525–567.

Parker, H., & Parker, S. (1986). Father-daughter sexual abuse: An emerging perspective. *American Journal of Orthopsychology, 56*, 531–549.

Parsons, T. (1951). *The social system.* New York: The Free Press.

Parsons, T. (1966). *Societies: Evolutionary and comparative perspectives.* Englewood Cliffs, NJ: Prentice-Hall.

Parsons, T. (1971). *The system of modern societies.* Englewood Cliffs, NJ: Prentice-Hall.

Parsons, T. (1978). *Action theory and the human condition.* New York: Free Press.

Parsons, T. (1990). Prolegomena to a theory of social institutions. *American Sociology Review, 55*, 319–333. (Original work published in 1935)

Parsons, T., & Shils, E. A. (1951). *Toward a general theory of action.* Cambridge, MA: Harvard University Press.

Pastner, C. M. (1986). The Westermarck hypothesis and first coursin marriage: The cultural modification of negative sexual imprinting. *Journal of Anthropoligical Research, 24,* 573–586.

Pavlov, I. P. (1960). *Conditioned reflexes: An investigation of physiological activity in the cerebral cortex.* New York: Dover.

Pearson, K. (1900). *The grammar of science.* London: Macmillan.

Perner, J. (1991). *Understanding the representational mind.* Cambridge; MA: MIT Press.

Perner, J., Leekam, S. R., & Wimmer, H. M. (1987). Three-year olds' difficulty with false belief: The case for a conceptual deficit. *British Journal of developmental Psychology, 5,* 125–127.

Perrett, D., Rolls, E., & Caan, W. (1982). Visual neurons responsive to faces in monkey temporal cortex. *Experimental Brain Research, 47,* 329–342.

Perusse, D. (1992a). Cultural and reproductive success in industrial societies: Testing the relationship at the proximate and ultimate levels. *Behavioral and Brain Sciences, 16,* 267–322.

Perusse, D. (1992b). Specific versus general adaptations: Another unnecessary dichotomy? *Behavioral and Brain Sciences, 15,* 399–400.

Pfeiffer, C., & Oswald, M. (Eds.). (1989). *Strafzumessung, Empirische Forschung und Strafrechtsdogmatik im Dialog [Determination of penalty. Dialogue on empirical research and dogmatic of penalty].* Stuttgart: Enke.

Piaget, J. (1940/1967). *Six psychological studies* (A. Tenzer and D. Elkind, Transl.). New York: Random House.

Pinker, S. (1984). *Language learnability and language development.* Cambridge, MA: Harvard University Press.

Pinker, S. (1991). Rules of language. *Science, 253,* 530–535.

Pinker, S. (1994). *The language instinct.* New York: Morrow.

Pinker, S., & Prince, A. (1988). On language and connectionism: Analysis of a parallel distributed processing model of language acquisition. *Cognition, 28,* 73–193.

Pinker, S., & Bloom, P. (1990). Natural language and natural selection. *Behavioral and Brain Sciences, 13,* 707–784.

Platnick, N., & Cameron, D. (1977). Cladistic methods in textual, linguistic, and phylogenetic analysis. *Systematic Zoology, 26,* 380–385.

Plomin, R., & Bergeman, C. S. (1991). The nature of nurture: Genetic influence on "environmental" measures. *Behavioral and Brain Sciences, 14,* 373–427.

Plutchik, R. (1980). *Emotion: A psychoevolutionary synthesis.* New York: Harper & Row.

Plutchik, R. (1984). Emotions: A general psychoevolutionary theory. In K. R. Scherer & P. Ekman (Eds.), *Approaches to emotion.* Hillsdale, NJ:Lawrence Erlbaum Associates.

Poizner, H., Bellugi, U., & Klima, E. (1990). Biological foundations of language, *Annual Review of Neurosciences, 13,* 283–307.

Pollard, P. (1990). Natural selection for the selection task: Limits to social exchange theory. *Cognition, 36,* 195–204.

Posner, R. (1992). *Sex and reason.* Cambridge, MA: Harvard University Press.

Premack, D., & Woodruff, G. (1978). Does the chimpanzee have a theory of mind? *Behavioral and Brain Sciences, 3,* 111–132; *4,* 515–526.

Preuschoft, S., & van Hooff, J. A. R. A. M. (1997) The social function of 'smile' and 'laughter': Variations across primate species and societies. In U. Segerstråle & P. Molnár (Eds.), *Nonverbal communication: Where nature meets culture* (pp. 171–189). Mahwah, NJ: Lawrence Erlbaum Associates.

Provine, W. (1973). Geneticists and the biology of race crossing. *Science, 182,* 790–796.

Pugh, G. E. (1977). *The biological origin of human values.* New York: Basic Books.

Pulliam, H. R., & Dunford, C. (1980). *Programmed to learn: An essay in the evolution of culture.* New York: Columbia University Press.

Pusey, A., & Packer, C. (1987). Dispersal and philopatry. In B. Smuts, D. Cheney, R. Seyfarth, R. Wrangham, & T. Struhsaker (Eds.), *Primate societies* (pp. 250–266). Chicago: University of Chicago Press.

Putnam, H. (1988). *Representation and reality.* Cambridge, MA: MIT Press.

Pylyshyn, W. Z. (Ed.). (1987). *The robot's dilemma: The frame problem in artificial intelligence.* Norwood, NJ: Ablex.

R

Radcliffe-Brown, A. R. (1935). On the concept of function in social science (reply to Lesser, 1935). *American Anthropologist, 37,* 394–402.

Radcliffe-Brown, A. R. (1952). *Structure and function in primitive society.* London: Cohen & West.

Ramachandran, V. (1990). Visual perception in people and machines. In A. Blake & T. Troscianko (Eds.), *AI and the eye* (pp. 21–77). New York: Wiley.

Rappaport, R. A. (1979). *Ecology, meaning and religion.* Richmond, CA: North Atlantic.

Ratzenhofer, G. (1881). *Die Staatswehr [The state's armed forces].* Stuttgart: Cotta.

Renfrew, C. (1987). *Archaeology and language: The puzzle of Indo–European origins.* London: Cape.

Reynolds, V. (1980). *The biology of human action.* Oxford, England: Freedman.

Richards, R. J. (1987). *Darwin and the emergence of evolutionary theories of mind and behavior.* Chicago: University of Chicago Press.

Richerson, P. J., & Boyd, R. (1978). A dual inheritance model of the human evolutionary process I: Basic postulates and a simple model. *Journal of Social and Biological Structures, 1,* 127–154.

Richerson, P. J., & Boyd, R. (1984). Natural selection and culture. *BioScience, 34,* 430–434.

Richerson, P. J., & Boyd, R. (1987). Simple models of complex phenomena: the case of cultural evolution. In J. Dupré (Ed.), *The latest on the best: Essays on Evolution and optimality* (pp. 27-52). Cambridge, MA: MIT Press.

Richerson, P. J., & Boyd, R. (1989). A Darwinian theory for the evolution of symbolic cultural traits. In M. Freilich (Ed.), *The relevance of culture* (pp. 120–142). New York: Bergin & Garvey.

Richerson, P. J., & Boyd, R. (1992). Cultural inheritance and evolutionary ecology. In E. A. & B. Winterhalder (Eds.), *Evolutionary ecology and human behavior.* New York: Aldine.

Ridley, M. (1985). *The problems of evolution.* Oxford, England: Oxford University Press.

Ridley, M. (1986). *Evolution and classification: The reformation of cladism.* London: Longman.

Rindos, D. (1985). Darwinian selection, symbolic variation, and the evolution of culture. *Current Anthropology, 26*(1), 65–88.

Rindos, D. (1986). The evolution of the capacity for culture: Sociobiology, structuralism, and cultural selectionism. *Current Anthropology, 27*(4), 315–332.

Ristau, C. A. (Ed.). (1991). *Cognitive ethology: The minds of other animals.* Hillsdale, NJ: Lawrence Erlbaum Associates.

Ritvo, H. (1987). *The animal estate: The English and other creatures in the Victorian Age.* Cambridge, MA: Harvard University Press.

Robinson, P. (1977). *The modernization of sex. Havelock Ellis, Alfred Kinsey, William Masters and Virginia Johnson.* New York: Harper & Row.

Rogers, A. R. (1988). Does biology constrain culture? *American Anthropologist, 90,* 819–831.

Rogers, E. M. (1983). *Diffusion of innovations.* New York: The Free Press.

Rogers, E. M., & Shoemaker, F. F. (1971). *The communication of innovations: A cross-cultural approach.* New York: The Free Press.

Romanes, G. (1883). *Mental evolution in animals.* London: Kegan Paul.

Romanes, G. (1898). *Mental evolution in animals.* New York: Appleton-Century Crofts.

Romer, P. (1993, June 25). *A taste for violence. Plenary address. Evolution and the human sciences.* London: London School of Economics.

Rose, S. (Ed.). (1982a). *Against biological determinism.* New York: Allison & Busby, Schocken.

Rose, S. (Ed.). (1982b). *Toward a liberatory biology.* New York: Allison & Busby, Schocken.

Rosenberg, H. (1976). *Grosse Depression und Bismarckzeit. Wirtschaftsablauf, Gesellschaft und Politik in Mitteleuropa [Economic Depression in the era of Bismarck. Economy, society, and politics in middle Europe].* Frankfurt a.M., Berlin, Wien: Ullstein.

Rosenthal, T. L., & Zimmerman, B. J. (1979). *Social learning and cognition.* New York: Academic Press.

Roth, E. A. (1993). A reexamination of Rendille population regulation. *American Anthropologist, 95,* 597–611.

Roth, G., & Wake, D. B. (Eds.). (1989, August–September). *Complex organismal functions: Integration and evolution in vertebrates.* Report on the Dahlem Workshop on "Complex Organismal Functions: Integration and Evolution in Vertebrates". Berlin.

Rothschild, M. (1992). *Bionomics: Economy as ecosystem.* New York: Holt.

Rozin, P. (1976). The evolution of intelligence and access to the cognitive unconscious. In J. M. Sprague & A. N. Epstein (Eds.), *Progress in psychobiology and physiological psychology* (pp. 245–280). New York. Academic Press.

Runciman, W. G. (1989). *A treatise on social theory: Vol. 2. Substantive social theory.* Cambridge, England: University of Cambridge Press.

Ruse, M. (1979). *The Darwinian revolution. Science red in tooth and claw.* Chicago, IL: University of Chicago Press.

Ruse, M. (1988). Molecules to man: The concept of evolutionary biology. In M. Nitecki (Ed.), *Evolutionary progress* (pp. 97–128). Chicago: University of Chicago Press.

Ruse, M. (1993). Evolution and progress. *Tree, 8,* 55–60.

Rushforth, S., & Chisholm, J. S. (1991). *Cultural persistence: Continuity in meaning and moral responsibility among Bearlake Athapaskans.* Tucson: University of Arizona Press.

S

Sackett, G. (1966). Monkeys reared in isolation with pictures as visual input: Evidence for an innate releasing mechanism. *Science, 154,* 1468–1473.

Sacks, O. (1993, April 8). Making up the mind. *New York Review of Books,* 42–49.

Sadalla, E. K., Kenrick, D. T., & Vershure, B. (1987). Dominance and heterosexual attraction. *Journal of Personality and Social Psychology, 52,* 730–738.

Sahlins, M. D. (1976a). *Culture and practical reason.* Chicago: University of Chicago Press.

Sahlins, M. D. (1976b). *The use and abuse of biology: An anthropological critique of sociobiology.* Ann Arbor, MI: University of Michigan Press.

Salthe, S. N. (1985). *Evolving hierarchical systems: Their structure and representation.* New York: Columbia University Press.

Samelson, F. (1978). From "race psychology" to "studies in prejudice." *Journal of the History of the Behavioral Sciences, 17,* 265–278.

Samelson, F. (1979). Putting psychology on the map: Ideology and intelligence testing. In A. Buss (Ed.), *Psychology in social context* (103–168). New York: Irvington.

Sanderson, S. K. (1990). *Social evolutionism: A critical history.* Oxford, England: Basil Blackwell.

Sapir, E. (1949). *Selected writings in language, culture and personality.* Berkeley: University of California Press.

Sapp, J. (1987). *Beyond the gene.* New York: Oxford University Press.

de Saussure, F. (1959). *Course in general linguistics.* New York: McGraw-Hill.

Savage-Rumbaugh, S., Murphy, J., Seveik, R., Brakke, D., Williams, G. S., & Rumbaugh, D. M. (1993). Language comprehension in the ape and child. *Monographs of the Society for Research in Child Development, 58*(3–4).

Scarr, S. (1989). Sociobiology: The psychology of sex, violence, and oppression? *Contemporary Psychology, 34,* 440–443.

Schachter, S., & Singer, J. (1962). Cognitive, social, and psychological determinants of emotional state. *Psychological Review, 69,* 379–399.

Schäffle, A. G. F. (1875–1878). *Bau und Leben des Socialen Körpers [Construction and life of the social body].* Tübingen, Germany: Laupp.

van Schajk, C. P. (1983). Why are diurnal primates living in groups? *Behaviour, 87,* 120–144.

Schallmayer, W. (1918). *Vererbung und Auslese. Grundriß der Gesellschaftsbiologie und der Lehre vom Rassedienst (Inheritance and selection. Outline of the biology of society and the theory of race service].* Jena, Germany: Fischer.

Scheff, T. J. (1990). *Microsociology: Discourse, emotion and social structure.* Chicago: University of Chicago Press.

Scheff, T. J., & Retzinger, S. M. (1991). *Emotion and violence: Shame/rage in interminable conflicts.* Boston, MA: Lexington.

Scheflen, A. (1973). *Communicational structure: Analysis of a psychotherapy transaction.* Bloomington, IN: Indiana University Press.

Scherer, K. R., & Ekman, P. (Eds.). (1984). *Approaches to emotion.* Hillsdale, NJ: Lawrence Erlbaum Associates.

Schiefenhövel, W. (1992). Signale zwischen Menschen. Formen nichtsprachlicher Kommunikation [Signals among people. Forms of nonverbal communication]. *Funkkolleg, Studienheft 11, Der Mensch.* Tübingen, Germany: Deutsches Institut für Fernstudien.

Schiefenhövel, W. (1997). Universals in interpersonal interactions. In U. Segerstråle & P. Molnár (Eds.), *Nonverbal communication: Where nature meets culture* (pp. 61–79). Mahwah, NJ: Lawrence Erlbaum Associates.

Schiffer, S. (1987). *Remnants of meaning.* Cambridge, MA: MIT Press.

Schmid, M. (1982). *Theorie sozialen Wandels [The theory of social change].* Opladen: Westdeutscher Verlag.

Schmid, M., & Wuketits, F. M. (Eds.). (1987). *Evolutionary theory in social science.* Boston, MA: Kluwer.

Schmidt, S. J. (1980). *Grundriß der empirischen Literaturwissenschaft: Vol. 1. Der gesellschaftliche Handlungsbereich Literatur [Outline of the empirical science of literature: Vol. 1. The action range of social literature].* Braunschweig, Wiesbaden, Germany: Vieweg.

Schmookler, A. B. (1984). *The parable of the tribes: The problem of power in social evolution.* Boston: Houghton Mifflin.

Schneider, D. M. (1956). Attempts to account for the incest taboo. Unpublished manuscript.

Schneider, K. (1997) Development of emotions and their expression in task-oriented situations in infants and pre-school children. In U. Segerstråle & P. Molnár (Eds.), *Nonverbal communication: Where nature meets culture* (pp. 109–130). Mahwah, NJ: Lawrence Erlbaum Associates.

Schumpeter, J. A. (1939). *Business cycles: A theoretical, historical, and statistical analysis of the capitalist process.* New York: McGraw-Hill.

Schumpeter, J. A. (1954). *History of economic analysis.* New York: Oxford University Press.

Schwegler, H., & Roth, G. (1992). Steuerung, Steuerbarkeit und Steuerungsfähigkeit komplexer Systeme [Control, controllability, and capability to control complex systems]. In H. Busshoff (Ed.), *Politische Steuerung [Political control]* (pp. 11–50). Baden-Baden, Germany: Nomos.

Scribner, S., & Cole, M. (1991). *The psychology of literacy.* Cambridge, MA: Harvard University Press.

Sebeok, T. A., & Umiker-Sebeok, J. (Eds.). (1980). *Speaking of apes: A critical anthology of two-way communication with man.* New York: Plenum.

Seeley, T. D., Camazine, S., & Sneyd, J. (1992). Collective decision-making in honey bees: How colonies chose among nectar sources. *Behavioral Ecology and Sociobiology, 28,* 277–290.

Segerstråle, U. (1983). *Whose truth shall prevail? Moral and scientific interests in the sociobiology controversy.* Unpublished doctoral dissertation, Department of Sociology, Harvard University.

Segerstråle, U. (1986). Colleagues in conflict: An "in vivo" analysis of the sociobiology controversy. *Biology and Philosophy, 1*(1), 53–87.

Segerstråle, U. (1992). Reductionism, "bad science," and politics: A critique of anti-reductionist reasoning. *Politics and the Life Sciences, 11,* 199–214.

Segerstråle, U. (1993). Review of Elazar Barkan, the retreat of scientific racism. *American Journal of Sociology, 99,* 3.

Segerstråle, U., & Molnár, P. (Eds.) (1997). *Nonverbal communication: Where nature meets culture.* Mahwah, NJ: Lawrence Erlbaum Associates.

Service, E. R. (1962). *Primitive social organisation.* New York: Random House.

Shannon, C. E., & Weaver, W. (1949). *The mathematical theory of communication.* Urbana, IL: University of Illinois Press.

Sheehan, T. (1980). Paris: Moses and polytheism. In A. Montagu (Ed.), *Sociobiology examined* (pp. 342–355). Oxford, England: Oxford University Press.

Shepher, J. (1971). *Self-imposed incest avoidance and exogamy in second generation Kibbutz adults.* Ann Arbor: University Microfilms.

Shepher, J. (1983). *Incest: The biosocial view.* New York: Academic Press.

Sherfey, M. J. (1972). *The nature and evolution of female sexuality.* New York: Random House.

Sherman, P. (1988). The levels of analysis. *Animal Behavior, 36,* 616–619.

Sherry, D. F., & Schacter, D. L. (1987). The evolution of multiple memory systems. *Psychological Review, 94,* 439–454.

Shott, S. (1979). Emotion and social life: A symbolic interactionist analysis. *American Journal of Sociology 84,* 1317–1334.

Shott, S. (1980). Reply to Kemper. *American Journal of Sociology, 85,* 1423–1426.

Shweder, R. A., & LeVine, R. A. (Eds.). (1984). *Culture theory: Essays on mind, self, and emotion.* Cambridge, England: Cambridge University Press.

Sieff, D. F. (1990). Explaining biased sex ratios in human populations. *Current Anthropology, 31,* 25–48.

Silk, J. B. (1992). The patterning of intervention among male Bonnet macaques: Reciprocity, revenge, and loyalty. *Current Anthropology, 33,* 318–325.

Simberloff, D. S. (1983). Competition theory, hypothesis testing, and other community ecological buzzwords. *American Naturalist, 122,* 626–635.

Simon, H. A. (1970). *Sciences of the artificial.* Cambridge, MA: MIT Press.

Simon, H. A. (1990). A mechanism for social selection and successful altruism. *Science, 250,* 1665–1668.

Simoons, F. J. (1969). Primary adult lactose intolerance and the milding habit: A problem in biological and cultural interrelations: I. Review of the medical research. *American Journal of Digestive Diseases, 14*, 819–836.

Singer, P. (1976). *Animal liberation. Towards an end to man's inhumanity to animals.* London: Jonathan Cape.

Singer, W. (1986). The brain as a self-organizing system. *European Archives of Psychiatry and Neurological Sciences, 236*, 4–9.

Sinnott, E. W., Dunn, L. C., & Dobzhansky, T. (1958). *Principles of genetics.* New York: McGraw-Hill.

Skinner, B. F. (1953). *Science and human behavior.* New York: Macmillan.

Sloep, P. B. (1993). Methodology revitalized? *British Journal for the Philosophy of Science, 44*, 231–249.

Sluckin, W. (Ed.). (1979). *Fear in animals and man.* New York: Van Nostrand Reinhold.

Small, A. (1905). *General sociology.* Chicago: University of Chicago Press.

Smith, A. (1937). *An inquiry into the nature and causes of the wealth of nations.* New York: Random House. (Original work published in 1776)

Smith, A. (1976a). *The theory of moral sentiments.* Oxford, England: Clarendon. (Original work published in 1759)

Smith, A. (1976b). *An inquiry into the nature and causes of the wealth of the nations.* London: Methuen. (Original work published in 1776)

Smith, E. A. (1984). Anthropology, evolutionary ecology, and the explanatory limitations of the ecosystem concept. In E. F. Moran (Ed.), *The ecosystem concept in anthropology* (pp. 51–85). Boulder, CO: Westview.

Smith, E. A. (1992). Human behavioral ecology: 1 & 2. *Evolutionary Anthropology, 1*, 20–25, 50–55.

Smith, E. A., & Winterhalder, B. (Eds.). (1992a). *Evolutionary ecology and human behavior.* New York: Aldine de Gruyter.

Smith, E. A., & Winterhalder, B. (1992b). Natural selection and decision making: Some fundamental principles. In E. A. Smith & B. Winterhalder (Eds.), *Evolutionary ecology and human behavior* (pp. 25–60). New York: Aldine de Gruyter.

Smuts, B. B. (1985). *Sex and friendship in baboons.* New York: Aldine de Gruyter.

Sober, E. (1984). *The nature of selection.* Cambridge, MA, London: MIT Press.

Sober, E. (1987). What is adaptationism? In J. Dupré (Ed.), *The latest on the best* (pp. 105–118). Cambridge, MA: MIT Press.

Sociobiology Study Group of Science For The People. (1976). Sociobiology—Another biological determinism. *BioScience, 26*(3), 182, 184–186.

Soltis, J., Boyd, R., & Richerson, P. J. (1994). Can group-functional behaviors evolve by cultural group selection? An empirical test. *Current Anthropology, 36*, 473–494.

Spain, D. H. (1987). The Westermarck–Freud incest–theory debate: An evaluation and reformulation. *Current Anthropology, 28*(5), 623–645.

Spelke, E. S. (1990). Priciples of object perception. *Cognitive Science, 14*, 29–56.

Spence, K. W. (1956). *Behavior theory and conditioning.* New Haven, NJ: Yale University Press.

Spencer, C. S. (1993). Human agency, biased transmission and the cultural evolution of chiefly authority. *Journal of Anthropological Archaeology, 12*, 41–74.

Spencer, H. (1852/1888). *Social statics.* New York: Appleton-Century-Crofts.

Spencer, H. (1854–1855 [1898]). *Principles of psychology.* New York: Appleton-Century-Crofts.

Spencer, H. (1862/1898). *First principles.* New York: Appleton-Century-Crofts.

Spencer, H. (1864–1867 [1887]). *The principles of biology*, 2 volumes. New York: Appleton-Century-Crofts.

Spencer, H. (1873). *The study of sociology.* London: Routledge & Kegan Paul.

Spencer, H. (1874–1896 [1898]). *The Principles of Sociology,* 3 volumes. New York: Appleton-Century-Crofts.

Sperber, D. (1985). Anthropology and psychology: Towards an epidemiology of representations. *Man, 20,* 73–89.

Sperber, D. (1996). *Explaining Culture.* Cambridge, MA: MIT Press.

Stammbach, E. (1988). Group responses to specially skilled individuals in a macaca fascicularis group. *Behaviour, 107,* 241–266.

Stearns, S. C. (1989). *The evolution of life histories.* Oxford, England: Oxford University Press.

Steklis, H., & Erwin, J. (Eds.). (1988). *Neuroscience* (Volume 4) . New York: Alan R. Liss.

Steward, J. (1955). *Theory of culture change: The methodology of multilinear evolution.* Urbana: University of Illinois Press.

Stinson, S. (1992). Nutritional adaptation. *Annual Review of Ecology and Systematics, 21,* 143–170.

Strong, D. R. (1980). Null hypotheses in ecology. *Synthese, 43,* 271–285.

Strum, S. C. (1987). *Almost human. A journey into the world of baboons.* New York: Random House.

Stuart-Fox, M. (1986). The unit of replication in sociocultural evolution. *Journal of Social and Biological Structures, 9,* 67–89.

Sugden, R. (1986). *The economics of rights, co-operation and welfare.* Oxford, England: Blackwell.

Sulloway, F. J. (1982). Freud and biology: The hidden legacy. In W. R. Woodward & M. G. Ash (Eds.), *The problematic science. Psychology in nineteenth-century thought* (pp. 198–227). New York: Praeger.

Sumner, W. G. (1906). *Folkways.* Boston: Ginn.

Sumner, W. G. (1914). *The challenge of facts and other essays.* New Haven, CT: Yale University Press.

Sumner, W. G., Galloway Keller, A. (1927). *The science of society,* 4 volumes. New Haven: Yale University Press.

Suomi, S. (1997). Nonverbal communication in nonhuman primates: Implications for the emergence of culture. In U. Segerstråle & P. Molnár (Eds.), *Nonverbal communication: Where nature meets culture* (pp. 131–146). Mahwah, NJ: Lawrence Erlbaum Associates.

Sutherland, A. (1898). *The origin and growth of moral instincts,* 2 volumes. London: Longman.

Swanson, C. (1983). *Ever-expanding horizons.* Amherst, MA: University of Massachusetts Press.

Symonds, N. (1991, September, 21). A fitter theory of evolution? *New Scientist,* 30–34.

Symons, D. (1979). *The evolution of human sexuality.* Oxford, England: Oxford University Press.

Symons D. (1987). If we're all Darwinians what's the fuss about? In C. B. Crawford, M. F. Smith, & D. L. Krebs (Eds.), *Sociobiology and psychology* (pp. 121–146). Hillsdale, NJ: Lawrence Erlbaum Associates.

Symons D. (1989). A critique of Darwinian anthropology. *Ethology and Sociobiology, 10,* 131–144.

Symons, D. (1992). On the use and misuse of Darwinism in the study of human behavior. In J. H. Barkow, L. Cosmides, & J. Tooby (Eds.), *The adapted mind: Evolutionary psychology and the generation of culture* (pp. 137–159). New York: Oxford University Press.

T

Terrace, H. S. (1985). In the beginning was the name. *American Psychologist, 40,* 1011–1028.

Terrell, J. (1986). *Prehistory of the Pacific Islands: A study of variation in language, customs, and human biology*. Cambridge, MA: Cambridge University Press.

Teubner, G. (1984). Das regulatorische Trilemma, Zur Diskussion um post-instrumentale Rechtsmodelle [The regulatory trilemma. On the discussion on post-instrumental models of law]. *Quaderini Fiorentini, 13*, 109–149.

Thomas, B. (1991). Alfred Marshall on economic biology. *Review of Political Economy, 3*, 1–14.

Thomason, S. G., & Kaufman, T. (1991). *Language contact, creolization, and genetic linguistics*. Berkeley: University of California Press.

Thompson, P. (1989). *The structure of biological theories*. New York: SUNY Press.

Thorndike, E. L. (1898). Animal intelligence: An experimental study of associative processes in animals. *Psychological Review Monograph (Suppl. 2*.

Thorndike, E. L. (1932). *The fundamentals of learning*. New York: Harper & Row.

Thorndike, E. L. (1941). *A history of magic and experimental science, 8 volumes*. New York: Columbia University Press.

Thornhill, N. W. (1987). *Rules of mating and marriage pertaining to relatives: An evolutionary biological analysis*. Unpublished doctoral dissertation. Albuquerque: University of Mexico.

Thornhill, N. W. (1990a). The comparative method of biology in the study of the societies of history. *The International Journal of Comparative Sociology, 27*, 7–78.

Thornhill, N. W. (1990b). An evolutionary analysis of incest rules. *Ethology and Sociobiology, 11*, 113–129.

Thornhill, N. W. (1991). An evolutionary analysis of rules regulating inbreeding and marriage. *Behavioral and Brain Sciences, 14*, 247–293.

Thornhill, N. W. (1996). Psychological adaptation to sexual coercion in victims and offenders. In D. Buss & N. Malamuth (Eds.), *Sex, power, and conflict: Evolutionary and feminist perspectives* (pp. 90–104). New York: Oxford University Press.

Thornhill, N. W., & Thornhill, R. (1983). Human rape: An evolutionary analysis. *Ethology and Sociobiology, 4*, 137–173.

Thornhill, N. W., & Thornhill, R. (1985). Matriliny, sexual selection, and conflict. *Behavioral and Brain Sciences, 8*, 679–680.

Thornhill, N. W., & Thornhill, R. (1987). Rules of mating and marriage pertaining to relatives. In C. Crawford, M. Smith, & C. Krebs (Eds.), *Psychology and sociobiology: Ideas, issues and applications* (pp. 151–180). Hillsdale, NJ: Lawrence Erlbaum Associates.

Thornhill, R. (1990). The study of adaptation. In M. Beckoff & D. Jamieson (Eds.), *Interpretation and explanation in the study of animal behavior* (Vol. II). (pp. 31–62). Boulder, CO: Westview.

Thornhill, R., & Alcock, J. (1983). *The evolution of inset mating systems*. Cambridge, MA: Harvard University Press.

Thornhill, R., & Thornhill, N. W. (1987). Human rape: The strength of the evolutionary perspective. In C. Crawford, M. Smith, & D. Krebs (Eds.), *Sociobiology and psychology* (pp. 291–269). Hillsdale, NJ: Lawrence Erlbaum Associates.

Thornhill, R., & Thornhill, N. W. (1991). Coercive sexuality of men as evolutionary adaptation. In E. Grauerholz & M. Koralewski (Eds.), *Sexual coercion* (pp. 91–107). Lexington, MA: Lexington Books.

Tinbergen, N. (1951). *The study of instinct*. New York: Oxford University Press.

Tinbergen, N. (1963). On aims and methods of ethology. *Zeitschrift für Tierpsychologie, 20*, 410–433.

Tobias, P. (1987). The brain of *Homo Habilis*: A new level. *Journal of Human Evolution, 16*, 741–761.

Tobias, P. (Ed.) (1985). *Hominoid evolution: Past, present and future.* New York: Alan Liss.

Tobisson, E. (1986). *Family dynamics among the Kuria.* Gothenburg: University of Gothenburg Press.

Tofts, C., & Franks, N. R. (1992, October). Doing the right thing: Ants, honey bees, and naked mole-rats. *TREE, 7,* 346–349.

Tomasello, M. (1996). Do apes ape? In C. M. Heyes & B. G. Galef, Jr. (Eds.), *Social learning in animals* (pp. 319–346). San Diego, CA: Academic Press.

Tomasello, M., Krueger, A. C., & Ratner, H. H. (1993). Cultural learning. *Behavioral and Brain Sciences, 16,* 495–552.

Tomkins, S. S. (1962). *Affect, imagery, consciousness. Vol. 1.* New York: Springer.

Tomkins. S. S. (1963). *Affect, imagery, consciousness. Vol. 11.* New York: Springer.

Tompa, F. (1962). Territorial behavior: The main controlling factor of a local song sparrow population. *Auk, 79,* 687–697.

Tooby, J. (1982). Pathogens, polymorphisms, and the evolution of sex. *Journal of Theoretical Biology, 97,* 557–576.

Tooby, J. (1985). The emergence of evolutionary psychology. In D. Pines (Ed.), *Emerging synthese in science.* Proceedings of the Founding Workshops of the Santa Fe Institute, Santa Fe, NM: Santa Fe Institute.

Tooby, J., & Cosmides, L. (1989a). Evolutionary psychology and the generation of culture: Part I. Theoretical considerations. *Ethology and Sociobiology, 10,* 29–49.

Tooby, J., & Cosmides, L. (1989b, August). *The logic of threat.* Paper presented at the annunal Meeting of the Human Behavior and Evolution Society, Evanston, IL.

Tooby, J., & Cosmides, L. (1989c). Adaptation versus phylogeny: The role of animal psychology in the study of human behavior. *International Journal of Comparative Psychology, 2,* 105–118.

Tooby, J., & Cosmides, L. (1990a). The past explains the present: Emotional adaptations and the structure of ancestral environments. *Ethology and Sociobiology, 11,* 375–424.

Tooby, J., & Cosmides, L. (1990b). On the universality of human nature and the uniqueness of the individual: The role of genetics and adaptation. *Journal of Personality, 58,* 17–67.

Tooby, J., & Cosmides, L. (1992). The psychological foundations of culture. In J. Barkow, L. Cosmides, & J. Tooby (Eds.), *The Adapted Mind* (pp. 19–136). New York: Oxford University Press.

Townsend, J. M. (1987). Sex differences in sexuality among medical students: Effects of increasing socioeconomic status. *Archives of Sexual Behavior, 16,* 425–441.

Trager, G. L. (1958). Paralanguage: A first approximation. *Studies in Linguistics, 13,* 1–12.

Traweek, S. (1988). *Beamtimes and lifetimes. The world of high energy physicists.* Cambridge, MA: Harvard University Press.

Trevarthen, C. (1977). Descriptive analyses of infant communicative behavior. In H. R. Schaffer (Ed.), *Studies in mother–infant interaction* (pp. 227–270). London: Academic Press.

Trivers, R. L. (1971). The evolution of reciprocal altruism. *Quarterly Review of Biology, 46*(4). 35–57.

Trivers, R. L. (1972). Parental investment and sexual selection. In B. Cambell (Ed.), *Sexual selection and the descent of man, 1871–1971* (pp. 136–179). Chicago: Aldine de Gruyter.

Trivers, R. L. (1974). Parent–offspring conflict. *American Zoologist, 14,* 249–264.

Tullock, G. (1979, September). Sociobiology and economics. *Atlantic Economic Journal,* 1–10.

Turke, P. W. (1990). Which humans behave adaptively, and why does it matter? *Ethology and Sociobiology, 11,* 305–339.

Turner, J. H. (1972). *Patterns of social organization.* New York: McGraw-Hill.

Turner, J. H. (1984). *Societal stratification: A theoretical analysis.* New York: Columbia University Press.

Turner, J. H. (1991). *The structure of sociological theory.* Belmont, CA: Wadsworth.

Turner, J. H. (1994a). The ecology of macrostructure. *Advances in Human Ecology, 3,* 113–131.

Turner, J. H. (1994b). The assembling of human populations. *Advances in Human Ecology, 3,* 65–91.

Turner, J. H. (1995). *Macrodynamics: Toward a theory on the organization of human populations.* New Brunswick, NJ: Rutgers University Press.

Turner, J. H. (1997a). *The institutional order.* New York: Longman.

Turner, J. H. (1997b) The evolution of emotions: The nonverbal basis of human social organization. In U. Segerstråle & P. Molnár (Eds.), *Nonverbal communication: Where nature meets culture* (pp. 211–223). Mahwah, NJ: Lawrence Erlbaum Associates.

Turner, J. H., & Maryanski, A. M. (1979). *Functionalism.* Menlo Park: Benjamin-Cummings.

Turner, V. (1977). Process, system and symbol: A new anthropological synthesis. *Daedalus, I,* 61–80.

Tversky, A., & Kahneman, D. (1974). Judgment under uncertainty: Heuristics and biases. *Science, 183,* 1124–1131.

Tylor, E. B. (1871). *Primitive cultures,* 2 volumes. London: Macmillan.

Tylor, E. B. (1888). On a method of investigating the development of institutions: Applied to laws of marriage and descent. *Journal of Royal Anthropological Institute, 18,* 245–269.

V

Vansina, J. (1990). *Paths in the rainforests: Toward a history of political tradition in Equatorial Africa.* Madison, WI: University of Wisconsin Press.

Vayda, A. P., & Rappaport, R. A. (1968). Ecology, cultural and non-cultural. In J. A. Clifton (Ed.), *Introduction to cultural anthropology* (pp. 477–497). Boston, MA: Houghton Mifflin.

Veblen, T. B. (1898). Why is economics not an evolutionary science? *Quartely Journal of Economics, 12,* 373–397.

Veblen, T. B. (1899). *The theory of the leisure class: An economic study of institutions.* New York: Macmillan.

Veblen, T. B. (1919). *The place of science in modern civilisation and other essays.* New York: Huebsch.

Velichkovsky, B. M. (1994). The levels endeavour in psychology and cognitive science. In P. Bertelson, P. Eelen, & G. d'Ydewalle (Eds.), *International perspectives on psychological science: Leading themes* (pp. 143–162). Hillsdale, NJ: Lawrence Erlbaum Associates

Velichkovsky, B. M., & Rumbaugh, D. M. (1996). *Communicating meaning: The evolution and development of language.* Mahwah, NJ: Lawrence Erlbaum Associates.

Verral, R. (1979). Sociobiology: The instinct in our genes. *March 1979 issue of* Spearhead (cited in J. Beckwith, 1981/1982, p. 316).

Via, S. (1993). Adaptive phenotypic plasticity: Target or by-product of selection in a variable environment? *American Nature, 42,* 352–365.

Visalberghi, E. D. F., & Fragaszy, D. M. (1990). Do monkeys ape? In S. Parker & K. Gibson, (Eds.), *Comparative developmental psychology and intelligence in primates* (pp. 146–173). Cambridge, England: Cambridge University Press.

Vogt, E. Z. (1964). The genetic model and Maya cultural development. In E. Z. Vogt & A. L. Ruz (Eds.), *Desarrollo cultural de los Mayas* (pp. 9–48). Mexico DF: University Nac. Autonomade Mexico.

Voland, E. (1990). Differential reproductive success within the Krummhörn population (Germany, 18th and 19th centuries). *Behavioral Ecology and Sociobiology, 26,* 65–72.

Voland, E. (1995). Reproductive decisions viewed from an evolutionarily informed historical demography. In R. I. M. Dunbar (Ed.), *Human reproductive decisions—biological and social perspectives* (pp. 137–159). London/Houndsmills: MacMillan; New York: St. Martin's.

Voland, E., & Dunbar, R. I. M. (1997). The impact of social status and migration on female age at marriage in an historical population. *Journal of Biosocial Science, 29*(2).

Voland E., & Engel, C. (1990). Female choice in humans: A conditional mate selection strategy of the Krummhörn women (Germany, 1720–1874). *Ethology, 84*, 144–154.

Voland, E., Siegelkow, E., & Engel, C. (1991). Cost/benefit orientated parental investment by high status families: The Krummhörn case. *Ethology and Sociobiology, 12*, 105–118.

Voland, E., Dunbar, R. I. M., Engel, C., & Stephan, P. (1997). Population increase and sex-biased parental investment in humans: Evidence from 18th and 19th century Germany. *Current Anthropology, 38*, 129–135.

Vygotsky, L. S. (1985). *Mind in society.* Cambridge, MA: Harvard University Press.

W

de Waal, F. B. M. (1982). *Chimpanzee politics.* London: Jonathan Cape.

de Waal, F. B. M. (1989). *Peacemaking among primates.* Cambridge, MA: Harvard University Press.

Waddington, C. H. (1961). The human evolutionary system. In M. Banton (Ed.), *Darwinism and the study of society* (pp. 63–81). Chicago: Quadrangle Books.

Wade, M. S. (1987). Measuring sexual selection. In J. W. Bradbury & M. B. Andersson (Eds.), *Sexual selection; testing the alternatives* (pp. 197–207). New York: Wiley.

Wahlsten, D. (1990). Insensitivity of the analysis of variance to heredity–environment interaction. *Behavioral and Brain Sciences, 13*, 109–161.

Wallace, A. R. (1904). *Man's place in the universe.* London: Chapman & Hall.

Waller, R. (1986). Ecology, migration, and expansion in East Africa. *African Affairs, 85*, 347–370.

Wang, X. T. (1992, July). *An evolutionary analysis of the framing effect in decision making.* Paper presented at the fourth annual meeting of the Human Behavior and Evolution Society, Albuquerque, NM.

Ward, L. (1903). *Pure sociology.* New York: Macmillan.

Wardhaugh, R. (1992). An introduction to sociolinguistics. Oxford, England: Blackwell.

Wason, P. (1966). Reasoning. In B. M. Foss (Ed.), *New horizons in psychology.* New York: Penguin.

Weaver, W. (1949). Recent contributions to the mathematical theory of communication. In C. E. Shannon & W. Weaver (Eds.), *The mathematical theory of communication* (pp. 1–28). Urbana, IL: University of Illinois Press.

Weinberg, S. (1992). *Dreams of a final theory.* New York: Pantheon.

Weingart, P. (1988). Close encounters of the third kind. Science and the context of relevance. *Poetics Today, 9*, 1.

Weingart, P. (1994). Biology as social theory. In D. Ross (Ed.), *Modernist impulses in the human sciences.* Baltimore: Johns Hopkins University Press

Weingart, P. (1995). Struggle for existence—selection and retention of a metaphor. In S. Maasen, E. Mendelsohn, & P. Weingart (Eds.), *Biology as society—society as biology. Metaphors. Yearbook Sociology of the Sciences (Vol. XIX)* (pp. 127–151). Dordrecht, Holland: Kluwer.

Weingart, P., Kroll, G., & Bayertz, K. (1988). *Rasse, Blut und Gene [Race, blood, and genes].* Frankfurt a.M.: Suhrkamp.

Weiss, R. (1979). Ethnicity and reform: Minorities and the ambience of the depression years. *Journal of American History, 66*, 575.

Weiss, R. (1988). Discriminating neurons pick the right face (monkey temporal lobe facial recognition cells; work of Michael E. Hasselmo and Gordon Bayliss). *Science News, 134,* November 19, 326.

Wells, R. S., Scott, M. D., & Irvine, A. B. (1987). The social structure of free-ranging bottlenose dolphins. *Current Mammalogy, 1,* 247–305.

Werskey, P. G. (1978). *The visible college: A study of left–wing scientists in Britain, 1918–1939.* New York: Holt, Rinehart & Winston.

Wertheimer, M. (1925). *Drei Abhandlungen zur Gestalttheorie [Three studies on Gestalttheory].* Erlangen, Germany: Verlag der Philosophischen Akademie.

Westermarck, E. (1922). *The history of human marriage.* London: Macmillan. (Original work published in 1891)

White, D. R. (1988). Rethinking polygyny: Co-wives, codes, and cultural systems. *Current Anthropology, 29,* 529–572.

White, L. A. (1948). The definition and prohibition of incest. *American Anthropologist, 50,* 416–435.

White, L. A. (1949). *The science of culture.* New York: Farrar Straus.

White, L. A. (1959). *The evolution of culture: The development of civilization to the fall of Rome.* New York: McGraw-Hill.

White, L., Jr. (1962). *Medieval technology and social change.* Oxford, England: Clarendon.

Whiten, A., & Byrne, R. W. (1988). Tactical deception in primates. *Behavioral and Brain Sciences, 2,* 233 273.

Whitley, R. (1984). *Intellectual and social organisation of the sciences.* Oxford, England: Clarendon.

Whorf, B. L. (1956). *Language, thought and reality.* Cambridge, MA: MIT Press.

Wiegele, T. C. (Ed.). (1979). *Biopolitics: Search for a more human political science.* Boulder, CO: Westview.

Williams, G. C. (1966). *Adaptation and natural selection.* Princeton, NJ: Princeton University Press.

Williams, G. C. (1985). A defense of reductionism in evolutionary biology. *Oxford Surveys in Evolutionary Biology, 2,* 1–27.

Williamson, O. E. (1975). *Markets and hierarchies: Analysis and anti–trust implications. A study in the economics of international organization.* New York: The Free Press.

Wilson, E. B. (1896). *The cell in development and inheritance.* New York: Macmillan.

Wilson, E. O. (1971a). *The insect societies.* Cambridge, MA: Harvard University Press.

Wilson, E. O. (1971b). The prospects for a unified sociobiology. *American Scientist, 59,* 400–403.

Wilson, E. O. (1975). *Sociobiology: The new synthesis.* Cambridge, MA: Harvard University Press.

Wilson, E. O. (1975a). For Sociobiology, *New York Review of Books, December 11, 20,* 60–61.

Wilson, E. O. (1976). Academic vigilantism and the political significance of sociobiology. *BioScience, 26,* 183–190.

Wilson, E. O. (1978). *On human nature.* Cambridge, MA: Harvard University Press.

Wilson, E. O. (1981). Genes and racism. *Nature, 289,* 627.

Wilson, E. O. (1994). *Naturalist.* Washington, DC: Island Press.

Wilson, E. O., & Hölldobler, H. (1988). Dense heterarchies and mass communication as the basis of organization in ant colonies. *Trends in Ecology and Evolution, 3,* 65–67.

Wilson, M., & Daly, M. (1992). The man who mistook his wife for a chattel. In J. Barkow, L. Cosmides, & J. Tooby (Eds.), *The adapted mind, evolutionary psychology and the generation of culture* (pp. 289–324). New York: Oxford University Press.

Wimmer, H. M., & Perner, J. (1983). Beliefs about beliefs: Representation and constraining function of wrong beliefs in young children's understanding of deception. *Cognition, 13,* 103–128.

Wimmer, H. M., Gruber, S., & Perner, J. (1984). Young children's conception of lying: lexical realism–moral subjectivism. *Journal of Experimental Child Psychology, 37,* 1–30.

Wimsatt, W. C. (1987). False models as means to truer theories. In M. H. Nitecki & A. Hoffman (Eds.), *Neutral models in biology* (pp. 23–55). Oxford, England: Oxford University Press.

Winterhalder, B., & Smith, E. A. (1981). *Hunter–gatherer foraging strategies.* Chicago: University of Chicago Press.

Wirth, L. (1928). *The ghetto.* Chicago: University of Chicago Press.

Witt, U. (1991). Economics, sociobiology, and behavioral psychology on preferences. *Journal of Economic Psychology, 12,* 557–573.

Wolf, A. P., & Huang, C. (1980). *Marriage and adaptation in China, 1845–1945.* Stanford, CA: Stanford University Press.

Wolfe, A. (1993). *The human difference. Animals, computers, and the necessity of the social sciences.* Berkeley: University of California Press.

Worms, R. (1896). *Organicisme et société [Organicism and society].* Paris: Giard and Brière.

Wrangham, R. W. (1980). An ecological model of female–bonded primate groups. *Behaviour, 75,* 262–300.

Wright, S. (1969). *Evolution and the genetic of populations: Vol. 2. The theory of gene frequencies.* Chicago: University of Chicago Press.

Wundt, W. (1916). *Elements of folk psychology.* London: George Allen.

Wuthnow, R. (1987). *Meaning and moral order: Explorations in cultural analysis.* Berkeley, CA: University of California Press.

Wynne-Edwards, V. C. (1962). *Animal dispersion in relation to social behavior.* London: Oliver & Boyd.

Wynne-Edwards, V. C. (1986). *Evolution through group selection.* Oxford, England: Blackwell.

Y

Young, M. P., & Yamane, S. (1992). Sparse population coding of faces in the inferotemporal cortex (macaques). *Science, 256,* 1327–1331.

Young, R. M. (1971). Darwin's methapor: Does nature select? *Monist, 55,* 442–503.

Young, R. M. (1985). *Darwin's metaphor: Nature's place in Victorian culture.* Cambridge, England: Cambridge University Press.

Z

Zajonc, R. (1980). Feeling and thinking: Preferences need no inferences. *American Psychologist, 35,* 151–175.

Zorbaugh, H. W. (1926). The natural areas of the city. *Publications of the American Sociological Society, 20,* 188–197.

Zuckerman, L. (1991, May 30). Apes not us. *New York Review of Books,* 43–49.

AUTHOR INDEX*

---

*Page numbers in italic refer to reference pages.

SUBJECT INDEX

LIST OF AUTHORS

Monique Borgerhoff Mulder, Department of Anthropology, University of California at Davis, Davis, CA 95616, USA

Robert Boyd, Department of Anthropology, University of California Los Angeles, Los Angeles, CA 90024 , USA

Leda Cosmides, Department of Psychology, University of California, Santa Barbara, CA 93106, USA

Lorraine Daston, Max Planck Institute for the History of Science, Wilhelmstraße 44, D-10117 Berlin, Germany

William H. Durham, Department of Anthropology, Stanford University, Stanford, CA 94305-2145, USA

Raphael Falk, Department of Genetics, The Hebrew University of Jerusalem, Givat Ram Campus, Jerusalem 91904, Israel

Bernhard Giesen, Institut für Soziologie, Justus-Liebig-Universität, Karl-Glöckner-Straße 21E, D-35394 Giessen, Germany

Gerd Gigerenzer, Center for Adaptive Behavior and Cognition, Max Planck Institute for Psychological Research, Leopoldstraße 24, D-80802 Munich, Germany

Peter M. Hejl, Institut für empirische Literatur- und Medienforschung, University of Siegen, Postfach 10 12 40, D-57068 Siegen, Germany

Hubert Hendrichs, Department of Biology, University of Bielefeld, P.O. Box 10 01 31, D-33501 Bielefeld, Germany

Geoffrey Hodgson, The Judge Institute of Management Studies, University of Cambridge, Trumpington Street, Cambridge CB2 1AG, England

Eva Jablonka, The Cohn Institute for the History and Philosophy of Science and Ideas, Tel Aviv University, Tel Aviv 69978, Israel

Hans Kummer, Gartendörfliweg 8, CH-8135 Langnau a. A., Switzerland

Sabine Maasen, Max Planck Institute for Psychological Research, Leopoldstraße 24, D-80802 Munich, Germany

Alexandra Maryanski, Department of Sociology, University of California at Riverside, Riverside, CA 92521-0419, USA

Peter Meyer, Department of Economics and Social Sciences, University of Augsburg, Universitätsstr. 16, D-86159 Augsburg, Germany

Sandra D. Mitchell, Department of Philosophy, B-0119, University of California, San Diego, 9500 Gilman Drive, La Jolla, CA 92093-0119, USA

Peter Molnár, Department of Medical Anthropology, Institute of Behavioural Sciences, Semmelweis University Medical School, Nagyvarad sq. 4, H-1089 Budapest, Hungary

Peter J. Richerson, Department of Environmental Biology and Management, University of California at Davis, Davis, CA 95616, USA

Ullica Segerstråle, Department of Social Sciences, Illinois Institute of Technology, 3255 S. Dearborn, 214 Wishnick Hall, Chicago, IL 60616, USA

Neven Sesardic, Miyazaki International College, 1405 Kano Kiyotake-cho, Miyazaki 889-16, Japan

Stephen J. Shennan, Department of Archaeology, University College London, 31-34 Gordon Sq., London, WC1H 0PY, England

Joan B. Silk, Department of Anthropology, University of California, Los Angeles, CA 90095, USA

Peter B. Sloep, Science Faculty, Open Universiteit, P.O. Box 29 60, NL-6401 DL Heerlen, The Netherlands

Nancy W. Thornhill, Department of Anthropology, University of Southern California, Los Angeles, CA 90089, USA

John Tooby, Department of Anthropology, University of California, Santa Barbara, CA 03106, USA

Jonathan H. Turner, Department of Sociology, University of California at Riverside, Riverside, CA 92521-0419, USA

Boris M. Velichkovsky, Department of Psychology, Dresden University of Technology, Mommsenstraße 13, D-01062 Dresden, Germany

Eckart Voland, Zentrum für Philosophie und Grundlagen der Wissenschaft, Justus-Liebig-Universität Giessen, Otto-Behaghel-Straße 10 C II, D-35394 Giessen, Germany

Peter Weingart, Department of Sociology, University of Bielefeld, P.O. Box 10 01 31, D-33501 Bielefeld, Germany